COGNITIVE NEUROSCIENCE
OF AGING

COGNITIVE NEUROSCIENCE OF AGING

Linking Cognitive and Cerebral Aging

Edited by
Roberto Cabeza, Lars Nyberg,
and Denise Park

UNIVERSITY PRESS

2005

OXFORD
UNIVERSITY PRESS

Oxford   New York
Auckland   Bangkok   Buenos Aires   Cape Town   Chennai
Dar es Salaam   Delhi   Hong Kong   Istanbul   Karachi   Kolkata
Kuala Lumpur   Madrid   Melbourne   Mexico City   Mumbai   Nairobi
São Paulo   Shanghai   Taipei   Tokyo   Toronto

Copyright © 2005 by Oxford University Press, Inc.

Published by Oxford University Press, Inc.
198 Madison Avenue, New York, New York 10016

www.oup.com

Oxford is a registered trademark of Oxford University Press.

Library of Congress Cataloging-in-Publication Data

Cognitive neuroscience of aging : linking cognitive and cerebral aging
/ edited by Roberto Cabeza, Lars Nyberg, and Denise Park.
      p. cm.
   Includes bibliographical references and index.
   ISBN 0-19-515674-9
   1. Brain—Aging.   2. Cognitive neuroscience.   I. Cabeza, Roberto.
II. Nyberg, Lars, 1966–   III. Park, Denise C.
   QP356.25.C64   2005
   153—dc22   2004004716

*We dedicate this book to Alma and Maia (RC), Erica, Isak, and Samuel
(LN), and Bill, Rob, and Colleen (DCP).*

9 8 7 6 5 4 3 2 1

Printed in the United States of America
on acid-free paper

Contents

Contributors

LARS BÄCKMAN
Aging Research Center
Division of Geriatric Epidemiology
Neurotec
Karolinska Institute
Stockholm Gerontology Research
  Center
Stockholm, Sweden

RANDY L. BUCKNER
Departments of Psychology,
  Radiology and Anatomy, and
  Neurobiology
Howard Hughes Medical Institute at
  Washington University
St. Louis, Missouri, United States

ROBERTO CABEZA
Center for Cognitive Neuroscience
Duke University
Durham, North Carolina, United
  States

MARK D'ESPOSITO
Henry H. Wheeler Jr. Brain Imaging
  Center
Helen Wills Neuroscience Institute
Department of Psychology
University of California, Berkeley
Berkeley, California, United States

SANDER DASELAAR
Center for Cognitive Neuroscience
Duke University
Durham, North Carolina, United
  States

MONICA FABIANI
Department of Psychology and
  Beckman Institute
University of Illinois at Urbana-
  Champaign
Urbana-Champaign, Illinois, United
  States

LARS FARDE
Department of Clinical Neuroscience
Section of Psychiatry
Karolinska Institute
Stockholm, Sweden

ADAM H. GAZZALEY
Henry H. Wheeler Jr. Brain Imaging
  Center
Helen Wills Neuroscience Institute
Department of Psychology
University of California, Berkeley
Berkeley, California, United States

CHERYL L. GRADY
Rotman Research Institute
Baycrest Centre for Geriatric Care
University of Toronto
Toronto, Ontario, Canada

GABRIELE GRATTON
Department of Psychology and
  Beckman Institute
University of Illinois at Urbana-
  Champaign
Urbana-Champaign, Illinois, United
  States

ANGELA H. GUTCHESS
University of Michigan, Ann Arbor
Ann Arbor, Michigan, United States

SCOTT A. HUETTEL
Duke University Medical Center
Durham, North Carolina, United
  States

SHU-CHEN LI
Center for Lifespan Psychology
Max Planck Institute for Human
  Development
Berlin, Germany

DAVID J. MADDEN
Duke University Medical Center
Durham, North Carolina, United
  States

ALEXA M. MORCOM
Brain Mapping Unit
Department of Psychiatry
University of Cambridge
Cambridge, England

LARS NYBERG
Umeå University
Umeå, Sweden

DENISE C. PARK
University of Illinois at Urbana-
  Champaign
Urbana-Champaign, Illinois, United
  States

NAFTALI RAZ
Wayne State University
Detroit, Michigan, United States

PATRICIA A. REUTER-LORENZ
Department of Psychology
University of Michigan, Ann Arbor
Ann Arbor, Michigan, United States

MICHAEL D. RUGG
Institute of Cognitive Neuroscience
University College London
London, England

CHING-YUNE C. SYLVESTER
Department of Psychology
University of Michigan, Ann Arbor
Ann Arbor, Michigan, United States

ROBERT WEST
Department of Psychology
University of Notre Dame
Notre Dame, Indiana, United States

WYTHE L. WHITING
Duke University Medical Center
Durham, North Carolina, United
  States

COGNITIVE NEUROSCIENCE
OF AGING

1

Cognitive Neuroscience of Aging
Emergence of a New Discipline

Roberto Cabeza

Lars Nyberg

Denise C. Park

Until recently, the cognitive and neural mechanisms of age-related changes in cognition were usually studied independently of each other. On one hand, studies in the domain of *cognitive psychology of aging* investigated the effects of aging on behavioral measures of cognition and characterized a variety of age-related deficits in memory, attention, and the like. On the other hand, studies in the domain of *neuroscience of aging* investigated the effects of aging on the anatomy and physiology of the brain and described forms of age-related neural decline, such as cerebral atrophy and synaptic loss. Although it is reasonable to assume that cognitive aging is largely a consequence of cerebral aging, the relationships between these two phenomena are still largely unknown. Fortunately, this void is being rapidly resolved by studies focusing on the relationships between the effects of aging on the cognition and on the brain. This group of studies constitutes the new discipline of cognitive neuroscience of aging (CNA). Although CNA has a long past, only lately has it achieved the critical mass to be considered an autonomous discipline. The main goal of this book is to provide an introduction to this exciting new field.

To describe the issues addressed by CNA, it is useful to start with a simple model that includes the basic components of the problem. In the model in figure 1.1, aging is assumed to affect structures and processes both in the brain and regarding cognition. Although artificial, the distinctions between brain and cognition and between structures and processes are useful for conceptual purposes. Likewise, even though any change in cognition implies a change in the brain, it is useful to distinguish between neurogenic and psychogenic effects. *Neurogenic effects* (solid arrows in figure 1.1) occur when a change in the brain causes a change in cognition. For example, age-related atrophy of prefrontal gray matter may lead to decline in work-

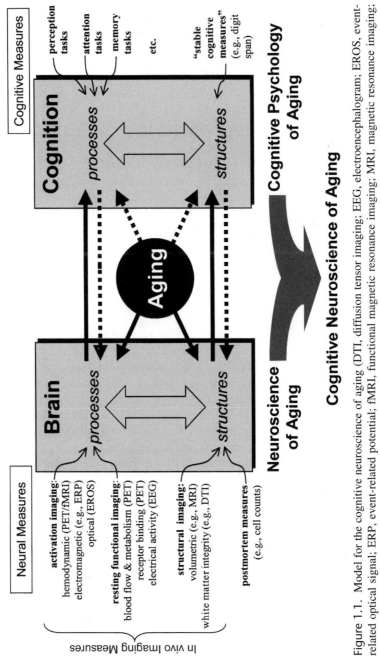

Figure 1.1. Model for the cognitive neuroscience of aging (DTI, diffusion tensor imaging; EEG, electroencephalogram; EROS, event-related optical signal; ERP, event-related potential; fMRI, functional magnetic resonance imaging; MRI, magnetic resonance imaging; PET, positron emission tomography).

ing memory function. *Psychogenic effects* (dashed arrows in figure 1.1) occur when a change in cognition causes a change in the brain. For instance, older adults who do not use certain cognitive processes may suffer greater cerebral atrophy in the brain regions that mediate these processes, or older adults who received a cognitive intervention may show improvements in cognitive function and changes in neural networks. As illustrated by figure 1.1, neurogenic effects may lead to psychogenic effects and vice versa. For instance, a decline in neural function may originate a compensatory change in cognitive strategies, which in turn may initiate a change in brain function.

The main goal of CNA is to link the effects of aging on cognition to the effects of aging on the brain. The effects of aging on cognition are assessed with cognitive measures (right side of figure 1.1), such as accuracy and RT data from perceptual tasks, attention tasks, and the like. The effects of aging on the brain are assessed with neural measures (left side of figure 1.1), such as postmortem and in vivo imaging measures. Postmortem data provide much greater spatial resolution (e.g., dendrite morphology), but in vivo imaging measures can be more directly linked to cognitive performance in living human participants. This is the main reason why the development of imaging methods and their application to the study of aging were the main forces behind the birth of CNA. At present, imaging is the dominant CNA approach, which is a trend clearly reflected in the contents of this first introduction to CNA. As CNA develops, future books are likely to cover other methodological approaches.

This book has four main sections. The first section describes the main imaging methods, including structural imaging (chapter 2 by Raz), resting functional imaging (chapter 3 by Bäckman and Farde), and activation imaging (chapter 4 by Fabiani and Gratton, chapter 5 by Gazzaley and D'Esposito, and chapter 6 by Rugg and Morcom). The second section reviews imaging findings about specific cognitive functions, including perception and attention (chapter 7 by Madden, Whiting, and Huettel), working memory (chapter 8 by Reuter-Lorenz and Sylvester), episodic memory (chapter 9 by Park and Gutchess), and prospective memory (chapter 10 by West). The third section focuses on clinical and applied issues, including causal mechanisms in healthy and pathological aging (chapter 11 by Buckner), functional connectivity in healthy and pathological aging (chapter 12 by Grady), and the combination of imaging and cognitive rehabilitation methods (chapter 13 by Nyberg). The last section of the book focuses on CNA models, including empirical models of the effects of aging on lateralization (chapter 14 by Daselaar and Cabeza) and a computational model of the effects of aging on the dopaminergic system (chapter 15 by Li). The contents of the four sections of the book are summarized and discussed next.

Imaging Measures

The chapters in the first section of the book describe the use in CNA of imaging measures, including structural, resting functional, and activation imaging. Structural imaging consists mainly of magnetic resonance imaging (MRI) measures of gray and white matter volume and integrity. Resting functional imaging measures include positron emission tomography (PET) and MRI measures of blood flow and metabolism, scalp recordings of electrical brain activity (electroencephalogram, EEG), and PET measures of receptor binding. Activation imaging is comprised of measures taken while participants are actively engaged in performing a cognitive task; these measures include electromagnetic measures such as event-related potentials (ERPs), optical measures such as event-related optical signal (EROS), and hemodynamic measures such as PET and functional MRI (fMRI). The five chapters in the first section of the book focus on the use of different imaging techniques in CNA, including empirical findings and methodological issues.

The use of structural imaging in CNA is described by Raz in chapter 2, which reviews cross-sectional and longitudinal approaches in MRI studies of aging. These two approaches have different weaknesses: Cross-sectional data may be confounded by cohort effects, secular trends, and selection criteria differences, whereas longitudinal data may be contaminated by sampling bias caused by differences in mortality, morbidity, and mobility (the three *M*s of longitudinal research). These problems may be attenuated by combining both approaches.

The results of cross-sectional studies suggest that the volume of gray matter declines linearly with aging, whereas white matter increases during young age, plateaus during young adulthood and the middle age, and declines during old age (an inverted U function). The prefrontal cortex (PFC) is the region that shows greatest age-related differences, followed by the putamen and the hippocampus. There is substantial variability across studies because of differences in subject selection criteria, measurement methods, and definitions of regions of interest (ROIs). This kind of problem is attenuated by automated methods, such as voxel-based morphometry (VBM), but these methods have their own problems (e.g., sensitivity to fluctuations in MRI signal, partial-volume errors).

The number of published longitudinal studies increased during the last three years. However, most of these studies covered relatively short intervals (e.g., 1–2 years), with only a few spanning intervals up to 5 years. In these studies, the expansion of cerebral ventricles with age is nonlinear, with little change in young adults, but rapid change in older adults. Cortical regions show a linear decline with age, and consistent with cross-sectional data, it is more pronounced in PFC. In contrast, medial temporal lobe (MTL) regions show a nonlinear decline, possibly reflecting cumulative pathological effects. MTL atrophy may provide important information for the diagnosis of Alzheimer's disease (AD), which is associated with a faster atrophy rate in these regions. In general, the results of longitudinal studies tend to agree with those of cross-sectional studies, but when they disagree it is usually because the latter underestimates the magnitude of true change.

Chapter 2 reviews also a few recent studies using diffusion tensor and diffusion weighted imaging (DTI and DWI, respectively) to investigate age-related changes in white matter integrity. Finally, Raz considers modifiers of age-related neural decline, including those that bring bad news (hypertension), good news (aerobic exercise), and mixed news (hormone replacement therapy).

The use of resting functional imaging in CNA is described by Bäckman and Farde, whose chapter 3 reviews receptor imaging studies of dopamine (DA) function. There is abundant evidence that DA systems play an important role not only in motor functions, but also in higher order cognitive functions. For example, cognitive functions are often impaired in patients (with Huntington's or Parkinson's disease) and animals with DA deficits and can be modulated by DA agonists and antagonists. The role of DA in cognition is also supported by computational models and by ontogenetic and phylogenetic evidence.

There are two main DA systems, nigrostriatal and mesolimbic, and two families of DA receptors, D_1 and D_2. Located in the presynaptic terminal, the DA transporter (DAT) protein regulates the synaptic DA concentration. DA function can be measured in vivo using PET and SPECT (single-photon emission computed tomography) and special ligands. Different ligands have been developed for measuring D_1 and D_2 receptor binding, the synthesis of DA in presynaptic neurons, and the DAT. There is strong evidence of age-related losses in post- and presynaptic DA markers, which may reflect decreases in the number of neurons, the number of synapses per neurons, and/or the expression of receptor proteins in each neuron. D_1 and D_2 receptor binding declines from early adulthood at a rate of 4% to 10% per decade, and this decline is correlated with the decline of DAT, possibly reflecting a common causal mechanism.

From the point of view of CNA, the most important finding is that age-related DA decline is associated with age-related cognitive decline. Given the cognitive role of fronto-striatal loops, age-related striatal DA deficits could also account for age-related cognitive deficits associated with PFC dysfunction. Moreover, age-related DA binding deficits have been observed in PFC and in posterior cortical and hippocampal regions.

The use of activation imaging in CNA is described in chapter 4 by Fabiani and Gratton, chapter 5 by Gazzaley and D'Esposito, and chapter 6 by Rugg and Morcom. Chapter 4 by Fabiani and Gratton considers the advantages and disadvantages of different functional imaging methods, reviews the main findings of ERP studies of aging, and describes novel optical imaging methods and their application to aging research. Whereas hemodynamic imaging measures such as PET and fMRI have excellent spatial resolution but poor temporal resolution, electrophysiological measures such as ERPs have poor spatial resolution but excellent temporal resolution. Optical methods can provide good spatial and temporal resolution, but have limited penetration and a low signal-to-noise ratio.

Given that the strengths and weaknesses of these techniques are complementary, combining these methods is probably the best strategy to address their respective limitations. With their exquisite temporal resolution, ERPs are ideal to investigate one of the most prominent features of cognitive aging: the age-related slowing in information processing. Whereas in cognitive research the only direct measure of processing speed is reaction time (RT) and the duration of the various processing stages constituting the RT can only be inferred, ERPs provide a direct measure of these processing stages. For example, ERP studies have shown that age-related slowing affects the evaluation rather than the response stage, inconsistent with the notion of generalized slowing. ERPs can also assess the integrity of inhibitory processes by measuring neural responses to irrelevant and novel stimuli, and available results are consistent with the idea that aging impairs inhibitory control processes.

Optical imaging methods provide greater spatial resolution and yield both hemodynamic measures (near-infrared spectroscopy, NIRS) and neuronal measures (EROS) of brain activity. Optical imaging has already been applied to investigate cognitive aging and could provide critical information concerning the effect of aging on the coupling between neuronal function and hemodynamic responses. This effect is one of the main topics of chapter 5 by Gazzaley and D'Esposito.

Chapter 5 focuses on hemodynamic measures, particularly potential confounding factors in the interpretation of the blood oxygen level dependent (BOLD) signal in fMRI studies of cognitive aging. These studies generally attribute age-related changes in BOLD signal to age-related changes in neural activity, thereby assuming that the coupling between BOLD signal and neural activity is the same for young and older adults. However, this coupling may be altered by age-related changes in the neurovascular system and by comorbidities associated with aging. Age-related changes of the neurovascular system likely to affect the BOLD signal include changes in ultrastructure (e.g., sclerosis), resting cerebral blood flow (CBF), vascular reactivity, and cerebral metabolic rate of oxygen consumption. The BOLD signal may also be affected by comorbidities associated with aging, such as leukoariosis and small strokes, and by medications.

Given all of these potentially confounding factors, several fMRI studies directly investigated the coupling of BOLD signal and neural activity in young and older adults. These studies investigated simple sensory and motor tasks assumed to be unaffected by aging and measured the similarity of the hemodynamic response function (HRF) in younger and older adults. Overall, the results suggested that although the signal-to-noise ratio may be smaller in older adults, the overall shape, refractoriness, and summation of the HRF are similar in young and older adults. These findings are encouraging and support the feasibility of using fMRI to investigate age-related changes in neural activity. At the same time, differences in signal-to-noise ratio suggest caution when interpreting the results of studies in which the level of activity is generally weaker in the older group. Gazzaley and D'Esposito provide very useful recommendations on how to address potential confounds in imaging studies of cognitive aging.

Useful recommendations are also provided by Rugg and Morcom in chapter 6, which provides guidelines for avoiding potential confounds in fMRI and ERP studies of cognitive aging. After describing a series of general issues regarding brain activity measures and subject selection, Rugg and Morcom discuss a series of confounding variables when imaging the effects of aging on episodic memory encoding and retrieval. Regarding encoding, the authors emphasize the need for controlling study processing by using incidental study tasks that recruit qualitatively similar cognitive processes in young and older adults and measures of performance that allow the rejection of failed encoding trials. Another encoding-related issue is the potential confound between task-related and encoding-related activity, which can be partly addressed by analyzing encoding activity on the basis of later memory performance (subsequent memory paradigm). When using this method, it is also important to control for differences in the type of memory measured by the subsequent memory task (e.g., recollection vs. familiarity). Even if the type of memory measured is controlled, there is a chance that age effects may be confounded with differences in item memorability. The authors illustrate the control of these various encoding-related issues by describing an fMRI study of encoding and aging.

Regarding retrieval, Rugg and Morcom note that control over study processing is critical not only in encoding studies, but also in retrieval studies. They also emphasize the need for unconfounding the effects of aging on retrieval attempt and retrieval success; this can be accomplished by using event-related designs. Imaging studies should also make sure that young and older adults are using equivalent forms of memory, for example avoiding a greater implicit memory component in older adults. Finally, the authors underscore the need for distinguishing activations caused by age differences from activations caused by performance differences. If memory performance is lower in older adults, age-related activity will be confounded with differences in effort, differences in the proportion of guessing trials, differences in monitoring caused by lower confidence, and differences in the type of items retrieved (hard- vs. easy-to-retrieve items). Rugg and Morcom illustrate the control over some of these retrieval issues by describing an ERP study of retrieval and aging.

In summary, there is today a wealth of neuroimaging methods available to CNA researchers; these methods include structural imaging, resting functional imaging, and activation imaging techniques. These various imaging techniques have complementary strengths and weaknesses, which are partly a consequence of the level of neural phenomena they measure. As illustrated by figure 1.2, neural structure is a prerequisite for resting neural function, and resting neural function is a prerequisite for cognition-related neural activity. Thus, the three types of imaging measures provide access to different but interconnected aspects of the neural bases of cognitive aging. Structural imaging measures have the advantage being closer to the original neurobiological mechanisms of cognitive aging and being primarily sensitive to neurogenic effects (e.g., it is more likely that atrophy causes cognitive deficits than the other way around). On the other hand, structural imaging measures are only indirectly related to behavior and cannot easily identify compensatory changes in the aging brain.

The advantages and disadvantages of activation imaging are a virtual mirror image of those of structural imaging. Activation imaging measures are directly related

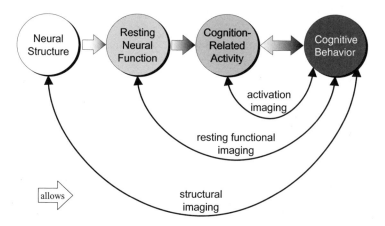

Figure 1.2. Imaging techniques link behavior to different kinds of neural phenomena.

behavior and are ideally suited for investigating reorganization of function and possible compensatory changes in the aging brain. On the other hand, activation imaging measures are removed from the original neurobiological mechanisms of aging and cannot easily distinguish between neurogenic and psychogenic effects (Do older adults perform differently because their brain activity is dissimilar, or is their brain activity dissimilar because they perform differently?). Finally, the strengths and weaknesses of resting functional imaging fall somewhere between those of structural and activation imaging. Thus, the three imaging techniques provide different and complementary information; hence, an exciting challenge for CNA researchers is to combine these techniques and integrate their findings to achieve a clearer picture of the neural correlates of cognitive aging.

Basic Cognitive Processes

There has been rapid growth in linkage between cognitive processes and neural function in older adults, and the integration of these domains has provided stunning insight into the dynamic interplay between neurobiological and cognitive processes across the life span. It is clear that, with age, frontal and hippocampal structures that are central structures to higher order cognition show a decrease in volume, particularly in frontal areas. It appears, however, that these decreases in volume do not map directly onto decreases in attention and memory function. Based on early findings in the CNA, it appears that, in response to these neural insults, the brain retains a certain amount of residual plasticity and may remodel or reorganize activation patterns and neural networks to partially mitigate the effects of the decreasing integrity of the aging brain. Thus, a key question in the CNA regards the extent that differences in neural activity between young and old reflect adaptive neural activations compensatory for decreased volume. Other questions focus on the nature of neural activations that underlie areas of preserved cognitive function with age and, as the field develops, the specific nature of remodeled neural networks. In this section, we include chapter reviews of visual perception and attention, working memory, longterm memory, and prospective memory.

   In chapter 7 by Madden, Whiting, and Huettel on visual perception and attention, the authors provide a comprehensive overview of age-related changes in sensory systems that alter the identification of objects and events in the environment. A thorough review of the behavioral literature on perception and attention is provided, documenting decreases in sensory function with age and the centrality of theories of decreased speed of processing in accounting for many age differences in perception and attention. This is followed by a discussion of age differences in attention, as well as the instances when some types of attentional processes remain age invariant. Then there is a review of the neurobiological underpinnings of attention and perception in young adults. This sets the stage for a detailed discussion of what has been learned about age differences in neural activation and pathways for object recognition and attention. The picture presented is one of decreased efficiency and less differentiation of neural pathways mediating object recognition and higher order visual processes, along with instances of compensatory activation. The authors discuss the importance of understanding the nature of age differences in the hemodynamic response, assessing criteria for evaluating whether data are supportive of compensatory recruitment with age, and the authors also suggest that there may be age differences in baseline neural activity that color the interpretation in subtraction analyses of attention and perception.

Chapter 8, authored by Reuter-Lorenz and Sylvester, reviews what is known about working memory and aging and the neural underpinnings of working memory as revealed by functional neuroimaging studies. The chapter is organized with an initial section on behavioral work that isolates the structure and function of working memory in young adults. This is followed by a review of the literature on aging, which suggests that although maintenance functions are relatively preserved in working memory with age, executive processing components exhibit substantial declines in late adulthood. From this point, the chapter addresses the neural circuitry of working memory with an initial focus on findings in young adults, followed by what is known about aging. There is a thorough discussion of the meaning of increased frontal activations in older adults and an evaluation of arguments suggesting that the increased activation is compensatory; there are suggestions for directions and questions that future research should address.

Park and Gutchess address in chapter 9 the topic of the cognitive neuroscience of long-term memory. They review findings from the behavioral literature that indicate that long-term memory declines with age, although there are also areas of preserved function, such as that observed for recognition of complex pictures. In this chapter, neuroimaging findings are organized around the hypothesis that increased activation in frontal areas with age during encoding of long-term memory is observed in response to decreased hippocampal activations. A lengthy section on the encoding of information addresses age differences in neural activations associated with intentional versus incidental memory, pictures compared to words, and differences in neural activations associated with remembered compared to forgotten items. Contextual manipulations, as well as neural activations associated with retrieval, are also studied, with evidence that patterns of neural differences with age are larger for encoding in comparison to retrieval manipulations. The final section of the chapter examines patterns of neural activations as a function of individual differences, such as for high versus low performers. The results from these studies do not provide convincing evidence at this time regarding the compensatory value of increased frontal activations with age. The authors nevertheless conclude that the study of individual differences and aging has the potential to resolve arguments about the compensatory value of increased neural activation in older adults.

The final chapter in this section is authored by West and focuses on neural activations associated with prospective memory, that is, remembering to carry out planned intentions or actions. There is a large body of behavioral literature on age differences in prospective memory, and important distinctions are made between event-based and time-based prospective memories. Models of prospective memory are compared in chapter 10, including the multicomponent model, the automatic associative model, and the controlled attention model. Functional imaging and ERP studies have revealed a distributed network of structures that support prospective memory, including the frontal and parietal lobes, as well as the thalamus and hippocampus. Nevertheless, research in this domain is limited; at the time of this writing, there were only two functional imaging studies and three ERP studies on prospective memory. Decreases in prospective memory with age are isolated because of inefficient encoding of intentions and the inability to maintain those intentions over time, with these functions residing primarily in the frontal lobes, brain structures that show decreased integrity in late adulthood.

The four chapters in this section provide a complete overview of behavioral findings on age differences in perception and attention, working memory, long-term memory, and prospective memory, along with a thorough integration of the neural mechanisms governing these fundamental aspects of cognitive function. Perhaps the single most consistent theme throughout these chapters is the meaning of increased neural activation in frontal areas with age, along with the great promise that larger studies that examine individual differences hold for resolving this issue. The chapters in this section represent the most complete integration of behavioral data with neuroscientific findings on basic cognitive processes and aging that presently exist.

Clinical and Applied Issues

As noted at the beginning of this chapter, the main goal of CNA is to link the effects of aging on cognition to the effects of aging on the brain. If the knowledge generated by studies within this field can help us understand the basis for the cognitive problems that often accompany normal aging as well as pathological forms of aging (notably Alzheimer's disease), then it may in turn have relevance for attempts at developing means by which age-related cognitive deficits can be compensated for. In particular, it is possible that knowledge about age-related brain changes can inform us about the constraints we may be facing in trying to boost the memory performance of older and demented adults. In turn, this could put focus on the avenues by which various forms of compensation are most likely to have an impact. The chapters in the section on clinical and applied issues speak to these significant issues.

Chapter 11 by Buckner begins by asking the fundamental question of why there is so much variability in the age of onset of prominent cognitive decline. Buckner presents a thought-stimulating discussion of possible answers to this question. The discussion is organized around three basic principles. The first principle holds that multiple, co-occurring causal mechanisms contribute to cognitive decline in aging. The second principle states that variability exists in the expression of causal mechanisms across individuals and in the responses of individuals to them. This principle is of critical importance to various attempts at supporting impaired cognition as it stresses the role of the active mechanisms of compensation and responses that individuals adopt. The third and final principle is that causal mechanisms should be studied within integrative theories that span different levels of organization, from the genetic to the behavioral. This final principle not only is relevant in this particular section, but also is closely related to issues discussed in the following section on CNA models.

In chapter 12, Grady presents a review of functional neuroimaging studies of memory in young adults, older adults, and patients with dementia. A special focus is on changes involving the PFC and the hippocampus as these areas have been suggested as particularly vulnerable to aging, and much of the neuroimaging literature on memory has indeed focused on these particular regions. The first review section is concerned with studies using the traditional univariate subtraction approach to identify brain regions in which age-related differences in the magnitude of activation changes exist.

In the next section of chapter 12, Grady introduces another important approach to the analysis of functional neuroimaging data: connectivity analyses. One form of connectivity analysis is referred to as *functional connectivity* and involves assessing how activity in a given region covaries with activity in other areas of the brain during a task. Another form of connectivity analysis, *effective connectivity*, models the way brain areas influence one another and tests whether the model fits the data at hand. It is illustrated in the chapter how connectivity analyses can be useful in identifying between-group differences not seen with univariate approaches.

Nyberg is concerned in chapter 13 with the topic of *plasticity*, defined as within-person variability designating the potential for various forms of behavior or development. A selective literature review is presented to address four related issues: (1) the potential for plasticity in older age, (2) limitations of plasticity in older age, (3) cognitive explanations of reduced plasticity in older age, and (4) neuroanatomical correlates of reduced plasticity in older age. Based on this review, the chapter concludes that there is indeed substantial potential for plasticity in older age. Nonetheless, there is much evidence to suggest that younger adults benefit more from training than older adults, and the reduction in plasticity in older age seems to reflect both a processing and a production deficit. Imaging studies provide some indication that the processing deficit can be linked to age-related changes in the frontal cortex, whereas the neural correlates of production deficits seem to be task specific. It is tentatively proposed that training aimed at overcoming production deficits in specific cognitive domains is the most fruitful strategy for attempts at improving the performance of older adults.

Taken together, the chapters in this and other sections demonstrate that today there is some knowledge about the basis for impaired cognitive performance in older age. The chapters also suggest that future CNA studies, using imaging techniques as well as other methodological approaches, can yield additional important information. The transformation of knowledge about brain–cognition relations in adulthood and aging into various compensatory actions for age-associated cognitive impairment is still a relatively little examined area, but an area that holds promise for the future.

Models in Cognitive Neuroscience of Aging

Perhaps the most salient aspect of the discipline of CNA is its integrative nature (see figure 1.1). That is, we strongly emphasize the need to consider changes at multiple levels of examination (see also chapter 11). Naturally, in a specific study, it is not realistic to think that all the relevant theoretical and methodological aspects of a problem can be considered. Instead, cross-level integration will typically be realized in efforts to link related findings from multiple studies. The section on CNA models presents two such efforts.

Chapter 14 by Daselaar and Cabeza relates recent behavioral and neuroimaging findings on hemispheric lateralization and aging to general ideas about hemispheric organization. The chapter has three sections. In the first section, anatomical differences between the left and right hemispheres and various accounts of hemispheric specialization are introduced together with three models of hemispheric interaction (insulation, inhibition, and cooperation). In the second section, two models of age-related changes in hemispheric lateralization are presented: the right hemi-aging model and the hemispheric asymmetry reduction in older adults (HAROLD) model. The former model states that the right hemisphere is most sensitive to the harmful effects of aging, resulting in a greater dependence on left hemisphere processing in elderly adults. By contrast, the HAROLD model states that elderly are more likely to rely on both hemispheres in conditions in which unilateral recruitment is sufficient in young adults. In the final section, three different accounts of age-related asymmetry reductions are discussed in relation to the different hemispheric interaction models addressed at the beginning of chapter 14 (dedifferentiation, competition, and compensation).

Chapter 15 by Li is concerned with neurocomputational approaches that examine the relation between cognitive aging deficits and aging-related attenuation of neuromodulation that can have effects on neural representations and information transfer within and between cortical regions. A selective review of recent computational approaches to neuromodulation and their applications in cognitive aging research is presented. It is proposed that cognitive aging may be related to declines in dopaminergic modulation in the PFC and in various subcortical regions. A cross-level integrative theoretical link is highlighted: Deficient neuromodulation leads to noisy neural information processing, which in turn might result in less-distinctive cortical representation and various subsequent behavioral manifestations of commonly observed cognitive aging deficits. It is emphasized that the brain is an open system, and life span cognitive development is a dynamic, cumulative process that shapes the neurocognitive representations of ongoing interactions with the environment and sociocultural contexts through experiences. From this position, it follows that not only feed-upward effects from neural mechanisms to cognition and behavior must be considered, but also downward contextual and experiential influences on neurocognitive processing.

These chapters jointly span the levels from neurochemical modulation to evolutionary and cultural influences. It may strike the reader as an overwhelming task to consider data from such a multitude of sources. However, given the complexity of the substantive issues, a full understanding of how brain–cognition relationships are affected by aging will most likely require that (directly or indirectly) happenings at the molecular level are interrelated with changes that take place at the societal level.

Conclusion

This volume is designed as a handbook to represent state-of-the-art knowledge about the CNA. Leading researchers have provided detailed and thoughtful consideration of the theoretical, methodological, and empirical knowledge and challenges facing the emerging discipline of the CNA. It is likely that progress in this field will be rapid and, 5 years from now when a new edition of this volume will likely be available, that many of the puzzles raised in this book will have been solved. We feel relatively certain that a central question raised in this volume—whether increased frontal activations in older adults that occur across a range of demanding cognitive tasks are compensatory—will have been answered. The theoretical and methodological tools to address the compensation issue empirically are available. All that remains is for a large, carefully controlled and executed study to be conducted to address this issue across fundamental domains of attention, working memory, and long-term memory.

Even as we see that a deeper understanding of compensatory neural mechanisms is within reach, we recognize as well that unlocking this puzzle will lead to many new questions. We expect that new techniques and methodologies will evolve at a rapid rate, resulting in a new set of issues and challenges facing researchers in the CNA. If we were to guess, we would expect that studies of tensor imaging, connectivity analyses, and transcranial magnetic stimulation (TMS) will play a more prominent role in the next volume than in this present version. We also believe that imaging techniques will provide a gold standard for evaluating the efficacy of cognitive interventions, both pharmacological and behavioral. Moreover, we expect that the study of individual differences with age will move beyond behavioral measures of performance into the dynamic field of neurogenetics, resulting in an important new subdiscipline within the CNA.

In closing, we have high hopes for the promise of the CNA to provide the framework necessary for understanding both neurological health and disease as it unfolds across the human life span. We are hopeful that the research and ideas contained in this volume serve as an important springboard for better understanding of the aging mind, as well as provide the information needed to further the maintenance of health and vitality into the later years of our older citizens.

I

IMAGING MEASURES

2

The Aging Brain Observed in Vivo
Differential Changes and Their Modifiers

Naftali Raz

Thoughts of a dry brain in a dry season.

—T. S. Eliot, *Gerontion*

Aging is a manifold of universal biological processes that, with passage of time, profoundly alter anatomy, neurochemistry, and physiology of all organisms. Although no organs or systems escape the impact of aging, its effects on the central nervous system (CNS) are especially dramatic. The brains of older people can be distinguished from those of their younger peers in many ways and on many levels, from mitochondria to gross anatomy. So numerous and diverse are the changes that encompassing the totality of brain aging in one survey would be too daunting an objective. Thus, for comprehensive up-to-date accounts of neurobiology and neurophysiology of aging as well as surveys of the classic postmortem findings the reader is directed to readily available recent reviews (Arendt, 2001; Rosenzweig & Barnes, 2003; Uylings & de Brabander, 2002; Kemper, 1994; Giannakopoulos et al., 1997). On the other pole of the cell-to-thought continuum, several concise appraisals of functional brain aging have appeared (Cabeza, 2002; Reuter-Lorenz, 2002; Grady, 2000), and those accounts are augmented by several chapters of this volume.

My intent, therefore, is to concentrate on a relatively narrow, albeit rapidly developing, field: *in vivo* neuroanatomy of aging. Even in that narrow domain, it would be too ambitious (and somewhat redundant) to cover all the literature from the inception of *in vivo* imaging of the aging brain. Therefore, this review should be read in conjunction with the surveys of brain aging available in the extant literature. In particular, this chapter is intended as an update of a previous review (Raz, 2000) in which age-related brain differences were surveyed in the context of cognitive aging.

Cross-Sectional Studies

When the advent of magnetic resonance imaging (MRI) provided an opportunity to observe age-related differences in the human brains *in vivo*, the universal signs of brain aging became clearly evident. However, recognition of profound gross anatomical discrepancies between the brains of ostensibly healthy older people and those of their younger peers was accompanied by a realization of the individual differences within the narrow age range. A comparison of three brains in figure 2.1 is instructive. Although some signs of the advanced age, such as white matter hyperintensities, enlarged ventricles, and expanded sulci, are clearly visible, so are the individual

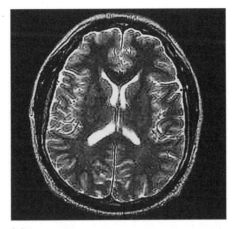

(a)

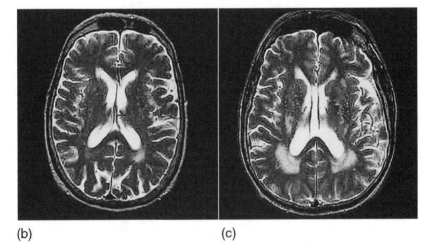

(b)   (c)

Figure 2.1. Age-related and individual differences in white matter hyperintensities (WMH) in *a*, 24-year old; *b*, 80-year-old; *c*, and 79-year-old men.

differences between two brains that belong to cognitively intact individuals of the same age.

It is clear that research on brain aging cannot be confined to identification of the qualitative age-related differences and establishment of diagnostic categories. As the continuum of aging is expressed in a continuum of biological changes, research on brain aging must be quantitative in its methods and noncategorical in interpretation of its findings. Of course, continuity of age-related changes does not imply linearity. Change can present itself as linear, accelerating, decelerating, or threshold phenomena of almost categorical steepness. Establishing the specific trajectories of age-related changes in specific systems and structures as well as gauging their dependence on pathological age-associated processes and their implications for cognitive functions is the goal of brain exploration through neuroimaging.

White versus Gray Matter

The question of differential effects of age on white versus gray matter was raised by earlier postmortem investigations; Miller, Alston, and Corsellis (1980) revealed contrasting age trends for white and gray matter. Regression of gray matter volume on age suggested a steady decline between the 20s and the 50s, with a later plateau of the age trend, whereas the volume of the white matter increased between young adulthood and middle age only to evidence a decline in older brains. On the basis of those findings, Miller and Corsellis concluded in 1977 that the white matter is more vulnerable to aging than the gray matter.

The issue of differential gray–white vulnerability was revisited in several *in vivo* investigations. In comprehensive life span studies (Pfefferbaum et al., 1994; Sullivan et al., 2004; Courchesne et al., 2000), the investigators examined subjects from infancy to 70–80 years of age. They found that, although gray matter might decline in a linear fashion from childhood to old age, white matter followed a different trajectory. In white matter volume, the initial linear increase up to the early 20s is followed by a plateau stretching into the 60s, with a linear declining branch of the curve appearing in the oldest old. A similar pattern of results was observed in a sample of subjects ranging in age between 14 and 77 years (Liu et al., 2003), although the peak of white matter volume in that study was estimated at about 38 years of age.

In a study specifically devoted to assessment of age effects on prefrontal and temporal regions (Bartzokis et al., 2001), the investigators showed a similar pattern of differential white versus gray matter aging within a narrower age range (19–76 years). A linear decline in neocortical gray volume (more in prefrontal than in temporal) was contrasted to an inverted U relationship between the white matter volume in both regions. A somewhat different nonlinear trajectory of age-related differences in the white matter volume was suggested in another sample with an age range between 30 and 99 years (Jernigan et al., 2001). Notably, approximately the same age for the beginning of white matter volume decline (mid-40s) was estimated in all samples that revealed nonlinear trends.

An inverted U pattern of age differences in white matter volume was replicated with automated voxel-based morphometry (VBM) methods of analysis, although only in female participants (Good et al., 2001). It must be noted, however, that in that carefully screened large sample only about 5% of the participants were older than 60 years. A substantial age-related shrinkage of the gray matter volume was noted in the same sample (Good et al., 2001). In another VBM study, a significant age-related shrinkage of the gray matter was accompanied by a lack of difference in the bulk of the white matter (Van Laere & Dierckx, 2001). Finally, a study using voxel-based automated estimation of tissue density revealed a linear decline in gray matter density from the teens into the late 60s, with flattening of the decline curve in the range 70–90 years (Sowell et al., 2003). By contrast, that investigation revealed an inverted U curve of age-related dependence of the white matter density, with rapid increase during adolescence and young adulthood, a plateau during middle age, and a precipitous decline during the senium.

Thus, because of variations in the shape of age–volume relations among the regions, studies that examine samples restricted to older adults (over 60 years of age) may be likely to find trends toward significant shrinkage of the white matter along with relative stability of the gray matter volume. Apparently, the wider the age range and the greater the proportion of younger adults included in the sample, the higher the chances for the study to reveal only very weak association between age and white matter volume. For example, age-related differences in prefrontal volume are uniformly strong across the adult age span (Raz et al., 1997; Raz, Gunning-Dixon, et al., 2004a; Jernigan et al., 2001). However, when age range is curtailed and restricted to the last decades of the normal life span, the estimated declines in the prefrontal cortical volume do not differ from those in the other neocortical regions (Resnick et al., 2000) or may even show smaller declines (Salat et al., 1999). In sum, it appears that when a sufficiently large sample with a wide age range is employed, the pattern of age-related differences observed in vivo conforms to the postmortem findings (Miller, Alston, & Corsallis, 1980).

Why is the inverted U or inverted J pattern not observed in all studies? Several reasons can be offered. First, nonlinearity of volume relationship with age is not easy to prove because the logic of statistical hypothesis testing requires proceeding in a hierarchical fashion, with the null hypothesis for the linear slope rejected first, and all higher order components tested as an addition above and beyond the linear one. For example, no significant nonlinearity in age-related differences in the white matter volumes was observed in two relatively large independent samples (Raz et al., 1997; Raz, Gunning-Dixon, et al., 2004a), yet a smaller sample of very healthy adults followed up for five years exhibited an inverted U pattern in the relationship between the prefrontal white matter volume and age (Raz et al., submitted).

Another possibility is that inclusion of older participants with cardiovascular disease and risk factors (e.g., hypertension) increases the likelihood of finding age-related declines in white matter volume. Samples that include older subjects with cardiovascular disease tend to show larger age-related differences in white matter volumes (Guttmann et al., 1998; Resnick et al., 2000; Jernigan et al., 2001; Salat et al., 1999). When a subsample of "superhealthy" older persons is considered, the correlations between age and white matter volume tend to drop (Resnick et al., 2000). Comparison of well-matched groups of otherwise healthy adults differing only in the presence of a diagnosis of hypertension revealed that prefrontal volumes are the only among those of seven examined regions to exhibit significant shrinkage in the hypertensive group (Raz, Rodrigue, & Acker, 2003a). Notably, in case of hypertension, unlike in normal aging, the prefrontal white matter is as vulnerable as the prefrontal cortex (PFC). Nonlinearity of white matter aging is probably not unique because a nonlinear pattern of age-related differences has been observed in other regions. Relative plateau in the young age group and age-related acceleration in the older subjects was observed for the hippocampal volume in some samples (Jernigan et al., 2001; Raz, Gunning-Dixon, et al., 2004a), with the estimated volume declines becoming apparent, as in the white matter, in the mid-40s.

Regional Variations in the Magnitude of Age-Related Differences

Because of the greater number of anatomically diverse components involved, the landscape of age-related differences is more complicated than a contrast between the white and the gray matter discussed above. In addition to the differences between age trends in gray and white matter volume, strength and shape of age–volume associations varies among the brain regions; see Raz (2000) for a review. Studies published since that review (tables 2.1–2.4) are in general consistent with the reported pattern of differential aging. However, substantial variability is apparent in the magnitude of age differences across the brain regions and across studies, as illustrated in a box-and-whisker plot in figure 2.2.

The observed variability across studies is not surprising and most likely stems from the variability in criteria for subject selection, measurement approaches, and definitions of the regions of interest (ROIs) that characterize this literature. However, when those variations are controlled, age-related differences appear reasonably stable. Stability of the differential aging pattern was examined by comparing the magnitude of the negative age–volume associations observed in two samples ($N = 148$ and 200, respectively) drawn from the same population (Raz et al., 1997; Raz, Gunning-Dixon, et al., 2004a). In those samples, the subjects were recruited from the same population according to the same criteria. Although the images were acquired on the same scanner, and regional volumes were measured according to the same set of rules (with some notable exceptions), the software, measurement equipment, and operators who performed the tracing varied between the studies. The results of that study demonstrated that the pattern of regional age-related differences in brain volumes is a consistent and replicable phenomenon. Of 13 brain regions examined in both samples, 12 showed no significant differences in age effect size. The only region to evidence a significantly different age effect was the precentral gyrus, which was defined in the second study (Raz, Gunning-Dixon, et al., 2004a) by an altered set of rules. The magnitude of age differences was particularly stable in the prefrontal, fusiform, and visual cortices. Notably, the observed stability of age differences contrasts to the lack thereof in sex differences and hemispheric asymmetry.

This comparison showed that manual volumetry allows reliable estimation of regional brain volumes by specific landmark-based rules. In that respect, it is an in vivo extension of traditional anatomic methods. However, manual volumetric measures have to be executed reliably by human operators. When an ROI cannot be reliably

Table 2.3 Age-Related Differences in the Volume of the Basal Ganglia and the Thalamus

Study/Author/Year	Age range (years)	N	Structure			
			Caudate	Putamen	Globus Pallidus	Thalamus
Studies reviewed in Raz, 2000		46	−.48	−.41	−.22	−.17
Van Der Werf et al., 2001	21–82	57				−.28
Jernigan et al., 2001	30–99	78	−.35			−.13
Sullivan et al., 2003	23–85	100				−.56
Raz et al., 2003, unpublished data	18–81	200	−.29	−.41	−.14	
Xu et al., 2000	30–79	331				−.30
Median		46	−.36	−.43	−.19	−.26

defined, it cannot be measured. In addition, only a few ROIs can be measured within reasonable time limits. Therefore, manual studies examine a limited number of ROIs selected on the basis of hypotheses generated from the extant literature.

There are several potential sources of variations among the volumetric studies: image acquisition with respect to the natural orientation of specific ROIs, segmentation and pixel counting software, degree of operator skill, and definition and demarcation of the ROIs (Jack et al., 1995). Definitions of ROIs are usually aimed at maximizing both anatomical validity and reliability of measurement, and the resulting rules reflect a compromise between those demands. For instance, in most studies the term *caudate nucleus* refers to the head of that structure and covers less than its actual anatomical totality. In a similar fashion, definitions of the hippocampus (HC), probably the most frequently measured structure in the brain, vary mostly regarding

Table 2.4 Regional Volumes: Cerebellum and Pons

Study/Author/Year	Age range (years)	N	Effect Size (r)							
			Hemispheres			Vermis				
			Total	Gray	White	Total	Superior	DFT	Posterior	Pons
Studies reviewed in Raz (2000), median			−.29			−.34	−.31	−.40	−.35	
Rhyu et al., 1999	20–79	124	−.02			−.07				
Sullivan et al., 2000	23–72	61	−.17	−.43	.10	−.41	−.44	−.34	−.19	
Jernigan et al., 2001	30–99	78	−.52	−.56	−.49					
Xu et al., 2000	30–79	331	−.15							
Sullivan et al., 2003	20–85	100								.08
Liu et al., 2003	14–77	90	−.37							
Pfefferbaum et al., 1998	22–65									−.10
Raz et al., 2001	18–81	190	−.32			−.32	−.24	−.29	−.25	−.01
Median		64	−.30			−.33	−.31	−.39	−.33	.07

Note. DFT, declive-folium-tuber.

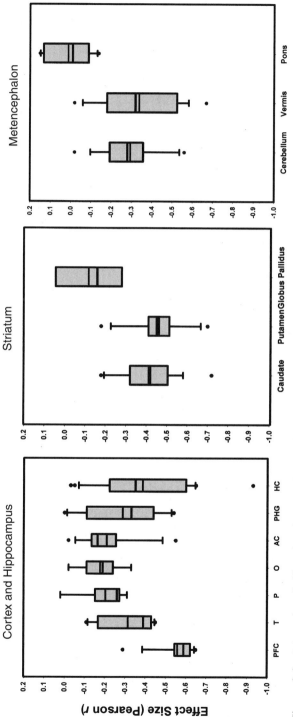

Figure 2.2. A box plot of effect sizes for age-related differences in regional brain volumes. The magnitude of the effect is expressed as Pearson *r* between age and volume. AC, anterior cingulate cortex; HC, hippocampus; O, occipital cortex; P, parietal cortex; PFC, prefrontal cortex; PHG, parahippocampal gyrus; T, temporal cortex. Thin horizontal line in the box designates the median, and the thick horizontal line is the mean effect size for a given region of interest. The bars indicate the interquartile range.

how much of its most anterior part is included, although sometimes the head of the HC is also excluded (see Jack et al., 1995, for a methodological review).

A decision to begin measurement at the most anterior slice on which the HC appears separated from the amygdala entails a possibility of bias in favor of the older subjects, whose enlarged inferior horn of the ventricles may facilitate drawing a distinction on a more rostral slice than in younger subjects. That may potentially introduce bias in measuring a cognitively valuable target (i.e., the head of the HC) (Hackert et al., 2002; Sullivan et al., 1995). Because the head is an HC part with the largest cross section, even a difference in one slice may introduce a significant bias. Using the alveus, a narrow but distinct high-intensity area on T1-weighted images, may improve the demarcation. A possible alternative may be to use a more stable (although not entirely age-invariant) landmark, such as the mammillary bodies (e.g., Raz, Gunning-Dixon, et al., 2004a). Yet another alternative may be to use additional projections for HC identification, as indeed is done in some studies (e.g., Moffat et al., 2000). Such a procedure, however, prolongs the time of tracing and does not add to reliability of the volume estimation. Although a well-reasoned and concise account of methodological differences is available (Jack et al., 1995), the empirical evaluation of the described alternatives may be useful.

The greatest discrepancies are found in the definition of the cortical regions with the region demarcation rules ranging from the most coarse (grossly defined lobes; e.g., Lim et al., 1992), to restricted slabs that include parts of several gyri (Raz et al., 1997; Raz, Gunning-Dixon, et al., 2004a), to measurements of specific gyri (e.g., Convit et al., 2001). Because of discrepancy between age differences in gray and white matter, lumping white and gray matter together in an ROI definition may reduce the estimated age effect, hence *caveat lector*, let the reader beware. Examine the definitions of the regions that bear common anatomical labels but may represent slightly (and in some cases not so slightly) different entities. Nonetheless, reviews of the extant literature indicated a reasonably good correspondence among the volumes of the HC (Pruessner et al., 2001) and the cerebellum (Courchesne, Townsend, & Saitoh, 1994) across samples and methods.

The magnitude of regional age differences may vary within grossly defined lobar regions. Within the PFC, there may be a differential effect of age on specific subdivisions. Raz et al. (1997) found age differences in the dorsolateral PFC exceeded those in the orbital frontal regions. In the Xu et al. (2000) study, the estimated age effect on the posterior and lateral frontal regions was moderate ($r = -.32$), whereas the age differences in the anterior and orbital regions were small ($r = -.15$). Bartzokis et al. (2001), who observed differentially stronger age–volume correlations in the PFC, also sampled mostly mid-to-posterior lateral regions of the PFC. Tisserand and colleagues (2002) found stronger age–volume correlations in the dorsolateral, inferior, and lateral-orbital frontal regions (range from $r = -.62$ to $r = -.66$) than in the frontal pole ($-.42$). Middle temporal regions in the Xu et al. (2000) study exhibited larger differences for age than the rest of the temporal lobe.

Thus, although the general trends of differential aging may be reliable, there is little consistency in observed differences within regions. Unless there is an agreement among the research regarding definitions and measurement rules for specific brain regions, the observed variability among the studies is likely to persist. Variability of that sort may be not an entirely negative feature of structural brain aging literature because it is unclear how well localized the true age-related changes are. If the actual change in area 46, for example, is the same as in area 9, then by virtue of averaging out the random error, the measurement of a larger region that encompasses both areas provides a closer approximation to reality than more precise (but less-reliable) measures of specific regions.

Automated voxel-based methods (Ashburner et al., 2003) were designed to overcome the outlined limitations of manual methods. Although not entirely automated and by no means assumption free (Bookstein, 2001), voxel-based techniques are well suited for hypothesis-free data mining from the vast data sets generated by MRI. Computerized brain volumetry develops rapidly, and a wide variety of approaches and software tools have been generated to date. However, the core idea is the same. Automatically segmenting the acquired volume into gray matter, white matter, and cerebrospinal fluid (CSF); registration of the segmented images to a standard template; and smoothing-filtering to create normally distributed fields of gray scale values. After those manipulations, the gray scale intensity value of every voxel is examined and used as the dependent variable in a group comparison or age regression models. In some approaches, deformation field algorithms are used to create the voxel maps, and the deformation field variables are used in voxel-by-voxel analysis (Fox & Freeborough, 1997). The assumption is that an altered signal reflects a difference in tissue density, which can be used to declare the ROI and to estimate its volume.

The VBM methods have several obvious advantages. First, they are perfectly reliable; that is, computer-based estimates of the regional tissue density and regional volumes can be repeated an unlimited number of times by any operator who is trained in executing the program and on any platform on which the software runs. Second, in one sweep a whole-brain map of local densities and volumes can be generated. Third, no specific hypotheses about the relations between given brain locales and the independent variables are made. Fourth, the structural density maps can be coregistered with functional images acquired on the same subjects and analyzed with the same software.

Like any other technique, however, VBM is no panacea, and it has several significant limitations. First, because it is "assumption (i.e., hypothesis) free," it is prone to spurious findings and works better as an exploratory tool rather than as an instrument for testing specific hypotheses. The claims of being assumption free have been criticized by Bookstein (2001) on statistical grounds.

Second, in analyzing the voxel-by-voxel differences in signal intensity, the technique dispenses with several advantages of human observers. The algorithm makes decisions exclusively on the basis of local information without the benefit of "top-down" knowledge that guides and informs perceptual–motor behavior of human tracers. As such, it is susceptible to meaningless fluctuations of signal intensity that may present a distorted view of some brain structures. The smaller and the more irregular the structures are, the greater is the likelihood of misrepresentation.

Third, it must be noted that, although a typical VBM analysis starts with acquisition of a high-resolution volume image (ideally with an isotropic voxel), its resolution is significantly (almost 10-fold) degraded by filtering and template matching.

Fourth, the templates employed by most of the VBM programs were derived from young brains and may result in underestimation of gray matter volume (Panzer et al., 2003).

Fifth (and this is not specific to VBM, but is a common limitation of all automatic segmentation methods), at the segmentation stage, errors arise from partial voluming. More important is the fact that a substantial amount of filtering and smoothing inherent in automated methods may introduce disproportionately greater inaccuracies in volumes of small structures than in the global measures (Scahill et al., 2002). Indeed, a direct comparison of VBM methods with manual volumetry in an investigation of age-related differences revealed notable discrepancies (along with some significant areas of agreement) between the two classes of methods (Tisserand et al., 2002). Thus, the VBM approach is not likely to replace manual volumetry, although it may prove to be a valuable source of hypotheses generated with relative ease and in a reasonably short time.

Although VBM studies of brain aging are still relatively scarce, they already have produced several important findings. The VBM studies revealed significant age-related differences in the superior parietal (Good et al., 2001; Ohnishi et al., 2001); inferior parietal (Good et al., 2001; Van Laere & Dierckx, 2001; Ohnishi et al., 2001); inferior frontal (Van Laere & Dierckx, 2001; Ohnishi et al., 2001; Tisserand et al., 2002); orbital frontal (Tisserand et al., 2002); middle frontal (Good et al., 2001; Ohnishi et al., 2001; Tisserand et al., 2002); straight (Ohnishi et al., 2001); superior temporal (Good et al., 2001; Van Laere & Dierckx, 2001; Ohnishi et al., 2001); and anterior cingulate (Good et al., 2001; Ohnishi et al., 2001; Tisserand et al., 2002); gyri, insula (Good et al., 2001; Ohnishi et al., 2001); cerebellum (Good et al., 2001; Van Laere & Dierckx, 2001); as well as perirolandic territories (Good et al., 2001). Thus, in overall agreement with the results of volumetric investigations, the VBM findings support the notion that association cortices are more vulnerable to aging than are primary sensory regions.

There are, however, some significant discrepancies between volumetric and VBM studies of the aging brain. The major point of disagreement is in the findings pertaining to the anterior cingulate gyrus. Age differences in density consistently found in that region stand in contrast to its relative volumetric stability (Raz, 2000). Interestingly, that particular region was noted as an example of VBM sensitivity to errors of registration and spatial deformation by the neighboring structures (e.g., corpus callosum) in critical comments on VBM validity (Bookstein, 2001). Thus, in volumetric measures of a relatively small structure, age-related variance may be overwhelmed by significant individual differences, whereas VBM errors of registration may exaggerate the effect of age. Therefore, the true magnitude of age effects on the anterior cingulate may lie somewhere between those estimates and amount to a moderate effect.

All things considered, the extant cross-sectional studies of normal aging (volumetric and voxel based alike) supported a conclusion that aging is associated with differential effects on specific cortical and subcortical structures. The question, however, is whether and to what extent cross-sectional estimates reflect the real *change*. Until recently, the understanding of human brain aging was based almost entirely on cross-sectional studies and, among those, on a substantial subset of investigations in which only extreme age groups were examined. Such approaches have several advantages: They allow relatively rapid, cheap, and logistically manageable tests of hypotheses about age differences in brain structure and its links to cognition. For instance, in a span of several months, a cross-sectional study can cover an age range of six or seven decades and examine multiple measurement domains. However, the convenience of a cross-sectional approach comes at a price. Cohort effects and secular trends may confound the cross-sectional findings, an extreme group approach leaves researchers in the dark with respect to true age trajectories, and in partitioning of the variance, individual differences compete with age-related variability and may undermine the true age effects. Moreover, when healthy aging is concerned, cross-sectional studies posit a conundrum. Although older participants are screened for age-related diseases and recruited into the studies, their younger counterparts are admitted more or less on the basis of their youth. Because it may take years for most age-related conditions to develop, the younger component of the sample may actually be less healthy than its more explicitly selected older part. On the other hand, older participants, no matter how healthy at the time of testing, may harbor preclinical forms of debilitating conditions to be expressed shortly after completion of the study.

An obvious answer to the failings of cross-sectional studies is a longitudinal approach. In longitudinal studies, subjects serve as their own comparison cases, and the confounding influence of the individual differences, cohort effects, and secular trends is controlled. Unfortunately, longitudinal designs harbor their own ghosts, which are just as difficult to exorcise as their cross-sectional counterparts. For one, the aging and mortality of the investigators limit the calendar period that can be observed longitudinally. Even when the baton can be safely passed from one generation of scientists to another, the technological advances in measurements erect obstacles in the path of a reliable follow-up. Subjects' attrition is a serious concern, and even the most diligently followed samples lose more than half of their participants between the measures because of mortality, morbidity, and mobility—the three *M*s of longitudinal research. To make matters worse, each of the three *M* factors affects specific age segments differentially, with the older subjects dying, the middle aged getting sick, and the young moving out of researchers' reach. Even the most stringently screened cross-sectional samples are less selective than the longitudinal ones. Participants in longitudinal studies are healthier, more intelligent, and less depressed than those who drop out (McArdle et al., 1991; Lindenberger, Singer, & Baltes, 2002). Thus, both types of investigations—cross-sectional and longitudinal—are necessary for developing a more lucid view of brain aging, and the combination of the two in a cross-sequential design is probably the most desirable approach of all (Schaie & Strother, 1968).

Certain methodological limitations are common to longitudinal and cross-sectional studies alike. When the objective is to study healthy aging, highly selected nonrepresentative samples are employed. The participants are well educated and highly motivated healthy volunteers who represent a relatively small fraction of the general population of older adults, and people who suffer from common age-related diseases are usually excluded from the analysis. The last is a potential source of differences among the samples. No health screening—by a questionnaire, an interview, or actual medical tests and examinations—is perfect. Samples are likely to vary in the proportion of subjects who suffer from prodromal conditions that are clinically silent, but neuroanatomically and neurophysiologically influential. Moreover, there is no consensus among the researchers regarding specific conditions to be excluded from studies of healthy aging. Although virtually all studies screen out patients with identifiable strokes, only some samples exclude subjects with depressed mood or history of depression, diabetes, and cardiovascular disease. Diabetes is associated with significant increase in white matter abnormalities (Taylor et al., 2003), and even relatively mild forms of cardiovascular conditions are associated with significant (although circumscribed) neuroanatomical differences (Raz, Rodrigue, & Acker, 2003a). Thus, the presence of diabetic or hypertensive participants in the sample may produce a more negative picture of brain aging than is really warranted.

One of the most significant methodological problems in MRI volumetry, manual and semiautomatic alike, is the lack of clear understanding of the relationship between the appearance of the brain on the image and its actual anatomy. With all its exquisitely realistic anatomical appearance, MRI is just a computerized map of local properties of the brain water. The apparent density and volume in any given region depend on the signal intensity, which is a relatively simple exponential function of two relaxation time constants. These time constants characterize two processes: spin–lattice relaxation ($T1$) and spin–spin relaxation ($T2$). Any alterations in the system of physical and chemical factors that affect concentration and motility of brain water inevitably affect the appearance of MRI-rendered anatomy. Thus, local increases in free water, loss of large molecules that restrict water motility (e.g., myelin), or accumulation of solids such as iron and calcium change the relaxation times and consequently modify the value of pixels in the computer-reconstructed brain image. The validity of measures of age differences in brain volumes or density is threatened by age-related changes in $T1$ and $T2$ relaxation times (Cho et al., 1997). These localized changes alter image contrast and may make the brains of the older individuals appear different from those of their younger counterparts. The age–$T1$ relationship is curvilinear (quadratic), and it predicts progressively smaller decrements of $T1$ with age. The local minimum of $T1$ is reached at different ages in different brain structures. The cortex shows a decline into the 60s, whereas $T1$ shortening in the putamen levels off at the end of the third decade. In older brains, age-related shortening of the gray matter $T1$ time constant may cause gray matter pixels to appear more similar to their white matter neighbors than in younger brains. This confound may cause the structures with earlier expected minima of $T1$ to appear more age stable than those in which $T1$ continues to decline until later age. The impact of this potential confound is unclear and merits further investigation.

Longitudinal Studies

Whole Brain Shrinkage and Ventricular Expansion

Since the introduction of the first in vivo imaging techniques, such as computerized tomography (CT), several attempts have been made to assess longitudinal changes in the brain. The physical constraints of early CT studies limited anatomical resolution and forced the investigators to focus on the changes in CSF-filled spaces. However, differential as well as global changes were noted in these studies, which reported moderate expansion of the ventricular system and the prefrontal (but not occipital, parietal, or temporal) sulci (see Fox & Schott, 2004, for a review). The advent of MRI allowed a more anatomically detailed account of brain aging. However, most of the longitudinal MRI studies of healthy brain aging were aimed at understanding brain changes that may lead to Alzheimer's disease (AD). As a result, longitudinal studies were restricted primarily to the global brain changes and to the temporal and medial temporal structures considered especially relevant to that malady.

Global changes in the brain are assessed in two ways: by gauging the actual loss of tissue in the parenchyma and by measuring the addition of CSF in the cerebral ventricles. Visualization of cerebral ventricles and reliable estimation of their volume can be accomplished with relative ease. Global assessment of brain tissue without commitment to evaluation of small structures lends itself to automated computerized methods. These considerations have led to the frequent use of ventricular and global brain volumes as indices of brain change. To date, ventricular expansion has been observed in eighteen longitudinal studies (table 2.5). The results of those studies revealed significant ventricular expansion in older adults (although not in their younger counterparts; Cahn et al., 2002). The median rate of ventricular enlargement (annual percentage change, APC) across nine studies was 2.9% per annum. How-

Table 2.5 Longitudinal Changes in the Cerebral Ventricles and Total Brain Tissue

Study	N	Age	Method	Interval	Ventricles	Total Brain
Mueller et al., 1998	46	81	Manual	3.5	4.25	
Schott et al., 2003	20	46	BBSI	1.4		0.12
DeLisi et al., 1997	20	28	Manual	4.3	1.03	0.16
Chan et al., 2001	27	60	Automated	1		0.47
Hu et al., 2001	10	72	Automated	1.5	4.54	0.06
Tang et al., 2001	66	79	Manual	4.4	5.56	2.13
Ho et al., 2003	23	26	Automated	3	0.35	+0.11
Cahn et al., 2002	36	24	Automated	1.1	0	+1.00
Thompson et al., 2003	14	71	Warping	2		0.88
Sullivan et al., 2002	215	72	Manual	4	2.90	
Saijo et al., 2001	12	37	Manual	10	0.51	
Lieberman et al., 2001	15	31	Manual	1.8	1.33	
R. M. Cohen et al., 2001[b]	9	60	Manual	2		0.04
Liu et al., 2003	90	38	Manual	3.5		0.14
Resnick et al., 2003	92	70	RAVENS	4	4.00	0.50
Scahill et al., 2003	37	52	Manual	1.7		0.32
Wang and Doddrell, 2002	15	72	Automated	1		0.37
Cardenas et al., 2003	16	76	BBSI/Manual	2.6		0.20

Note. BBSI, boundary shift interval; RAVENS, regional analysis of volumes examined in normalized space.
[a]Right > left (1.67 vs. 0.67).
[b]Only apolipoprotein E ε4– subjects included.

ever, for five studies limited to older subjects (mean age 70–81 years), the median annual rate of expansion was 4.25% (2.90%–5.56%), whereas for four samples composed of younger subjects (range of mean age 24 to 37 years) the median value of annual ventricular expansion was 0.43%. Scahill et al. (2003) also reported a significant increase in the rate of ventricular expansion with age without providing the percentage values. Thus, the longitudinal data suggested a nonlinear course of change in the volume of cerebral ventricles throughout the adult life span.

Reduction of the total brain parenchyma is considerably milder. For 14 studies that investigated longitudinal change in total brain volume, the median value was a meager 0.18% per annum. As in the case of ventricular expansion, the observed magnitude of parenchymal shrinkage depends on the age of the participants in the study. In four samples composed of younger adults (the range of mean age was between 24 and 46 years), shrinkage of cerebral tissue was only 0.12%. In the samples that consisted of older subjects (mean age range between 52 and 79 years), modest shrinkage was observed, 0.35% per annum. Notably, steeper volume declines were noted in two studies that considered gray and white matter separately. Incidentally, both employed automated methods of tissue classification and measurement. In one of those studies, a substantial decline was found in gray and white matter of older individuals, 1.17% and 2.52% per annum, respectively (Thompson et al., 2003). In the other, the decline of gray matter volume was more the four times faster than the total parenchymal shrinkage: 0.90% versus 0.20%, respectively (Cardenas et al., 2003).

Regional Cortical Changes

The data on regional cortical changes are even scarcer than the findings on the total brain parenchyma and the ventricular system (see table 2.6). The first study of that kind was actually not designed as a study of aging, but reported brain changes in a group of controls who served in a study of alcoholism (Pfefferbaum et al., 1998). In that study, the authors measured gray and white matter in grossly defined lobes. The study was conducted on a small sample of healthy adults; measures were separated

Table 2.6 Longitudinal Changes in Cortical Regions and Adjacent White Matter Volume

Study	N	Age (years)	Method	Interval	PFC	T	P	O
Pfefferbaum et al., 1998	28	51	Manual	5	1.50	0.05	0.34	0.45
Resnick et al., 2003	92	70	RAVENS	4	1.15	0.55	0.90	0.34
Scahill et al., 2003	39	52	Manual	1.7		0.68		
Mueller et al., 1998	46	81	Manual	3.5				
Raz et al., submitted	72	53	Manual	5.3	0.91	0.59[a]	0.87	0.10
Schott et al., 2002	20	46	BBSI	1.4		0.04		
Ho et al., 2003	23	27	Semiautomated	3.4	+0.80	+0.19	+1.06	
DeLisi et al., 1997	20	28	Manual	4.3		0.30		

Note. BBSI, boundary shift interval; O, occipital lobe; P, parietal lobe; PFC, prefrontal cortex; RAVENS, regional analysis of volumes examined in normalized space; T, temporal lobe.
[a]Inferior temporal and fusiform gyri averaged.

by a 5-year interval. Pfefferbaum and colleagues observed significant shrinkage only in the prefrontal region.

In the same year, Mueller and colleagues (1998) published their findings on a sample of 46 super-healthy older volunteers who were followed for about 3.5 years in the Oregon Brain Aging Study. Although longitudinal declines were found in the medial temporal structures of those subjects (see table 2.7), no changes were detected in the grossly defined cortical regions (with the adjacent white matter). However, breaking the sample by age into young-, middle-, and old-old reveals that nonsignificant but positive change in the medial temporal lobes of the young-old was offset by a mild decline in the older groups. By contrast, in other lobes, no longitudinal declines were observed, and even some (nonsignificant) enlargements of local brain parenchyma were registered.

Two longitudinal studies of healthy adults were published. In one, 92 older adults underwent successive MRI imaging with an interval of 4 years (Resnick et al., 2003). White and gray matter were segmented and measured separately in several brain regions. The results revealed differential longitudinal declines in local brain volumes, with frontal lobes showing the steepest rate of shrinkage, closely followed by the parietal regions. Occipital lobes evidenced little change. Within frontal and parietal cortices, the inferior frontal and inferior parietal regions exhibited the steepest decline. Notably, the estimated magnitude of change was reduced when only very healthy participants were considered, with the greatest attenuation exhibited by the frontal gray matter rates.

The second of the most recent studies was conducted on 39 healthy adults followed for 1.7 years on average (Scahill et al., 2003). In that study, only one cortical region—the temporal lobes—was examined, and a mild decline was observed. In

Table 2.7 Longitudinal Changes in the Volume of Medial Temporal Lobe Structures, Annual Percentage of Change

Study	N	Age (years)	Method	Interval	HC	EC
Mueller et al., 1998	46	81	Manual	3.5	1.69	
Jack et al., 1998	24	70–89	Manual	1	1.60	
Jack et al., 2000	48	80	Manual	3	1.70	
Laakso, Lehtovirta, et al., 2000	8	70	Manual	3	1.60	
Scahill et al., 2003	39	52	Manual	1.7	0.82	
Schott et al., 2002	20	46	BBSI	1–4	+0.12	1.58
Du et al., 2003[a]	23	76.5	Manual	1.8		1.40
Cardenas et al., 2003[a]	16	76	Manual	2.6	1.80	2.60
Moffat et al., 2000[b]	13	70	Manual	2.7	1.85	
R. M. Cohen et al., 2001[b]	9	60	Manual	2	0.77	
Liu et al., in press	90	38	Manual	3.5	0.11	
DeLisi et al., 1997	20	28	Manual	4.3	0.37	
Raz et al., 2004b	54	52	Manual	5	0.86	0.37

Note. BBSI, boundary shift interval; EC, entorhinal cortex; HC, hippocampus.
[a]About 25% overlap between the samples.
[b]Only apolipoprotein E ε4− subjects included.

that sample, the rate of temporal lobe shrinkage appeared to accelerate in older participants, although between-subject variance in annual change also dramatically increased with age. An important finding in that study was that cross-sectional estimates of age-related shrinkage were below the figures obtained in the longitudinal study.

Although significant progress has been made in longitudinal research of brain aging, information on regional differences is still very scarce. To address the question of regional differences in brain aging and to provide a comparison between cross-sectional and longitudinal estimates of shrinkage, we measured a number of cortical regions and adjacent white matter in 72 healthy adults who at baseline spanned an age range between 20 and 77 years (Raz et al., submitted). In that sample, a significant longitudinal decline was observed across a 5-year period. The PFC exhibited the fastest annual shrinkage (0.91% per annum or a 5-year drop of $d = .91$ standard deviations). Temporal cortices (inferior temporal and fusiform) showed slower volume declines (0.69% and 0.48% per annum or $d = .67$ and .56, respectively). The occipital (pericalcarine) cortex revealed no significant decline (APC = 0.10%, $d = .18$). All of the listed regions except the occipital cortex evidenced steeper longitudinal declines predicted by the estimates derived from cross-sectional data.

In a sharp contrast to those findings, the inferior parietal lobule (IPL), which showed no cross-sectional age-related differences, displayed a significant longitudinal decline of 0.87% per year and $d = .86$ for a 5-year period (Raz et al., submitted). Notably, among all measured regions, the IPL was the region with the highest inter-subject variability. In all likelihood, the individual differences obscured age effects in both waves of cross-sectional measurement. However, when those differences were controlled in the repeated measures design, the longitudinal changes became apparent. In all examined cortical regions, the rate of decline did not differ with age. Notably, a similar pattern of longitudinal decline was observed in adolescents. Frontal and parietal (but not occipital) gray matter volume declined after the early teens into young adulthood (Giedd et al., 1999).

In contrast to the gray matter, prefrontal white matter evidenced a nonlinear pattern of age differences at baseline as well as at follow-up. As in the Bartzokis et al. (2001) and Jernigan et al. (2001) cross-sectional studies, no age-related differences were observed among younger participants (under 50 years of age), but significant linear slope was found in a subsample of older adults. Moreover, a significant Age × Time interaction observed in that sample indicated that the magnitude of white matter shrinkage depended on age. Beginning at about the fifth decade of life, the white matter of the participants showed significant shrinkage, whereas their younger counterparts showed no 5-year change. A pattern of steady increase in white matter volume between childhood and young adulthood was observed in a longitudinal study of healthy development (Giedd et al., 1999).

Changes in Medial Temporal Structures

Medial temporal structures—the HC and the entorhinal cortex (EC)—attracted special attention of the researchers. Both regions are involved in episodic memory, a faculty that declines with age (Verhaeghen, Marcoen, & Goossens, 1993) and is especially impaired in AD (Corey-Blum, Galasko, & Thal, 1994). The EC is believed to be the first cerebral structure to show AD pathology (Braak & Braak, 1991; Gomez-Isla et al., 1996), and in postmortem material from very old nondemented persons, it showed a predilection to neurofibrillary tangles characteristic of AD (Troncoso et al., 1996). Moreover, unlike the PFC, which displays significant amyloid burden in the brains of nondemented elderly, the EC is almost exclusively affected in those who died with a diagnosis of AD (Bussière et al., 2002).

In normal aging, the extent and the role of EC pathology is less clear. The research findings from several methodologically distinct paradigms converge onto the notion of EC pathology as a harbinger of incipient dementia, a sort of neuropathological canary in the mineshaft. Loss of neurons in lamina II of the EC and reduction of cortical volume are more likely to be discovered on autopsy in nondemented adults with impaired antemortem cognition than in their counterparts who died before exhibiting signs of cognitive decline (Kordower et al., 2001). Metabolically compromised EC in normal elderly predicts onset of memory declines 3 years later (de Leon et al., 2001). In contrast, the effects of normal aging on EC volume (Insausti et al., 1998) and neuron number (Gazzaley et al., 1997; Merrill, Roberts, & Tuszynski, 2000) are virtually nil.

In attempts to identify reliable preclinical signs of AD, a number of researchers measured volumes of the HC and EC in vivo in subjects with various degrees of cognitive pathology. The results indicated that, although HC is a very good predictor of concurrent AD (Jack et al., 1992; Xu et al., 2000; Laakso, Frisoni, et al., 2000) and of AD-type pathology in nondemented individuals (Gosche et al., 2002), the volume of the EC may fare better as a prospective predictor of conversion from mild impairment to AD (Killiany et al., 2000, 2002; Dickerson et al., 2001). A discriminant analysis indicated that, although HC volume is the best among the structural variables in distinguishing between AD patients and controls, the volume of EC performed better in discriminating normal elderly from those who fit the criteria for mild cognitive impairment (Pennanen et al., 2004).

To date, HC of normal adults has been measured in at least a dozen longitudinal studies, and, in four longitudinal studies, EC volumes in normal subjects have been reported (table 2.7). Almost without exception, manual tracing was used, and generally comparable rules were applied to demarcation and tracing of the structures, although some important variations are apparent (Jack et al., 1995). An important methodological difference among the studies, as discussed in the first few sections of this chapter, was the definition of the anterior borders of the HC. With some methods that rely on visualization of separation between HC and the amygdala, a slice or two may be added to the HC volume of the older subjects, and the age-related effects may be reduced.

Because the anterior HC has been suspected as more vulnerable to AD (Petersen et al., 1998) than the body and the tail of the structure and because there is at least one report on the role of the HC head in age-related memory deficits (Hackert et al., 2002), it is important to take the border definition rules into account. Yet, some reports indicated that, in contrast to the whole or posterior HC, reliability of the anterior HC is rather low (Colchester et al., 2001; Goodwin & Ebmeier, 2002), and there are no clear anatomical landmarks for demarcating the anterior HC as a distinct region.

The overall results of the longitudinal studies of HC indicated that the structure shrinks at a median rate of 1.23% per annum. There is also a trend for samples with younger subjects to show slower (if any) decline of the HC volume (1% per year or less). Notably, the studies that restricted subject selection to people in the seventh decade of life and older produced a remarkably stable set of estimates, ranging between 1.6% and 1.85% per annum. Within-sample comparisons revealed that even among very healthy adults, the shrinkage rate (Raz, Rodrigue, et al., 2004b; Liu et al., 2003). A similar pattern was observed within a sample of older adults ranging in age between the seventh and the tenth decades (Mueller et al., 1998). It is worth mentioning, however, that the rates of HC shrinkage in normal individuals are considerably slower than 3%–4% shrinkage rate observed in those with AD (Jack et al., 2000) and almost an order of magnitude smaller than in people with a genetic variety of AD, for whom they reach 8% per annum (Fox et al., 1996).

Given the importance of EC in genesis of AD, it is surprising that only four longitudinal studies of healthy adults examined changes in that structure. A significant reduction in the volumes of the parahippocampal gyrus (which includes the EC) was observed in one of the first longitudinal studies of healthy brain aging (Kaye et al., 1997). Two samples (with about 25% overlap) evidenced a significant decline in EC volume that ranged between 1.4% and 2.6% per year (Du et al., 2003; Cardenas et al., 2003). In one of those studies (Cardenas et al., 2003), the HC was measured as well, and the rate of shrinkage in that region was smaller than in the EC, but somewhat greater than in the other reported EC studies (see table 2.7). Both samples included subjects in their 80s and 80s and followed them for a relatively short period (1–3 years).

Two samples of broader age range revealed conflicting findings. In a small sample with a mean age of 46 years, no HC changes were found; a decline of 1.6% per annum was observed in the EC (Schott et al., 2003). In a larger sample of healthy adults whose HC and EC were measured with an interval of 5 years, we observed a different pattern (Raz, Rodrigue, et al., 2004b). A significant decline in HC volume was accompanied by minimal shrinkage of the EC. Interestingly, the rate of decline in both structures accelerated with age, more so in the HC. Whereas for the younger participants (age younger than 50 years) no EC shrinkage and only mild HC shrinkage were observed, for their older counterparts the EC shrinkage was greater than zero and about at the magnitude of HC shrinkage observed for the younger adults (approximately 0.5% per year). The findings of the latter study converge with metabolic data. A study of hemodynamic properties of the medial temporal regions in healthy adults revealed a similar pattern of significant age-related decline in two hippocampal regions (the subiculum and the dentate gyrus), with no age-related differences in the EC (Small et al., 2000). Notably, a significant decline of basal metabolism was observed in the EC only in the oldest participants (70–88 years of age).

Changes in Striatum and Its Components

To date, five longitudinal MRI studies have addressed some aspects of age-related changes in the adult human striatum. Most of these studies were limited to small samples ($N = 10$–20) of younger normal controls who were compared to patients with first episodes of schizophrenia. In three studies restricted to assessment of the caudate nucleus (Chakos et al., 1994; DeLisi et al., 1997; Tauscher-Wisniewski et al., 2002), a 1-year change in all three striatal nuclei was measured in one study (Lang et al., 2001). Only one study examined long-term changes in striatal volume in a sample of healthy adults covering six decades of age (Raz, Rodrigue, et al., 2003c).

Among younger adults, the findings are mixed. Two studies (Chakos et al., 1994; Tauscher-Wisniewski et al., 2002) revealed significant shrinkage of the caudate nucleus even at a relatively young age, with annual percentage of change exceeding 1%. By contrast, another study of young adults (DeLisi et al., 1997) revealed no longitudinal shrinkage over a 5-year period. In a 5-year follow-up of 53 healthy adults whose ages ranged from 20 to 77 years at baseline, we found linear declines in all striatal nuclei. However, the rate of decline varied across the nuclei. The caudate nucleus evidenced the fastest decline (0.83% per annum), with the putamen and the globus pallidus showing lesser rates of decline (0.73% and 0.51%, respectively).

It is noteworthy that annual percentage of decline—a frequently used measure of change—is deficient in one important aspect: It ignores variability. When the change over 5 years is assessed by the effect size index d, the mean difference normalized by the pooled standard deviation (SD), the differential change becomes even clearer. In 5 years, the caudate shrunk by 1.2 SD, compared to only 0.85 SD for the putamen and 0.55 SD for the globus pallidus. The observed shrinkage was linear and unrelated to age; that is, the striatal nuclei shrunk in young adults at roughly the same rate as in their older counterparts. The results of the surveyed studies are presented in table 2.8.

Changes in the Cerebellum and Other Metencephalic Structures

Nine longitudinal studies (see table 2.9) examined changes in the cerebellar volume, and in one report longitudinal course of volume in the cerebellar vermis and the ventral pons was examined as well. All but one published longitudinal studies of the cerebellum were conducted on samples with severely restricted age ranges, either

Table 2.8 Longitudinal Changes in the Volume of Basal Ganglia

Study	N	Age (years)	Method	Interval	Cd	Pt	GP
Lieberman et al., 2001	15	31	Manual	2.1	1.52		
Lang et al., 2001	17	28	Manual	1	1.10	0.20	+4.22
Tauscher-Wisniewski et al., 2002	10	29	Manual	4.9	1.90		
Raz et al., 2003c	53	52	Manual	5.25	.83	0.73	0.51
DeLisi et al., 1997	20	28	Manual	4.3	.37		

Note. Cd, caudate nucleus; GP, globus pallidus; Pt, putamen.

Table 2.9 Longitudinal Changes in the Volume of Metencephalic Structures
and Corpus Callosum

Study	N	Age (years)	Method	Interval	Cerebellum	Vermis	Corpus Callosum	Pons
Tauscher-Wisniewski et al., 2002	10	29	Manual	4.9	1.86			
Raz et al., 2003b	53	52	Manual	5.25	0.64	0.41		0.16
Cahn et al., 2002	36	24	Automated	1.1	+1.0			
Tang et al., 2001	66	79	Manual	4.4	1.2			
Liu et al., in press	90	38	Manual	3.5	0.13			
Ho et al., 2003	23	27	Automatic	3	1.71			
DeLisi et al., 1997	20	28	Manual	4.3	0.49		0.18	
Sullivan et al., 2002	215	72	Manual	4			0.90	
Teipel et al., 2002	10	65	Manual	2			0.90	

young adults or the elderly. The results of the fourth longitudinal investigation demonstrated that all metencephalic structures shrink with age. However, the rate of shrinkage differs among these structures. The annual shrinkage of the cerebellar hemispheres was somewhat greater than that of the vermis, whereas the ventral pons exhibited minimal volumetric change. As in the case of the basal ganglia, when the variability was taken into account, the magnitude of 5-year change in the cerebellum was substantial (1.19 SD). The vermis evidenced less decline (0.68 to 0.84 SD, depending on the region), whereas little change was noted in the pons (0.29 SD).

Changes in Corpus Callosum

Although cross-sectional studies revealed little if any shrinkage of corpus callosum in normal aging (Driesen & Raz, 1995), longitudinal investigations indicated that a significant reduction in the total callosal size occurs (e.g., Sullivan et al., 2002). The mean annual shrinkage rate across the studies was 0.90%. The same magnitude of age-related shrinkage was found in another, much smaller, sample of healthy elderly (Teipel et al., 2002). The results of all longitudinal studies of regional brain volumetry are summarized in figure 2.3.

In Vivo Studies of Age-Related Differences in Microstructure of the White Matter

Although the white matter volume remains relatively stable across most of adulthood, significant age-related differences in its microstructure have been observed (Peters & Sethares, 2002; Kemper, 1994). Small connecting fibers of the anterior corpus callosum have been noted for their particular vulnerability to aging (Aboitiz et al., 1996; Meier-Ruge et al., 1992; see Sullivan & Pfefferbaum, 2003, for a review). Although microstructural changes in the white matter cannot be observed on high-resolution MRI employed in regional volumetry studies, new approaches such

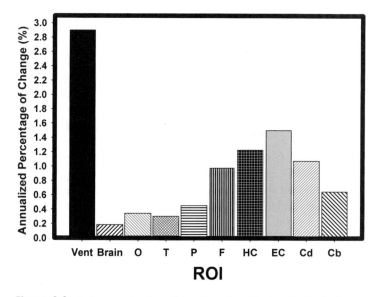

Figure 2.3. A bar graph of median effect sizes for longitudinal changes of brain regions. The index of effect is annual percentage of change (APC) across studies. APC was either reported in the study or computed from mean change data and mean interval between the scans. Cb, cerebellum; Cd, caudate nucleus; EC, entorhinal cortex; F, frontal lobe; HC, hippocampus; O, occipital lobe; P, parietal lobe; ROI, region of interest; T, temporal lobe; Vent, cerebral ventricles.

as diffusion tensor imaging (DTI) and diffusion weighted imaging (DWI) promise to open a window into that aspect of brain aging. For a more detailed account of the methods, there are a number of available reviews (e.g., Moseley, Bammer, & Isles, 2002; Sullivan & Pfefferbaum, 2003).

In brief, both approaches are based on sensitivity of the MR signal to movement of water molecules. Specifically, DTI takes advantage of the diffusion anisotropy phenomenon. In the intact myelinated fibers, the molecules of water are much more likely to drift along the internal membrane of the fibers than across the thick wall of proteins and lipids. The likelihood of bidirectional diffusion along three main axes within each space element can be described by a 3×3 matrix of values, the diffusion tensor. As the integrity of the myelin sheath becomes compromised in the process of normal aging, the differences in probability and speed of diffusion across and along the fiber walls diminish. Hence, a reduction in fractional anisotropy (FA) can be used to gauge white matter deterioration. At the same time, a summary index (trace or mean eigenvalue) of the diffusion tensor, the apparent diffusion coefficient (ADC), increases with deterioration of the white matter. Thus, both FA and ADC can describe age-related differences in regional white matter.

At the time of this writing, only a handful of studies of age-related differences in brain water diffusion and age-related alteration of the white matter microstructure were available. Because the studies are not numerous and because their results are mixed, it is too early to draw conclusions. There are some commonalities in findings. In some small samples of healthy volunteers with ages that cover adult life span, average brain ADC showed significant increase with age ($r = .74$) (Nusbaum et al., 2001), and anisotropy decreased with age in centrum semiovale and parietal perical-losal regions, with weaker trends in the same direction observed at the both ends of the corpus callosum (Pfefferbaum et al., 2000).

In a sample of 50 healthy adults (aged 21–69 years), diffusion increased with age in frontal white matter and lentiform nucleus, but not in the parietal white matter, posterior limb of internal capsule, thalamus, and corpus callosum. In the same sample, anisotropy (FA) declined with age only in the genu of the corpus callosum (Abe et al., 2002). Pfefferbaum and Sullivan (2003) used DTI to study regional age-related differences in white matter. In general, they found that ADC increased with age ($r = 0.24$ to 0.58, depending on the region); anisotropy (FA) decreased ($r = -0.29$ to -0.79, depending on the region). However, in at lest one carefully screened sample of 80 healthy adults (aged 22–85 years), no age differences in diffusion (ADC) were found in 36 regions that included cortex and subcortical white matter, the basal ganglia, and the metencephalon (Helenius et al., 2002). In part, the variability among the studies may stem from methodological differences. For instance, in their review of the DTI methodology, Sullivan and Pfefferbaum (2003) cautioned against reliance on VBM in regional analysis of diffusion-based images because of its increased susceptibility to partial voluming and resultant distortions.

An attempt to apply DWI to diagnostic classification of AD, mildly cognitively impaired (MCI) adults, and normal controls revealed a pattern of deterioration similar to the one shown by the volumetric measures. The hippocampal ADC is higher in AD than in mildly impaired elderly, and the latter in turn exhibit higher ADC values than normal controls (Kantarci et al., 2001). Increased diffusion in the posterior cingulate, parietal, occipital, and temporal white matter distinguished between the AD and the preclinical cases, but not between MCI and normal individuals, whereas no differences were observed in the frontal lobe and the thalamus. It is unclear whether diffusion indices are more sensitive than volumetry to age-related changes.

The integrity of white matter was assessed by multiple MRI methods (diffusion, $T1$, and $T2$ weighted) in a relatively large sample ($N = 89$) of healthy volunteers spanning the age range between 11 and 76 years (Rovaris et al., 2003). In that study, all indices of white matter integrity (number of white matter hyperintensities [WMHs], ADC, and FA) correlated with age. However, the best nonredundant predictors of age were WMH number and total brain volume. Thus, although diffusion-based indices of white matter integrity show age-related declines, they may not add much information to what is known from other sources, at least as long as they are used globally. It is possible that local differences and longitudinal changes in ADC or FA can prove more useful. However, such studies have not been conducted at the time of this writing, although in a small sample of older patients with cerebrovascular disease, ADC was shown to be at least as sensitive a measure of white matter changes as the whole brain volume index (Mascalchi et al., 2003).

Modifiers of Brain Aging: The Good News and the Bad News

Multiple factors affect brain development and aging. Some of them act as accelerators of age-related declines, and others display a potential for slowing age-related deterioration and delaying its advancement to pathological levels. In this discussion of the good news–bad news message, the bad news is presented first.

Hypertension and Other Cardiovascular Risk Factors

Cerebrovascular disease, stroke, and diabetes exert a negative influence on cerebral structure and functions in older adults (for reviews, see Pantoni, Inzitari, & Wallin, 2001; Gunning-Dixon and Raz, 2000). Failure to account for these factors may bias the results of studies that are focused on healthy aging but fail to screen the subjects adequately. In most studies, however, subjects suffering from debilitating cardiovascular or neurological illness are excluded from the sample. On the other hand, pathological factors that are highly prevalent among active adults and that are relatively silent clinically are likely to confound the results of the studies of healthy brain aging. One such factor is hypertension, a chronic, age-related condition associated with multiple changes in the vascular system (Marin & Rodriguez-Martinez, 1999). Even when defined conservatively by systolic blood pressure in excess of 160 mm Hg or diastolic pressure greater than 90 mm Hg, hypertension affects over 55% of Americans (Burt et al., 1995).

Chronic elevation of blood pressure augments the effects of aging on brain structure (Carmelli et al., 1999; de Leeuw et al., 2001; Salerno et al., 1992; Schmidt et al., 1996; Strassburger et al., 1997; Raz, Rodrigue, & Acker, 2003a). Exclusion of medically treated hypertensive participants from a sample can bring a significant reduction in age effects on brain and cognition (Head et al., 2002). Relatively small increases in blood pressure may be associated with generalized brain atrophy (Goldstein et al., 2002). Some reports suggest that even treated hypertension may be associated with higher prevalence of white matter abnormalities than observed in matched normotensive controls (van Swieten et al., 1991; Raz, Rodrigue, & Acker, 2003a). We reported that treated (and reasonably well-controlled) hypertension is associated with increased prevalence of white matter abnormalities and shrinkage of the prefrontal gray and white matter (Raz, Rodrigue, & Acker, 2003a). Thus, early detection and uncompromising control of blood pressure may modify the currently observed pattern of brain aging. In particular, successful treatment and prevention of hypertension may reduce the differential significance of age-related changes in the PFC and especially in the prefrontal white matter.

Aerobic Fitness

As a counterweight to the bad news about brain aging surveyed in the previous section, some good news, or at least some hopeful findings that suggest that pathological influence of cardiovascular risk factors on the aging brain can be alleviated and even prevented, can be cautiously offered. A growing body of studies indicates that aerobic fitness positively affects a wide variety of variables linked to brain health (van Praag, Kempermann, & Gage, 1999; Cotman & Berchtold, 2002). Until recently, studies on brain aging and exercise were based on indirect measurements of brain structure and function such as global electrical activity (electroencephalogram) and cognitive performance on tasks with known sensitivity to brain lesions (Churchill et al., 2002). Nonetheless, the general direction of the findings was toward the assertion that executive functions and, by inference, brain structures that support them are especially sensitive to beneficial effects of aerobic fitness (Colcombe & Kramer, 2003).

A confirmation of the benefits of aerobic fitness for brain aging was presented in a cross-sectional study (Colcombe et al., 2003). Aerobic fitness of 55 highly educated, cognitively normal persons (aged 55–79 years) was assessed by estimating maximal oxygen uptake (VO_{2max}). Brain integrity was assessed from MRI scans using VBM methodology. The analysis revealed a typical pattern of age-related differences: reduced brain tissue density in association with cortical regions (prefrontal, superior and inferior parietal, and inferior temporal) and in the prefrontal (but not posterior) white matter, accompanied by no age effects on occipital and motor regions. However, an important finding in that study was that the pattern of brain aging was altered by fitness: The regions that showed age-related decline in the whole sample were those that exhibited the greatest attenuation of age effects by fitness. Thus, aerobic fitness emerged as a potential modifier of brain aging. Although the physiological underpinnings of that effect are unclear, it is most likely that it is mediated by cardio- and cerebrovascular benefits of aerobic training, including its well-documented effects on blood pressure (Lesniak & Dubbert, 2001).

Hormone Replacement Therapy

Hormone replacement therapy (HRT) has generated significant debate and controversy among researchers of brain aging. A significant body of animal (mainly rodent) research suggests that estrogen may have multiple beneficial effects on the CNS. Estrogen was reported to enhance plasticity, to reduce β-amyloid deposits, and contravene the oxidative action of free radicals (see van Amelsvoort, Compton, & Murphy, 2001, for a concise review).

Several human studies produced encouraging results. In a comparison from the Austrian Stroke Prevention Study of 70 women receiving HRT and 140 women not receiving HRT, the HRT group evidenced fewer silent strokes, and the duration of HRT was inversely related to the burden of WMH (Schmidt et al., 1996). In a longitudinal study of 15 women receiving HRT, the progression of gross brain changes was slowed compared to progression in the control group (Cook et al., 2002). In a sample of Mexican American women, 13 women on HRT showed significantly larger right hippocampi and larger anterior hippocampi (right and left) than 46 women who were not taking estrogen supplements (Eberling et al., 2003). In another sample, 12 women who were taking HRT were compared to 16 controls during a period of 2 years (Maki & Resnick, 2000). Women on HRT therapy showed longitudinal increases in regional cerebral blood flow (rCBF) of the right HC, right entorhinal and posterior parahippocampal gyri, middle temporal gyrus, right inferior frontal and insular regions, and medial frontal gyrus, that is, the regions in which significant age-related differences in local volumes have been observed. Although the implications of such change in activation for cognitive functions are unclear, the distinct pattern of results observed for women on HRT is intriguing.

Although animal investigations and small-sample human studies of HRT generated significant enthusiasm, the positive expectations have been tempered by some negative findings. In a large-scale study of 2133 women (aged 65–95 years), no effect of current or past HRT on prevalence of cerebral infarcts was observed (Luoto et al., 2000). However, women who took estrogen had significantly greater brain atrophy than their HRT-naïve peers. In a sample of 837 Japanese American women (aged 55–101 years), a 2-year follow-up study of unopposed estrogen therapy revealed modest cognitive benefits, but in the same sample, modest detrimental effects of estrogen–progestin combination have been reported as well (Rice et al., 2000).

We examined whether participation in HRT explains part of variability to brain volumes (Raz, Gunning-Dixon, et al., 2004a). Twenty-one women who reported receiving estrogen replacement therapy were closely matched on age (±1 year), hypertension status, and race to 21 women who received no supplementary estrogen. The average age of the groups was 60 years, and each group included 5 women who were taking antihypertensive medication. The comparison of regional volumes and regional proportional measures in 13 brain regions (including the HC and the PFC) revealed no differences related to the estrogen supplementation status, all $Fs < 1$.

Too much estrogen is not necessarily a benefit. In a sample of 210 older women (aged 60 to 90 years), higher total estradiol levels and bioavailable and free estradiol levels were associated with smaller hippocampal volumes and poorer memory (den Heijer et al., 2003). This finding contradicts the report of Drake and colleagues (Drake et al., 2000), who found a moderate positive correlation between bioavailability of estradiol and memory performance in a sample of 39 women. Notably, performance on visual reproduction tests was negatively correlated with estradiol levels and bioavailability. Recent animal studies also revealed a potentially harmful side of the HRT. In a rodent model, a harmful interaction between HRT and induced neuroinflammation was observed (Marriott et al., 2002). Because pathological age-related changes and AD pathology have been attributed to neuroinflammation, such interaction may act to offset the potential benefits of HRT.

The most recent report of potentially harmful effects of HRT came from the Women Health Initiative (WHI) study, a multicenter, double-blind, placebo-controlled, randomized clinical trial involving almost 17,000 women aged 50–79 years who were followed-up for more than 5 years (Wassertheil-Smoller et al., 2003; Shumaker et al., 2003). The results of the WHI study showed that therapy with estrogen plus progesterone is associated with excessive risk for strokes (Wassertheil-Smoller et al., 2003). The diagnoses were made on the basis of standard clinical data, including MRI scans, but no specific brain measures were available. With respect to preventing or slowing the transition from mild cognitive impairment to dementia, the therapy also failed. Moreover, the members of the treatment group exhibited an increased risk for developing dementia (Shumaker et al., 2003).

It must be noted that, unlike the rigorously planned WHI study, all studies that examined the effects of HRT on regional brain aging were retrospective. A wide variety of doses was used, and women were not classified according to the reasons for HRT. Prospective studies with controlled levels of hormonal intervention and carefully described samples may help clarify the question of estrogen's potential for neuroprotection in humans.

Conclusions

A survey of a relatively limited sample of longitudinal studies of healthy brain aging led to several tentative conclusions.

1. Age-related brain shrinkage is a real phenomenon and not an artifact of cohort differences and secular trends.
2. Brain shrinkage is differential; that is, the rate of shrinkage varies spatially (across brain regions, structures, and compartments) and temporally (along the age continuum). Brain aging appears not only as a spatially distributed patch-work but as a sequence of temporally arranged windows of vulnerability as well. (a) The aspect of the brain that changes with the greatest speed is the ventricular system. This is not surprising because cerebral ventricles are a part of a closed fluid system that encompasses the CNS. Thus, with all other factors equal, loss in any region of CNS changes the external pressure and allows fluid expansion, both locally and eventually globally. In a way, the ventricular system represents a whole-market index of the brain and conveys important information about the general health of the system, but is not particularly informative about the specific regions. In that context, ventricular expansion is sensitive to accumulation of brain changes, but not at all specific to their location. (b) In contrast, the total volume of brain parenchyma is a poor index of normal brain aging: If some regions shrink and others do not, the average result is a reduced, diluted, measure that glosses over differences and presents an underestimation of brain aging. Within the cerebral cortex, prefrontal regions exhibit a steeper decline than other brain areas, whereas temporal and occipital regions evidence only mild declines. (c) The caudate nucleus evidences a rate of decline similar to that of the tertiary association cortices, and the cerebellar hemispheres exhibit a somewhat slower decline. The caudate nuclei, the cerebellum, and the cortex appear to shrink in a linear manner. The observed linear (but heterochronous) volume reduction in both regions is not an exclusive phenomenon of aging, but a process that begins early in adolescence and proceeds at a steady clip into ripe old age. (d) Across the extant studies, shrinkage of the medial temporal structures (the HC and the EC) appears greater than that of the other brain regions. However, closer examination of the findings reveals that such a conclusion would be misleading. Whereas both structures show an age-dependent course of decline, volume loss in young and middle-aged adults is minimal in the HC and nonexistent in the EC. Hippocampal shrinkage is restricted to older adults and, in the case of EC, to the oldest of them. Thus, it appears that middle-temporal structures, in contrast to the neocortex, show nonlinear decline trajectories. Such differences evoke a

possibility of different factors underpinning brain shrinkage in those groups of regions. Neocortical shrinkage may be driven mainly by programmed time-dependent processes, whereas in the medial temporal structures, cumulative pathological effects may play a greater role.

3. Cross-sectional estimates of brain shrinkage do not necessarily agree with the longitudinal measures. However, in cases of disagreement, the cross-sectional measures almost always underestimate the magnitude of the true change.

4. Structural brain aging can be differentially modified by disease and environmental manipulations. The possibility exists of therapeutic intervention that would retard the aging process, thus affording an additional period of high-quality cognitive life to the older adults.

Future Directions

Although there is a reasonable consensus that the human brain shrinks with age, many important questions remain open. Even though the cross-sectional and longitudinal literature indicates that brain aging is differential, the exact pattern of heterochronous brain decline is unclear. Do the anterior frontal regions bear the brunt of age-related changes? Are all tertiary cortices disproportionately vulnerable to the effects of senescence? What is the role of vascular risk factors in differential aging of the brain? Can specific interventions such as increase in aerobic fitness, early and aggressive treatment of cardiovascular disease, or hormone therapy combined with blockers of unwanted side effects alleviate the differential vulnerability but not the general declines?

One of the foremost goals is the understanding of the neurobiological underpinnings of age-related changes observed on MRI. To date, the invasive methodology available for animal studies revealed important information about mammalian brain aging. However, very few in vivo imaging data are available in nonhuman organisms. In humans, invasive studies are unavailable, and acquisition of healthy brain material from subjects who underwent premortem MRI is logistically and ethically complicated. Although some information about pathophysiological and histological correlates of MR-derived brain measures are available in stroke and AD, little is known about the neurobiological meaning of MR changes observed in healthy aging. Combining invasive and noninvasive methods in established primate and rodent models of physiological aging may be a realistic way to shed light on neuroanatomical correlates of specific MR changes. Animal models that allow a relatively cheap and reliable application of high-field MRI and postmortem histology may be critical to future understanding of mammalian brain aging.

In brain aging, changes in structure, neurochemistry, metabolism, and electrophysiology occur within the same time window. Sometimes, a specific change in one aspect of the system precedes the others, but by and large a complex pattern of mutual influences prevails. Although significant progress has been achieved in describing age-related differences in brain structure (described in this chapter) and function (see chapters 3, 5, and 7 in this volume), these lines of research seem to run almost perfectly in parallel. The relationship between local changes in brain parenchyma, deterioration in the microstructure of connecting fibers, alterations of regional cerebral blood flow, loss of neurotransmitter functions, and modification in the pattern of task-related activation that are observed in aging have not been tied together in one sample. Given the magnitude of individual differences, such a study, no matter how daunting, is highly desirable. Tracking structural and functional changes over time in addition to examination of age-related differences is also necessary.

Acknowledgments This study was supported in part by the National Institutes of Health (AG-11230). I am grateful to Roberto Cabeza, David Madden, and Edie Sullivan for helpful comments on a draft of this chapter and to Donna Lang and Jeff Kaye for providing unpublished and supplemental data for their published studies.

References

Abe O, Aoki S, Hayashi N, Yamada H, Kunimatsu A, Mori H, Yoshikawa T, Okubo T, Ohtomo K. (2002). Normal aging in the central nervous system: Quantitative MR diffusion-tensor analysis. *Neurobiology of Aging, 23*, 433–441.

Aboitiz F, Rodriguez E, Olivares R, Zaidel E. (1996). Age-related changes in fibre composition of the human corpus callosum: Sex differences. *Neuroreport, 7*, 1761–1764.

Arendt T. (2001). Alzheimer's disease as a disorder of mechanisms underlying structural brain self-organization. *Neuroscience, 102*, 723–765.

Ashburner J, Csernansky JG, Davatzikos C, Fox NC, Frisoni GB, Thompson PM. (2003). Computer-assisted imaging to assess brain structure in healthy and diseased brains. *Lancet Neurology, 2*, 79–88.

Bartzokis G, Beckson M, Lu PH, Nuechterlein KH, Edwards N, Mintz J. (2001). Age-related changes in frontal and temporal volume in men: A magnetic resonance imaging study. *Archives of General Psychiatry, 58*, 461–465.

Bookstein FL. (2001) "Voxel-based morphometry" should not be used with imperfectly registered images. *Neuroimage, 14*, 1454–1462.

Braak H, Braak E. (1991). Neuropathological staging of Alzheimer-related changes. *Acta Neuropathologica, 82*, 239–259.

Burt VL, Cutler JA, Higgins M, Horan MJ, Labarthe D, Whelton P, Brown C, Roccella EJ. (1995). Trends in the prevalence, awareness, treatment, and control of hypertension in the adult US population. Data from the health examination surveys, 1960 to 1991. *Hypertension, 26*, 60–69.

Bussière T, Friend PD, Sadeghi N, Wicinski B, Lin GI, Bouras C, Giannakopoulos P, Robakis NK, Morrison JH, Perl DP, Hof PR. (2002). Stereologic assessment of the total cortical volume occupied by amyloid deposits and its relationship with cognitive status in aging and Alzheimer's disease. *Neuroscience, 112*, 75–91.

Cabeza R. (2002). Hemispheric asymmetry reduction in older adults: The HAROLD model. *Psychology and Aging, 17*, 85–100.

Cahn W, Pol HE, Lems EB, van Haren NE, Schnack HG, van der Linden JA, Schothorst PF, van Engeland H, Kahn RS. (2002). Brain volume changes in first-episode schizophrenia: A 1-year follow-up study. *Archives of General Psychiatry, 11*, 1002–1010.

Cardenas VA, Du AT, Hardin D, Ezekiel F, Weber P, Jagust WJ, Chui HC, Schuff N, Weiner MW. (2003). Comparison of methods for measuring longitudinal brain change in cognitive impairment and dementia. *Neurobiology of Aging, 24*, 537–544.

Carmelli D, Swan GE, Reed T, Wolf PA, Miller BL, DeCarli C. (1999). Midlife cardiovascular risk factors and brain morphology in identical male twins. *Neurology*, *52*, 1119–1124.

Chakos MH, Lieberman JA, Bilder RM, Borenstein M, Lerner G, Bogerts B, Wu H, Kinon B, Ashtari M. (1994). Increase in caudate nuclei volumes of first-episode schizophrenic patients taking antipsychotic drugs. *American Journal of Psychiatry*, *151*, 1430–1436.

Chan D, Fox NC, Jenkins R, Scahill RI, Crum WR, Rossor MN. (2001). Rates of global and regional cerebral atrophy in AD and frontotemporal dementia. *Neurology*, *57*, 1756–1763.

Cho S, Jones D, Reddick WE, Ogg RJ, & Steen RG. (1997). Establishing norms for age-related changes in proton T1 of human brain tissue in vivo. *Magnetic Resonance Imaging*, *15*, 1133–1143.

Churchill JD, Galvez R, Colcombe S, Swain RF, Kramer AF, Greenough WT. (2002). Exercise, experience and the aging brain. *Neurobiology of Aging*, *23*, 941–955.

Cohen RM, Small C, Lalonde F, Friz J, Sunderland T. (2001). Effect of apolipoprotein E genotype on hippocampal volume loss in aging healthy women. *Neurology*, *57*, 2223–2228.

Colchester A, Kingsley D, Lasserson D, Kendall B, Bello F, Rush C, Stevens TG, Goodman G, Heilpern G, Stanhope N, Kopelman MD. (2001). Structural MRI volumetric analysis in patients with organic amnesia, 1: Methods and comparative findings across diagnostic groups. *Journal of Neurology, Neurosurgery, and Psychiatry*, *71*, 13–22.

Colcombe S, Erickson KI, Raz N, Webb AG, Cohen NJ, McAuley E, Kramer AF. (2003). Aerobic fitness reduces brain tissue loss in aging humans. *Journal of Gerontology, A: Biological Sciences and Medical Sciences*, *58A*, 176–180.

Colcombe S, Kramer AF. (2003). Fitness effects on the cognitive function of older adults: A meta-analytic study. *Psychological Science*, *4*, 125–130.

Convit A, Wolf OT, de Leon MJ, Patalinjug M, Kandil E, Caraos C, Scherer A, Saint Louis LA, Cancro R. (2001). Volumetric analysis of the pre-frontal regions: Findings in aging and schizophrenia. *Psychiatry Research*, *107*, 61–73.

Cook IA, Morgan ML, Dunkin JJ, David S, Witte E, Lufkin R, Abrams M, Rosenberg S, Leuchter AF. (2002). Estrogen replacement therapy is associated with less progression of subclinical structural brain disease in normal elderly women: A pilot study. *International Journal of Geriatric Psychiatry*, *17*, 610–618.

Corey-Bloom J, Galasko D, Thal LJ. (1994). Clinical features and natural history of Alzheimer's disease. In Calne DB (Ed.), *Neurodegenerative diseases* (pp. 631–645). Philadelphia: WB Saunders.

Cotman CW, Berchtold NC. (2002). Exercise: A behavioral intervention to enhance brain health and plasticity. *Trends in Neurosciences*, *25*, 295–301.

Courchesne E, Chisum HJ, Townsend J, Cowles A, Covington J, Egaas B, Harwood M, Hind S, Press GA. (2000). Normal brain development and aging: Quantitative analysis at in vivo MR imaging in healthy volunteers. *Radiology*, *216*, 672–682.

Courchesne E, Townsend J, Saitoh O. (1994). The brain in infantile autism: Posterior fossa structures are abnormal. *Neurology*, *44*, 214–223.

Csernansky JG, Wang L, Jones D, Rastogi-Cruz D, Posener JA, Heydebrand G, Miller JP, Miller MI. (2002). Hippocampal deformities in schizophrenia characterized by high dimensional brain mapping. *American Journal of Psychiatry*, *159*, 2000–2006.

de Leeuw FE, De Groot JC, Breteler MMB. (2001). White matter changes: Frequency and risk factors. In Pantoni L, Inzitari D, Wallin A (Eds.), *The matter of white matter: Clinical and pathophysiological aspects of white matter disease related to cognitive decline and vascular dementia* (pp. 19–33). Utrecht, The Netherlands: Academic Pharmaceutical Productions.

de Leon MJ, Convit A, Wolf OT, Tarshish CY, DeSanti S, Rusinek H, Tsui W, Kandil E, Scherer AJ, Roche A, Imossi A, Thorn E, Bobinski M, Caraos C, Lesbre P, Schlyer D, Poirier J, Reisberg B, Fowler J. (2001). Prediction of cognitive decline in normal elderly subjects with 2-[^{18}F]fluoro-2-deoxy-D-glucose/positron-emission tomography (FDG/PET). *Proceedings of National Academy of Sciences of the United States of America, 98*, 10966–10971.

DeLisi LE, Sakuma M, Tew W, Kushner M, Hoff AL, Grimson R. (1997). Schizophrenia as a chronic active brain process: a study of progressive brain structural change subsequent to the onset of schizophrenia. *Psychiatry Research, 74*, 129–140.

den Heijer T, Geerlings MI, Hofman A, de Jong FH, Launer LJ, Pols HA, Breteler MM. (2003). Higher estrogen levels are not associated with larger hippocampi and better memory performance. *Archives of Neurology, 60*, 213–220.

Dickerson BC, Goncharova I, Sullivan MP, Forchetti C, Wilson RS, Bennett DA, Beckett LA, deToledo-Morrell L. (2001). MRI-derived entorhinal and hippocampal atrophy in incipient and very mild Alzheimer's disease. *Neurobiology of Aging, 22*, 747–754.

Drake EB, Henderson VW, Stanczyk FZ, McCleary CA, Brown WS, Smith CA, Rizzo AA, Murdock J, Buckwalter GA. (2000). Associations between circulating sex steroid hormones and cognition in normal elderly women. *Neurology, 54*, 599–603.

Driesen NR, Raz N. (1995). Sex-, age-, and handedness-related differences in human corpus callosum observed in vivo. *Psychobiology, 23*, 240–247.

Du AT, Schuff N, Zhu XP, Jagust WJ, Miller BL, Reed BR, Kramer JH, Mungas D, Yaffe K, Chui HC, Weiner MW. (2003). Atrophy rates of entorhinal cortex in AD and normal aging. *Neurology, 60*, 481–486.

Eberling JL, Wu C, Haan MN, Mungas D, Buoncore M, Jagust WJ. (2003). Preliminary evidence that estrogen protects against age-related hippocampal atrophy. *Neurobiology of Aging, 24*, 725–732.

Fox NC, Freeborough PA. (1997). Brain atrophy progression measured from registered serial MRI: Validation and application to Alzheimer's disease. *Journal of Magnetic Resonance Imaging, 7*, 1069–1075.

Fox NC, Schott JM. (2004). Imaging cerebral atrophy: Normal ageing to Alzheimer's disease. *Lancet, 363*, 392–394.

Fox NC, Warrington EK, Freeborough PA, Hartikainen P, Kennedy AM, Stevens JM, Rossor MN. (1996). Presymptomatic hippocampal atrophy in Alzheimer's disease. A longitudinal MRI study. *Brain, 119*, 2001–2007.

Gazzaley AH, Thakker MM, Hof PR, Morrison JH. (1997). Preserved number of entorhinal cortex layer II neurons in aged macaque monkeys. *Neurobiology of Aging, 18*, 549–553.

Giannakopoulos P, Hof PR, Michel JP, Guimon J, Bouras C. (1997). Cerebral cortex pathology in aging and Alzheimer's disease: A quantitative survey of large hospital-based geriatric and psychiatric cohorts. *Brain Research: Brain Research Reviews, 25*, 217–245.

Giedd JN, Blumenthal J, Jeffries NO, Castellanos FX, Liu H., Zijdenbos A, Paus T, Evans AC, Rapoport JL. (1999). Brain development during childhood and adolescence: A longitudinal MRI study. *Nature Neuroscience, 2*, 861–863.

Goldstein IB, Bartzokis G, Guthrie D, Shapiro D. (2002). Ambulatory blood pressure and brain atrophy in the healthy elderly. *Neurology, 59*, 713–719.

Gomez-Isla T, Price JL, McKeel DW Jr, Morris JC, Growdon JH, Hyman BT. (1996). Profound loss of layer II entorhinal cortex neurons occurs in very mild Alzheimer's disease. *Journal of Neuroscience, 16*, 4491–4500.

Good C, Johnsrude IS, Ashburner J, Henson RNA, Friston KJ, and Frackowiak RSJ. (2001). A voxel-based morphometric study of ageing in 465 normal adult human brains. *Neurolmage, 14*, 21–36.

Goodwin GM, Ebmeier KP. (2002). Chronic, treatment-resistant depression and right fronto-striatal atrophy. *The British Journal of Psychiatry*, *180*, 434–440.

Gosche KM, Mortimer JA, Smith CD, Markersbery WR, Snowdon DA. (2002). Hippocampal volume as an index of Alzheimer neuropathology: Findings from the Nun Study. *Neurology*, *58*, 1476–1482.

Grady CL. (2000). Functional brain imaging and age-related changes in cognition. *Biological Psychology*, *54*, 259–281.

Gunning-Dixon FM, Raz N. (2000). The cognitive correlates of white matter abnormalities in normal aging: A quantitative review. *Neuropsychology*, *14*, 224–232.

Guttmann CR, Jolesz FA, Kikinis R, Killiany RJ, Moss MB, Sandor T, Albert MS. (1998). White matter changes with normal aging. *Neurology*, *50*, 972–978.

Hackert VH, den Heijer T, Oudkerk M, Koudstaal PJ, Hofman A, Breteler MM. (2002). Hippocampal head size associated with verbal memory performance in nondemented elderly. *Neuroimage*, *17*, 1365–1372.

Head D, Raz N, Gunning-Dixon F, Williamson A, Acker JD. (2002). Age-related shrinkage of the prefrontal cortex is associated with executive, but not procedural aspects of cognitive performance. *Psychology and Aging*, *17*, 72–84.

Helenius J, Soinne L, Perkiö J, Salonen O, Kangasmäki A, Kaste M, Carano RAD, Aronen HJ, Tatlisumak T. (2002). Diffusion-weighted MR imaging in normal human brains in various age groups. *AJNR American Journal of Neuroradiology*, *23*, 194–199.

Ho BC, Andreasen NC, Nopoulos P, Arndt S, Magnotta V, Flaum M. (2003). Progressive structural brain abnormalities and their relationship to clinical outcome: A longitudinal magnetic resonance imaging study early in schizophrenia. *Archives of General Psychiatry*, *60*, 585–594.

Hu MT, White SJ, Chaudhuri KR, Morris RG, Bydder GM, Brooks DJ. (2001). Correlating rates of cerebral atrophy in Parkinson's disease with measures of cognitive decline. *Journal of Neural Transmission*, *108*, 571–580.

Insausti R, Jouttonen K, Soininen H, Insausti AM, Partanen K, Vainio P, Laakso MP, Pitkä-nen A. (1998). MR volumetric analysis of the human entorhinal, perirhinal, and temporo-polar cortices. *American Journal of Neuroradiology*, *19*, 659–671.

Jack CR Jr, Petersen RC, O'Brien PC, Tangalos EG. (1992). MR-based hippocampal volume-try in the diagnosis of Alzheimer's disease. *Neurology*, *42*, 183–188.

Jack CR Jr, Petersen RC, Xu Y, O'Brien PC, Smith GE, Ivnik RJ, Boeve BF, Tangalos EG, Kokmen E. (2000). Rates of hippocampal atrophy correlates with change in clinical status in aging and AD. *Neurology*, *55*, 484–489.

Jack CR Jr, Petersen RC, Xu Y, O'Brien PC, Smith GE, Ivnik RJ, Tangalos EG, Kokmen E. (1998). Rate of medial temporal lobe atrophy in typical aging and Alzheimer's disease. *Neurology*, *51*, 993–999.

Jack CR Jr, Theodore WH, Cook M, McCarthy G. (1995) MRI-based hippocampal volumet-rics: Data acquisition, normal ranges, and optimal protocol. *Magnetic Resonance Imaging*, *13*, 1057–1064.

Jernigan TL, Archibald SL, Fenema-Notestine C, Gamst AC, Stout JC, Bonner J, Hesselink JR. (2001) Effects of age on tissues and regions of the cerebrum and cerebellum, *Neurobiology of Aging*, *22*, 581–594.

Kantarci K, Jack CR Jr, Xu YC, Campeau NG, O'Brien PC, Smith GE, Ivnik RJ, Boeve BF, Kokmen E, Tangalos EG, Petersen RC. (2001). Mild cognitive impairment and Alzheimer disease: Regional diffusivity of water. *Radiology*, *219*, 101–107.

Kaye JA, Swihart T, Howieson D, Dame A, Moore MM, Karnos T, Camicioli R, Ball M, Oken B, Sexton G. (1997). Volume loss of the hippocampus and temporal lobe in healthy elderly persons destined to develop dementia. *Neurology*, *48*, 1297–1304.

Kemper T. (1994). Neuroanatomical and neuropathological changes during aging and dementia. In Albert ML, Knoefel J (Eds.), *Clinical neurology of aging* (pp. 3–67) New York: Oxford University Press.

Killiany RJ, Gomez-Isla T, Moss M, Kikinis R, Sandor T, Jolesz F, Tanzi R, Jones K, Hyman BT, Albert MS. (2000). Use of structural magnetic resonance imaging to predict who will get Alzheimer's disease. *Annals of Neurology, 47,* 430–439.

Killiany RJ, Hyman BT, Gomez-Isla T, Moss MB, Kikinis R, Jolesz F, Tanzi R, Jones K, Albert MS. (2002). MRI measures of entorhinal cortex vs hippocampus in preclinical AD. *Neurology, 58,* 1188–1196.

Kordower JH, Chu Y, Stebbins GT, DeKosky ST, Cochran EJ, Bennett D, Mufson EJ. (2001). Loss and atrophy of layer II entorhinal cortex neurons in elderly people with mild cognitive impairment. *Annals of Neurology, 49,* 202–213.

Laakso MP, Frisoni GB, Kononen M, Mikkonen M, Beltramello A, Geroldi C, Bianchetti A, Trabucchi M, Soininen H, Aronen HJ. (2000). Hippocampus and entorhinal cortex in frontotemporal dementia and Alzheimer's disease: A morphometric MRI study. *Biological Psychiatry, 47,* 1056–1063.

Laakso MP, Lehtovirta M, Partanen K, Riekkinen PJ, Soininen H. (2000). Hippocampus in Alzheimer's disease: A 3-year follow-up MRI study. *Biological Psychiatry, 47,* 557–561.

Lang DJ, Kopala LC, Vandorpe RA, Rui Q, Smith GN, Goghari VM, Honer WG. (2001). An MRI study of basal ganglia volumes in first-episode schizophrenia patients treated with risperidone. *American Journal of Psychiatry, 158,* 625–631.

Lesniak KT, Dubbert PM. (2001). Exercise and hypertension. *Current Opinion in Cardiology, 16,* 356–359.

Lieberman J, Chakos M, Wu H, Alvir J, Hoffman E, Robinson D, Bilder R. (2001). Longitudinal study of brain morphology in first episode schizophrenia. *Biological Psychiatry, 49,* 487–499.

Lim KO, Zipursky RB, Watts MC, Pfefferbaum A. (1992). Decreased gray matter in normal aging: An in vivo magnetic resonance study. *Journal of Gerontology, 47,* B26–B30.

Lindenberger U, Singer T, Baltes PB. (2002). Longitudinal selectivity in aging populations: Separating mortality-associated versus experimental components in the Berlin Aging Study (BASE). *Journal of Gerontology B: Psychological Science, 57,* P474–P482.

Liu RSN, Lemieux L, Bell GS, Sisodiya SM, Shovron SD, Sander JWAS, Duncan JS. (2003). A longitudinal study of brain morphometrics using quantitative magnetic resonance imaging and difference image analysis. *NeuroImage, 20,* 22–33.

Luoto R, Manolio T, Meilahn E, Bhadelia R, Furberg C, Cooper L, Kraut M. (2000). Estrogen replacement therapy and MRI-demonstrated cerebral infarcts, white matter changes, and brain atrophy in older women: The Cardiovascular Health Study. *Journal of American Geriatric Society, 48,* 467–472.

Maki PM, Resnick SM. (2000). Longitudinal effects of estrogen replacement therapy on PET cerebral blood flow and cognition. *Neurobiology of Aging, 21,* 373–383.

Marin J, Rodriguez-Martinez MA. (1999). Age-related changes in vascular responses. *Experimental Gerontology, 34,* 503–512.

Marriott LK, Hauss-Wegrzyniak B, Benton RS, Vraniak PD, Wenk GL. (2002). Long-term estrogen therapy worsens the behavioral and neuropathological consequences of chronic brain inflammation. *Behavioral Neuroscience, 116,* 902–911.

Mascalchi M, Moretti M, Della Nave R, Lolli F, Tessa C, Carlucci G, Bartolini L, Pracucci G, Pantoni L, Filippi M, Inzitari D. (2003). Longitudinal evaluation of leukoaraiosis with whole brain ADC histograms. *Neurology, 59,* 938–940.

McArdle JJ, Hamagami F, Elias MF, Robbins MA. (1991). Structural modeling of mixed longitudinal and cross-sectional data. *Experimental Aging Research, 17,* 29–51.

Meier-Ruge W, Ulrich J, Bruhlmann M, Meier E. (1992). Age-related white matter atrophy in the human brain. *Annals of New York Academy of Sciences, 673,* 260–269.

Merrill DA, Roberts JA, Tuszynski MH. (2000). Conservation of neuron number and size in entorhinal cortex layers II, III, and V/VI of aged primates. *Journal of Comparative Neurology, 422,* 396–401.

Miller AK, Alston RL, Corsellis JA. (1980). Variation with age in the volumes of grey and white matter in the cerebral hemispheres of man: Measurements with an image analyser. *Neuropathology and Applied Neurobiology, 6,* 119–132.

Miller AK, Corsellis JA. (1977). Evidence for a secular increase in human brain weight during the past century. *Annals of Human Biology, 4,* 253–257.

Moffat SD, Szekely CA, Zonderman AB, Kabani NJ, Resnick SM. (2000). Longitudinal change in hippocampal volume as a function of apolipoprotein E genotype. *Neurology, 55,* 134–136.

Moseley M, Bammer R, Illes J. (2002). Diffusion-tensor imaging of cognitive performance. *Brain and Cognition, 50,* 396–413.

Mu Q, Xie J, Wen Z, Weng Y, Shuyun Z. (1999). A quantitative MR study of the hippocampal formation, the amygdala, and the temporal horn of the lateral ventricle in healthy subjects 40 to 90 years of age. *American Journal of Neuroradiology, 20,* 207–211.

Mueller EA, Moore MM, Kerr DC, Sexton G, Camicioli RM, Howieson DB, Quinn JF, Kaye JA. (1998). Brain volume preserved in healthy elderly through the eleventh decade. *Neurology, 51,* 1555–1562.

Nusbaum AO, Tang CY, Buchsbaum MS, Wei TC, Atlas SW. (2001). Regional and global changes in cerebral diffusion with normal aging. *AJNR American Journal of Neuroradiology, 22,* 136–142.

Ohnishi T, Matsuda H, Tabira T, Asada T, Uno M. (2001). Changes in brain morphology in Alzheimer disease and normal aging: Is Alzheimer disease an exaggerated aging process? *AJNR American Journal of Neuroradiology, 22,* 1680–1685.

Pantoni L, Inzitari D, Wallin A (Eds.). (2001). The matter of white matter: Clinical and pathophysiological aspects of white matter disease related to cognitive decline and vascular dementia. Utrecht, The Netherlands: Academic Pharmaceutical Productions.

Panzer V, VanMeter J, Stevens M, Beckley D, Wolfson L. (2003, November). Effects of aging on automated segmentation of brain MRI. Paper presented at the Society for Neuroscience meeting; New Orleans, LA, Program 863.17.

Pennanen C, Kivipelto M, Tuomainen S, Hartikainen P, Hänninen T, Laakso MP, Hallikainen M, Vanhanen M, Nissinen A, Helkala EL, Vainio P, Vanninen R, Partanen K, Soininen H. (2004). Hippocampus and entorhinal cortex in mild cognitive impairment and early AD. *Neurobiology of Aging, 25,* 303–310.

Peters A, Sethares C. (2002). Aging and the myelinated fibers in prefrontal cortex and corpus callosum of the monkey. *Journal of Comparative Neurology, 442,* 277–291.

Petersen RC, Jack CR, Smith GE, Waring SC, Ivnik RJ. (1998). MRI in the diagnosis of mild cognitive impairment and Alzheimer's disease [abstract]. *Journal of the International Neuropsychological Society, 4,* 22.

Pfefferbaum A, Mathalon DH, Sullivan EV, Rawles JM, Zipursky RB, Lim KO. (1994). A quantitative magnetic resonance imaging study of changes in brain morphology from infancy to late adulthood. *Archives of Neurology, 51,* 874–887.

Pfefferbaum A, Sullivan EV. (2003). Increased brain white matter diffusivity in normal adult aging: Relationship to anisotropy and partial voluming. *Magnetic Resonance in Medicine, 49,* 953–961.

Pfefferbaum A, Sullivan EV, Hedehus M, Lim KO, Adalsteinsson E, Moseley M. (2000). Age-related decline in brain white matter anisotropy measured with spatially corrected echo-planar diffusion tensor imaging. *Magnetic Resonance in Medicine, 44,* 259–268.

Pfefferbaum A, Sullivan EV, Rosenbloom MJ, Mathalon DH, Lim KO. (1998). A controlled study of cortical gray matter and ventricular changes in alcoholic men over a 5-year interval. *Archives of General Psychiatry, 55,* 905–912.

Pruessner JC, Collins DL, Pruessner M, Evans AC. (2001). Age and gender predict volume decline in the anterior and posterior hippocampus in early adulthood. *Journal of Neuroscience, 21,* 194–200.

Raz N. (2000). Aging of the brain and its impact on cognitive performance: Integration of structural and functional findings. In Craik FIM, Salthouse TA (Eds.), *Handbook of aging and cognition II* (pp. 1–90). Mahwah, NJ: Erlbaum.

Raz N, Gunning FM, Head D, Dupuis JH, McQuain JD, Briggs SD, Loken WJ, Thornton AE, Acker JD. (1997). Selective aging of the human cerebral cortex observed in vivo: Differential vulnerability of the prefrontal gray matter. *Cerebral Cortex, 7,* 268–282.

Raz N, Gunning-Dixon F, Head D, Williamson A, Acker JD. (2001). Age and sex differences in the cerebellum and the ventral pons: A prospective MR study of healthy adults. *American Journal of Neuroradiology, 22,* 1161–1167.

Raz N, Gunning-Dixon F, Head D, Williamson A, Rodrigue K, Acker JD. (2004a). Aging, sexual dimorphism, and hemispheric asymmetry of the cerebral cortex: Replicability of regional differences in volume. *Neurobiology of Aging, 25,* 377–396.

Raz N, Lindenberger U, Rodrigue KM, Kennedy KM, Head D, Williamson A, Dahle C, Acker, JD. (submitted). General trends, individual differences, and modifiers of regional brain shrinkage in healthy adults.

Raz N, Rodrigue KM, Acker, JD. (2003a). Hypertension and the brain: Vulnerability of the prefrontal regions and executive functions. *Behavioral Neuroscience, 17,* 1169–1180.

Raz N, Rodrigue KM, Head D, Kennedy KM, Acker JD. (2004b). Differential aging of the medial temporal lobe: A study of a five-year change. *Neurology, 62,* 433–439.

Raz N, Rodrigue K, Kennedy K, Head D, Dahle C, Acker JD. (2003b). Differential age-related changes in the regional metencephalic volumes: A 5-year follow-up. *Neuroscience Letters, 349,* 163–166.

Raz N, Rodrigue KM, Kennedy KM, Head D, Gunning-Dixon FM, Acker JD. (2003c). Differential aging of the human striatum: Longitudinal evidence. *American Journal of Neuroradiology, 24,* 1849–1856.

Resnick SM, Goldszal AF, Davatzikos C, Golski S, Kraut MA, Metter EJ, Bryan RN, Zonderman AB. (2000). One-year age changes in MRI brain volumes in older adults. *Cerebral Cortex, 10,* 464–472.

Resnick SM, Pham DL, Kraut MA, Zonderman AB, Davatzikos C. (2003). Longitudinal magnetic resonance imaging studies of older adults: A shrinking brain. *Journal of Neuroscience, 23,* 3295–3301.

Reuter-Lorenz P. (2002). New visions of the aging mind and brain. *Trends in Cognitive Science, 6,* 394–400.

Rhyu IJ, Cho TH, Le NJ, Uhm CS, Kim H, Suh YS. (1999). Magnetic resonance image-based cerebellar volumetry in healthy Korean adults. *Neuroscience Letters, 270,* 149–152.

Rice MM, Graves A, McCurry SM, Gibbons LE, Bowen JD, McCormick WC, Larson EB. (2000). Postmenopausal estrogen and estrogen-progestin use and 2-year rate of cognitive change in a cohort of older Japanese American women: The Kame project. *Archives of Internal Medicine, 160,* 1641–1649.

Rosenzweig ES, Barnes CA. (2003). Impact of aging on hippocampal function: Plasticity, network dynamics, and cognition. *Progress in Neurobiology, 69,* 143–179.

Rovaris M, Iannucci G, Cercignani M, Sormani MP, De Stefano N, Gerevini S, Comi G, Filippi M. (2003). Age-related changes in conventional, magnetization transfer, and diffusion-tensor MR imaging findings: Study with whole-brain tissue histogram analysis. *Radiology, 227*, 731–738.

Saijo T, Abe T, Someya Y, Sassa T, Sudo Y, Suhara T, Shuno T, Asai K, Okubo Y. (2001). Ten year progressive ventricular enlargement in schizophrenia: An MRI morphometrical study. *Psychiatry and Clinical Neurosciences, 55*, 41–47.

Salat DH, Kaye JA, Janowsky JS. (1999). Prefrontal gray and white matter volumes in healthy aging and Alzheimer disease. *Archives of Neurology, 56*, 338–344.

Salerno JA, Murphy DG, Horwitz B, DeCarli C, Haxby JV, Rapoport SI, Schapiro MB. (1992). Brain atrophy in hypertension. A volumetric magnetic resonance imaging study. *Hypertension, 20*, 340–348.

Scahill RI, Frost C, Jenkins R, Whitwell JI, Rossor MN, Fox NC. (2003). A longitudinal study of brain volume changes in normal aging using serial registered magnetic resonance imaging. *Archives of Neurology, 60*, 989–994.

Scahill RI, Schott JM, Stevens JM, Rossor MN, Fox NC. (2002). Mapping the evolution of regional atrophy in Alzheimer's disease: Unbiased analysis of fluid-registered serial MRI. *Proceedings of National Academy of Science of the United States of America, 99*, 4703–4707.

Schaie KW, Strother CR. (1968). A cross-sequential study of age changes in cognitive behavior. *Psychological Bulletin, 70*, 671–680.

Schmidt R, Fazekas F, Reinhart B, Kapeller P, Fazekas G, Offenbacher H, Eber B, Schumacher M, Freidl W. (1996). Estrogen replacement therapy in older women: A neuropsychological and brain MRI study. *Journal of American Geriatric Society, 44*, 1307–1313.

Schott JM, Fox NC, Frost C, Scahill RI, Janssen JC, Chan D, Jenkins R, Rossor MN. (2003). Assessing the onset of structural change in familial Alzheimer's disease. *Annals of Neurology, 53*, 181–188.

Schretlen D, Pearlson GD, Anthony JC, Aylward EH, Augustine AM, Davis A, Barta P. (2000). Elucidating the contributions of processing speed, executive ability, and frontal lobe volume to normal age-related differences in fluid intelligence. *Journal of International Neuropsychological Society, 6*, 52–61.

Schuff N, Amend DL, Knowlton R, Norman D, Fein G, Weiner MW. (1999). Age-related metabolite changes and volume loss in the hippocampus by magnetic resonance spectroscopy and imaging. *Neurobiology of Aging, 20*, 279–285.

Shumaker SA, Legault C, Thal L, Wallace RB, Ockene JK, Hendrix SL, Jones BN III, Assaf AR, Jackson RD, Kotchen JM, Wassertheil-Smoller S, Wactawski-Wende J, WHIMS Investigators. (2003). Estrogen plus progestin and the incidence of dementia and mild cognitive impairment in postmenopausal women: The Women's Health Initiative Memory Study: A randomized controlled trial. *Journal of the American Medical Association, 289*, 2651–2662.

Small SA, Nava AS, Perera GM, Delapaz R, Stern Y. (2000). Evaluating the function of hippocampal subregions with high-resolution MRI in Alzheimer's disease and aging. *Microscopy Research and Technique, 51*, 101–108.

Sowell ER, Peterson BS, Thompson PM, Welcome SE, Henkenius AL, Toga AW. (2003). Mapping cortical change across the human life span. *Nature Neuroscience, 6*, 309–315.

Strassburger TL, Lee HC, Daly EM, Szczepanik J, Krasuski JS, Mentis MJ, Salerno JA, DeCarli C, Schapiro MB, Alexander GE. (1997). Interactive effects of age and hypertension on volumes of brain structures. *Stroke, 28*, 1410–1417.

Sullivan EV, Deshmukh A, Desmond JE, Lim KO, Pfefferbaum A. (2000). Cerebellar volume decline in normal aging, alcoholism, and Korsakoff's syndrome: relation to ataxia. *Neuropsychology, 14*, 341–352.

Sullivan EV, Marsh L, Mathalon DH, Lim KO, Pfefferbaum A. (1995). Anterior hippocampal volume deficits in nonamnesic, aging chronic alcoholics. *Alcohol: Clinical and Experimental Research, 19*, 110–122.

Sullivan EV, Pfefferbaum A. (2003). Diffusion tensor imaging in normal aging and neuropsychiatric disorders. *European Journal of Radiology, 45*, 244–255.

Sullivan EV, Pfefferbaum A, Adalsteinsson E, Swan GE, Carmelli D. (2002). Differential rates of regional brain change in callosal and ventricular size: A 4-year longitudinal MRI study of elderly men. *Cerebral Cortex, 12*, 438–445.

Sullivan EV, Rosenbloom M, Serventi KL, Pfefferbaum A. (2004). Effects of age and sex on volumes of the thalamus, pons, and cortex. *Neurobiology of Aging, 25*, 185–192.

Tang Y, Whitman GT, Lopez I, Baloh, RW. (2001). Brain volume changes on longitudinal magnetic resonance imaging in normal older people. *Journal of Neuroimaging, 11*, 393–400.

Tauscher-Wisniewski S, Tauscher J, Logan J, Christensen BK, Mikulis DJ, Zipursky RB. (2002). Caudate volume changes in first episode psychosis parallel the effects of normal aging: A 5-year follow-up study. *Schizophrenia Research, 58*, 185–188.

Taylor WD, MacFall JR, Provenzale JM, Payne ME, McQuoid DR, Steffens DC, Krishnan KR. (2003). Serial MR imaging of volumes of hyperintense white matter lesions in elderly patients: Correlation with vascular risk factors. *AJR American Journal of Roentgenology, 81*, 571–576.

Teipel SJ, Bayer W, Alexander GE, Zebuhr Y, Teichberg D, Kulic L, Schapiro M, Möller H-J, Rapoport SI, Hampel H. (2002). Progression of corpus callosum atrophy in Alzheimer disease. *Archives of Neurology, 59*, 243–248.

Thompson PM, Hayashi KM, de Zubicaray G, Janke AL, Rose SE, Semple J, Herman D, Hong MS, Dittmer SS, Doddrell DM, Toga AW. (2003). Dynamics of gray matter loss in Alzheimer's disease. *Journal of Neuroscience, 23*, 994–1005.

Tisserand DJ, Pruessner JC, Sanz Arigita EJ, van Boxtel MP, Evans AC, Jolles J, Uylings HB. (2002). Regional frontal cortical volumes decrease differentially in aging: An MRI study to compare volumetric approaches and voxel-based morphometry. *Neuroimage, 17*, 657–669.

Tisserand DJ, Visser PJ, van Boxtel, MPJ, Jolles J. (2000). The relation between global and limbic brain volumes on MRI and cognitive performance in healthy individuals across the age range. *Neurobiology of Aging, 21*, 569–576.

Troncoso JC, Martin LJ, Dal Forno G, Kawas CH. (1996). Neuropathology in controls and demented subjects from the Baltimore Longitudinal Study of Aging. *Neurobiology of Aging, 17*, 365–371.

Uylings HB, de Brabander JM. (2002). Neuronal changes in normal human aging and Alzheimer's disease. *Brain and Cognition, 49*, 268–276.

van Amelsvoort T, Compton J, Murphy D. (2001). In vivo assessment of the effects of estrogen on the human brain. *Trends in Endocrinology and Metabolism, 12*, 273–276.

Van Der Werf YD, Tisserand DJ, Visser PJ, Hofman PAM, Vuurman E, Uylings HBM, Jolles J. (2001). Thalamic volume predicts performance on tests of cognitive speed and decreases in healthy aging—A magnetic resonance imaging-based volumetric analysis. *Cognitive Brian Research, 11*, 377–385.

Van Laere KJ, Dierckx RA. (2001). Brain perfusion SPECT: Age- and sex-related effects correlated with voxel-based morphometric findings in healthy adults. *Radiology, 221*, 810–817.

van Praag H, Kempermann G, Gage FH. (1999). Running increases cell proliferation and neurogenesis in the adult mouse dentate gyrus. *Nature Neuroscience, 2*, 266–270.

van Swieten JC, Geyskes GG, Derix MM, Peeck BM, Ramos LM, van Latum JC, van Gijn

J. (1991). Hypertension in the elderly is associated with white matter lesions and cognitive decline. *Annals of Neurology, 30*, 825–830.

Verhaeghen P, Marcoen A, Goossens L. (1993). Facts and fiction about memory aging: A quantitative integration of research findings. *Journal of Gerontology, 48*, P157–P171.

Wang D, Doddrell DM. (2002). MR image-based measurement of rates of change in volumes of brain structures. Part I: method and validation. *Magnetic Resonance Imaging, 20*, 27–40.

Wassertheil-Smoller S, Hendrix SL, Limacher M, Heiss G, Kooperberg C, Baird A, Kotchen T, Curb JD, Black H, Rossouw JE, Aragaki A, Safford M, Stein E, Laowattana S, Mysiw WJ, WHI Investigators. (2003). Effect of estrogen plus progestin on stroke in postmenopausal women: the Women's Health Initiative: A randomized trial. *Journal of the American Medical Association, 289*, 2673–2684.

Xu Y, Jack CR Jr, O'Brien PC, Kokmen E, Smith GE, Ivnik RJ, Boeve BF, Tangalos RG, Petersen RC. (2000). Usefulness of MRI measures of entorhinal cortex versus hippocampus in AD. *Neurology, 54*, 1760–1767.

3

The Role of Dopamine Systems
in Cognitive Aging

Lars Bäckman
Lars Farde

In this chapter, we review the extant literature on the influence of age-related changes in the nigrostriatal dopamine (DA) system on age-related cognitive changes. In so doing, we draw primarily on research using molecular imaging modalities to quantify DA biomarkers in the living human brain. The chapter is organized as follows: First, we provide an empirical and theoretical rationale for the cognitive relevance of DA. This is followed by an overview of the organization of DA systems in the brain. Next, we describe the basic principles for imaging of the DA system. We then discuss evidence for an influence of adult age on various DA markers. Following this, the major findings in behavioral research on cognitive aging are reviewed. The sections converge into a review of research examining the correlative triad among age, DA markers, and cognitive performance. The findings from this research are then positioned in relation to other theory and data in the cognitive neuroscience of aging. Finally, we conclude by suggesting avenues for future empirical research on DA functions and cognitive aging.

Dopamine and Cognitive Functioning

A key role of the nigrostriatal DA system in efficient motor functioning has long been known, mainly from observations of patients with degenerative brain disorders affecting the striatum (e.g., Freed & Yamamoto, 1985; McEntee, Mair, & Langlais, 1987). However, several lines of evidence from more recent studies suggested that DA is also critically involved in many higher order cognitive functions.

First, studies on subject populations with severe alterations of the DA system, such as patients with Huntington's disease (HD) and Parkinson's disease (PD), indicated deficits across multiple cognitive domains, including executive functions, visuospatial skill, episodic memory, verbal fluency, perceptual speed, and reasoning (e.g., Brandt & Butters, 1986; R. G. Brown & Marsden, 1990). Positron emission tomography (PET) studies have demonstrated a sizable relationship of DA D_1 and D_2 receptor binding as well as DA transporter (DAT) binding to performance in the aforementioned task domains in groups of mildly to moderately ill patients with HD (Bäckman et al., 1997; Lawrence et al., 1998). A similarly strong relationship between PET-derived measures of presynaptic kinetics of [^{18}F]DOPA and executive functioning has been documented in PD (Remy et al., 2000). The role of DA losses in the cognitive deficits associated with PD has been further substantiated by experimental studies in monkeys (Burns et al., 1983; Langston & Irwin, 1986) and clinical studies in human subjects (Stern & Langston, 1985; Stern et al., 1990), showing that methyl-phenyl-tetrahydripyridine (MPTP), a specific neural toxin that kills neuronal cell bodies in the substantia nigra, results in cognitive deficits that parallel those occurring in PD (e.g., executive and visuospatial deficits).

Second, there is substantial evidence from animal studies that depletion of dopaminergic pathways is associated with cognitive deficits. For example, destruction of dopaminergic nerve terminals at different sites in the mesocorticolimbic system (e.g., septum, nucleus accumbens, prefrontal cortex) has been found to produce deficits across multiple cognitive domains in rodents and monkeys alike. This includes impairment in memory (Simon, Taghzouti, & Le Moal, 1986), inhibitory functions (G. H. Jones & Robbins, 1992), set shifting (Roberts et al., 1994), and spatial attention (Boussaoud & Kermadi, 1997). Relatedly, lesioning dopaminergic pathways at the level of the subthalamic nucleus, which leads to deprivation of nigral DA input, results in deficits in tasks that assess attentional as well as executive function and motor sequencing (Baunez, Nieoullon, & Amalric, 1995; Baunez & Robbins, 1999). In general, this research indicates a role of DA in regulating performance across a variety of higher order cognitive functions.

Third, there is evidence from animals and humans that pharmacological manipulations of DA transmission are related to cognitive performance. Administration of D-amphetamine (D-AMP) elevates the synaptic concentration of DA and may serve as a model for DA hyperactivity. Although research on the effects of D-AMP on cognition in humans has yielded somewhat equivocal results (see Kolega, 1993, for an overview), several studies have reported drug-related performance gains in tasks that assess information-processing speed (e.g., Halliday et al., 1994), discrimination (e.g., Kelly, Foltin, & Fischman, 1991), and vigilance (Spiegel, 1978). Relatedly, Servan-Schreiber, Carter, et al. (1998) reported beneficial effects of D-AMP regarding both latency and accuracy in a selective-attention task. Further, in a series of studies, Luciana and colleagues (Luciana & Collins, 1997; Luciana, Collins, & Depue, 1998; Luciana et al., 1992) found that bromocriptine, a D_2 receptor agonist, may facilitate delayed spatial working memory performance in healthy volunteers. An interesting feature of the Luciana, Collins, and Depue (1998) study was that fenfluramine, a serotonin agonist, impaired performance in the same task. These data suggest opposing roles for DA and serotonin in modulating working memory functions in humans. Of further note is that the pattern of findings in these studies suggests that the effects were not secondary to changes in basic sensorimotor, attentional, or global arousal processes. Rather, they seem to reflect changes in the temporal integration between a sensory cue and the requested response.

Williams and Goldman-Rakic (1995) found that injections of D_1 and D_2 receptor agonists into the prefrontal cortex facilitated working memory performance in nonhuman primates. Interestingly, whereas the effects of the D_1 agonist appeared to be specific in modulating memory fields of locally active neurons, the D_2-related effects were more general, likely reflecting changes in the integration of motor, memory, and motivational capacities.

A critical question concerns whether the demonstrated stimulatory effects of DA agonists on cognitive performance represent functions that can be disturbed or hampered by DA antagonists. Indeed, Luciana and Collins (1997) demonstrated that administration of haloperidol, a D_2 receptor antagonist, worsened performance in a working-memory task in which beneficial effects were seen from a D_2 agonist. In a related study, Ramaekers et al. (1999) reported that a rather low dose of haloperidol impaired performance in tasks assessing multiple cognitive domains, including psychomotor speed and working memory. Likewise, several studies with monkeys (e.g., Sawaguchi & Goldman-Rakic, 1991) indicate that blockade of DA receptors resulted in reversible impairment in motor and cognitive tasks.

Although the pharmacological work reviewed in this section may appear consistent, there are equivocal findings in the extant literature. Inconsistent observations may depend on doses, preexperimental cognitive skill, or drug affinities for distinct DA receptor subtypes. Luciana and Collins (1997) reported a facilitative effect of bromocriptine on spatial working memory at lower, but not at the same, doses as initially reported by Luciana et al. (1992). Kimberg, D'Esposito, and Farah (1997) found that persons with low working memory capacity showed positive bromocriptine-related effects on working memory performance, whereas those with high working memory capacity showed negative effects (see also Mehta et al., 2000). In contrast, Kimberg and D'Esposito (2003) documented larger effects of pergolide, an agonist for both the D_1 and the D_2 receptor subtypes, on delayed working memory performance for persons with greater working memory capacity than for those with lower capacity. In this study, administration of pergolide also had some negative overall effects, namely, increases in susceptibility to interference and reduced verbal fluency.

Finally, although several studies (Kimberg, D'Esposito, & Farah, 1997; Luciana & Collins, 1997; Luciana et al., 1992) have implicated D_2 receptors in human working memory, Müller, von Cramon, and Pollmann (1998) found positive effects of pergolide, but not of bromocriptine, on visuospatial working memory performance. These data suggest that D_1 receptors have a preferential role in working memory modulation. Although the reasons for the mixed findings remain unclear, they may reflect yet poorly understood interactions between subject-related and drug-related factors that vary between receptor subtypes. Interestingly, similar inconsistencies have been observed at a neurophysiological level. There is evidence of an inverted U-shaped dose–response function with administration of DA agonists in monkeys (Cai & Arnsten, 1997). Thus, a DA agonist may promote or inhibit firing in the same neural circuitry, depending on both dosage and initial endogenous DA levels.

At a theoretical level, several models have been proposed postulating a key role for DA in modulating cognitive performance. Common to many of these models is that DA is assumed to facilitate switching between different targets within as well as between neural networks (e.g., Beninger, 1983; Oades, 1985). This role has been conceptualized in terms of enhancing the incoming neural signal relative to background noise (e.g., Cohen & Servan-Schreiber, 1992; Sawaguchi, Matsamura, & Kubota, 1988), with the notion that an increased signal-to-noise ratio should promote the firing frequency of innervated neurons (e.g., Daniel et al., 1991; Luciana, Collins, & Depue, 1998).

Servan-Schreiber, Bruno, et al. (1998) proposed a model that was specifically developed to come to grips with the effects of D-AMP on selective attention. In this model, DA effects are simulated as a change in gain of neural assemblies in the area of release. An interesting aspect of the model is that effects on motor performance are thought to result from gains over the response layer, resulting in increased speed but impaired accuracy. In contrast, attentional effects are simulated as a change in gains over the attention layer, resulting in improved speed and accuracy, particularly under demanding conditions. Results from a study that investigated the effects of D-AMP on motor and cognitive performance in a selective attention task were in excellent agreement with the proposed model (Servan-Schreiber, Carter, et al., 1998).

Of particular relevance to the current chapter is that neurocomputational work (Li, Lindenberger, & Sikström, 2001) has successfully modeled age-related cognitive deficits as a function of deficient dopaminergic modulation. Similar to general models of DA and cognition, Li and colleagues assumed that age-related loss of DA increases the neural noise, which in turn results in less-distinctive representations in the brain. These less-distinctive representations are hypothesized as a key determinant of age-related cognitive deficits across a variety of domains (e.g., working memory, executive functions).

Finally, there is both onto- and phylogenetic evidence suggesting a role for DA in cognitive development. The presence of dopaminergic cells in the first stages of embryogenesis in almost all species, including all vertebrae, suggests a role for DA in early neurodevelopment (e.g., Pendleton et al., 1998). A progressive postnatal maturation of dopaminergic cortical innervation has been demonstrated in the rhesus monkey (Goldman-Rakic & Brown, 1982). Further, reorganization of the superficial layers of the prefrontal cortex occurs in primates during the postnatal period, when the dopaminergic innervation is maximal. Thus, it has been suggested that DA innervation contributes to the organization of the prefrontal cortex. Specifically, given that cortical areas that are critical to higher order cognitive functions are far from fully developed at birth, DA may serve as one among several neurodevelopmental factors that regulate division, migration, and differentiation processes of cortical neurons (Nieoullon, 2002).

Regarding the role of DA in hominid evolution, it is interesting to note that dopaminergic terminals are restricted to the frontal lobes in rodents, although they innervate the entire cortical areas in monkeys and humans (R. M. Brown & Goldman, 1977; Gaspar et al., 1989). The expansion of DA innervation during evolution coincides with the increasing cortical involvement in sensory processing through the basal ganglia (Smeets, Marin, & Gonzales, 2000). Relatedly, the presence of dopaminergic fibers across different cortical layers is substantially more widespread in primates than in rodents. In humans, D_1 and D_2 receptors are distributed throughout the neocortex (e.g., Farde et al., 1987; Kessler et al., 1993). These observations provide converging evidence for increased dopaminergic cortical innervation in late-stage mammalian evolution.

In an intriguing article, Previc (1999) contended that the development of DA systems in the brain may have been pivotal in the evolution of human intelligence. In brief, given the role of DA in counteracting hyperthermia during endurance activity, Previc argued that a dopaminergic expansion during early hominid evolution might have resulted in successful chase hunting in the African savannas. Changes in physical activity and diet may have further increased cortical DA levels. These physiological and dietary changes may have contributed to the vertical elongation of the body, increased brain size, and increased cortical convolutedness.

Dopamine Systems in the Human Brain

The nigrostriatal and mesolimbic systems are two major DA systems. The cell bodies of the nigrostriatal DA system are located in the substantia nigra in ventral mesencephalon. The neurons project to the striatum, a region with dense dopaminergic innervation. The mesolimbic DA system originates from a more diffuse collection of dopaminergic neurons in ventral mesencephalon, medial to the substantia nigra. This region is called the ventral tegmental area. One portion of the neurons here projects to limbic regions, such as the nucleus accumbens, the amygdala, the hippocampus, and the anterior cingulate cortex. A third pathway also originates from the ventral tegmentum and projects to the neocortex. This pathway has been identified mainly in the primate brain and has been referred to as the mesocortical DA system. Figure 3.1 portrays the major dopaminergic pathways in the human brain.

Several proteins may serve as biochemical markers for the DA systems. The physiological effects of DA are mediated by binding to any of the five currently identified DA receptor subtypes (D_{1-5}). The DA receptor subtypes have distinct anatomical distributions in the brain (Meador-Woodruff, 1994) and can thus be viewed as markers for different clusters of DA-related functions. The five subtypes are grouped into two families on the basis of structural homology and biochemical characteristics. The family of D_1-like receptors includes the D_1 and D_5 subtypes and the family of D_2-like receptors includes the D_2, D_3, and D_4 subtypes. In the following, the two families are referred to as D_1 and D_2 receptors because these are the most highly expressed DA receptor subtypes in the human brain. In addition, most of the ligands currently used for receptor imaging do not differentiate among the family members.

The D_1 receptors are more abundant than the D_2 receptors, reflecting a high concentration not only in the striatum, but also throughout the neocortex (Hall et al., 1994). The D_2 receptors are highly concentrated in the striatum. Lower concentrations are expressed in the brain stem and the thalamus, and concentrations are minute throughout the neocortex (Kessler et al., 1993). Cortically, the D_2 receptors have a regional-specific laminar distribution, located in lamina 2 of the lower temporal cortex and in lamina 6 of the remaining neocortex (Kohler, Ericson, & Radesater, 1991).

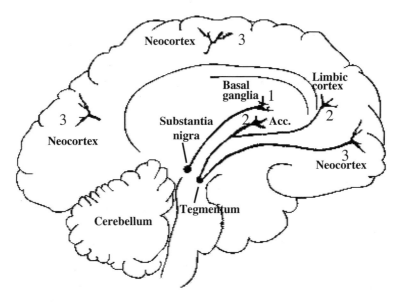

Figure 3.1. Major dopaminergic pathways in the human brain: 1, the nigro-striatal system projecting to the basal ganglia; 2, the mesolimbic system projecting to the accumbens (Acc) and the limbic cortex; 3, the mesocortical system projecting to the neocortex.

Early work with rodents suggested an anterior-to-posterior gradient of dopaminergic projections to the neocortex, with a preferential DA innervation of the frontal cortex (e.g., Ungerstedt, 1971). However, this generally accepted assumption has not been confirmed by more recent in vitro (e.g., Hall et al., 1994; Kessler et al., 1993) and in vivo (e.g., Farde et al., 1997) data. Specifically, these studies in human subjects demonstrated homogenous distribution of D_1 receptors across the neocortex and preferential localization of D_2 receptors in the ventral temporal cortex. The species differences in receptor distribution are consistent with findings that dopaminergic terminals are restricted to the frontal lobes in rodents, although they are distributed across the entire cortex in monkeys and humans (R. M. Brown & Goldman, 1977; Gaspar et al., 1989).

Most DA receptors are located on postsynaptic neurons, although a small proportion is expressed on DA cells. The autoreceptors presynaptically located on DA nerve terminals (Carlsson, 1975) regulate DA synthesis and release and belong to the family of D_2-like receptors (Roth, 1984). DA is synthesized at the presynaptic terminal, a process that is determined by the enzyme tyrosine hydroxylase (TH), which converts tyrosine to the DA precursor Dopa. The DAT is a membrane-bound protein that serves as a regulator of the synaptic concentration of DA at nerve terminals (Giros et al., 1992). The DAT provides a rapid and efficient mechanism for reuptake of synaptic DA and is essential for the regulation of DA neurotransmission (e.g., Giros et al., 1996). It has been suggested that the concentration of DAT may serve as a marker of the homeostatic tone of the DA system (Jaber et al., 1997;

S. R. Jones et al., 1998). That said, it should be noted that a small population of presynaptic D2 receptors also participates in the regulation of DA release (e.g., Roth, 1984). The highest concentration of the DAT is found in the striatum. The concentration is much lower in the brain stem and the thalamus. Importantly, the DAT is not expressed in the neocortex, in which the noradrenaline transporter serves as a regulator of the DA concentration. A schematic illustration of the striatal DA synapse is provided in plate 3.1 (see color insert).

Dopamine Imaging

About half of the genes in the human genome are expressed in the brain. However, the nanomolar range is the concentration range of most receptor proteins in the brain and such low concentrations cannot be detected using techniques based on magnetic resonance (MR). The nuclear medicine techniques PET and single-photon emission tomography (SPET) are ideal for this purpose and have a millionfold sensitivity advantage over MR-based techniques. PET and SPET use radioactive tracers that, after injection, pass the blood–brain barrier and bind selectively to specific target proteins in the brain. PET detects rather short-lived radionuclides that decay by release of a positron, whereas SPET detects more long-lived radionuclides that decay by release of a gamma ray.

PET studies of biochemical markers for specific neurotransmission systems are dependent on the availability of suitable ligands that can be rapidly labeled with short-lived radionuclides such as carbon-11, which has a half-life of 20.3 minutes. An advantage of radiolabeling with carbon-11 by substitution of the naturally occurring carbon-12 is that the structure and properties of the molecule remain unchanged. A tracer amount of about 1 μg of the radioligand is injected intravenously, and brain radioactivity is measured continuously for about 1 hour, during which time the subject lies on a scanner table with his or her head in a fixed position. The relatively long acquisition time is one reason for the excellent test–retest reproducibility, which is usually within 5% (e.g., Nordström et al., 1992). A drawback of the long acquisition time is that PET studies of neurotransmission have limited potential for assessment of rapid alterations in regional neurotransmitter binding resulting from changes in task demands. The binding potential (BP) is a commonly used parameter in PET research on neuroreceptor binding. This parameter represents the ratio B_{max}/K_d, where B_{max} is the concentration of a protein in a brain region, and K_d is the apparent in vivo affinity of the radioligand for the receptor.

Many radioligands have been developed for examination of DA markers in the human brain (for an overview, see Halldin et al., 2001). The benzazepine $[^{11}C]SCH23390$ was the first radioligand developed for PET visualization of the D_1 receptor (Farde et al., 1987) and has since been a reference ligand for this purpose. $[^{11}C]NNC112$ is a more recently developed ligand that provides a higher signal-to-noise ratio for cortical D_1 receptors (Halldin et al., 1998). The most commonly used radioligand for PET examination of D_2 receptors is $[^{11}C]raclopride$ (Farde et al., 1986). This radioligand is suitable for quantification in regions with a high density of D_2 receptors (i.e., the striatum; see plate 3.2 in color insert). The more recently developed radioligand [^{11}C]FLB457 has very high affinity for D_2 receptors and is one example of ligands suitable for visualization of low-density D_2 populations in the limbic system and the neocortex (Farde et al., 1997).

L-[^{18}F]DOPA was the first radiotracer developed for imaging of the presynaptic DA neuron (Garnett, Firnau, & Nahmias, 1983). PET studies with L-[^{18}F]DOPA provide the rate constant k3, which is assumed to serve as an index of DA synthesis. DAT is another marker for imaging of the presynaptic neuron. Different cocaine analogues have been developed for this purpose. Of these, [^{123}I]β-CIT is the most widely used ligand for SPET imaging of the DAT (Neumeyer et al., 1991). However, this ligand also has affinity for the serotonin and noradrenaline transporters. More recently, analogues such as [^{11}C]β-CIT-FE (Farde et al., 2000) and [^{11}C]PE2I (Halldin et al., 2003) have been shown to provide a more selective signal and are currently used in PET studies. In particular, [^{11}C]PE2I also is promising for detailed examination of extrastriatal DAT populations, such as those in the midbrain (see plate 3.3 in color insert).

Aging and Dopamine Functions

There is pervasive evidence for age-related losses in various biochemical markers of the nigrostriatal DA system. As noted, a characteristic feature of this system is the dense innervation of the caudate and the putamen in the striatal complex. A central question is how to interpret age-related losses of brain protein concentrations. In principle, the age-related decrease in pre- and postsynaptic DA markers may reflect any or a combination of (1) decrease in neuronal number, (2) decrease in the number of synapses per cell, and (3) decreased expression of receptor proteins in each neuron. There is evidence available for all these mechanisms.

First, postmortem evidence demonstrates an age-related reduction of neurons in substantia nigra, with an average loss of 3% per decade (Fearnley & Lees, 1991). In a PET study, Snow et al. (1993) examined patients with different neurodegenerative brain disorders using 6-[^{18}F]fluorodopa. In these patients, postmortem cell counts were later obtained for substantia nigra. The key finding was that uptake rate constants for 6-[^{18}F]fluorodopa were strictly proportional to cell densities in substantia nigra. This result suggests that neuronal number may determine the total synthesis rate of DA. Second, principal evidence for a decrease in the number of synapses per cell comes from observations supporting the theory of age-related synaptic pruning (Gopnick, Meltzoff, & Kuhl, 1999). At birth, each neuron in the cortex has approximately 2500 synapses. At 3 years of age, this number has increased to about 15,000. Importantly, the number of synapses per neuron is reduced to about half of that in early adulthood, and this reduction continues throughout adulthood and old age. Finally, evidence in favor of an age-related decrease in the number of proteins per cell comes primarily from experimental studies. Work with rodents has demonstrated substantial age-related losses in steady-state levels and synthesis of D_2 receptor messenger ribonucleic acid (mRNA; e.g., Mesco et al., 1993).

Much of the work on the relationship of age to DA function has targeted postsynaptic DA markers. Postmortem studies indicate losses of both D_1 (e.g., Cortes et al.,

1989; Rinne, Lönnberg, & Marjamäki, 1990) and D_2 (e.g., Seeman et al., 1987; Severson et al., 1982) receptor binding from early to later adulthood, with the rate of decline ranging from 4% to 8% per decade. Likewise, in vivo work using both PET and SPET demonstrate age-related decreases of 7%–10% per decade for D_1 (Suhara et al., 1991; Wang et al., 1998) and D_2 (e.g., Antonini et al., 1993; Ichise et al., 1998; Nordström et al., 1992) receptor binding.

In addition, postmortem studies indicated clear age-related losses of the DAT, with the average decrease mimicking that observed for postsynaptic markers (e.g., Allard & Marcusson, 1989; Bannon et al., 1992; Bannon & Whitty, 1997; Ma et al., 1999). These observations have been substantiated by PET and SPET studies, demonstrating marked decreases in DAT binding across the adult life span (e.g., Rinne et al., 1998; Van Dyck et al., 1995). The age-related decrease in DAT mRNA exceeded the extent of neuronal loss. Accordingly, age-related changes in DAT have been largely attributed to losses of DAT mRNA rather than to a decreased number of nerve terminals or neurons (De Keyser et al., 1990). This is an interesting observation in view of the fact that mRNA for TH is little affected by aging (e.g., Joyce, 2001). Thus, rather than suggesting a general age-related biochemical failure of DA neurons, the evidence indicates that these neurons are selectively downregulating the expression of DAT.

Replicating and extending animal studies (e.g., Herbert & Gerhardt, 1998; Irwin et al., 1994), Volkow, Wang, et al. (1998) found a sizable relationship between D_2 receptor binding and DAT binding in the striatum. Importantly, this association remained after partialing out age. This suggests that the expression of receptors and transporters may reflect functional demands on dopaminergic pathways. Indeed, work on DAT knockout mice shows a reduction of D_2 receptor mRNA in the postsynaptic medium spiny neurons (Gainetdinov, Jones, & Caron, 1999). Given that loss of DAT may initially result in increased DA (Shinkai et al., 1997), one possibility is that increased DA levels lead to functional downregulation of these neurons, contributing to the decline in D_2 receptor binding with advancing age (e.g., Sakata, Farooqui, & Prasad, 1992; Zhang et al., 1995).

In general, both the autopsy and the imaging findings suggest that the rate of the age-related loss of DA markers is similar in the caudate and the putamen. Another general observation is that the in vivo findings suggest a somewhat faster rate of age-related decline than the in vitro findings. This may reflect failure to correct for age-related striatal shrinkage in the brain imaging analyses (Morris et al., 1999). A reduction of volume may lead to lower concentration values because of partial volume effects related to the limited spatial resolution of PET. In a study involving 8000 brains, Eggers, Haug, and Fischer (1984) found an estimated decrease for caudate volume of approximately 3% per decade across the adult life span. However, the striatal nuclei are large in comparison with the resolution in PET imaging, which is 3–4 mm (full width at half maximum), and it is difficult to argue that a 3% volume reduction per decade should warrant significant correction of binding concentration values.

In accounting for the greater age-related loss for biochemical DA markers compared with striatal volumes, it is important to consider the fact that a sizable portion of structural volumes represents glia cells rather than neurons. Thus, if the loss of

DA markers reflects, in part, loss of neurons, this may be compensated by an increase of glia cells. In addition, loss of terminals may not influence volume measures greatly given that the neuronal cell bodies are preserved (Bäckman & Farde, 2001).

Although there is agreement that the age-related decrease of pre- and postsynaptic DA markers starts in early adulthood and proceeds throughout the life span, evidence is mixed regarding the exact nature of the age–DA relationship. Most studies have reported evidence for a linear relationship (for an overview, see Reeves, Bench, & Howard, 2002). However, for the D_2 receptor, an exponential loss has been observed, with increasing rate of decline after middle adulthood (e.g., Antonini et al., 1993; Rinne, Lönnberg, & Marjamäki, 1990). A similar exponential age trajectory has been reported for the DAT, with the most marked decline occurring after 55 years of age (e.g., Bannon & Whitty, 1997; Ma et al., 1999). In a SPET study involving 55 subjects between 19 and 74 years of age, P. D. Mozley et al. (1999) found considerably greater decline in DAT binding before than after 40 years of age. Although the reasons for the discrepant findings remain unclear, it should be noted that (1) most relevant studies involve relatively few subjects, (2) several studies may not have covered a sufficiently wide age range, and (3) there is considerable interindividual variability in DA receptor density within age-homogeneous samples (e.g., Farde et al., 1995). Conceivably, these factors underlie the different function forms relating age to DA markers in the extant literature.

Multiple causative mechanisms may contribute to the age-related reduction of DA markers (for an overview, see Reeves, Bench, & Howard, 2002). As noted, the age-independent relationship between DAT and receptor densities suggests that a common mechanism regulates their concentrations (Bäckman & Farde, 2001). This may reflect a mechanism regulating both pre- and postsynaptic maturation of the DA systems during neurodevelopment. It may also correspond to an age-related decrease in the functional demands on dopaminergic pathways. Another possibility is that it reflects age-related failure in responding to oxidative stress and cell damage (e.g., Joseph, Denisova, & Villalobos-Molina, 1996). Toward this end, animal research indicates a relationship among striatal DA levels, markers of oxidative damage, and motor function (Cardozo-Pelaez et al., 1999). Finally, it has been suggested that the expression of DA itself may contribute to degenerative processes through the production of neurotoxins during autooxidation (Luo & Roth, 2000).

General Trends in Cognitive Aging

Cognitive aging is characterized by large interindividual variability. Individual differences within multiple demographic (e.g., sex, education), lifestyle (e.g., activity patterns, substance use), health-related (e.g., vascular factors, vitamin status), and genetic (e.g., apolipoprotein E genotype) domains contribute to performance variability among older adults and may affect the size of the age-related deficit observed (for an overview, see Bäckman et al., 1999).

However, as indicated by the other chapters in this volume, systematic patterns are evident concerning the relationship between adult age and cognitive performance across different domains of functioning. For example, regarding memory, evidence suggests that age-related differences in primary memory (e.g., recency) and various forms of priming (e.g., word-stem completion priming) are small or nonexistent. For procedural (e.g., pursuit rotor task, mirror reading) and semantic (e.g., verbal fluency, monitoring of general knowledge) memory, age-related deficits may or may not be observed, depending on various demand characteristics. In contrast, tasks that assess working memory (e.g., reading span) and episodic memory (free recall) routinely exhibit a marked performance deterioration from early to late adulthood (for an overview, see Bäckman, Small, & Wahlin, 2001).

In addition, there is pervasive evidence that tests that reflect fluid aspects of intelligence (e.g., Digit Symbol, Block Design) reveal robust and gradual decline across the adult life span (for overviews, see Kausler, 1991; Salthouse, 1991). Such tests involve relatively unfamiliar material and require fast and efficient solutions to novel problems. Tests that draw on crystallized aspects of intelligence (e.g., vocabulary, comprehension) show relatively modest age-related changes across the adult life span. Tests of crystallized intelligence assess world knowledge in a broad sense; they draw on prior experience and have rather limited speed demands. Such tests may even show performance increases from early to middle adulthood (e.g., Nyberg et al., 2003), with no detectable decline until in very old age (Lindenberger & Baltes, 1997). Tasks derived from the experimental literature that tap related abilities (e.g., fact retrieval and object naming tasks vs. perceptual closure and syllogistic reasoning tasks) show similar performance trajectories from early to late adulthood (e.g., Bäckman & Nilsson, 1996; Mitchell, 1989; Salthouse, 1992).

Along with findings from research targeting other cognitive domains demonstrating age-related deficits (e.g., executive functioning), the pattern of results emerging from this brief review suggests that older adults are quite efficient in utilizing preexisting knowledge structures, but not when fast and efficient processing of novel information is required. Another observation is that, for many cognitive domains yielding robust age-related decline (e.g., perceptual speed, episodic memory), the onset of decline occurs earlier in life than perhaps commonly thought. In addition, the pattern of deterioration from early to late adulthood appears to proceed in a continuous rather than a discrete fashion (e.g., Nilsson et al., 1997; Park et al., 2002; Salthouse, 1998). The early onset and gradual nature of the age-related cognitive decline could inform attempts to determine its biological origins. Specifically, whatever the proposed origin may be, it would strengthen the case if the causative factor(s) would show a similar onset and trajectory as the behavioral data.

Given that we now have established evidence for a correlative triad among age, DA functions, and cognitive performance using theory and data from multiple lines of inquiry, research that specifically addressed this triad is reviewed in the next section.

Aging, Dopamine Markers, and Cognitive Performance

The decline of DA markers and cognitive functioning with advancing age along with the role of DA systems in many cognitive abilities have prompted researchers to examine the relationship of age-related changes in DA markers to age-related cognitive changes. Although only a handful of studies have addressed this issue, the pattern of findings is strikingly consistent, indicating a strong relationship among age, DA markers, and cognitive performance.

Wang and colleagues (1998) used PET to examine striatal D_1 receptors in normal adults ranging between 22 and 74 years of age. In addition, the Purdue Pegboard Test (PPBT) was used to assess psychomotor functioning. Results indicated a pronounced age-related decrease of D_1 binding in both the caudate ($r = -.86$) and the putamen ($r = -.88$). PPBT performance also declined with age ($r = -.57$), and there was a sizable relationship of D_1 binding in both the caudate ($r = .52$) and the putamen ($r = .68$) to PPBT performance. Although this pattern of findings indicates a strong correlative triad involving age, D_1 binding potential, and psychomotor functioning, the analytical strategy did not permit any firm conclusions concerning the influence of age-related dopaminergic losses on age-related slowing of psychomotor speed.

In another PET study, Volkow, Gur, et al. (1998) determined striatal D_2 binding potential in healthy adults ranging from 24 to 86 years of age. These investigators also administered a cognitive battery that included tests of executive (i.e., Wisconsin Card Sorting Test [WCST], Stroop Color–Word Test) and motor (i.e., finger tapping) functioning as well as perceptual speed (i.e., Digit Symbol), all of which are known to be sensitive to both aging and striatal dysfunction. In line with earlier studies, D_2 receptor binding decreased with advancing age in both the caudate ($r = -.62$) and the putamen ($r = -.70$). As predicted, there were also negative relationships between age and performance in the cognitive tests. In general, the magnitude of these relationships was the same as those observed between age and D_2 binding.

Perhaps the most interesting feature of the Volkow, Gur, et al. (1998) study was that partial correlations revealed moderate to strong relationships of D_2 binding to motor and cognitive performance also after controlling for age. Whereas D_2 binding in both the caudate and the putamen were related to motor performance, caudate D_2 binding emerged as the stronger correlate of cognitive performance. Thus, these results indicated that age-related decreases in DA function are associated with decline in both motor and cognitive functioning. In addition, the fact that the DA–performance relationships remained after partialing out age suggests that the activity of the DA system may influence motor and cognitive performance irrespective of age.

In a related PET study, Bäckman et al. (2000) examined striatal DA D_2 binding in adults between 21 and 68 years of age along with MR-based volumetric measurements of the caudate and the putamen. In this study, two cognitive domains were targeted, namely, episodic memory (word and face recognition) and perceptual speed (Trail Making-A and Dots). These cognitive domains are strongly affected by normal aging, and clear deficits in tasks that assess episodic memory and speed are routinely observed in persons with degeneration of the nigrostriatal DA system, such as patients with HD.

In agreement with Volkow, Gur, et al. (1998), Bäckman et al. (2000) observed systematic age-related reductions of D_2 binding in both the caudate ($r = -.75$) and the putamen ($r = -.87$). In contrast, age was only weakly related to striatal volumes.

These results provide further evidence that aging exerts stronger effects on markers of striatal DA innervation than on caudate and putaminal volumes. Another striking observation in this study was the nearly perfect correlation between D_2 binding in the caudate and the putamen ($r = .98$).

As expected, increasing age was negatively associated with performance in the two memory tasks as well as the two speed tasks. To examine the relative importance of age and DA markers for cognitive performance, Bäckman et al. (2000) conducted hierarchical regression analyses in which the order of entry of the independent variables (age vs. D_2 binding) was varied, and the four cognitive variables constituted the outcome measures. Because of the near-perfect correlation between D_2 binding in the caudate and the putamen, these data were aggregated to form a composite D_2 variable.

As can be seen from table 3.1, although age contributed strongly to performance when entered first, D_2 binding added substantial variance when entered second. However, the reverse was not true. Initial entry of the D_2 variable absorbed most of the cognitive variance and effectively eliminated the influence of age on performance. The fact that there was residual D_2-related cognitive variation after partialing out age is in agreement with the results reported by Volkow, Gur, et al. (1998). These findings suggest that the two- to threefold interindividual variability in D_2 demonstrated in samples of age-homogeneous normal adults (Farde et al., 1995) may be related to cognitive performance.

Table 3.1 Amount of Variance r^2 in Cognitive Performance Accounted for by Age and Dopamine D_2 Receptor Binding as a Function of Order of Entry

	Perceptual Speed		Episodic Memory	
	Dots	Trail Making	Word Recognition	Face Recognition
Age	.52	.34	.13	.27
D_2	.11	.22	.27	.24
Total	.63	.56	.40	.51
D_2	.61	.55	.38	.48
Age	.02	.01	.02	.03
Total	.63	.56	.40	.51
Percentage age-related variance accounted for by D_2	.96	.97	.85	.89
Percentage D_2-related variance accounted for by age	.81	.60	.29	.50

Source. Adapted from Bäckman et al., 2000.

In further analyzing these data, we used the decomposition procedure devised by Salthouse (1992) to estimate the amount of age-related cognitive variance that could be accounted for by the D_2 variable, and the amount of D_2-related cognitive variance that could be accounted for by age. As shown in the bottom of table 3.1, D_2 binding accounted for nearly all of the age-related cognitive variation, whereas age accounted for considerably less of the D_2-related cognitive variation.

The results from this study confirm and extend the correlative triad among age, DA activity, and cognitive performance observed by Wang et al. (1998) and Volkow, Gur, et al. (1998). Notably, although the four cognitive tasks were specifically selected because of their sensitivity to age, D_2 binding emerged as the stronger predictor of performance across all tasks.

In the three studies described above, postsynaptic markers of DA function were assessed. It has been suggested that the concentration of DAT, a presynaptic marker of DA function, is a more sensitive indicator of the activity of the dopaminergic system than postsynaptic receptor densities (P. D. Mozley et al., 1999). In a SPET study with persons ranging from 18 to 75 years of age, L. H. Mozley et al. (2001) reported marked age-related reductions of the DAT in caudate and putamen along with age-related deficits in verbal episodic memory. Importantly, DAT availability in the striatum was strongly associated with memory performance in both young and older adults. In addition, L. H. Mozley and colleagues (2001) found relationships of DAT density to motor and executive functioning in women, but not in men. The reasons for these sex-differential effects remain unclear.

Using PET, Erixon-Lindroth et al. (in press) also found an age-related decrease of DAT density in caudate and putamen in a group of individuals between 34 and 81 years of age. Consistent with expectations, age-related deficits were found in tests of episodic memory, working memory, and word fluency, but not in tests of vocabulary and general knowledge. Using the same analytical strategy as Bäckman et al. (2000), the results further indicated that the age-related cognitive deficits were completely mediated by DAT density, although DAT density contributed to the performance variation in memory and fluency over and above age. The last finding was substantiated by the result that DAT density was related to performance also in the vocabulary and knowledge tests, for which no age-related performance differences were observed.

In sum, the available evidence suggests that pre- and postsynaptic markers of the nigrostriatal DA system are powerful mediators of the cognitive changes that occur across adulthood and old age, as well as strong general correlates of cognitive performance. Regarding the apparent similarity in patterns of data for pre- and postsynaptic DA markers, it may be noted that Volkow, Wang, et al. (1998) demonstrated a sizable relationship between losses in DAT and D_2 receptors across adulthood. The DAT–D_2 association was independent of age, suggesting that common genetic or adaptive mechanisms may regulate the expression of DA receptors and transporters irrespective of age. Support for a genetic regulation of DA markers was provided in several studies (e.g., Jönsson et al., 1999) demonstrating an association between polymorphisms of the D_2 gene and the density of D_2 receptors. Thus, changes in pre- and postsynaptic DA function may be an interdependent and generalized phenomenon in human aging (Morgan & Finch, 1998).

Relationships to Other Findings in the Cognitive Neuroscience of Aging

As intriguing as the data reviewed in the preceding section may be, it is important to put findings on the influence of striatal DA markers on cognitive aging in the greater context of the cognitive neuroscience of aging. Numerous structural and functional brain parameters likely contribute to age-related cognitive difficulties. To mention a few among several possible examples, structural (e.g., Simic et al., 1997; West, 1993) and functional (e.g., Grady et al., 1995; Small et al., 1999) age-related changes in the medial-temporal lobe, age-related increases of white matter lesions (DeCarli et al., 1995; O'Sullivan et al., 2001), and cytokine dysregulation with advancing age (Wilson, Finch, & Cohen, 2002) have been successfully linked to cognitive aging.

However, much recent research on the neural underpinnings of cognitive aging has focused on age-related changes in the frontal, particularly the prefrontal, cortex. Structural imaging studies (e.g., Raz et al., 1993, 1997; for an overview, see Raz, 1999) indicate sizable relationships between age-related losses in frontal gray matter and age-related cognitive deficits. Relatedly, in functional imaging studies, an underrecruitment of task-relevant frontal regions has been associated with age-related deficits in tasks assessing working memory (e.g., Rypma et al., 2001; Rypma & D'Esposito, 2000) and episodic memory (e.g., Grady et al., 1995; Stebbins et al., 2002). Toward this end, it is of interest to note that several studies on DA and cognitive aging have used cognitively demanding tasks (e.g., executive tasks, episodic memory tasks) associated with prefrontal regions in functional imaging studies (for an overview, see Cabeza & Nyberg, 2000).

Further evidence for the role of frontal changes in age-related cognitive deficits comes from research indicating that patients with circumscribed frontal lesions may show patterns of cognitive deficits that resemble closely those observed in normal aging (e.g., Moscovitch & Winocur, 1992; Troyer et al., 1998; West, 1996).

Given (1) the relationship between age-related changes in striatal DA function and cognitive functioning and (2) the role of frontal alterations in cognitive aging, it is of interest to note that the striatum is topographically organized with abundant reciprocal connections to the neocortex (Graybiel & Ragsdale, 1979; Crosson, 1992) and the thalamus (Dom, Malfroid, & Barg, 1976; Jayarman, 1984). Specifically, there is a functional influence of dopaminergic neurotransmission through the parallel cortico-striato-pallido-thalamic circuits that form a fundamental basis for information processing in the brain (Alexander, DeLong, & Strick, 1986; Gerfen, 1989; Graybiel, 2000; Parent & Hazrati, 1995). Damage to a specific component in this network may result in functional and eventually structural changes in other components (Cummings, 1993; Wise, Murray, & Gerfen, 1996).

In the context of cognitive aging, it has been stressed that a declining nigrostriatal DA system may lead to impoverished inputs to the frontal lobes, thereby reducing the executive capacity of working memory (Prull, Gabrieli, & Bunge, 1999). Relatedly, a deficient DA–frontal mechanism has been proposed to underlie age-related changes in context processing, resulting in age decrements across several cognitive domains, such as attention, inhibition, and working memory (Braver et al., 2001).

Volkow and colleagues (2000) demonstrated age-related decreases in both D_2 receptor binding and glucose metabolism in the frontal cortex and the cingulate. Most interestingly, there was a strong relationship between D_2 binding and frontal and cingulate metabolism that was independent of age. These findings underscore the functional interrelatedness between striatal and neocortical brain regions. Thus, the results from the reviewed studies on the relationship among aging, striatal DA function, and cognitive performance may best be viewed as reflecting age-related alterations in the frontostriatal circuitry.

Additional evidence that it may be ill advised to overemphasize the role of the striatum in accounting for the relationship between DA losses and age-related cognitive deficits comes from studies that have investigated the influence of age on DA markers outside the basal ganglia. Studies on extrastriatal DA markers are rare because suitable radioligands for imaging of the sparse dopaminergic innervation of extrastriatal regions have been developed only recently.

An early PET study focusing on D_1 receptor binding found comparable rates of age-related loss in the striatum and the frontal cortex (Suhara et al., 1991). Postmortem evidence also demonstrated an age-related decrease of frontal D_1 receptor densities (de Keyser et al., 1990). These findings were extended to the D_2 receptor subtype in PET studies using [^{11}C]FLB457, a highly selective ligand for extrastriatal D_2 binding (Inoue et al., 2001; Kaasinen et al., 2000). These studies revealed clear age-related losses in D_2 binding not only in the frontal cortex, but also in the temporal, parietal, and occipital cortices, as well as in the hippocampus and the thalamus. The magnitude of these age differences in extrastriatal DA functions resembles closely those observed for the striatum. Thus, an age-related decrease of DA markers in a wide variety of brain regions appears to be part of the normal aging process.

Conclusions and Future Directions

A striking observation in the studies conducted on DA and cognitive aging is the similarity of the effects of different DA markers. As is true with corresponding research on patients with HD (e.g., Bäckman et al., 1997; Lawrence et al., 1998; for an overview, see Bäckman & Farde, 2001), markers of D_1, D_2, and DAT binding in both the caudate and the putamen show strong relationships to each other as well as to cognitive performance (Bäckman et al., 2000; Erixon-Lindroth et al., in press; L. H. Mozley et al., 2001; Volkow, Gur, et al., 1998; Wang et al., 1998).

These general patterns are observed despite postulated functional differences between the striatal structures. The caudate and the putamen receive dopaminergic input from the same region in the brain stem, but are part of different, albeit parallel, topographic frontostriatal circuits (Alexander & Crutcher, 1990; Parent & Hazrati, 1995). Traditionally, the caudate circuits are thought to be particularly relevant to complex cognitive functioning, whereas the putaminal circuits are primarily implicated in motor activity (Alexander, DeLong, & Strick, 1986; Bhatia & Marsden, 1994; Houk, Davis, & Beiser, 1995).

Biochemically, the D_1 and D_2 subtypes show preferential localization to certain striatal pathways. Although a proportion of the D_1 and D_2 receptors are co-localized on the same neurons, research on striatal organization indicates that D_1 receptors are mainly expressed in neurons in the "direct" striatal pathway, whereas D_2 receptors are expressed in "indirect" pathways that include interneurons (Gerfen, Keefe, & Gauda, 1995; Hersch et al., 1995). At a histological level, this differential organization corresponds to the observation that D_1 neurons are primarily located in striosomes, whereas D_2 neurons are preferentially found in the matrix component of the striatum (Graybiel et al., 1994; Joyce, Sapp, & Marshall, 1986).

The similar effects of different DA markers on age-related cognitive changes may appear counterintuitive in view of these structural and biochemical differences. However, as should be obvious from the current review, only a few age-comparative imaging studies have addressed the DA–cognition relationship, and the relevant studies are characterized by relatively small sample sizes. Thus, the general failure to obtain differential relationships among brain regions as well as different biochemical markers may reflect the limited nature of the database along with low statistical power. Future research using larger samples, multiple radioligands for distinct DA markers, and suitable approaches for parametric receptor imaging (Cselenyi et al., 2002) should provide more definite evidence concerning the extent to which the effects of DA losses on cognitive aging are global or can be attributed to specific markers in specific brain structures.

For example, could it be that DA losses in a particular brain area (e.g., putamen) are more critical than DA losses in other areas (e.g., frontal cortex) for certain domains of cognitive functioning (e.g., psychomotor speed), whereas the opposite pattern holds for other cognitive domains (e.g., working memory)? Alternatively, considering the integrated network of striatal and extrastriatal brain regions (e.g., Alexander, DeLong, & Strick, 1986; Graybiel, 2000), and given that pre- and postsynaptic DA markers appear to exhibit similar decline with age (Morgan & Finch, 1998; Reeves, Bench, & Howard, 2002) throughout the human brain (e.g., Kaasinen et al., 2000; Suhara et al., 1991), selective effects may be difficult to observe.

Another interesting avenue for future research concerns the relationship between age-related changes in neuromodulation and age-related decreases in task-specific brain activity during actual cognitive performance. It is tempting to relate findings of deficient DA neurotransmission to decreased levels of task-related brain activity (as reflected by regional blood flow), such that impaired neurotransmitter function underlies decreased activity. Indeed, findings of a strong relationship between striatal D_2 binding and frontal and cingulate resting state glucose metabolism (Volkow et al., 2000) provide support for a transmitter–activation relationship.

By collecting PET-based DA data and functional imaging data on the same individuals during task performance, several intriguing issues in the cognitive neuroscience of aging could be addressed. For example, in some task situations (e.g., episodic retrieval), older adults may exhibit higher activity than younger adults in specific brain regions (e.g., left prefrontal cortex). Such findings have been interpreted to reflect a reallocation of neural resources in old age that serves compensatory purposes (e.g., Cabeza, 2002; Cabeza, Grady, et al., 1997). According to this view, increased activity in the older person is assumed to be associated with better cognitive performance. However, it has also been proposed that greater regional activity of older adults may reflect lack of specificity of neural processing (as a function of age-related changes in neuromodulation; e.g., Li, Lindenberger, & Sikström, 2001). By the latter view, recruitment of more brain regions is thought to be associated with impaired neurotransmitter function. These theoretical alternatives can be evaluated by multimodal imaging, relating data on DA markers and regional blood flow to cognitive performance in young and older adults.

Another observation in age-comparative functional imaging studies is that increasing age may be associated with deficient integration across networks of brain regions (e.g., Cabeza, McIntosh, et al., 1997; Esposito et al., 1999). For example, Esposito and colleagues found alterations in the relationship between the dorsolateral prefrontal cortex and the hippocampal complex with advancing age during WCST performance. Relatedly, they observed age-related alterations in the relationship between the inferolateral temporal cortex and medial and polar portions of the prefrontal cortex during performance of Raven's Progressive Matrices. In general, these age differences in patterns of brain activation were characterized by failures to activate task-relevant brain regions and to suppress task-irrelevant brain regions in old age.

Disordered neural connectivity during cognitive processing in old age may have multiple origins, including disruption of white matter tracts (O'Sullivan et al., 2001). However, it is conceivable that age-related changes in DA functions contribute to altered connectivity. Specifically, the age-related changes in the relationships among brain regions observed by Esposito et al. (1999) could be conceptualized in terms of diminished signal-to-noise ratio. As noted in the section on DA and cognitive functioning, DA modulates the neural signal-to-noise ratio by suppressing spontaneous background firing and enhancing responses to relevant stimuli (e.g., Daniel et al., 1991; Sawaguchi, Matsumura, & Kubota, 1988). Direct evidence for the role of DA in neural connectivity comes from a study by Mattay and colleagues (1996). These investigators demonstrated increased activity in the dorsolateral prefrontal cortex (the signal) and decreased hippocampal activity (the noise) during WCST performance in young adults following the administration of D-AMP. Again, by collecting data on relevant biochemical DA markers, regional blood flow, and cognitive performance in persons from early to late adulthood, new insights may be gained pertaining to the relationship between neuromodulation and functional brain activation in cognitive aging.

Acknowledgments   Preparation of this chapter was supported by grants from the Swedish Research Council and the Bank of Sweden Tercentenary Foundation to Lars Bäckman and from the Swedish Research Council to Lars Farde.

References

Alexander, G. E., & Crutcher, M. D. (1990). Functional architecture of basal ganglia circuits: Neural substrates of parallel processing. *Trends in Neuroscience, 13*, 266–271.

Alexander, G. E., DeLong, M. R., & Strick, P. L. (1986). Parallel organization of functionally segregated circuits linking basal ganglia and cortex. *Annual Review of Neuroscience, 9*, 357–381.

Allard, P., & Marcusson, J. (1989). Age-correlated loss of dopamine uptake sites labeled with [³H]GBR-12935 in human putamen. *Neurobiology of Aging, 10*, 661–664.

Antonini, A., Leenders, K. L., Reist, H., Thomann, R., Beer, H.-F., & Locher, J. (1993). Effect of age on D_2 dopamine receptors in normal human brain measured by positron emission tomography and [^{11}C] raclopride. *Archives of Neurology, 50*, 474–480.

Bäckman, L., & Farde, L. (2001). Dopamine and cognitive functioning: Brain imaging findings from Huntington's disease and normal aging. *Scandinavian Journal of Psychology, 42*, 287–296.

Bäckman, L., Ginovart, N., Dixon, R. A., et al. (2000). Age-related cognitive deficits mediated by changes in the striatal dopamine system. *American Journal of Psychiatry, 157*, 635–637.

Bäckman, L., & Nilsson, L.-G. (1996). Semantic memory functioning across the adult life span. *European Psychologist, 1*, 27–33.

Bäckman, L., Robins-Wahlin, T.-B., Lundin, A., Ginovart, N., & Farde, L. (1997). Cognitive deficits in Huntington's disease are predicted by dopaminergic PET markers and brain volumes. *Brain, 120*, 2207–2217.

Bäckman, L., Small, B. J., & Wahlin, Å. (2001). Aging and memory: Cognitive and biological perspectives. In J. E. Birren & K. W. Schaie (Eds.), *Handbook of the psychology of aging* (5th ed., pp. 349–377). San Diego, CA: Academic Press.

Bäckman, L., Small, B. J., Wahlin. Å, & Larsson, M. (1999). Cognitive functioning in very old age. In F. I. M. Craik & T. A. Salthouse (Eds.), *Handbook of aging and cognition* (Vol. 2, pp. 499–558). Mahwah, NJ: Erlbaum.

Bannon, M. J., Poosch, M. S., Xia, Y., Goebel, D. J., Cassin, B., & Kapatos, G. (1992). Dopamine transporter mRNA content in human substantia nigra decreases precipitously with age. *Proceedings of the National Academy of Sciences of the United States of America, 89*, 7095–7099.

Bannon, M. J., & Whitty, C. J. (1997). Age-related and regional differences in dopamine mRNA expression in human midbrain. *Neurology, 48*, 969–977.

Baunez, C., Nieoullon, A., & Amalric, M. (1995). Dopamine and complex sensorimotor integration: Further studies in a conditioned motor task in the rat. *Neuroscience, 65*, 375–384.

Baunez, C., & Robbins, T. W. (1999). Effects of dopamine depletion of the dorsal striatum and further interaction with subthalamic nucleus lesions in an attentional task in the rat. *Neuroscience, 92*, 1343–1356.

Beninger, R. J. (1983). The role of dopamine in locomotor activity and learning. *Brain Research and Reviews, 6*, 173–196.

Bhatia, K. P., & Marsden, C. D. (1994). The behavioral and motor consequences of focal lesions of the basal ganglia in man. *Brain, 117*, 859–876.

Boussaoud, D., & Kermadi, I. (1997). The primate striatum: Neuronal activity in relation to spatial attention versus motor preparation. *European Journal of Neuroscience, 9*, 2152–2162.

Brandt, J., & Butters, N. (1986). The neuropsychology of Huntington's disease. *Trends in Neuroscience, 9*, 118–120.

Braver, T. S., Barch, D. M., Keys, B. A., et al. (2001). Context processing in older adults: Evidence for a theory relating cognitive control to neurobiology in healthy aging. *Journal of Experimental Psychology: General, 130*, 746–763.

Brown, R. G., & Marsden, C. D. (1990). Cognitive function in Parkinson's disease: From description to theory. *Trends in Neuroscience, 13*, 21–29.

Brown, R. M., & Goldman, P. S. (1977). Catecholamines in neocortex of rhesus monkey: Regional distribution and ontogenetic development. *Brain Research, 124*, 576–580.

Burns, R. S., Chieuh, C. C., Markey, S. P., Ebert, M. H., Jacobowitz, D. M., & Kopin, I. J. (1983). A primate model of Parkinsonism: Selective destruction of dopaminergic neurons in the pars compacta of the substantia nigra by *N*-methyl-4-phenyl-1,2,3,6-tetrahydropyridine. *Proceedings of the National Academy of Sciences of the United States of America, 80*, 4546–4550.

Cabeza, R. (2002). Hemispheric asymmetry reduction in older adults: The HAROLD model. *Psychology and Aging, 17*, 85–100.

Cabeza, R., Grady, C. L., Nyberg, L., et al. (1997). Age-related differences in neural activity during memory encoding and retrieval: A positron emission tomography study. *Journal of Neuroscience, 17*, 391–400.

Cabeza, R., McIntosh, A. R., Tulving, E., Nyberg, L., & Grady, C. L. (1997). Age-related differences in effective neural connectivity during encoding and recall. *NeuroReport, 8*, 3479–3483.

Cabeza, R., & Nyberg, L. (2000). Imaging cognition II: An empirical review of 275 PET and fMRI studies. *Journal of Cognitive Neuroscience, 12*, 1–47.

Cai, J. X., & Arnsten, A. F. (1997). Dose-dependent effects of the dopamine receptor agonists A77636 and SKF81297 on spatial working memory in aged monkeys. *Journal of Pharmacology and Experimental Therapeutics, 283*, 183–189.

Cardozo-Pelaez, F., Song, S., Partasarathy, A., et al. (1999). Oxidative damage in the aging mouse brain. *Movement Disorders, 14*, 972–980.

Carlsson, A. (1975). Drugs acting through dopamine release. *Pharmacological Therapy, 1*, 401–405.

Cohen, J. D., & Servan-Schreiber, D. (1992). Context, cortex, and dopamine: A connectionist approach to behavior and biology in schizophrenia. *Psychological Review, 99*, 45–77.

Cortes, R., Gueye, B., Pazos, A., & Palacios, J. M. (1989). Dopamine receptors in human brain: Autoradiographic distribution of D_1 sites. *Neuroscience, 28*, 262–273.

Crosson, B. (1992). *Subcortical functions in language and memory.* New York: Guilford.

Cselenyi, Z., Olsson, H., Farde, L., & Gulyas, B. (2002). Wavelet-aided parametric mapping of cerebral dopamine D_2 receptors using the high-affinity ligand [^{11}C]FLB 457. *Neuroimage, 17*, 47–60.

Cummings, J. L. (1993). Frontal-subcortical circuits and human behavior. *Archives of Neurology, 50*, 873–880.

Daniel, D. G., Weinberger, D. R., Jones, D. W., et al. (1991). The effect of amphetamine on regional cerebral blood flow during cognitive activation in schizophrenia. *Journal of Neuroscience, 11*, 1907–1917.

DeCarli, C., Murphy, D. G. M., Tranh, M., et al. (1995). The effect of white-matter hyperintensity volume on brain structure, cognitive performance, and cerebral metabolism of glucose in 51 healthy adults. *Neurology, 45*, 2077–2084.

de Keyser, J., De Backer, J. P., Vauquelin, G., & Ebinger, G. (1990). The effect of aging on the D_1 dopamine receptors in human frontal cortex. *Brain Research, 528*, 308–310.

Dom, R., Malfroid, M., & Barg, F. (1976). Neuropathology of Huntington's chorea: Cytometric studies of the ventrobasal complex of the thalamus. *Neurology, 26*, 64–68.

Eggers, R., Haug, H., & Fischer, D. (1984). Preliminary report on macroscopic age changes in the human prosencephalon: A stereologic examination. *Journal für Hirnforschung, 25*, 129–139.

Erixon-Lindroth, N., Farde, L., Halldin, C., Robins Wahlin, T.-B., Sovago, J., Halldin, C., & Bäckman, L. (in press). The role of the striatal dopamine transporter in cognitive aging. *Psychiatry Research: Neuroimaging.*

Esposito, G., Kirby, G. S., Van Horn, J. D., Ellmore, T. M., & Faith Berman, K. (1999). Context-dependent, neural system-specific neurophysiological concomitants of aging: Mapping PET correlates during cognitive activation. *Brain, 122*, 963–979.

Farde, L., Ginovart, N., Halldin, C., Chou, Y., Olsson, H., & Swahn, C. (2000). A PET-study of [^{11}C]β-CIT-FE binding to the dopamine transporter in the monkey and human brain. *International Journal of Clinical Neuropsychopharmacology*, *3*, 203–214.

Farde, L., Hall, H., Ehrin, E., & Sedvall, G. (1986). Quantitative analysis of D$_2$ dopamine receptor binding in the living human brain by PET. *Science*, *231*, 258–261.

Farde, L., Hall, H., Pauli, S., & Halldin, C. (1995). Variability in D$_2$ dopamine receptor density and affinity: A PET study with [^{11}C] raclopride in man. *Synapse*, *20*, 200–208.

Farde, L., Halldin, C., Stone-Elander, S., & Sedvall, G. (1987). PET analysis of human dopamine receptor subtypes using ^{11}C-SCH 23390 and ^{11}C-raclopride. *Psychopharmacology*, *92*, 278–284.

Farde, L., Suhara, T., Nyberg, S., et al. (1997). A PET-study of [^{11}C]FLB 457 binding to extrastriatal D$_2$-dopamine receptors in healthy subjects and antipsychotic drug treated patients. *Psychopharmacology*, *133*, 396–404.

Fearnley, J. M., & Lees, A. J. (1991). Aging and Parkinson's disease: Substantia nigra regional selectivity. *Brain*, *114*, 2283–2301.

Freed, C. R., & Yamamoto, B. K. (1985). Regional brain dopamine metabolism: A marker for the speed, direction, and posture of moving animals. *Science*, *229*, 62–65.

Gainetdinov, R. R., Jones, S. R., & Caron, M. G. (1999). Functional hyperdopaminerga in dopamine transporter knock-out mice. *Biological Psychiatry*, *46*, 303–311.

Garnett, E. S., Firnau, G., & Nahmias, C. (1983). Dopamine visualized in the basal ganglia of living man. *Nature*, *305*, 137–138.

Gaspar, P., Berger, B., Febvret, A., Vigny, A., & Henry, J. P. (1989). Catecholamine innervation of the human cerebral cortex as revealed by comparative immunohistochemistry of tyroxine-hydroxylase and dopamine-beta-hydroxylase. *Journal of Comparative Neurology*, *279*, 249–271.

Gerfen, C. R. (1989). The neostriatal mosaic: Striatal-patch matrix organization is related to cortical lamination. *Science*, *246*, 385–388.

Gerfen, C. R., Keefe, K. A., & Gauda, E. B. (1995). D$_2$ and D$_2$ dopamine receptor function in the striatum: Coactivation of D$_1$- and D$_2$-dopamine receptors on separate populations of neurons results in potentiated immediate early gene response in D$_1$-containing neurons. *Journal of Neuroscience*, *15*, 8167–8176.

Giros, B., El Mestikawy, S., Godinot, N., et al. (1992). Cloning, pharmacological characterization, and chromosome assignment of the human dopamine transporter. *Molecular Pharmacology*, *3*, 383–390.

Giros, B., Jaber, M., Jones, S. R., Wightman, R. M., & Caron, M. G. (1996). Hyperlocomotion and indifference to cocaine and amphetamine in mice lacking the dopamine transporter. *Nature*, *379*, 606–612.

Goldman-Rakic, P. S., & Brown, R. M. (1982). Post-natal development of monoamine content and synthesis in the cerebral cortex of rhesus monkey. *Developmental Brain Research*, *4*, 339–349.

Gopnic, A., Meltzoff, A., & Kuhl, P. (1999). *The scientist in the crib: What early learning tells us about the mind.* New York: HarperCollins.

Grady, C. L., McIntosh, A. R., Horwitz, B., et al. (1995). Age-related reductions in human recognition memory due to impaired encoding. *Science*, *269*, 218–221.

Graybiel, A. M. (2000). The basal ganglia and adaptive motor control. *Current Biology*, *10*, 509–511.

Graybiel, A. M., Aosaki, T., Flaherty, A. W., & Kimura, M. (1994). The basal ganglia and adaptive motor control. *Science*, *265*, 1826–1831.

Graybiel, A., & Ragsdale, C. W, Jr. (1979). Fiber connections of the basal ganglia. In M. Cuenod, G. Kreutzbarg, & F. Bloom F (Eds.), *Progress in brain research* (pp. 239–283). Amsterdam, The Netherlands: North-Holland.

Hall, H., Sedvall, G., Magnusson, O., Kopp, J., Halldin, C., & Farde, L. (1994). Distribution of D₁- and D₂-dopamine receptors and dopamine and its metabolites in the human brain. *Neuropsychopharmacology, 11,* 245–256.

Halldin, C., Erixon-Lindroth, N., Pauli, S., et al. (2003). [¹¹C]PE2I: A highly selective radioligand for PET examination of the dopamine transporter in monkey and human brain. *European Journal of Nuclear Medicine, 30,* 1220–1230.

Halldin, C., Foged, C., Karlsson, P., Swahn, C.-G., Sedvall, G., & Farde, L. (1998). [¹¹C]NNC 112: A radioligand for PET examination of striatal and extrastriatal D₂-dopamine receptors. *Journal of Nuclear Medicine, 39,* 2061–2068.

Halldin, C., Gulyas, B., Langer, O., & Farde, L. (2001). Brain radioligands—State of the art and new trends. *Quarterly Journal of Nuclear Medicine, 45,* 139–152.

Halliday, R., Naylor, H., Brandeis, D., Callaway, E., Yano, L., & Herzig, K. (1994). The effect of d-amphetamine, clonidine, and yohimbine on human information processing. *Psychophysiology, 31,* 331–337.

Herbert, M. A., & Gerhardt, G. A. (1998). Normal and drug-induced locomotor behavior in aging: Comparison to evoked DA release and tissue content in Fischer 344 rats. *Brain Research, 797,* 42–54.

Hersch, S. M., Ciliax, B. J., Gutekunst, C. A., et al. (1995). Electron microscope analysis of D₁ and D₂ dopamine receptor proteins in the dorsal striatum and their synaptic relationships with motor corticostriatal afferents. *Journal of Neuroscience, 15,* 5222–5237.

Houk, J. C., Davis, J. L., & Beiser, D. G. (Eds.). (1995). *Models of information processing in the basal ganglia.* Cambridge, MA: MIT Press.

Ichise, M., Ballinger, J. R., Tanaka, F., et al. (1998). Age-related changes in D₂ receptor binding with Iodine-123-iodobenzofuran SPECT. *Journal of Nuclear Medicine, 39,* 1511–1518.

Inoue, M., Suhara, T., Sudo, Y., et al. (2001). Age-related reduction of extrastriatal dopamine D₂ receptor measured by PET. *Life Sciences, 69,* 1079–1084.

Irwin, I., DeLanney, L. E., McNeill, T., et al. (1994). Aging and the nigrostriatal dopamine system: A nonhuman primate study. *Neurodegeneration, 3,* 251–265.

Jaber, M., Jones, S., Giros, B., & Caron, M. G. (1997). The dopamine transporter: A crucial component regulating dopamine transmission. *Movement Disorders, 12,* 629–633.

Jayarman, A. (1984). Thalamostriate projections: An overview. In J. McKenzie, R. Klemm, & L. Wilcock (Eds.), *The basal ganglia: Advances in behavioral biology* (pp. 69–86). New York: Plenum.

Jones, G. H., & Robbins, T. W. (1992). Differential effects of mesocortical. Mesolimbic, and mesostriatal dopamine depletion on spontaneous, conditioned, and drug-induced locomotor activity. *Pharmacology, Biochemistry, and Behavior, 43,* 883–895.

Jones, S. R., Gainetdinov, R. R., Jaber, M., Giros, B., Wightman, R. M., & Caron, M. G. (1998). Profound neural plasticity in response to inactivation of the dopamine transporter. *Proceedings of the National Academy of Sciences of the United States of America, 95,* 4029–4034.

Jönsson, E. G., Nothen, M. M., Grunhage, F., et al. (1999). Polymorphisms in the dopamine D₂ receptor gene and their relationships to striatal dopamine receptor density of healthy volunteers. *Molecular Psychiatry, 4,* 290–296.

Joseph, J. A., Denisova, N., & Villalobos-Molina, R. (1996). Oxidative stress and age-related neuronal deficits. *Molecular Chemistry and Neuropathology, 28,* 35–40.

Joyce, J. N. (2001). The basal ganglia dopaminergic systems in normal aging and Parkinson's disease. In P. R. Hof & C. V. Mobbs (Eds.), *Functional neurobiology of aging* (pp. 689–709). San Diego, CA: Academic Press.

Joyce, J. N., Sapp, D. W., & Marshall, J. F. (1986). Human striatal dopamine receptors are organized in compartments. *Proceedings of the National Academy of Sciences of the United States of America, 83,* 8002–8006.

Kaasinen, V., Vilkman, H., Hietala, J., et al. (2000). Age-related D$_2$/D$_3$ receptor loss in extrastriatal regions of the human brain. *Neurobiology of Aging, 21,* 683–688.

Kausler, D. H. (1991). *Experimental psychology, cognition, and human aging* (2nd ed.). New York: Springer-Verlag.

Kelly, T. H., Foltin, R. W., & Fischman, M. W. (1991). The effects of repeated amphetamine exposure on multiple measures of human behavior. *Pharmacology, Biochemistry, and Behavior, 38,* 417–426.

Kessler, R. M., Whetsell, W. O., Ansari, M. S., et al. (1993). Identification of extrastriatal dopamine D$_2$ receptors in post mortem human brain with [^{125}I]epidepride. *Brain Research, 609,* 237–243.

Kimberg, D. Y., & D'Esposito, M. (2003). Cognitive effects of the dopamine receptor agonist pergolide. *Neuropsychologia, 41,* 1020–1027.

Kimberg, D. Y., D'Esposito, M., & Farah, M. J. (1997). Effects of bromocriptine on human subjects depend on working memory capacity. *NeuroReport, 8,* 3581–3585.

Kohler, C., Ericson, H., & Radesater, A. C. (1991). Different laminar distributions of dopamine D$_1$ and D$_2$ receptors in the rat hippocampal region. *Neuroscience Letters, 126,* 107–109.

Kolega, H. S. (1993). Stimulant drugs and vigilance performance: A review. *Psychopharmacology, 11,* 1–16.

Langston, J. W., & Irwin, I. (1986). MPTP-Current concepts and controversies. *Clinical Neuropharmacology, 9,* 485–507.

Lawrence, A. D., Weeks, R. A., Brooks, D. J., et al. (1998). The relationship between dopamine receptor binding and cognitive performance in Huntington's disease. *Brain, 121,* 1343–1355.

Li, S.-C., Lindenberger, U., & Sikström, S. (2001). Aging cognition: From neuromodulation to representation to cognition. *Trends in Cognitive Sciences, 5,* 479–486.

Lindenberger, U., & Baltes, P. B. (1997). Intellectual functioning in old and very old age: Cross-sectional results from the Berlin Aging Study. *Psychology and Aging, 12,* 410–432.

Luciana, M., & Collins, P. F. (1997). Dopamine modulates working memory for spatial but not object cues in normal humans. *Journal of Cognitive Neuroscience, 9,* 330–347.

Luciana, M., Collins, P. F., & Depue, R. A. (1998). Opposing roles for dopamine and serotonin in the modulation of human spatial working memory functions. *Cerebral Cortex, 8,* 218–226.

Luciana, M., Depue, R. A., Arbisi, P., & Leon, A. (1992). Facilitation of working memory in humans by a D$_2$ dopamine receptor agonist. *Journal of Cognitive Neuroscience, 4,* 58–68.

Luo, Y., & Roth, G. S. (2000). The roles of dopamine oxidative stress and dopamine receptor signaling in aging and age-related neurodegeneration. *Antioxidants & Redox Signaling, 2,* 1549–1559.

Ma, S. Y., Ciliax, B. J., Stebbins, G., et al. (1999). Dopamine transporter-immunoreactive neurons decrease with age in the human substantia nigra. *Journal of Comparative Neurology, 409,* 25–37.

Mattay, V. S., Berman, K. F., Ostrem, J. L., et al. (1996). Dextroamphetamime enhances "neural network-specific" physiological signals: A positron emission tomography rCBF study. *Journal of Neuroscience, 16,* 4816–4822.

McEntee, W. J., Mair, R. G., & Langlais, P. J. (1987). Neurochemical specificity of learning: Dopamine and motor learning. *Yale Journal of Biology and Medicine, 60,* 187–193.

Meador-Woodruff, J. H. (1994). Update on dopamine receptors. *Annals of Clinical Psychiatry, 6,* 79–90.

Mehta, M. A., Owen, A. M., Sahaikan, B. J., et al. (2000). Methylphenidate enhances working memory by modulating discrete frontal and parietal lobe regions in the human brain. *Journal of Neuroscience Online, 20,* RC 65.

Mesco, E. R., Carlsson, S. G., Joseph, J. A., & Roth, G. S. (1993). Decreased striatal D_2 dopamine receptor mRNA synthesis during aging. *Molecular Brain Research, 17,* 160–162.

Mitchell, D. B. (1989). How many memory systems? Evidence from aging. *Journal of Experimental Psychology: Learning, Memory, & Cognition, 15,* 31–49.

Morgan, D. G., & Finch, C. E. (1998). Dopaminergic changes in the basal ganglia: A generalized phenomenon of aging in mammals. *Annals of the New York Academy of Sciences, 515,* 145–160.

Morris, E. D., Chefer, S. I., Lane, M. A., et al. (1999). Loss of D_2 receptor binding with age in rhesus monkeys: Importance of correction for differences in striatal size. *Journal of Cerebral Blood Flow and Metabolism, 19,* 218–229.

Moscovitch, M., & Winocur, G. (1992). The neuropsychology of memory and aging. In F. I. M. Craik & T. A. Salthouse (Eds.), *The handbook of aging and cognition* (pp. 315–372). Hillsdale, NJ: Erlbaum.

Mozley, L. H., Gur, R. C., Mozley, P. D., & Gur, R. E. (2001). Striatal dopamine transporters and cognitive functioning in healthy men and women. *American Journal of Psychiatry, 158,* 1492–1499.

Mozley, P. D., Acton, P. D., Barraclough, E. D., et al. (1999). Effects of age on dopamine transporters in healthy humans. *Journal of Nuclear Medicine, 40,* 1812–1817.

Müller, U., von Cramon, D. Y., & Pollmann, S. (1998). D_1- versus D_2-receptor modulation of visuospatial working memory in humans. *Journal of Neuroscience, 18,* 2720–2728.

Neumeyer, J. L., Wang, S., Milius, R. A., et al. (1991). [^{123}I]-2-β-carbomethoxy-3β-(4-iodophenyl)-tropane: High-affinity SPECT radiotracer of monoamine reuptake sites in brain. *Journal of Medicinal Chemistry, 34,* 3144–3146.

Nieoullon, A. (2002). Dopamine and the regulation of cognition and attention. *Progress in Neurobiology, 67,* 53–83.

Nilsson, L.-G., Bäckman, L., Erngrund, K., et al. (1997). The Betula prospective cohort study: Memory, health, and aging. *Aging, Neuropsychology, and Cognition, 4,* 1–32.

Nordström, A. L., Farde, L., Pauli, S., Litton, J. E., & Halldin, C. (1992). PET analysis of [^{11}C] raclopride binding in healthy young adults and schizophrenic patients: Reliability and age effects. *Human Psychopharmacology, 7,* 157–165.

Nyberg, L., Maitland, S. B., Rönnlund, M., Bäckman, L., Dixon, R. A., & Nilsson, L.-G. (2003). Selective adult age differences in an age-invariant multi-factor model of declarative memory. *Psychology and Aging, 18,* 149–160.

Oades, R. D. (1985). The role of noradrenaline in tuning and dopamine in switching between signals in the CNS. *Neuroscience and Biobehavioral Reviews, 9,* 261–282.

O'Sullivan, M., Jones, D. K., Summers, P. E., Morris, R. G., Williams, S. C. R., & Markus, H. S. (2001). Evidence for cortical "disconnection" as a mechanism of age-related cognitive decline. *Neurology, 57,* 632–638.

Parent, A., & Hazrati, L. N. (1995). Functional anatomy of the basal ganglia. I. The cortico-basal ganglia-thalamo-cortical loop. *Brain Research Review, 20,* 91–127.

Park, D. C., Lautenschlager, G., Hedden, T., Davidson, N. S., Smith, A. D., & Smith, P. K. (2002). Models of visuospatial and verbal memory across the adult life span. *Psychology and Aging, 17,* 299–320.

Pendleton, R. G., Rasheed, A., Roychowdhury, R., & Hillman, R. (1998). A new role for catecholamines: Ontogenesis. *Trends in Pharmacological Sciences, 19,* 248–251.

Previc, F. H. (1999). Dopamine and the origins of human intelligence. *Brain and Cognition*, *41*, 299–350.

Prull, M. W., Gabrieli, J. D. E., & Bunge, S. A. (1999). Age-related changes in memory: A cognitive neuroscience perspective. In F. I. M. Craik & T. A. Salthouse (Eds.), *The handbook of aging and cognition* (Vol. 2, pp. 91–153). Mahwah, NJ: Erlbaum.

Ramaekers, J. G., Louwerens, J. W., Muntjewerff, N. D., et al. (1999). Psychomotor, cognitive, extrapyramidal and affective functions of healthy volunteers during treatment with an atypical (amisulpiride) and a classic (haloperidol) antipsychotic. *Journal of Clinical Psychopharmacology*, *19*, 209–221.

Raz, N. (1999). Aging of the brain and its impact on cognitive performance: Integration of structural and functional findings. In F. I. M. Craik & T. A. Salthouse (Eds.), *The handbook of aging and cognition* (Vol. 2, pp. 1–90). Mahwah, NJ: Erlbaum.

Raz, N., Gunning-Dixon, F., Head, D., et al. (1997). Selective aging of human cerebral cortex observed in vivo: Differential vulnerability of the prefrontal gray matter. *Cerebral Cortex*, *7*, 268–282.

Raz, N., Torres, I. J., Spencer, W. D., Baertschie, J. C., Millman, D., & Sarpel, G. (1993). Neuroanatomical correlates of age-sensitive and age-invariant cognitive abilities: An in vivo MRI investigation. *Intelligence*, *17*, 407–422.

Reeves, S., Bench, C., & Howard, R. (2002). Aging and the nigrostriatal dopamine system. *International Journal of Geriatric Psychiatry*, *17*, 359–370.

Remy, P., Jackson, P. L., Ribeiro, M. J., et al. (2000). Relationships between cognitive deficits and dopaminergic function in the striatum of Parkinson's disease patients. *Neurology*, *54*(Suppl.), 372.

Rinne, J. O., Lönnberg, P., & Marjamäki, P. (1990). Age-dependent decline of dopamine-D_1 and dopamine-D_2 receptor. *Brain Research*, *508*, 349–352.

Rinne, J. O., Sahlberg, N., Ruottinen, H., Nagren, K., & Lehikoinen, P. (1998). Striatal uptake of the dopamine reuptake ligand [^{11}C]β-CFT is reduced in Alzheimer's disease assessed by positron emission tomography. *Neurology*, *50*, 152–156.

Roberts, A. C., De Salvia, M. A., Wilkinson, L. S., Collins, P., Buir, J. L., Everitt, B. J., et al. (1994). 6-Hydroxydopamine lesions of the prefrontal cortex in monkeys enhance performance on an analog of the Wisconsin Card Sort Test: Possible interactions with subcortical dopamine. *Journal of Neuroscience*, *14*, 2531–2544.

Roth, R. H. (1984). CNS dopamine autoreceptors: Distribution, pharmacology, and function. *Annals of the New York Academy of Sciences*, *430*, 27–53.

Rypma, B., & D'Esposito, M. (2000). Isolating the neural mechanisms of age-related changes in human working memory. *Nature Neuroscience*, *3*, 509–515.

Rypma, B., Prabhakaran, V., Desmond, J. D., & Gabrieli, J. D. E. (2001). Age differences in prefrontal cortical activity in working memory. *Psychology and Aging*, *16*, 371–384.

Sakata, M., Farooqui, S. M., & Prasad, C. (1992). Post-transcriptional regulation of loss of rat striatal D_2 dopamine receptor during aging. *Brain Research*, *575*, 309–314.

Salthouse, T. A. (1991). *Theoretical perspectives on cognitive aging*. Hillsdale, NJ: Erlbaum.

Salthouse, T. A. (1992). *Mechanisms of age-cognition relations in adulthood*. Hillsdale, NJ: Erlbaum.

Salthouse, T. A. (1998). Independence of age-related influences on cognitive abilities across the life span. *Developmental Psychology*, *34*, 851–864.

Sawaguchi, T., & Goldman-Rakic, P. S. (1991). D_1 dopamine receptors in prefrontal cortex: Involvement in working memory. *Science*, *251*, 947–950.

Sawaguchi, T., Matsamura, M., & Kubota, K. (1988). Dopamine enhances the neuronal activity of spatial short-term memory in the primate prefrontal cortex. *Neuroscience Research*, *5*, 465–473.

Seeman, P., Bzowej, N. H,, Guan, H. C., et al. (1987). Human brain dopamine receptors in children and aging adults. *Synapse, 1*, 399–404.

Servan-Schreiber, D., Bruno, R. M., Carter, C. S., & Cohen, J. D. (1998). Dopamine and the mechanisms of cognition: Part I. A neural network model predicting dopamine effects on selective attention. *Biological Psychiatry, 43*, 713–722.

Servan-Schreiber, D., Carter, C. S., Bruno, R. M., & Cohen, J. D. (1998). Dopamine and the mechanisms of cognition: Part II. D-Amphetamine effects in human subjects performing a selective attention task. *Biological Psychiatry, 43*, 723–729.

Severson, J. A., Marcusson, J., Winblad, B., & Finch, C. E. (1982). Age-correlated loss of dopaminergic binding sites in human basal ganglia. *Journal of Neurochemistry, 39*, 1623–1631.

Shinkai, T., Zhang, L., Mathias, S. A., & Roth, G. S. (1997). Dopamine induces apoptosis in cultured rat striatal neurons: Possible mechanism of D_2-dopamine receptor neuron loss during aging. *Journal of Neuroscience Research, 47*, 393–399.

Simic, G., Kostovic, I., Winblad, B., & Bogdanovic, N. (1997). Volume and number of neurons of the human hippocampal formation in normal aging and Alzheimer's disease. *Journal of Comparative Neurology, 379*, 482–494.

Simon, H., Taghzouti, K., & Le Moal, M. (1986). Deficits in spatial-memory tasks following lesions of septal dopaminergic terminals in the rat. *Behavioral and Brain Research, 19*, 7–16.

Small, S. A., Perera, G. M., DeLaPaz, R., Mayeux, R., & Stern, Y. (1999). Differential regional dysfunction of the hippocampal formation among elderly with memory decline and Alzheimer's disease. *Annals of Neurology, 45*, 466–472.

Smeets, W. J., Marin, O., & Gonzales, A. (2000). Evolution of the basal ganglia: New perspectives through a comparative approach. *Journal of Anatomy, 196*, 501–517.

Snow, B. J., Tooyama, I., McGeer, E. G., et al. (1993). Human positron emission tomographic [^{18}F]fluorodopa studies correlate with dopamine cell counts and levels. *Annals of Neurology, 34*, 324–330

Spiegel, R. (1978). Effects of amphetamines on performance and on polygraphic sleep parameters in man. *Advances in Bioscience, 21*, 189–201.

Stebbins, G. T., Carrillo, M. C., Dorfman, J., et al. (2002). Aging effects on memory encoding in the frontal lobes. *Psychology and Aging, 17*, 44–55.

Stern, Y., & Langston, J. W. (1985). Intellectual changes in patients with MPTP-induced Parkinsonism. *Neurology, 35*, 1506–1509.

Stern, Y., Tetrud, J. W., Martin, W. R., Kutner, S. J., & Langston, J. W. (1990). Cognitive change following MPTP exposure. *Neurology, 40*, 261–264.

Suhara, T., Fukuda, H., Inoue, O., et al. (1991). Age-related changes in human D_1 dopamine receptors measured by positron emission tomography. *Psychopharmacology, 103*, 41–45.

Troyer, A. K., Moscovitch, M., Winocur, G., Alexander, M. P., & Stuss, D. (1998). Clustering and switching on verbal fluency: The effects of focal frontal- and temporal-lobe lesions. *Neuropsychologia, 36*, 499–504.

Ungerstedt, U. (1971). *On the anatomy, pharmacology, and function of the nigrostriatal dopamine system.* Stockholm: Norstedts.

Van Dyck, C. H., Seibyl, J. P., Malison, R. T., et al. (1995). Age-related decline in striatal dopamine transporter binding with iodine-123-β-CIT. *Journal of Nuclear Medicine, 36*, 1175–1181.

Volkow, N. D., Gur, R. C., Wang, G.-J., et al. (1998). Association between decline in brain dopamine activity with age and cognitive and motor impairment in healthy individuals. *American Journal of Psychiatry, 155*, 344–349.

Volkow, N. D., Logan, J., Fowler, J. S., et al. (2000). Association between age-related decline in brain dopamine activity and impairment in frontal and cingulate metabolism. *American Journal of Psychiatry, 157,* 75–80.

Volkow, N. D., Wang, G.-J, Fowler, J. S., et al. (1998). Parallel loss of presynaptic and postsynaptic dopamine markers in normal aging. *Annals of Neurology, 44,* 143–147.

Wang, Y., Chan, G. L. Y., Holden, J. E., et al. (1998). Age-dependent decline of dopamine D_1 receptors in human brain: A PET study. *Synapse, 30,* 56–61.

West, M. J. (1993). Regionally specific loss of neurons in the aging human hippocampus. *Neurobiology of Aging, 14,* 287–293.

West, R. L. (1996). An application of prefrontal cortex function theory to cognitive aging. *Psychological Bulletin, 120,* 272–292.

Williams, G. V., & Goldman-Rakic, P. S. (1995). Modulation of memory fields by dopamine D_1 receptors in prefrontal cortex. *Nature, 376,* 572–575.

Wilson, C. J., Finch, C. E., & Cohen, H. J. (2002). Cytokines and cognition—The case for a head-to-toe inflammatory paradigm. *Journal of the American Geriatrics Society, 50,* 2041–2056.

Wise, S. P., Murray, E. A., & Gerfen, C. R. (1996). The frontal cortex-basal ganglia system in primates. *Critical Reviews in Neurobiology, 10,* 317–356.

Zhang, L., Ravipati, A., Joseph, J., & Roth, G. S. (1995). Aging-related changes in rat striatal D_2 dopamine receptor mRNA-containing neurons: A quantitative nonradioactive in situ hybridization study. *Journal of Neuroscience, 15,* 1735–1740.

4

Electrophysiological and Optical Measures of Cognitive Aging

Monica Fabiani
Gabriele Gratton

As exemplified by the first *Symposium on Neuroscience, Aging, and Cognition*, of which this book is an outcome, the last decade has seen an explosion of research in the cognitive neuroscience of aging. Human aging is characterized by changes in cognition within a context of changes in both structural and functional anatomy. The biggest challenge facing researchers in this area is to understand the relationships among cognitive, anatomical, and physiological changes and to reconcile discrepancies between these levels of analysis. The availability of a number of imaging methods that allow for the noninvasive study of brain function during the performance of cognitive tasks has allowed investigators to explore a number of questions that previously could only be tackled indirectly.

In this chapter, we review two of these methods (optical brain imaging and electrophysiology) in the context of other available methodologies as they apply to aging research. Both of these methods emphasize the temporal aspects of the brain phenomena underlying cognition and thus allow for a closer parallel with cognitive studies using a mental chronometry approach to the study of aging. However, these two methods differ in the amount of localization information they provide, with electrophysiological methods yielding a coarser spatial description of brain activity and optical imaging meshing temporal and spatial information at a finer level. In fact, the spatial resolution of optical imaging may be close to that reached with functional magnetic resonance imaging (fMRI) or positron emission tomography (PET), especially when data from a number of subjects are combined, which leads to a loss of resolution for all techniques.

Neuronal and Hemodynamic Measures of Brain Function

There are two general classes of noninvasive methods that are widely available for human brain research. Hemodynamic/metabolic methods, such has ^{15}O-PET and, more recently, fMRI are based on imaging some of the consequences of neuronal activity, such as the increased blood flow to active areas of the brain (Toga & Mazziotta, 1996; Raichle, 1998). These methods have very good localization power and, in the case of fMRI, have the advantage of being able to provide a functional map that can be plotted on the anatomical image, collected during the same session, of the participant's brain. Studies of aging using these methods (and reviewed in chapters 8, 9, 11, 12, and 14, this volume) show that more structures are activated in the older adult's brain than in the younger adult's brain, especially in working memory tasks. This has led to the formulation of a dedifferentiation or widespread activation hypothesis, with the exact functional significance of this more extended brain involvement in older adults (compensation vs. lack of differentiation) still under debate (see Cabeza, 2002; Logan et al., 2002; Colcombe et al., 2004).

The main limitation of hemodynamic methods is their poor temporal resolution, which is more severe for PET, but still quite substantial for fMRI. This is not because of technical constraints, but the intrinsic nature of the hemodynamic signal, which lags the corresponding neuronal signal by several seconds. This is particularly a problem in aging studies because the signal lag may be larger and more variable in older than in younger adults. Another factor limiting temporal resolution in fMRI is the relatively low sampling rate (typically 0.5 Hz, although in some cases a sampling rate as high as 10 Hz is possible). Although algorithms exist for providing trial-by-trial indices of event-related activity (Dale & Buckner, 1997; Buckner, 1998), these methods do not provide a breakdown of processing within trials. A related limitation is that, by virtue of imaging the vascular response that follows the neuronal signal of interest, hemodynamic methods possess some inherent ambiguities: (1) changes in the cardiovascular response (which often occur in aging) may alter these measures without necessarily reflecting a proportional change in the corresponding neuronal signal (D'Esposito et al., 1999; Huettel, Singerman, & McCarthy, 2001); and (2) these measures integrate information over time (because of their slow time course) and therefore may potentially confound time on task with magnitude of activation (e.g., Logothetis et al., 2001; Martinez et al., 1999).

The second class of methods comprises electrophysiological techniques, such as event-related brain potentials (ERPs; for a review see Fabiani, Gratton, & Coles, 2000) and magnetoencephalography (MEG; Hari, Levanen, & Raij, 2000). These methods are based on measuring neuronal activity, mostly postsynaptic potentials that can be recorded at the scalp in response to (or in preparation for) specific events. The advantage of these methods is their excellent temporal resolution, which allows for imaging brain activity in the millisecond range. The main limitation of these methods is their poor spatial resolution (although modeling algorithms are available to address localization issues; Scherg & Von Cramon, 1986; Simpson et al., 1995; Bonmassar et al., 2001).

Electroencephalogram (EEG) studies of aging have been conducted for a long time and have often shown slowing of basic rhythms, especially the alpha rhythm (Obrist, Henry, & Justiss, 1961), as well as variations in spatial and coherence patterns (e.g., G. Gratton et al., 1992). The interpretation of EEG studies is complicated by the relative lack of control of cognitive processes in these paradigms. Therefore, in this chapter we focus on ERP studies in which specific tasks are given to the subjects. The main results obtained in these studies emphasize the slowing of several ERP components in aging (Goodin et al., 1978). In addition, recent emphasis has been on the persistent occurrence of "normal" responses at seemingly inappropriate times in older adults, such as the persistence of frontal P300 responses typically elicited by novel stimuli even in conditions in which the eliciting stimuli are no longer novel (Fabiani & Friedman, 1995; Fabiani, Friedman, & Cheng, 1998). This phenomenon bears similarities to the dedifferentiation/widespread activation hypothesis outlined above, although it underscores the dynamic aspects of this phenomenon, with rapid changes over time in younger adults that fail to occur in older adults.

Since the mid-1990s, a third class of noninvasive brain imaging methods—optical methods, based on imaging the properties of light propagation in tissue—has begun to emerge (G. Gratton & Fabiani, 1998, 2001; Villringer & Chance, 1997; Fabiani, Gratton, & Corballis, 1996). These methods differ in a number of ways from the hemodynamic and electrophysiological methods described above in that they can provide both neuronal and hemodynamic information with a combination of spatial and temporal resolution.

We have begun to explore the application of these methods to the study of cognitive aging (Wee et al., 2001). The questions we are addressing include (1) the localization of processing delays within the context of the network of brain areas involved in information processing (Wee et al., 2000, 2001); (2) integration and extension of information obtained with different methodologies, particularly with respect to the persistence in older adults of processes that are apparently no longer needed (Low et al., 2001), and the possible relationship of this phenomenon to the dedifferentiation/widespread activation hypothesis (Wee at al., 2003); and (3) the study of neurovascular coupling in young and older adults, exploiting the sensitivity of these measures to both neuronal and hemodynamic events (G. Gratton, Goodman-Wood, & Fabiani, 2001). Currently, the two main limitations of these methods are the limited penetration (making them suitable only for cortical rather than sub-cortical measures) and the low signal-to-noise ratio, which requires the recording of a large number of trials. The latter problem may be considerably eased by a new instrumental design currently in progress.

It should be apparent from the above description that different imaging methods provide complementary views of the brain functions that underlie cognitive aging. This also points to the potential advantages of combining different methods to obtain a more complete picture of age-related changes. This combined approach may be methodologically complex, but its feasibility is documented in a number of publications, including some chapters of this book (chapter 6, this volume; Bonmassar et al., 2001; G. Gratton et al., 1997; G. Gratton, Goodman-Wood, & Fabiani, 2001; Fabiani et al., 2003).

In the remainder of this chapter, we briefly review some age-related findings obtained with electrophysiological methods and highlight some of the insights and unresolved issues emanating from this research. We then describe optical imaging methods, with particular emphasis on their applications to aging research. We then conclude by discussing advantages, methodological constraints, and possible future directions of aging research work based on imaging methods with high temporal resolution.

Selective Review of Age-Related Event-Related Potential Research: Insights and Unresolved Issues

ERPs have been used to study aspects of brain cognitive aging since the mid-1970s. Part of this research is focused on the idea of using ERPs to decompose the time between stimulus and response to identify which stages of processing are most affected by aging (for reviews, see Fabiani, Gratton, & Coles, 2000; Fabiani & Wee, 2001). This is done in the context of the theories of aging, emphasizing the slowing of information processing (Salthouse, 1996).

Initially, Goodin et al. (1978) showed that the latency of the P300 component of the ERPs, which is considered an index of the duration of stimulus evaluation processes, increases by approximately 1.5 ms per year between young adulthood and old age. This effect is smaller than the increase in reaction time (RT), leading to the interpretation that both pre- and poststimulus evaluation processes slow with age, consistent with a generalized slowing account of aging. Similar results were reported by Ford et al. (1979, 1982); Strayer, Wickens, and Braune, 1987; and Strayer and Kramer (1994; see also Bashore, Osman, & Heffley, 1989, for a meta-analytic study).

Some researchers have begun to apply the Lateralized Readiness Potential (LRP; G. Gratton et al., 1988) to study response-related processes in aging. This component of the ERP provides an on-line index of the preferential activation of one motor response over another and can therefore be used to separate premotor from motor processes using LRP onset as a demarcation between these two as well as the subthreshold activation of motor responses. The main finding of this research with respect to aging is that much, if not all, of the slowing is observed before the LRP onset (premotor period, with the timing between LRP onset and overt movement remaining constant with age) (Jurkowski, Hackley, & Gratton, 2002). This contrasts with effects obtained with patients with Parkinson's disease compared to age-matched controls, for whom the delay is localized to the period between LRP onset and overt response (Low, Miller, & Vierck, 2002; Jurkowski, Hackley, & Gratton, 2002).

The specificity of these effects to either the premotor or the motor period is not consistent with a generalized slowing account of aging and highlights the insights that can be obtained using methods that allow for a fine-grained temporal decomposition of information processing. Further, these data indicate that the effects of Parkinson's disease on RT are not merely an amplification of the effects of aging because they seem to affect different component processes—a conclusion that would be difficult to draw on the basis of RT data alone. In fact, these data are consistent with the view that aging may influence decision processes, perhaps because of problems dealing with conflict or inhibition, rather than motoric processes. This is largely consistent with an extensive meta-analysis of chronometric ERP data carried out by Bashore et al. (1997). These authors analyzed a number of studies of aging effects on the latency of ERP activity as well as of overt responses in a variety of tasks and concluded that "generalized slowing" cannot account for the variety of effects observed, which in fact appear to be both process specific and task dependent.

Several theories of cognitive aging also emphasize the reduced ability of older adults to control their attention/working memory and inhibit responses to irrelevant information (Craik & Byrd, 1982; Hasher & Zacks, 1988; for a review see Park, 2000). In the context of these theories, age-related slowing is explained by competition between processes and/or memory representations. A number of ERP components are exquisitely sensitive to differential preattentive and attentive processes and have been exploited in the context of this research.

Much of this research has been based on the examination of the brain responses to stimuli in series intermixing target and distractor information. Three main findings have been reported in this context. First, the amplitude of the auditory N100 elicited by irrelevant stimuli is larger in older than younger adults (Low et al., 2001; Chao & Knight, 1997; Alain & Woods, 1999). The N100 is considered an index of early sensory attention gating processes (Hillyard et al., 1973). This suggests that attention gating of irrelevant information is compromised in older adults (Chao & Knight, 1997).

A second finding is that the amplitude of the mismatch negativity (MMN) is reduced in aging, at least under conditions of divided attention and/or when the interstimulus intervals are long (over 4 s; Pekkonen et al., 1996; Czigler, Csibra, & Csontos, 1992; Gaeta et al., 1998; Kazmerski, Friedman, & Ritter, 1997; Woods, 1992; Alain & Woods, 1999). The MMN is an ERP component obtained by subtracting the waveforms elicited by standard stimuli from those elicited by deviant stimuli in an unattended condition (Ritter et al., 1995) and is considered an index of sensory memory. These results suggest that there may be problems with the deployment of sensory memory in aging. However, recent work suggested that the phenomenon may still be largely caused by increased processing of irrelevant information by the older adults, even at this early sensory-memory level (Wee et al., 2001; Alain & Woods, 1999).

A third set of results is focused on changes in the scalp distribution of the P300 response to target (attended) stimuli. Specifically, several studies have shown that the P300 (also called P3 or P3b) has a more frontal distribution (i.e., is relatively larger at frontal than at parietal recording sites) in older adults compared to younger adults (e.g., Fabiani & Friedman, 1995; Friedman, Simpson, & Hamberger, 1993). This finding, by itself, suggests that a different set of brain structures is active at this latency in younger and older subjects.

To understand better this phenomenon, it is important to note that a frontal distribution of activity is observed in both younger and older adults in response to novel (i.e., never presented before) and unexpected stimuli. However, in young subjects, the frontally distributed response is suppressed after a few presentations of the novel stimuli. In contrast, in older subjects this frontal response persists after many presentations of the novel stimuli (Friedman & Simpson, 1994; Fabiani & Friedman, 1995). This frontal activity has been interpreted as an index of the automatic orienting of attention toward novel stimuli, a response that is normally lost after a few stimulus repetitions in young but not older adults.

Evidence from lesion studies suggests that this frontal activity requires an intact dorsolateral prefrontal cortex (DLPFC) for its generation (Knight, 1984). In addition, Fabiani, Friedman, and Cheng (1998) found that the scalp distribution of P300 is more variable in older than in younger subjects. They observed that older individuals with sustained frontal responses to repeated stimuli over time were also impaired in neuropsychological tests of frontal function with respect to age- and IQ-matched subjects showing a "younger looking" parietal maximum response. These results are shown in figure 4.1a and 4.1b.

This research and the work on N1 and MMN described here suggest that older subjects may have problems in the deployment of attention to irrelevant and/or repeated stimuli. This work is in line with both cognitive work on the lack of inhibition of prepotent responses in aging (Hasher & Zacks, 1988; for a review, see Fabiani & Wee, 2001) or with lack of habituation and with neuroimaging evidence of more widespread activity in older adults (dedifferentiation/widespread activation hypothesis). Whether these effects are caused by attempts at compensation (Cabeza et al., 2002; Reuter-Lorentz, 2002) or are indices of the underlying processing problems (Logan et al., 2002; Colcombe et al., 2004) is still to be determined.

The chronometric and sequential analyses discussed in this section take advantage of the high temporal resolution of electrophysiological methods and provide insights about possible mechanisms underlying cognitive aging. Although this research approach is useful in a number of contexts, the limited spatial resolution of ERP measures poses limitations on the conclusions that can be drawn from these data. In fact, as there is extensive cross talk between scalp-recorded brain responses, it is difficult to attribute a particular ERP measure to a specific brain generator, sometimes even in the presence of corroborating evidence from modeling, lesion data, and combined recording approaches with hemodynamic measures. In the next section, we describe a new imaging method that combines spatial and temporal specificity and thus potentially will allow investigators to address some of these issues.

Optical Imaging and Its Applications to Aging Research

The use of light for the investigation of the inner aspects of the human body has a relatively long history (Cutler, 1929, 1931; Isard, 1981; Chance, 1989; Andersson-Engels et al., 1990; Yamashita & Kaneko, 1993). Optical imaging methods include several techniques that involve measuring the parameters of light propagation (absorption and scattering) through tissue to estimate the functional activity occurring within the tissue (G. Gratton et al., 2003). Whereas changes in optical properties of exposed brain tissue can be measured relatively easily (as demonstrated by exposed cortex studies; Bonhoeffer & Grinvald, 1996), noninvasive measurement of these properties in "deep" tissue, such as the brain, is more complex. This is partly because of the presence of hemoglobin, a strong absorber of visible light.

However, as shown in plate 4.1 (see color insert), hemoglobin is a weaker absorber of near-infrared (NIR) light (600–1300 nm), and scattering becomes the dominant factor in determining light propagation through the head (by a factor of approximately 20–100). NIR light penetrates several centimeters into the head, thus allowing the noninvasive measurement of some of the optical properties of the brain (or at least of the cortex). In addition, by properly placing NIR light sources and detectors on the surface of the head, it is possible to select different tissue volumes (G. Gratton et al., 2000). Understanding how light propagates in strongly scattering media allows the description of the paths followed by photons from the source to

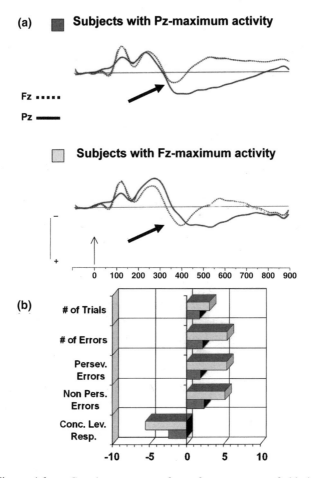

Figure 4.1. *a*, Grand average waveforms for two groups of elderly subjects classified on the basis of their P3 scalp maxima. The waveforms elicited by the target stimuli during an oddball task are plotted. Pz is indicated by the solid line and Fz by the dotted line. Time (milliseconds) is on the abscissa, and amplitude (microvolts) is on the ordinate. *b*, Older adults with Pz maximum activity (which is typical of younger adults) were less impaired in their performance of the Wisconsin Card Sorting Test (WCST; dark gray bars) with respect to older adults with Fz maximum activity (light gray bars). Scores were plotted as a function of their deviation from the scores of young subjects (*z* transformation). # of Trials, total number of trials to complete test; # of Errors, total number of errors; Persev. Errors, percentage perseverative errors; Non Pers. Errors, percentage nonperseverative errors; Conc. Lev. Resp., percentage conceptual level responses (i.e., runs of three or more correct responses divided by the total number of trials times 100). (Data adapted from Fabiani, Friedman, & Cheng, 1998.)

the detector and thus provides the basis for the localization power of these methods (Maier & Gratton, 1993; E. Gratton et al., 1993; G. Gratton et al., 1994; Fantini et al., 1994).

Scattering and absorption interact in a complex manner in determining how NIR light propagates through the head. However, it is now apparent that modeling of the optical properties of tissue and appropriate recording techniques may lead to measures that are recorded from volumes with diameters of just a few millimeters. This makes the localization power of optical methods roughly comparable to that of PET and only slightly inferior to that of fMRI. However, different from PET and fMRI, NIR measurements are limited to relatively shallow areas, with a maximum penetration of 3–5 cm from the surface of the head. Here, we describe two specific types of noninvasive optical imaging: near-infrared spectroscopy (NIRS) and the event-related optical signal (EROS), with particular focus on EROS measures.

Near-Infrared Spectroscopy

As mentioned in the section on neuronal and hemodynamic measures of brain function, optical imaging allows investigators to collect both neuronal and hemodynamic data in parallel and within the same experimental session. Hemodynamic information is typically obtained using a spectroscopic measurement approach (NIRS) based on the in vivo quantification of the concentration of significant substances using NIR light of different wavelengths (see Villringer & Chance, 1997; see also Jobsis, 1977).

This technique is possible because several substances of metabolic importance, including oxy- and deoxyhemoglobin, have characteristic and distinctive absorption spectra in the NIR range (see plate 4.1, right panel). In fact, NIRS is the only available method for measuring the absolute concentration of oxy- and deoxyhemoglobin in a selected area of the body in a noninvasive fashion. Several investigators have used this approach to measure regional changes in the concentration of oxy- and deoxyhemoglobin in the brain during visual stimulation (Kato et al., 1993; Meek et al., 1995; Wenzel et al., 1996), somatosensory stimulation (Obrig et al., 1996), motor tasks (Hirth et al., 1997), and cognitive tasks (Hoshi & Tamura, 1993). An example of data obtained with NIRS is presented in plate 4.2 (see color insert).

The Event-Related Optical Signal

EROS (G. Gratton, Corballis, et al., 1995; G. Gratton & Fabiani, 1998, 2001) has been proposed as a noninvasive brain imaging tool that combines spatial specificity (i.e., the signal observed can be ascribed to localized cortical areas extending less than 1–2 cm^2; G. Gratton et al., 1997; G. Gratton & Fabiani, 2003) with good temporal resolution (i.e., responses occurring several times per second can be measured independently; G. Gratton, Goodman-Wood, & Fabiani, 2001). Additional advantages of EROS (as well as of NIRS) include relatively low cost, portability, repeatability of the measurement, and compatibility for concurrent recording with other techniques, such as fMRI, MEG, and ERPs. EROS measurements are conducted using the same type of device used for recording NIRS signals.

There are two major differences between the hemodynamic signals measured with NIRS and the neuronal signals measured with EROS. First, the two signals are carried by different frequency bands (3–50 Hz for the neuronal signal, 0.1–0.3 Hz for the hemodynamic signals); second, the hemodynamic signals are mostly caused by absorption changes, and scattering appears to play a major role in the generation of the EROS signal. The apparatus and procedures used to derive the EROS signal are graphically depicted in plate 4.3 (see color insert).

As shown in plate 4.3, the fast optical signals measured with EROS are derived using procedures (such as signal averaging) that isolate very rapid responses to stimulation. Data showed that the use of high-pass filters cutting off frequencies of less than 3 Hz may markedly improve the signal-to-noise ratio of fast optical measures (Wolf, Wolf, Choi, Toronov, et al., 2003; Maclin, Gratton, & Fabiani, 2003), presumably because they eliminate the influence of slower signals (such as slow hemodynamic changes, vascular pulsation, and respiration). The fast effects are not likely caused by changes in the concentration of major absorbers in the brain (e.g., oxy- and deoxyhemoglobin, water). Rather, they probably are caused by changes in scattering properties of tissue with neuronal activity.

Substantial evidence based on studies of isolated neurons (Cohen, 1972), invertebrate animals (Stepnoski et al., 1991), hippocampal and cortical slices (Frostig et al., 1990), as well as implanted optical probes (Rector et al., 1997; Rector, Harper, & George, 2002) supports the idea that changes in light-scattering properties of neural tissue occur simultaneously with electrical activity. For instance, Rector et al. (1997) recorded parameters of light transmission in the hippocampus with implanted probes and found that activation of the Schaeffer's collateral leads to light-scattering changes in CA1, which has a time course that is similar to that of electrical evoked activity. These changes are commonly attributed to either conformational change in the neuronal membrane (Stepnoski et al., 1991) or to volumetric and osmolar changes associated with the movement of ions and water across the membrane as a function of neuronal activity (Cohen, 1972; Andrew & MacVicar, 1994).

The light-scattering signal identified by the animal work described above can be useful for functional brain imaging because (1) it is temporally concurrent with the neuronal activity itself, (2) it is spatially well localized, and (3) it is an "intrinsic" signal (i.e., it does not require the introduction of external tracers into the tissue). In the last 7 years, we have collected a substantial amount of data indicating that it is possible to record noninvasively in humans a signal with similar characteristics. The results have been replicated in other laboratories (Steinbrink et al., 2000; Wolf, Wolf, Choi, Toronov, et al., 2003; Wolf, Wolf, Choi, Gupta, et al., 2003).

Our initial studies were conducted in the visual (G. Gratton, Corballis, et al., 1995) and motor (G. Gratton, Fabiani, et al., 1995) modalities. They showed that unilateral activity over occipital and precentral areas was observed, respectively, after visual stimulation of the opposite hemifield or in association with movement of the contralateral hand. The activity consisted of changes (increases) in the photon transit time. In the visual stimulation experiment (Gratton, Corballis, et al., 1995), the latency of this response was approximately 100 ms. We labeled this type of short-latency optical response the EROS. Our data indicated that the localization of the EROS response was not only hemispherically specific, but could also reliably distinguish between cortical activation of medial occipital areas associated with stimulation of the top and bottom quadrants of the visual field (located just a few millimeters from each other) in a manner consistent with the known representation of the visual field in occipital cortex.

We have compared the localization of the EROS activity observed in our original study with that of the fMRI activity observed in similar conditions on the same subjects and its time course with that of ERP activity (also recorded in similar conditions on the same subjects; G. Gratton et al., 1997). The results indicated a good spatial overlap between EROS and fMRI responses and a good temporal overlap between the EROS and the ERP activity. Similar spatial and temporal overlaps across techniques have also been obtained in subsequent studies (e.g., DeSoto et al., 2001; G. Gratton et al., 2000; G. Gratton, Goodman-Wood, & Fabiani, 2001; Rinne et al., 1999).

In summary, fast optical signals have been recorded by us and other groups in several different modalities and brain regions, including medial occipital areas for the visual modality (G. Gratton, 1997; G. Gratton et al., 1998, 2000; G. Gratton, Goodman-Wood, & Fabiani, 2001; Wolf, Wolf, Choi, Toronov, et al., 2003); superior temporal areas for the auditory modality (Rinne et al., 1999); parietal areas for the somatosensory modality (Steinbrink et al., 2000); and precentral areas for the movement-related activity (DeSoto et al., 2001; Wolf, Wolf, Choi, Gupta, et al., 2003). These data support the claim that fast optical signals related to neural activity can be recorded noninvasively in a variety of brain regions. These signals are localized to areas not greater than a few millimeters in diameter, consistent with fMRI observations, and have a time course comparable to that of electrophysiological signals. Thus, fast optical signals can be used to provide measures of the time course of neuronal activity in localized cortical areas.

Optical Imaging in Aging: Preliminary Data

Work in our laboratory using optical imaging (EROS) measures and concurrent recording of ERPs demonstrated the feasibility of obtaining these measures in older adults (Wee et al., 2001). In this work, young (18–30 years old) and older (65 years or older) adults were examined in a replication and extension of a paradigm previously employed with young adults (Rinne et al., 1999). A "passive oddball" paradigm was used in which series of sounds were presented binaurally to the subjects while they were reading a book of their choice. The sounds (harmonically enriched tones with a basic frequency of 500 Hz) varied in duration: 80% of them were 75 ms long (frequent), and 20% were 25 ms long. Subjects' hearing was tested at 500 Hz, and the volume of the tones was increased proportional to hearing loss.

EROS and ERPs were recorded concurrently. The EROS recordings were taken from the auditory cortex. Both EROS and ERPs showed that responses could be recorded in the period immediately following the stimuli. In particular, both EROS and ERP measures showed a response to the frequent stimuli with a peak latency of 100; for both measures, the response was particularly large for the first few stimuli in the series (warm-up trials), but then declined somewhat in amplitude. Responses to the deviant items were also obtained, and the locations of the largest EROS responses to the frequent and deviant items were different. These responses could be recorded in both young and old subjects.

The location of the EROS response (as well as its latency) was similar in young and old subjects; in both cases, the response was easily distinguishable from the noise (see plate 4.4 in color insert). Although the absolute amplitude of the response was somewhat reduced in the older subjects, the signal-to-noise ratio was at least as high (if not higher) in the older than in the younger subjects. This occurs because the head tissues in older subjects tend to be more transparent to NIR light than that of the younger subjects. Note that, for both young and old and as reported previously (e.g., Chao & Knight, 1996), the N1 component in response to frequent stimuli appeared larger in older adults.

Neurovascular Coupling in Aging and Related Issues

We briefly reviewed two types of optical measures of brain activity that can be taken concurrently: NIRS (based on hemodynamic signals) and EROS (based on neuronal signals). The possibility of concurrent recording of these two types of signals from the same volume presents a unique opportunity for addressing a crucial issue in brain aging research, namely, whether the relationship between these two signals (*neurovascular coupling*; Villringer & Dirnagl, 1995) remains constant with age or whether it changes depending on the brain areas under study and on the age and health status of the individual.

An understanding of neurovascular coupling has both theoretical and methodological implications for aging research. In fact, as mentioned here, neuroimaging techniques such as fMRI and PET are based on measuring phenomena associated with local hemodynamic and metabolic changes occurring in the brain a few seconds after the beginning of neuronal activity (Grinvald et al., 1986; Malonek & Grinvald, 1996). Specifically, for reasons not yet completely understood, blood flow increases quite significantly in active regions of the brain, a phenomenon that was observed 100 years ago (Sherrington, 1906).

The increase in blood flow leads to a change in the concentration of critical substances, such as oxy- and deoxyhemoglobin, which occur naturally within the body (and brain). For instance, the concentration of deoxyhemoglobin drops in active cortical areas, beginning a couple of seconds after the onset of neuronal activity (Malonek & Grinvald, 1996). This is presumably because of increased blood flow, which flushes venous blood away from active cortical areas.

Deoxyhemoglobin has pronounced paramagnetic properties and therefore can influence the MR signal. This effect provides the basis for blood oxygen level dependent (BOLD) fMRI recording. Ogawa et al. (1992) and Kwong et al. (1992; see also Turner, 1995) showed that it is possible to use this phenomenon to infer which areas of the brain are active without introducing external tracers.

Typically, it is assumed that the relationship between the hemodynamic data provided by these brain imaging methods and the underlying neuronal phenomena is approximately linear, so that changes in one reflect proportional changes in the other (Buckner et al., 2000; Dale & Buckner, 1997; D'Esposito et al., 1999; Huettel, Singerman, & McCarthy, 2001; Miezin et al., 2000). In fact, the assumption of linearity is at the basis of linear decomposition methods of the fMRI signal, such as statistic parametric mapping (SPM) and fast event-related fMRI analyses (see D'Esposito et al., 1999; Friston et al., 1995, 1998; Menon & Kim, 1999; Rosen, Buckner, & Dale, 1998, for reviews).

The linearity assumption has been examined in several studies (Dale & Buckner, 1997; Huettel, Singerman, & McCarthy, 2001; Fox & Raichle, 1985), which have used systematic manipulations of stimulus conditions to test whether they elicit proportional (i.e., linear) increments in the magnitude of the signal. Although support for linearity has been found in studies involving high-contrast stimulation of visual areas in young adults (Dale & Buckner, 1997; Fox & Raichle, 1985; Pollman et al., 2000; Wobst et al., 2001), nonlinear effects have also been reported when examining activity in different brain areas or under different stimulation conditions in visual areas (Binder et al., 1994; Birn, Saad, & Bandettini, 2001; Friston et al., 1998; Liu & Gao, 2000; Rees et al., 1997; Vazquez & Noll, 1998). In addition, one significant limitation of these studies is that only the hemodynamic signal is manipulated and measured, without an independent measure of neuronal activity.

A few studies have indeed compared the BOLD signal with electrical measures (Janz et al., 2001; Arthurs et al., 2000; Logothetis et al., 2001), but the results of these studies are conflicting, so that linear relationships were found in some cases but not others. A problem in comparing hemodynamic and neuronal measures is that an appropriate comparison should be based on hemodynamic and neuronal measurements taken simultaneously from the same volume of the brain. Thus, surface electrophysiological measures of neuronal activity are not well suited for this comparison because it is difficult (but not necessarily impossible; e.g., Pascual-Marqui, Michel, & Lehman, 1994) to determine the contribution of a specified volume to the overall observed surface activity. Because the human body conducts electricity, the difference in potential measured at any pair of scalp electrodes can potentially be generated everywhere inside the head (or even inside the body in general).

Another problem with surface electrophysiological measures is that they can only be produced by neurons or dendritic fields organized in an open field configuration, that is, all oriented in the same direction. This occurs because the electric fields generated by individual neurons sum vectorally to produce the electric field observed at the surface of the head (Allison et al., 1986). If the orientations of the individual fields are random, they will cancel. Because this cancellation does not occur for hemodynamic imaging measures, it is likely that there will be significant dissociations between these two sets of measures (i.e., for instance, there might be conditions in which BOLD responses may occur in the absence of ERP activity).

These issues may create problems in the interpretation of hemodynamic data, especially when young and older adults are compared. Typically, the magnitude of the fMRI signal is smaller and more variable in older adults (D'Esposito et al., 1999; Huettel, Singerman, & McCarthy, 2001). However, it is not clear whether these differences should be attributed to (1) an age-related reduction in the neuronal signal; (2) a reduction in the dynamic range of the hemodynamic signal (i.e., to age-related changes in neurovascular coupling); or (3) peripheral changes in the sensory function tested. In addition, the overall conditions of the cardiovascular system vary widely across older adults, depending on their state of health and level of aerobic fitness

(Goldberg, Dengel, & Hagberg, 1996; Yerg et al., 1985), further complicating the problem of interpreting and comparing hemodynamic imaging data obtained in different age groups (see Kramer et al., 1999). We are currently running a series of studies systematically exploring the relationship between neuronal and hemodynamic signals in young and older adults.

In summary, direct data on the relationship between neuronal and vascular signals in older adults are scarce. In addition, research on cardiopulmonary fitness indicates that sedentary older adults may have difficulty adapting their hemodynamic response to task demands, especially under high-load conditions, suggesting an increase in the variability of responses with age. Optical methods appear particularly suited for studying this relationship because they can be used to index both fast (neuronal, EROS) and slow (hemodynamic, NIRS) signals in localized cortical areas. Further, both hemodynamic and neuronal optical measures can be related to the same volume of tissue, something that is difficult to achieve with other methods (G. Gratton, Goodman-Wood, & Fabiani, 2001). The G. Gratton, Goodman-Wood, and Fabiani (2001) study provided support for the use of hemodynamic data in the analysis of brain activity. However, it should be viewed with caution with respect to aging research because the subjects were all young adults. Therefore, more studies are needed to elucidate this relationship further and test it with other brain areas, subject groups, and experimental conditions.

Discussion

In this chapter, we reviewed the possible contributions of techniques with high temporal resolution to the understanding of the neurophysiological phenomena underlying cognitive aging. In particular, we have considered two sets of techniques: electrophysiological methods, more specifically ERPs, and optical methods (EROS and NIRS). Electrophysiological methods have been used extensively and have provided a variety of data that can be used to identify age-related processing bottlenecks and to suggest possible underlying mechanisms for age-related deficits. Optical methods are very new to this field, and only preliminary data have been obtained so far. However, these data suggest that optical imaging has a combination of spatial and temporal resolution ideally suited to address age-related research questions in humans, including chronometric aspects of processing as well as the relationship between neuronal and vascular signals.

A number of issues should be considered when applying these methods to cognitive aging research. First, all functional imaging data need to take into account the fact that age-related changes in function occur within the context of a changing anatomy (chapter 2, this volume). For instance, we have observed that interindividual anatomical differences may be greater in older than in younger subjects. This may lead to possible confounding in interpreting brain activation differences and emphasizes the need for the development and application of appropriate alignment and volumetric correction methods (see figure 4.2).

In figure 4.2, optical activity (EROS) elicited by auditory stimuli in the temporal cortex for younger and older adults are shown in two analysis conditions. In the left

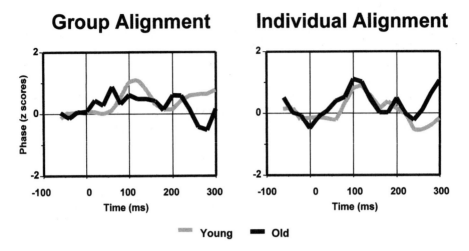

Group Alignment   Individual Alignment

Young   Old

Figure 4.2. Talairach coordinates corresponding to area 42; event-related optical signal (EROS) time course in younger (gray line) and older (black line) adults. The data in the left panel are aligned on one standard brain, whereas the data in the right panel are aligned based on each individual subject's anatomy. Improved similarity between the two groups is obtained with individual alignment.

panel, data from different locations and subjects were aligned based on one standard brain. In the right panel, the same data were analyzed by aligning each subject to his or her own anatomy. As can be seen, differences between groups are much reduced once differences in anatomy are taken into consideration.

Second, although most of our current descriptions of brain activity tend to emphasize the specific role of individual brain areas, brain function may be more fully represented by an examination of the functional connectivity among brain areas (Della-Maggiore et al., 2000; Grady et al., 1999; chapter 12, this volume). Functional connectivity may be examined in a number of ways, including elaborate statistical methods (such as linear equation modeling), as well as by recording techniques that allow visualization of the integrity of fiber tracts (such as diffusion tensor imaging; Moseley, 2002). However, methods combining high temporal and spatial resolution, such as EROS, may provide a unique opportunity to study functional connectivity by examining the relative order of activation and the cross-correlation function between different areas. Note that work by G. Gratton and Fabiani (2003) showed that EROS, without requiring any mathematical modeling, can provide independent information about the activity of areas located as close as 1.5 cm from each other with virtually no cross talk.

Third, it appears that different methods for studying brain function provide complementary (and not necessarily overlapping) views of the aging brain. Whereas fMRI and PET can provide detailed pictures of the anatomical structures involved in cognitive processing, ERPs and EROS provide a more dynamic account of brain function. It is therefore particularly important to combine these different methods. There are a number of problems inherent in this integration process, including (1) whether different techniques reflect the activity of the same neuronal populations, (2) whether they can be related to the same brain volume, and (3) whether they are equally sensitive to various experimental and physiological phenomena. Because of the possibility of concurrently recording both neuronal and hemodynamic signals, optical imaging may be particularly useful for providing a bridge between methods emphasizing spatial and temporal resolution. In addition, because optical data recording involves the use of nonmagnetic glass fibers as sensors, it is feasible to record concurrently optical and fMRI data (Toronov et al., 2001) and optical and ERP data (G. Gratton et al., 2000; DeSoto et al., 2001).

Acknowledgments   This work was supported by grants from the National Institute on Aging (AG21887–01; M. Fabiani, primary investigator); National Institutes of Mental Health (MH57125; G. Gratton, primary investigator) and Defense Advanced Research Projects Agency (NSF EIA 00–79800; G. Gratton & M. Fabiani, primary investigators). We wish to thank Paul Corballis for comments on an earlier draft of this chapter.

References

Alain, C., & Woods, D. L. (1999). Age-related changes in processing auditory stimuli during visual attention: evidence for deficits in inhibitory control and sensory memory. *Psychology of Aging, 14*, 507–519.

Allison, T., Wood, C. C., & McCarthy, G. (1986). The central nervous system. In M. G. H. Coles, S. W. Porges, & E. Donchin (Eds.), *Psychophysiology: Systems, processes, and applications* (pp. 5–25). New York: Guilford.

Andersson-Engels, S. R., Berg, R., Svanberg, S., & Jarlman, O. (1990). Time-resolved transillumination for medical diagnostic. *Optics Letters, 15*, 1179–1181.

Andrew, R. D., & MacVicar, B. A. (1994). Imaging cell volume changes and neuronal excitation in the hippocampal slice. *Neuroscience, 62*, 371–383.

Arthurs, O. J., Williams, E. J., Carpenter, T. A., Pickard, J. D., & Boniface, S. J. (2000). Linear coupling between functional magnetic resonance imaging and evoked potential amplitude in human somatosensory cortex. *Neuroscience, 101*, 803–806.

Bashore, T. R., Osman, A., & Heffley, E. F. (1989). Mental slowing in elderly persons: A cognitive psychophysiological analysis. *Psychology and Aging, 4*, 235–244.

Bashore, T. R., van der Molen, M. W., Ridderinkhof, K. R., & Wylie, S. A. (1997). Is the age-complexity effect mediated by reductions in a general processing resource? *Biological Psychology, 45*, 263–282.

Binder, J. R., Rao, S. M., Hammeke, T. A., Frost, J. A., Bandettini, P. A., & Hyde, J. S. (1994). Effects of stimulus rate on signal response during functional magnetic resonance imaging of auditory cortex. *Brain Research. Cognitive Brain Research, 2*, 31–38.

Birn, R. M., Saad, Z. S., & Bandettini, P. A. (2001). Spatial heterogeneity of the nonlinear dynamics in the fMRI bold response. *NeuroImage, 14*, 817–826.

Bonhoeffer, T., & Grinvald, A. (1996). Optical imaging based on intrinsic signals. In A. W. Toga & J. C. Mazziotta (Eds.), *Brain mapping: The methods* (pp. 55–97). San Diego, CA: Academic Press.

Bonmassar, G., Schwartz, D. P., Liu, A. K., Kwong, K. K., Dale, A. M., & Belliveau, J. W. (2001). Spatiotemporal brain imaging of visual-evoked activity using interleaved EEG and fMRI recordings. *Neuroimage, 13(6, Part 1)*, 1035–1043.

Buckner, R. L. (1998). Event-related fMRI and the hemodynamic response. *Human Brain Mapping, 6,* 373–377.

Buckner, R. L., Snyder, A. Z., Sanders, A. I., Raichle, M. E., & Morris, J. C. (2000). Functional brain imaging of young, nondemented, and demented older adults. *Journal of Cognitive Neuroscience, Supplement 2, 12,* 24–34.

Cabeza, R. (2002). Hemispheric asymmetry reduction in older adults: The HAROLD model. *Psychology and Aging, 17,* 85–110.

Cabeza, R., Anderson, N. D., Locantore, J. K., & McIntosh, A. R. (2002). Aging gracefully: Compensatory brain activity in high-performing older adults. *Neuroimage, 17,* 1394–1402.

Chance, B. (1989). Time resolved spectroscopic (TRS) and continuous wave spectroscopic (CWS) studies of photon migration in human arms and limbs. *Advances in Experimental and Medical Biology, 248,* 21–31.

Chao, L. L., & Knight, R. T. (1996). Age-related prefrontal alterations during auditory memory. *Neurobiology of Aging, 18,* 87–95.

Chao, L. L., & Knight, R. T. (1997). Prefrontal deficits in attention and inhibitory control with aging. *Cerebral Cortex. 7,* 63–69.

Cohen, L. B. (1972). Changes in neuron structure during action potential propagation and synaptic transmission. *Physiological Review, 53,* 373–417.

Colcombe, S. J., Kramer, A. F., Erickson, K. I., Scalf, P., McAuley, E., Cohen, N. J., et al. (2004). Cardiovascular fitness, cortical plasticity, and aging. *Proceedings of the National Academy of Sciences USA, 101*(9), 3316–3321.

Craik, F. I., & Byrd, M. (1982). Aging and cognitive deficits: The role of attentional resources. In F. I. Craik & S. Trehub (Eds.), *Aging and cognitive processes* (pp. 191–211). New York: Plenum Press.

Cutler, M. (1929). Transillumination as an aid in the diagnosis of breast lesions. With special reference to its value in case of bleeding nipple. *Surgery in Gynecology and Obstetrics, 48,* 721–729.

Cutler, M. (1931). Transillumination of the breast. *Annals of Surgery, 93,* 223–234.

Czigler, I., Csibra, G., & Csontos, A. (1992). Age and inter-stimulus interval effects on event-related potentials to frequent and infrequent auditory stimuli. *Biological Psychology, 33*(2–3), 195–206.

Dale, A. M., & Buckner, R. L. (1997). Selective averaging of rapidly presented individual trials using fMRI. *Human Brain Mapping, 5,* 329–340.

Della-Maggiore, V., Sekuler, A. B., Grady, C. L., Bennett, P. J., Sekuler, R., & McIntosh, A. R. (2000). Corticolimbic interactions associated with performance on a short-term memory task are modified by age. *Journal of Neuroscience, 20,* 8410–8416.

DeSoto, M. C., Fabiani, M., Geary, D. L., & Gratton, G. (2001). When in doubt, do it both ways: Brain evidence of the simultaneous activation of conflicting responses in a spatial Stroop task. *Journal of Cognitive Neuroscience, 13,* 523–536.

D'Esposito, M., Zarahan, E., Aguirre, G. K., & Rympa, B. (1999). The effect of normal aging on the coupling of neural activity to the bold hemodynamic response. *Neuroimage, 10,* 6–14.

Fabiani, M., & Friedman, D. (1995). Changes in brain activity patterns in aging: The novelty oddball. *Psychophysiology, 32,* 579–594.

Fabiani, M., Friedman, D., & Cheng, J. C. (1998). Individual differences in P3 scalp distribution in old subjects and their relationship to frontal lobe function. *Psychophysiology, 35,* 1–11.

Fabiani, M., Gratton, G., & Coles, M. G. H. (2000). Event-related brain potentials: Methods, theory, and applications. In J. Cacioppo, L. Tassinary, & G. Berntson (Eds.), *Handbook of psychophysiology* (pp. 114–205). New York: Cambridge University Press.

Fabiani, M., Gratton, G., & Corballis, P. M. (1996). Non-invasive NIR optical imaging of human brain function with sub-second temporal resolution. *Journal of Biomedical Optics*, *1*, 387–398.

Fabiani, M., Ho, J., Stinard, A., & Gratton, G. (2003). Multiple visual memory phenomena in a memory search task. *Psychophysiology*, *40*, 472–485.

Fabiani, M., & Wee, E. (2001). Age-related changes in working memory function: A review. In C. Nelson & M. Luciana (Eds.), *Handbook of developmental cognitive neuroscience* (pp. 473–488). Cambridge, MA: MIT Press.

Fantini, S., Franceschini, M. A., Maier, J. S., Walker, S. A., Barbieri, B., & Gratton, E. (1994). Frequency-domain multichannel optical detector for non-invasive tissue spectros-copy and oximetry. *Optical Engineering*, *34*, 32–42.

Ford, J. M., Pfefferbaum, A., Tinklenberg, J. R., & Kopell, B. S. (1982). Effects of perceptual and cognitive difficulty on P3 and RT in young and old adults. *Electroencephalography and Clinical Neurophysiology*, *54*, 311–321.

Ford, J. M., Roth, W. T., Mohs, R. C., Hopkins, W. F. D., & Kopell, B. S. (1979). Event-related potentials recorded from young and old adults during a memory retrieval task. *Electroencephalography and Clinical Neurophysiology*, *47*, 450–459.

Fox, P. T., & Raichle, M. E. (1985). Stimulus rate determines regional brain blood flow in striate cortex. *Annals of Neurology*, *17*, 303–305.

Friedman, D., & Simpson, G. V. (1994). ERP amplitude and scalp distribution to target and novel events: Effects of temporal order in young, middle-aged and older adults. *Brain Research: Cognitive Brain Research*, *2*, 49–63.

Friedman, D., Simpson, G., & Hamberger, M. (1993). Age-related changes in scalp topography to novel and target stimuli. *Psychophysiology*, *30*(4), 383–396.

Friston, K. J., Fletcher, P., Josephs, O., Holmes, A., Rugg, M. D., & Turner, R. (1998). Event-related fMRI: Characterizing differential responses. *Neuroimage*, *7*, 30–40.

Friston, K. J., Holmes, A. P., Poline, J. B., Grasby, P. J., Williams, S. C., Frackowiak, R. S., & Turner, R. (1995). Analysis of fMRI time-series revisited. *Neuroimage*, *2*, 45–53.

Frostig, R. D., Lieke, E. E., Ts'o, D. Y., & Grinvald, A. (1990). Cortical functional architecture and local coupling between neuronal activity and the microcirculation revealed by in vivo high-resolution optical imaging of intrinsic signals. *Proceedings of the National Academy of Sciences of the United States of America*, *87*, 6082–6086.

Gaeta, H., Friedman, D., Ritter, W., & Cheng, J. (1998). An event-related potential study of age-related changes in sensitivity to stimulus deviance. *Neurobiology of Aging*, *19*(5), 447–459.

Goldberg, A., Dengel, D., & Hagberg, J. M. (1996). Exercise physiology and aging. In E. Schneider & J. Rowe (Eds.), *Handbook of the biology of aging* (pp. 331–354). New York: Academic Press.

Goodin, D. S., Squires, K. C., Henderson, B. H., & Starr, A. (1978). Age-related variations in evoked potentials to auditory stimuli in normal human subjects. *Electroencephalography and Clinical Neurophysiology*, *44*, 447–458.

Grady, C. L., McIntosh, A. R., Rajah, M. N., Beig, S., & Craik, F. I. (1999). The effects of age on the neural correlates of episodic encoding. *Cerebral Cortex*, *9*, 805–814.

Gratton, E., Mantulin, W. W., van de Ven, M. J., Fishkin, J. B., Maris, M. B., & Chance, B. (1993). A novel approach to laser tomography. *Bioimaging*, *1*, 40–46.

Gratton, G., Coles, M. G. H., Sirevaag, E., Eriksen, C. W., & Donchin E. (1988). Pre- and poststimulus activation of response channels: A psychophysiological analysis. *Journal of Experimental Psychology: Human Perception and Performance*, *11*, 331–344.

Gratton, G., Corballis, P. M., Cho, E., Fabiani, M., & Hood, D. (1995). Shades of gray matter: Noninvasive optical images of human brain responses during visual stimulation. *Psychophysiology*, *32*, 505–509.

Gratton, G., & Fabiani, M. (1998). Dynamic brain imaging: Event-related optical signal (EROS) measures of the time course and localization of cognitive -related activity. *Psychonomic Bulletin and Review, 5*, 535–563.

Gratton, G., & Fabiani, M. (2001). Shedding light on brain function: The event-related optical signal. *Trends in Cognitive Sciences, 5*, 357–363.

Gratton, G., & Fabiani, M. (2003). The event-related optical signal (EROS) in visual cortex: Replicability, consistency, localization and resolution. *Psychophysiology, 40*, 561–571.

Gratton, G., Fabiani, M., Corballis, P. M., Hood, D. C., Goodman-Wood, M. R., Hirsch, J., Kim, K., Friedman, D., & Gratton, E. (1997). Fast and localized event-related optical signals (EROS) in the human occipital cortex: Comparison with the visual evoked potential and fMRI. *NeuroImage, 6*, 168–180.

Gratton, G., Fabiani M., Elbert, T., & Rockstroh, B. (Eds.). (2003). Optical imaging. *Psychophysiology, 40*(4, special issue), 487–571.

Gratton, G., Fabiani, M., Friedman, D., Franceschini, M. A., Fantini, S., Corballis, P. M., & Gratton, E. (1995). Rapid changes of optical parameters in the human brain during a tapping task. *Journal of Cognitive Neuroscience, 7*, 446–456.

Gratton, G., Fabiani, M., Goodman-Wood, M. R., & DeSoto, M. C. (1998). Memory-driven processing in human medial occipital cortex: An event-related optical signal (EROS) study. *Psychophysiology, 38*, 348–351.

Gratton, G., Goodman-Wood, M. R., & Fabiani, M. (2001). Comparison of neuronal and hemodynamic measure of the brain response to visual stimulation: An optical imaging study. *Human Brain Mapping, 13*, 13–25.

Gratton, G., Maier, J. S., Fabiani, M., Mantulin, W., & Gratton, E. (1994). Feasibility of intracranial near-infrared optical scanning. *Psychophysiology, 31*, 211–215.

Gratton, G., Sarno, A. J., Maclin, E., Corballis, P. M., & Fabiani, M. (2000). Toward non-invasive 3-D imaging of the time course of cortical activity: Investigation of the depth of the event-related optical signal (EROS). *NeuroImage, 11*, 491–504.

Gratton, G., Villa, A. E. P., Fabiani, M., Colombis, G., Palin, E., Bolcioni, G., & Fiori, M. G. (1992). Functional correlates of a three-component spatial model of the alpha rhythm. *Brain Research, 582*, 159–162.

Grinvald, A., Lieke, E., Frostig, R. D., Gilbert, C. D., & Wiesel, T. N. (1986). Functional architecture of cortex revealed by optical imaging of intrinsic signals. *Nature, 324*, 361–364.

Hamberger, M. (1993). Age-related changes in scalp topography to novel and target stimuli. *Psychophysiology, 30*, 383–396.

Hari, R., Levanen, S., & Raij, T. (2000). Timing of human cortical functions during cognition: Role of MEG. *Trends in Cognitive Sciences, 4*, 455–462.

Hasher, L., & Zacks, R. T. (1988). Working memory, comprehension, and aging: A review and a new view. In G. H. Bower (Ed.), *The psychology of learning and motivation: Advances in research and theory* (Vol. 22, pp. 193–225). San Diego, CA: Academic Press.

Hillyard, S. A., Hink, R. F., Schwent, V. L., & Picton, T. W. (1973). Electrical signs of selective attention in the human brain. *Science, 182*, 177–180.

Hirth, C., Obrig, H., Valdueza, J., Dirnagl, U., & Villringer, A. (1997). Simultaneous assessment of cerebral oxygenation and hemodynamics during a motor task. A combined near infrared and transcranial Doppler sonography study. *Advances in Experimental Medicine and Biology, 411*, 461–469.

Hoshi, Y., & Tamura, M. (1993). Dynamic multichannel near-infrared optical imaging of human brain activity. *Journal of Applied Physiology, 75*, 1842–1846.

Huettel, S. A., Singerman, J. D., & McCarthy, G. (2001). The effects of aging upon the hemodynamic response measured by functional MRI. *NeuroImage, 13*, 161–175.

Isard, H. J. (1981). Diaphanography: transillumination of the breast revisited. In G. F. Schwartz & D. Marchant (Eds.), *Breast disease: Diagnosis and treatment* (pp. 67–70). North Holland, The Netherlands: Elsevier.

Janz, C., Heinrich, S. P., Kornmayer, J., Bach, M., & Hennig, J. (2001). Coupling of neural activity and BOLD fMRI response: New insights by combination of fMRI and VEP experiments in transition from single events to continuous stimulation. *Magnetic Resonance in Medicine, 46,* 482–486.

Jobsis, F. F. (1977). Noninvasive, infrared monitoring of cerebral and myocardial oxygen sufficiency and circulatory parameters. *Science, 198,* 1264.

Jurkowski, A. J., Hackley, S. A., & Gratton, G. (2002). Dissociation of age and Parkinson's disease effects in a response conflict paradigm. *Psychophysiology Supplement, 39,* S8.

Kato, T., Kamei, A., Takashima, S., & Ozaki, T. (1993). Human visual cortical function during photic stimulation monitoring by means of near-infrared spectroscopy. *Journal of Cerebral Blood Flow and Metabolism, 13,* 516–520.

Kazmerski, V. A., Friedman, D., & Ritter, W. (1997). Mismatch negativity during attend and ignore conditions in Alzheimer's disease. *Biological Psychiatry, 42*(5), 382–402.

Knight, R. T. (1984). Decreased response to novel stimuli after prefrontal lesions in man. *Electroencephalography and Clinical Neurophysiology, 59,* 9–20.

Kramer, A. F., Hahn, S., Cohen, N., Banich, M., McAuley, E., Harrison, C., Chason, J., Vakil, E., Bardell, L., Boileau, R. A., & Colcombe, A. (1999). Aging, fitness, and neurocognitive function. *Nature, 400,* 418–419.

Kwong, K. K., Belliveau, J. W., Chesler, D. A., Goldberg, I. E., Weisskoff, R. M., Poncelet, B. P., Kennedy, D. N., Hoppel, B. E., Cohen, M. S., Turner, R., Cheng, H.-M., Brady, T. J., & Rosen, B. R. (1992). Dynamic magnetic resonance imaging of human brain activity during primary sensory stimulation. *Proceedings of the National Academy of Sciences of the United States of America, 89,* 5675–5679.

Liu, H., & Gao, J. (2000). An investigation of the impulse functions for the nonlinear BOLD response in functional MRI. *Magnetic Resonance Imaging, 18,* 931–938.

Logan, J. M., Sanders, A. L., Snyder, A. Z., Morris, J. C., & Buckner, R. L. (2002). Underrecruitment and nonselective recruitment: Dissociable neural mechanisms associated with aging. *Neuron, 33,* 827–840.

Logothetis, N. K., Pauls, J., Augath, M., Trinath, T., & Oeltermann, A. (2001). Neurophysiological investigation of the basis of the fMRI signal. *Nature, 412,* 150–157.

Low, K. A., Miller, J., & Vierck, E. (2002). Response slowing in Parkinson's disease: A psychophysiological analysis of premotor and motor processes. *Brain, 125*(Part 9), 1980–1994.

Low, K. A., Wee, E., Sable, J. J., Gratton, G., & Fabiani, M. (2001). Effects of interstimulus delay on the mismatch negativity in young and older adults. *Psychophysiology, 38,* S62.

Maclin, E., Gratton, G., & Fabiani, M. (2003). Optimum filtering for EROS measurements. *Psychophysiology, 40,* 542–547.

Maier, J. S., & Gratton, E. (1993). Frequency-domain methods in optical tomography: Detection of localized absorbers and a backscattering reconstruction scheme. *Proceedings of the Society of Photo-optical Instrumentation Engineers, 1888,* 440–451.

Malonek, D., & Grinvald, A. (1996). Interactions between electrical activity and cortical microcirculation revealed by imaging spectroscopy: Implications for functional brain mapping. *Science, 272,* 551–554.

Martinez, A., Anllo-Vento, L., Sereno, M. I., Frank, L. R., Buxton, R. B., Dubowitz, D. J., Wong, E. C., Hinrichs, H., Heinze, H. J., & Hillyard, S. A. (1999). Involvement of striate and extrastriate visual cortical areas in spatial attention. *Nature Neuroscience, 2,* 364–369.

Meek, J. H., Elwell, C. E., Khan, M. J., Romaya, J., Wyatt, J. S., Delpy, D. T., & Zeki, S. (1995). Regional changes in cerebral haemodynamics as a result of a visual stimulus measured by near infrared spectroscopy. *Proceedings of the Royal Society of London. Series B. Biological Sciences, 261*, 351–356.

Menon, R. S., & Kim, S. G. (1999). Spatial and temporal limits in cognitive neuroimaging with fMRI. *Trends in Cognitive Sciences, 3*, 207–216.

Miezin, F. M., Maccotta, L., Ollinger, J. M., Petersen, S. E., & Buckner, R. L. (2000). Characterizing the hemodynamic response: Presentation rate, sampling procedure, and the possibility of ordering brain activity based on relative timing. *NeuroImage, 11*, 735–759.

Moseley, M. (2002). Diffusion tensor imaging and aging—a review. *NMR in Biomedicine, 15*, 553–560.

Obrig, H., Wolf, T., Doge, C., Hulsing, J. J., Dirnagl, U., & Villringer, A. (1996). Cerebral oxygenation changes during motor and somatosensory stimulation in humans, as measured by near-infrared spectroscopy. *Advances in Experimental Medicine and Biology, 388*, 219–224.

Obrist, W. D., Henry, C. E., & Justiss, W. A. (1961). Longitudinal study of EEG in old age. *Excerpta Medical International Congress, Serial 37*, 180–181.

Ogawa, S., Tank, D. W., Menon, R., Ellermann, J. M., Kim, S. G., Merkle, H., & Ugurbil, K. (1992). Intrinsic signal changes accompanying sensory stimulation: Functional brain mapping with magnetic resonance imaging. *Proceedings of the National Academy of Sciences of the United States of America, 89*, 5951–5955.

Park, D. C. (2000). The basic mechanisms accounting for age-related decline in cognitive function. In D. C. Park and N. Schwarz (Eds.), *Cognitive aging. A primer* (pp. 3–21). Philadelphia, PA: Psychology Press.

Pascual-Marqui, R. D., Michel, C. M., & Lehmann, D. (1994). Low resolution electromagnetic tomography: A new method for localizing electrical activity in the brain. *International Journal of Psychophysiology, 18*, 49–65.

Pekkonen, E., Rinne, T., Reinikainen, K., Kujala, T., Alho, K., & Näätänen, R. (1996). Aging effects on auditory processing: An event-related potential study. *Experimental Aging Research, 22*, 171–184.

Pollmann, S., Dove, A., Yves von Cramon, D., & Wiggins, C. J. (2000). Event-related fMRI: Comparison of conditions with varying BOLD overlap. *Human Brain Mapping, 9*, 26–37.

Raichle, M. E. (1998). Behind the scenes of functional brain imaging: A historical and physiological perspective. *Proceedings of the National Academy of Sciences of the United States of America, 95*, 765–772.

Rector, D. M., Harper, R. M., & George, J. S. (2002). In vivo observations of rapid scattered-light changes associated with electrical events. In R. Frostig (Ed.), *Methods for in vivo optical imaging of the central nervous system* (pp. 93–112). Boca Raton, FL: CRC Press.

Rector, D. M., Poe, G. R., Kristensen, M. P., & Harper, R. M. (1997). Light scattering changes follow evoked potentials from hippocampal Schaeffer collateral stimulation. *Journal of Neurophysiology, 78*, 1707–1713.

Rees, G., Howseman, A., Josephs, O., Frith, C. D., Friston, K. J., Frackowiak, R. S., & Turner, R. (1997). Characterizing the relationship between BOLD contrast and regional cerebral blood flow measurements by varying the stimulus presentation rate. *NeuroImage, 6*, 270–278.

Reuter-Lorenz, P. (2002). New visions of the aging mind and brain. *Trends in Cognitive Sciences, 6*, 394–400.

Rinne, T., Gratton, G., Fabiani, M., Cowan, N., Maclin, E., Stinard, A., Sinkkonen, J., Alho, K., & Näätänen, R. (1999). Scalp-recorded optical signals make sound processing from the auditory cortex visible. *NeuroImage, 10*, 620–624.

Ritter, W., Deacon, D., Gomes, H., Javitt, D. C., & Vaughan, H. G., Jr. (1995). The mismatch negativity of event-related potentials as a probe of transient auditory memory: A review. *Ear and Hearing, 16*, 52–67.

Rosen, B. R., Buckner, R. L., & Dale, A. M. (1998). Event-related functional MRI: Past, present, and future. *Proceedings of the National Academy of Sciences of the United States of America, 95*, 773–780.

Salthouse, T. A. (1996). The processing-speed theory of adult age differences in cognition. *Psychological Review, 103*, 403–428.

Scherg, M., & von Cramon, D. (1986). Evoked dipole source potentials of the human auditory cortex. *Electroencephalography and Clinical Neurophysiology, 65*, 344–360.

Sherrington, C. (1906). *The integrative action of the nervous system.* New Haven, CT: Yale University Press.

Simpson, G. V., Pflieger, M. E., Foxe, J. J., Ahlfors, S. P., Vaughan, H. G., Jr., Hrabe, J., Ilmoniemi, R. J., & Lantos, G. (1995). Dynamic neuroimaging of brain function. *Journal of Clinical Neurophysiology, 12*, 432–449.

Steinbrink, J., Kohl, M., Obrig, H., Curio, G., Syré, F., Thomas, F., Wabnitz, H., Rinneberg, H., & Villringer, A. (2000). Somatosensory evoked fast optical intensity changes detected non-invasively in the adult human head. *Neuroscience Letters, 291*, 105–108.

Stepnoski, R. A., LaPorta, A., Raccuia-Behling, F., Blonder, G. E., Slusher, R. E., & Kleinfeld, D. (1991). Noninvasive detection of changes in membrane potential in cultured neurons by light scattering. *Proceedings of the National Academy of Sciences of the United States of America, 88*, 9382–9386.

Strayer, D. L., & Kramer, A. F. (1994). Aging and skill acquisition: Learning-performance distinctions. *Psychology and Aging, 9*, 589–605.

Strayer, D. L., Wickens, C. D., & Braune, R. (1987). Adult age differences in the speed and capacity of information processing: II. An electrophysiological approach. *Psychology and Aging, 2*, 99–110.

Toga, A. W., & Mazziotta, J. C. (Eds.). (1996). *Brain mapping. The methods.* San Diego, CA: Academic Press.

Toronov, V., Webb, A., Choi, J. H., Wolf, M., Michalos, A., Gratton, E., & Huber, D. (2001). Investigation of human brain hemodynamics by simultaneous near infrared spectroscopy and functional magnetic resonance imaging. *Medical Physics, 28*, 521–527.

Turner, R. (1995). Functional mapping of the human brain with magnetic resonance imaging. *Seminars in the Neurosciences, 7*, 179–194.

Vazquez, A. L., & Noll, D. C. (1998). Nonlinear aspects of the BOLD response in functional MRI. *NeuroImage, 7*, 108–118.

Villringer, A., & Chance, B. (1997). Non-invasive optical spectroscopy and imaging of human brain function. *Trends in Neurosciences, 20*, 435–442.

Villringer, A., & Dirnagl, U. (1995). Coupling of brain activity and cerebral blood flow: Basis of functional neuroimaging. *Cerebrovascular and Brain Metabolism Reviews, 7*, 240–276.

Wee, E., Leaver, E., Rowley, T., Gratton, G., & Fabiani, M. (2003). Age-related effects in task switching in a spatial Stroop task. *Cognitive Neuroscience Society Abstracts*, 27.

Wee, E., Low, K. A., Sable, J. J., Gratton, G., & Fabiani, M. (2000). Optical response in auditory cortex to standard and deviant stimuli: A replication. *Psychophysiology, Supplement 1*, S103.

Wee, E., Low, K. A., Sable, J. J., Gratton, G., & Fabiani, M. (2001). Optical responses in auditory cortex to standard and deviant stimuli: An aging study. *Journal of Cognitive Neuroscience, Supplement*, 87.

Wenzel, R., Obrig, H., Ruben, J., Villringer, K., Thiel, A., Bernarding, J., Dirnagl, U., &

Villringer, A. (1996). Cerebral blood oxygenation changes induced by visual stimulation in humans. *Journal of Biomedical Optics, 1,* 399–404.

Wobst, P., Wenzel, R., Kohl, M., Obrig, H., & Villringer, A. (2001). Linear aspects of changes in deoxygenated hemoglobin concentration and cytochrome oxidase oxidation during brain activation. *NeuroImage, 13,* 520–530.

Wolf, M., Wolf, U., Choi, J. H., Gupta, R., Safonova, L. P., Paunescu, L. A., Michalos, A., & Gratton, E. (2003). Detection of the fast neuronal signal on the motor cortex using functional frequency domain near infrared spectroscopy. *Advances in Experimental and Medical Biology, 510,* 193–197.

Wolf, M., Wolf, U., Choi, J. H., Toronov, V., Paunescu, L. A., Michalos, A., & Gratton, E. (2003). Fast cerebral functional signal in the 100 ms range detected in the visual cortex by frequency-domain near-infrared spectrophotometry. *Psychophysiology, 40,* 521–528.

Woods, D. L. (1992). Auditory selective attention in middle-aged and elderly subjects: An event-related brain potential study. *Electroencephalography and Clinical Neurophysiology, 84*(5), 456–468.

Yamashita, Y., & Kaneko, M. (1993). Visible and infrared diaphanoscopy for medical diagnosis. *Society of Photo-optical Instrumentation Engineers, 11,* 283–316.

Yerg, J., Seals, D., Hagberg, J., & Holloszy, J. (1985). Effect of endurance exercise training on ventilatory function in older individuals. *Journal of Applied Physiology, 58,* 791–794.

5

BOLD Functional MRI
and Cognitive Aging

Adam H. Gazzaley
Mark D'Esposito

The emergence of functional neuroimaging technology such as positron emission tomography (PET) and functional magnetic resonance imaging (fMRI) and its associated analytical methods has ushered in a new stage in the study of cognitive aging, allowing a unique appreciation of the complexity of this evolving process (Cabeza, 2002; Gazzaley & D'Esposito, 2003; Grady, 2000; Reuter-Lorenz, 2002). These new techniques have complemented the traditional method for exploring the neural basis of age-associated cognitive deficits, which involves the behavioral testing of older patients with neuropsychological tasks to tap specific cortical functions. Conclusions regarding the link between a particular neuropsychological test and its neural substrate rely on data derived from the performance of patients with defined structural lesions, such as those secondary to stroke or trauma (Stuss et al., 1996). This approach has been largely responsible for the development of the frontal hypothesis of cognitive aging, in which cognitive deficits in older adults are often comparable, although usually milder, than the impairments documented in patients with frontal lobe damage (Moscovitch & Winocur, 1995).

Using the "lesion" method to generate hypotheses about the neural mechanisms underlying cognitive aging raises several important issues. For example, is the neural mechanism underlying the proposed frontal lobe dysfunction in normal aging comparable to the mechanism that leads to frontal lobe dysfunction after damage to this area from a stroke (Greenwood, 2000)? Clearly, significant differences likely exist in the mechanism, extent of dysfunction, and time course of neural changes that occur during the normal aging process compared to those that occur during pathological processes such as stroke, trauma, or neurodegenerative disease. In stroke, the onset of frontal lobe damage is acute, and neuronal death occurs; patients are typically tested behaviorally within a few months and rarely more than a year or two postinjury. In contrast, the effect of normal aging on brain function is a lifelong process that will presumably lead to differences in the reorganization that may result. Functional neuroimaging studies provide an opportunity to make direct comparisons between the normal aging brain and the normal younger brain, avoiding potential confounds that may exist in making comparison to patients with disease.

Another method that has frequently been used to explore the neural basis of cognitive aging is event-related potential (ERP) recording (Chao & Knight, 1997; West & Covell, 2001). Although ERP is a powerful method that, unlike fMRI or PET, directly measures neural activity, it cannot precisely localize evoke potentials to neuroanatomical structures and therefore lacks the spatial resolution of fMRI. Structural imaging with computerized tomography (CT) or MRI, coupled with newer volumetric techniques (Salat, Kaye, & Janowsky, 2001; Tisserand et al., 2002), also provides an opportunity to link age-related regional cortical or subcortical changes with specific cognitive deficits (Sullivan et al., 2002; Tisserand et al., 2000; Ylikoski et al., 2000).

Such studies have also supported the frontal hypothesis of cognitive aging (Raz et al., 1997; West, 1996). However, accumulating evidence suggests that normal aging is more likely to be accompanied by chemical and physiological changes than gross structural alterations such as neuronal loss (Gazzaley et al., 1996, 1997; Morrison & Hof, 1997). Structural imaging only indexes the former type of change, whereas fMRI is ideally suited to investigate age-related physiological changes with superb spatial resolution. Although if the application of this new technology is exciting and promising, it is important to be cautious given its increasing availability. We must critically examine the signal derived from fMRI and the potential of misinterpretation of results and overstatement of conclusions that might occur as a result of the extension of fMRI to an older population.

In this chapter, we focus exclusively on potential confounding factors in the interpretation of the blood oxygen level dependent (BOLD) signal in fMRI studies of cognitive aging. A common approach when using BOLD fMRI in the study of the aging brain has been to compare BOLD signal patterns in a group of healthy young individuals (usually in the age range of 18–25 years) and a group of healthy older individuals (usually in the age range of 65–85 years) during the performance of a task that taps a cognitive process or ability that shows age-related decline in behavioral tests. Virtually all conclusions generated from such experiments equate changes in the BOLD signal, both magnitude and anatomical distribution, with age-associated changes in neural activity. The first step in considering how these results might be misinterpreted is to address exactly what is measured by BOLD fMRI and how it might differ between these two populations.

The Blood Oxygen Level Dependent Signal

An important consideration when interpreting changes in the BOLD signal is that it is not a direct reflection of neural activity, but rather it is usually an indication of local changes in cerebral blood flow (CBF). Specifically, the BOLD signal is a reflection of the ratio of diamagnetic oxyhemoglobin, which in relative terms raises the BOLD signal, to paramagnetic deoxyhemoglobin, which reduces the BOLD signal (Thulborn et al., 1982; Turner et al., 1991). Neural activity leads to a change in this ratio by influencing several factors: CBF, cerebral blood volume (CBV), and cerebral metabolic rate of oxygen consumption ($CMRO_2$) (Buxton & Frank, 1997). Neural activity induces mediators that are still under characterization (Bonvento, Sibson, & Pellerin, 2002; Lindauer et al., 1999) to generate a local hemodynamic response that increases the CBF and CBV, resulting in an elevation in the supply of oxyhemoglobin within a local region of brain tissue.

The process by which neural activity influences the hemodynamic properties of the surrounding vasculature is known as *neurovascular coupling*. Neural activity also raises local metabolic demands, which in turn results in an increase in the $CMRO_2$ and a resultant elevation in the level of deoxyhemoglobin. Although all of these factors increase in response to neural activity, the magnitude of the CBF increase far exceeds the $CMRO_2$ increase (Fox & Raichle, 1986; Fox et al., 1988). This results in an excess of oxyhemoglobin localized to the activation site, an imbalance that is then detected as an increase in the BOLD signal. Thus, under most conditions, neural activity results in a positive BOLD signal that is primarily a reflection of increased local CBF.

When comparing changes in BOLD signal levels within the brain of an individual subject across different cognitive tasks and making conclusions regarding changes in neural activity and the pattern of activity, numerous assumptions are made regarding the steps comprising neurovascular coupling (stimulus → neural activity → hemodynamic response → BOLD signal) and the regional variability of the metabolic and vascular parameters influencing the BOLD signal. This in itself is an area of intensive research and debate (Mechelli, Price, & Friston, 2001; K. L. Miller et al., 2001; Rees et al., 1997).

These confounding factors are further amplified when comparing between subjects within a population and even more so when comparing across groups of different populations of subjects. This concern is especially relevant to studies involving an aging population, in which structural changes in cerebral vasculature, such as local vascular compromise or diffuse vascular disease, can alter the vascular response to neural activity. For example, a vascular disparity in the absence of a difference in neural activity may alter the neurovascular coupling and thus affect a component of the hemodynamic response to neural activity, such as the CBF. This will in turn alter the influx of oxyhemoglobin into the region, thus modifying the BOLD signal and resulting in the potential misinterpretation of a signal change as a difference in neural activity.

It is clear that an evaluation of BOLD signal differences in the aging population is dependent on an understanding of alterations in the aging neurovascular system, including vascular pathology, changes in vascular reactivity, and CBF. Although this chapter focuses on vascular changes and their impact on the BOLD signal, it should be recognized that changes in the levels of any of the mediators of the neurovascular response, including neurotransmitters, during aging and disease are important considerations.

Review of Age-Related Influences on the Blood Oxygen Level Dependent Signal

The Aging Neurovascular System and Its Influence on the Blood Oxygen Level Dependent Signal

Extensive research on the aging neurovascular system has revealed that it undergoes significant changes in multiple domains in a continuum throughout the human life span, probably as early as the fourth decade (for review, see Farkas & Luiten, 2001). These changes affect the vascular ultrastructure, the resting CBF, and the vascular responsiveness of the vessels in older brains.

Ultrastructure

The compromise to the ultrastructural integrity of the cerebral vasculature in aging is largely the result of arteriosclerotic changes, principally fibrohyaline thickening of the vessel wall (Furuta et al., 1991), smooth muscle cell necrosis (Masawa et al., 1994), and thickening of the basement membrane (Nagasawa et al., 1979), which gradually increases with age. Although sclerotic changes correlate with the degree of hypertension (Furuta et al., 1991), age itself appears to be an independent risk factor (Knox et al., 1980; Masawa et al., 1994). It is a general consensus that these changes result in a decrease in the elasticity and compliancy of affected vessels, which include the capillaries, the larger arterioles, and the cerebral arteries (for a review, see Kalaria, 1996). Venous alterations that accompany aging, known as peri-ventricular venous collagenosis (PVC), have also been observed in 65% of subjects over 60 years old, and in severe cases can completely occlude veins (Moody et al., 1997). In addition to ultrastructural changes of the vessels, there is also an increase in the tortuosity of some vessels with aging, most notably in the arteriole-venous-capillary bed (Fang, 1976), as well as changes in the density of capillaries and arterioles (Abernethy et al., 1993) that has not been observed in venules (Sonntag et al., 1997).

The presence of such diverse pathological changes that differentially affect the various components of the vascular system of the brain may influence the interpretation of age-related BOLD signal changes when comparing results between studies using different strength magnets and different pulse sequences. Stronger magnets, such as those used in 4-tesla systems, are more sensitive to influences from capillaries (Menon et al., 1995) compared to weaker magnets, which are influenced more by the magnetic properties of blood within venules and draining veins (Gati et al., 1997). In addition, gradient-echo echo-planar imaging (EPI) generates a significant portion of its signal from large veins, with contributions from capillaries (Song, Fichtenholtz, & Woldorff, 2002), whereas spin-echo EPI exhibits a higher degree of spatial resolution and receives a greater contribution from smaller vessels (Norris et al., 2002). Although the impact of disparate pathology across vascular populations on the interpretation of BOLD signal obtained from different fMRI systems is still unclear, it is becoming increasingly obvious that vascular pathology may have a large impact on BOLD signal interpretations secondary to their influence on baseline CBF and vascular reactivity (Kawamura et al., 1993; Kuwabara et al., 1996).

Resting Cerebral Blood Flow

The primary techniques used to determine the presence of changes in the resting CBF in the microvasculature of the cortex are PET, single-photon emission computed tomography (SPECT), and gas inhalation contrast CT. Arterial spin labeling (ASL) is an fMRI technique that allows the determination of CBF with high anatomic resolution, but it has not yet been applied to aging (Detre & Alsop, 1999; Lia et al., 2000). Multiple studies using PET, SPECT, and CT have compared resting CBF between old and young groups, as well as CBF changes with age as a continuum, and have observed that aging is associated with a significant decrease in resting CBF in cortical and subcortical parenchyma (Bentourkia et al., 2000; Kawamura et al., 1993; Madden & Hoffman, 1997; Reich & Rusinek, 1989; Schultz et al., 1999). Similar findings have also been reported for blood flow in large cerebral arteries, such as decreases in blood flow velocity in the middle, posterior, and anterior cerebral arteries with advancing age (Krejza et al., 1999).

Measurement of the resting CBF is an important, but usually unaddressed, issue when interpreting BOLD signal changes. The BOLD signal is not an absolute value, but rather a value that represents a relative ratio of oxy- to deoxyhemoglobin concentration. An assumption that the baseline CBF is the same between two populations, if it actually is not, may lead to incorrect conclusions when forming direct comparisons between those populations. An additional note of caution is that the baseline CBF may not only be influenced by age, but also by different physiological states. For instance, fluctuating carbon dioxide (CO_2) levels such as those influenced by the breathing rate have been shown both to affect the BOLD signal baseline and alter the magnitude of the BOLD response to visual stimulation (Cohen, Ugurbil, & Kim, 2002).

Vascular Reactivity

In addition to a decline in resting CBF in aging, there also seems to be an age-associated decrease in the vascular reactivity of cerebral vessels to various chemical modulators, including the concentration of CO_2. This is particularly relevant to the discussion of the BOLD signal because a local change in pCO_2 associated with increased metabolism is believed to be one of the chemical mediators responsible for neurovascular coupling.

Two techniques frequently used to assess vascular reactivity are the induction of hypercapnia by breath holding or inhalation of high CO_2 gas, which results in increased CBF, and the induction of hypocapnia with hyperventilation, which results in decreased CBF. Decreased vascular responsiveness to hypercapnia has been observed in aged rats (Tamaki et al., 1995) and humans with and without risk factors for atherosclerosis (Yamamoto et al., 1980). In another study of elderly subjects, regional CBF (rCBF) changes monitored with PET revealed a significant deficit in the total vascular response from a hypocapnic to a hypercapnic state in comparison to young adults (Ito et al., 2002).

Of significant importance in the interpretation of regional BOLD changes is an assessment of age-related changes in vascular reactivity across different brain regions. A study comparing the resting and stimulus-evoked rCBF in rats revealed that basal forebrain stimulation elicited ipsilateral increases in CBF in both the parietal and frontal cortex of young rats, but only the frontal cortex of the aged rats (Linville & Arneric, 1991). Regional variability in vascular factors is clearly an important issue for functional imaging studies of cognitive aging because many hypotheses are likely to include comparison between different neural systems.

Photic stimulation has also been applied as a robust cortical stimulator; when coupled with trancranial Doppler sonography of CBF velocities, it has been used to detect alterations in neurovascular coupling in a number of different conditions (Diehl et al., 1998; Urban et al., 1995). Using this technique, Niehaus et al. (2001) reported an age-related reduction in blood flow velocity in the posterior cerebral artery in response to photic stimulation. This change, however, cannot be attributed with certainty to an alteration of neurovascular coupling because a change in neural activity was not ruled out.

The exact mechanisms of age-related changes in resting CBF and vascular reactivity have not been completely elucidated, although it is often suggested that they are secondary to the increased stiffness and lack of compliance of the aging vasculature. Several studies of rats have concluded that the decline in vasoreactivity may be the result of impaired vasodilatory mechanisms, as determined by a significantly reduced degree of vasodilation in older rats in response to cerebrospinal fluid perfusion of vasodilators adenosine (Jiang et al., 1992), acetylcholine, and bradykinin (Mayhan et al., 1990). Regardless of the mechanism of these changes, it is clear that their presence should invoke a high degree of caution in researchers who attempt to directly compare BOLD signal changes between two age groups.

Cerebral Metabolic Rate of Oxygen Consumption

We have discussed the multiple age-related changes in vascular parameters occurring with aging that may alter the BOLD signal in a neural activity independent manner, but have not considered the possibility of changes in cerebral oxygen metabolism. The importance of identifying age-related changes in cerebral oxygen metabolism and studying its influence on the BOLD signal should not be underestimated. The BOLD signal is not only dependent on the level of oxyhemoglobin as regulated by CBF, but also on the level of deoxyhemoglobin, which is largely influenced by the $CMRO_2$. Although the hemodynamic effects on the BOLD signal appear to be dominant, increasing neural activity results in increased $CMRO_2$, leading to increased levels of deoxyhemoglobin and a significant decrease in BOLD signal (Schwarzbauer & Heinke, 1999).

An effect of aging on $CMRO_2$ has been appreciated for some time. Two PET studies have revealed a significantly lower resting $CMRO_2$ in cortical and subcortical regions of older subjects compared with younger subjects; this value actually exceeded age-related changes in CBF (Takada et al., 1992; Yamaguchi et al., 1986).

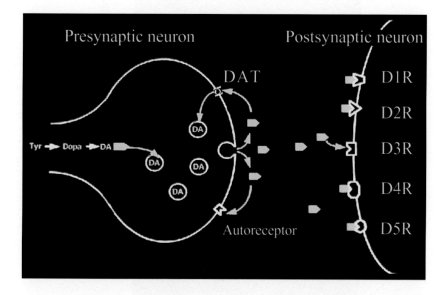

Plate 3.1. A schematic dopaminergic synapse in the striatum. Dopamine (DA) is synthesized from tyrosine (Tyr), stored in vesicles, and released into the synaptic cleft. In the synaptic cleft, DA can bind to postsynaptic receptors (D1R–D5R) or to the presynaptic autoreceptor, which regulates DA release. The dopamine transporter (DAT) is a presynaptic protein that regulates the synaptic concentration of DA. All five DA receptors are not expressed in the same postsynaptic neuron, but are so indicated in the figure for didactic reasons.

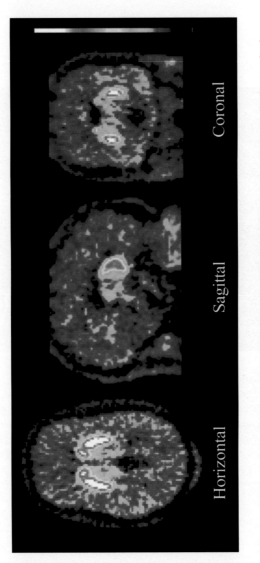

Horizontal   Sagittal   Coronal

Plate 3.2. The anatomical distribution of [11C]raclopride binding to D2 DA receptors in the human brain. The images represent horizontal, coronal, and sagittal sections through the striatum.

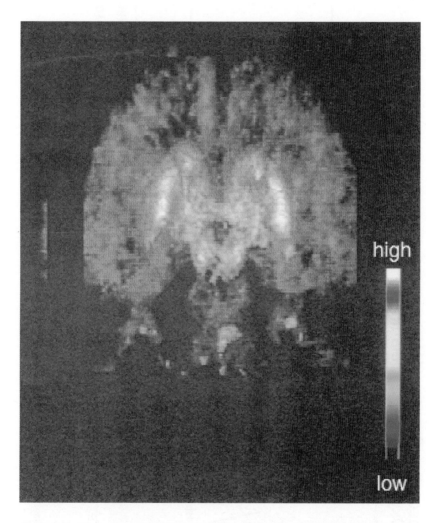

Plate 3.3. Three-dimensional volume rendering showing [11C]PE2I binding to the DA transporter in the human brain viewed from a posterior angle. (Adapted from Halldin et al., 2003.)

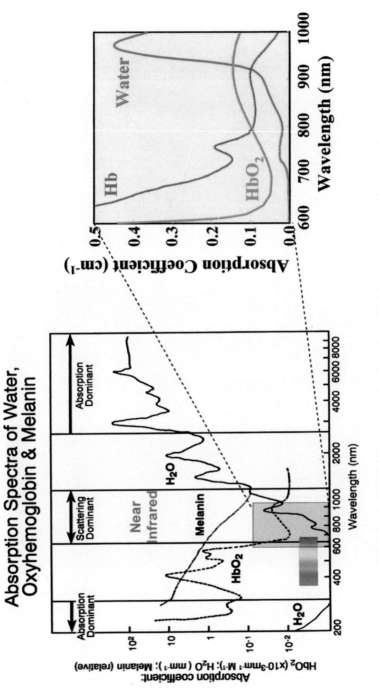

Plate 4.1. Left, absorption spectra. (After Wilson et al., 1989.) Right, inset (gray area in left graph) of absorption spectra for near-infrared region.

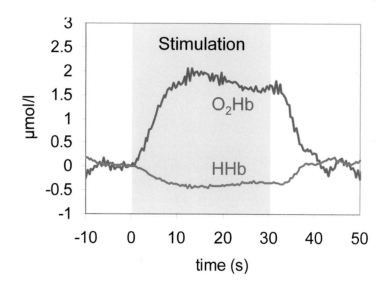

Plate 4.2. Changes in the concentration of oxy- (red line) and deoxyhemoglobin (blue line) in occipital areas during visual stimulation (light blue area) measured with near-infrared spectroscopy (NIRS). (Figure courtesy of M. Wolf [from Wolf, Wolf, Choi, Toronov, et al., 2003]; reprinted with permission of the author and Blackwell Publishing, Ltd.)

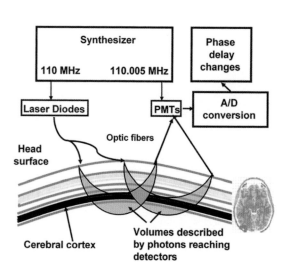

Plate 4.3. Schematic representation of event-related optical signal (EROS) derivation and main analysis steps. A/D, analog-to-digital; PMTs, photo-multiplier tubes; MR, magnetic resonance.

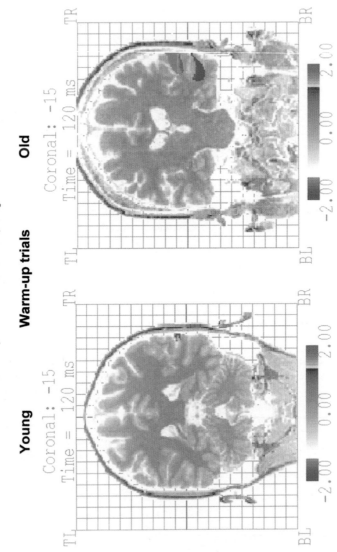

Plate 4.4. Optical (event-related optical signal [EROS]) data (collected simultaneously with event-related potentials [ERPs]) are shown for the same trial type for area 42 at a latency of 120 ms (pick of the electrical N1) from right auditory cortex of younger (left) and older adults (right).

A | B

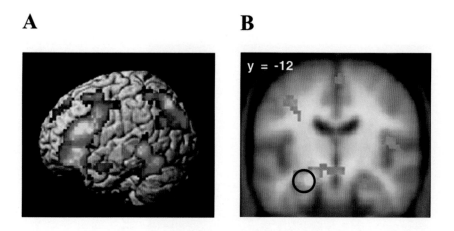

Plate 6.1. Main effect of subsequent memory common to young and older age groups in the study of Morcom et al. (2003). a, Key left hemisphere regions showing subsequent memory effects are rendered onto a canonical brain. b, The left hippocampal effect is shown on an across-subject averaged coronal structural image.

A | B

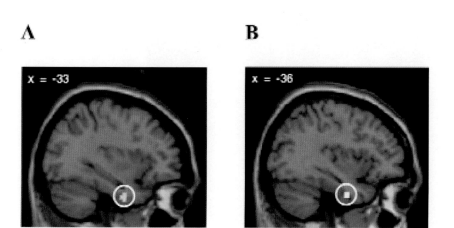

Plate 6.2. Interaction of age group with subsequent memory in the anterior temporal cortex in the study of Morcom et al. (2003). a, Analysis collapsed over study-test delay; younger subjects showed a greater subsequent memory effect than older subjects. b, Analysis matching memory performance (see text); younger subjects again showed a greater subsequent memory effect than older subjects in the region indicated. Activations are displayed on an across-subject averaged smoothed structural image.

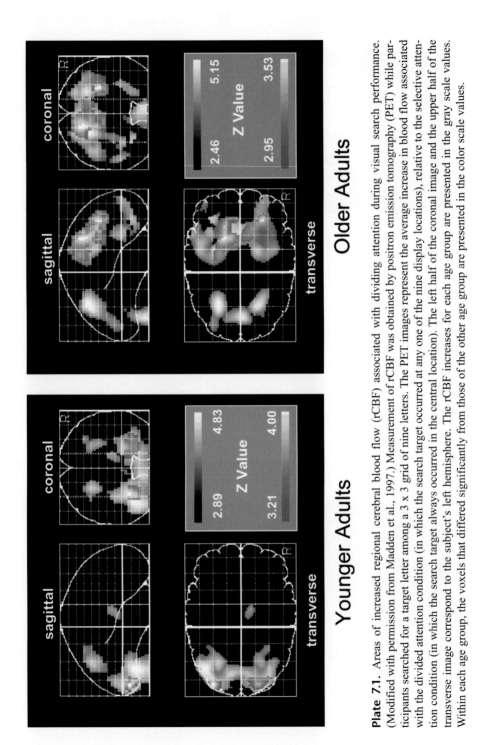

Plate 7.1. Areas of increased regional cerebral blood flow (rCBF) associated with dividing attention during visual search performance. (Modified with permission from Madden et al., 1997.) Measurement of rCBF was obtained by positron emission tomography (PET) while participants searched for a target letter among a 3 x 3 grid of nine letters. The PET images represent the average increase in blood flow associated with the divided attention condition (in which the search target occurred at any one of the nine display locations), relative to the selective attention condition (in which the search target always occurred in the central location). The left half of the coronal image and the upper half of the transverse image correspond to the subject's left hemisphere. The rCBF increases for each age group are presented in the gray scale values. Within each age group, the voxels that differed significantly from those of the other age group are presented in the color scale values.

Younger Adults　　　　　　**Older Adults**

Conjunction minus Feature

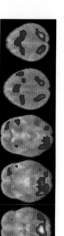 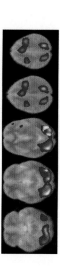 

	2.33	7.18
	Z	
	2.33	3.84

Conjunction minus Guided

	2.33	5.29
	Z	
	2.33	3.97

Guided minus Feature

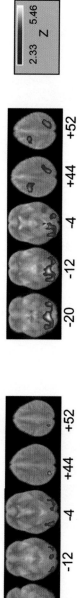

-20　-12　-4　+44　+52

| | 2.33 | 5.46 |
| | Z | |

Plate 7.2. Areas of increased regional cerebral blood flow (rCBF) associated with different levels of visual search complexity. (Modified with permission from Madden, Turkington, et al., 2002.) Measurement of rCBF was obtained by positron emission tomography (PET), while participants searched for an upright L among rotated L distractors. Each display contained 18 items, distributed in a 5 × 5 grid. The PET images represent rCBF differences between pairs of task conditions. In the most difficult condition (conjunction search), the display items were divided equally between black and white Ls. In the easiest condition (feature search), the target always differed from the distractors in color (i.e., a difference in color specified the presence of a target). In an intermediate condition (guided search), there was a subset of three display items with the target-relevant color. The PET images are in standard neurological orientation (right = right; anterior = top). The rCBF increases for each age group are presented in the blue color scale values. Within each age group, the voxels that differed significantly from those of the other age group are presented in the red color scale values.

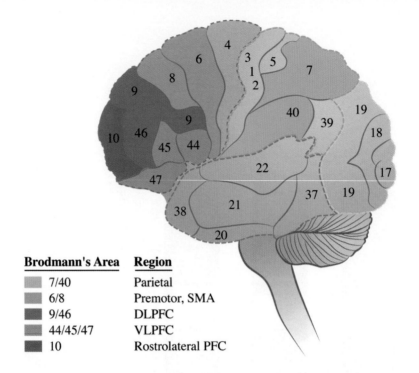

Brodmann's Area	Region
7/40	Parietal
6/8	Premotor, SMA
9/46	DLPFC
44/45/47	VLPFC
10	Rostrolateral PFC

Plate 8.1. Lateral view of the left hemisphere indicating the Brodmann's areas and the major cortical regions that are part of the working memory system.

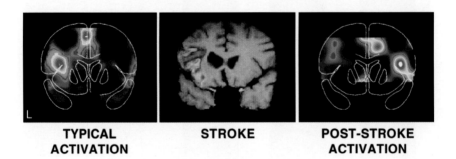

TYPICAL ACTIVATION   STROKE   POST-STROKE ACTIVATION

Plate 11.1. Evidence consistent with increased activation associated with compensation. Left panel: Strong left-lateralized activation during word generation is shown for typical, healthy young adults. Middle panel: Magnetic resonance image (MRI) shows the location of a stroke in patient LF1 that damaged his left frontal cortex. Surprisingly, LF1 could complete many forms of word generation task that typically activated his damaged cortex. Right panel: Strong right-lateralized activation is present in patient LF1, consistent with the possibility that contralateral recruitment associates with compensation. (Adapted from Buckner et al., 1996.)

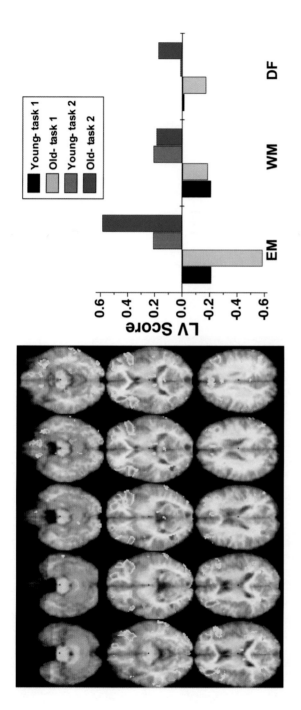

Plate 12.1. On the left of the figure, the brain areas with differential activity during face-processing tasks in three separate experiments are shown on a standard magnetic resonance image (MRI; slices ranging from −28 mm to +28 mm relative to the anterior-posterior commissure [AC-PC] line; the left side of the brain is seen on the left side of the images). In the episodic memory (EM) experiment, task 1 was a face-matching task, and task 2 was a recognition task. In the working memory (WM) experiment, task 1 was a matching task, and task 2 was a delayed matching task (6-s delay). In the degraded face (DF) experiment, task 1 was nondegraded face matching, and task 2 was degraded face matching (50% degradation). The graph on the right shows the mean scores (LV or latent variable scores) for young and old adults for each task condition from a multivariate analysis. Positive scores for a condition indicate that activity was increased in all of the brain regions shown in red and yellow, and negative scores for a condition indicate that activity was increased in the brain regions shown in blue. Thus, the old group showed increased prefrontal activity across all of the more difficult tasks, whereas young adults showed prefrontal activity only in the memory tasks. (Data from Grady, 2002.)

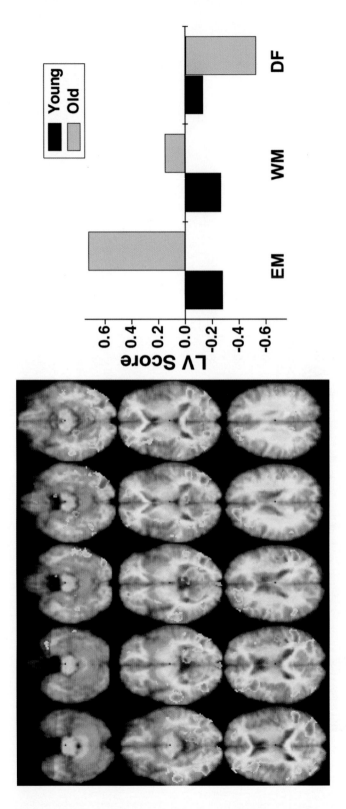

Plate 12.2. On the left of the figure are the brain areas where activity was correlated with reaction time (RT) during the face memory and degraded perception tasks (seen in plate 12.1). Areas are shown on a standard magnetic resonance image (MRI) as in figure 12.1. The graph on the right shows the mean scores for young adults (black bars) and old adults (gray bars) for each task condition. If the scores are positive for a condition, it indicates that RT was positively correlated with activity in the brain regions shown in yellow and red and negatively correlated with activity in the blue regions. If the scores are negative for a condition, it indicates that RT was positively correlated with activity in the brain regions shown in blue and negatively correlated with activity in the red regions. Thus, the older adults had positive correlations between activity in frontal areas and RT, whereas these correlations in young adults were negative. Abbreviations are the same as in plate 12.1. (Data from Grady, 2002.)

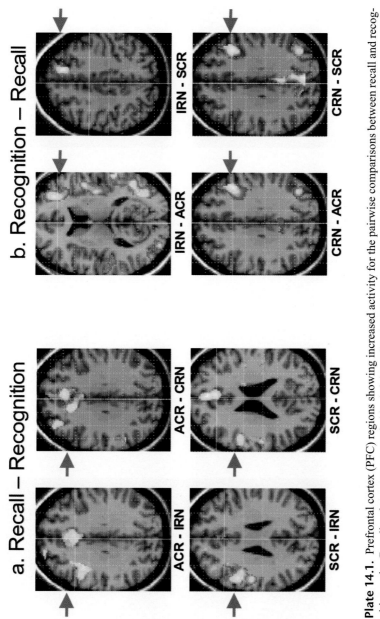

Plate 14.1. Prefrontal cortex (PFC) regions showing increased activity for the pairwise comparisons between recall and recognition tasks. Recall tasks are accompanied by left lateralized PFC activity, whereas recognition tasks induce activity in the right PFC. ACR, associative cued recall; CRN, context recognition; IRN, item recognition; SCR, stem cued recall. (Data from Cabeza, Locantore, & Anderson, 2003.)

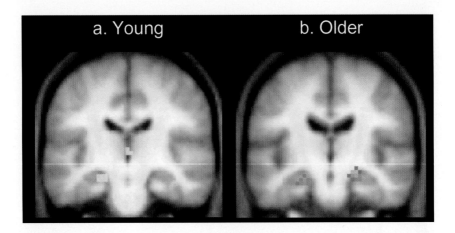

Plate 14.2. Medial temporal lobe activity during retrieval of autobiographical memory: a, for young subjects, there was increased activation of the left hippocampus; b, for older subjects, there was increased activation of both left and right hippocampi. (From Maguire & Frith, 2003.)

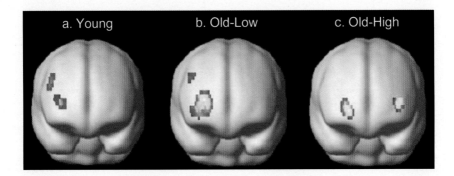

Plate 14.3. Prefrontal cortex activity during memory retrieval was right-lateralized in young and old-low participants, but bilateral in old-high subjects.

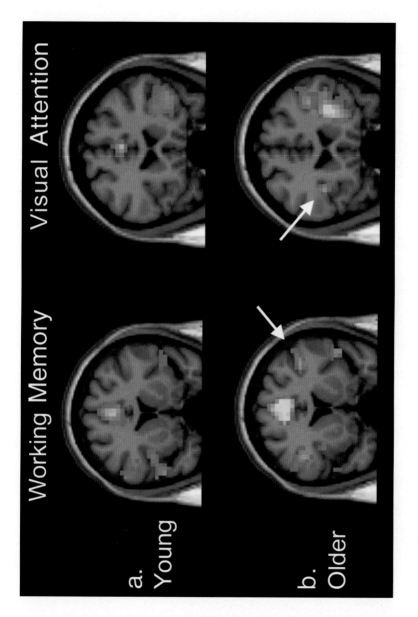

Plate 14.4. Older adults show contralateral recruitment in right prefrontal cortex (PFC) during working memory and in left PFC during visual attention. As a result of these changes, activity in the PFC was more bilateral in older than in younger adults. (From Cabeza et al., 2004.)

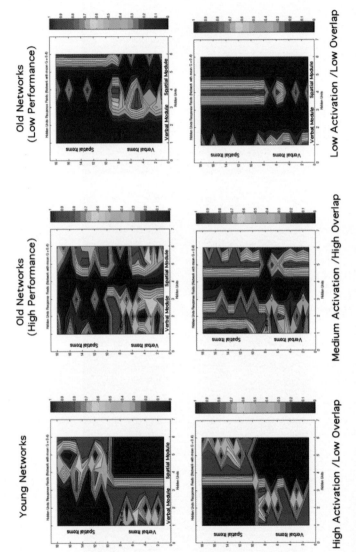

Plate 15.1. Simulation results obtained from networks with two modules designated for verbal and spatial processing. Plotted are internal activation patterns of two young networks (mean G = 1.3), two old networks with high performance (mean G = 0.4), and two old networks with low performance (mean G = 0.4). The range of the color legend from dark blue to dark red indicates activation levels from 0 to 1, respectively. a, Overall, the young networks show intense and distinct activation patterns in the two separate processing modules. b, High-performance old networks show median level of activation, with clear patterns of cross-module coactivation. c, Low-performance old networks show low level of activation, but do not show cross-module activation.

This finding, however, has not yet been extended to consider the presence of age-related changes in activity-induced $CMRO_2$ or its potential implications on BOLD signal interpretations in older populations.

The Influence of Age-Associated Comorbidities on the Blood Oxygen Level Dependent Signal

Aging is frequently associated with comorbidities such as diabetes, hypertension, and hyperlipidemia, all of which may affect the BOLD signal by affecting CBF and neurovascular coupling (Claus et al., 1998). The importance of screening older patients for these commonly associated conditions has unfortunately been underemphasized in functional neuroimaging studies of cognitive aging. In addition to the independent influences of these conditions on the vascular parameters, the conditions are also risk factors for vascular disease and arteriosclerosis (Shantaram, 1999). Vascular disease is a prevalent finding in the older population; aside from clinically significant stroke and transient ischemic attack, it can result in clinically silent small-vessel disease, large-vessel disease, and lacunar infarcts, all of which have been shown to alter CBF, neurovascular coupling, or the BOLD signal. Although any of these pathologies may be present without the knowledge of the subjects or the researcher, they are not routinely screened prior to fMRI studies of older populations.

Leukoaraiosis

White matter lucencies (leukoaraiosis) are common findings on CT and MRI scans of older patients, often found without other evidence of vascular disease and associated with large-vessel atherosclerosis (Bots et al., 1993) and hypertension (Dufouil et al., 2001). Most, but not all, areas of lucency are believed associated with small-vessel disease, and microscopic evaluation of these regions reveals arteriolar hyalinization and arteriosclerotic changes (Fazekas et al., 1993; George et al., 1986). The severity of leukoaraiosis has been shown to directly correlate with a reduction in CBF (Hatazawa et al., 1997), cerebral perfusion within the white matter areas (Kawamura et al., 1993; Kobari, Meyer, & Ichijo, 1990; Marstrand et al., 2002), and a decreased cerebrovascular response to hypercapnia (Kuwabara et al., 1996) and acetazolamide (Marstrand et al., 2002).

Stroke/Lacunes

In addition to the presence of small-vessel disease that may have been unnoticed, older subjects may have had small strokes and lacunes that were never clinically recognized. There has been limited research to investigate whether structural lesions secondary to stroke might influence the BOLD signal in a manner unrelated to changes in neural activity. Despite this lack of research, there have been multiple fMRI studies that have made statements regarding functional reorganization in stroke populations (Cao et al., 1999; Feydy et al., 2002; Small et al., 2002; Thirumala, Hier, & Patel, 2002; Thulborn, Carpenter, & Just, 1999). Ignoring these issues can lead to gross misinterpretations because there is probably no other study population in which the potential confounding effects of changes in neurovascular coupling on interpretations of BOLD signal changes is more apparent than in the stroke population.

An fMRI study by Piniero et al. (2002) addressed the issue of the influence of vascular factors on the BOLD signal in a symptomatic stroke population. The study analyzed the time course of the BOLD hemodynamic response function (HRF) in the sensorimotor cortex of patients with an isolated subcortical lacunar stroke compared to a group of age-matched controls. Piniero et al. found a decrease in the rate of rise and the maximal BOLD HRF to a finger- or hand-tapping task in the sensorimotor cortex of both the hemisphere affected by the stroke and the unaffected hemisphere (see figure 5.1a). The authors suggested that, given the widespread changes of these BOLD signal differences, the change was unlikely a direct consequence of the subcortical lacunar stroke, but rather a manifestation of preexisting diffuse vascular pathology. Furthermore, the assumption was made that the BOLD change was secondary to an alteration in the CBF because the other contributing factors to the HRF, the CBV and $CMRO_2$, were unlikely to be different between the two groups.

Given that changes in vascular parameters will alter the BOLD signal, we believe it is necessary to carefully screen structural MRIs in all experimental subjects for leukoaraiosis, or lacunar infarcts, that may be clinically silent. Unfortunately, most fMRI protocols do not collect images with appropriate pulse sequences for detecting white matter lesions (i.e., T2 weighted). It is also critical to obtain a comprehensive medical and neurological history to look for the past occurrence of possible transient ischemic attacks or stroke. Again, most subjects in cognitive aging studies are not screened by neurologists, who have the expertise to determine if the subject has had a vascular event in the past that may not necessarily be detected by routine screening questionnaires.

Extracranial Disease

In addition to screening for the presence of small-vessel disease and lacunar strokes, future studies of cognitive aging should consider the use of Doppler ultrasound and magnetic resonance angiography in evaluating the extracranial vasculature for the presence of significant occlusion. An fMRI study concluded that severe extracranial carotid stenosis in a patient without MRI evidence of an infarct led to neurovascular uncoupling that presented as a negative BOLD signal response during a motor task (Rother et al., 2002) (see figure 5.1b). Furthermore, this negative BOLD response occurred in only the affected hemisphere and correlated with a severely impaired hemodynamic response to hypercapnia isolated to that hemisphere. Given that there was no reason to suspect an abnormality in neural activity in this patient with normal motor performance, the finding was interpreted as a local activity-driven increase in deoxyhemoglobin, secondary to oxygen consumption, in the absence of an accompanying increase in CBF. Although this was a rather extreme example of the effect of impaired autoregulation on the BOLD response, it serves as an important illustration that extracranial vascular disease can impair this process and alter the BOLD response.

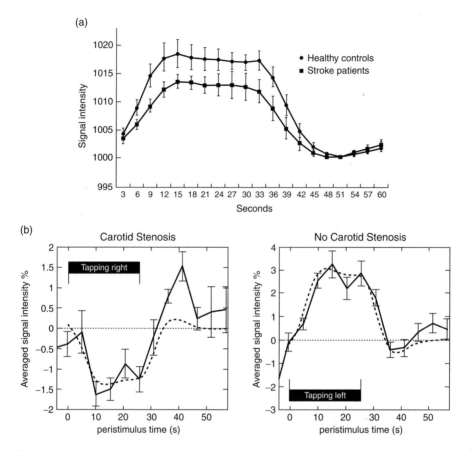

Figure 5.1. *a*, Blood oxygen level dependent (BOLD) signal time course in sensorimotor cortex opposite to hand movements during a sequential finger-tapping task in healthy controls and patients. The time course started with the stimulus for movement. (Adapted from Pineiro et al., 2002.) *b*, BOLD signal time course during tapping task in a single patient from motor cortex on the same side as (left) carotid stenosis and (right) no carotid stenosis (right). The fit (dotted line) and the averaged stimulus response (solid line) are shown. Activation on the side of carotid stenosis revealed a negative BOLD response lasting for the whole period of finger-tapping. (Adapted from Rother et al., 2002.)

Medications

Aside from the presence and influence of pathological processes, most patients are prescribed medications for the prevention or treatment of these conditions. Few studies strictly screen subjects for the use of all medications, including estrogen replacement therapy and common nonprescription drugs such as nonsteroidal antiinflammatory drugs (e.g., aspirin), which inhibit the cycloxygenase pathway of arachidonic acid and may alter neurovascular coupling and thus the BOLD signal independent of the pathological influence. There are very few studies that have investigated the effect of medications on CBF (Bednar & Gross, 1999; D. D. Miller et al., 1997; Nobler, Olvet, & Sackeim, 2002) or the BOLD signal (Neele et al., 2001; Pariente et al., 2001). The necessity to increase the understanding of the effects of medications, such as aspirin or hypertensive and hyperlipidemic medications, on the BOLD signal will continue to escalate as groups of older patients with diseases are studied and require control data. In addition, we need to be cognizant of and control for the potential effects on the BOLD signal of frequently used substances, such as caffeine and nicotine, which may have independent vascular effects and/or effects on neural activity (Jacobsen et al., 2002; Laurienti et al., 2002; Mulderink et al., 2002; Stein et al., 1998).

Hemodynamic Response Characteristics Determined by Blood Oxygen Level Dependent Functional Magnetic Resonance Imaging

Several researchers have recognized the potential for confounding results using BOLD fMRI to study cognitive aging and have designed fMRI experiments in an attempt to study this issue. One method is to study the spatial and temporal characteristics of the BOLD HRF during a stimulation that is expected to result in equivalent neural activity in young and old subjects, such as a simple motor task (Buckner et al., 2000; D'Esposito et al., 1999; Hesselmann et al., 2001; Mattay et al., 2002; Taoka et al., 1998) or a simple visual stimulation task (Buckner et al., 2000; Huettel, Singerman, & McCarthy, 2001; Ross et al., 1997) (see table 5.1). If there are changes in the HRF in response to a task that is assumed to induce no age-related change in neural activity, then it can be attributed to an alteration in another contributor to the HRF, such as a change in CBF or neurovascular coupling. The limitation of these fMRI studies is that the absence of an age-related change in neural activity is an assumption that is not directly recorded, and it is possible that motor and sensory processes are affected by aging (Lindenberger & Baltes, 1994).

Our laboratory compared the HRF characteristics in the sensorimotor cortex of young and older subjects in response to a simple motor reaction time task (D'Esposito et al., 1999). The provisional assumption was made that there was identical neural activity between the two populations based on physiological findings of equivalent movement-related electrical potentials in subjects under similar conditions (Cunnington et al., 1997). Thus, we presumed that any changes that we observed in BOLD fMRI signal between young and older individuals in the motor cortex would be because of vascular and not neural activity changes in normal aging. Several important similarities and differences were observed between age groups. Although there was no significant difference in the shape of the hemodynamic response curve or peak amplitude of the signal, we found a significantly decreased signal-to-noise ratio in the BOLD signal in older individuals compared to young individuals. This was attributed to a greater level of noise in the older individuals (see figure 5.2a). We also observed a decrease in the spatial extent of the BOLD signal in the sensorimotor cortex (i.e., the median number of suprathreshold voxels) in older individuals compared to younger individuals. These findings suggest that

Table 5.1 Functional Magnetic Resonance Imaging Studies of the Blood Oxygen Level Dependent Hemodynamic Response in Aging

Study	Age (years)	Stimulus/Task	Cortical Area Examined	Spatial Extent	Peak Amplitude	Form of HRF	Other Findings
Ross et al., 1997	Y: 24 (20–36) O: 71 (57–84)	Flashlight	Visual	↔	↓	NA	
Taoka et al., 1998	All: 20–76	Hand grasp	Motor	NA	NA	↑ Rise time ↔ Return to baseline	↑ Noise
D'Esposito et al., 1999	Y: 22.9 (18–32) O: 71.3 (61–82)	Button press	Sensorimotor	↓	↔	↔	
Buckner et al., 2000	Y: 21.1 (18–24) O: 74.9 (66–89)	Button press Checkerboard	Sensorimotor Visual	↓ ↓	↔ ↓	NA	↔ Summation
Huettel, Singerman, and McCarthy, 2001	Y: 23 (18–32) O: 66 (57–76)	Checkerboard	Visual	↓	↔	↔ Rise time Peaked earlier	↔ Refractoriness ↑ Noise
Hesselmann et al., 2001	All: 20–83	Finger-thumb opposition	Sensorimotor	↓	↓	NA	
Mattay et al., 2002	Y: 30 (24–34) O: 59 (50–74)	Button press	Sensorimotor	↑	↑	NA	↑ Extent and amplitude in multiple regions

Note. All results are changes observed in the older age group relative to the younger group. ↔, no change; NA, not analyzed; O, old; Y, young.

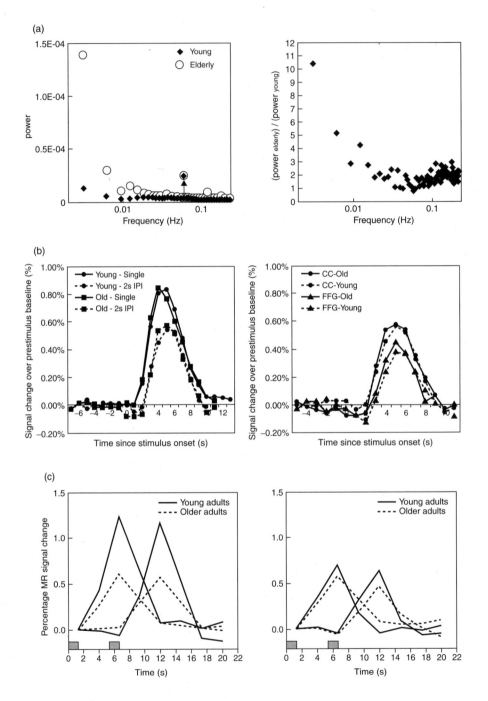

there is some property of the coupling between neural activity and BOLD signal that changes with age.

Several other studies have also investigated the HRF characteristics in response to simple motor tasks and have reached similar conclusions (Buckner et al., 2000; Hesselmann et al., 2001; Taoka et al., 1998); and one study revealed disparate findings (Mattay et al., 2002). Taoka et al. found an age-associated time lag in the BOLD signal to reach half maximum in the precentral gyrus between the start and end of a 10-s hand-grasping task. They proposed that this lag may be attributable to arteriolar changes such as vascular stiffening. Hesselman et al. observed a decrease in both the signal amplitude and the number of activated voxels with age during a finger-tapping task and suggested the possibility of a deterioration of neurovascular coupling or an impairment of vascular supply.

Other studies have analyzed the HRF characteristics in the visual cortex in response to simple visual stimuli. A study by Buckner et al. (2000) revealed the presence of an age-associated, regional difference in the BOLD signal between the motor and visual cortex. Hemodynamic response characteristics were examined in young and older adults as they viewed a large-field flickering checkerboard. They were

---

Figure 5.2. (Facing Page) *a*, Functional magnetic resonance imaging (fMRI) signal noise in young and old subjects. On the left side of the figure, the average power spectra of the fMRI signal for the young and elderly groups during a simple sensorimotor task are shown. It can be seen that power at the fundamental frequency of the behavioral paradigm (marked by the arrow) is nearly identical in the two groups. On the right side of the figure, the ratio of the average elderly group power spectrum to the average young group power spectrum is shown. It can be seen that the greatest disparity between noise in the young and elderly groups is at the lowest frequencies, although the noise tends to be greater in the elderly group throughout the spectrum. (Adapted from D'Esposito et al., 1999.) *b*, Refractory effects for young and old subjects. On the left side of the figure, the hemodynamic response function (HRF) is plotted for single-stimulus trials (solid lines) and for the second stimulus in a pair with a 2-s intrapair interval (IPI) (dashed lines). For both younger (circles) and older (squares) subjects, there were significant attenuations in amplitude and increases in latency in the HRF to the second stimulus in a pair. These refractory effects were similar between the subject groups. On the right side of the figure, the HRF to the second stimulus in a pair is plotted for calcarine cortex (CC) (circles) and fusiform gyrus (FFG) (triangles) for both young and old subjects. As the amplitude of the HRF to a single stimulus was not significantly different across these conditions, differences in the response to the second stimulus in a pair reflect differences in proportional recovery (not initial amplitude). (Adapted from Huettel, Singerman, & McCarthy, 2001.) *c*, Summation effects for young and old subjects. The selectively averaged blood oxygen level dependent (BOLD) signal is shown for visual (left) and motor (right) regions to illustrate the linear summation of the HRF. The gray boxes at the bottom of each panel represent when the two visual stimuli were present. The lines in each panel that show a peak to the left represent the selectively averaged data from the isolated trial events, and the peak to the right represents the added contributions of the second (summated) trials in the two-trial condition. Note the near linear summation across all groups for both regions, as indicated by similar amplitudes for the left and right peaks. (Adapted from Buckner et al., 2000.)

also instructed to make a key press on stimulus presentation so that motor cortex responses could be examined simultaneously. They recorded a decrease in BOLD signal amplitude in the visual cortex, in concordance with the findings of Ross et al. (1997) on a flashlight stimulation task, and no change in the BOLD signal amplitude in the motor cortex, a finding consistent with our results from the motor cortex (D'Esposito et al., 1999). The authors proposed that these findings might represent a regional difference in the deterioration of neurovascular coupling with age, but they also conceded that the findings in the visual cortex might very well be a corre-late of regionally reduced neural activity. Another study addressing the characteris-tics of a visually evoked HRF to checkerboard stimuli found a decrease in spatial extent, similar amplitudes, and increased noise levels in the older visual cortex (Huettel, Singerman, & McCarthy, 2001). These findings were consistent with our observations in the motor cortex (D'Esposito et al., 1999) and questioned the pres-ence of regional variability.

There are other aspects of the BOLD signal that have been studied in young adults, such as refractoriness and summation, which have also been analyzed in the aging brain. *Refractoriness* refers to the finding of an attenuated HRF amplitude evoked by a second stimulus that is spaced close (1–2 s) to the first stimulus. The degree of attenuation of the amplitude correlates with the length of the interval between the paired stimuli (Huettel & McCarthy, 2000). *Summation* is the property by which a paired group of stimuli will summate in a roughly linear fashion when presented at intervals of 5–6 s or greater (Miezin et al., 2000). It was determined that there was no age-related effect on the refractoriness (Huettel, Singerman, & McCarthy, 2001) or the ability of the HRF to summate (Buckner et al., 2000) (see figure 5.2b and 5.2c). These are encouraging findings for continued use of event-related fMRI designs in the study of aging. If the relationship of the coupling is similar between young and old adults even in the setting of decreased signal or increased noise, it bodes well for the ability to study within-group interactions, as we discuss next.

Recommendations

Implications for Blood Oxygen Level Dependent Functional Magnetic Resonance Imaging Design, Analysis, and Interpretation

The presence of alterations in vascular ultrastructure, resting CBF, vascular respon-siveness, and BOLD HRF characteristics associated with aging leads to limitations in conclusions about the link between neural activity and behavior derived from directly comparing the BOLD response between populations of young and old adults. Such comparisons assume that the absolute levels of hemodynamic response and the baseline CBF are the same between the two study groups, and as we have discussed, there is considerable evidence to question this assumption. The design, analysis, and interpretation of BOLD experiments aimed at the study of age-related changes in neural activity must consider these relationships.

It should be noted that the vascular pathology described in this chapter is a very common feature in the aging brain, and it is possible that age-related cognitive changes might be based on such vascular changes. We are therefore not recommending excluding all subjects with significant vascular changes from aging investigations. Rather, we stress the necessity of identifying vascular changes in all older subjects (i.e., T2 sequences and breath-holding trials) and to consider these data when interpreting fMRI data and behavioral changes.

There have been very few studies of cognitive aging that have used fMRI (Krause et al., 1999; Logan et al., 2002; Milham et al., 2002; Mitchell et al., 2000; Rypma & D'Esposito, 2000; Stebbins et al., 2002) because most studies have used PET. The issues regarding age-related changes in the hemodynamic coupling of neural activity to fMRI signal may not necessarily generalize to other imaging methods based on blood flow, such as PET. In fact, one study comparing fMRI and PET suggested that the transform between blood flow to imaging signal between these methods may differ (Rees et al., 1997). Nevertheless, examination of the results of fMRI studies of cognitive aging that have been published provides a forum for considering the issues raised in this chapter and a foundation for assisting in the design, analysis, and interpretation of future studies of cognitive aging.

Logan et al. (2002) formed direct comparisons between BOLD signal levels from young and old study groups in a memory paradigm. They stated that by "using younger adults' mean regional activity levels as a baseline, under-recruitment was defined as less activity in older adults compared to younger adults" (p. 3). They determined that there was a main effect of age in decreasing the BOLD signal amplitude in certain frontal regions. Such an effect is often interpreted as underrecruitment of neural systems. As mentioned here, a decreased age-related BOLD signal could be caused by an age-related decrease in neurovascular reactivity or a decrease in the baseline CBF and not a decrease in neural activity. However, Logan et al. also identified new areas of significant BOLD activity in old subjects that were not present in young adults, as well as regions that did not seem to change from the young adult baseline. Thus, the overall finding of a network of brain regions in which some brain regions exhibit decreased age-related activity, some have increased age-related activity, and some show no change between old and young groups is unlikely to be accounted for by a global change in neurovascular coupling in the aging brain (see figure 5.3). Also, the finding of recruitment of brain regions in older individuals that are not recruited in younger individuals during a particular cognitive task cannot likely be accounted for by age-related changes in neurovascular coupling.

In studies in which only underrecruitment is observed (Jonides et al., 2000), the possible interpretation that the change is because of vascular causes and not neural changes is unavoidable. However, there are several approaches that may address this potential confound. For example, we have proposed that greater levels of noise per voxel in the sensorimotor cortex in the aging brain will lead to erroneous inferences when comparing younger and older adults based on statistical maps that rely on scaling of signal components by noise. However, if the magnitude of voxelwise task-related signal is not different between age groups, then one approach may be to analyze the signal component of fMRI data separate from the noise component. For example, we investigated (Rypma and D'Esposito, 2000) age-related differences in

Young   Elderly

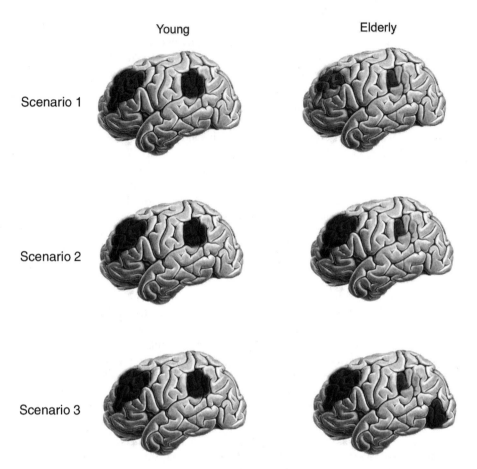

Scenario 1

Scenario 2

Scenario 3

Figure 5.3. Three scenarios depicting potential age-related changes in the blood oxygen level dependent (BOLD) signal. Scenario 1 illustrates a decrease in the magnitude and extent in the elderly brain in both regions that exhibited a significant task-correlated activation in the young brain. This finding could result from age-related vascular as well as neural changes. Scenario 2 illustrates an age-related decrease in activation in one region, but comparable activity between younger and older groups in another region. Scenario 3 illustrates one region with an age-related decrease in activation, one region without age-related changes, and a newly identified region of activity in the older group. Scenarios 2 and 3 are more likely to be attributable to age-related changes in neural activity.

prefrontal neural activity with random effects tests of age differences in the mean parameter estimates (i.e., the β values derived from the least-squares solution of a linear model of the dependent data) that characterized the fMRI signal during each task component. These parameter estimates were not scaled by the model error term (which would typically be used to obtain t statistics for each voxel). This method avoided use of the noise component of the fMRI signal.

then be extended to the population, for whom comparisons should have a reduced contribution of vascular changes.

By studying interactions of age with behavioral condition, all of the analysis options we discussed will reduce the possibility that nonneural changes such as a global decrease in CBF or vascular responsiveness account for BOLD signal changes between age groups. However, the success of all of these options in accurately describing changes in neural activity relies on assumptions of limited regional variability in vascular changes and preserved linearity of neurovascular coupling with aging. It is encouraging that the processes of summation and refractoriness of the HRF seem to be age independent, and that similar HRF characteristics have been observed in both the motor and the visual cortex, although this was not a consistent finding. Clearly, more studies need to be performed to specifically address linearity and regional variability of vascular changes during aging.

Conclusions

The use of functional neuroimaging has the potential to revolutionize the understanding of the neural basis of cognitive aging. Its high spatial resolution coupled with its ability to assess correlates of neural activity while subjects are performing cognitive tasks make its role invaluable. However, caution must be taken to avoid misinterpreting the results of BOLD fMRI studies. The BOLD signal usually reflects the influence of neural activity on CBF, and therefore age-related changes in resting CBF or neurovascular coupling may influence the ability to attribute BOLD signal changes to alterations in neural activity. Until new methods are developed to more closely link functional imaging to neural activity, care must be taken at all levels of study design, analysis, and interpretation to maximize the ability to continue to contribute valuable insights to the literature on the neural mechanisms of cognitive aging.

References

Abernethy, W. B., Bell, M. A., Morris, M., & Moody, D. M. (1993). Microvascular density of the human paraventricular nucleus decreases with aging but not hypertension. *Exp Neurol, 121*, 270–274.

Bednar, M. M., & Gross, C. E. (1999). Aspirin reduces experimental cerebral blood flow in vivo. *Neurol Res, 21*, 488–490.

Bentourkia, M., Bol, A., Ivanoiu, A., Labar, D., Sibomana, M., Coppens, A., et al. (2000). Comparison of regional cerebral blood flow and glucose metabolism in the normal brain: Effect of aging. *J Neurol Sci, 181*, 19–28.

Bonvento, G., Sibson, N., & Pellerin, L. (2002). Does glutamate image your thoughts? *Trends Neurosci, 25*, 359–364.

Bots, M. L., van Swieten, J. C., Breteler, M. M., de Jong, P. T., van Gijn, J., Hofman, A., et al. (1993). Cerebral white matter lesions and atherosclerosis in the Rotterdam Study. *Lancet, 341*, 1232–1237.

Buckner, R. L., Snyder, A. Z., Sanders, A. L., Raichle, M. E., & Morris, J. C. (2000). Functional brain imaging of young, nondemented, and demented older adults. *J Cogn Neurosci, 12(Suppl 2)*, 24–34.

Buxton, R. B., & Frank, L. R. (1997). A model for the coupling between cerebral blood flow and oxygen metabolism during neural stimulation. *J Cereb Blood Flow Metab, 17,* 64–72.

Cabeza, R. (2002). Hemispheric asymmetry reduction in older adults: The HAROLD model. *Psychol Aging, 17,* 85–100.

Cabeza, R., McIntosh, A. R., Tulving, E., Nyberg, L., & Grady, C. L. (1997). Age-related differences in effective neural connectivity during encoding and recall. *Neuroreport, 8,* 3479–3483.

Cao, Y., Vikingstad, E. M., George, K. P., Johnson, A. F., & Welch, K. M. (1999). Cortical language activation in stroke patients recovering from aphasia with functional MRI. *Stroke, 30,* 2331–2340.

Chao, L. L., & Knight, R. T. (1997). Prefrontal deficits in attention and inhibitory control with aging. *Cereb Cortex, 7,* 63–69.

Claus, J. J., Breteler, M. M., Hasan, D., Krenning, E. P., Bots, M. L., Grobbee, D. E., et al. (1998). Regional cerebral blood flow and cerebrovascular risk factors in the elderly population. *Neurobiol Aging, 19,* 57–64.

Cohen, E. R., Ugurbil, K., & Kim, S. G. (2002). Effect of basal conditions on the magnitude and dynamics of the blood oxygenation level-dependent fMRI response. *J Cereb Blood Flow Metab, 22,* 1042–1053.

Cunnington, R., Iansek, R., Johnson, K. A., & Bradshaw, J. L. (1997). Movement-related potentials in Parkinson's disease. Motor imagery and movement preparation. *Brain, 120(Part 8),* 1339–1353.

D'Esposito, M., Zarahn, E., Aguirre, G. K., & Rypma, B. (1999). The effect of normal aging on the coupling of neural activity to the bold hemodynamic response. *Neuroimage, 10,* 6–14.

Detre, J. A., & Alsop, D. C. (1999). Perfusion magnetic resonance imaging with continuous arterial spin labeling: Methods and clinical applications in the central nervous system. *Eur J Radiol, 30,* 115–124.

Diehl, B., Stodieck, S. R., Diehl, R. R., & Ringelstein, E. B. (1998). The photic driving EEG response and photoreactive cerebral blood flow in the posterior cerebral artery in controls and in patients with epilepsy. *Electroencephalogr Clin Neurophysiol, 107,* 8–12.

Dufouil, C., de Kersaint-Gilly, A., Besancon, V., Levy, C., Auffray, E., Brunnereau, L., et al. (2001). Longitudinal study of blood pressure and white matter hyperintensities: The EVA MRI Cohort. *Neurology, 56,* 921–926.

Fang, H. C. H. (1976). Observations on aging characteristics of cerebral blood vessels, macroscopic and microscopic features. In Samuel Gershon & R. D. Terry (Eds.), *Neurobiology of aging* (pp. 155–166). New York: Raven.

Farkas, E., & Luiten, P. G. (2001). Cerebral microvascular pathology in aging and Alzheimer's disease. *Prog Neurobiol, 64,* 575–611.

Fazekas, F., Kleinert, R., Offenbacher, H., Schmidt, R., Kleinert, G., Payer, F., et al. (1993). Pathologic correlates of incidental MRI white matter signal hyperintensities. *Neurology, 43,* 1683–1689.

Feydy, A., Carlier, R., Roby-Brami, A., Bussel, B., Cazalis, F., Pierot, L., et al. (2002). Longitudinal study of motor recovery after stroke: Recruitment and focusing of brain activation. *Stroke, 33,* 1610–1617.

Fox, P. T., & Raichle, M. E. (1986). Focal physiological uncoupling of cerebral blood flow and oxidative metabolism during somatosensory stimulation in human subjects. *Proc Natl Acad Sci U S A, 83,* 1140–1144.

Fox, P. T., Raichle, M. E., Mintun, M. A., & Dence, C. (1988). Nonoxidative glucose consumption during focal physiologic neural activity. *Science, 241,* 462–464.

Furuta, A., Ishii, N., Nishihara, Y., & Horie, A. (1991). Medullary arteries in aging and dementia. *Stroke, 22*, 442–446.

Gati, J. S., Menon, R. S., Ugurbil, K., & Rutt, B. K. (1997). Experimental determination of the BOLD field strength dependence in vessels and tissue. *Magn Reson Med, 38*, 296–302.

Gazzaley, A., & D'Esposito, M. (2003). The contribution of functional brain imaging to our understanding of cognitive aging. *Science's SAGE KE, 4*, PE2.

Gazzaley, A. H., Siegel, S. J., Kordower, J. H., Mufson, E. J., & Morrison, J. H. (1996). Circuit-specific alterations of N-methyl-D-aspartate receptor subunit 1 in the dentate gyrus of aged monkeys. *Proc Natl Acad Sci U S A, 93*, 3121–3125.

Gazzaley, A. H., Thakker, M. M., Hof, P. R., & Morrison, J. H. (1997). Preserved number of entorhinal cortex layer II neurons in aged macaque monkeys. *Neurobiol Aging, 18*, 549–553.

George, A. E., de Leon, M. J., Gentes, C. I., Miller, J., London, E., Budzilovich, G. N., et al. (1986). Leukoencephalopathy in normal and pathologic aging: 1. CT of brain lucencies. *AJNR Am J Neuroradiol, 7*, 561–566.

Grady, C. L. (2000). Functional brain imaging and age-related changes in cognition. *Biol Psychol, 54*, 259–281.

Greenwood, P. M. (2000). The frontal aging hypothesis evaluated. *J Int Neuropsychol Soc, 6*, 705–726.

Hatazawa, J., Shimosegawa, E., Satoh, T., Toyoshima, H., & Okudera, T. (1997). Subcortical hypoperfusion associated with asymptomatic white matter lesions on magnetic resonance imaging. *Stroke, 28*, 1944–1947.

Hesselmann, V., Zaro Weber, O., Wedekind, C., Krings, T., Schulte, O., Kugel, H., et al. (2001). Age related signal decrease in functional magnetic resonance imaging during motor stimulation in humans. *Neurosci Lett, 308*, 141–144.

Huettel, S. A., & McCarthy, G. (2000). Evidence for a refractory period in the hemodynamic response to visual stimuli as measured by MRI. *Neuroimage, 11*(5, Part 1), 547–553.

Huettel, S. A., Singerman, J. D., & McCarthy, G. (2001). The effects of aging upon the hemodynamic response measured by functional MRI. *Neuroimage, 13*, 161–175.

Ito, H., Kanno, I., Ibaraki, M., & Hatazawa, J. (2002). Effect of aging on cerebral vascular response to Paco2 changes in humans as measured by positron emission tomography. *J Cereb Blood Flow Metab, 22*, 997–1003.

Jacobsen, L. K., Gore, J. C., Skudlarski, P., Lacadie, C. M., Jatlow, P., & Krystal, J. H. (2002). Impact of intravenous nicotine on BOLD signal response to photic stimulation. *Magn Reson Imaging, 20*, 141–145.

Jiang, H. X., Chen, P. C., Sobin, S. S., & Giannotta, S. L. (1992). Age related alterations in the response of the pial arterioles to adenosine in the rat. *Mech Ageing Dev, 65*, 257–276.

Jonides, J., Marshuetz, C., Smith, E. E., Reuter-Lorenz, P. A., Koeppe, R. A., & Hartley, A. (2000). Age differences in behavior and PET activation reveal differences in interference resolution in verbal working memory. *J Cogn Neurosci, 12*, 188–196.

Kalaria, R. N. (1996). Cerebral vessels in ageing and Alzheimer's disease. *Pharmacol Ther, 72*, 193–214.

Kawamura, J., Terayama, Y., Takashima, S., Obara, K., Pavol, M. A., Meyer, J. S., et al. (1993). Leuko-araiosis and cerebral perfusion in normal aging. *Exp Aging Res, 19*, 225–240.

Knox, C. A., Yates, R. D., Chen, I., & Klara, P. M. (1980). Effects of aging on the structural and permeability characteristics of cerebrovasculature in normotensive and hypertensive strains of rats. *Acta Neuropathol (Berl), 51*, 1–13.

Kobari, M., Meyer, J. S., & Ichijo, M. (1990). Leuko-araiosis, cerebral atrophy, and cerebral perfusion in normal aging. *Arch Neurol, 47*, 161–165.

Krause, B. J., Horwitz, B., Taylor, J. G., Schmidt, D., Mottaghy, F. M., Herzog, H., et al. (1999). Network analysis in episodic encoding and retrieval of word-pair associates: A PET study. *Eur J Neurosci, 11*, 3293–3301.

Krejza, J., Mariak, Z., Walecki, J., Szydlik, P., Lewko, J., & Ustymowicz, A. (1999). Transcranial color Doppler sonography of basal cerebral arteries in 182 healthy subjects: Age and sex variability and normal reference values for blood flow parameters. *AJR Am J Roentgenol, 172*, 213–218.

Kuwabara, Y., Ichiya, Y., Sasaki, M., Yoshida, T., Fukumura, T., Masuda, K., et al. (1996). Cerebral blood flow and vascular response to hypercapnia in hypertensive patients with leukoaraiosis. *Ann Nucl Med, 10*, 293–298.

Laurienti, P. J., Field, A. S., Burdette, J. H., Maldjian, J. A., Yen, Y. F., & Moody, D. M. (2002). Dietary caffeine consumption modulates fMRI measures. *Neuroimage, 17*, 751–757.

Lia, T. Q., Guang Chen, Z., Ostergaard, L., Hindmarsh, T., & Moseley, M. E. (2000). Quantification of cerebral blood flow by bolus tracking and artery spin tagging methods. *Magn Reson Imaging, 18*, 503–512.

Lindauer, U., Megow, D., Matsuda, H., & Dirnagl, U. (1999). Nitric oxide: A modulator, but not a mediator, of neurovascular coupling in rat somatosensory cortex. *Am J Physiol, 277*(2, Part 2), H799–H811.

Lindenberger, U., & Baltes, P. B. (1994). Sensory functioning and intelligence in old age: A strong connection. *Psychol Aging, 9*, 339–355.

Linville, D. G., & Arneric, S. P. (1991). Cortical cerebral blood flow governed by the basal forebrain: Age-related impairments. *Neurobiol Aging, 12*, 503–510.

Logan, J. M., Sanders, A. L., Snyder, A. Z., Morris, J. C., & Buckner, R. L. (2002). Underrecruitment and nonselective recruitment: Dissociable neural mechanisms associated with aging. *Neuron, 33*, 827–840.

Madden, D. J., & Hoffman, J. M. (1997). Application of positron emission tomography to age-related cognitive changes. In K. R. R. Krishmann & P. M. Doraiswamy (Eds.), *Brain Imaging in clinical psychiatry* (pp. 575–613). New York: Marcel Dekker.

Marstrand, J. R., Garde, E., Rostrup, E., Ring, P., Rosenbaum, S., Mortensen, E. L., et al. (2002). Cerebral perfusion and cerebrovascular reactivity are reduced in white matter hyperintensities. *Stroke, 33*, 972–976.

Masawa, N., Yoshida, Y., Yamada, T., Joshita, T., Sato, S., & Mihara, B. (1994). Morphometry of structural preservation of tunica media in aged and hypertensive human intracerebral arteries. *Stroke, 25*, 122–127.

Mattay, V. S., Fera, F., Tessitore, A., Hariri, A. R., Das, S., Callicott, J. H., et al. (2002). Neurophysiological correlates of age-related changes in human motor function. *Neurology, 58*, 630–635.

Mayhan, W. G., Faraci, F. M., Baumbach, G. L., & Heistad, D. D. (1990). Effects of aging on responses of cerebral arterioles. *Am J Physiol, 258*(4, Part 2), H1138–H1143.

McIntosh, A. R. (1999). Mapping cognition to the brain through neural interactions. *Memory, 7*, 523–548.

Mechelli, A., Price, C. J., & Friston, K. J. (2001). Nonlinear coupling between evoked rCBF and BOLD signals: A simulation study of hemodynamic responses. *Neuroimage, 14*, 862–872.

Menon, R. S., Ogawa, S., Hu, X., Strupp, J. P., Anderson, P., & Ugurbil, K. (1995). BOLD based functional MRI at 4 Tesla includes a capillary bed contribution: Echo-planar imaging correlates with previous optical imaging using intrinsic signals. *Magn Reson Med, 33*, 453–459.

Miezin, F. M., Maccotta, L., Ollinger, J. M., Petersen, S. E., & Buckner, R. L. (2000). Characterizing the hemodynamic response: Effects of presentation rate, sampling procedure, and the possibility of ordering brain activity based on relative timing. *Neuroimage*, *11*(6, Part 1), 735–759.

Milham, M. P., Erickson, K. I., Banich, M. T., Kramer, A. F., Webb, A., Wszalek, T., et al. (2002). Attentional control in the aging brain: Insights from an fMRI study of the stroop task. *Brain Cogn*, *49*, 277–296.

Miller, D. D., Andreasen, N. C., O'Leary, D. S., Rezai, K., Watkins, G. L., Ponto, L. L., et al. (1997). Effect of antipsychotics on regional cerebral blood flow measured with positron emission tomography. *Neuropsychopharmacology*, *17*, 230–240.

Miller, K. L., Luh, W. M., Liu, T. T., Martinez, A., Obata, T., Wong, E. C., et al. (2001). Nonlinear temporal dynamics of the cerebral blood flow response. *Hum Brain Mapp*, *13*, 1–12.

Mitchell, K. J., Johnson, M. K., Raye, C. L., & D'Esposito, M. (2000). fMRI evidence of age-related hippocampal dysfunction in feature binding in working memory. *Brain Res Cogn Brain Res*, *10*, 197–206.

Moody, D. M., Brown, W. R., Challa, V. R., Ghazi-Birry, H. S., & Reboussin, D. M. (1997). Cerebral microvascular alterations in aging, leukoaraiosis, and Alzheimer's disease. *Ann N Y Acad Sci*, *826*, 103–116.

Morrison, J. H., & Hof, P. R. (1997). Life and death of neurons in the aging brain. *Science*, *278*, 412–419.

Moscovitch, M., & Winocur, G. (1995). Frontal lobes, memory, and aging. *Ann N Y Acad Sci*, *769*, 119–150.

Mulderink, T. A., Gitelman, D. R., Mesulam, M. M., & Parrish, T. B. (2002). On the use of caffeine as a contrast booster for BOLD fMRI studies. *Neuroimage*, *15*, 37–44.

Nagasawa, S., Handa, H., Okumura, A., Naruo, Y., Moritake, K., & Hayashi, K. (1979). Mechanical properties of human cerebral arteries. Part 1: Effects of age and vascular smooth muscle activation. *Surg Neurol*, *12*, 297–304.

Neele, S. J., Rombouts, S. A., Bierlaagh, M. A., Barkhof, F., Scheltens, P., & Netelenbos, J. C. (2001). Raloxifene affects brain activation patterns in postmenopausal women during visual encoding. *J Clin Endocrinol Metab*, *86*, 1422–1424.

Niehaus, L., Lehmann, R., Roricht, S., & Meyer, B. U. (2001). Age-related reduction in visually evoked cerebral blood flow responses. *Neurobiol Aging*, *22*, 35–38.

Nobler, M. S., Olvet, K. R., & Sackeim, H. A. (2002). Effects of medications on cerebral blood flow in late-life depression. *Curr Psychiatry Rep*, *4*, 51–58.

Norris, D. G., Zysset, S., Mildner, T., & Wiggins, C. J. (2002). An investigation of the value of spin-echo-based fMRI using a Stroop color-word matching task and EPI at 3 T. *Neuroimage*, *15*, 719–726.

Pariente, J., Loubinoux, I., Carel, C., Albucher, J. F., Leger, A., Manelfe, C., et al. (2001). Fluoxetine modulates motor performance and cerebral activation of patients recovering from stroke. *Ann Neurol*, *50*, 718–729.

Pineiro, R., Pendlebury, S., Johansen-Berg, H., & Matthews, P. M. (2002). Altered hemodynamic responses in patients after subcortical stroke measured by functional MRI. *Stroke*, *33*, 103–109.

Raz, N., Gunning, F. M., Head, D., Dupuis, J. H., McQuain, J., Briggs, S. D., et al. (1997). Selective aging of the human cerebral cortex observed in vivo: Differential vulnerability of the prefrontal gray matter. *Cereb Cortex*, *7*, 268–282.

Rees, G., Howseman, A., Josephs, O., Frith, C. D., Friston, K. J., Frackowiak, R. S., et al. (1997). Characterizing the relationship between BOLD contrast and regional cerebral blood flow measurements by varying the stimulus presentation rate. *Neuroimage*, *6*, 270–278.

Reich, T., & Rusinek, H. (1989). Cerebral cortical and white matter reactivity to carbon dioxide. *Stroke, 20,* 453–457.

Reuter-Lorenz, P. (2002). New visions of the aging mind and brain. *Trends Cogn Sci, 6,* 394.

Ross, M. H., Yurgelun-Todd, D. A., Renshaw, P. F., Maas, L. C., Mendelson, J. H., Mello, N. K., et al. (1997). Age-related reduction in functional MRI response to photic stimulation. *Neurology, 48,* 173–176.

Rother, J., Knab, R., Hamzei, F., Fiehler, J., Reichenbach, J. R., Buchel, C., et al. (2002). Negative dip in BOLD fMRI is caused by blood flow–oxygen consumption uncoupling in humans. *Neuroimage, 15,* 98–102.

Rypma, B., & D'Esposito, M. (2000). Isolating the neural mechanisms of age-related changes in human working memory. *Nat Neurosci, 3,* 509–515.

Salat, D. H., Kaye, J. A., & Janowsky, J. S. (2001). Selective preservation and degeneration within the prefrontal cortex in aging and Alzheimer disease. *Arch Neurol, 58,* 1403–1408.

Schultz, S. K., O'Leary, D. S., Boles Ponto, L. L., Watkins, G. L., Hichwa, R. D., & Andreasen, N. C. (1999). Age-related changes in regional cerebral blood flow among young to mid-life adults. *Neuroreport, 10,* 2493–2496.

Schwarzbauer, C., & Heinke, W. (1999). Investigating the dependence of BOLD contrast on oxidative metabolism. *Magn Reson Med, 41,* 537–543.

Shantaram, V. (1999). Pathogenesis of atherosclerosis in diabetes and hypertension. *Clin Exp Hypertens, 21,* 69–77.

Small, S. L., Hlustik, P., Noll, D. C., Genovese, C., & Solodkin, A. (2002). Cerebellar hemispheric activation ipsilateral to the paretic hand correlates with functional recovery after stroke. *Brain, 125*(Part 7), 1544–1557.

Song, A. W., Fichtenholtz, H., & Woldorff, M. (2002). BOLD signal compartmentalization based on the apparent diffusion coefficient. *Magn Reson Imaging, 20,* 521–525.

Sonntag, W. E., Lynch, C. D., Cooney, P. T., & Hutchins, P. M. (1997). Decreases in cerebral microvasculature with age are associated with the decline in growth hormone and insulin-like growth factor 1. *Endocrinology, 138,* 3515–3520.

Stebbins, G. T., Carrillo, M. C., Dorfman, J., Dirksen, C., Desmond, J. E., Turner, D. A., et al. (2002). Aging effects on memory encoding in the frontal lobes. *Psychol Aging, 17,* 44–55.

Stein, E. A., Pankiewicz, J., Harsch, H. H., Cho, J. K., Fuller, S. A., Hoffmann, R. G., et al. (1998). Nicotine-induced limbic cortical activation in the human brain: A functional MRI study. *Am J Psychiatry, 155,* 1009–1015.

Stuss, D. T., Craik, F. I., Sayer, L., Franchi, D., & Alexander, M. P. (1996). Comparison of older people and patients with frontal lesions: Evidence from world list learning. *Psychol Aging, 11,* 387–395.

Sullivan, E. V., Pfefferbaum, A., Adalsteinsson, E., Swan, G. E., & Carmelli, D. (2002). Differential rates of regional brain change in callosal and ventricular size: A 4-year longitudinal MRI study of elderly men. *Cereb Cortex, 12,* 438–445.

Takada, H., Nagata, K., Hirata, Y., Satoh, Y., Watahiki, Y., Sugawara, J., et al. (1992). Age-related decline of cerebral oxygen metabolism in normal population detected with positron emission tomography. *Neurol Res, 14*(2, Suppl), 128–131.

Tamaki, K., Nakai, M., Yokota, T., & Ogata, J. (1995). Effects of aging and chronic hypertension on cerebral blood flow and cerebrovascular CO_2 reactivity in the rat. *Gerontology, 41,* 11–17.

Taoka, T., Iwasaki, S., Uchida, H., Fukusumi, A., Nakagawa, H., Kichikawa, K., et al. (1998). Age correlation of the time lag in signal change on EPI-fMRI. *J Comput Assist Tomogr, 22,* 514–517.

Thirumala, P., Hier, D. B., & Patel, P. (2002). Motor recovery after stroke: Lessons from functional brain imaging. *Neurol Res, 24*, 453–458.

Thulborn, K. R., Carpenter, P. A., & Just, M. A. (1999). Plasticity of language-related brain function during recovery from stroke. *Stroke, 30*, 749–754.

Thulborn, K. R., Waterton, J. C., Matthews, P. M., & Radda, G. K. (1982). Oxygenation dependence of the transverse relaxation time of water protons in whole blood at high field. *Biochim Biophys Acta, 714*, 265–270.

Tisserand, D., Pruessner, J., Sanz Arigita, E., van Boxtel, M., Evans, A., Jolles, J., et al. (2002). Regional frontal cortical volumes decrease differentially in aging: An MRI study to compare volumetric approaches and voxel-based morphometry. *Neuroimage, 17*, 657.

Tisserand, D. J., Visser, P. J., van Boxtel, M. P., & Jolles, J. (2000). The relation between global and limbic brain volumes on MRI and cognitive performance in healthy individuals across the age range. *Neurobiol Aging, 21*, 569–576.

Turner, R., Le Bihan, D., Moonen, C. T., Despres, D., & Frank, J. (1991). Echo-planar time course MRI of cat brain oxygenation changes. *Magn Reson Med, 22*(1), 159–166.

Urban, P. P., Allardt, A., Tettenborn, B., Hopf, H. C., Pfennigsdorf, S., & Lieb, W. (1995). Photoreactive flow changes in the posterior cerebral artery in control subjects and patients with occipital lobe infarction. *Stroke, 26*, 1817–1819.

West, R., & Covell, E. (2001). Effects of aging on event-related neural activity related to prospective memory. *Neuroreport, 12*, 2855–2858.

West, R. L. (1996). An application of prefrontal cortex function theory to cognitive aging. *Psychol Bull, 120*, 272–292.

Yamaguchi, T., Kanno, I., Uemura, K., Shishido, F., Inugami, A., Ogawa, T., et al. (1986). Reduction in regional cerebral metabolic rate of oxygen during human aging. *Stroke, 17*, 1220–1228.

Yamamoto, M., Meyer, J. S., Sakai, F., & Yamaguchi, F. (1980). Aging and cerebral vasodilator responses to hypercarbia: responses in normal aging and in persons with risk factors for stroke. *Arch Neurol, 37*, 489–496.

Ylikoski, R., Salonen, O., Mantyla, R., Ylikoski, A., Keskivaara, P., Leskela, M., et al. (2000). Hippocampal and temporal lobe atrophy and age-related decline in memory. *Acta Neurol Scand, 101*, 273–278.

6

The Relationship Between Brain Activity, Cognitive Performance, and Aging
The Case of Memory

Michael D. Rugg
Alexa M. Morcom

As indexed by performance on a variety of different memory tasks, episodic memory (memory for unique events) declines quite markedly as a function of advancing age, even in individuals seemingly free from age-associated pathology. The question of how best to account for this decline in functional terms is a long-standing one (for review, see Light, 1991). In particular, it has been much debated whether the decline is attributable predominantly to a deficit in the initial encoding of information into memory or in its subsequent retrieval (e.g., Perfect, Williams, & Anderton-Brown, 1995; see also chapter 9). With the development of noninvasive methods for measuring task-related brain activity, the question whether the neural substrates of episodic memory vary with age has also become prominent.

In this chapter, we discuss some of the methodological issues that arise when using noninvasive measures of neural activity (specifically, functional magnetic resonance imaging [fMRI] and event-related potentials [ERPs]) to address these and related questions. The focus of the chapter is on how studies can be designed to identify age-related differences in brain activity associated with memory processes free from the influence of confounding variables that, by virtue of their correlation with age, might masquerade as differences inherent to the aging process. Whereas some of these variables are relevant to fMRI and ERP studies of aging in any cognitive domain, others are more specific to studies of episodic memory, and it is to these latter variables that we devote most attention.

As noted above, we focus here on the use of fMRI and ERPs to investigate the neural correlates of age-related changes in episodic memory. The signals detected by both methods appear predominantly to reflect—directly in the case of ERPs, indirectly in the case of fMRI—the aggregated postsynaptic activity of relatively large neuronal populations (Wood, 1987; Logothetis et al., 2001; Attwell & Iadecola, 2002). Whereas fMRI has far better spatial resolution than the ERP method, the sluggishness of the hemodynamic response means that the temporal resolution of fMRI responses (even when obtained in "event-related" designs) is typically of the order of hundreds of milliseconds. This compares unfavorably with the millisecond-level resolution that can be attained with ERPs. Thus, the two methods provide broadly complementary perspectives on brain activity related to cognitive function (see Rugg, 1998, for further discussion of the relative strengths and weaknesses of the two methodologies in the context of memory research).

In considering the neural correlates of cognitive function, it is important to distinguish between transient changes in neural activity that follow a specific event such as the presentation of a stimulus (*item-related* activity) and more sustained modulations of activity that accompany engagement in a specific task and are unaffected by the presentation of specific items (*state-related* activity) (Rugg & Wilding, 2000). These two classes of neural activity have been linked to quite different kinds of cognitive process: associated with on-line stimulus processing in the case of item-related activity and associated with the maintenance of a specific cognitive set or mode in the case of state-related activity (Donaldson et al., 2001; Otten, Henson, & Rugg, 2002).

In functional neuroimaging studies employing blocked experimental designs (which include the overriding majority of studies of memory and aging), item- and state-related activity are inextricably confounded. In principle, however, age-related differences in neural correlates of memory could be reflected in either class of activity. For example, the finding of reduced left inferolateral prefrontal activity in older adults performing intentional as opposed to semantically oriented incidental encoding tasks (Logan et al., 2002) could be caused by either a failure to maintain an appropriate task set or a failure spontaneously to process study items semantically. Relatively recently, methods have been developed that allow fMRI data to be obtained in a manner analogous to that employed to record ERPs (Dale & Buckner, 1997; Josephs, Turner, & Friston, 1997; Zarahn, Aguirre, & D'Esposito, 1997). As with ERPs, event-related fMRI allows item-related activity to be identified independent of the influence of state-related activity.

Event-related methods have advantages other than just the capacity to detect item-related activity unequivocally. Of particular relevance to memory studies, the methods permit experimental trials to be allocated to different experimental conditions post hoc on the basis of behavioral performance. Thus, it is possible to compare brain activity elicited by, say, "old" items in a recognition memory test according to whether the items were correctly detected or misclassified as new.

General Issues

Three important general issues concern the aims and interpretation of neuroimaging studies of cognitive aging, the comparability of measures of brain activity obtained from different age groups, and the choice of the study populations used to assess aging effects on the neural correlates of memory.

Aims of Aging Studies

Cognitive neuroimaging studies can be undertaken for a variety of purposes. Within-group studies, which typically employ samples of young healthy subjects, have three primary objectives (Rugg, 1999): identification of the regions and circuits engaged by a specific cognitive operation or function; dissociation of different cognitive operations through the demonstration that they have distinct neural correlates; and the covert monitoring or measurement of a cognitive process. We argue that, in studies of aging, it is the first of these applications that is the most important. This stems from our conviction that the key question at present is whether there are systematic differences as a function of age in the neural correlates of specific cognitive functions. In other words, to what extent do the patterns of neural activity associated with the engagement of a given cognitive operation vary with age? To address this question, considerable care is required with study design to ensure that age-related differences in neural activity are not the result of confounding variables such as differences in performance levels or cognitive strategy. We discuss in some detail how this might be achieved in the context of studies of episodic encoding and retrieval (see the sections on encoding and retrieval).

Given that the ultimate goal of the study of cognitive aging is an explanation of why and how certain cognitive functions, episodic memory among them, decline with age, why is the above question so important? Our view is that, until it has been answered satisfactorily for a given cognitive domain, findings of age-related differences in the neural correlates of task performance within the domain are likely to be very difficult to interpret. This is because it will often be unclear whether such differences should be interpreted as evidence that the neural correlates of functionally equivalent cognitive operations differ in young and older individuals or as evidence that performance is supported by functionally (and neurally) distinct operations in the two groups. These alternative interpretations lead to very different theoretical perspectives on age-related changes in cognitive performance. The first interpretation implies that such changes result from age-related decline in the efficiency of a common cognitive operation or set of operations. In contrast, an implication of the second interpretation is that performance changes are associated with, and possibly result from, a shift to a less-efficient cognitive strategy.

Measures of Brain Activity

The question of the comparability of measures of brain activity over the life span is both crucial and difficult to address. Arguably, the issue is more problematic for hemodynamic measures such as the fMRI blood oxygen level dependent (BOLD) response, which index neural activity indirectly via a complex and incompletely understood neurovascular coupling mechanism (Attwell & Iadecola, 2002), than it is for more direct measures such as ERPs. This is not to say that the interpretation of direct measures of neural activity is free of difficulty. It is unclear, for example, what should be made of the frequent observation (see figure 6.1 for an example) that the morphology and scalp distribution of ERP waveforms differ according to age and whether such findings are of functional significance or merely reflect age-correlated changes in, say, brain morphology.

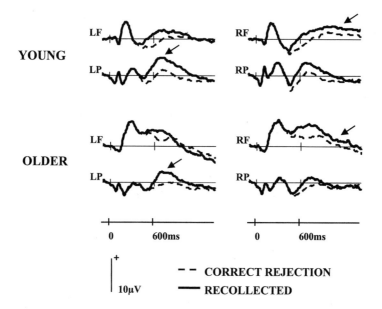

Figure 6.1. Grand average waveforms for young and older subjects, collapsed across task. Waveforms are shown from left frontal (LF), right frontal (RF), left parietal (LP), and right parietal (RP) electrodes for event-related potentials (ERPs) elicited by correctly rejected new items (broken lines) and by correctly judged old items receiving either an accurate source judgement or a remember response (unbroken lines). Left parietal and right frontal old/new effects are indicated by arrows. (Adapted from Mark & Rugg, 1998).

As we discuss in more detail in this chapter, we have tried to minimize the impact of this issue in our research by focusing not on main effects of age, but on age-by-condition interactions, that is, on age-related differences in the modulation of ERP waveforms. This does not eschew the problem entirely, however; differences in the scalp distribution of ERP modulations may themselves reflect age-related differences in generator geometry secondary to changes in brain morphology rather than evidence for the engagement of different neural systems. Parenthetically, it should be noted that morphological differences may also be relevant for the interpretation of age-related differences in hemodynamic signals.

A second problem—shared equally by hemodynamic and electrophysiological measures—arises when the signal-to-noise ratio (SNR) of a measure differs according to age. One reason why the SNR might decline with advancing age that is particularly relevant to memory research employing event-related designs is the greater likelihood of error trials in older subjects. All other things equal, this will result in event-related responses (for correct trials) estimated from fewer trials in older than in younger subjects. Although this will not lead to systematic bias in estimates of response magnitude, it will lead to across-group differences in their reliability (that is, their associated standard errors). In particular, because the SNR is roughly proportional to the square root of the number of trials over which a response is estimated, the effects of unequal trial numbers across groups could lead to marked differences in the power of within-group contrasts when trial numbers are relatively low (e.g., Huettel & McCarthy, 2001; Desmond & Glover, 2002).

A related issue arises from the finding that response times (RTs) may show more within-subject variability with increasing age (e.g., Hultsch, MacDonald, & Dixon, 2002). In such circumstances, neural responses correlated with RT will demonstrate more temporal jitter in older subjects. As the peak amplitude of an across-trial average is inversely proportional to degree of jitter, such age-related differences in jitter will lead to the relative underestimation of the amplitude of older subjects' averaged responses. This problem is well recognized in the ERP field (Picton et al., 2000), but its impact on the estimation of event-related BOLD responses has yet to be assessed.

The foregoing problems are exacerbated by other factors likely to reduce the SNR in older subjects, such as greater incidence of extraneous artifacts (e.g., eye-movement in ERP studies, head movement in fMRI) and possibly a signal that is inherently noisier or more variable with increasing age (see D'Esposito et al., 1999, and Huettel, Singerman, & McCarthy, 2001, for examples relevant to fMRI; but see also Morcom, Henson, et al., 2003). Thus, unless steps have been taken to ensure that the SNRs are equivalent, considerable caution is needed in the interpretation of ERP or fMRI studies that find null or attenuated effects in one age group relative to the other. In fMRI studies, this caution appears to be especially warranted in the interpretation of age-related differences in the spatial extent of an experimental effect (i.e., the number of voxels in which the effect crosses a given significance threshold) (Huettel & McCarthy, 2001; Huettel, Singerman, & McCarthy, 2001).

As mentioned, additional complexity is introduced into the interpretation of hemodynamic measures such as the BOLD response because of their indirect nature. Specifically, if the coupling between neural and hemodynamic activity varies with age (for example, because of the effects of aging on vascular elasticity; see Kalaria, 1996, for review), it may be difficult to determine whether age-related differences in a hemodynamic measure should be attributed to neural activity or to the associated vascular response. It is important to note, however, that even if the coupling is not constant with age, there remain circumstances in which meaningful conclusions can be still drawn on the basis of age-related differences in hemodynamic responses. In particular, there are certain kinds of dissociation that are difficult, if not impossible, to account for in purely vascular terms.

Two examples of such dissociations are illustrated in figure 6.2. Figure 6.2a depicts a hypothetical scenario in which responses in the same brain region show opposite aging effects in each of two experimental conditions. Crossover interactions such as this can confidently be interpreted in neural terms. Figure 6.2b illustrates differential effects found in homotopic regions of each hemisphere. Under the plausible assumption that age-related changes in vascular reactivity are not systematically lateralized, this scenario also is unlikely to be explicable in terms of differential vascular responses. These two examples highlight the importance of designing functional neuroimaging studies so that the crucial predictions are expressed in terms of age-by-condition interactions rather than main effects. In general, the more convinc-

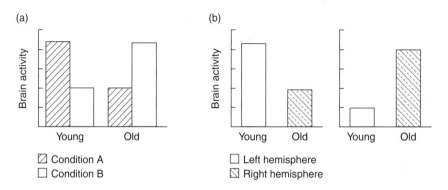

Figure 6.2. Idealized dissociations between measurements of brain activity in younger and older subjects; the *y* axes show estimated brain activity (arbitrary units). *a*, Age group by condition interaction within a region. This pattern, with no significant main effects of age or of task, allows the uniquivocal interpretation of group differences in neural as opposed to hemodynamic terms. (For a discussion of the interpretation of interactions in the presence of main effects, for which the scaling between neural and blood oxygen level dependent [BOLD] responses may differ between groups, see Shallice's 1988 discussion of analogous issues in the interpretation of data from neuropsychological lesion studies.) *b*, Age group-by-hemisphere interactions, for which the same argument applies (given that assumptions about vascular reactivity within a region also hold across homotopic regions; see text).

ingly an aging effect on a hemodynamic measure can be demonstrated as condition specific, the more immune it is from a nonneural interpretation (see D'Esposito et al., 1999, and Buckner et al., 2000, for further discussion of the value of interactions in neuroimaging research on aging).

Subject Selection

Turning to the question of subject populations, we believe that an important current priority is to identify neural correlates of cognitive aging that are unlikely to be attributable either to frank age-associated pathology or, inasmuch as this is possible, to cognitive decline of more subtle pathological origin. Thus, not only should subjects be screened for such conditions as Alzheimer's disease and other dementing illnesses, but also efforts should be made to exclude individuals with risk factors or medical histories associated with other conditions that might have cognitive impairment as a concomitant. Of course, one might plausibly argue that all age-related changes in cognitive performance result from pathology. From this perspective, the strategy advocated above would lead ultimately to the selection of older individuals whose cognitive functioning was the equivalent of that in young subjects and would provide no insights into the nature of cognitive aging. In our view, the strength of this argument turns on the definition of pathology that is employed, specifically, whether the term is used to refer to *any* form of age-associated biological degradation or is reserved instead for age-associated biological changes that are abnormally accelerated or part of a disease process. We believe that, for the time being at least, the latter definition is the more useful.

In our own work described below, the samples of older subjects consist of individuals—typically retired professionals—who, in addition to meeting the above criteria, are well matched to university students regarding educational history and indices of crystallized intelligence. Such individuals (sometimes referred to as the *superelderly*) are of course by no means typical of similarly aged members of the general population (any more than undergraduates are representative of young people generally). In our view, the value of research with such individuals is that any age-related differences observed likely represent the lower bound of effects that can be attributed to nonpathological aging. The extent to which such differences are exaggerated or accompanied by additional effects in less highly selected older individuals can be addressed subsequently.

Issues Specific to Aging Effects on Episodic Memory

As has been noted many times, one advantage of functional imaging studies of memory (regardless of method) over purely behavioral investigations lies in the fact that data can be obtained separately at the time information is initially encoded into memory as opposed to when it is subsequently retrieved. Thus, questions such as whether age-related effects on memory performance are attributable more to differences in encoding or retrieval operations in principle can be addressed directly. It is important, however, not to lose sight of the fact that, although encoding and retrieval can be operationalized in the laboratory as separate stages in memory processing, this does not necessarily mean that they do not share processes in common or interact in important ways.

For example, as was pointed out by Tulving and colleagues, among others (Tulving et al., 1994), inasmuch as a stimulus event is interpreted in terms of its meaning, its encoding is intimately associated with retrieval of information, albeit from semantic rather than episodic memory. Also, the retrieval of episodic information and, indeed, the mere presentation of a stimulus that triggers a retrieval attempt (a retrieval cue), are events that may themselves be subject to episodic encoding

Encoding

We define *encoding* as processing engaged at the time an event is experienced that renders it accessible on a later memory test. A key question concerns how such processing and its neural correlates differ with age. We start by discussing what we view as the criteria that should ideally be met by studies addressing this question and then describe an fMRI study in which an attempt was made to fulfill these methodological requirements.

Criteria

Control Over Study Processing   A number of studies have suggested that younger and older individuals spontaneously adopt different encoding strategies in intentional memory tasks in that younger subjects are more likely to encode items elaboratively in terms of their semantic attributes, whereas older individuals are more likely to employ nonelaborative, rote-based strategies (Craik & Simon, 1980). These findings are of obvious relevance to the broader question of the factors contributing to age-related changes in memory function. In the present context, however, they serve to emphasize the importance of effecting control over study processing; there is little to be gained from encoding studies in which age-related neural differences are confounded with, say, the adoption of elaborative versus nonelaborative processing strategies (see the introductory section).

We suggest that studies of encoding should employ (1) incidental study tasks that are sufficiently constrained to ensure qualitatively similar cognitive processes are engaged in different age groups and (2) measures of performance that permit the rejection of study trials associated with errors or other evidence of a failure to engage fully in the study task (e.g., atypical RTs).

Unconfound Task- and Encoding-Related Activity   A number of studies investigating the neural correlates of memory encoding have done so by contrasting the activity associated with engagement in tasks chosen because of their differential effects on subsequent memory (e.g., deep vs. shallow tasks; see Buckner, Kelley, & Petersen, 1999, for a review). Such contrasts are likely to confound differences in activity because of differential encoding with differences associated with the myriad other processes that differ between any pair of tasks (Otten, Henson, & Rugg, 2001). This is problematic for the interpretation of findings in aging studies, for which the contribution to an age-by-task interaction of neural activity directly related to encoding will be difficult, if not impossible, to separate from the contribution of other aspects of differential task-related activity and may be confounded with group differences in memory performance.

This problem can be avoided by identifying encoding-related activity within rather than across tasks. This can be achieved with the subsequent memory procedure (see Paller & Wagner, 2002, for a review). In this procedure, event-related activity elicited by a series of study items is contrasted according to whether the items were remembered or forgotten on a subsequent memory test; the assumption is that differences in activity that predict successful versus unsuccessful memory reflect the differential engagement of processes supporting effective encoding.

Clearly, there are circumstances when this assumption is likely to be invalid or when such differences would convey only trivial information about memory encoding. For example, if subjects attended to only some study items while ignoring others, there likely would be a strong correlation between the engagement of attentional processes and subsequent memory performance. Thus, the resulting subsequent memory effects would largely reflect differences in neural activity related to differential allocation of attention rather than to differences connected more directly to memory encoding.

The likelihood of such factors contributing to subsequent memory effects can be assessed by comparing study task performance according to subsequent memory; for example, if subsequently remembered items were found to attract shorter RTs than forgotten items, this would constitute evidence in favor of an attentional effect of the kind outlined here. Assuming that effects such as these can be discounted, studies employing the subsequent memory procedure offer what is arguably the most direct means of identifying the neural correlates of successful encoding and of determining how these correlates differ according to age.

Contrast Equivalent Forms of Memory in Older and Younger Individuals   Memory tests are not necessarily "process pure" and can instead reflect the influence of multiple, functionally distinct forms of memory (Jacoby & Kelley, 1992). When comparing the neural correlates of memory-related processing across different age groups, it is therefore necessary to ensure that like is compared with like, in other words, that there is no confound between age and the kind of memory supporting test performance.

Of particular relevance in this regard is the large body of evidence (reviewed in Yonelinas, 2001) suggesting that recognition memory—tests of which are widely employed in functional neuroimaging studies—is supported by two forms of memory, only one of which can properly be considered episodic. The two types of memory are the retrieval of contextually specific information about a test item's study episode (episodic retrieval or recollection) and an undifferentiated, acontextual sense of familiarity (providing a nonepisodic basis for judging prior occurrence). Because recollection and familiarity make independent contributions to recognition, there is no guarantee that the recognition performance of older and younger individuals will reflect equivalent contributions from these two forms of memory even when performance is matched.

This has important implications for the use of recognition memory to study subsequent memory effects. Because recollection appears to decline more rapidly with age than familiarity (Yonelinas, 2001), subsequent memory effects in young and older individuals will be weighted in favor of activity associated with recognition based on recollection in the young, but in favor of familiarity-based recognition in older groups. In turn, this will compromise the identification of age-related differences in neural activity associated specifically with episodic encoding.

This problem can largely be avoided by the employment of procedures that allow recollection-based recognition judgments (i.e., judgments associated with episodic retrieval) to be identified. This can be achieved in a variety of ways, for example, by requiring positive recognition responses to be accompanied by a subsequent remember/know or source memory judgment (e.g., Friedman & Trott, 2000). A difficulty with the former procedure, however, is that younger and older adults may employ different criteria when making remember versus know judgments (see the section on retrieval and Mark & Rugg, 1998). Another approach is to use confidence ratings, although this procedure also is less than ideal (see the section on retrieval).

Unconfound Effects Caused by Age and Performance   For any particular study task, older subjects will usually remember fewer items than young subjects, likely reflecting, at least in part, less-effective encoding on the part of the older individuals. Thus, if brain activity elicited by study items is not segregated according to subsequent memory, age-related differences will be confounded with the neural correlates of effective versus ineffective encoding. This problem is ameliorated by the use of event-related designs, which enable a comparison of the neural correlates specifically of successful memory encoding across age groups.

However, a subtler problem remains. If subsequent memory performance is worse in older than younger individuals, the items remembered by the older group may be comparable only to a subset of the items remembered by the younger subjects. For example, older subjects might tend to retrieve only those items that are particularly memorable, perhaps because they are easy to image or to associate with other information in memory. Under such circumstances, age-related differences in encoding-related activity run the risk of being confounded with differences because of item effects. One way to overcome this problem is to incorporate a difficulty manipulation into the experimental design, allowing differences in subsequent memory effects caused by variation in item memorability to be dissociated from differences caused by aging.

Age and Episodic Encoding: A Functional Magnetic Resonance Imaging Study

In a recent study we attempted to adhere to the criteria in the preceding section (Morcom, Good, et al., 2003). Young (mean age 21 years) and older (mean age 68 years) subjects ($N = 14$ in each group) made animate/inanimate judgments on a series of words as fMRI images were obtained. Subsequent memory was tested with yes/no recognition using two levels of response confidence. Memory for half of the study items was tested approximately 10 min after the end of the study phase (short delay), and memory for the remainder of the items was tested some 30 min later (long delay).

The rationale for the delay manipulation was twofold. First, it allowed an assessment of whether subsequent memory effects vary according to the difficulty of the retrieval task. Second, it permitted the effects of age to be investigated under conditions for which memory performance was matched across groups, achieved by contrasting the older subjects' subsequent memory effects for the short delay with the effects obtained for the younger subjects at the long delay. The validity of this contrast and the effects of the difficulty manipulation are both apparent in figure 6.3, in which it can be seen that recognition performance for confident judgments demonstrated additive effects of age and delay. Nonconfident recognition barely exceeded chance levels of performance.

fMRI subsequent memory effects were obtained by contrasting the activity elicited by study items that were subsequently confidently recognized with the activity elicited by items that were recognized nonconfidently or misclassified as new. By defining confident recognition judgments as remembered and all other responses to study words as forgotten, we aimed to bias the subsequent memory effects in favor of episodic remembering (recollection is almost invariably associated with highly confident responding; Yonelinas, 2001). However, because familiarity alone can also support confident recognition (Yonelinas, 2001), we concede that this procedure is not as satisfactory as more direct methods for identifying recognition judgments associated with recollection (see the section on encoding criteria). Study trials associated with incorrect animacy decisions were excluded.

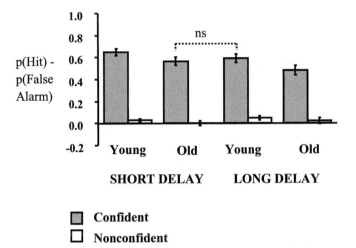

Figure 6.3. Subsequent memory performance in the study of aging and episodic encoding of Morcom, Good, et al. (2003). Across both delays, recognition memory was significantly more accurate for the younger than for the older group, and this effect of age was unmodified by confidence or test delay. Comparison of recognition performance for younger subjects at the long memory test delay with that of older subjects at the short delay confirmed that there was no significant age difference in the accuracy of confident responses. ns, nonsignificant.

Age-invariant subsequent memory effects are illustrated in plate 6.1 (see color insert). These effects were identified by collapsing data across age groups and test delay and excluding any voxels for which subsequent memory effects interacted either with age or delay. As is evident from the figure, effects were found in widespread cortical regions, including much of the left inferior frontal gyrus. Age-invariant effects were also observed in the left anterior medial temporal lobe (MTL), including the hippocampus. Prior studies investigating the neural correlates of the encoding of visually presented words in young subjects also identified subsequent memory effects in these regions (left inferior prefrontal cortex: Wagner et al., 1998; Kirchhoff et al., 2000; Baker et al., 2001; Otten & Rugg, 2001; Otten, Henson, & Rugg, 2001; left MTL: Kirchhoff et al., 2000; Otten, Henson, & Rugg, 2001). The present findings replicate these results and suggest that they hold equally in older subjects. Thus, there is no evidence that successful episodic encoding in older individuals involves the relative disengagement of regions that are thought to play a core role in (semantically mediated) episodic encoding in the young.

Plate 6.2 (see color insert) illustrates an anterior temporal region in which subsequent memory effects were found to vary with age. Plate 6.2a shows the outcome of an analysis that identified voxels demonstrating an interaction between subsequent memory and age unmodified by the delay factor. Plate 6.2b illustrates the outcome of the contrast between the subsequent memory effects in each age group for the two cells in which performance was matched (i.e., short delay in the older subjects, long delay in the young). This contrast identified a cluster of voxels overlapping the cluster revealed by the full analysis.

On the basis of neuroimaging findings and the observation that degeneration of this region is an early correlate of semantic dementia, Price (2000) proposed that the temporal region highlighted in plate 6.2 supports cognitive operations necessary for highly differentiated semantic processing. It is possible, therefore, that the present findings indicate that, despite the imposition of an incidental task, the older individuals subjected the study items to less-differentiated processing than the young subjects did (cf. Craik, 2000). Thus, in the younger group only, items subjected to differentiated semantic processing were encoded more effectively (as evidenced by the subsequent memory effects in the anterior temporal region). Importantly, the present findings suggest that this age-related encoding effect is not a consequence of differential memory performance, implying that it does not merely reflect a difference confined to items that are relatively hard to remember.

A final issue arising from these data relates to age-related differences in the lateralization of subsequent memory effects. In studies investigating a variety of different tasks, prefrontal activation has been reported to be more bilateral in older than in younger individuals (the so-called HAROLD [hemispheric asymmetry reduction in older adults] pattern; see Cabeza, 2002, and chapter 15 for review and discussion). To investigate this question, we compared the magnitudes of the prefrontal subsequent memory effects from each hemisphere of our younger and older subjects. To avoid bias in the selection of the regions in which to make these measurements, three homotopic pairs of voxels were selected, each corresponding to one of the three left prefrontal locations where subsequent memory effects were maximal in a previous study (Otten, Henson, & Rugg, 2001). The data are illustrated in figure 6.4, in which it can be seen that they clearly exhibit the general pattern reported in previous studies: Subsequent memory effects are strongly left lateralized in the young subjects, but are bilateral in older individuals. Moreover, this pattern was unmodified by the factor of task difficulty.

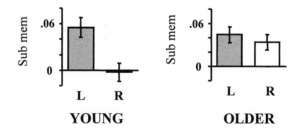

Figure 6.4. Lateralization of subsequent memory (Sub mem) effects in prefrontal cortex according to age in aging and encoding study. Graphs show subsequent memory effects, that is, difference in activity elicited by remembered versus forgotten items, averaged across 3 voxels in left (L)/right (R) Brodmann area (BA) 47, BA 45, and BA 9/44.

These findings extend previous results in two ways. First, they demonstrate that HAROLD applies to item-related activity (previous studies reporting this pattern have invariably employed blocked designs, thus confounding item- with state-related activity; see the introductory section). Second, they indicate that the HAROLD principle extends beyond across-task differences to encompass within-task effects that are correlated with the efficiency of a specific cognitive operation or operations (in the present case, operations linked to episodic encoding).

With reference to the criteria outlined in the section on the encoding criteria, there are three important caveats to the interpretation of these findings. One has been alluded to already: Because confident recognition judgments are not associated invariably with episodic retrieval, it is possible that some of the age-related differences noted here reflect a greater reliance in older than younger individuals on familiarity-based memory. To address this concern, it will be necessary to repeat the study using a more selective procedure for identifying items subsequently recognized on the basis of recollection.

A second problem arises out of the proposed interpretation given to the finding of greater anterior temporal subsequent memory effects in the young subjects. If, as implied by this interpretation, study items were processed differently by the young and older subjects (i.e., the items were subject to more semantic differentiation by the young), then the experiment failed to equate study processing in the two age groups.

The third caveat arises out of the difficulty manipulation that was employed. A crucial assumption underlying this manipulation is that, in each age group, qualitatively equivalent encoding operations supported memory at the two delays such that all that varied between the delays was the accessibility of the study items. If this assumption is invalid, the rationale for the contrast between the older subjects' subsequent memory effects at the short delay and the young subjects' effects at the long delay no longer holds. The failure to find any theoretically relevant differences in subsequent memory effects as a function of delay does, however, lend support to the assumption.

Retrieval

Retrieval from episodic memory involves an interaction between a retrieval cue (either self-generated or provided by the environment) and a memory trace (Tulving, 1983), leading to the reconstruction of aspects of the episode represented by the trace. The retrieval of episodic information provides the rememberer with knowledge about both the content of a prior event and contextual information such as where and when the event was experienced. Whether an episodic retrieval attempt is successful is influenced by numerous factors, not least how the event was initially encoded into memory (Craik & Lockhart, 1972; see the preceding section). Also important are the cues available and the processes engaged during the retrieval attempt.

According to Rugg and Wilding (2000), episodic retrieval depends on the engagement of several functionally distinct processes. Rugg and Wilding identified three kinds of preretrieval process: (1) retrieval mode, a cognitive state that causes events to be processed specifically as episodic retrieval cues (Wheeler, Stuss, & Tulving, 1997); (2) retrieval effort, the mobilization of processing and attentional resources in service of a retrieval attempt; and (3) retrieval orientation, the bias to process retrieval cues to meet the demands of a given retrieval task (e.g., Rugg, Allen, & Birch 2000; Robb & Rugg, 2002). These three kinds of process are held to operate regardless of whether a retrieval attempt is successful. In addition, there exist post-retrieval processes that support the recovery and representation of episodic information and its subsequent evaluation. These processes are engaged primarily when a retrieval attempt is successful, that is, when a cue initiates "synergistic ecphory" (Tulving, 1983) and, consequently, a consciously accessible representation of a prior episode.

Studies of the effects of age on retrieval processing have to deal with many of the same issues noted in the section on encoding. A number of other considerations must also be borne in mind. These arise because of the complexity of the retrieval process and the ensuing multiplicity of ways in which age-related differences in retrieval processing might be manifest. Within the framework outlined here, for example, aging effects might be found in the adoption of an appropriate task set, in cue processing, in ecphoric processes, or in postretrieval processing. Distinguishing between these different processes requires careful attention to experimental design and is difficult to achieve without recourse to event-related methods. As in the case of encoding, we find it helpful to consider systematically the criteria that we think need to be met by aging studies of episodic retrieval.

Criteria

Control Over Study Processing   As with encoding studies, it is important to exercise tight control over study processing, ensuring, as much as possible, that items are processed to a common representational level. In the absence of such control, there is a risk that young and older individuals will encode study items in ways that are qualitatively different. Age differences in neural correlates of retrieval may then say more about the retrieval of different kinds of memory representations than about the effects of age per se.

Unconfound the Neural Correlates of Retrieval Attempt and Retrieval Success
Neural activity associated with a retrieval cue varies markedly according to whether the cue elicits successful retrieval (Rugg & Wilding, 2000). Thus, in designs in which cue-related activity is not assessed separately for trials associated with successful and unsuccessful retrieval, the activity will vary according to performance. This is likely to prove particularly problematic in aging studies, for which it is not uncommon for older subjects to exhibit lower levels of retrieval than young individuals. In such cases, age effects on retrieval-related activity will be confounded with the differential contribution of the effects of retrieval success. This problem can be overcome by the employment of event-related designs, which allow cue-related activity to be separated according to whether retrieval is successful. That said, it is important nonetheless to control for age differences in the level of task performance (see "Unconfound Effects Caused by Age and Performance").

Contrast Equivalent Forms of Memory in Older and Younger Individuals   As noted in the section on contrasting equivalent forms of memory in older and younger individuals, not all direct memory tests are process pure. The case of recognition memory and the importance of distinguishing between recollection- and familiarity-based responding have been discussed. Another important example of an impure test is word stem cued recall, for which partial retrieval cues (e.g., MOT__) are employed to cue memory for study items. It has been demonstrated that cued recall performance is influenced not only by intentional, explicit memory, but also by the same kind of implicit memory that supports priming on word stem completion tasks (Jacoby, Toth, & Yonelinas, 1993).

Age effects on the neural correlates of cued recall, therefore, may merely reflect the differential contribution to performance in the two groups of the two different kinds of memory, of which only one kind corresponds to true episodic memory. One way to obviate this difficulty is to modify the cued recall procedure so that subjects explicitly judge whether each stem completion was a word from the study list. Word stems that are completed by a studied word but judged as unstudied can be assumed to have been completed as a result of either priming or a lucky guess (see Allan & Rugg, 1997; Schott et al., 2002, for examples of the employment of this procedure in neuroimaging contexts).

Unconfound Effects Caused by Age and Performance   The issue of unconfounding effects caused by age and performance was discussed in relation to encoding. In the context of retrieval studies, differential performance raises several problems. First, to the extent that performance differences are associated with inequalities in the subjective experience of the difficulty of the retrieval task, there is a risk that aging effects will be confounded with the effects of differential retrieval effort. For example, if older individuals perceive a retrieval task as more difficult than young subjects do, they may allocate more effort to it, which in turn may add to or masquerade as age differences in retrieval-related activity.

Second, as performance declines, the proportion of trials on which a correct response was caused by chance or very weak memory is likely to increase. On the plausible assumption that trials on which a correct response was because of a lucky guess will not be associated with the neural correlates of successful retrieval, it follows that the trial-averaged neural correlates of retrieval success will be diluted to a greater extent when performance is relatively poor (as in older people) than when it is relatively good (as in young subjects). Thus, even when event-related methods are employed to isolate trials associated with successful retrieval, it is necessary to take the potential influence of this diluting effect into account when there are age-related differences in performance.

Third, it is possible that when only a few items are successfully retrieved, the items are processed differently from when memory is relatively good. For example, postretrieval monitoring may be engaged to a greater extent because of lower confidence (Henson et al., 2000).

Finally, a parallel argument to that outlined in the section on unconfounding these effects for studies of memory encoding applies with respect to item differences.

When older adults retrieve fewer items than younger adults, the neural correlates of successful retrieval may differ between the groups because of the different characteristics of hard- versus easy-to-retrieve items.

Age and Episodic Retrieval: An Event-Related Potential Study

We describe here a study (Mark & Rugg, 1998) that went some way to meet the criteria discussed above. The aim was to investigate whether the neural correlates of successful episodic retrieval, as reflected in ERPs, differ either quantitatively or qualitatively according to age. The study took as its starting point previous research on young subjects that suggested that recollection of a prior episode and the use of the content of recollection to guide a discriminative response are associated with a characteristic pattern of ERP modulation (Allan, Wilding, & Rugg, 1998). Relative to ERPs elicited by correctly rejected test items, ERPs elicited by recollected items elicit a phasic positivity with a left parietal maximum and a more sustained positivity with a maximum over the right frontal scalp. The first of these effects is thought to reflect the retrieval and initial representation of episodic information, whereas the second effect has been interpreted as evidence for the engagement of postretrieval evaluation and monitoring processes that operate on the products of a successful retrieval attempt. On the basis of closely analogous fMRI findings, it has been suggested that these two effects originate from the lateral parietal and right prefrontal cortex, respectively (Rugg, Otten, & Henson, 2002).

The study employed young and older subjects ($N = 16$ per group) selected according to the same criteria employed in the encoding experiment described in this chapter. A series of four study–test cycles were undertaken, each comprising an identical study phase and one of two different retrieval tasks. Study items were words presented auditorily in either a male or a female voice. In an effort to ensure uniformity of encoding in the two subject groups and to promote good memory, the requirement on hearing each word was to repeat it aloud, name the gender of the voice, and perform one of two judgments ("pleasant/unpleasant" or "active/passive") depending on gender.

At test, studied and unstudied words were presented visually, each requiring a yes/no recognition response. In the source task, an item judged old then required a second response to indicate in which context (male vs. female) it had been studied. In the remember/know task, subjects judged whether their recognition response was accompanied (remember response) or unaccompanied (know response) by recollection of any aspect of the study episode.

As can be seen in table 6.1, the two age groups performed at equivalent levels on the initial recognition task and showed equivalent levels of remembering. In keeping with previous findings (Spencer & Raz, 1995), however, the older subjects demonstrated lower levels of source memory.

ERP waveforms for each group are shown in figure 6.1 for correctly rejected new items, and for studied items that were both recognized and recollected (as in Rugg, Schloerscheidt, & Mark, 1998), there were no differences according to whether recollection was defined as a remember response or a correct source judgment). The

Table 6.1 Behavioral Performance of Young and Older
Subjects in the Study of Rugg and Mark (1988)

Accuracy	Correct Rejection	Hit	Correct Source/ Remember
Young			
Source task	93	85	89
R/K task	95	84	77
Older			
Source task	90	81	72
R/K task	91	84	76

Correct Rejection and Hit refer to percentage of items correctly classified as
unstudied and studied, respectively. Correct source/remember refers to percentage of hits for which a correct source assignment was made on the source task
or that were endorsed as Remembered in the remember/know (R/K) task.

waveforms from the young subjects demonstrated the left parietal and right frontal
effects characteristically observed in tasks such as these. Qualitatively similar modulations were evident in the older individuals' waveforms, although these effects are
obscured somewhat at frontal electrodes by the marked age-related differences that
exist in general waveform morphology. Statistical analysis revealed that neither the
magnitude nor onset latency of the frontal effect differed between the groups. The
same held true for the magnitude of the left parietal effect; its onset latency, however, was delayed by around 100 ms in the older subjects.

These findings can be well appreciated in figure 6.5, which displays the relevant
subtraction waveforms. The scalp distributions of the effects are illustrated in figure

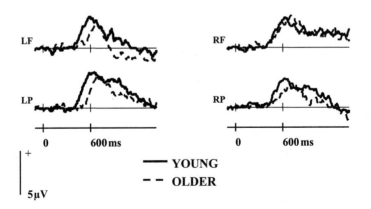

Figure 6.5. Grand average subtraction waveforms for young and
older subjects in the retrieval study of Mark and Rugg (1998). Waveforms represent the difference between event-related potentials (ERPs)
elicited by recollected items and those elicited by correctly classified
items for the same electrode sites as in figure 6.1. LF, left frontal; LP,
left parietal; RF, right frontal; RP, right parietal.

6.6. The transition over time from a left parietal to a right frontal maximum is clearly evident in the data from the young subjects. A very similar pattern can be seen for the older subjects, and there was no evidence that the distribution of these effects differed according to age.

These findings suggest that the neural correlates of recollection can be remarkably similar in younger and older subjects. Thus, when encoding is sufficiently elaborate and the test task designed to identify trials associated specifically with recollection, there was no evidence that older subjects are disadvantaged relative to the young in respect to their ability to engage processes related to either the representation of retrieved episodic information or its postretrieval processing. Of particular note, in light of other findings in favor of the HAROLD pattern (see the section on age and episodic encoding and chapter 15), was the failure to find any evidence of reduced lateralization in either the left parietal or the right frontal effect in the older subjects.

As with our encoding study, these findings are subject to several caveats. First, the study can be criticized on the grounds that, on one of our measures of recollection, the older subjects performed less well. This raises the possibility that recollection-related effects were to some extent diluted in this group, implying that the magnitude of the effects was underestimated. It is conceivable, therefore, that the neural correlates of retrieval success are actually of greater magnitude in older individuals than in the young.

Second, whereas the findings reported in the present study for the left parietal effect have also been described by others (Trott et al., 1999; Wegesin et al., 2002), this is not the case for the frontal effects. Trott et al. and Wegesin et al. both reported a diminution in the amplitude of these effects in older subjects. Whereas it is currently unclear which of the numerous differences between those studies and the present one is responsible for this disparity, their findings substantially qualify our conclusion that frontally mediated, recollection-related processing is unaffected by age.

Finally, it is important to note that our findings do not necessarily imply that the age-related decline in episodic memory function is primarily attributable to an impairment in encoding (despite the suggestion to this effect in Mark & Rugg, 1998). Even if it transpires that the cognitive operations engaged when retrieval is successful differ little with age, other aspects of retrieval processing may nonetheless undergo important age-related changes. In particular, studies such as that described here give no insight into possible changes in the way retrieval cues are processed. The probability of successful retrieval depends to a large extent on whether the processing applied to a retrieval cue overlaps with or recapitulates the processing engaged at the time of encoding (Morris, Bransford, & Franks, 1977; Tulving & Thomson, 1973). ERP evidence suggests that young subjects vary the way they process retrieval cues according to the nature of the information sought (Robb & Rugg, 2002; Herron & Rugg, 2003). We have found that these ERP retrieval orientation effects are delayed and attenuated in older subjects (Morcom & Rugg, in press) suggesting that the capacity to adjust cue processing to meet different retrieval demands declines with age. We think it is likely that the investigation of cue processing will prove a fertile area to further the understanding of age-related differences in memory retrieval.

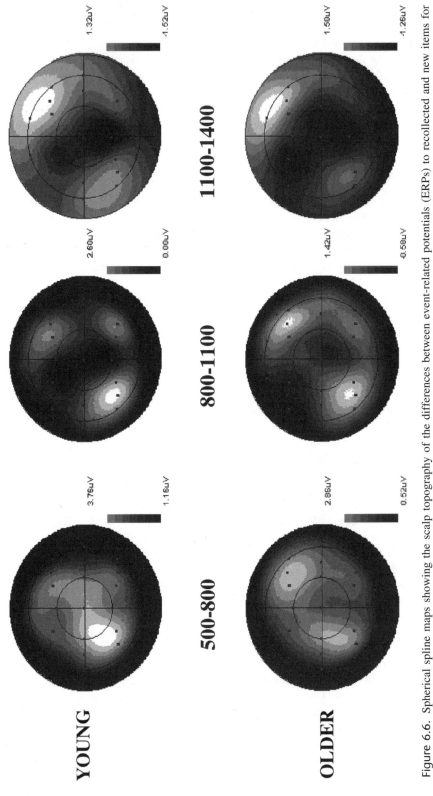

Figure 6.6. Spherical spline maps showing the scalp topography of the differences between event-related potentials (ERPs) to recollected and new items for younger and older groups in the study of Mark and Rugg (1998).

Conclusions

We have outlined what we believe to be some of the important issues in the design of studies investigating age-related changes in the neural correlates of episodic memory. We hope that the general principles that lie behind our specific proposals are useful for the study of aging in other cognitive domains. Motivating the criteria outlined in the section on issues specific to aging effects on episodic memory is the view that elucidation of how the neural correlates of a cognitive function differ with age is not well served by studies in which age is confounded with variables that independently affect task-related neural activity, such as cognitive strategy or level of performance. When such confounding occurs, findings of age-related effects may shed light on how cognitive processes change in efficiency with age and how the cognitive system adapts to these changes. They are unlikely, however, to give more than limited insight into the primary neurobiological changes that underlie cognitive aging.

Acknowledgments   We and our research were supported by the Wellcome Trust.

References

Allan, K., & Rugg, M. D. (1997). An event-related potential study of explicit memory on tests of cued recall and recognition. *Neuropsychologia, 35,* 387–397.

Allan, K., Wilding, E. L., & Rugg, M. D. (1998). Electrophysiological evidence for dissociable processes contributing to recollection. *Acta Psychologica (Amsterdam), 98,* 231–252.

Attwell, D., & Iadecola, C. (2002). The neural basis of functional brain imaging signals. *Trends in Neurosciences, 5,* 621–625.

Baker, J. T., Sanders, A. L., Maccotta, L., & Buckner, R. L. (2001). Neural correlates of verbal memory encoding during semantic and structural processing tasks. *Neuroreport, 12,* 1251–1256.

Buckner, R. L., Kelley, W. M., & Petersen, S. E. (1999). Frontal cortex contributes to human memory formation. *Nature Neuroscience, 2,* 311–314.

Buckner, R. L., Snyder, A. Z., Sanders, A. L., Raichle, M. E., & Morris, J. C. (2000). Functional brain imaging of young, nondemented, and demented older adults. *Journal of Cognitive Neuroscience, 12*(Suppl. 2), 24–34.

Cabeza, R. (2002). Hemispheric asymmetry reduction in older adults: The HAROLD model. *Psychology and Aging, 17,* 85–100.

Craik, F. I. M. (2000). Human memory and aging. In L. Backman & C. von Hofsten (Eds.), *Psychology at the turn of the millennium. Volume 1: Cognitive, biological and health perspectives* (pp. 261–280). Stockholm: Psychology Press.

Craik, F. I. M., & Lockhart, R. S. (1972). Levels of processing: A framework for memory research. *Journal of Verbal Learning and Verbal Behaviour, 11,* 671–684.

Craik, F. I. M., & Simon, H. (1980). Age differences in memory: The roles of attention and depth of processing. In L. W. Poon, J. L. Fozard, L. Cermak, D. Arenberg, & L. W. Thompson (Eds.), *New directions in memory and aging: Proceedings of the George A. Talland Memorial Conference* (pp. 95–112). Hillsdale, NJ: Erlbaum.

Dale, A. M., & Buckner, R. L. (1997). Selective averaging of rapidly presented individual trials using fMRI. *Human Brain Mapping, 5,* 329–340.

Desmond, J. E., & Glover, G. H. (2002). Estimating sample size in functional MRI (fMRI) neuroimaging studies: Statistical power analyses. *Journal of Neuroscience Methods, 118,* 115–128.

D'Esposito, M., Zarahn, E., Aguirre, G. K., & Rypma, B. (1999). The effect of normal aging on the coupling of neural activity to the bold hemodynamic response. *Neuroimage, 10,* 6–14.

Donaldson, D. J., Petersen, S. E., Ollinger, J. M., & Buckner, R. L. (2001). Separating state and item related processing during recognition memory using functional MRI. *Neuroimage, 13,* 129–142.

Friedman, D., & Trott, C. (2000). An event-related potential study of encoding in young and older adults. *Neuropsychologia, 38,* 542–557.

Henson, R. N. A., Rugg, M. D., Shallice, T., & Dolan, R. J. (2000). Confidence in recognition memory for words: Dissociating right prefrontal roles in episodic retrieval. *Journal of Cognitive Neuroscience, 12,* 913–923.

Herron, J. E., & Rugg, M. D. (2003). Retrieval orientation and the control of recollection. *Journal of Cognitive Neuroscience, 15,* 843–854.

Huettel, S. A., & McCarthy, G. (2001). The effects of single-trial averaging upon the spatial extent of fMRI activation. *Neuroreport, 12,* 2411–2416.

Huettel, S. A., Singerman, J. D., & McCarthy, G. (2001). The effects of aging upon the hemodynamic response measured by functional MRI. *Neuroimage, 13,* 161–175.

Hultsch, D. F., MacDonald, S. W., & Dixon, R. A. (2002). Variability in reaction time performance of younger and older adults. *Journal of Gerontology B: Psychological Science and Social Science, 57,* 101–115.

Jacoby, L. L., & Kelley, C. (1992). Unconscious influences of memory: Dissociations and automaticity. In A. D. Milner & M. D. Rugg (Eds.), *The neuropsychology of consciousness* (pp. 201–233). London: Academic Press.

Jacoby, L. L., Toth, J. P., & Yonelinas, A. P. (1993). Separating conscious and unconscious influences of memory—Measuring recollection. *Journal of Experimental Psychology: General, 122,* 139–154.

Josephs, O., Turner, R., & Friston, K. (1997). Event-related fMRI. *Human Brain Mapping, 5,* 243–248.

Kalaria, R. N. (1996). Cerebral vessels in ageing and Alzheimer's disease. *Pharmacology and Therapeutics, 72,* 193–214.

Kirchhoff, B. A., Wagner, A. D., Maril, A., & Stern, C. E. (2000), Prefrontal-temporal circuitry for episodic encoding and subsequent memory. *Journal of Neuroscience, 20,* 6173–6180.

Light, L. L. (1991). Memory and aging, four hypotheses in search of data. *Annual Review of Psychology, 42,* 333–376.

Logan, J. M., Sanders, A. L., Snyder, A. Z., Morris, J. C., & Buckner, R. L. (2002). Under-recruitment and nonselective recruitment, dissociable neural mechanisms associated with aging. *Neuron, 33,* 827–840.

Logothetis, N. K., Pauls, J., Augath, M., Trinath, T., & Oeltermann, A. (2001). Neurophysiological investigation of the basis of the fMRI signal. *Nature, 412,* 150–157.

Mark, R. E., & Rugg, M. D. (1998) Age effects on brain activity associated with episodic memory retrieval, an electrophysiological study. *Brain, 121,* 861–873.

Morcom, A. M., Good, C. D., Frackowiak, R. S. J., & Rugg, M. D. (2003). Age effects on the neural correlates of successful memory encoding. *Brain, 126,* 213–229.

Morcom, A. M., Henson, R. N. A., Frackowiak, R. S. J., & Rugg, M. D. (2003, June). Measuring the BOLD response in young and older subjects. Poster presented at 2003 Conference on Human Brain Mapping, New York.

Morcom, A. M., & Rugg, M. D. (in press). Effects of age on retrieval procession as revealed by ERPs. *Neuropsychologia.*

Morris, C. D., Bransford, J. D., & Franks, J. J. (1977). Levels of processing versus transfer appropriate processing. *Journal of Verbal Learning and Verbal Behavior, 16,* 519–533.

Otten, L. J., Henson, R. N. A., & Rugg, M. D. (2001). Depth of processing effects on neural correlates of memory encoding, relationship between findings from across- and within-task comparisons. *Brain, 124,* 399–412.

Otten, L. J., Henson, R. N. A., & Rugg, M. D. (2002). State-related and item-related neural correlates of successful memory encoding. *Nature Neuroscience, 5,* 1339–1344.

Otten, L. J., & Rugg, M. D. (2001). Task-dependency of the neural correlates of episodic encoding as measured by fMRI. *Cerebral Cortex, 11,* 1150–1160.

Paller, K. A., & Wagner, A. D. (2002). Observing the transformation of experience into memory. *Trends in Cognitive Sciences, 6,* 93–102.

Perfect, T. J., Williams, R. B., & Anderton-Brown, C. (1995). Age differences in reported recollective experience are due to encoding effects, not response bias. *Memory, 3,* 169–186.

Picton, T. W., Bentin, S., Berg, P., Donchin, E., Hillyard, S. A., Johnson, R. Jr., Miller, G. A., Ritter, W., Ruchkin, D. S., Rugg, M. D., & Taylor, M. J. (2000). Guidelines for using human event-related potentials to study cognition, recording standards and publication criteria. *Psychophysiology, 37,* 127–152.

Price, C. J. (2000). The anatomy of language, contributions from functional neuroimaging. *Journal of Anatomy, 197,* 335–359.

Robb, W. G. K., & Rugg, M. D. (2002). Electrophysiological dissociation of retrieval orientation and retrieval effort. *Psychonomic Bulletin and Review, 9,* 583–589.

Rugg, M. D. (1998). Convergent approaches to electrophysiological and hemodynamic investigations of memory. *Human Brain Mapping, 6,* 394–398

Rugg, M. D. (1999). Functional neuroimaging in cognitive neuroscience. In C. M. Brown, & P. Hagoort (Eds.), *The neurocognition of language* (pp. 15–36). Oxford: Oxford University Press.

Rugg, M. D., Allan, K., & Birch, C. S. (2000). Electrophysiological evidence for the modulation of retrieval orientation by depth of study processing. *Journal of Cognitive Neuroscience, 12,* 664–678.

Rugg, M. D., Mark, R. E., Walla, P., Schloerscheidt, A. M., Birch, C. S., & Allan, K. (1998). Dissociation of the neural correlates of implicit and explicit memory. *Nature, 392,* 595–598.

Rugg, M. D., Otten, L. J., & Henson, R. N. (2002). The neural basis of episodic memory, evidence from functional neuroimaging. *Philosophical Transactions of the Royal Society of London B: Biological Science, 357,* 1097–1110.

Rugg, M. D., Schloerscheidt, A. M., & Mark, R. E. (1998). An electrophysiological study of two indices of recollection. *Journal of Memory and Language, 39,* 47–49.

Rugg, M. D., & Wilding, E. L. (2000). Retrieval processing and episodic memory. *Trends in Cognitive Sciences, 4,* 108–115.

Schott, B., Richardson-Klavehn, A., Heinze, H. J., & Duzel, E. (2002). Perceptual priming versus explicit memory, dissociable neural correlates at encoding. *Journal of Cognitive Neuroscience, 14,* 578–592.

Shallice, T. (1988). *From neuropsychology to mental structure.* New York: Cambridge University Press.

Spencer, W. D., & Raz, N. (1995). Differential effects of aging on memory for content and context, a meta-analysis. *Psychology and Aging, 10,* 527–539.

Trott, C. T., Friedman, D., Ritter, W., Fabiani, M., & Snodgrass, J. G. (1999). Episodic priming and memory for temporal source, event-related potentials reveal age-related differences in prefrontal functioning. *Psychology and Aging, 14,* 390–413.

Tulving, E. (1983). *Elements of episodic memory.* Oxford, U.K.: Oxford University Press.

Tulving, E., Kapur, S., Craik, F. I. M., Moscovitch, M., & Houle, S. (1994). Hemispheric encoding/retrieval asymmetry in episodic memory, positron emission tomography findings. *Proceedings of the National Academy of Science of the United States of America, 91,* 2016–2020.

Tulving, E., & Thomson, D. M. (1973). Encoding specificity and retrieval processes in episodic memory. *Psychological Review, 80,* 353–373.

Wagner, A. D., Schacter, D. L, Rotte, M. Koustaal, W., Maril, A., Dale, A. M., Rosen, B. R., & Buckner, R. L. (1998). Building memories, remembering and forgetting of verbal experiences as predicted by brain activity. *Science, 21,* 188–191.

Wegesin, D. J., Friedman, D., Varughese, N., & Stern, Y. (2002). Age-related changes in source memory retrieval, an ERP replication and extension. *Brain Research and Cognitive Brain Research, 13,* 323–338.

Wheeler, M. E., Stuss, D. T., & Tulving, E. (1997). Toward a theory of episodic memory: The frontal lobes and autonoetic consciousness. *Psychological Bulletin, 121,* 331–354.

Wood, C. C. (1987). Generators of event-related potentials. In A. M. Halliday, S. R. Butler, & R. Paul (Eds.), *A textbook of clinical neurophysiology* (pp. 535–567). New York: Wiley.

Yonelinas, A. P. (2001). Components of episodic memory, the contribution of recollection and familiarity. *Philosophical Transactions of the Royal Society of London B: Biological Science, 356,* 1363–1374.

Zarahn, E., Aguirre, G., & D'Esposito, M. (1997). A trial-based experimental design for fMRI. *Neuroimage, 6,* 122–138.

II

BASIC COGNITIVE PROCESSES

7

Age-Related Changes in Neural Activity During Visual Perception and Attention

David J. Madden
Wythe L. Whiting
Scott A. Huettel

The identification of objects and events in the environment depends on a variety of information-processing mechanisms that extend over time, however briefly. Consequently, there is not a complete dichotomy between perception and attention. Perceptual processing is initiated at the level of sensory receptors, but the contribution of attention is evident even at the earliest stages of identification. Psychophysical studies, for example, have demonstrated that attending to a specific display location facilitates both threshold-level detection and contextual integration (between a target and surrounding stimuli). These findings imply a modulating role of attention in what are usually considered early-level perceptual processes (Cameron, Tai, & Carrasco, 2002; Freeman, Sagi, & Driver, 2001).

Changes in Early Visual Processing

Age-related change typically occurs in several aspects of perceptual and attentional functioning, even for individuals who are in good health (Madden & Whiting, 2004; McDowd & Shaw, 2000; B. A. Schneider & Pichora-Fuller, 2000). In this chapter, we are concerned primarily with the visual system, although changes occur in the auditory and other sensory systems as well (Fozard & Gordon-Salant, 2001; Kline & Scialfa, 1996). The visual sensory system undergoes several age-related changes, leading to a degradation of the retinal image, including an increase in the density and hardness of the crystalline lens, a decrease in the resting diameter of the pupil, increased opacification of the lens, and loss of receptor cells within the retina (Scialfa, 2002). The result is increased scatter of light within the eye and substantial loss of retinal illuminance. The amount of light reaching a 60-year-old retina may be only one-third the amount reaching a 20-year-old retina (Weale, 1961).

As a consequence of these changes in sensory functioning with age, the initial stages of visual information processing are noisier for older adults than for younger adults. There is an age-related decrease in the rate at which the elementary visual features can be distinguished (Ellis, Goldberg, & Detweiler, 1996; Madden & Allen, 1991), which slows the identification of individual characters. When the presentation duration of a display is limited, the age difference in accuracy is magnified as the number of items in the display increases, reflecting the older adults' slower rate of search through the display items (Davis, Fujawa, & Shikano, 2002; Zacks & Zacks, 1993). This age-related decline in visual feature extraction also interacts with later processing stages, including response selection (Harpur, Scialfa, & Thomas, 1995).

Influence of Perceptual Speed

A prominent theme in behavioral research on aging is that slowing at the perceptual level shares a substantial portion of age-related variance in higher order cognitive measures, such as memory and reasoning, suggesting that a generalized slowing of information processing may underlie many of the observed age-related changes in perceptual and cognitive performance (Madden, 2001; Salthouse, 1996, 2000). Two methodologies have played a particularly important role in the investigation of generalized age-related slowing: Brinley plots and hierarchical regression.

In the Brinley plot methodology (also known as the method of systematic relations), the mean performance of older adults in each task condition is plotted as a function of the corresponding mean for younger adults (Brinley, 1965). When mean reaction time (RT) is the dependent variable, this function has been observed to be highly monotonic, with a slope between 1.5 and 2.0, across a variety of contexts, for the conditions within individual tasks (e.g., Madden, 1988; Salthouse & Somberg, 1982), as well as for meta-analyses of different tasks (Cerella, 1985; Verhaeghen & De Meersman, 1998). Brinley (1965) also applied this methodology to accuracy measures, but subsequent research has focused almost exclusively on RT, and the monotonic relation between the task condition means for older and younger adults has been interpreted as evidence for a generalized age-related slowing of information processing (Cerella, 1990; Myerson et al., 1990).

This conclusion is also supported by the results of hierarchical regression and related techniques (Salthouse, 1985, 1992). In this approach, a measure of elementary perceptual processing, such as digit symbol coding speed, is used as a covariate in the analysis of age–performance relations (i.e., entered before age as an independent variable in the regression model for estimating cognitive performance). That is, the age-related influence on cognitive performance is measured after controlling statistically the age-related variance shared between the cognitive measure and elementary perceptual processing. This research has suggested that perceptual speed is a pervasive underlying dimension of cognitive performance, and that the unique influences of age, independent of the speed dimension, are relatively few in number and small in magnitude (Salthouse, 2000; Verhaeghen & Salthouse, 1997). Alternative interpretations of the data obtained from Brinley plots and hierarchical regression have been discussed by Fisk and Fisher (1994), Allen et al. (2001), and Piccinin and Rabbitt (1999).

The relation between sensory functioning and higher order cognitive abilities has provided additional evidence for a single underlying dimension to cognitive aging. In the context of a large-scale longitudinal study of adults 70–103 years of age, visual and auditory acuity accounted for 93% of the age-related variance on a battery of cognitive tests representing speed, reasoning, knowledge, memory, and fluency (Baltes & Lindenberger, 1997; Lindenberger & Baltes, 1994). Interestingly, this result emerged even though the sensory measures were obtained while participants used their best current corrections for visual and auditory deficits (i.e., glasses and hearing aids). Further analyses indicated that balance and gait were as effective as vision and hearing in accounting for age-related variance in the cognitive measures, whereas general health and education were less successful as predictors. Salthouse et al. (1996) corroborated these results and demonstrated that nearly 89% of the age-related variance in working memory and other cognitive measures was shared with both corrected visual acuity and perceptual speed. This pattern of results suggests that age-related changes in sensory functioning, perceptual speed, and cognitive performance all derive from a "common cause" that is most likely a general decline in the efficiency of central nervous system functioning.

One manifestation of this general age-related change is that visuospatial abilities are less differentiated for older adults than for younger adults. Principal components analyses of younger adults' performance on a battery of speeded cognitive tests suggested that tasks that involve the identification of visual features of objects rely on a different set of abilities than tasks that involve the spatial relations among objects (Chen et al., 2000). This pattern of individual differences in behavioral measures corresponds to the distinction between ventral (object identification) and dorsal (spatial localization) pathways in visual cortical regions, which have been identified on the basis of anatomical and neuroimaging research (Ungerleider & Mishkin, 1982). Chen, Myerson, and Hale (2002) reported that a principal components analysis of older adults' performance on a battery of visual tests yielded only a single common factor rather than a differentiation into object identification and spatial tasks as in the younger adults' data. These results suggest that aging is associated with a dedifferentiation of visuospatial abilities, that is, a decrease in the extent to which these abilities are mediated by distinct neural pathways.

Attention

It has been long recognized that attentional tasks are particularly difficult for older adults (Rabbitt, 1965). Tasks that involve either dividing attention among multiple display items (Madden, Pierce, & Allen, 1996; Plude & Hoyer, 1986) or switching between different types of decisions on successive trials (Kramer, Hahn, & Gopher, 1999; Mayr, 2001) are fairly consistent in eliciting age-related decline. Several theories have been developed regarding age-related changes in attentional abilities. An active area of investigation currently is executive control, which includes a variety of processes such as updating and maintaining information in working memory, shifting mental sets, and the intentional inhibition of irrelevant information (Miyake et al., 2000). The relevant abilities form a disparate set, however, and it is difficult to determine the boundary that distinguishes executive control from related perceptual and memory abilities.

One commonality among executive control processes is that they are the types of abilities particularly vulnerable to disruption by damage to prefrontal cortical regions (Duncan et al., 1997). West and colleagues have proposed that age-related changes in many forms of attention may be the result of an age-related decline in the functioning of the prefrontal cortex (West, 1996; West et al., 2002). These authors reported considerable evidence in support of a prefrontal theory, but one difficulty in testing this theory with behavioral measures is that neuropsychological tests designed to assess prefrontal functioning share substantial variance with tests designed to assess other cortical regions (Salthouse, Fristoe, & Rhee, 1996). Similarly, because executive control processes are diverse, it is difficult to distinguish age-related changes in these processes from the generalized slowing discussed previously (McDowd & Craik, 1988; Salthouse & Miles, 2002). The close relation between executive functioning and speed suggests that deep gray matter regions related to sensory–motor integration, such as the basal ganglia and thalamus, may be at least as important as the frontal lobe in relation to age-related cognitive change (Hicks & Birren, 1970; Rubin, 1999).

Age-related decline in a specific component of executive control, inhibitory functioning, has also been an active area of investigation. Hasher, Zacks, and colleagues have proposed that an age-related decline in the ability to inhibit irrelevant information is a determinant of age differences in several types of cognitive tasks, especially those relying on working memory (Hasher & Zacks, 1988; May, Kane, & Hasher, 1995). As for executive control functions in general, it is difficult to distinguish age-related changes in inhibition from those associated with perceptual speed (Shilling, Chetwynd, & Rabbitt, 2002). Evidence suggesting a specific age-related inhibitory decline has been obtained in some experiments estimating the time required to inhibit currently activated responses using a stop-signal paradigm (Bedard et al., 2002; Kramer, Humphrey, Lavish, Logan, & Stayer, 1994).

The evidence that is perhaps most widely regarded as supporting an age-related decline in inhibition has been obtained from investigations of the Stroop task. In this task, participants attempt to name colors of display items, and in an interference condition, the display items are color words that conflict with the correct naming response (e.g., the word *red* printed in green). Several experiments have reported that Stroop interference is disproportionately greater for older adults than for younger adults (Brink & McDowd, 1999; Hartley, 1993; Spieler, Balota, & Faust, 1996). A Brinley plot analysis of 20 studies of age differences in Stroop interference, however, suggested that the age-related changes in this task are consistent with generalized age-related slowing (Verhaeghen & De Meersman, 1998). Other measures of distraction by irrelevant information during perceptual tasks (e.g., negative priming, inhibition of return) have not varied reliably as a function of adult age, as would be predicted from an inhibitory-deficit model (Kramer et al., 1994; Kramer, Hahn, Irwin, & Theeuwes, 1999).

Experiments investigating dual-task performance suggested that processes related to response selection represent an attentional bottleneck that is particularly affected by aging. In this approach, two stimuli requiring separate responses are presented in close succession (e.g., a shape discrimination response to the first stimulus, followed by a lexical decision response to the second stimulus), and interpretation focuses on the change in RT to the second stimulus as a function of its temporal interval between the stimuli (Pashler, 1994). The results indicate that attention cannot be allocated to a second response until a first response is completed. This psychological refractory period effect tends to be greater in magnitude for older adults than for younger adults, suggesting that a response selection bottleneck is vulnerable to age-related decline (Allen et al., 1998; Hartley & Little, 1999). The age difference can be eliminated, however, if the two responses use different modalities (e.g., vocal and manual), implying that the attentional bottleneck is localized to the generation of a specific motor program (Hartley, 2001).

Age Constancy in Attentional Functioning

Although we have focused primarily on age-related decline, several aspects of attentional functioning appear to exhibit a constancy during adulthood. Surprisingly, some exceptions to age-related decline are evident in measures of processing speed, which as noted in this section is also the category of measures exhibiting the most reliable age-related change. An age constancy has been observed in several RT experiments that have varied the temporal interval between a task-relevant cue and a subsequent visual display. RT to the display typically decreases as the cue–display interval increases (to some asymptote determined by specific task demands), representing a time course of attentional preparation.

Hartley, Kieley, and Slabach (1990) examined several different types of cues and found that, although RT was higher overall for older adults than for younger adults, the time course associated with the cuing effects was comparable for the two age groups. Similar findings have been reported by Nissen and Corkin (1985) and Folk and Hoyer (1992). In these experiments, the metric for the time course effects was an independent variable manipulated by the investigators (cue–display interval) rather than a dependent variable, RT, associated with participants' responses. Thus, the overall higher RT for older adults may be in large part caused by encoding and response selection processes discussed here. These processes are nonetheless attentional, but distinct from the preparatory component defined by the cue–display time course.

The allocation of attention to spatial location also exhibits some degree of age constancy. When a cue indicates the spatial location of a target item in a visual display, the overall magnitude of improvement in RT (as well as the time course), associated with the presence of a valid cue, is frequently comparable for younger and older adults (Madden & Plude, 1993; Madden & Whiting, 2004; Plude & Hoyer, 1986). Similarly, estimates of the time required to shift attention across multiple display locations are similar for younger and older adults, although age-related slowing tends to increase as additional demands are placed on visual feature discrimination and eye movements (Madden, 1990, 1992; Scialfa, Thomas, & Joffe, 1994). The age constancy in the spatial allocation of attention in addition can modulate the age effects in other attentional demands. Hartley (1993) demonstrated that when the conflicting elements of a Stroop task display were separated spatially (i.e., the conflicting color word was located either directly above or below a to-be-named block of color), the age-related increase in Stroop interference was virtually eliminated. The opportunity to engage spatial selective attention in this instance can reduce the task demands that lead to age-related performance decline.

This age constancy in spatial selective attention is related to the more general issue of attentional control in the sense of observers using various aspects of a visual display to guide performance (Wolfe, 1998). When, for example, multiitem displays can be segregated into subsets on the basis of color (Nebes & Madden, 1983; Plude & Doussard-Roosevelt, 1989), shape (Madden, Pierce, & Allen, 1996), motion (Kramer et al., 1996), or apparent depth (Atchley & Kramer, 1998, 2000), older adults are frequently as successful as younger adults in using these display properties to improve the search for a target item. These forms of attentional guidance rely heavily on local changes in the physical properties of the display and are thus primarily "bottom-up" processes. Some evidence suggests that when selective attention relies on "top-down" processes that are dependent on participants' knowledge of the task structure, older adults are less efficient than younger adults in using the relevant information to improve performance (Folk & Lincourt, 1996). Although little research is available on this issue currently, an age-related decline in top-down selective attention would be consistent with the research on executive control discussed here.

Neuroimaging of Visual Perception and Attention

Neuroimaging Studies of Younger Adults

Neuroimaging studies of visual perception and attention have used positron emission tomography (PET) and functional magnetic resonance imaging (fMRI) to measure task-related changes in brain metabolic activity (regional cerebral blood flow [rCBF] in the case of PET and the blood oxygen level dependent [BOLD] signal in the case of fMRI). Two key themes have emerged from this research with the younger adult population. First, functionally distinct neural pathways in the occipital, temporal, and parietal lobes modulate different aspects of bottom-up visual perception, consistent with single-unit studies in animal models. Second, attentional control systems located primarily in prefrontal and parietal cortical regions exert top-down influence in the visual cortical pathways, demonstrating the integration of attentional and perceptual systems in the brain. The interplay between determinate, bottom-up perceptual mechanisms and goal-directed, top-down attentional mechanisms forms the basis for visual experience.

Perception

Evidence from anatomical and single-unit electrophysiological studies, primarily of nonhuman primates, suggests that the visual system exhibits both small-scale (local) and large-scale (global) organization. At the local level, individual neurons respond selectively to specific object properties such as shape, color, and texture (Desimone

& Ungerleider, 1989). Both the receptive field size and the complexity of the relevant feature tend to increase between primary visual cortex (V1, or Brodmann area [BA] 17) and the more anterior regions of the occipitotemporal pathway, suggesting a neural mechanism for bottom-up processing of visual object identification.

At the global level, the processing of distinct object attributes is mediated by two posterior cortical pathways that diverge from primary visual cortex: a ventral, occipitotemporal pathway and a dorsal, occipitoparietal pathway. One characterization of these pathways is that they represent the differential processing of information for object identity (ventral) and spatial location (dorsal) or "what" versus "where" processing, respectively (Ungerleider & Mishkin, 1982). An alternative characterization of the two pathways emphasizes the role of visual information in movement control (Goodale, 2000; Goodale & Milner, 1992). In this last theory, both pathways process identity and spatial information but use the information differently. In both of these differing interpretations of the global organization of visual cortex, connections from prefrontal cortex to both the dorsal and ventral pathways, as well as reciprocal connections within the pathways, provide a basis for top-down attentional control of perceptual processing.

Neuroimaging investigations have confirmed the global distinction between the dorsal and ventral processing pathways, and individual experiments lend support to the interpretation of this distinction in terms of both what/where processing (Haxby et al., 1991) and movement control (Passingham & Toni, 2001). Neuroimaging experiments have also provided extensive evidence of local organization within the ventral and dorsal pathways. Studies using PET demonstrated that changes in elementary sensory variables of a visual display, such as stimulus intensity and rate, affect activation of primary visual cortex selectively (Fox & Raichle, 1984, 1985), and these results were confirmed and extended with fMRI (W. Schneider, Noll, & Cohen, 1993; W. Schneider, Casey, & Noll, 1994).

Within the ventral pathway, a number of regions downstream from the primary visual cortex are selective for higher order visual features. The lateral occipital cortex has been shown to be preferentially active to actual objects compared to nonobjects with similar basic features (Grill-Spector et al., 1999; Malach et al., 1995). The fusiform gyrus has been identified as a key region associated with the perception of faces (Kanwisher, McDermott, & Chun, 1997; Puce et al., 1995; Sergent, Ohta, & MacDonald, 1992). This finding has been challenged by fMRI studies suggesting that what appears to be face-specific activation may instead represent level of processing differences within a general object identification system (Gauthier et al., 1997). Converging evidence from intracranial electrode recordings, however, supports the idea of focal regions in the fusiform gyrus associated with face processing (Allison et al., 1999; McCarthy et al., 1999). The visual identification of words is mediated primarily by a left hemisphere system, including prefrontal and occipitotemporal regions (Binder & Price, 2001).

In addition to spatial localization and movement control processing, regions in the dorsal, occipitoparietal pathway also respond differentially when target items can be distinguished from distractors only on the basis of conjunction of component features, as compared to targets that can be identified from a single feature (Donner et al., 2002). When the number of objects (generally more than four items) in a visual display cannot be apprehended as a single group, counting the number of display items activates the dorsal pathway (Piazza et al., 2002; Sathian et al., 1999). Motion is an identifiable feature of objects, but is a spatial property, and motion discrimination activates a lateral occipitotemporal region (V5) near the border with the dorsal pathway (Watson et al., 1993; Zeki et al., 1991). Similarly, motion of biologically relevant objects, including faces, evokes activity in the superior temporal sulcus (Allison, Puce, & McCarthy, 2000). The most widely investigated functions of the dorsal pathway, however, are related more closely to the allocation of spatial attention than to the discrimination of static features of visual displays.

Attention

A distributed network of regions in parietal and prefrontal cortex appears to be particularly important for the top-down control of visual perception. Kastner et al. (1999), for example, demonstrated that covert attention to a peripheral spatial location (with fixation maintained centrally) led to an increase in the BOLD signal in a network of areas, including the superior parietal lobule, frontal eye fields, and supplementary eye fields. This attentional effect also occurred in the extrastriate cortex (V4), but the magnitude was not as pronounced as in the parietal and prefrontal regions. In addition, the onset of the visual display led to a further increase in the BOLD signal in V4, but not in the parietal and prefrontal regions, suggesting that the activity in these last regions reflected the source of the attentional operations rather than visual sensory processing. Hopfinger, Buonocore, and Mangun (2000) have also reported activation within prefrontal and parietal cortical regions in response to a centrally presented cue indicating the spatial location of an upcoming target.

Activation in this frontoparietal network occurs in a variety of visual search and discrimination tasks that involve shifting attention spatially (Corbetta, 1998; Handy, Hopfinger, & Mangun, 2001; Kastner & Ungerleider, 2000), and the pattern of activation does not differ substantially as a result of whether the shift of attention is triggered exogenously by a visual transient at a peripheral display location or endogenously by the observer's interpretation of a centrally presented symbolic cue (Nobre et al., 1997; Rosen et al., 1999). Some specialization of function, however, is evident.

Regions within the parietal lobe are activated differentially by specific components of attention, such as the transient shift of spatial attention versus the maintenance of attention at a particular display location (Hopfinger, Buonocore, & Mangun, et al., 2000; Yantis et al., 2002). The role of the prefrontal regions is related primarily to the less spatially dependent, executive control aspects of attention, such as the adoption of a task set, sensorimotor monitoring, and inhibitory functions (Brass & von Cramon, 2002; Konishi et al., 1999; Pollmann et al., 2000), although executive control processing also leads to activation in parietal regions (Rushworth, Paus, & Sipila, 2001; Shulman et al., 2002). This pattern reflects both the close resemblance between attention and working memory at the behavioral level and the central role of prefrontal regions, especially the dorsolateral prefrontal cortex, in working memory performance (Cohen et al., 1997; D'Esposito et al., 1998; Huettel, Mack, & McCarthy, 2002; Jha & McCarthy, 2000; Rowe & Passingham, 2001).

When compared directly, working memory and visuospatial attention tasks evoke activity in an overlapping set of frontoparietal regions, suggesting that common cognitive processes are active in both paradigms (LaBar et al., 1999).

Two other central components of the attentional network include the anterior cingulate gyrus and deep gray matter structures (basal ganglia and thalamus). The anterior cingulate, like dorsolateral prefrontal regions, is frequently activated in response to working memory and sensorimotor control (Paus et al., 1998). There is evidence for an additional, specific role of the anterior cingulate in the resolution of conflict between incongruent sources of information (MacDonald et al., 2000; Miller & Cohen, 2001). The specific role of the basal ganglia is less clear, but there are extensive and topographically organized projections from the basal ganglia to both prefrontal and motor cortical regions (Middleton & Strick, 2002). Huettel, Güzeldere, and McCarthy (2001), using an fMRI methodology that separated visual search and response generation processes, found that phasic activation in the basal ganglia and thalamus was associated with the execution of a manual response to a visual display. Thalamic activation has been observed across different types of visual task conditions related by the common factor of attentional engagement (Kinomura et al., 1996; Shulman et al., 1997), and LaBerge (2000) proposed that attentional states depend on the operation of a triangular circuit, in which the thalamus modulates activity in the posterior sensory cortex (e.g., extrastriate) on the basis of top-down signals from prefrontal regions.

What are the effects of attention on activity in visual cortical regions? One important mechanism is the enhancement of the neural response to stimuli appearing at an attended location. In the absence of attention, multiple visual stimuli interact competitively for limited processing resources. Single-unit electrophysiological studies have demonstrated that the response of a neuron to multiple stimuli presented simultaneously within a receptive field is a weighted average of the responses to the same stimuli presented individually, suggesting a mutually suppressive, bottom-up interaction among items during simultaneous presentation (Reynolds, Chelazzi, & Desimone, 1999). Similarly, stimulus-dependent activation in visual cortical regions as measured from fMRI is greater for display items presented sequentially than for those presented simultaneously (Kastner et al., 1998).

As noted in this section, covert attention to a peripheral display location increases stimulus-related BOLD signal in extrastriate cortex (Kastner et al., 1999). This attentional effect is greater with the simultaneous presentation of the display items than with sequential presentation, implying that directed spatial attention, by enhancing the neural response to the attended item, can counteract the (bottom-up) suppressive influence among multiple stimuli. This top-down form of attentional control is more pronounced in the extrastriate regions mediating later stages of visual processing than in primary visual cortex, but the enhancement associated with spatial attention is organized retinotopically (Heinze et al., 1994; Woldorff et al., 1997), and attentional enhancement has been observed for other display features such as color, speed, and motion (Corbetta, 1998).

Some degree of the attentional enhancement of neural responses occurs in the absence of visual stimulation as a result of expecting an upcoming display (Kastner et al., 1999). Thus, top-down attentional control also operates by increasing the baseline activity in the relevant cortical region. This baseline shift, unlike the effect of directed spatial attention, is evident in the primary visual cortex as well as in extrastriate regions (Gandhi, Heeger, & Boynton, 1999; Somers et al., 1999), enhancing responses to entire objects rather than isolated features (O'Craven, Downing, & Kanwisher, 1999). There are consequently multiple components in the neural activity for an attended visual item, including a level of baseline activity determined by the degree of expectation or arousal, the perceptual salience of the individual display items in the context of bottom-up interference from competing distractors, and the specific neural response to the attended item or spatial location as enhanced by top-down control.

Neuroimaging Studies of Adult Age Differences

Sensory-Level Changes

Evidence from neuroimaging investigations suggests that, consistent with findings from behavioral research, there is an age-related decline in the activation of visual cortical regions during the early stages of perceptual processing. The first of these was an fMRI study by Ross et al. (1997), which reported that the amplitude of the BOLD signal for visual cortex (BA 17 and 18), in response to a red diffuse flash, was lower for older adults than for younger adults. The spatial extent of the activation was similar for the two age groups. Two fMRI studies of age differences in visual perception (Buckner et al., 2000; Huettel, Singerman, & McCarthy, 2001) used an event-related design that allowed a more complete estimation of the time course of the BOLD signal in response to checkerboard stimuli. Like Ross et al., Buckner et al. found that the signal amplitude in visual cortex was lower for healthy older adults than for younger adults, although in contrast to the findings of Ross et al., Buckner et al. also noted that the spatial extent of the activation was decreased for older adults. Huettel et al. confirmed that the spatial extent of checkerboard-related activation in primary (calcarine) and secondary (fusiform) visual cortical regions was relatively lower for the older adults. Unlike both the Ross et al. and Buckner et al. results, however, Huettel, Singerman, and McCarthy found that the BOLD signal amplitude was similar for younger and older adults.

These results suggest that some aspect of neural activation in visual cortical regions, either the amplitude or number of activated voxels, is reduced for older adults relative to younger adults. The variability across the different neuroimaging studies may be related to age-related changes in the properties of the hemodynamic response underlying the BOLD signal (see the section on current issues).

Perception of Nonverbal Stimuli

Neuroimaging investigations of age differences in higher order perceptual processes have demonstrated functional changes in the ventral and dorsal processing pathways. Grady and colleagues (Grady, 2002; Grady et al., 1992, 1994, 2000) conducted an extensive series of PET experiments using the nonverbal tasks of face matching and location judgment that led to task-specific rCBF activation in ventral and dorsal pathways, respectively. Grady et al. (1992, 1994) found that in the face-matching task, older adults exhibited relatively less activation of the ventral pathway mediating visual feature extraction (BA 18) and relatively more activation of extrastriate and parietal cortical regions outside this pathway. In the location judgment task, older adults also tended to activate cortical regions outside the dorsal pathway, especially prefrontal regions. That is, the differentiation of the ventral and dorsal pathways from task-specific activation was less evident for older adults than for younger adults.

This pattern of neural activation resembles the behavioral results of Chen et al. (2002; Chen, Myerson, & Hale, 2002), who found that covariation in speeded task performance, representing separate underlying dimensions of visual object identification and spatial localization, was less pronounced for older adults than for younger adults. Grady et al. (1992, 1994) concluded that the age-related increase in prefrontal activation may represent a compensatory mechanism in response to a decline in the efficiency of the neural systems that mediate visual feature extraction.

Grady (2002) performed a meta-analysis of three PET studies of face perception and memory tasks and proposed that prefrontal activation for younger adults was task specific, whereas for older adults this activation (especially in left prefrontal regions) occurred in response to increasing task difficulty, regardless of specific task demands. Thus, the age-related decrease in differentiation of dorsal and ventral pathway activation (Grady et al., 1992, 1994) may be because of older adults' increased reliance on prefrontal regions as a common compensatory mechanism across different nonverbal perceptual tasks.

Perception of Verbal Stimuli

The findings from perceptual tasks with verbal stimuli have supported the age-related decline in activation in the ventral pathway noted by Grady and colleagues, although an age-related increase in prefrontal activation has not been prominent. Madden et al. (1996), using PET, reported that rCBF activation in the left extrastriate cortex (BA 18), in a lexical decision (word/nonword discrimination) task, was greater for younger adults than for older adults. Madden, Langley, et al. (2002) also used a lexical decision task (with a different baseline comparison condition) and found that activation in left striate cortex (BA 17) was relatively greater for younger adults, whereas activation in the more anterior region of the left hemisphere ventral pathway (inferior temporal gyrus; BA 37) was relatively greater for older adults. Activation of left prefrontal cortical regions was comparable for the two age groups.

In further analyses of the Madden, Langley, et al. (2002) data, Whiting et al. (2003) demonstrated that, for older adults, increasing neural activity (normalized PET radioactivity counts) in both BA 17 and BA 37 was associated with a more pronounced effect of word frequency on RT, suggesting that the activation represents the activation or retrieval of semantic (lexical) information. These lexical decision data thus agree with the Grady et al. (1992, 1994, 2000) face-matching data in suggesting that age-related compensation for decreased efficiency of visual feature extraction may be expressed as an increased reliance on later visual processing stages. The lexical decision data also imply that this compensation may be expressed through a differential pattern of activation within regions of the task-relevant pathway rather than through the recruitment of prefrontal regions.

Attention

Several neuroimaging experiments have addressed age differences in various aspects of attention, especially selective attention, executive control, and inhibition. As noted in the introduction, age-related deficits in behavioral performance are elicited by the requirement to divide attention among multiple display items and are minimized when attention can be allocated selectively to specific display locations. Madden et al. (1997) examined age differences in visual search performance and rCBF activation in a selective attention condition (discrimination of a target letter located consistently in the center of a nine-letter display) and in a divided attention condition (discrimination of a target letter located at any of the nine display positions). Divided attention was associated with greater rCBF activation (relative to selective attention) in the extrastriate cortex (BA 18) for younger adults, whereas the requirement to divide attention led to activation of prefrontal cortex bilaterally for older adults (plate 7.1; see color insert). Further, age differences in RT were most pronounced in the divided attention condition, and activation covaried positively with RT for both age groups. Thus, as in the Grady et al. (1992, 1994, 2000) studies of face matching, older adults appeared to respond to decreased efficiency of ventral pathway processing by recruiting prefrontal regions.

In the type of search task used by Madden et al. (1997), selective attention to spatial location is a form of attentional control in which participants use a spatial property of the display, a predefined location, to guide attention to the target item. A PET study conducted by Madden, Turkington, et al. (2002) demonstrated that both younger and older adults were able to use a different property, color, as a means of improving search performance (detection of an upright *L* among rotated *L*s). Target detectability was lower for older adults than for younger adults, but both groups exhibited substantially higher accuracy for detection of a black *L* among rotated white *L* distractors (feature search) than for detection of a black *L* among an equal number of black and white rotated *L* distractors (conjunction search), even though the location of the target in the display was not predictable in either condition. Activation in the ventral pathway associated with the most difficult condition (conjunction search) was more pronounced for younger adults than for older adults, consistent with an age-related decline in the efficiency of visual identification processes mediated by the ventral processing pathway (plate 7.2; see color insert). Activation of prefrontal regions, however, was comparable for the two age groups, and there was consequently no evidence for compensation of the form described by Grady et al. (1992, 1994) and Madden et al. (1997). A condition that allowed the selection of a subset of display items based on color (guided search), however, led to a higher level of ventral pathway activation for older adults than for younger adults, which may reflect different levels of baseline activation for the two age groups (see the section on current issues).

Age differences in aspects of attention relating to executive control, such as task switching and active inhibition of irrelevant information, have also been the focus of neuroimaging studies. DiGirolamo et al. (2001) reported an fMRI experiment in which participants performed two different types of numerical judgments, a digit value task and a digit numerosity task. Both younger and older adults found a condition that switched between the two tasks every few trials more difficult than a non-switch condition. There was a trend toward a greater difference in RT between the task conditions for older adults, consistent with previous reports of age-related decline in executive control. The activation data indicated that both age groups activated medial and dorsolateral prefrontal cortex during the task-switching condition, but older adults also showed prefrontal activation during the nonswitch trials (relative to fixation); younger adults' prefrontal activation was minimal during the nonswitch trials. The spatial extent of the prefrontal activation, in terms of the percentage of active voxels within a delimited prefrontal region, was greater for older adults than for younger adults, which DiGirolamo et al. interpreted as a compensatory recruitment.

The efficiency with which older adults can successfully inhibit irrelevant information was critically evaluated in two fMRI studies (Milham et al., 2002; Nielson, Langenecker, & Garavan, 2002). Milham et al. used a choice-RT version of the Stroop color-naming paradigm in which the irrelevant sources of color information could be congruent, incongruent, or neutral. The behavioral data revealed a trend toward an age-related decline in performance when the word's identity was incongruent with the printed color. Overall, competing sources of color information (whether congruent or incongruent) were associated with an age-related reduction in the activation of parietal and dorsolateral prefrontal cortical regions, suggesting an age-related decrease in the efficiency of the neural systems mediating attentional control. When conflicting (incongruent) color information was present, older adults exhibited relatively greater activation in the extrastriate and inferior temporal regions and increased activation of anterior inferior regions of prefrontal cortex, consistent with an increased level of processing of irrelevant information. In addition, the presence of irrelevant color information (either congruent or incongruent) was associated with activation in the anterior cingulate cortex for older adults, whereas only conflicting information clearly led to anterior cingulate activation for younger adults. Milham et al. proposed that this anterior cingulate activation was also consistent with an age-related decline in attentional control in the sense that the range of activity over which this cortical region operates is more limited for older adults. Thus, for older adults, activation in this area was maximal in the presence of irrelevant information regardless of whether incongruent responses were also involved.

Nielson, Langenecker, and Garavan (2002) examined age differences in inhibition using a go/no go version of two-choice letter identification in which a sequence of individual letters was presented visually. Participants responded when either one of two target letters occurred, but only when the current target was an alternation (i.e., the current target letter was different from the most recent target letter). When the current target was a repetition of the most recent target letter, the goal was to refrain from responding (lure trials). There were four groups of individuals spanning 18 to 78 years of age, and the ability to inhibit responding on the repetition lure trials declined with age. Successful inhibition trials were associated with right prefrontal activation for all age groups, but were also associated with left prefrontal activation for older adults, consistent with a compensatory recruitment of prefrontal regions on these attention-demanding trials. In addition, when older adults were divided into subgroups on the basis of performance, activation of the presupplementary motor area (BA 6) of the right hemisphere was greatest for the least accurate participants. This last effect was greater in the oldest adults, which Nielson et al. argued as additional support for a compensatory model.

Although relatively few neuroimaging investigations of age-related changes in perception and attention have been conducted, several themes have emerged consistently. One of these is the age-related decline in the functional efficiency of the neural systems that mediate visual information processing (Buckner et al., 2000; Huettel, Singerman, & McCarthy, 2001; Ross et al., 1997). A similar theme is evident in higher order perceptual tasks, in which the age-related decrease in both ventral and dorsal pathway activation has been associated with a corresponding decline in the quality (speed and accuracy) of task performance (Grady et al., 1992, 1994, 2000; Madden et al., 1996, 1997; Madden, Langley, et al., 2002; Madden, Turkington, et al., 2002). In some tasks, the age-related decline in activation in these posterior cortical regions is accompanied by an age-related increase in prefrontal activation, which may represent a compensatory recruitment of an anterior attentional network (Grady, 2002; Madden et al., 1997). In other tasks, however, older adults exhibit a different pattern of activation within the task-relevant neural pathways rather than a recruitment of other cortical regions (Madden, Langley, et al., 2002; Madden, Turkington, et al., 2002), and the task features that are necessary to elicit prefrontal recruitment are not currently known. One critical feature of prefrontal recruitment may be the successful inhibition of a response (Nielson, Langenecker, & Garavan, 2002), but recruitment may also represent more general features of executive control (DiGirolamo et al., 2001; Milham et al., 2002).

Current Issues

Neuroimaging research has begun to clarify the age-related changes that occur in the neural systems that mediate perception and attention, but many fundamental issues remain to be addressed. Consider, for example, the interaction between top-down and bottom-up processing influences in visual perception, in which top-down processing can counteract the mutually suppressive influence among multiple display items (Kastner & Ungerleider, 2000). Although age-related changes in the frontoparietal network for attention have been demonstrated, it is not known whether these changes are associated differentially with top-down or bottom-up processes. Similarly, whether the neural systems that mediate the top-down control of spatial attention (Handy, Hopfinger, & Mangun, 2001) change with age are unknown.

In further research on these and other questions, it will also be essential to remain aware of methodological issues that influence the interpretation of age differences in neural activation. Three particularly relevant issues are the nature of the hemodynamic response, the interpretation of compensatory recruitment, and the level of baseline neural activity.

Age-Related Changes in the Hemodynamic Response

Research investigating adult age differences in measures of brain activation typically assumes that the metabolic measure of interest, whether the rCBF or the BOLD signal, has comparable properties for younger and older adults. That is, the coupling between neural activity and measured response should be the same for the two age groups. If this assumption is not valid, then the interpretation of the age differences in neuroimaging measures is more difficult (chapter 5, this volume; D'Esposito et al., 1999). If there is an age-related increase in activation, the interpretative problem is less critical because it is unlikely that there are age-related changes in the central nervous system that would lead to an increase in the strength of the coupling between a neural signal and the hemodynamic response. When, however, the neuroimaging task yields an age-related decline in activation, the neural coupling assumption is more problematic. In many experiments, the neuroimaging data are either smoothed or averaged across a spatial extent, and thus an age-related decrease in the coupling between the neural signal and the hemodynamic response might yield what appears to be an age-related decrease in activation even though the strength of individual neural signals is comparable for the two age groups. That is, an age difference in variability or noise might be expressed as an age difference in activation.

Data obtained from the primary motor cortex (D'Esposito et al., 1999) and visual cortical regions (Huettel, Singerman, & McCarthy, 2001) suggest that the form and amplitude of the hemodynamic response, as determined by event-related fMRI, are similar for younger and older adults. Huettel Singerman, and McCarthy also included paired stimuli and obtained significant BOLD signal refractory effects for the second stimulus in a pair, similar to previous studies (Huettel & McCarthy, 2000), and the refractory effects were comparable for younger and older adults. In both the D'Esposito et al. and Huettel, Singerman, and McCarthy studies, however, there was evidence for an age-related decline in the coupling between the neural signal and hemodynamic response, in terms of a relatively higher voxelwise noise level for older adults, that was not attributable to head motion (but cf. Buckner et al., 2000). As a result, the voxelwise signal-to-noise ratio was lower for older adults than for younger adults. The physiological changes associated with increased age-related fMRI variability are unknown, and evidence from other techniques (e.g., spectroscopy; Hock et al., 1995; Mehagnoul-Schipper et al., 2002) will be necessary to identify possible mechanisms. In view of the apparent age-related increase in voxelwise noise, event-related analyses of potential age differences in the form and time course of the hemodynamic response will be particularly useful.

Interpreting Compensatory Recruitment

In several of the neuroimaging studies of age differences in perception and attention reviewed in this chapter, older adults exhibited a more extensive activation of prefrontal regions than did younger adults (e.g., Grady et al., 1992, 1994; Madden et al., 1997; Nielson, Langenecker, & Garavan, 2002). These authors, as well as those investigating age differences in memory (e.g., Cabeza et al., 1997), have suggested that older adults may activate prefrontal regions in compensation for a decline in the efficiency of processing in task-relevant neural regions. Behavioral studies of neuropsychological test performance (see the section on attention) suggest that age-related changes in cognitive functioning are the result of differential changes in the frontal lobe (West, 1996; West et al., 2002). To what extent do the neuroimaging findings provide support for the frontal lobe hypothesis? As a compensatory strategy, it would not appear adaptive to increase reliance on those cortical systems that are the most vulnerable to age-related decline.

In addition, it is not clear what the expected relation between compensatory activation and behavioral performance should be. One logical interpretation of compensation is that it should benefit performance and thus be more clearly demonstrated by higher performing older adults than by lower performing older adults (Cabeza et al., 2002). On the other hand, it would also be reasonable to predict that compensatory prefrontal activation should be more pronounced for those older adults exhibiting the lower levels of performance, that is, those individuals who would benefit most from assistance in performing the task (Nielson, Langenecker, & Garavan, 2002). These issues are related to the more general questions of what is the relation between neural activation and behavioral performance and whether this relation changes as a function of age (Madden et al., 1999; chapter 9, this volume; Rypma & D'Esposito, 2000; Whiting et al., 2003).

Cabeza (2001, 2002) and Daselaar and Cabeza (chapter 14, this volume) viewed compensation as a specific interpretation within a more general theoretical framework, the hemispheric asymmetry reduction in older adults (HAROLD) model. In this model, the basic phenomenon is an age-related shift from a localized neural representation of a cognitive function to a more differentiated representation. From the perspective of the HAROLD model, the age-related increase in prefrontal activation not only may be compensatory, but also may represent a decrease in the level of functional differentiation of the task-relevant neural systems (Chen, Myerson, & Hale, 2002).

Interpretation of compensatory recruitment has been developed primarily in the context of tasks leading to age-related changes in prefrontal activation. Perceptual and attentional tasks mediated by posterior cortical regions have also yielded another pattern, in which older adults activate the same task-relevant neural pathways as younger adults, but exhibit more anterior foci. Regarding the ventral visual pathway, studies of both face matching (Grady et al., 1994, 2000) and word processing (Madden, Langley, et al., 2002; Milham et al., 2002) have shown that whereas younger adults activate the posterior (striate or extrastriate) regions of the pathway, older adults' activation is diminished in these areas and is instead focused in the more anterior occipitotemporal regions. Grady et al. (2000) found that posterior extrastriate activation was associated with more accurate facial discrimination. Thus, compensation for age-related decline in visual cortical functioning may not always entail recruiting prefrontal regions, but may also be expressed as an increased reliance on downstream occipitotemporal regions mediating higher order identification processes.

Whiting et al. (2003) developed a similar argument in interpreting age-related changes in the relation between word frequency effects in RT and the magnitude of rCBF activation. This relation was evident for activation foci in both earlier (BA

17) and later (BA 37) stages of the ventral occipitotemporal pathway for older adults, but not for younger adults, suggesting that older adults may rely to a greater degree on lexical-level processing mediated by this neural pathway.

Other forms of compensatory recruitment may also be possible. In an fMRI study of executive control during visual target detection, for example, we observed an age-related increase in BOLD signal amplitude in deep gray matter nuclei (Madden et al., 2004). Younger and older adults performed a visual oddball task in which they pressed the same response key at the appearance of standards (squares; 87% of trials) and novels (pictures of objects; 6% of trials), but pressed a different response key at the appearance of targets (circles; 7% of trials). Both age groups exhibited greater activation of the extrastriate cortex (lateral occipital gyrus) for novels than for standards, reflecting the visual complexity of the novels (figure 7.1). This extrastriate activation also was more extensive spatially for younger adults than for older adults, confirming the age-related decline in the activation of the ventral occipitotemporal pathway reported previously (Buckner et al., 2000; Huettel, Singerman, & McCarthy, 2001).

We also found that both age groups exhibited greater activation of deep gray matter structures, such as the caudate nucleus of the thalamus, for targets than for standards, which was likely a result of the response selection processing required by the targets (Huettel, Güzeldere, & McCarthy, 2001). This last activation was greater in amplitude for older adults than for younger adults (figure 7.2), and there was a trend toward an age-related increase in the extent of activation as well. The targets also led to activation of prefrontal regions (e.g., middle frontal gyrus and anterior cingulate), but the age-related changes in the prefrontal BOLD signal were less consistent than those associated with the deep gray matter regions.

The reason for the increased amplitude of the older adults' caudate activation is not entirely clear, but in view of the central role of the basal ganglia and thalamus in motor control and the substantial contribution of a slowing in information processing (especially at response stages) to age differences in cognitive performance, it is possible that as a compensatory mechanism older adults are devoting additional attentional resources to response selection. Our findings are also consistent with the involvement of the thalamus and other subcortical regions in attentional control (LaBerge, 2000; Shulman et al., 1997) and highlight the potential role of these deep gray matter regions in age-related cognitive changes (Hicks & Birren, 1970; Rubin, 1999).

Age Differences in Baseline Neural Activity

A central assumption in the interpretation of age differences in activation measures obtained from neuroimaging is that an age-related decline in activation in fact represents a lower level of task-related metabolic activity for older adults than for younger adults. Although this would seem at face value to be a safe assumption, it may not always be valid, especially if age-related changes in baseline neural activity exist. This issue arises because neural activation is frequently estimated from a subtraction analysis in which metabolic activity during a perceptual or cognitive task is compared to a sensorimotor control condition. That is, neural activation is typically as-

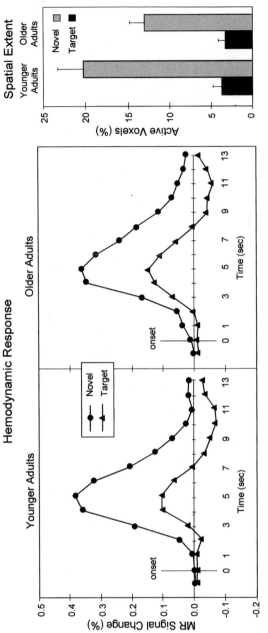

Figure 7.1. Changes in blood oxygen level dependent (BOLD) signal measured by functional magnetic resonance imaging (fMRI) during a visual oddball task. (Modified with permission from Madden et al., 2004.) Participants pressed the same response key at the appearance of standards (squares; 87% of trials) and novels (pictures of objects; 6% of trials), but pressed a different response key at the appearance targets (circles; 7% of trials). Data are presented for the time course of the active voxels and the spatial extent of activation (percentage of active voxels) in the lateral occipital gyrus as a function of age group and task condition.

174

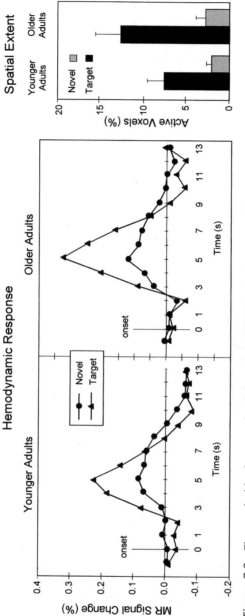

Figure 7.2. Changes in blood oxygen level dependent (BOLD) signal measured by functional magnetic resonance imaging (fMRI) during a visual oddball task, as described in the legend to figure 7.1. Data are presented for the time course of the active voxels and the spatial extent of activation (percentage of active voxels) in the caudate nucleus of the thalamus as a function of age group and task condition.

sessed as relative change. The measurement of metabolic activity in absolute (quanti-tative) values (e.g., rCBF values in milliliters per 100 g of tissue per min) requires more invasive procedures, such as arterial blood sampling. The subtraction method-ology is a hallmark of PET designs because the radiotracer half-life causes the rCBF estimation to be based on blocks of trials that integrate activity over at least several minutes. The use of event-related measurement of the BOLD signal in fMRI reduces the reliance on subtraction, but even the event-related approach estimates signal change relative to a prestimulus baseline. Thus, if older adults exhibit a higher level of neural activity in the baseline condition than younger adults but a comparable level of event- or task-related activity, then the result will be a smaller degree of relative change expressed as an age-related decline in task-related activation.

Evidence for age differences in baseline neural activity has appeared in several experiments. Madden, Turkington, et al. (2002), for example, used PET to measure rCBF activation for younger and older adults across three visual search task condi-tions that varied in complexity. In each condition, participants performed the same type of search task, detection of an upright target L among rotated L distractors. In the least difficult condition (feature search), the target differed from all of the dis-tractors in color (e.g., a black target among 17 white distractors), whereas in the most difficult condition (conjunction search), half of the display items contained the target's color (e.g., a black target among 8 black distractors and 9 white distractors). The guided search condition was an intermediate level of difficulty and included a subset of three items that shared the target's color (e.g., a black target among 2 black distractors and 15 white distractors). Interestingly, occipitotemporal activation related to the guided search condition was similar to that associated with the feature search condition for younger adults, whereas activation in the guided search condi-tion resembled conjunction search activation for older adults (plate 7.2). Thus, the age-related decline in occipitotemporal activation associated with the difficult search condition may to some extent be the result of older adults' maintaining a higher level of neural activity in the easier (baseline) task conditions. Age-related increases in activation in easier task conditions have also been reported for the anterior cingu-late (Milham et al., 2002) and dorsolateral prefrontal cortex (DiGirolamo et al., 2001).

An age-related change in baseline neural activity may have a compensatory func-tion, perhaps representing a top-down attentional enhancement with a goal to offset a reduction in information-processing efficiency. Whiting et al. (2003) noted that those older adults who exhibited more efficient processing of the visual features of words (in terms of a decreased reliance of RT on word length) also showed higher levels of activity in the primary visual cortex (BA 17). In addressing the baseline activity issue, it will be helpful to incorporate neuroimaging designs that include both event-related and blocked conditions (Donaldson et al., 2001), an approach that can potentially dissociate the neural activity related to individual items from that related to sustained cognitive states.

Acknowledgments   Preparation of this chapter was supported by research grants from the National Institute on Aging (R01 AG11622) and the National Institute on Drug Abuse (R03

DA016214). We are grateful to Susanne Harris, Leslie Crandell Dawes, Sara Moore, and Niko Harlan for technical assistance.

References

Allen, P. A., Hall, R. J., Druley, J. A., Smith, A. F., Sanders, R. E., & Murphy, M. D. (2001). How shared are age-related influences on cognitive and non-cognitive variables? *Psychology and Aging, 16,* 532–549.

Allen, P. A., Smith, A. F., Vires-Collins, H., & Sperry, S. (1998). The psychological refractory period: Evidence for age differences in attentional time-sharing. *Psychology and Aging, 13,* 218–229.

Allison, T., Puce, A., & McCarthy, G. (2000). Social perception from visual cues: Role of the STS region. *Trends in Cognitive Sciences, 4,* 267–278.

Allison, T., Puce, A., Spencer, D. D., & McCarthy, G. (1999). Electrophysiological studies of human face perception. I: Potentials generated in occipitotemporal cortex by face and non-face stimuli. *Cerebral Cortex, 9,* 415–430.

Atchley, P., & Kramer, A. F. (1998). Spatial cuing in a stereoscopic display: Attention remains "depth-aware" with age. *Journal of Gerontology: Psychological Sciences, 53B,* P318–P323.

Atchley, P., & Kramer, A. F. (2000). Age-related changes in the control of attention in depth. *Psychology and Aging, 15,* 78–87.

Baltes, P. B., & Lindenberger, U. (1997). Emergence of a powerful connection between sensory and cognitive functions across adult life span: A new window to the study of cognitive aging? *Psychology and Aging, 12,* 12–21.

Bedard, A.-C., Nichols, S., Barbosa, J. A., Schachar, R., Logan, G. D., & Tannock, R. (2002). The development of selective inhibitory control across the life span. *Developmental Neuropsychology, 21,* 93–111.

Binder, J., & Price, C. J. (2001). Functional neuroimaging of language. In R. Cabeza & A. Kingstone (Eds.), *Handbook of functional neuroimaging of cognition* (pp. 187–251). Cambridge, MA: MIT Press.

Brass, M., & von Cramon, D. Y. (2002). The role of the frontal cortex in task preparation. *Cerebral Cortex, 12,* 908–914.

Brink, J. M., & McDowd, J. M. (1999). Aging and selective attention: An issue of complexity or multiple mechanisms? *Journal of Gerontology: Psychological Sciences, 54B,* P30–P33.

Brinley, J. F. (1965). Cognitive sets, speed and accuracy of performance in the elderly. In A. T. Welford & J. E. Birren (Eds.), *Behavior, aging, and the nervous system* (pp. 114–149). Springfield, IL: Thomas.

Buckner, R. L., Snyder, A. Z., Sanders, A. L., Raichle, M. E., & Morris, J. C. (2000). Functional brain imaging of young, nondemented, and demented older adults. *Journal of Cognitive Neuroscience, 12*(Suppl. 2), 24–34.

Cabeza, R. (2001). Functional neuroimaging of cognitive aging. In R. Cabeza & A. Kingstone (Eds.), *Handbook of functional neuroimaging of cognition* (pp. 331–377). Cambridge, MA: MIT Press.

Cabeza, R. (2002). Hemispheric asymmetry reduction in old adults: The HAROLD model. *Psychology and Aging, 17,* 85–100.

Cabeza, R., Anderson, N. D., Locantore, J. K., & McIntosh, A. R. (2002). Aging gracefully: Compensatory brain activity in high-performing older adults. *NeuroImage, 17,* 1394–1402.

Cabeza, R., Grady, C. L., Nyberg, L., McIntosh, A. R., Tulving, E., Kapur, S., et al. (1997). Age-related differences in neural activity during memory encoding and retrieval: A positron emission tomography study. *Journal of Neuroscience, 17,* 391–400.

Cameron, E. L., Tai, J. C., & Carrasco, M. (2002). Covert attention affects the psychometric function of contrast sensitivity. *Vision Research, 42,* 949–967.

Cerella, J. (1985). Information processing rates in the elderly. *Psychological Bulletin, 98,* 67–83.

Cerella, J. (1990). Aging and information-processing rate. In J. E. Birren & K. W. Schaie (Eds.), *Handbook of the psychology of aging* (3rd ed., pp. 201–221). San Diego, CA: Academic Press.

Chen, J., Myerson, J., & Hale, S. (2002). Age-related dedifferentiation of visuospatial abilities. *Neuropsychologia, 40,* 20–50.

Chen, J., Myerson, J., Hale, S., & Simon, A. (2000). Behavioral evidence for brain-based ability factors in visuospatial information processing. *Neuropsychologia, 38,* 380–387.

Cohen, J. D., Perlstein, W. M., Braver, T. S., Nystrom, L. E., Noll, D. C., Jonides, J., et al. (1997). Temporal dynamics of brain activation during a working memory task. *Nature, 386,* 604–608.

Corbetta, M. (1998). Functional neuroanatomy of visual attention in the human brain: Studies with positron emission tomography. In R. Parasuraman (Ed.), *The attentive brain* (pp. 95–122). Cambridge, MA: MIT Press.

Davis, E. T., Fujawa, G., & Shikano, T. (2002). Perceptual processing and search efficiency of young and older adults in a simple-feature search task: A staircase approach. *Journal of Gerontology: Psychological Sciences, 57B,* P324–P337.

Desimone, R., & Ungerleider, L. G. (1989). Neural mechanisms of visual processing in monkeys. In F. Boller & J. Grafman (Eds.), *Handbook of neuropsychology* (Vol. 2, pp. 267–299). Amsterdam, The Netherlands: Elsevier.

D'Esposito, M., Aguirre, G. K., Zarahn, E., Ballard, D., Shin, R. K., & Lease, J. (1998). Functional MRI studies of spatial and nonspatial working memory. *Cognitive Brain Research, 7,* 1–13.

D'Esposito, M., Zarahn, E., Aguirre, G. K., & Rypma, B. (1999). The effect of normal aging on the coupling of neural activity to the BOLD hemodynamic response. *NeuroImage, 10,* 6–14.

DiGirolamo, G. J., Kramer, A. F., Barad, V., Cepeda, N. J., Weissman, D. H., Milham, M. P., et al. (2001). General and task-specific frontal lobe recruitment in older adults during executive processes: A fMRI investigation of task-switching. *NeuroReport, 12,* 2065–2071.

Donaldson, D. I., Petersen, S. E., Ollinger, J. M., & Buckner, R. L. (2001). Dissociating state and item components of recognition memory using fMRI. *NeuroImage, 13,* 129–142.

Donner, T. H., Kettermann, A., Diesch, E., Ostendorf, F., Villringer, A., & Brandt, S. A. (2002). Visual feature and conjunction searches of equal difficulty engage only partially overlapping frontoparietal networks. *NeuroImage, 15,* 16–25.

Duncan, J., Johnson, R., Swales, M., & Freer, C. (1997). Frontal lobes after head injury: Unity and diversity of function. *Cognitive Neuropsychology, 14,* 713–741.

Ellis, R. D., Goldberg, J. H., & Detweiler, M. C. (1996). Predicting age-related differences in visual information processing using a two-stage queuing model. *Journal of Gerontology: Psychological Sciences, 51B,* P155–P165.

Fisk, A. D., & Fisher, D. L. (1994). Brinley plots and theories of aging: The explicit, muddled, and implicit debates. *Journal of Gerontology: Psychological Sciences, 49,* P81–P89.

Folk, C. L., & Hoyer, W. J. (1992) Aging and shifts of visual spatial attention. *Psychology and Aging, 7,* 453–465.

Folk, C. L., & Lincourt, A. E. (1996). The effects of age on guided conjunction search. *Experimental Aging Research, 22,* 99–118.

Fox, P. T., & Raichle, M. E. (1984). Stimulus rate dependence of regional cerebral blood flow in human striate cortex demonstrated by positron emission tomography. *Journal of Neurophysiology, 51,* 1109–1120.

Fox, P. T., & Raichle, M. E. (1985). Stimulus rate determines regional cerebral blood flow in striate cortex. *Annals of Neurology, 17,* 303–305.

Fozard, J. K., & Gordon-Salant, S. (2001). Changes in vision and hearing with aging. In J. E. Birren & K. W. Schaie (Eds.), *Handbook of the psychology of aging* (5th ed., pp. 241–266). San Diego, CA: Academic Press.

Freeman, E., Sagi, D., & Driver, J. (2001). Lateral interactions between targets and flankers in low-level vision depend on attention to flankers. *Nature Neuroscience, 4,* 1032–1036.

Gandhi, S. P., Heeger, D. J., & Boynton, G. M. (1999). Spatial attention affects brain activity in human primary visual cortex. *Proceedings of the National Academy of Sciences of the United States of America, 96,* 3314–3319.

Gauthier, I., Anderson, A. W., Tarr, M. J., Skudlarski, P., & Gore, J. C. (1997). Levels of categorization in visual recognition studied using functional magnetic resonance imaging. *Current Biology, 7,* 645–651.

Goodale, M. A. (2000). Perception and action in the human visual system. In M. S. Gazzaniga (Ed.), *The new cognitive neurosciences* (2nd ed., pp. 365–377). Cambridge, MA: MIT Press.

Goodale, M. A., & Milner, A. D. (1992). Separate visual pathways for perception and action. *Trends in Neuroscience, 15,* 20–25.

Grady, C. L. (2002). Age-related differences in face processing: a meta-analysis of three functional neuroimaging experiments. *Canadian Journal of Experimental Psychology, 56,* 208–220.

Grady, C. L., Haxby, J. V., Horwitz, B., Schapiro, M. B., Rapoport, S. I., Ungerleider, L. G., et al. (1992). Dissociation of object and spatial vision in human extrastriate cortex: Age-related changes in activation of regional cerebral blood flow measured with [^{15}O] water and positron emission tomography. *Journal of Cognitive Neuroscience, 4,* 23–34.

Grady, C. L., Maisog, J. M., Horwitz, B., Ungerleider, L. G., Mentis, M. J., Salerno, J. A., et al. (1994). Age-related changes in cortical blood flow activation during visual processing of faces and location. *Journal of Neuroscience, 14,* 1450–1462.

Grady, C. L., McIntosh, A. R., Horwitz, B., & Rapoport, S. I. (2000). Age-related changes in the neural correlates of degraded and nondegraded face processing. *Cognitive Neuropsychology, 17,* 165–186.

Grill-Spector, K., Kushnir, T., Edelman, S., Avidan, G., Itzchak, Y., & Malach, R. (1999). Differential processing of objects under various viewing conditions in the human lateral occipital complex. *Neuron, 24,* 187–203.

Handy, T., Hopfinger, J. B., & Mangun, G. R. (2001). Functional neuroimaging of attention. In R. Cabeza & A. Kingstone (Eds.), *Handbook of functional neuroimaging of cognition* (pp. 75–108). Cambridge, MA: MIT Press.

Harpur, L. L., Scialfa, C. T., & Thomas, D. M. (1995). Age differences in feature search as a function of exposure duration. *Experimental Aging Research, 21,* 1–15.

Hartley, A. A. (1993). Evidence for the selective preservation of spatial selective attention in old age. *Psychology and Aging, 8,* 371–379.

Hartley, A. A. (2001). Age differences in dual-task interference are localized to response-generation processes. *Psychology and Aging, 16,* 47–54.

Hartley, A. A., Kieley, J. M., & Slabach, E. H. (1990). Age differences and similarities in the effects of cues and prompts. *Journal of Experimental Psychology: Human Perception and Performance, 16,* 523–537.

Hartley, A. A., & Little, D. M. (1999). Age-related differences and similarities in dual-task interference. *Journal of Experimental Psychology: General, 128,* 416–449.

Hasher, L., & Zacks, R. T. (1988). Working memory, comprehension, and aging: A review and a new review. In G. H. Bower (Ed.) *The psychology of learning and motivation* (Vol. 22, pp. 193–225). Orlando, FL: Academic Press.

Haxby, J., Grady, C., Horwitz, B., Ungerleider, L., Mishkin, M., Carson, R., et al. (1991). Dissociation of object and spatial visual processing pathways in human extrastriate cortex. *Proceedings of the National Academy of Sciences of the United States of America, 88,* 1621–1625.

Heinze, H. J., Mangun, G. R., Burchert, W., Hinrichs, H., Scholz, M., Münte, T. F., et al. (1994). Combined spatial and temporal imaging of brain activity during visual selective attention in humans. *Nature, 372,* 543–546.

Hicks, L. H., & Birren, J. E. (1970). Aging, brain damage, and psychomotor slowing. *Psychological Bulletin, 74,* 377–396.

Hock, C., Muller-Spahn, F., Schuh-Hofer, S., Hofmann, M., Dirnagl, U., & Villringer, A. (1995). Age dependency of changes in cerebral hemoglobin oxygenation during brain activation: A near-infrared spectroscopy study. *Journal of Cerebral Blood Flow and Metabolism, 15,* 1103–1108.

Hopfinger, J. B., Buonocore, M. H., & Mangun, G. R. (2000). The neural mechanisms of top-down attentional control. *Nature Neuroscience, 3,* 284–291.

Huettel, S. A., Güzeldere, G., & McCarthy, G. (2001). Dissociating the neural mechanisms of visual attention in change detection using functional MRI. *Journal of Cognitive Neuroscience, 13,* 1006–1018.

Huettel, S. A., Mack, P. B., & McCarthy, G. (2002). Perceiving patterns in random series: Dynamic processing of sequence in prefrontal cortex. *Nature Neuroscience, 5,* 485–490.

Huettel, S. A., & McCarthy, G. (2000). Evidence for a refractory period in the hemodynamic response to visual stimuli as measured by MRI. *NeuroImage, 11,* 547–553.

Huettel, S. A., Singerman, J. D., & McCarthy, G. (2001). The effects of aging upon the hemodynamic response measured by functional MRI. *NeuroImage, 13,* 161–175.

Jha, A. P., & McCarthy, G. (2000). The influence of memory load upon delay-interval activity in a working-memory task: An event-related functional MRI study. *Journal of Cognitive Neuroscience, 12*(Suppl. 2), 90–105.

Kanwisher, N., McDermott, J., & Chun, M. M. (1997). The fusiform face area: A module in human extrastriate cortex specialized for face perception. *Journal of Neuroscience, 17,* 4302–4311.

Kastner, S., De Weerd, P., Desimone, R., & Ungerleider, L. G. (1998, October 2). Mechanisms of directed attention in the human extrastriate cortex as revealed by functional MRI. *Science, 282,* 108–111.

Kastner, S., Pinsk, M. A., De Weerd, P., Desimone, R., & Ungerleider, L. G. (1999). Increased activity in human visual cortex during directed attention in the absence of visual stimulation. *Neuron, 22,* 751–761.

Kastner, S., & Ungerleider, L. G. (2000). Mechanisms of visual attention in the human cortex. *Annual Review of Neuroscience, 23,* 315–341.

Kinomura, S., Larsson, J., Gulyas, B., & Roland, P. E. (1996). Activation by attention of the human reticular formation and thalamic intralaminar nuclei. *Science, 271,* 512–515.

Kline, D. W., & Scialfa, C. T. (1996). Visual and auditory aging. In J. E. Birren & K. W. Schaie (Eds.), *Handbook of the psychology of aging* (4th ed., pp. 181–203). San Diego, CA: Academic Press.

Konishi, S., Nakajima, K., Uchida, I., Kikyo, H., Kameyama, M., & Miyashita, Y. (1999).

Common inhibitory mechanism in human inferior prefrontal cortex revealed by event-related functional MRI. *Brain, 122*, 981–991.

Kramer, A. F., Hahn, S., & Gopher, D. (1999). Task coordination and aging: Explorations of executive control processes in the task switching paradigm. *Acta Psychologica, 101*, 339–78.

Kramer, A. F., Hahn, S., Irwin, D. E., & Theeuwes, J. (1999). Attentional capture and aging: Implications for visual search performance and oculomotor control. *Psychology and Aging, 14*, 135–154.

Kramer, A. F., Humphrey, D. G., Larish, J. F., Logan, G. D., & Strayer, D. L. (1994). Aging and inhibition: Beyond a unitary view of inhibitory processing in attention. *Psychology and Aging, 9*, 491–512.

Kramer, A. F., Martin-Emerson, R., Larish, J. F., & Anderson, G. J. (1996). Aging and filtering by movement in visual search. *Journal of Gerontology: Psychological Sciences, 51B*, P201–P216.

LaBar, K. S., Gitelman, D. R., Parrish, T. B., & Mesulam, M.-M. (1999). Neuroanatomic overlap of working memory and spatial attention networks: A functional MRI comparison within subjects. *NeuroImage, 10*, 695–704.

LaBerge, D. (2000). Networks of attention. In M. S. Gazzaniga (Ed.), *The new cognitive neurosciences* (2nd ed., pp. 711–723). Cambridge, MA: MIT Press.

Lindenberger, U., & Baltes, P. B. (1994). Sensory functioning and intelligence in old age: A strong connection. *Psychology and Aging, 9*, 339–355.

MacDonald, A. W., III, Cohen, J. D., Stenger, V. A., & Carter, C. S. (2000). Dissociating the role of the dorsolateral prefrontal and anterior cingulate cortex in cognitive control. *Science, 288*, 1835–1838.

Madden, D. J. (1988). Adult age differences in the effects of sentence context and stimulus degradation during visual word recognition. *Psychology and Aging, 3*, 167–172.

Madden, D. J. (1990). Adult age differences in the time course of visual attention. *Journal of Gerontology: Psychological Sciences, 45*, P9–P16.

Madden, D. J. (1992). Selective attention and visual search: Revision of an allocation model and application to age differences. *Journal of Experimental Psychology: Human Perception and Performance, 18*, 821–836.

Madden, D. J. (2001). Speed and timing of behavioral processes. In J. E. Birren & K. W. Schaie (Eds.), *Handbook of the psychology of aging* (5th ed., pp. 288–312). San Diego, CA: Academic Press.

Madden, D. J., & Allen, P. A. (1991). Adult age differences in the rate of information extraction during visual search. *Journal of Gerontology: Psychological Sciences, 46*, P124–P126.

Madden, D. J., Gottlob, L. R., Denny, L. L., Turkington, T. G., Provenzale, J. M., Hawk, T. C., & Coleman, R. E. (1999). Aging and recognition memory: Changes in regional cerebral blood flow associated with components of reaction time distributions. *Journal of Cognitive Neuroscience, 11*, 511–520.

Madden, D. J., Langley, L. K., Denny, L. L., Turkington, T. G., Provenzale, J. M., & Hawk, T. C. (2002). Adult age differences in visual word identification: Functional neuroanatomy by positron emission tomography. *Brain and Cognition, 49*, 297–321.

Madden, D. J., Pierce, T. W., & Allen, P. A. (1996). Adult age differences in the use of distractor homogeneity during visual search. *Psychology and Aging, 11*, 454–474.

Madden, D. J., & Plude, D. J. (1993). Selective preservation of selective attention. In J. Cerella, J. Rybash, W. Hoyer, & M. L. Commons (Eds.), *Adult information processing: Limits on loss* (pp. 273–300). San Diego, CA: Academic Press.

Madden, D. J., Turkington, T. G., Coleman, R. E., Provenzale, J. M., DeGrado, T. R., & Hoffman, J. M. (1996). Adult age differences in regional cerebral blood flow during visual word identification: Evidence from $H_2^{15}O$ PET. *NeuroImage, 3,* 127–142.

Madden, D. J., Turkington, T. G., Provenzale, J. M., Denny, L. L., Langley, L. K., Hawk, T. C., et al. (2002). Aging and attentional guidance during visual search: Functional neuroanatomy by positron emission tomography. *Psychology and Aging, 17,* 24–43.

Madden, D. J., Turkington, T. G., Provenzale, J. M., Hawk, T. C., Hoffman, J. M., & Coleman, R. E. (1997). Selective and divided visual attention: Age-related changes in regional cerebral blood flow measured by $H_2^{15}O$ PET. *Human Brain Mapping, 5,* 389–409.

Madden, D. J., & Whiting, W. L. (2004). Age-related changes in visual attention. In P. T. Costa & I. C. Siegler (Eds.), *Recent advances in psychology and aging* (pp. 41–88). Amsterdam, The Netherlands: Elsevier.

Madden, D. J., Whiting, W. L., Provenzale, J. M., & Huettel, S. A. (2004). Age-related changes in neural activity during visual target detection measured by fMRI. *Cerebral Cortex, 14,* 143–155.

Malach, R., Reppas, J. B., Benson, R. R., Kwong, K. K., Jiang, H., Kennedy, W. A., et al. (1995). Object-related activity revealed by functional magnetic resonance imaging in human occipital cortex. *Proceedings of the National Academy of Sciences of the United States of America, 92,* 8135–8139.

May, C. P., Kane, M. J., & Hasher, L. (1995). Determinants of negative priming. *Psychological Bulletin, 118,* 35–54.

Mayr, U. (2001). Age differences in selection of mental sets: The role of inhibition, stimulus ambiguity, and response-set overlap. *Psychology and Aging, 16,* 96–109.

McCarthy, G., Puce, A., Belger, A., & Allison, T. (1999). Electrophysiological studies of human face perception. II: Response properties of face-specific potentials generated in occipitotemporal cortex. *Cerebral Cortex, 9,* 431–444.

McDowd, J. M., & Craik, F. I. M. (1988). Effects of aging and task difficulty on divided attention performance. *Journal of Experimental Psychology: Human Perception and Performance, 14,* 267–280.

McDowd, J. M., & Shaw, R. J. (2000). Attention and aging: A functional perspective. In F. I. M. Craik & T. A. Salthouse (Eds.), *The handbook of aging and cognition* (2nd ed., pp. 221–292). Hillsdale, NJ: Erlbaum.

Mehagnoul-Schipper, D. J., van der Kallen, B. F., Colier, W. N., van der Sluijs, M. C., van Erning, L. J., Thijssen, H. O., et al. (2002). Simultaneous measurements of cerebral oxygenation changes during brain activation by near-infrared spectroscopy and functional magnetic resonance imaging in healthy young and elderly subjects. *Human Brain Mapping, 16,* 14–23.

Middleton, F. A., & Strick, P. L. (2002). Basal-ganglia "projections" to the prefrontal cortex of the primate. *Cerebral Cortex, 12,* 926–935.

Milham, M. P., Erickson, K. I., Banich, M. T., Kramer, A. F., Webb, A., Wszalek, T., et al. (2002). Attentional control in the aging brain: Insights from an fMRI study of the Stroop task. *Brain and Cognition, 49,* 277–296.

Miller, E. K., & Cohen, J. D. (2001). An integrative theory of prefrontal cortex function. *Annual Review of Neuroscience, 24,* 167–202.

Miyake, A., Friedman, N. P., Emerson, M. J., Witzki, A. H., Howerter, A., & Wager, T. D. (2000). The unity and diversity of executive functions and their contributions to complex "frontal lobe" tasks: A latent variable analysis. *Cognitive Psychology, 41,* 49–100.

Myerson, J., Hale, S., Wagstaff, D., Poon, L. W., & Smith, G. A. (1990). The information loss model: A mathematical theory of age-related cognitive slowing. *Psychological Review, 97,* 475–487.

Nebes, R. D., & Madden, D. J. (1983). The use of focused attention in visual search by young and old adults. *Experimental Aging Research, 9*, 139–143.

Nielson, K. A., Langenecker, S. A., & Garavan, H. (2002). Differences in the functional neuroanatomy of inhibitory control across the adult life span. *Psychology and Aging, 17*, 56–71.

Nissen, M. J., & Corkin, S. (1985). Effectiveness of attentional cueing in older and younger adults. *Journal of Gerontology, 40*, 185–191.

Nobre, A. C., Sebestyen, G. N., Gitelman, D. R., Mesulam, M.-M., Frackowiak, R. S. J., & Frith, C. D. (1997). Functional localization of the system for visuospatial attention using positron emission tomography. *Brain, 120*, 515–533.

O'Craven, K. M., Downing, P. E., & Kanwisher, N. (1999). fMRI evidence for objects as the units of attentional selection. *Nature, 401*, 584–587.

Pashler, H. (1994). Dual-task interference in simple tasks: Data and theory. *Psychological Bulletin, 116*, 220–244.

Passingham, R. E., & Toni, I. (2001). Contrasting the dorsal and ventral visual systems: Guidance of movement versus decision making. *NeuroImage, 14*, S125–S131.

Paus, T., Koski, L., Caramanos, Z., & Westbury, C. (1998). Regional differences in the effects of task difficulty and motor output on blood flow response in the human anterior cingulate cortex: A review of 107 PET activation studies. *NeuroReport, 9*, R37–R47.

Piazza, M., Mechelli, A., Butterworth, B., & Price, C. J. (2002). Are subitizing and counting implemented as separate or functionally overlapping processes? *NeuroImage, 15*, 435–446.

Piccinin, A. M., & Rabbitt, P. M. (1999). Contribution of cognitive abilities to performance and improvement on a substitution coding task. *Psychology and Aging, 14*, 539–551.

Plude, D. J., & Doussard-Roosevelt, J. A. (1989). Aging, selective attention, and feature integration. *Psychology and Aging, 4*, 98–105.

Plude, D. J., & Hoyer, W. J. (1986). Age and the selectivity of visual information processing. *Psychology and Aging, 1*, 4–10.

Pollmann, S., Weidner, R., Müller, H. J., & von Cramon, D. Y. (2000). A fronto-posterior network involved in visual dimension changes. *Journal of Cognitive Neuroscience, 12*, 480–494.

Puce, A., Allison, T., Gore, J. C., & McCarthy, G. (1995). Face-sensitive regions in human extrastriate cortex studied by functional MRI. *Journal of Neurophysiology, 74*, 1192–1199.

Rabbitt, P. (1965). Age and discrimination between complex stimuli. In A. T. Welford & J. E. Birren (Eds.), *Behavior, aging, and the nervous system* (pp. 35–53). Springfield, IL: Thomas.

Reynolds, J. H., Chelazzi, L., & Desimone, R. (1999). Competitive mechanisms subserve attention in macaque areas V2 and V4. *Journal of Neuroscience, 19*, 1736–1753.

Rosen, A. C., Rao, S. M., Caffarra, P., Scaglioni, A., Bobholz, J. A., Woodley, S. J., et al. (1999). Neural basis of endogenous and exogenous spatial orienting. A functional MRI study. *Journal of Cognitive Neuroscience, 11*, 135–152.

Ross, M. H., Yurgelun-Todd, D. A., Renshaw, P. F., Maas, L. C., Mendelson, J. H., Mello, N. K., et al. (1997). Age-related reduction in functional MRI response to photic stimulation. *Neurology, 48*, 173–176.

Rowe, J. B., & Passingham, R. E. (2001). Working memory for location and time: Activity in prefrontal area 46 relates to selection rather than maintenance in memory. *NeuroImage, 14*, 77–86.

Rubin, D. C. (1999). Frontal-striatal circuits in cognitive aging: Evidence for caudate involvement. *Aging, Neuropsychology, and Cognition, 6*, 241–259.

Rushworth, M. F., Paus, T., & Sipila, P. K. (2001). Attention systems and the organization of the human parietal cortex. *Journal of Neuroscience, 21,* 5262–5271.

Rypma, B., & D'Esposito, M. (2000). Isolating the neural mechanisms of age-related changes in human working memory. *Nature Neuroscience, 3,* 509–515.

Salthouse, T. A. (1985). *A theory of cognitive aging.* North Holland, The Netherlands: Elsevier.

Salthouse, T. A. (1992). *Mechanisms of age-cognition relations in adulthood.* Hillsdale, NJ: Erlbaum.

Salthouse, T. A. (1996). The processing-speed theory of adult age differences in cognition. *Psychological Review, 103,* 403–28.

Salthouse, T. A. (2000). Aging and measures of processing speed. *Biological Psychology, 54,* 35–54.

Salthouse, T. A., Fristoe, N., & Rhee, S. H. (1996). How localized are age-related effects on neuropsychological measures? *Neuropsychology, 10,* 272–285.

Salthouse, T. A., Hancock, H. E., Meinz, E. J., & Hambrick, D. Z. (1996). Interrelations of age, visual acuity, and cognitive functioning. *Journal of Gerontology: Psychological Sciences, 51B,* 317–330.

Salthouse, T. A., & Miles, J. D. (2002). Aging and time-sharing aspects of executive control. *Memory & Cognition, 30,* 572–582.

Salthouse, T. A., & Somberg, B. L. (1982). Isolating the age deficit in speeded performance. *Journal of Gerontology, 37,* 59–63.

Sathian, K., Simon, T. J., Peterson, S., Patel, G. A., Hoffman, J. M., & Grafton, S. T. (1999). Neural evidence linking visual object enumeration and attention. *Journal of Cognitive Neuroscience, 11,* 36–51.

Schneider, B. A., & Pichora-Fuller, M. K. (2000). Implication of perceptual deterioration for cognitive aging research. In F. I. M. Craik & T. A. Salthouse (Eds.), *The handbook of aging and cognition* (2nd ed., pp. 155–219). Mahwah, NJ: Erlbaum.

Schneider, W., Casey, B. J., & Noll, D. (1994). Functional MRI mapping of stimulus rate effects across visual processing stages. *Human Brain Mapping, 1,* 117–133.

Schneider, W., Noll, D. C., & Cohen, J. D. (1993). Functional topographic mapping of the cortical ribbon in human vision with conventional MRI scanners. *Nature, 365,* 150–153.

Scialfa, C. T. (2002). The role of sensory factors in cognitive aging research. *Canadian Journal of Experimental Psychology, 56,* 153–163.

Scialfa, C. T., Thomas, D. M., & Joffe, K. M. (1994). Age differences in the useful field of view: An eye movement analysis. *Optometry and Vision Science, 71,* 736–742.

Sergent, J., Ohta, S., & MacDonald, B. (1992). Functional neuroanatomy of face and object processing: A positron emission tomography study. *Brain, 115,* 15–36.

Shilling, V. M., Chetwynd, A., & Rabbitt, P. M. (2002). Individual inconsistency across measures of inhibition: An investigation of the construct validity of inhibition in older adults. *Neuropsychologia, 40,* 605–619.

Shulman, G. L., Corbetta, M., Buckner, R. L., Fiez, J. A., Miezin, F. M., Raichle, M. E., et al., (1997). Common blood flow changes across visual tasks: I. Increases in subcortical structures and cerebellum but not in nonvisual cortex. *Journal of Cognitive Neuroscience, 9,* 624–647.

Shulman, G. L., d'Avossa, G., Tansy, A. P., & Corbetta, M. (2002). Two attentional processes in the parietal lobe. *Cerebral Cortex, 12,* 1124–1131.

Somers, D. C., Dale, A. M., Seiffert, A. E., & Tootell, R. B. (1999). Functional MRI reveals spatially specific attentional modulation in human primary visual cortex. *Proceedings of the National Academy of Sciences of the United States of America, 96,* 1663–1668.

Spieler, D. H., Balota, D. A., & Faust, M. E. (1996). Stroop performance in healthy younger and older adults and in individuals with dementia of the Alzheimer's type. *Journal of Experimental Psychology: Human Perception and Performance, 22*, 461–479.

Ungerleider, L. G., & Mishkin, M. (1982). Two cortical visual systems. In D. J. Ingle, M. A. Goodale, & R. J. W. Mansfield (Eds.), *Analysis of visual behavior* (pp. 549–586). Cambridge, MA: MIT Press.

Verhaeghen, P., & De Meersman, L. (1998). Aging and the Stroop effect: A meta-analysis. *Psychology and Aging, 13*, 120–126.

Verhaeghen, P., & Salthouse, T. A. (1997). Meta-analysis of age-cognition relations in adulthood: Estimates of linear age effects and structural models. *Psychological Bulletin, 122*, 231–249.

Watson, J. D. G., Myers, R., Frackowiak, R. S. J., Hajnal, J. V., Woods, R. P., Mazziotta, J. C., et al. (1993). Area V5 of the human brain: Evidence from a combined study using positron emission tomography and magnetic resonance imaging. *Cerebral Cortex, 3*, 79–94.

Weale, R. A. (1961). Retinal illumination and age. *Transactions of the Illuminating Engineering Society, 26*, 95–100.

West, R. L. (1996). An application of prefrontal cortex function theory to cognitive aging. *Psychological Bulletin, 120*, 272–292.

West, R. (L.), Murphy, K. J., Armilio, M. L., Craik, F. I. M., & Stuss, D. T. (2002). Lapses of intention and performance variability reveal age-related increases in fluctuations of executive control. *Brain and Cognition, 49*, 402–419.

Whiting, W. L., Madden, D. J., Langley, L. K., Denny, L. L., Turkington, T. G., Provenzale, J. M., et al. (2003). Lexical and sublexical components of age-related changes in neural activation during visual word identification. *Journal of Cognitive Neuroscience, 15*, 475–487.

Woldorff, M. G., Fox, P. T., Matzke, M., Lancaster, J. L., Veeraswamy, S., Zamarripa, F., et al. (1997). Retinotopic organization of early visual spatial attention effects as revealed by PET and ERPs. *Human Brain Mapping, 5*, 280–286.

Wolfe, J. M. (1998). Visual search. In H. Pashler (Ed.), *Attention* (pp. 13–73). East Sussex, U.K.: Psychology Press.

Yantis, S., Schwarzbach, J., Serences, J. T., Carlson, R. L., Steinmetz, M. A., Pekar, J. J., et al. (2002). Transient neural activity in human parietal cortex during spatial attention shifts. *Nature Neuroscience, 5*, 995–1002.

Zacks, J. L., & Zacks, R. T. (1993). Visual search times assessed without reaction times: A new method and an application to aging. *Journal of Experimental Psychology: Human Perception and Performance, 4*, 798–813.

Zeki, S., Watson, J. D. G., Lueck, C. J., Friston, K. J., Kennard, C., & Frackowiak, R. S. J. (1991). A direct demonstration of functional specialization in human visual cortex. *Journal of Neuroscience, 11*, 641–649.

8

The Cognitive Neuroscience
of Working Memory and Aging

Patricia A. Reuter-Lorenz
Ching-Yune C. Sylvester

Since its introduction in the 1970s, the concept of working memory has been a catalyst for research (Baddeley & Hitch, 1974). Working memory is a powerful explanatory construct that accords with our subjective experience: Introspection reveals a kind of mental workspace in which our current thoughts (information) can be maintained (rehearsed) in the fore. We sense that we accomplish this with inner speech (the phonological loop) or mental images (the visuospatial sketchpad). We can hold in mind this limited amount of information and discard it once our goal is completed (short-term memory). We can also reorganize, sort through, or otherwise work with the briefly retained information (executive processes). However, as with most introspective evidence, these experiences of "working memory" hint at, but do little to reveal, its inner workings and complex structure.

Several decades of behavioral and neuroscience research have provided these insights. Indeed, the construct of working memory has become such a mainstay of cognitive psychology that it figures prominently in major theories of cognition (e.g., Anderson, 1983; Schneider, 1993; D. E. Meyer & Kieras, 1997; Newell, 1990) and has been closely linked to language comprehension, reasoning and problem solving, and even the hallowed intelligence factor g (Spearman, 1927; Daneman & Carpenter, 1980; Turner & Engle, 1989; Engle et al., 1999). Specifically, research has documented that individual differences in the fortitude, or capacity, of working memory are strongly related to variations in performance on measures such as the Verbal Scholastic Aptitude Test, the Tower of Hanoi, and Ravens Progressive Matrices (Carpenter, Just, & Shell, 1990; see Jonides, 1995, for a review). It should not be surprising, then, that changes in working memory during the course of normal aging are a pivotal determinant of more general age-related declines in cognitive performance (Salthouse, 1995; Park et al., 2002).

The goal of this chapter is to review current knowledge about the effects of normal aging on working memory and its neural underpinnings as revealed by functional neuroimaging. The cognitive neuroscience approach has brought the study of aging to an exciting crossroad with great potential for new discoveries about cognitive aging in general and about working memory in particular (Reuter-Lorenz, 2002). The tools of cognitive neuroscience provide a new source of evidence to test and revise hypotheses about aging that were founded on purely behavioral results. At the same time, neuroimaging studies are raising completely new questions about aging and the potential for lifelong plasticity. Moreover, we believe that a cognitive neuroscience approach to aging can yield new insights into the structure of cognition in the youthful brain. This chapter examines these possibilities as they relate to the structure and function of working memory.

We begin with a general overview of working memory, how it is measured by different tasks, and a controversy that pertains to theoretical claims about the organization of working memory. We then review behavioral evidence indicating how working memory changes because of normal aging. This section is organized around three issues central to behavioral studies of aging working memory: (1) the effects of aging on maintenance versus maintenance plus processing tasks; (2) the role of attentional and inhibitory declines in aging working memory; and (3) the effects of aging on verbal versus nonverbal working memory. After an overview of the working memory circuitry in younger adults, we take an in-depth look at neuroimaging studies of aging and working memory published to date, and we examine how this literature can clarify each of the three issues emerging from the behavioral studies. Our conclusions describe what the infusion of neuroimaging has taught us about aging working memory, revisit the controversy about the organization of working memory, and point to directions for future research.

What Is Working Memory?

The working memory construct as proposed by Baddeley (Baddeley & Hitch, 1974; Baddeley, 1986), includes some of the fundamental properties of its progenitor, *short-term memory*, a limited capacity store that keeps information active via rehearsal processes for a brief period of time, on the order of 3–30 s (cf. Atkinson & Shiffrin, 1971; Murdock, 1974). Baddeley's system expanded on the notion of a short-term store in two key ways. First, he proposed the existence of different storage mechanisms specialized for verbal or phonological materials (phonological loop) on the one hand and for visuospatial material (visuospatial sketchpad) on the other. Each of these stores are separate and are associated with their own rehearsal processes. Second, he included the processes required to use the contents of these stores in the service of complex cognitive tasks. So, for example, the ability to retain a series of digits, identify the largest, multiply each in the series by it, and sum the products would require memory, ordering, calculations, and storage of intermediate products. These task requirements extend well beyond the capabilities ascribed to short-term memory and necessitate a kind of superordinate control system to orchestrate the dynamic execution of this series of operations. Enter the central executive, a sphere of cognitive processes that control the sequencing, selection, and flow of mental operations applied to the stored information. Thus, the working memory scheme proposed by Baddeley and widely adopted by the cognitive psychology community includes short-term memory stores, rehearsal processes that maintain information in an active state, and executive processes that enable work to be done with the stored contents (see Miyake & Shah, 1999).

Three decades of research on working memory have largely upheld these basic claims. Nevertheless, the construct of working memory continues to evolve. For example, there is evidence to suggest that there may be more than two stores, with the proposal of additional modality and material specific and episodic stores (Baddeley, 2003; Haxby et al., 2000; Smith, Jonides, & Koeppe, 1996; Potter, 1993). In addition, substantial effort is currently focused on defining the mental operations that make up the central executive (e.g., Smith & Jonides, 1999; Goldman-Rakic, 1995; Petrides, 1994).

Although different taxonomies of executive functions have been proposed (e.g., Smith & Jonides, 1999), at least four key processes appear crucial to the operation of working memory. One of them is *executive attention*, a term that refers to processes mediated by the so-called "anterior attention system" (Posner & Peterson, 1990; Engle, 2002). Executive attention focuses resources on task-relevant information and is the source of expectancies and priority setting. A second executive process, *inhibition*, is closely related to executive attention. Inhibitory processes serve to suppress irrelevant information, and to resolve interference and conflict. Another is *task management*, which refers to the ability to maintain a goal while organizing subgoals and intermediate solutions to the task at hand. The fourth is *set shifting*, which refers to the ability to rapidly change rule states and decision criteria. One of the field's current challenges is to define the precise role of such executive operations in working memory and the tasks that measure it.

Measuring Working Memory

The literature on working memory has drawn a distinction between tasks that emphasize the storage or maintenance of information versus those that include additional processing of the stored contents. Tasks that fall into the former category are thought to measure short-term memory, whereas tasks that fall into the latter category are thought to measure working memory (Engle et al., 1999; Park et al., 2002). For example, the letter, word, and digit span tasks emphasize rote maintenance and have thus been considered measures of short-term memory capacity. In these tasks, a string of items is presented either auditorily or visually and the participant recalls the series verbally or on paper. The capacity of such memory, long honored by the memorable phrase "7 plus or minus 2" (Miller, 1956), refers to the number of such items that can be accurately maintained over a brief retention interval.

Delayed matching to sample tasks, also referred to as item recognition tasks, is another class of tasks that emphasizes storage (Jacobsen, 1931; Goldman-Rakic, 1992; Sternberg, 1966). These tasks involve the presentation of up to seven items (the memory set) followed by a delay interval that lasts up to 20 s. A probe is then presented, and participants indicate yes or no whether the probe is an item in their memory set. Memory for spatial locations, faces, nonverbal sounds, and even emotions can be tested using these types of procedures (Smith et al., 1995; Haxby et al., 2000; Chao & Knight, 1997a, 1997b; Mikels, 2003). Note that this simple task can be described by three separate stages: the encoding stage, in which the memory set is perceived and encoded into working memory; the rehearsal stage, in which the information is maintained in an active state; and the recognition stage, in which the probe item is matched (or not) to one of the items retrieved from the memory set.

Maintenance tasks can be distinguished from tasks that explicitly require the manipulation or recoding of stored information, so-called maintenance-plus-processing tasks. The most widely used measures of working memory capacity are the reading span task developed by Daneman and Carpenter (1980) and the operation span task developed by Turner and Engle (1989). Both measures require the performance of two concurrent tasks and thus engage the executive processes of task management and set shifting in addition to executive attention. The reading span task requires participants to listen to a sequence of sentences and remember the final word of each sentence. At the same time, they must also pay attention to the meaning of the sentence itself because their comprehension of each sentence is tested as well. Working memory span is defined as the number of final words correctly remembered as the number of sentences in each sequence increases from two to six. Operation span is similar except that it requires the completion of mental calculations alternating with words that must be read and remembered, such as "$(5 \times 1) - 4 = 2$? beach."

Reading span and operation span are clearly more complex and place greater explicit demands on executive processing operations than do rote maintenance tasks. But, do these different kinds of tasks measure different kinds of memory? Several findings from the behavioral literature suggest that they do. First, working memory span, as measured by either the reading or operation span tasks, correlates highly with a number of measures of higher cognition, including tests of reading comprehension for which correlations measured by Pearson's r range from .72 to .90 (Daneman & Carpenter, 1980; Turner & Engle, 1989). Rote maintenance tasks do not correlate with such measures of higher cognition. Second, as described in the section that follows on working memory function in older adults, aging seems to spare performance on rote maintenance tasks while leading to marked declines on working memory tasks that explicitly require executive processes (maintenance-plus-processing tasks; Craik & Jennings, 1992). Thus, the apparent selectivity of age-related changes also argues for a fundamental difference between these two types of memory.

However, primary support for the distinction between short-term and working memory has been drawn from behavioral evidence. Taking into account more recent neuroimaging data, we argue in this chapter that these two types of memory differ only in degree rather than in kind. That is, all tasks requiring the on-line, short-term storage of limited amounts of information are measures of working memory, with the difference existing only in the demands they place on executive processing operations. Thus, our view places working memory measures along a continuum in which the degree of involvement of executive processing operations is what varies for each task. Toward one end of the continuum are the rote maintenance tasks, for which executive demands are minimally involved; toward the opposite end of the continuum are the reading and operation span tasks because of their considerable demands on executive processes.

However, neuroimaging of younger and older adults reveals a crucial property of working memory and the organization of this continuum. A task's position on the continuum of executive involvement is not fixed. It can vary depending on the size of the memory set, the context of the task, and the performance level and age of the performer. So, for example, as we show in this chapter, an item recognition task with a set size of six recruits executive processes more than the same task with a set size of three. Likewise, for any given working memory task, older adults may be more likely to recruit executive processes than younger adults. This means that a rigid taxonomy of tasks based on behavioral evidence alone can be misleading and incomplete. On this cautionary note, we turn to an examination of the behavioral evidence for age-related declines in working memory.

Working Memory Function in Older Adults

Because the behavioral literature on working memory and cognitive aging is vast, we focus our review around three major issues prominent in this literature and for which some progress has been made with neuroimaging: maintenance versus processing operations; attention, inhibition, and interference in working memory; and material-specific buffers and aging.

Maintenance Versus Processing Operations

Cognitive aging research reveals that performance differences between older and younger adults generally increase with greater task complexity (e.g., Salthouse & Babcock, 1991). This pattern holds for studies of working memory as well. In one well-cited study by Dobbs and Rule (1989), five groups ranging in age from 30 to over 70 years were compared on working memory tasks that differed in their storage and processing requirements. Dobbs and Rule found only slight age differences in forward and backward digit span tasks (storage), and age did not predict performance on these tasks. However, for the *n*-back task (storage plus processing), in which participants heard a continuous string of digits and had to repeat the digit 0, 1, or 2 back from the current digit, age differences were pronounced, and age did predict performance. The authors concluded that aging is more detrimental to the processing components of working memory than to the components responsible for information storage.

Besides using the number and kind of operations applied to stored information, there are other ways to define complexity. Gick, Craik, and Morris (1988) varied the grammatical complexity of the sentences in the sentence verification component of the reading span task. They found that the working memory accuracy of older adults suffered more from increased sentence complexity than that of young adults. Again, such findings have fostered the view that executive components of working memory are more affected by aging than working memory maintenance operations.

Indeed, a small-scale meta-analysis by Babcock and Salthouse (1990) confirmed greater processing than maintenance costs for older than younger adults across a corpus of 18 published reports (for an opposing view, see Craik, Morris, & Gick, 1990; Salthouse, Babcock, & Shaw, 1991). In addition, there are numerous reports of reliable age differences on working memory tasks that emphasize maintenance plus executive processing operations (Belleville, Rouleau, & Caza, 1998; Chao & Knight, 1997a, 1997b; Daigneault & Braun, 1993; Hartman, Dumas, & Nielson, 2001; Shimamura & Jurica, 1994; West et al., 1998; Van der Linden, Brédart, & Beerten, 1994; see also Hasher & Zacks, 1988, for a review), although direct experimental comparisons with simpler maintenance tasks are not always included. Moreover, reliable age differences have been documented on tests of executive processing that require minimal storage, including dual task coordination and task switching (Glass et al., 2000; Kramer, Hahn, & Gopher, 1999), Wisconsin Cart Sorting (Hartman, Bolton, & Fehnel, 2001), and Stroop (Verhaegen & De Meersman, 1998). A review of this literature is beyond the scope of this chapter, but can be found in a volume by U. Meyer, Spieler, and Kliegl (2001).

At face value, the behavioral data thus suggest the following proposal about working memory and aging: Rote maintenance abilities, and presumably their underlying neural substrates, are relatively spared in normal aging. In contrast, executive processing components of working memory and their neural substrates are affected disproportionately. This proposal implies that encoding, maintenance/rehearsal, and retrieval operations are relatively free from age-related decline. We have presented an alternative account we refer to as the selective compensation hypothesis (Reuter-Lorenz et al., 2001; Reuter-Lorenz, 2002) and for which we argue further in this chapter.

We propose that age-related declines in rote maintenance operations merely escape detection with the use of behavioral measures alone. Instead, both maintenance and processing operations decline with age; however, executive processes can compensate for declining maintenance operations, which reduces performance declines. The compensation is selective because the reverse does not occur: maintenance operations are unable to assume executive functions, so consequently executive declines are more evident. Moreover, the increased reliance on executive operations in the service of simpler storage tasks means that less executive resource is available to meet increased task demands. We return to these issues in our subsequent review of the neuroimaging literature.

Attention, Inhibition, and Interference in Working Memory

The executive processes of selective attention and inhibitory control have figured prominently in several accounts of aging and working memory decline (Hasher & Zacks, 1988; Engle, 2002; McDowd & Shaw, 2000). Although the details of these accounts differ, the basic idea is that age-related changes in executive attentional control and inhibition increase vulnerability to interference, resulting in declines in working memory.

Interference can influence working memory performance in multiple ways. During encoding, for example, distracting, irrelevant information may make its way into working memory. This can be referred to as a breakdown in selective attention (Hasher & Zacks, 1988; West, 1996). During the retention interval, irrelevant material could also be inadvertently encoded and then interfere with the material that is stored. This is a form of retroactive interference (RI), by which new material disrupts the retention of previously encoded information.

In addition, material encoded on a previous trial may interfere with material stored from the current trial and indeed decrease the storage capacity of working memory in that the antecedent representations remain active. This form of interference is known as proactive interference (PI), by which prior memory items disrupt the ability to remember a current set.

Interference effects can also emerge at retrieval, by the presence of extraneous probe items that must be ignored, or by a retrieval probe that activates competing candidate representations that must be vetoed in favor of the correct response. One can ask whether any or all of these forms of interference are greater in older than younger adults, and if so, why?

Several studies suggested that older adults have particular difficulty with selective attention and are thus more vulnerable to interference. For example, R. L. West (1999) studied younger and older adults in a version of the *n*-back task both with and without distracters on each trial. Older adults were more impaired by distracters than were young adults. Likewise, Connelly, Hasher, and Zacks (1991) found that older adults were less able to ignore irrelevant text in a reading comprehension test than young adults.

RI effects are also greater in older than younger adults according to some reports. Chao and Knight (1997a, 1997b) used an auditory memory task requiring the short-term maintenance and recognition of a single tone. The memory interval was either empty or filled with distracting tones. According to their electrophysiological results, older adults showed larger auditory evoked responses to the distracters than did young adults, suggesting they were less able to inhibit processing of these events. Moreover, older adults showed greater interference from these distracters, resulting in poorer performance in the filled versus the empty interval compared to the performance of young adults (see also Hartman, Dumas, & Nielson, 2001).

Hedden and Park (2001) found a similar result using lists of word pairs. Participants had to remember a list of three word pairs, after which they read three new pairs, which they were told to forget. During the recognition phase, older adults were more likely than young adults to mistake the "read items" for the to-be-remembered items, although age did not affect memory performance for the latter items. One possible explanation for the Hedden and Park result is that older adults have a more difficult time encoding or accessing information about the source or context in which they encountered a particular item (see also Braver et al., 2001; Mitchell, Johnson, Raye, Mather, et al., 2000). Indeed, they confirmed this interpretation in a subsequent study (Hedden & Park, 2003). Impaired encoding of contextual cues may reduce the distinctiveness of remembered items, making them more vulnerable to interference.

In contrast to the clear age-related deficits in selective attention and RI, results from studies on age differences in PI are mixed. One approach is to use variants of the rote maintenance task and to measure PI by comparing performance on early trials, for which interference is presumably low, to performance on later trials, for which interference has built up. This index of PI yields minimal to nonexistent age differences (Craik, 1977; see also Hedden & Park, 2001, for a review), with the exception of a study by Parkin and Walter (1991), which reported greater PI in older adults, who also scored poorly on a test of frontal lobe function (i.e., the Wisconsin Card Sorting Test).

On the other hand, robust age differences in PI have been found with a clever manipulation of the reading span task (May, Hasher, & Kane, 1999; see also Shimamura & Jurica, 1994). Typically, this task is administered so that the number of sentences to verify (and corresponding to-be-remembered final words) progressively increases. With this procedure, the later trials are not only more difficult (longer) trials, but also have been preceded by more material than the earlier trials and thus are more subject to PI.

To test whether age differences in susceptibility to PI underlie age differences in reading span, May et al. (1999) administered this task both in the canonical ascending order and in descending order (i.e., presenting the longer lists first and thus reducing the potential for PI). The results were striking: The standard administration yields significantly larger memory span in younger than in older adults. The descending order eliminates this age difference. This result, which was replicated in a large sample of 250 participants (Lustig, May, & Hasher, 2001), indicated that an important source of age-related working memory decline is increased vulnerability to PI.

The behavioral tasks reviewed in this section, primarily variations of the rote maintenance task with interfering material, revealed age differences in performance. It is likely that, in the absence of such interfering material, these same tasks would show little or no age differences. We infer then that aging compromises the efficiency of processes that mediate interference resolution, presumably executive attention, contextual coding, and inhibitory control. As we shall see, neuroimaging has the potential to reveal the neural basis for this decline.

Material-Specific Buffers and Aging

Baddeley's innovation of hypothesizing material-specific buffers for verbal and nonverbal material has been amply substantiated over several decades of research. With respect to a multiple buffer architecture, the effects of aging center on two main questions. First, does aging affect all buffers equally? Second, do the buffers maintain their functional (and structural) independence in older age as they do in younger adults?

The working memory issues surrounding the first question also relate to the wellestablished finding that verbal intelligence or crystallized knowledge shows greater preservation across the life span than nonverbal intelligence measures such as the Wechsler Adult Intelligence Scale (WAIS) Performance IQ (Albert & Kaplan, 1979; Arenberg, 1978; Botwinick, 1977; Park et al., 2002; Schaie & Schaie, 1977; see Reuter-Lorenz, 2000, for a review). Does this dissociation reveal fundamental differences in the aging of verbal versus nonverbal cognitive mechanisms? Does it arise from a differential decline of the left and right cortical hemispheres? Or, does it stem from some failure to equate the verbal and nonverbal measures on some other variable, such as familiarity of materials or their reliance on processing speed? Several studies have gone to great lengths to rule out such confounding effects and have converged on the conclusion that nonverbal cognition is disproportionately impaired by aging (Jenkins et al., 2000; Myerson et al., 1999; Tubi & Calev, 1989; however, see Park et al., 2002, & Salthouse, 1995).

The general age-related dissociation between verbal and nonverbal cognition appears to apply to age-related changes in verbal and nonverbal working memory as well. In a series of experiments comparing verbal and spatial memory spans with and without an intervening interference task, Myerson, Hale and their colleagues concluded that spatial span suffers more from normal aging than does verbal span (Jenkins et al., 1999, 2000; Myerson et al., 1999). Convergence with this conclusion comes from a cross-sectional study that compared working memory for letters, faces, and doors in participants ranging in age from 20 to 70 years (Leonards, Ibanez, & Giannakopoulos, 2002). This n-back study found greater age-related declines in two-back accuracy for faces and doors than for letters; age effects on detection or one-back accuracy for all three materials were minimal.

Thus, when well-matched verbal and nonverbal (i.e., spatial, pictorial) working memory tasks are compared, age differences are more likely to emerge on the nonverbal tasks. Note that some investigators reported equivalent declines in verbal and nonverbal working memory (Salthouse, 1995; Park et al., 2002); greater verbal than nonverbal decline has never been reported. Neuroimaging can reveal whether there are age differences in the neural circuitry for verbal and nonverbal tasks and whether such differences depend on age-related variations in performance.

The second major question is whether verbal and spatial working memory subsystems retain their dissociability across the life span. To address this question, Myerson and colleagues (1999) evaluated the selectivity of interference effects in verbal and spatial working memory in younger and older adults. In younger adults, the separability of verbal and spatial working memory was established by a double dissociation: A verbal secondary task interferes more with verbal than with nonverbal working memory, and the opposite is true for a spatial secondary task. Are these interference effects equally selective in older adults? The answer from Myerson et al. is "yes." Despite the greater decline in spatial than verbal span for older adults, the magnitude and selectivity of interference effects are equivalent to the younger group, indicating that verbal and spatial working memory subsystems retain their separability in older age. Park and colleagues (2002) have reached a similar conclusion using a structural equation modeling approach across a sample ranging in age from 20 to 80 years. The models that best fit their data required separate constructs of verbal and spatial working memory, and this fit was equivalent across the life span.

Summary of Behavioral Evidence

Our review of the behavioral evidence highlights three issues that can be addressed with neuroimaging. First, to what extent is aging accompanied by the preservation, decline, or reorganization of the mechanisms that subserve rote maintenance and executive processing in working memory? Second, can we identify the neural under-pinnings of age-related declines in executive processing operations of working mem-ory, particularly those associated with interference resolution and attentional control? Third, does evidence from the neuroimaging domain support the differential decline of verbal and spatial working memory and their maintained separability in older age?

Neural Architecture of Working Memory

By approximately 1990, neuropsychological studies of patients with focal lesions had established several facts about the neural architecture of working memory. First, medial temporal regions, such as the hippocampus, are not essential for the integrity of rote verbal and spatial maintenance tasks because profoundly amnesic patients such as HM have normal digit and spatial spans (Ogden, 1996).

Second, the left hemisphere is critical to verbal working memory, whereas visual-spatial working memory relies more on the right hemisphere. This double dissocia-tion between verbal and visual-spatial working memory was established through contrasting case studies of patients with left or right hemisphere lesions, as well as larger scale group studies of patients with lateralized damage (see Jonides et al., 1996; see Vallar & Shallice, 1990, for reviews).

Third, the left perisylvian region extending into the parietal cortex is critical for verbal working memory because damage to it can reduce memory span to one or two items (Warrington & Shallice, 1969; Vallar & Shallice, 1990). Fourth, regions of lateral prefrontal cortex (PFC), especially Brodmann's areas (BAs) 46 and 9 (plate 8.1; see color insert) are critical components of the working memory circuitry in that damage to these regions impairs delayed response-type tasks (e.g., Goldman-Rakic, 1987), especially when the retention interval includes distraction (Baldo & Shimamura, 2000; D'Esposito & Postle, 1999) and when the damage to this area is bilateral (Owen et al., 1995; see Reuter-Lorenz et al., 2001, for a review).

Neuroimaging studies using positron emission tomography (PET) or more re-cently functional magnetic resonance imaging (fMRI) have largely confirmed these basic facts while providing greater anatomical and functional specificity about the network of regions involved in working memory. Nonetheless, these imaging tech-niques and their interpretation are still evolving. The emerging neurocognitive pic-ture of working memory should thus be considered a work in progress. With that said, we now turn to a brief overview of the brain regions involved in working memory as revealed by neuroimaging in young adults.

Working Memory Circuitry in Younger Adults

One of the most popular tasks used for neuroimaging studies of working memory is that of item recognition. In this task, a small set of items (e.g., two to six letters, words, locations, etc., depending on the condition or the study) appears for a second or two, followed by a blank delay, and then a probe item appears to which the participant responds yes or no. The initial studies using PET compared the brain activation from this memory condition to activity produced by a control condition with matched perceptual and response requirements, but minimal working memory demands.

When the activations from the control condition are subtracted from those in the memory condition, the remaining activations should reflect the working memory demands of the task (Posner et al., 1988). When letters are the items to be remembered, the most prevalent sites of cortical activity are in left Broca's area (BA 44 and 45; also referred to as ventrolateral prefrontal cortex, or VLPFC), supplementary motor cortex area (SMA; BA 6), and parietal areas (BA 40 and 7) (see Cabeza & Nyberg, 2000, for a synopsis). However, when locations are the memoranda, SMA and parietal areas 40 and 7 are activated along with occipital sites; activation is no longer seen in BA 44. Moreover, spatial working memory activation tends to be right dominant or bilateral. With faces and objects as stimuli, the network of active sites overlaps to some extent with the activations observed in both verbal and location/spatial memory, with the addition of activation in the inferior temporal cortex (BA 37), an area involved in object processing (Smith et al., 1995).

Such rote maintenance tasks used with this subtraction methodology and PET have not reliably activated the dorsolateral prefrontal cortex (DLPFC; BA 46/9), at least with memory loads of four items or fewer (see Cabeza & Nyberg, 2000; D'Esposito et al., 1998; and Smith & Jonides, 1999, for reviews). However, when the executive processing demands of the task are increased, for example, using an n-back task or requiring item manipulation, DLPFC is activated along with the frontopolar cortex (BA 10) in some studies (Owen et al., 1995; Smith et al., 1995; see Cabeza & Nyberg, 2000; D'Esposito et al., 1998, 1999; Fletcher & Henson, 2001; Smith & Jonides, 1999, for reviews).

Interestingly, DLPFC activation has also been found with PET for verbal memory loads greater than four items, suggesting that executive processes are recruited to meet these higher task demands (e.g., Rypma et al., 1999). The laterality of DLPFC activation is less clear cut, although there have been reports that left hemisphere activation is greater than the right for verbal stimuli, whereas the opposite is true for spatial stimuli (Smith, Jonides, & Koeppe, 1996). The extent to which lateral prefrontal activation is material specific versus process specific is a matter of ongoing debate (Johnson et al., 2003).

More recent studies using fMRI have corroborated these working memory patterns and provided greater temporal resolution that permits regions of activation to be linked to specific task components. That is, activity associated with encoding, maintenance, and retrieval stages of working memory can be examined independently, unlike PET for which activations reflect the combined activity of these processes. One major difference from PET findings that are emerging with fMRI concerns activation in DLPFC. Using fMRI, several studies of item maintenance-type tasks reported activation in BA 46/9 and in some cases BA 10 (Rypma et al., 2001). This result contrasts with the PET results, for which activation in these sites is unlikely unless the task has explicit executive processing demands.

Conflicting outcomes of this sort could be caused by the differential sensitivity of PET and fMRI measures. Event-related fMRI has revealed that the DLPFC activations in question tend to be more prominent during encoding and retrieval phases of working memory than during the maintenance/rehearsal phase (e.g., Rowe & Passingham, 2001; Rypma & D'Esposito, 2000). Because encoding and retrieval phases typically consume less time per trial than the maintenance/rehearsal phase and PET methodology requires averaging across all three epochs, activation patterns revealed by PET are more heavily weighted by maintenance/rehearsal processes. PET activity in this case is thus more reflective of storage processes of working memory and is less sensitive to activation during the encoding or retrieval stages that may include DLPFC.

To summarize, there is general agreement from lesion studies, PET, and fMRI that, for tasks that emphasize rote maintenance, activation in the VLPFC and parietal cortex tends to be lateralized according to the type of material. In addition, DLPFC sites may be recruited during encoding and retrieval, but appear to be less involved during maintenance per se. Tasks with higher memory loads, and item manipulation produce stronger activations in DLPFC.

Age-Related Changes in the Working Memory Circuitry

In studies of working memory, as with most other cognitive domains studied to date, age differences in brain activation fall into three categories, with multiple patterns often emerging within the same data set: (1) age-equivalent activity in which there are no age differences in the magnitude of activation, (2) age-related underactivation in which older adults activate an area less than younger adults, and (3) age-related overactivation in which older adults activate an area more than younger adults (Cabeza et al., 1997; Reuter-Lorenz, 2002). The third category of results is the most provocative and has led to several alternative interpretations.

Grady and colleagues (1994), who first reported age-related overactivation, suggested that it may be compensatory, a view supported by evidence from more recent studies (Cabeza, 2002; Reuter-Lorenz et al., 2000, 2001; see also Reuter-Lorenz, Stanczak, & Miller, 1999; Reuter-Lorenz & Stanczak, 2000). Others have suggested that overactivation could be a sign of dysfunction (Logan et al., 2002) and have referred to it as *nonselective* activation. This term implies that the recruitment of the referent area is activated arbitrarily or the result of a breakdown in selectivity of recruitment. We prefer to use the more neutral term, overactivation, because the basis for this activation pattern is presently uncertain.

We have identified 16 functional neuroimaging reports of working memory, published in refereed journals, that included a sample of older adults (at least 55 years of age). Some reports included multiple experiments, and others reported different features or analyses of a data set common with another article. So, altogether there are 10 analyses of verbal working memory tasks, 5 of visual working memory, 2 of working memory for faces, and 1 of working memory for spatial locations. All but 4 of these studies used rote maintenance tasks, and all but 7 used PET.

We review this body of work in some detail to describe both the general patterns emerging thus far and the potential sources of inconsistency. Then, we consider how and to what extent the neuroimaging data we have in hand addresses the questions and issues raised through several decades of behavioral studies of older adults. We include two tables that summarize these reports. Table 8.1 provides basic information about the methodologies used in each study, and table 8.2 summarizes key behavioral and neuroimaging results.

Maintenance of Verbal Material

We begin with the working memory tasks that emphasized maintenance of verbal materials. Six data sets reported in six articles fall into this category (Johnson et al., 2004; Reuter-Lorenz et al., 2000, 2001; Rypma et al., 2001; Rypma & D'Esposito, 2000, 2001). Let us look at these studies in greater detail.

In a blocked design using PET, Reuter-Lorenz et al. (2000) compared a four-item letter recognition task with a long delay to a single-item (repeated four times in a single display to match perceptual load) recognition baseline task with a minimal delay. Although both older and younger participants performed the memory task with high accuracy (92% and 97% accurate, respectively), the older group was significantly slower and less accurate than the younger group. A region of interest (ROI) analysis yielded similar sites of activation in both groups; these sites included the left VLPFC (BA 44), left premotor cortex (lateral BA 6), and left parietal areas (BA 40/7). Marked age differences were found for anterior sites, with older adults showing higher activation in right frontal regions (VLPFC and DLPFC) compared to young adults. In particular, older adults activated BA 44 bilaterally and showed greater right than left activation in DLPFC. The younger adults showed left lateralized activation in both areas. In contrast, age-equivalent activation was observed in parietal working memory regions.

In a follow-up experiment with new samples from each age group, these prefrontal patterns were replicated, and bilateral activation emerged for older participants in parietal sites as well (Reuter-Lorenz et al., 2001). The combined power of the two experiments revealed a reliable relationship between performance speed and activation of right DLPFC: Faster older adults activated this area more than slower-performing older adults. This pattern supported the interpretation offered by Reuter-Lorenz and colleagues that bihemispheric activation in older adults may be serving a compensatory role (Reuter-Lorenz et al., 1999, 2000, 2001). Because these studies used PET, the spatial resolution of the imaging data is limited, and the blocked methodology makes it difficult to isolate the age differences to encoding, rehearsal, or retrieval components of the working memory task. Subsequent studies using fMRI can offer these benefits.

Using fMRI in a similar letter recognition task, Rypma and colleagues (Rypma & D'Esposito, 2000, 2001; Rypma et al., 2001) also found prominent age differences in frontal areas, although the details of their results differed from those of Reuter-Lorenz and colleagues. Using a blocked fMRI design to compare younger and older adults, a six-item working memory task was compared to a one-item memory task, both with a long delay interval (Rypma et al., 2001). Six letters appeared in the encoding phase of both conditions, but in the one-item condition, five of the letters were to be ignored. Again, older adults were slower and less accurate than young adults, especially in the six-item task, but none of these effects reached statistical significance. The imaging data showed that both groups activated the same prefrontal and parietal sites reported by Reuter-Lorenz et al. (2000), but with several important differences. Both groups showed bilateral activation in many of these regions, and both groups showed activation of the DLPFC in addition to more extensive activation of the VLPFC that included areas 45 and 47. In general, older adults showed less activation than younger adults, but the most pronounced age differences emerged in the right DLPFC. The only site that older adults activated more than young adults was the left rostral PFC in BA 10.

The selective attention demands introduced by the requirement to ignore five of the letters appearing in the one-item condition raise the possibility that some of these activations and the age-differential effects are not because of working memory per se. However, two subsequent event-related fMRI experiments by Rypma and D'Esposito suggested that this is not the case (reported in both 2000 and 2001). Both experiments used a six-item versus a two-item letter recognition task with a 12-s retention interval. The event-related design permitted the separate assessment of brain activation associated with encoding, maintenance, and retrieval. The primary result to emerge from this pair of experiments was that younger adults showed greater activation in the right DLPFC than the older adults, and this difference was restricted to the retrieval stage. This pattern was significant in the six-item task, but was also evident for two items. Although these results appear to diverge considerably from those reported by Reuter-Lorenz et al. (2000, 2001), Rypma and D'Esposito reported an important correlation between right DLPFC activation and performance that complements these other reports. For older adults, greater activation in the right DLPFC was associated with faster performance, which is the same relationship found by Reuter-Lorenz et al. Interestingly, Rypma and D'Esposito found the opposite pattern for younger adults.

One further study published by Johnson and colleagues (2004) deserves mention in this section even though the task is not strictly a measure of verbal maintenance. Johnson et al. examined age differences in a process referred to as *refreshing*. In this task, the participant reads a single word and, when signaled by the appearance of a dot 500 ms later, thinks of that word again (i.e., refreshes it). This simple process activates a network of parietal and temporal areas in addition to activating the left DLPFC in younger adults (Raye et al., 2002). Older adults showed equivalent activation to young adults in all regions except the DLPFC, in which they showed significantly less activity.

Although refreshing bears some similarities to information maintenance in more canonical working memory tasks, its precise role in working memory will require additional research. When these links are established, the simplicity of the approach used by Johnson and colleagues (2004) can potentially shed new light on the elementary operations underlying mnemonic processing.

There are several consistent patterns across these studies despite variations in the task designs and imaging methods. First, the most reliable and consistent age differences are localized to prefrontal sites. Second, some activation differences are correlated with performance differences in the older group. These correlations are consistent with the idea that, in the aging brain, recruiting additional prefrontal areas can be beneficial to performance (i.e., compensatory in function). Note, however, that performance levels were not well matched in these studies, and no formal measures

Table 8.1 Aging, Working Memory, and Neuroimaging: Task Summary

	Technique	Material Type	WM Task	Baseline Task	Ages (years)*		Sample Size	
					Y	O	Y	O
Verbal maintenance								
Reuter-Lorenz et al., 2000	PET	Letters (4)	Maintenance (3 s); recog. task	Letter (1); 300-ms delay	21–30	65–75	8	16
Reuter-Lorenz et al., 2001	PET	Letters (4)	Maintenance (3 s); recog. task	Letter (1); 300-ms delay	19–30	61–72	12	12
Rypma et al., 2001	fMRI (block)	Letters (6)	Maintenance (3 s); recog. task	Letter (1); 5-s delay	22–29	62–73	6	6
Rypma and D'Esposito, 2000, 2001	fMRI (ER)	Letters (6 and 2)	Maintenance (12 s); recog. task	None; ITI used	21–30	61–82	6	6
	fMRI (ER)	Letters (6 and 2)	Maintenance (12 s); recog. task	None; ITI used	19–26	55–83	6	6
Johnson et al., in press	fMRI (ER)	Word (1)	Maintenance (550 ms); refresh at cue	None; ITI used	19.6	65.3	7	7
Visual maintenance								
McIntosh et al., 1999 Della-Maggione et al., 2000	PET	Gratings (2)	Maintenance (4 s); discrimination task	Gratings (2); varied short delay	20–30	60–79	10	9
Bennet et al., 2001	fMRI (ER)	Object and location (3)	Maintenance; recog. task	None; ITI used	20–29	66–71	6	6
Rypma and D'Esposito, 2000, 2001 Park et al., in press	fMRI (ER)	Outdoor scenes (1)	Maintenance (4 s); fragment recog. task	Outdoor scenes (1); no delay	20.6	67	11	10
Mitchell, Johnson, Raye, and D'Esposito, 2000	fMRI (ER)	Object and location (3)	Maintenance (4 s); fragment recog. task	None; ITI used	23.7	67	6	6

Face maintenance								
Grady et al., 1998	PET	Faces (1)	Maintenance; recog. task	Visual noise (3), random response	25	66	13	16
Grady et al., 2001	PET	Faces (1)	Maintenance; recog. task	Visual noise (3), random response	—	66.1	—	21
Location maintenance								
Reuter-Lorenz et al., 2000	PET	Dots (3)	Maintenance; recog. task	Dot (1); short delay	18–25	62–73	10	10
Verbal maintenance plus processing								
Jonides et al., 2000	PET	Letters (4)	Rejecting high-conflict probe	Rejecting low-conflict probe	19–30	61–72	12	12
Haut et al., 2000	PET	Numbers (Y: 6, O: 10)	Generate vs. monitor random sequence	Counting numbers (Y: 6, O: 10)	30–58	60–69	6	6
Grossman et al., 2002	fMRI (block)	Sentences (long noun-gap)	Sentence comprehension	Sentences (short noun–gap)	22.6	64.5	13	11
Smith et al., 2001	PET	Math problems and sentences (Y: 5, O: 4)	Operation span	Math alone and sentence memory alone (Y: 5, O: 4)	18–29	65–72	12	12

Note. fMRI, functional magnetic resonance imaging; ITI, intertrial interval; O, older; PET, positron emission tomography; recog. task, recognition task; Y, young.

Table 8.2 Aging, Working Memory, and Neuroimaging: Results Summary

	Behavioral Performance		Parietal		Premotor/ SMA		VLPFC		DLPFC		Rostrolateral PFC		DLPFC performance correlations	
	Speed	Accuracy	Left	Right	Left	Right	Left	Right	Left	Right	Left	Right	Y	O
Verbal maintenance														
Reuter-Lorenz et al., 2000	Y faster	Y more accurate	=	=	>		=	>	<	>				⋁
Reuter-Lorenz et al., 2001	Y faster	Y more accurate	n.e.		n.e.		<*	>*		>*		n.e.		⋁
Rypma et al., 2001	n.s.	n.s.	<*		<*		=*		<*	<*		>*	n.r.	
Rypma and D'Esposito, 2000, 2001	Y faster	n.s.	n.e.		n.e.				<*a	<*a	n.e.		△	⋁
	Y faster	n.s.	n.e.		n.e.				<*a	<*a	n.e.		△	⋁
Johnson et al., in press	n.r.	n.s.							<*b				n.r.	
Visual maintenance														
McIntosh et al., 1999														
Della-Maggiore et al., 2000														
Bennett et al., 2001	n.s.	n.s.	n.e.		n.e.			<*	>*				△	⋁
Rypma and D'Esposito, 2000, 2001	Y faster	n.s.							<*a	<*a		n.e.		⋁
Park et al., in press	Y faster	n.s.	>*a				>*a	>*a					n.s.	

Face maintenance										
Grady et al., 1998	Y faster	n.s.	>	>	<*	<*	>*	<	>	∟
Grady et al., 2001	n.a.[c]	n.a.[c]	n.a.		n.a.	n.a.	n.a.			⅃
Location maintenance										
Reuter-Lorenz et al., 2000	Y faster	n.s.	=	=	=	>	>	<	n.s.	
Verbal maintenance plus processing										
Jonides et al., 2000	Y better than O[c]				<*	<*	>			
Haut et al., 2000										
S-C contrast (i.e., self-ordered vs. control)	n.r.	n.s.	<*	=*	=*	<*	=*	<*	n.r.	
E-C contrast (i.e., experiment ordered vs. control)		=*	>*	=*	<*	>*	>*	=*	n.r.	
Grossman et al., 2002	Y faster	n.s.	<*	>	>*	>*	>*	>*	n.r.	
Smith et al., 2001 (seniors vs. good young)	Y faster	n.s.	=	>	>	^	^	<	Low accuracy Y and all O, greater left PFC activation than high accuracy Y	

Note. DLPFC, dorsolateral prefrontal cortex; n.a., no young participants for comparison; n.e., area not examined for activation differences, implies use of region of interest analysis for other regions; n.r., not reported; n.s., not significant; O, older; PFC, prefrontal cortex; SMA, supplementary motor cortex area; VLPFC, ventrolateral prefrontal cortex; Y, young; =, significant activation in both groups, no difference reported; >, significant activation in older subjects, not in younger subjects; <, significant activation in younger subjects, not in older subjects; no direct comparison between groups; =*, direct comparison made—not significantly different; >*, significantly more activation for older subjects compared to younger subjects; <*, significantly more activation for younger subjects compared to older subjects; ∟, negative correlation between performance and activation; ⅃, positive correlation between performance and activation.

[a]During retrieval/probe.
[b]During refresh.
[c]Composite z of accuracy and speed.

of strategy use were obtained. Thus, the possibility remains that age differences in activation patterns could stem from age differences in performance or from differences in the way that younger and older adults approach these tasks.

Maintenance of Visual Material

Three experiments to date, reported in seven articles, have examined age differences in the circuitry associated with working memory in which visual identities of stimuli must be maintained over a delay and then matched to a subsequent probe. The first experiment reported by McIntosh and colleagues (1999) used sine-wave gratings. This study addressed an important issue that was unresolved in the verbal working memory imaging studies reviewed in the preceding section: The stimuli are elementary visual forms that do not readily lend themselves to verbal coding or other strategic transformations that could contribute to activation differences between the age groups. Furthermore, the performance levels of younger and older adults were more closely matched in this experiment than in the verbal studies, thus minimizing any confounding effects from performance. PET measurements were obtained while participants made same/different judgments about the frequency of two gratings (i.e., Gabor patches) presented successively with either a 500- or 4000-ms retention interval.

A variety of analyses performed on this data set led to three separate reports (Bennett et al., 2001; Della-Maggiore et al., 2000; McIntosh et al., 1999). Some of the most relevant highlights follow. First, both age groups activated a network of areas involved in working memory that included bilateral inferior prefrontal regions and the right inferior temporal cortex. Second, the interregional correlations were greater in the younger adults than in the older group, suggesting an age-related alteration in the functional connectivity among areas. Third, older adults activated the left DLPFC, which was not reliably engaged in the younger sample, and greater activation in this region was associated with better performance (see Bennett et al., 2001, for a summary of all analyses associated with this data set). These data therefore echo a pattern evident in the verbal maintenance tasks reviewed above: Increases in activation are associated with better performance in the older participants.

The correspondence between the verbal and visual memory results is reinforced by the results from another task requiring visual maintenance reported by Rypma and D'Esposito (2000, 2001). In this task, participants had to remember two features of each object in a sequence of briefly presented displays: the form of each object as well as its location. Note that this two-feature condition was actually a visual/spatial hybrid task because both visual identity and location memory were tested. The activation results mirrored their findings for verbal working memory (i.e., greater DLPFC activation during retrieval for young participants compared to older participants). Faster responses again were correlated with greater activation in the DLPFC for the older group, consistent with a beneficial impact of prefrontal recruitment.

Another way to think about the visual memory task discussed by Rypma and D'Esposito (2000, 2001) is in terms of the ability to bind together or form associations between different attributes of an item, in this case, its identity and its location.

Mitchell and colleagues have shown that older adults have difficulty with this aspect of encoding that can lead to performance deficits in both working memory and long-term memory for such information (Mitchell, Johnson, Raye, Mather, et al., 2000). To discover the neural correlates of this binding problem, they took another approach to the data set discussed by Rypma and D'Esposito by focusing specifically on brain regions that were more active when younger participants had to remember two attributes than when they had to remember either single attribute alone (Mitchell, Johnson, Raye, Mather, & D'Esposito, 2000). The anterior hippocampus was the site that most clearly distinguished these conditions; indeed, this was the region in which older adults showed age-related underactivation.

This result was corroborated in a study by Park and colleagues (2003) that examined the maintenance of complex visual scenes in younger and older adults. A condition in which the scenes were viewed continually rather than maintained in memory was also included. Younger adults showed more activity in anterior hippocampal regions compared to older adults, and older adults showed more activation than young adults in inferior prefrontal loci during the probe phase of the tasks. Interestingly, neither of these age differences was unique to the maintenance condition, and both appeared in the continual viewing condition as well. This result is important because it suggests that age differences associated with probe processing (e.g., linked to comparison, decision making, and response selection) may not be specific to age-related changes in working memory per se. Moreover, these results and those of Mitchell, Johnson, Raye, and D'Esposito (2000) implicate the hippocampus in working memory for complex visual material and suggest that age-related declines may be linked to underactivation of this brain region. (Hippocampal activity is rarely noted in working memory studies except when complex visual materials are used. This area therefore is not included in table 8.2.)

These studies examining the maintenance of visual material again point to prefrontal sites as an important locus for age-related changes and show that, in some cases, greater prefrontal activation is associated with better performance in the older groups. The network analyses used by McIntosh and colleagues suggest a possible breakdown in interregional activation patterns in the aging brain. This important possibility is one that warrants attention in future research.

Maintenance of Faces

Only one study to date has used neuroimaging to examine age differences in working memory for faces. In a delayed match-to-sample task using PET, Grady and colleagues (Grady et al., 1998; see also Grady et al., 2001) presented a single face that was retained for a variable delay ranging from 1 to 21 s. Younger and older adults performed this task with comparable accuracy at most delays (average accuracy of 98.5% and 94.7%, respectively), but with longer reaction times for older adults. Both groups revealed activation in the bilateral PFC, although the distribution of this activity varied with age. Specifically, younger adults activated the bilateral VLPFC (BA 45) more than older adults, and older adults activated the left DLPFC (BA 9) more than younger adults.

Several different correlational analyses revealed some opposite patterns of correlations for the younger and older groups that are noteworthy, but difficult to interpret. Increased activity in bilateral DLPFC, fusiform, and hippocampus was associated with poorer performance in older adults and better performance in younger adults. Conversely, right middle temporal and medial prestriate activation was associated with poorer performance in younger adults and better performance in older adults. Additional analyses of this data set reported in Grady et al. (2001) showed right prefrontal (BA 10) activity correlating with better performance in older adults. To summarize, this data set revealed both age-related underactivation and overactivation; again, prefrontal recruitment was a major source of variation because of age. In these results, however, not all prefrontal activity in the older group was related to better performance.

Maintenance of Spatial Locations

Only one study to date has examined location working memory as a function of age; this was done by Reuter-Lorenz and colleagues using PET (2000). Three locations were marked by briefly presented dots, followed by a 3-s delay and a probe that was either in a remembered location or not. The control task presented a single dot that varied between two locations, along with two constant markers and a minimal delay of 200 ms. The results from this experiment were complementary to those obtained from the verbal task described above. Young adults showed right lateralized activity in the SMA and VLPFC, with a trend toward right lateralization in the DLPFC, whereas older adults showed activation in both left and right prefrontal sites. It is important to note that the older adults who participated in the PET study had been preselected for their high performance. Consequently, the older and younger groups had equivalent accuracy, yet highly distinct patterns of activation associated with this task.

Summary of Maintenance Results

Despite the relatively small number of experiments on aging and working memory maintenance published to date, there are a number of consistent patterns that permit five tentative conclusions (see table 8.2). First, regardless of whether performance is matched across the two age groups, older and younger adults tend to activate different brain areas to perform the same task, indicating that they engage different neural circuitry. Thus, age differences that are invisible with behavioral measures are revealed by brain imaging. Second, prefrontal areas figure prominently, although by no means exclusively, as the site of age differences. Third, all forms of maintenance tested thus far are affected by aging. Fourth, evidence from performance/activation correlations is consistent with the possibility that recruitment of some brain regions by older adults is compensatory. Fifth, there are clear indications of increased bilaterality in older adults, although this appears to be only one of several signs of age-related alteration in neurocognitive processes.

Maintenance-plus-Processing Working Memory Tasks

There are only four published data sets from studies of working memory tasks that explicitly manipulate executive processing demands in younger and older adults. All four used verbal materials. They are organized here with respect to processing complexity because this dimension has been shown to influence age-related performance declines.

Jonides et al. (2000) added a high-interference condition to the standard letter recognition task to investigate the neural underpinnings of age-related decline in inhibition, or interference resolution. In the canonical version of this task, four target letters appear, followed by a delay, then a probe letter. Typically, the target and probe letters on each trail are drawn randomly from the set of candidate items. In the high-interference condition (modeled after Monsell, 1978), the negative probe letter on the current trial (probes to which the participant should answer "no") was one of the target letters of the immediately preceding trial. Such highly familiar probe letters should be harder to reject than unfamiliar ones. Indeed, they were for younger adults, as evidenced by their slower responses to these probes. These effects were significantly exacerbated in older adults (Jonides et al., 2000).

This behavioral age difference has a neural correlate. When the brain activation in blocks of trials with a high proportion of familiar negative probes is compared to blocks with a low proportion of such trials, younger adults activate a region in the left inferior frontal gyrus (BA 45). Older adults do not activate this area, suggesting that their performance deficit is related to the underrecruitment of this site in the inferior frontal gyrus (IFG). Support for this interpretation comes from a patient with damage to this site who also showed a very specific deficit, rejecting highly familiar negative probes (Thompson-Schill et al., 2002).

It is worth noting that these interference effects reported by Jonides et al. (2000) were based on the same data set used in the report by Reuter-Lorenz et al. (2001). Thus, older adults who show underactivation of BA 45 under conditions of high conflict show overactivation of the right DLPFC and right BA 44 in association with the maintenance demands of the same task. Thus, age-related underactivation can be associated with decline of specific executive processes, and concurrent overactivation may characterize the neural substrate of other processes engaged by that same task.

Another study used PET to investigate two tasks that required monitoring, updating, and ordering of a list of numbers held in working memory. The self-ordered task required young participants to generate a random sequence of the digits 1–10 and older adults to generate random sequences of the digits 1–6 (Haut et al., 2000). The experimenter-ordered task required participants to monitor a random sequence of these digits and to report which number was omitted. The baseline task required participants simply to count from 1 to 10 or 1 to 6 depending on the age group. Different sequence lengths were used to produce age-equivalent performance on both experimental and baseline tasks, especially because older adults perform poorly on tasks of self-ordering (Shimamura & Jurica, 1994). The neuroimaging results revealed similarities and differences between the two age groups. Both groups showed equivalent activation in a number of working memory areas in parietal and frontal cortices. However, in the self-ordered task, the younger group activated the right DLPFC and left inferior parietal cortex more than older adults; in the experimenter-ordered task, the older adults activated the left DLPFC and left temporal cortex more than did young adults. There is no clear explanation for why these tasks should produce differing results.

The third study, by Grossman and colleagues (2002), examined working memory during sentence comprehension. Working memory demands were varied by varying the structure of the sentences so that few or many words intervened (short or long gaps, respectively) between the subject–noun phrase and the subsequent pronoun that indexed that phrase. (For example, a short antecedent-gap sentence is "*The strange man* in black *who* adored Sue was rather sinister in appearance." A long antecedent-gap sentence is "*The cowboy* with the bright gold front tooth *who* rescued Julia was adventurous.). Participants were holding information in working memory while simultaneously processing the semantic and grammatical content of the relevant information. Both age groups activated a similar network of areas associated with the comprehension of written sentences, but the working memory manipulation activated different areas in the two age groups: Older adults showed less activation in left parietal sites, but more activation than younger adults in left lateral prefrontal, right temporal-parietal, and bilateral medial frontal sites (BA 10, 9). Older adults performed quite well on this task, leading the authors to suggest that the age differences in activation were compensatory.

The final experiment reviewed in this section studied working memory using the operation span task. As mentioned in the section on measuring working memory, this is a dual task in which a math problem is presented along with a word. The participant must judge whether the problem is solved correctly or not and then commit the word to memory. After a short sequence of these, the participant must recall the words in order. Smith and colleagues used PET to study younger and older adults performing this dual task, as well as math alone and word memory alone (Smith et al., 2001). The activations in the dual task were compared to the average activations from the math and memory combined. The objective of this approach was to determine if additional areas, presumably related to the executive demands of coordinating the two tasks, would be activated in the dual task relative to its constituents. The performance of the two age groups was equated by using several parametric adjustments, including use of a five-item sequence for the younger group and a four-item sequence for the older group. A variety of analyses performed on the PET data converged on the same conclusion: Older adults recruit left DLPFC (BA 9) during the performance of operation span; only a subgroup of the young adults showed activation in this site—those who performed most poorly on the operation span task relative to the constituent memory task.

Summary of Maintenance-Plus-Processing Changes in Working Memory

Given the importance of prefrontal regions to executive control, it should not be surprising that these regions of the cortex are the locus of age differences during tasks of maintenance plus processing. The most common pattern is for older adults to show greater PFC activation than younger adults. There, is however, an interesting and potentially important exception in the study by Jonides et al. (2000) that found age-related prefrontal underactivation in PFC. How do we explain this discrepancy? The first point to consider is that the Jonides et al. site was in the VLPFC rather than DLPFC, in which overactivation is often found. Moreover, the function served by this ventrolateral site appears to be strongly lateralized to the left hemisphere and specific to the selection of contextually appropriate representations. The absence of overactivation or bilateral recruitment in older adults suggests that this function may be less plastic than other executive processes and one for which compensation is less available.

With the sparse number of studies currently in the literature, no conclusions can be drawn yet about the relationship between activation of executive regions and performance on storage plus processing tasks. However, older adults appear more inclined to activate prefrontal areas at lower levels of task demand (see also DiGiralomo et al., 2001). This possibility urges caution in selecting the appropriate baseline condition. To the extent that the baseline comparison conditions recruit PFC in older adults, their activation of these sites will be underestimated in the task of interest.

Conclusions and Future Directions

Three main issues were posed by a review of the behavioral evidence from the cognitive aging literature on working memory. The first concerned the differential age-related decline of maintenance versus executive processes. Neuroimaging studies reveal unequivocal age-related alterations in the neural substrates recruited during tasks that emphasize maintenance. This class of tasks is by no means spared from the effects of aging. Indeed, based on activation patterns alone, which indicate age-related increases in PFC activation, to perform optimally the older brain appears to be treating these tasks as maintenance-plus-processing tasks.

To explain the age-related behavioral dissociation, we have proposed the selective compensation hypothesis (see also Reuter-Lorenz et al., 2001; Reuter-Lorenz, 2002). According to this proposal, both storage and executive processes decline with age. However, to perform storage operations, the older brain recruits additional brain areas, including executive processing areas. This pattern of overactivation serves a compensatory function, thereby reducing the behavioral expression of age-related alterations in storage operations. As a result of overrecruitment at relatively low levels of task demand, older adults have fewer available resources to meet the requirements of more demanding tasks, and the associated performance declines on tasks that explicitly require executive processing are more robust (Reuter-Lorenz et al., 2001; Reuter-Lorenz, 2002). Although we have focused on selective compensation within the domain of working memory, we speculate that this principle, whereby executive processes compensate for other cognitive operations, could extend to the neural substrates underlying other domains as well (e.g., Li et al., 2001).

The second issue concerned the question of age-related proneness to interference in working memory and the decline of attentional and inhibitory mechanisms that resolve interference. The study by Jonides et al. (2000) linked focal age-related underactivation in IFG (or VLPFC) to increased interference effects. Future work is needed to establish whether altered function of this region is related more generally to interference proneness in older adults.

The third issue concerns the differential decline of verbal and nonverbal working memory and their separability in older age. The neural substrates of both general types of working memory change with age. The two reports that included both verbal and nonverbal tasks did not test the same older adults in both tasks, therefore precluding any direct assessment of relative verbal and nonverbal declines. Reuter-Lorenz et al. (2000) did find, however, that older adults showed greater overlap in the regions activated by the verbal and spatial tasks than did younger adults, as might be expected given that both tasks produced greater bilateral activation in the older group. This result raises the possibility that there is declining differentiation of verbal and spatial subsystems with age (see Park et al., 2001; Reuter-Lorenz, 2002). Neuroimaging results also implicated the hippocampus as a substrate underlying greater decline of nonverbal than verbal working memory with age. In particular, the studies by Park et al. (2003) and Mitchell, Johnson, Raye, and D'Esposito (2000) found age-related underactivation of the hippocampus during demanding visual encoding (complex scenes and object/location binding, respectively). To the extent that nonverbal encoding relies more on the hippocampus than verbal encoding, age-related declines in hippocampal function could have a greater impact on working memory for nonverbal than for verbal materials.

It is clear from this review that a full agenda awaits future neuroimaging research on aging and working memory. Many stones remain unturned. In addition to the need to address more fully the questions from the behavioral literature, cognitive neuroscience has contributed an agenda of its own. The functional consequences of age-related under- and overactivation need to be more clearly defined. Are overactivations compensatory, and if so what operations are mediated by this activity? How do functional alterations relate to structural changes that accompany normal aging (Raz et al., 1997)?

New issues are emerging as well. For example, there is increasing evidence that the same prefrontal regions are activated by long-term and working memory tasks. This kind of evidence will prompt us to reconsider the extent to which long-term memory and working memory are separable systems and to examine age-related covariations in these processes (e.g., Fletcher & Henson, 2001; Raganath, Johnson, & D'Esposito, 2003; Nyberg et al., 2003).

The neuroimaging evidence reviewed here also has implications for theoretical claims about the distinction between short-term memory as measured by rote maintenance tasks and working memory as measured by maintenance-plus-processing tasks. The distinction between these task types is not upheld at the neural level: Executive processing areas are readily activated by older adults in maintenance-only tasks, and young adults activate these sites during encoding and retrieval as well. Moreover, high-performing young adults show less activation in executive processing areas on tasks such as operation span compared to their low-performing counterparts or older adults. Thus, the idea that executive processes are reserved for working memory tasks that explicitly require them (i.e., maintenance-plus-processing tasks) appears to be incorrect at the neural level. Working memory measures may be more properly viewed along a continuum in which the degree and kind of executive process recruited depends not only on the task demands, but also on the age and performance level of the participant. As a result, older adults may be able to recruit executive processes to assist with maintenance operations and thereby compensate for some functional consequences of age-related decline.

Acknowledgments   This chapter is dedicated to the memory of Patricia Goldman-Rakic. We thank Kathryn M. Welsh for her valuable assistance with the preparation of this chapter and the members of the Cognitive and Affective Neuropsychology Laboratory for helpful discussions of this work. Preparation of this chapter was supported by National Institutes of Health grant AG18286.

References

Albert, M. S., & Kaplan, E. (1979). Organic implications of neuropsychological deficits in the elderly. In L. W. Poon, J. L. Fozard, L. S. Cermak, D. Ehrenberg, & L. W. Thompson (Eds.), *New directions in memory and aging*: *Proceedings of the George Talland Memorial Conference* (pp. 406–432). Hillsdale, NJ: Erlbaum.

Anderson, J. R. (1983). *The architecture of cognition*. Cambridge, MA: Harvard University Press.

Arenberg, D. (1978). Differences and changes with age in the Benton Visual Retention Test. *Journal of Gerontology, 33*, 534–540.

Atkinson, R. C., & Schiffrin, R. M. (1971). The control of short-term memory. *Scientific American, 225*, 82–95.

Babcock, R. L., & Salthouse, T. A. (1990). Effects of increased processing demands on age differences in working memory. *Psychology and Aging, 5*, 421–428.

Baddeley, A. (2003). Working memory: Looking forward and looking back. *Nature Reviews*: *Neuroscience, 4*, 829–839.

Baddeley, A. D. (1986). *Working memory*. Oxford, U.K.: Oxford University Press.

Baddeley, A. D., & Hitch, G. J. (1974). Working memory. In G. H. Bower (Ed.), *The psychology of learning and motivation* (Vol. 8, pp. 47–89). New York: Academic Press.

Baldo, J. V., & Shimamura, A. P. (2000). Spatial and color working memory in patients with lateral prefrontal cortex lesions. *Psychobiology 28*, 156–167

Belleville, S., Rouleau, N., & Caza, N. (1998). Effect of normal aging on the manipulation of information in working memory. *Memory and Cognition, 26*, 572–583.

Bennett, P. J., Sekuler, A. B., McIntosh, A. R., & Della-Maggiore, V. (2001). The effects of aging on visual memory: Evidence for functional reorganization of cortical networks. *Acta Psychologica, 107*, 249–273.

Botwinick, J. (1977). Intellectual abilities. In J. E. Birren & K. W. Schaie (Eds.), *Handbook of the psychology of aging* (pp. 580–605). New York: Van Nostrand Reinhold.

Braver, T. S., Barch, D. M., Keys, B. A., Carter, C. S., Kaye, J. A., Janowsky, J. S., Taylor, S. F., Yesavage, J. A., Mumenthaler, M. S., Jagust, W. J., & Reed, B. R. (2001). Context processing in older adults: Evidence for a theory relating cognitive control to neuroaging. *Journal of Experimental Psychology*: *General, 130*, 746–763.

Cabeza, R. (2002). Hemispheric asymmetry reduction in older adults: The HAROLD model. *Psychology and Aging, 17*, 85–110.

Cabeza, R., Grady, C. L., Nyberg, L., McIntosh, A. R., Tulving, E., Kapur, S., Jennings, J. M., Houle, S., & Craik, F. I. M. (1997). Age-related differences in neural activity during memory encoding and retrieval: A positron emission tomography study. *Journal of Neuroscience, 17*, 391–400.

Cabeza, R., & Nyberg., L. (2000). Imaging cognition II: An empirical review of 275 PET and fMRI studies. *Journal of Cognitive Neuroscience, 12*, 1–47.

Carpenter, P. A., Just, M. A., & Shell, P. (1990). What one intelligence test measures: A theoretical account of the processing in the Raven Progressive Matrices Test. *Psychological Review, 97*, 404–431.

Chao, L. L., & Knight, R. T. (1997a). Age-related prefrontal alterations during auditory memory. *Neurobiology of Aging, 18*, 87–95.

Chao, L. L., & Knight, R. T. (1997b). Prefrontal deficits in attention and inhibitory control with aging. *Cerebral Cortex, 7*, 63–69.

Connelly, S. L., Hasher, L., & Zacks, R. T. (1991). Age and reading: The impact of distraction. *Psychology & Aging, 6*, 533–541.

Craik, F. I. M. (1977). Age differences in human memory. In J. E. Birren & K. W. Schaie (Eds.), *Handbook of the psychology of aging* (pp. 384–420). Englewood Cliffs, NJ: Prentice-Hall.

Craik, F. I. M., & Jennings, J. M. (1992). Human memory. In F. I. M. Craik & T. A. Salthouse (Eds.), *Handbook of aging and cognition* (pp. 51–109). Hillsdale, NJ: Erlbaum.

Craik, F. I. M., Morris, R. G., & Gick, M. L. (1990). Adult age differences in working memory. In G. Vallar & T. Shallice (Eds.), *Neuropsychological impairments of short-term memory* (pp. 247–267). New York: Cambridge University Press.

Daigneault, S., & Braun, C. M. J. (1993). Working memory and the self-ordered pointing task: Further evidence for early prefrontal decline in normal aging. *Journal of Clinical and Experimental Neuropsychology, 15*, 881–895.

Daneman, M., & Carpenter, P. A. (1980). Individual differences in working memory and reading. *Journal of Verbal Learning and Verbal Behavior, 19*, 450–466.

Della-Maggiore, V., Sekuler, A. B., Grady, C. L., Bennett, P. J., Sekuler, R., & McIntosh, A. R. (2000). Corticolimbic interactions associated with performance on a short term memory task are modified by age. *Journal of Neuroscience, 16*, 8410–8416.

D'Esposito, M., Aguirre, G. K., Zarahn, E., Ballard, D., Shin, R. K., & Lease, J. (1998). Functional MRI studies of spatial and nonspatial working memory. *Cognitive Brain Research, 7*, 1–13.

D'Esposito, M., & Postle, B. R. (1999). The dependence of span and delayed-response performance on prefrontal cortex. *Neuropsychologia, 37*, 1303–1315.

D'Esposito, M., Postle, B. R., Ballard, D., & Lease, J. (1999). Maintenance versus manipulation of information held in working memory: An event-related fMRI study. *Brain and Cognition, 41*, 66–86.

DiGirolamo, G. J., Kramer, A. F., Barad, V., Cepeda, N. J., Weissman, D. H., Milham, M. P., Wszalek, T. M., Cohen, N. J., Banich, M. T., Webb, A., Belopolsky, A. V., & McAuley, E. (2001). General and task-specific frontal lobe recruitment in older adults during executive processes: A fMRI investigation of task-switching. *Neuroreport, 12*, 2065–2071.

Dobbs, A. R., & Rule, B. G. (1989). Adult age differences in working memory. *Psychology and Aging, 4*, 500–503.

Engle, R. W. (2002). Working memory capacity as executive attention. *Current Directions in Psychological Science, 11*, 19–24.

Engle, R. W., Tuholski, S. W., Laughlin, J. E., & Conway, A. R. A. (1999). Working memory, short-term memory, and general fluid intelligence: A latent-variable approach. *Journal of Experimental Psychology, 128*, 309–331.

Fletcher, P. C., & Henson, R. N. A. (2001). Frontal lobes and human memory: Insights from functional neuroimaging. *Brain, 124*, 849–881.

Gick, M. L., Craik, F. I., & Morris, R. G. (1988). Task complexity and age differences in working memory. *Memory and Cognition, 16*, 353–361.

Glass, J. M., Schumacher, E. H., Lauber, E. J., Zurbriggen, E. L., Gmeindl, L., Kieras, D. E., & Meyer, D. E. (2000). Aging and the psychological refractory period: Task-coordination strategies in young and old adults. *Psychology and Aging, 15*, 571–595.

Goldman-Rakic, P. S. (1987). Circuitry of the primate prefrontal cortex and the regulation of behavior by representational memory. In F. Plum (Ed.), *Handbook of physiology, the nervous systems, higher functions of the brain* (Section I, Vol. 5, pp. 373–417). Bethesda, MD: American Physiological Society.

Goldman-Rakic, P. S. (1992). Working memory and the mind. *Scientific American, 267*, 110–117.

Goldman-Rakic, P. S. (1995). Architecture of the prefrontal cortex and the central executive. *Annals of the New York Academy of Sciences, 769*, 71–83.

Grady, C. L., Furey, M. L., Pietrini, P., Horwitz, B., & Rapoport, S. I. (2001). Altered brain functional connectivity and impaired short-term memory in Alzheimer's disease. *Brain, 124*, 739–756.

Grady, C. L., Maisog, J. M., Horwitz, B., Ungerleider, L. G. Mentis, M. J., Salerno, J. A., Pietrini, P., Wagner, E., & Haxby, J. V. (1994). Age-related changes in cortical blood flow activation during visual processing of faces and location. *Journal of Neuroscience, 14*(3, Part 2), 1450–1462.

Grady, C. L., McIntosh, A. R., Bookstein, F., Horwitz, B., Rapoport, S. I., & Haxby, J. V. (1998). Age-related changes in regional cerebral blood flow during working memory for faces. *Neuroimage, 8*, 409–425.

Grossman, M., Cooke, A., DeVita, C., Alsop, D., Detre, J., Chen, W., & Gee, J. (2002) Age-related changes in working memory during sentence comprehension: An fMRI study. *Neuroimage, 15*, 302–317.

Hartman, M., Bolton, E., & Fehnel, S. E. (2001). Accounting for age differences on the Wisconsin Card Sorting Test: Decreased working memory, not inflexibility. *Psychology and Aging, 16*, 385–399.

Hartman, M., Dumas, J., & Nielsen, C. (2001). Age differences in updating working memory: Evidence from the Delayed Matching-to-Sample Test. *Aging, Neuropsychology, and Cognition, 8*, 14–35.

Hasher, L., & Zacks, R. T. (1988). Working memory, comprehension, and aging: A review and a new view. In G. H. Bower (Ed.), *The psychology of learning and motivation: Advances in research and theory* (pp. 193–225) San Diego, CA: Academic Press.

Haut, M. W., Kuwabara, H., Leach, S., & Callahan, T. (2000). Age-related changes in neural activation during working memory performance. *Aging, Neuropsychology, and Cognition, 7*, 119–129.

Haxby, J. V., Petit, L., Ungerleider, L. G., & Courtney, S. (2000). Distinguishing the functional roles of multiple regions in distributed neural systems for visual working memory. *Neuroimage, 11*, 380–391.

Hedden, T., & Park, D. C. (2001). Aging and interference in verbal working memory. *Psychology and Aging, 16*, 666–681.

Hedden, T., & Park, D. C. (2003). Contributions of source and inhibitory mechanisms to age-related retroactive interference in verbal working memory. *Journal of Experimental Psychology: General, 132*, 93–112.

Jacobsen, C. F. (1931). The functions of frontal association areas in monkeys. *Comparative Psychology Monographs, 13*, 1–60.

Jenkins, L., Myerson, J., Hale, S., & Fry, A. F. (1999). Individual and developmental differences in working memory across the life span. *Psychonomic Bulletin and Review, 6*, 28–40.

Jenkins, L., Myerson, J., Joerding, J. A., & Hale, S. (2000). Converging evidence that visuospatial cognition is more age-sensitive than verbal cognition. *Psychology and Aging, 15*, 157–175.

Johnson, M. K., Raye, C. L., Mitchell, K. J., Greene, E. J., and Anderson, A. W. (2003). FMRI evidence for an organization of prefrontal cortex by both type of process and type of information. *Cerebral Cortex, 13*, 265–273.

Johnson, M. K., Raye, C. L., Mitchell, K. J., Greene, E. J., & Anderson, A. W. (2004). *Psychological Science, 15*, 127–132.

Jonides, J. (1995). Working memory and thinking. In D. Osherson & E. E. Smith (Eds.), *An invitation to cognitive science*. Cambridge, MA: MIT Press.

Jonides, J., Marshuetz, C., Smith, E. E., Reuter-Lorenz, P. A., & Koeppe, R. A. (2000). Age differences in behavior and PET activation reveal differences in interference resolution in verbal working memory. *Journal of Cognitive Neuroscience, 12*, 188–196.

Jonides, J., Reuter-Lorenz, P. A., Smith, E. E., Awh, E., Barnes, L. L., Drain, M., Glass, J., Lauber, E. J., Patalano, A. L., & Schumacher, E. H. (1996). Verbal and spatial working memory in humans. In D. L. Medin (Ed.), *The psychology of learning and motivation: Advances in research and theory* (Vol. 35, pp. 43–88). San Diego, CA: Academic Press.

Kramer, A. F., Hahn, S., & Gopher, D. (1999). Task coordination and aging: Explorations of executive control processes in the task switching paradigm. *Acta Psychologica, 101*: 339–378.

Leonards, U., Ibanez, V., & Giannakopoulos, P. (2002). The role of stimulus type in age-related changes of visual working memory. *Experimental Brain Research, 146*, 172–183.

Li, K. Z. H, Lindenberger, U., Freund, A. M., & Baltes, P. B. (2001). Walking while memorizing: Age-related differences in compensatory behavior. *Psychological Science, 12*, 230–237.

Logan, J. M., Sanders, A. L., Synder, A. Z., Morris, J. C., & Buckner, R. L. (2002). Under-recruitment and non-selective recruitment: Dissociable neural mechanisms associated with aging. *Neuron, 33*, 827–840.

Lustig, C., May, C. P., & Hasher, L. (2001). Working memory span and the role of proactive interference. *Journal of Experimental Psychology, 130*, 199–207.

May, C. P., Hasher, L., & Kane, M. J. (1999). The role of interference in memory span. *Memory and Cognition, 27*, 759–767.

McDowd, J. M., & Shaw, R. J. (2000). Attention and aging: A functional perspective. In F. I. M. Craik (Ed.), *The handbook of aging and cognition* (2nd ed., pp. 221–292). Mahwah, NJ: Erlbaum.

McIntosh, A. R., Sekuler, A. B., Penpeci, C., Rajah, M. N., Grady, C. L., Sekuler, R., & Bennett, P. J. (1999). Recruitment of unique neural systems to support visual memory in normal aging. *Current Biology, 9*, 1275–1278.

Meyer, D. E., & Kieras, D. E. (1997). A computational theory of executive cognitive processes and multiple-task performance: I. Basic mechanisms. *Psychological Review, 104*, 3–65.

Meyer, U., Spieler, D., & Kliegl, R. (Eds.). (2001). *Ageing and Executive Control* (pp. 257–278). East Essex, U.K.: Psychology Press.

Mikels, J. A. (2003). Hold on to that feeling: Working memory and emotion from a cognitive neuroscience perspective. Unpublished doctoral dissertation, University of Michigan, Ann Arbor.

Miller, G. A. (1956). The magical number seven, plus or minus two: Some limits on our capacity for processing information. *The Psychological Review*, *63*, 81–97.

Mitchell, K. J., Johnson, M. K., Raye, C. L., & D'Esposito, M. (2000). fMRI evidence of age-related hippocampal dysfunction in feature binding in working memory. *Cognitive Brain Research*, *10*, 197–206.

Mitchell, K. J., Johnson, M. K., Raye, C. L., Mather, M., & D'Esposito, M. (2000). Aging and reflective processes of working memory: Binding and test load deficits. *Psychology and Aging*, *15*, 527–541.

Miyake, A., & Shah, P. (1999). *Models of working memory: Mechanisms of active maintenance and executive control*. New York: Cambridge University Press.

Monsell, S. E. (1978). Recency, immediate recognition memory, and reaction time. *Cognitive Psychology*, *10*, 465–507.

Murdock, B. B. (1974). *Human memory: Theory and data*. Potomac, MD: Erlbaum.

Myerson, J., Hale, S., Rhee, S.H., & Jenkins, L. (1999). Selective interference with verbal and spatial working memory in young and older adults. *Journals of Gerontology*, *54B*, 161–164.

Newell, A. (1990). *Unified theories of cognition*. Cambridge, MA: Harvard University Press.

Nyberg, L., Marklund, P., Persson, J., Cabeza, R., Forkstam, C., Petersson, K. M., & Ingvar, M. (2003). Common prefrontal activations during working memory, episodic memory, and semantic memory. *Neuropsychologia*, *41*, 371–377

Ogden, J. A. (1996). *Fractured minds*. New York: Oxford University Press.

Owen, A. M., Sahakian, B. J., Semple, J., Polkey, C. E., & Robbins, T. W. (1995). Visuo-spatial short-term recognition memory and learning after temporal lobe excisions, frontal lobe excisions or amygdalo-hippocampectomy in man. *Neuropsychologia*, *33*, 1–24.

Park, D. C., Lautenschlager, G., Hedden, T., Davidson, N. S., Smith, A. D., & Smith, P. K. (2002). Models of visuospatial and verbal memory across the adult life span. *Psychology and Aging*, *17*, 299–320.

Park, D. C., Polk, T.A., Mikels, J. A., Taylor, S. F., & Marshuetz, C. (2001). Cerebral aging: Integration of brain and behavioral models of cognitive function. *Dialogues in Clinical Neuroscience: Cerebral Aging*, *3*, 151–165.

Park, D. C., Welsh, R. C., Marshuetz, C., Gutchess, A. H., Mikels, J., Polk, T. A., Noll, D. C., & Taylor, S. F. (2003). Working memory for complex scenes: Age differences in frontal and hippocampal activations. *Journal of Cognitive Neuroscience*, *15*, 1122–1134.

Parkin, A. J., & Walter, B. M. (1991). Aging, short-term memory, and frontal dysfunction. *Psychobiology*, *19*, 175–179.

Petrides, M. (1994). Frontal lobes and working memory: Evidence from investigations of the effects of cortical excisions in nonhuman primates. In F. Boller & J. Grafman (Eds.), *Handbook of neuropsychology* (Vol. 9, pp. 59–82). Amsterdam, The Netherlands: Elsevier.

Posner, M. I., & Peterson, S. E. (1990). The attention system of the human brain. *Annual Review of Neuroscience*, *13*, 25–42.

Posner, M. I., Peterson, S. E., Fox, P. T., and Raichle, M. (1988). Localization of cognitive functions in the human brain. *Science*, *240*, 1627–1631.

Potter, M. C. (1993). Very short-term conceptual memory. *Memory and Cognition*, *21*, 156–161.

Ranganath, C., Johnson, M. K., & D'Esposito, M. (2003). Prefrontal activity associated with working memory and episodic long-term memory. *Neuropsychologia*, *41*, 378–389.

Raye, C. L., Johnson, M. K., Mitchell, K. J., Reeder, J. A., & Greene, E. J. (2002). Neuroimaging a single thought: Dorsolateral PFC activity associated with refreshing just-activated information. *Neuroimage*, *15*, 447–453.

Raz, N., Gunning, F. M., Head, D., Dupuis, J. H., McQuain, J., Briggs, S. D., Loken, W. J., Thornton, A. E., & Acker, J. D. (1997). Selective aging of the human cerebral cortex observed in vivo: Differential vulnerability of the prefrontal gray matter. *Cerebral Cortex, 7*, 268–282.

Reuter-Lorenz, P. A. (2000). The cognitive neuropsychology of aging. In D. Park & N. Schwarz (Eds.), *Aging and cognition: A student primer* (pp. 93–113). Philadelphia, PA: Psychology Press.

Reuter-Lorenz, P. A. (2002). New visions of the aging mind and brain. *Trends in Cognitive Sciences, 6*, 394–400.

Reuter-Lorenz, P. A., Jonides, J., Smith, E. E., Hartley, A., Miller, A., Marshuetz, C., & Koeppe, R. A. (2000). Age differences in the frontal lateralization of verbal and spatial working memory revealed by PET. *Journal of Cognitive Neuroscience, 12*, 174–187.

Reuter-Lorenz, P. A., Marshuetz, C., Jonides, J., Hartley, A., & Smith, E. E. (2001). Neurocognitive ageing of storage and executive processes. *European Journal of Cognitive Psychology, 13*, 257–278.

Reuter-Lorenz, P. A., & Stanczak, L. (2000). Differential effects of aging on the functions of the corpus callosum. *Developmental Neuropsychology, 18*, 113–137.

Reuter-Lorenz, P. A., Stanczak, L., & Miller, A. (1999). Neural recruitment and cognitive aging: Two hemispheres are better than one especially as you age. *Psychological Science, 10*, 494–500.

Rowe, J. B., & Passingham, R. E. (2001). Working memory for location and time: Activity in prefrontal area 46 relates to selection rather than maintenance in memory. *Neuroimage, 14*, 77–86.

Rypma, B., & D'Esposito, M. (2000). Isolating the neural mechanisms of age-related changes in human working memory. *Nature Neuroscience, 3*, 509–515.

Rypma, B., & D'Esposito, M. (2001). Age-related changes in brain-behavior relationships: Evidence from event-related functional MRI studies. *European Journal of Cognitive Psychology, 13*, 235–256.

Rypma, B., Prabhakaran, V., Desmond, J. E., & Gabrieli, J. D. E. (2001). Age differences in prefrontal cortical activity in working memory. *Psychology and Aging, 6*, 371–384.

Rypma, B., Prabhakaran, V., Desmond, J. E., Glover, G. H., & Gabrieli, J. D. E. (1999). Load-dependent roles of frontal brain regions in the maintenance of working memory. *Neuroimage, 9*, 216–226.

Salthouse, T. A. (1991). Mediation of adult age differences in cognition by reductions in working memory and speed of processing. *Psychological Science, 2*, 179–183.

Salthouse, T. A. (1995). Differential age-related influences on memory for verbal-symbolic information and visual-spatial information. *Journal of Gerontology, 50B*, 193–201.

Salthouse, T. A., & Babcock, R. L. (1991). Decomposing adult age differences in working memory. *Developmental Psychology, 27*, 763–776.

Salthouse, T. A., Babcock, R. L., & Shaw, R. J. (1991). Effects of adult age on structural and operational capacities in working memory. *Psychology and Aging, 6*, 118–127.

Schaie, K. W., & Schaie, J. P. (1977). Clinical assessment and aging. In J. E. Birren & K. W. Schaie (Eds.), *Handbook of the psychology of aging* (pp. 692–723). New York: Van Nostrand Reinhold.

Schneider, W. (1993). Varieties of working memory as seen in biology and in connectionist/control architectures. *Memory and Cognition, 21*, 184–192.

Shimamura, A. P., & Jurica, P. J. (1994). Memory interference effects and aging: Findings from a test of frontal lobe function. *Neuropsychology, 8*, 408–412.

Smith, E. E., Geva, A., Jonides, J., Miller, A., Reuter-Lorenz, P. A., & Koeppe, R. A. (2001).

The neural basis of task-switching in working memory: Effects of performance and aging. *Proceedings of the National Academy of Sciences*, *98*, 2095–2100.

Smith, E. E., & Jonides, J. (1999). Storage and executive processes in the frontal lobes, *Science*, *283*, 1657–1661.

Smith, E. E., Jonides, J., & Koeppe, R. A. (1996) Dissociating verbal and spatial working memory using PET. *Cerebral Cortex*, *6*, 11–20.

Smith, E. E., Jonides, J., Koeppe, R. A., Awh, E., Schumacher, E. H., & Minoshima, S. (1995). Spatial versus object working memory: PET investigations. *Journal of Cognitive Neuroscience*, *7*, 337–356.

Spearman, E. (1927). *The abilities of man: Their nature and measurement*. New York: Macmillan.

Sternberg, S. (1966). High-speed scanning in human memory. *Science*, *153*, 562–654.

Thompson-Schill, S. L., Jonides, J., Marshuetz, C., Smith, E. E., D'Esposito, M., Kan, I. P., Knight, R. T., & Swick, D. (2002). Effects of frontal lobe damage on interference effects in working memory. *Journal of Cognitive, Affective & Behavioral Neuroscience*, *2*, 109–120.

Tubi, N., & Calev, A. (1989). Verbal and visuospatial recall by younger and older subjects: Use of matched tasks. Brief reports. *Psychology and Aging*, *4*, 493–495.

Turner, M. L., & Engle, R. W. (1989). Is working memory task dependent? *Journal of Memory and Language*, *28*, 127–154.

Vallar, G., & Shallice, T. (Eds). (1990). *Neuropsychological impairments of short-term memory*. New York: Cambridge University Press.

Van der Linden, M., Brédart, S., & Beerten, A. (1994). Age-related differences in updating working memory. *British Journal of Psychology*, *85*, 145–152.

Verhaeghen, P., & De Meersman, L. (1998). Aging and the Stroop effect: A meta-analysis. *Psychology and Aging*, *13*, 120–126.

Warrington, E. K., & Shallice, T. (1969). The selective impairment of auditory and verbal short-term memory. *Brain*, *92*, 885–896.

West, R., Ergis, A. M., Winocur, G., & Saint-Cyr, J. (1998). The contribution of impaired working memory monitoring to performance of the self-ordered pointing task in normal aging and Parkinson's disease. *Neuropsychology*, *12*, 546–554.

West, R. L. (1996). An application of prefrontal cortex function theory to cognitive aging. *Psychological Bulletin*, *120*, 272–292.

West, R. L. (1999). Visual distraction, working memory, and aging. *Memory and Cognition*, *27*, 1064–1072.

9

Long-Term Memory and Aging
A Cognitive Neuroscience Perspective

Denise C. Park
Angela H. Gutchess

There is little doubt that with age, long-term memory function declines. Countless behavioral studies have revealed significant differences in memory for lists of words (Smith, 1977), text (Dixon et al., 1982), contextual details (Park & Puglisi, 1985; Park, Puglisi, & Lutz, 1982), faces (Bartlett et al., 1989), abstract visual materials (Smith et al., 1990), and even television news (Frieske & Park, 1999). Although it is clear that memory decreases with age, there are a number of different views regarding the mechanisms underlying these age-related declines. Advances in neuroimaging have provided unprecedented opportunity to explore the neural underpinnings of behavioral theories of age-related memory decline and have resulted in new insights and neurally based theories accounting for memory phenomena associated with aging. In this chapter, we provide an updated view of what is known about aging and memory, integrating behaviorally based research with more recent neurally based findings.

Dominant views of causes of age-related declines in memory are varied in the cognitive aging literature. One broad theory is that there is a decline in processing resources, limiting the ability to encode and retrieve information. The clearest and perhaps earliest instantiation of this theory was presented by Craik and Byrd (1982). They argued that observed age-related declines in memory were caused by decreased "mental energy" or processing resource that limited the ability of older adults to engage in self-initiated processing. Later theorists have suggested that empirical measurement of processing resource could be represented by speed of information processing (Salthouse, 1994, 1996) or working memory capacity (Park et al., 1996, 2002; Salthouse et al., 1989; Salthouse & Babcock, 1991), both of which decline with age. Studies have conclusively demonstrated that both speed of processing and working memory mediate most, if not all, age-related variance in long-term memory

(Park et al., 1996, 2002; Salthouse & Babcock, 1991), demonstrating the utility of these constructs for understanding long-term memory.

In contrast to resource-based theories of speed and working memory, inhibition theory (Hasher & Zacks, 1988; Zacks & Hasher, 1997) suggests that older adults are less effective at gating or selecting information. Hence, they have less capacity available for effective encoding and retrieval of material, resulting in a long-term memory deficit. Other views of causes of memory decline with age include poor source memory (Johnson, Hashtroudi, & Lindsey, 1993), for which decreased ability to remember the context or source in which information is presented limits accurate recall of material with age.

Rather than focusing on age-related differences in difficulty recalling specific components of a memory such as context, Jacoby and colleagues (Jennings & Jacoby, 1993, 1997) suggested that there is an overall age impairment in recollection. They have argued that to understand age differences in memory, it is important to differentiate between memory processes that rely on explicit memory and memory based on feelings of familiarity. Jennings and Jacoby demonstrated convincingly that young adults rely on veridical explicit memory traces for memory performance, with some contributions from feelings of familiarity. In contrast, older adults' memory performance is dominated by automatically activated feelings of familiarity rather than explicit traces, resulting in degraded accuracy of their recall relative to young adults.

The connection of these cognitive theories of age-related decline in memory to neural function is one goal of this chapter, as is explicating new views of the aging memory that have resulted from neuroimaging studies. At the outset, it is important to note that the clarity and relative simplicity of behavioral theories are not mirrored in the neuroimaging literature. There are literally an infinite number of activation and deactivation patterns possible to be associated with memory function in a complex three-dimensional structure like the brain. Older adults may activate less, more, or even different neural structures to perform a memory task than young adults do (see Park et al., 2001; Cabeza, 2002; and chapter 2 of this volume for a more extended discussion of this issue). Further complicating interpretation of neural differences associated with aging on memory tasks are volumetric decreases in neural tissue that occur with age, with loss particularly marked in the frontal cortex (Raz, 2000; Raz et al., 1998). Nevertheless, despite these complications, neuroimaging studies have provided much insight into an understanding of aging and memory.

There are certain issues about memory that neuroimaging data are uniquely suited to answer. Behavioral measures of memory cannot ascertain if observed age differences result from strategy differences or mental effort exerted at encoding, as a result of differences in retrieval processes, or both. Neural activity, however, can be independently measured at encoding and retrieval, providing a unique window into processes that separately occur at these stages of memory.

In addition, neuroimaging allows a direct mapping of levels of activation in different brain sites to memory performance. Recall that Craik and Byrd (1982) suggested that decreased mental energy was the basis for age-related decline, which might lead one to expect consistently decreasing neural activation with age. However, neuroimaging studies suggest a different mapping. For example, Cabeza (2002) has argued that memory encoding and retrieval in older adults are often accompanied by increased activation relative to young in the frontal cortex. Specifically, he suggested that hemisphere-specific activations in young adults may be reorganized in old age so that bilateral activation occurs, that is, there is relatively equivalent engagement of frontal cortex in the left and right hemispheres. As will be discussed, this pattern of hemispheric asymmetry reduction in older adults (HAROLD) has been reported in several studies of memory and aging and is a recurring pattern in studies of working memory (see chapter 8, this volume). Further explicating the difficulties in mapping views of cognitive resource to neural activation are studies that demonstrated that low elder performers (Cabeza et al., 2002; Rosen et al., 2002; Daselaar, Veltman, Rombouts, Lazeron, et al., 2003) and even patients with early Alzheimer's disease have higher levels of frontal activations than young adults during encoding (Lustig et al., 2003).

It is also important to keep in mind some of the unique methodological limitations imposed by neuroimaging techniques when studying memory. Perhaps the most serious issue is the response limitations that occur when cognitive processes are studied using positron emission tomography (PET) or functional magnetic resonance imaging (fMRI). When in the scanner, subjects are usually restricted to making a button press to indicate their memory for a stimulus. As a result, PET and fMRI studies overwhelmingly involve the use of recognition memory compared to recall. Yet, the self-initiated processing demands of recognition compared to recall are considerably attenuated (Craik & McDowd, 1987), so researchers are typically studying tasks for which age differences in memory performance are minimized.

A second problem with studying memory using neuroimaging is that neural differences between groups are most readily interpreted when behavioral performance is equivalent between the groups, yet the most reliable finding about memory and age is that older adults perform more poorly than young. Hence, studies often involve differences in both recall and neural activation, making the activations more difficult to interpret, or studies involve the relatively small subset of memory tasks that are not age sensitive. Activations in these tasks are interpretable, but may not reflect neural activity that would occur with age on more demanding memory tasks.

Another concern is that, to detect adequate neural signal, it is often necessary to present relatively lengthy memory lists. There is some evidence that older adults are disproportionately sensitive to interference in memory paradigms (Hedden & Park, 2001, 2003; May, Hasher, & Kane, 1999), and these unusually long lists could result in age-related interference aggregated with other types of memory effects.

In this chapter, we frame our review around encoding and retrieval processes, context memory, and the study of individual differences. As depicted in table 9.1, the most dominant memory process studied has been encoding, with fewer studies focused on retrieval and effects of contextual support. A few studies have examined individual differences, which we argue provide some of the most compelling evidence to date to interpret the often-contradictory findings present in the literature, particularly with respect to frontal activations.

The study of the cognitive neuroscience of memory and aging is in its infancy, and these early studies in some ways parallel behavioral studies of memory and aging from the 1960s and 1970s, which had a more functional rather than theoretical focus. At the same time, the window neuroimaging studies provides into age differ-

Table 9.1 Study Characteristics of Neuroimaging Articles on Long-Term Memory and Aging

Reference	Method		Type of Memory		Stage of Memory		Memory Test Format		Material Type			
	PET	fMRI	Intentional	Incidental	Encoding	Retrieval	Recall	Recognition	Word	Face	Picture	Context
Grady et al., 1995	X		X	X	X	X		X		X		
Bäckman et al., 1997	X			X		X	X		X			
Schacter et al., 1996	X			X		X	X		X			
Cabeza, Grady, et al., 1997	X		X		X	X	X	X	X			
Grady et al., 1999	X		X	X	X			X	X		X	
Madden et al., 1999	X		X		X	X		X	X			
Cabeza et al., 2000	X		X			X		X	X			X
Anderson et al., 2000	X		X			X	X	X	X			
Iidaka et al., 2001		X	X		X			X			X	X
Logan et al., 2002		X	X	X	X			X	X	X		
Stebbins et al., 2002		X		X	X				X			
Grady et al., 2002	X		X	X	X	X				X		
Cabeza et al., 2002	X		X			X	X	X	X			X
Rosen et al., 2002		X		X	X			X	X			
Daselaar, Veltman, Rombouts, Lazeron, et al., 2003		X		X	X	X		X	X			
Morcom et al., 2003		X		X	X			X	X			
Maguire & Frith, 2003		X	X			X		X	X			
Daselaar, Veltman, Rombouts, Raaijmakers, et al., 2003		X		X	X				X			
Park et al., 2003		X		X	X			X			X	
Lustig et al., 2003		X		X				X	X			
Cabeza et al., 2004		X	X		X	X		X	X			
Gutchess et al., in press		X		X	X			X			X	

Note. fMRI, functional magnetic resonance imaging; PET, positron emission tomography.

ences in plasticity, strategy, and process is quite remarkable. These data are not only creating significant constraints for behavioral theories of aging, but are resulting in a tremendously fresh focus on new learning and strategy changes with age in the behavioral literature.

We also focus our review on neural activations in both frontal and hippocampal areas. Theorizing in the cognitive neuroscience of aging and memory has focused almost exclusively on frontal activation differences. The findings regarding age differences in engagement of the frontal cortex during memory processes are varied and often inconsistent. Cohen (Nystrom et al., 2000; Miller & Cohen, 2001) has argued that neural resources can be deployed flexibly by the frontal cortex, so that inconsistencies could result from strategy differences between subjects, particularly in memory tasks for which there may be multiple routes to successful encoding and retrieval. Furthermore, shrinkage of the prefrontal cortex and localization of compensatory sites could vary because of individual differences with aging, leading to difficulty interpreting group results.

In addition to focusing on the role of the frontal cortex in age differences in long-term memory, we also focus considerable attention on the hippocampus and related medial temporal structures, which are critically important for encoding and associating novel information into memory (Stern et al., 1996; Brewer et al., 1998; Wagner et al., 1998; Cohen et al., 1999). We propose that, with age, memory function is characterized by (1) decreased engagement of the hippocampus and other medial temporal areas; (2) relatively reliable age differences in left frontal activations, with some studies showing heightened activity and others less activity with age; (3) bilaterality in the frontal cortex in older adults when young adults show unilateral activity. Similar to the confusing picture with respect to left frontal activations, age-associated bilaterality sometimes results from increases in activation of the nondominant hemisphere by older adults (Cabeza, Grady, et al., 1997; Bäckman et al., 1997; Madden et al., 1999; Grady et al., 2002; Logan et al., 2002; Rosen et al., 2002); it also occurs as a result of less activation in the old in the dominant hemisphere activated by the young (Logan et al., 2002; Stebbins et al., 2002). Whether bilateral activations with age are compensatory for less-efficient neural function with age is not a question that is easily answered. Important tests would show increased activation in the contralateral hemisphere as a function of within-subject difficulty conditions and more contralateral activation at encoding on items that were remembered compared to those that were forgotten.

Encoding and Memory

There is a wealth of studies on the topic of encoding in both the behavioral and cognitive neuroscience literature of aging. Encoding has been isolated as a process that becomes impaired with aging because of numerous behavioral studies documenting age differences when subjects actively memorize materials (Smith, 1977) as well as under incidental conditions (Eysenck, 1974). There is good evidence that encoding is most impaired with age when the tasks demand substantial engagement of cognitive resources and there are relatively few cues or environmental supports to guide encoding (Craik, 1986; Park et al., 1990; Smith et al., 1998).

For example, Park et al. (1990) reported large age differences when old and young adults intentionally encoded pairs of unrelated pictures, but much smaller differences when the pictures were related because of more reliance in this last condition on world knowledge to support encoding and less reliance on basic processing mechanisms like speed and working memory. Similarly, Smith et al. (1998) found that elderly individuals integrate a target with a contextual cue effectively if there is a preexisting relationship among target and cue or an integration is provided by the experimenter. The elderly encounter difficulties with integration when the parts are seemingly unrelated, and they must engage in self-initiated processing, which draws heavily on cognitive resources.

Early Neuroimaging Studies of Encoding Processes With Age

The first published study of neuroimaging and aging (Grady et al., 1995) involved PET scanning of face encoding in young and old adults. Presenting findings that ultimately would be reported by many subsequent investigators, Grady and colleagues found that, during encoding, younger adults engaged more left prefrontal cortex than old and showed increased activation in medial temporal areas. There was also a striking correlation between hippocampal and prefrontal activation present in the young (.94), but not the old (.02). Based on these findings, Grady et al. concluded that encoding in late adulthood was characterized by less neural activity and decreased connectivity between the frontal and hippocampal areas.

In another early study that involved words instead of faces, Cabeza, Grady, et al. (1997), using PET, neuroimaged intentional encoding of words in young and old adults. Like Grady et al. (1995), they also reported decreased left prefrontal activations in older adults; in addition, they noted roughly equivalent levels of activation in the old in the left and right prefrontal cortex (bilaterality), whereas young adults showed a focal, unilateral pattern of left frontal activations. The compensation hypothesis emerged from these data as Cabeza, Grady, et al. suggested that the observed bilaterality in the old could be caused by a compensatory recruitment of the right hemisphere as a result of inadequate activations in the left hemisphere.

The findings from these two initial, pioneering studies proved to be reliable, and the observations from these seminal studies continue to be the basis for much theorizing. The notion that the aging brain was not simply characterized by linear declines in activity was provocative and convergent with the theorizing and findings of Reuter-Lorenz and colleagues (2000) on working memory. In an astonishingly short period of time, it became nearly obligatory for behavioral researchers reporting on memory function to integrate their behavioral findings with these seminal studies and with later neuroimaging work on aging and memory.

Other early findings were suggestive of the engagement of qualitatively different neural networks to perform encoding tasks. Madden et al. (1999) studied intentional word encoding and reported that regression analyses of reaction times and regional cerebral blood flow indicated that left prefrontal activations predicted young but not older adults' reaction times. Rather, for old adults, reaction times predicted left parahippocampal and right middle frontal activation, suggesting reorganization of neural systems with age. This conclusion was supported by a structural equation analysis of data from a PET study that also yielded evidence for reorganization of the neural systems in support of encoding and recall with age (Cabeza, McIntosh, et al., 1997).

Levels of Processing Manipulations at Encoding

In the behavioral literature, there is conflicting evidence about the impact of "deep" processing at encoding on subsequent memory of items. When older adults are presented with orienting tasks that require them to make semantic judgments about stimuli, deep encoding is induced (Craik & Lockhart, 1972). Generally, age differences persist under deep encoding and are of similar magnitude for incidental deep processing and intentional encoding (Eysenck, 1974; Smith, 1977; Simon, 1979; Mason, 1979), although there are exceptions for which deep encoding repairs older adults' memory to the level of young adults (Craik & Simon, 1980).

There are five neuroimaging studies of aging (Logan et al., 2002; Grady et al., 1999; Stebbins et al., 2002; Grady et al., 2002; Daselaar, Veltman, Rombouts, Raaijmakers, et al., 2003) that used levels of processing manipulations at encoding. All of these studies provided evidence for decreased activation of the left prefrontal cortex under intentional encoding compared to deep encoding, and all but one (Logan et al., 2002) showed evidence for decreased activations under deep-encoding conditions in the left inferior frontal cortex in old compared to young individuals; this area is associated with semantic processing (Demb et al., 1995; Poldrack et al., 1999). In addition, there is substantial evidence for decreased activation in older adults overall, as well as less medial temporal activation. Bilateral activations with age appear in many of the studies and generally occur as a result of less engagement of the left frontal cortex with age.

In an initial study, Grady et al. (1999), using PET, assessed the impact of shallow, deep, and intentional encoding of pictures and words in young and old adults. These investigators reported that young and old adults showed generally the same pattern of neural activations in response to the levels of processing manipulation, but that older adults' overall level of activation was attenuated compared to young adults. Deep encoding, when compared to intentional encoding, showed more activation of the left anterior prefrontal cortex and the hippocampus across subjects, but the old activated less in this area than the young. Interestingly, age differences in activation were larger for word encoding compared to pictures, just as memory differences as a function of age are larger for words than pictures. Because of the age differences in memory for words, it is not entirely clear whether the diminished neural activation drove poor memory or whether poor memory in older adults resulted in diminished activation.

In three subsequent levels of processing studies, deep encoding resulted in decreased left frontal activation in older adults compared to young adults. Stebbins et al. (2002) reported a study in which deep and shallow processing of words at encoding was examined in a young and old adult sample. They found evidence for increased activation in both old and young individuals under semantic encoding conditions. Congruent with the work of Grady et al. (1999), they reported decreased activation in left frontal areas in older adults compared to young adults during the deep semantic encoding condition. A bilateral activation pattern was observed in the frontal areas in old individuals, but it was because of decreased left frontal activation rather than an increase in right frontal activation above the level of young adults. In a later study, Grady et al. (2002) examined incidental shallow, incidental deep, and intentional encoding of faces, and as in the work of Stebbins et al. (2002), reported less left frontal activity in old individuals for deep encoding. There also was a correlation between frontal-hippocampal sites in young but not old adults, with a right prefrontal and parietal correlation in old adults. This finding demonstrated the use of different neural circuitry for task performance as a function of age and is suggestive of decreased hippocampal function in old adults. Finally, Daselaar, Veltman, Rombouts, Raaijmakers, et al. (2003) reported similar networks of activation in young and old individuals for a deep-processing task, with more left prefrontal activation and left hippocampal activation in young adults.

Thus, far, the studies reported are largely in agreement. The most global finding from these four levels of processing studies is that older adults remember less and show less neural activation. More specifically, the studies also demonstrated less left prefrontal activation in old individuals in semantic processing areas, particularly under intentional conditions.

In another study, using fMRI, Logan et al. (2002) studied encoding of words under three conditions: intentional memory, deep incidental processing (abstract vs. concrete judgments), and shallow incidental processing (temporal order of a letter). Behaviorally, both young and old showed a similar gain in memory for the items as a function of depth of processing. Memory was poorest for both age groups under phonemic encoding, intermediate for intentional encoding, and best for deep processing. Like the other studies described thus far, old adults had overall lower levels of activation across areas. Moreover, under intentional encoding conditions, as reported in the other studies, older adults showed less activation than young in left frontal cortex in Brodmann's areas 45 and 47, areas specialized for semantic processing (Demb et al., 1995; Poldrack et al., 1999).

The findings diverged from other studies in the deep-processing condition. Logan et al. (2002) reported that, under deep-encoding conditions, older adults showed left frontal activation at the same level as younger adults. They suggested that the difference in left frontal activations observed under intentional conditions between young and old was repaired or remediated by guiding older adults toward a deep encoding. Logan et al. also reported markedly less asymmetry of activation between hemispheres in old compared to young individuals, providing evidence for bilaterality. Logan et al. argued that older adults may have a production deficiency in use of strategies under intentional conditions, and that older adults are less selective in encoding operations in general. Older brains, however, activate more like younger brains under conditions of guided encoding for which strategies are controlled.

Superficially, it might appear that the Logan et al. (2002) findings are a fluke because four other studies found evidence for decreased left inferior frontal activations with age under deep-encoding instructions. However, in another study (also, like the Logan et al. study, conducted in the laboratory of Randy Buckner at Washington University, St. Louis, MO), Lustig et al. (2003) examined patterns of activation and deactivation in a large sample of young adults, healthy older adults, and older adults in early stages of Alzheimer's disease. This is not a true level-of-processing study because subjects only encoded words under deep-processing conditions. Nevertheless, these data are highly relevant to the issue of left frontal activations with age under deep-encoding conditions. As shown in figure 9.1a, Lustig et al. reported striking evidence for increased activations by both healthy and demented older adults in the left frontal cortex compared to young adults under deep-encoding conditions. The finding of equivalent or even higher levels of activation in older adults in left frontal areas under deep encoding is almost certainly reliable because the Lustig et al. (2003) study has one of the largest n's of studies to date (27 healthy old and 23 demented old), and the time course analysis displayed in figure 9.1 shows differences were maintained as a function of age over approximately a 25-s presentation block.

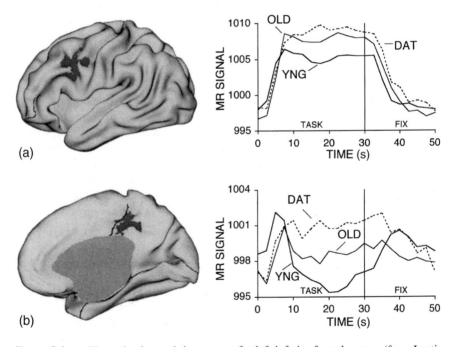

Figure 9.1. *a*, The activation and time course for left inferior frontal cortex. (from Lustig et al., 2003.) Note that both healthy and demented older adults showed increased activation compared to young (YNG) adults under deep-encoding conditions, and that activation was maintained over the entire task block before dropping off during fixation. *b*, Activations and time course for medial parietal/posterior cingulate cortex. Patients with dementia of the Alzheimer type (DAT) activated this region more than healthy elderly, who activated the region more than the young. (From "Adult Age Differences in Functional Neuroanatomy of Verbal Recognition Memory," by C. Lustig et al., 2003, *Proceedings of the National Academy of Sciences USA, 100,* 504–514. Copyright 2003 National Academy of Sciences, U.S.A.)

The data on levels of processing provide an inconsistent picture of encoding differences in neural activations as a function of age. Generally, the studies found consistent evidence for bilaterality in older adults, but it was often caused by decreased activation of the left frontal cortex relative to young adults rather than increased engagement beyond the level of younger adults, so it is harder (but not impossible) to make a compensation argument for this pattern than for a pattern in which activation increases above the level of young adults. Moreover, the data suggesting increased activation in left frontal areas in mildly demented subjects might be taken as evidence of a disinhibition or decreased selectivity rather than for the compensation argument, but it could also plausibly be that subjects with the poorest neural function showed the most activation, thus arguing that the pattern is supportive of compensation.

We believe that to reconcile whether deep encoding is characterized by more or less left frontal recruitment and whether the frontal recruitment is compensatory, it is important to demonstrate encoding conditions within subjects that increase or decrease engagement of left frontal areas in older adults. Relating such changes in frontal engagement to performance as well as to individual differences of subjects will bring much clarity to the issue of deep processing, aging, and left frontal activation.

The results of level-of-processing manipulations on medial temporal function are somewhat clearer. Of the three studies that examined activations in medial temporal areas, all reported some age differences in the role of the hippocampus in intentional versus deep incidental comparisons (Grady et al., 1999), deep versus shallow incidental encoding comparisons (Daselaar, Veltman, Rombouts, Raaijmakers, et al., 2003), or correlations of the hippocampus with behavior (Grady et al., 2002).

Finally, a methodological point worth noting is that, in a number of the studies (Stebbins et al., 2002; Daselaar, Veltman, Rombouts, Raaijmakers, et al., 2003), memory was not assessed or not reported. Future studies should include memory outcome measures because, without behavioral measures, it is difficult to interpret activation patterns, and actually, if there are no memory measures, it is uncertain whether these encoding conditions should be considered as memory studies. In closing this section, we should also note that the reports of the effects of deep versus intentional processing on memory in older adults in the behavioral literature are quite variable (see Kausler, 1990, for a review). Although the level-of-processing effect has proven to be one of the most reliable and integrative for the study of human memory, models that address changes in the quantity or engagement of processing resource with age have not been the most informative in understanding aging memory (e.g., Craik, 1986; Hasher & Zacks, 1979; see reviews in Hasher & Zacks, 1988, and Park, 2000). Hence, we suspect that confusion about engagement of neural resources will not be resolved by studying the depth of processing manipulations.

Differences in Encoding of Remembered Items

Since the seminal Grady et al. article on memory and aging was published in 1995, techniques for measuring neural signal have evolved. Event-related fMRI allows accurate recording of signal with a temporal resolution of as little as 2 s for whole brain coverage. Event-related designs are particularly useful for the study of memory because neural events associated with successful versus unsuccessful encoding of individual stimuli can be measured.

Using fMRI, Wagner et al. (1998) recorded event-related signal during encoding of words. Then, based on out-of-the-scanner recognition performance for the words, they sorted successfully encoded items (those recognized with high confidence) from those forgotten (those that were missed). The findings revealed that subjects were more likely to engage the parahippocampal gyrus for remembered compared to forgotten items, a finding also reported for pictures by Brewer et al. (1998).

There are three studies to date in the aging literature (Morcom et al., 2003; Daselaar, Veltman, Rombouts, Lazeron, et al., 2003; Gutchess et al., in press) that have used the subsequent memory paradigm to examine the neural signal at encoding associated with items that are remembered. These studies are particularly important as they may potentially provide insight into the difficult arguments regarding the relationship between heightened activation levels and compensation in older adults. If greater activation with age is compensatory, it would be expected to see more bilaterality and greater activation above perhaps young baseline levels for remembered versus forgotten items. Thus far, the findings are somewhat variable, with two of the three studies showing some evidence for decreased medial temporal activation for remembered items in old individuals and a mixed picture for frontal areas.

Morcom et al. (2003) studied word memory using an incidental, deep-processing task. When forgotten items were subtracted from remembered items, young and old adults showed equivalent levels of activation in the left inferior frontal cortex, supporting the findings of Logan et al. (2002) for deep processing. Old individuals showed enhanced activity for forgotten items compared to remembered items and, on query of frontal cortex in a regions-of-interest analysis, more bilateral anterior prefrontal activation for remembered items compared to young. Whether this additional recruitment is compensatory or merely decreased selectivity of encoding for old adults cannot be determined from the pattern of findings. In addition, both groups showed more hippocampal engagement for remembered items, although young individuals showed more activation of the left anterior inferior temporal cortex for remembered compared to forgotten items than old adults.

Daselaar, Veltman, Rombouts, Lazeron, et al. (2003) conducted a similar study, but due to an inadequate number of misses they compared remembered items to baseline rather than to forgotten items. Unlike Morcom et al. (2003), they observed equivalent amounts of lateralization between old and young individuals. The most interesting finding was related to hippocampal activation and occurred when older adults were divided into high-performing and low-performing memory groups based on recognition performance. The old-low individuals showed less medial temporal activation for remembered items than either old-high or young adults.

Finally, Gutchess et al. (in press) examined memory for pictures in an incidental deep-processing task. They reported more parahippocampal activation in young adults compared to old for remembered items, even when subjects were not divided into high and low performers. They also found significantly more recruitment of the left frontal cortex in old adults compared to young adults for remembered items. Given that pictures generally induce bilateral prefrontal activations (Kelley et al.,

1998), the older adults' increased recruitment of the left prefrontal cortex above the level of young adults suggests a selective activation that is potentially compensatory.

The subsequent memory paradigm is a potentially rich tool that, with sufficient *n*'s and varied encoding conditions, may permit disentangling functional from dysfunctional neural signal. At present, the findings have not yielded the clarity that one would hope for, but we believe that event-related designs that can separate the neural signal associated with remembered items from forgotten items offer a powerful tool that will yield a better understanding of memory function in late adulthood, particularly when individual differences in cognitive performance are examined, as demonstrated by Daselaar, Veltman, Rombouts, Lazeron, et al. (2003). Sorting remembered from forgotten items provides specificity at the level of process, and differentiating subjects based on cognitive performance provides specificity at the level of ability.

We should note that two of the three studies provided some evidence for decreased medial temporal activation with age for remembered items. The hippocampus is the primary structure that deteriorates with Alzheimer's disease. Alzheimer's disease is a ubiquitous disorder in later years; about 40% of older adults aged 85 years and older have frank Alzheimer's disease (Kukull et al., 2002; Launer et al., 1999). Given the disorder's long and slow progression, it is very plausible that decreased hippocampal activations in older adults may reflect early-stage Alzheimer's disease. If this is the case, apparent age differences in this region would be driven by a subset of subjects. The differences between old-high and old-low individuals found by Daselaar, Veltman, Rombouts, Lazeron, et al. (2003) are consistent with such an explanation.

Nonverbal Stimuli

The study of meaningful pictures is an ideal medium for understanding age differences in neural circuitry and potentially compensatory neural processes in older adults because it is often possible to equate performance between old and young adults on picture memory tasks (Park, Puglisi, & Smith, 1986; Park et al., 1988; Smith et al., 1990), permitting a clear interpretation of different patterns of neural signal. Moreover, the encoding of relational elements within meaningful scenes is particularly demanding of the hippocampus (Cohen et al., 1999; Stern et al., 1996), providing a strong medium for assessing medial temporal as well as frontal function in older adults. There are several studies that have used pictorial stimuli with older adults, and overall they present a strong picture of decreased hippocampal function with age, with a more variable pattern for frontal activations.

Grady et al. (1999) directly contrasted pictorial and verbal memory in young and old adults, presenting line drawings of objects as well as words for study. Generally, old adults showed similar patterns of neural circuitry, but decreased activation relative to young in frontal and medial temporal areas. The exception was a contrast between deep and shallow processing for pictures, for which older and younger adults showed relatively similar levels of activation increases in left prefrontal and medial temporal regions. It is important to note that these were line drawings of simple objects and probably made low demands on relational processes in the hippocampus. In a study of facial memory, Grady et al. (1995) reported less left prefrontal and medial temporal activations in old compared to young adults for encoding of faces; a later study suggested that the reduced activations in old individuals may occur primarily during shallow encoding and recognition processes rather than deep encoding (Grady et al., 2002).

Other work has focused exclusively on pictorial stimuli. Iidaka et al. (2001) examined neural activations when young and old adults encoded related and unrelated pictures as well as abstract pictures. Young adults showed bilateral activations in the prefrontal cortex for concrete unrelated pictures and abstract pictures, conditions more demanding of resource than the related picture condition. Overall, old adults showed lower activation levels than young for the unrelated and abstract pictures, with the main difference in the temporoparietal areas. Iidaka et al. noted that older adults showed significant left prefrontal activations, suggestive of intact semantic processing, and had particular decreases in temporoparietal activations, indicative of deficient visuospatial processing.

Decreased medial temporal activations were also observed during pictorial encoding in young and old adults by Park, Welsh, et al. (2003) in an event-related design. They reported significantly less left anterior hippocampal engagement in older adults compared to young during encoding. Older adults, however, showed heightened left and right frontal activations on a subsequent probe task that occurred after each encoding event, which may have been compensatory for the decreased hippocampal activation.

Gutchess et al. (in press) provided a fine-grain understanding of pictorial encoding operations in older adults by utilizing a subsequent memory paradigm for the encoding of complex pictures in young and old adults. As described in the subsequent memory section of this chapter, they reported that young and old adults showed bilateral prefrontal activations for remembered compared to forgotten pictures. However, older adults showed a somewhat different pattern in other regions, recruiting more left middle frontal cortex than young adults as well as showing less parahippocampal activation. The finding of increased left frontal activation in old individuals might be compensatory. It replicates findings from visuospatial studies in other domains, as Reuter-Lorenz et al. (2000) also reported increased left frontal activations for the maintenance of nonverbal materials in working memory. Moreover, Park, Welsh, et al. (2003) also found increased left and right frontal activations for old adults in a probe task following pictorial encoding.

To summarize, the literature on neural activation associated with pictorial encoding suggests that older adults show less engagement of medial temporal areas than young adults; this region has been strongly implicated in processing relationships among elements of meaningful scenes. Second, there were several studies showing age-equivalent activations in frontal areas under at least some conditions (Grady et al., 1999, 2002; Iidaka et al., 2001) and even some studies showing increased frontal activation for remembered pictures at encoding (Gutchess et al., in press). Finally, increased frontal function in old adults in studies of pictorial memory has most frequently occurred when meaningful scenes have been presented (Park, Welsh, et al., 2003; Gutchess et al., in press). Whether these increased frontal activations are indicative of compensatory activation cannot be determined from the findings and is an important area for future investigation. Evidence is accumulating to suggest that activations in medial temporal regions are decreased in old compared to young individuals (Grady et al., 2002; Gutchess et al., in press), and we speculate that the increased activation observed in other regions may be compensatory for the decreased medial temporal function.

Divided Attention at Encoding

Much of our everyday encoding processes occur against a background of distraction and ongoing activity. Moreover, we frequently perform or attempt to perform two or more tasks at the same time. Hence, an understanding of how encoding processes function in the context of distracting activity is an important issue to characterize memory effectively. There is strong evidence from the behavioral literature that encoding processes that occur when distracting tasks or information are present are more disadvantaged by age than retrieval processes (Anderson, Craik, & Naveh-Benjamin, 1998; Craik et al., 1996; Park et al., 1989). Hence, different age patterns of neural activation between divided and full-attention conditions might be expected.

Anderson et al. (2000) studied encoding of word pairs while subjects were making tone discriminations. They found that the divided attention task reduced memory equivalently in young and old adults and reduced left prefrontal and medial temporal activations at an equivalent level in young and old adults. Anderson et al. concluded that these data are confirmatory of the age encoding deficit hypothesis advanced by Craik (1986) because both age and divided attention decreased left prefrontal activations during encoding, suggesting that shared mechanisms are operating in these two conditions.

Retrieval and Memory

Older adults almost universally report problems with retrieval from both semantic and episodic memory. Nevertheless, the behavioral literature suggests that retrieval is much less impaired with age than encoding. Both Anderson, Craik, and Naveh-Benjamin (1998) and Park et al. (1989) demonstrated that older adults are disproportionately disadvantaged by interference at encoding but not retrieval when compared to younger adults. Craik et al. (1996) demonstrated a similar phenomenon and were able to show the automatic, obligatory nature of the retrieval operation—an operation that remains relatively unimpaired with age.

Neural Activations at Retrieval

There is a substantial body of literature on age differences in neural activation at retrieval. The HERA (Hemispheric Encoding/Retrieval Asymmetry) model suggests that retrieval is largely a right hemisphere activity (Tulving et al., 1994). Overall, age differences in neural activations at retrieval are most consistently focused on frontal areas, with medial temporal differences appearing less often. In an initial study, Grady et al. (1995) found that young individuals showed right prefrontal activity, as well as right parietal and bilateral occipital activations, when recognizing encoded faces, confirming the HERA model. Older adults also showed right prefrontal activations, but no significant activations in the other regions exhibited by the young. In addition, they reported a correlation of .94 between the activity in the frontal cortex and right hippocampal activity for young adults, but no relationship for older adults ($r = .02$).

These findings were replicated in a later study (Grady et al., 2002) and are suggestive of different retrieval networks with age, with young adults relying more on hippocampal circuitry than old adults. Madden et al. (1999) also confirmed the finding of engagement of different networks for recognition in old compared to young individuals. In this study, regression analyses of reaction time to regional cerebral blood flow suggested that memory retrieval networks encompass more regions (specifically in posterior cortex) in elderly adults. Thus, these studies suggested that retrieval may involve a qualitatively different neural network in old compared to young people.

Difficulty and Effort Manipulations at Retrieval

Behaviorally, performance differences as a function of age become larger as tasks require more directed retrieval (Light, 1991). For example, age differences are larger for explicit compared to implicit memory (LaVoie & Light, 1994; Park & Shaw, 1992) and for recall compared to recognition (Craik & McDowd, 1987; Rabinowitz, 1984, 1986; Schonfield & Robertson, 1966). Bäckman et al. (1997) measured neural activations in a PET scanner in young and old adults under different memory conditions. In the explicit condition, subjects were instructed to complete letter stems with studied words and with the first word that came to mind that completed the letter stem in the implicit condition. During explicit retrieval, both young and old adults showed increased activation of right prefrontal cortex when contrasted with implicit performance. Young adults showed unique activations as well in Wernicke's area and the left cerebellum for explicit retrieval, but the overall pattern was one of similar engagement of frontal systems for retrieval in young and old adults.

Cabeza, Grady, et al. (1997) conducted, using PET, one of the few studies contrasting verbal recall with recognition. They found decreased activation in the right frontal cortex with age, resulting in a pattern of bilateral activation for old and a more unilateral pattern for young adults. In addition, differences in activation patterns between recall and recognition were larger for young compared to old adults, suggesting less differentiation of neural activity in old individuals as a function of retrieval condition.

Schacter et al. (1996) varied how well subjects learned words at encoding for young and old adults. Using PET to image retrieval for the words, Schacter et al. found old and young individuals had equivalent hippocampal activations, and that these activations increased for better encoded words. Prefrontal activations, however, differed, with young adults showing typical increases in the anterior frontal cortex during retrieval, whereas older adults showed a more posterior pattern of frontal recruitment. This again supports the conclusion that older adults engage different networks at retrieval than young adults, although it is not clear whether the differential engagement reflects strategy differences or neural reorganization.

Anderson et al. (2000) manipulated divided attention at retrieval in young and old adults following the encoding of word pairs. They reported that divided attention had little effect at retrieval on either old or young adults, reflecting the obligatory nature of the retrieval process.

Finally, Daselaar, Veltman, Rombouts, Lazeron, et al. (2003) presented a pattern of findings that potentially account for inconsistencies in activation patterns among studies. They studied retrieval following semantic encoding of words and reported a pattern of decreased frontal activity in older adults. A split of high and low performers within the old group, however, revealed that low-performing elderly showed more prefrontal activations than young adults, whereas high-performing elderly showed the least, suggesting that disparate findings can be reconciled via the study of individual differences.

In general, neural patterns associated with episodic retrieval showed less-dramatic differences between old and young than encoding studies. Moreover, all studies noted frontal decreases, with considerably less evidence for hippocampal differences than is true in the encoding literature. Finally, there was considerable evidence for engagement of different networks with age, but whether these reflect neural reorganization or strategy differences is not clear from the present studies.

Recognition of Autobiographical Memories

Maguire and Frith (2003) examined the role of personally relevant information in recognition for young and old adults. They collected information from each subject regarding memory for specific autobiographical and public events prior to an experimental session and designed stimuli that were unique to the individual subject for presentation in an fMRI study. An intriguing pattern of age-related changes in hippocampal activations occurred. They found that elderly adults recruited the hippocampi bilaterally for autobiographical event retrieval trials, whereas young adults showed left-lateralized activations. Unlike the encoding studies reviewed, this study suggested that conditions do exist in which elderly adults activate the hippocampus more than young. Personally relevant or emotional information is likely part of an elaborate semantic network and may be less fragile than purely experimental/episodic information, thus eliciting robust hippocampal activations. Understanding whether rich, elaborated memories show different activation patterns than less-elaborated traces, at both encoding and retrieval, is an important issue for future research.

Context and Memory

There is a large body of behavioral literature on the benefits of contextual materials at encoding. In fact, some theorists argued that poor memory for contextual or source information is a fundamental mechanism accounting for poor memory in older adults (Johnson, Hashtroudi, & Lindsay, 1993). Findings indicated that older adults show larger differences for context memory than for item memory (Park & Puglisi, 1985; Park, Puglisi, & Lutz, 1982; Spencer & Raz, 1995) and have problems in binding target to context (Chalfonte & Johnson, 1996). Other behavioral work has focused on the potentially supportive role of context at encoding and retrieval and the working memory requirements of utilizing context. In paired associate tasks, when a target is unrelated to context and requires active integration and engagement of working memory, age differences are larger than when the context automatically activates an association through semantic relationships (Park et al., 1990; Smith et al., 1990, 1998).

At this point, there are only a few studies that have examined age differences in neural activations underlying contextual manipulations. Iidaka et al. (2001) studied age differences in encoding pairs of related and unrelated pictures. Both young and old adults showed increased left prefrontal activation for unrelated pictures compared to the control condition, reflecting the increased processing demands of utilizing the unrelated pictures as cues. At the same time, older adults showed less activation than young adults in right occipitotemporal areas, suggesting that they were less likely to encode the visuospatial features of the stimuli. No significant frontal activations were observed for young or old adults in the related-item condition, reflecting the relatively automatic encoding of related items; another possible cause is that the power in this study was low, even by imaging standards, with only seven subjects in each age group.

Two other studies of aging and context focused on retrieval of contextual information. First, Cabeza et al. (2000) used PET and studied item and order memory associated with the encoding of words. They reported that young adults showed increased activation in the right prefrontal cortex for order information compared to item information, whereas older adults did not, exhibiting less engagement of frontal areas in old compared to young individuals. This finding is consistent with reports of more impaired memory for context relative to item memory with age (Spencer & Raz, 1995). It is important to note as well that a pattern of activation suggestive of compensation for order information was observed in older adults. They showed weaker activations in the right prefrontal cortex compared to young adults, but greater activation in left prefrontal areas.

In a later study, Cabeza et al. (2002) presented subjects with words that were spoken aloud or presented visually and then measured neural activation at recognition for items and source. They again found that young adults showed lateralized activations in the right prefrontal cortex for source trials. High-performing, but not low-performing, old adults had bilateral activity in prefrontal areas, a finding consistent with compensatory activations in old individuals.

The data on utilization and memory for context are relatively sparse in the imaging literature. Cabeza et al. (2002) yielded patterns of compensatory, bilateral activation in high-performing old adults for contextual retrieval relative to young individuals, but the Iidaka et al. (2001) study, which focused on encoding, did not show a compensatory pattern and found decreased activations primarily in ventromedial temporal areas. Clearly, more studies are needed in the imaging literature on feature and contextual memory, particularly at encoding. We have a poor understanding of strategic differences for utilization of contextual information by older adults at encoding and the support that context may provide at retrieval. Neuroimaging studies have the potential to provide great insight into strategy differences at encoding and context utilization differences between young and old adults at both encoding and retrieval.

Individual Differences and Memory

Cognitive aging researchers have frequently used individual differences in various characteristics among subjects to explain sources of variance in memory function. For example, Lindenberger and Baltes (1994; Baltes & Lindenberger, 1997) reported that individual differences in sensory function (audition and vision) mediated substantial variance on a long-term memory task. Park et al. (1996, 2002) found that individual differences in speed and working memory accounted for age-related variance on many types of long-term memory tasks, including free recall, cued recall, and spatial recall. The importance of education and social context in response to environmental support has also been studied (Craik, Byrd, & Swanson, 1987; Cherry & Park, 1993). Work has even demonstrated that individuals' variability in performance on free-recall tasks over days may be an important predictor of later cognitive decline (Hultsch et al., 2000; Li et al., 2001).

Although the data on individual differences as predictors of patterns of neural function associated with memory are limited, the study of individual differences is a very powerful technique for understanding conflicting findings across studies. Characterizing subjects through neuropsychological batteries may provide substantive insight into the functional significance of different activation patterns. To the extent that bilateral patterns of activation are associated with good performance, it would suggest that recruitment of two hemispheres is likely compensatory for declining neural efficiency (Cabeza, 2002; Cabeza et al., 2002; Rosen et al., 2002).

On the other hand, if memory performance is poorer in individuals showing bilateral patterns of activation, the meaning of the pattern becomes somewhat harder to interpret. It may be that only low-memory subjects show bilateral recruitment patterns because only these subjects need the additional neural resources to perform the task (see the Daselaar and Cabeza walking stick argument in chapter 14 of this volume). At the same time, perhaps poor subjects are more disinhibited or increased activation is a marker of cognitive dysfunction. Note that the data presented in figure 1 of Lustig et al.'s 2003 work could support either argument.

At this time, there are six studies (Cabeza et al., 2002; Rosen et al., 2002; Logan et al., 2002; Lustig et al., 2003; Stebbins et al., 2002; Daselaar, Veltman, Rombouts, Lazeron, et al., 2003) relating individual differences in cognitive performance to patterns of neural activation. Of these, two suggested that bilateral activation patterns are associated with good performance; the other four reached the opposite conclusion. Cabeza et al. (2002) separated low- and high-memory subjects based on a battery developed by Glisky, Polster, and Routhicaux (1995). They imaged source retrieval using PET and reported that high-functioning old adults showed bilaterality, but that lower functioning old individuals exhibited changes in activation within sites in a single hemisphere. Cabeza et al. argued that contralateral recruitment in older adults is reflective of neural modification and reorganization over time to compensate for declining structural integrity of the nervous system.

In support of this finding, Rosen et al. (2002) also reported that older subjects who scored highly on a memory battery outside the scanner showed not only the typical left prefrontal activation pattern, but also greater right prefrontal activation than young adults. In contrast, low-performing elderly showed reduced activations in both left and right frontal regions.

These findings are generally supportive of a compensation view (Cabeza, Grady, et al., 1997; Cabeza et al., 2000, 2002; Cabeza, 2002). Unfortunately, other studies that have related individual differences in performance to patterns of neural activation yielded the opposite conclusion, that is, that bilaterality is more characteristic of poor performers. Logan et al. (2002) reported that bilaterality of the frontal cortex across a number of different encoding conditions was most likely to be evidenced by the oldest adults, whereas young adults and the younger subset of older adults showed a more selective (unilateral) recruitment pattern.

In a follow-up study, Lustig et al. (2003) considered healthy old and old adults in early stages of Alzheimer's disease. As displayed in figure 9.1a, both groups showed increased left frontal activation during encoding of words, suggesting increased activation in this area was characteristic of aging. More important for the present issue, however, is that there were differences between the healthy elderly and patients with early Alzheimer's disease in the medial parietal/posterior cingulate cortex (figure 9.1b). In this area, patients with Alzheimer's disease displayed more activation during encoding than healthy elderly, and healthy elderly exhibited more activation than young adults. This pattern of findings is strongly suggestive of increased activation as dysfunctional, although note that these activations were outside the prefrontal cortex. Perhaps activations in some frontal areas are compensatory for old individuals, and other areas are dysfunctional. We recognize, of course, that the argument cannot be ruled out that additional recruitment, such as that displayed in figure 9.1b, occurs because of its compensatory value for neural deterioration in patients with Alzheimer's disease.

Also reporting evidence for increased activation in poor performers, Stebbins et al. (2002) found that decreased performance on neuropsychological tests was correlated with decreased frontal lobe activation on a deep-encoding task, and that bilaterality in old adults resulted from reduced left hemisphere activation rather than increased right hemisphere activation.

Finally, Daselaar, Veltman, Rombouts, Lazeron, et al. (2003), using an incidental deep-encoding task followed by retrieval, separated subjects into old-high and old-low performers based on memory performance in the scanner. At encoding, old-high and young individuals showed greater medial temporal activations than old-low adults and relatively equivalent activation and lateralization of frontal activity. At retrieval, old-low adults exhibited widespread greater activation, although these differences vanished when only correct responses were included in the analysis.

How can these findings be reconciled? There is no apparent consistent thread to manipulations used in the studies. Of the four studies reporting evidence that high activation or bilaterality is characteristic of low performers (Daselaar, Veltman, Rombouts, Lazeron, et al., 2003; Logan et al., 2002, Lustig et al., 2003; Stebbins et al., 2002), all used deep-encoding tasks, but so did a study finding evidence for compensatory bilaterality (Rosen et al., 2002). The relationship of encoding and retrieval operations is also unclear because compensation was found in one encoding and one retrieval study even though all four studies that found evidence for dysfunctionality of increased recruitment studied encoding.

What is clear is that heightened activation in frontal areas relative to young individuals is significant for understanding the cognitive neuroscience of aging, and that there are conditions under which the activation is functional and others for which it is dysfunctional. It seems likely that carefully characterizing large numbers of subjects on multiple imaging and behavioral memory tasks, as well as relating performance to other domains of cognition such as attention and working memory, will provide tremendous insight into these provocative and important relationships.

Conclusions

At the end of each section of this chapter, we summarized findings and recommendations for future research in particular domains. We now adopt a broader view and conclude by addressing two issues. First, how consistent are current behavioral theories of memory with extant neuroimaging data? Second, how do neuroimaging findings and theories change our view of memory function with age?

Theories of Aging and Memory

Cognitive aging theories of memory are typically based on single-mechanism constructs, and the complexity of neuroimaging data does not readily map onto these theories. Nevertheless, some behavioral constructs and mechanisms are more successfully instantiated in the imaging literature than others. Theories of resource, such as views that suggest that decreases in speed of processing account for declines in fluid cognition with age (Salthouse, 1996), cannot directly account for the patterns of neural activation that occur with declines in memory performance in older adults. At present, the proposed causes of declines in speed with age are decreases in white matter integrity, dopamine receptors, and demyelination of axons (see Park et al., 2001, for a review). To support a view that speed changes are causal for age-related cognitive decline, it would be important to directly link decreased speed to these specific changes in the brain and then map these changes to memory function. This is an obviously tall order, and at this stage of development in the imaging literature, more proximal linkages between mechanisms and neural activations may be established more readily.

A simple version of the processing resource hypothesis accounting for age-related decline in memory (Park et al., 1996, 2002) is clearly problematic, but more complex versions of the working memory hypothesis may prove viable. In a simple form, it might be expected that availability of processing resources are reflected in level of activation of neural tissue. We have presented a number of studies indicating not only that sometimes lower functioning older adults, who presumably have less cognitive resource, show more activation (as in figure 1 in Lustig et al., 2003; Daselaar,

Veltman, Rombouts, Lazeron, et al., 2003; Logan et al., 2002, Stebbins et al., 2002), but also that older adults who are higher functioning show more activation (Cabeza et al., 2002; Rosen et al., 2002; Daselaar, Veltman, Rombouts, Lazeron, et al., 2003). Given these opposite patterns of findings, it is not possible that a simple mapping of activation levels to working memory capacity or speed of processing will be fruitful.

A more fertile approach may be to determine structures that are jointly or uniquely activated across tasks and/or categories of subjects (e.g., good or poor performers). As an example of this approach, Cabeza et al. (2004) examined activation patterns common to attention, working memory, and long-term memory. They reported that increases in prefrontal and parietal activations and decreases in hippocampal activations occurred with age across three different classes of tasks that tapped attention, working memory, and long-term memory, respectively. This particular finding suggests that increases in shared cross-task frontal, but not hippocampal, activation may be an important marker of cognitive resource with age. More studies are needed that examine broad classes of tasks or stimuli within the same subjects to secure a broader understanding of the relationship between neural activation in specific structures and performance.

Although the studies we presented in this chapter do not provide direct mapping to resource theories of memory, some findings map nicely onto inhibition theory. This view suggests that faulty inhibitory processes with age would result in increased neural activation when younger adults might show deactivations. There are several findings suggesting that older adults with the poorest memories (such as the patients with Alzheimer's disease depicted in figure 9.1b) show higher levels of neural activation, but as mentioned here, this does not necessarily mean that increased activation is dysfunctional, particularly because other studies show high-performing subjects sometimes show more activation. We also note that, despite the centrality of the construct of inhibition in cognitive aging (Hasher & Zacks, 1988; Zacks & Hasher, 1997), strong links in the behavioral literature between measures of inhibition and explicit memory have not been demonstrated. It may be, however, that neuroimaging may provide critical data connecting heightened activation to poor memory function with age, further establishing this view of cognitive aging.

Although the data are sparse, the neuroimaging literature does provide some confirmatory evidence that older adults' particularly poor source memory is mirrored in lower levels of neural activations for source compared to item memory (Cabeza et al., 2000). What remains to be established is that those older adults who show particularly large activation differences for source compared to item memory will also have the poorest item memory. The idea here would be that inefficient processing of, or decreased sensitivity to, contextual information reflects decrements in global memory function because source failures result from engaging fewer perceptual and reflective processes at encoding (Johnson, Hashtroudi, & Lindsay, 1993).

Finally, theories positing that older adults' memory function is more driven by familiarity than that of young adults (Jennings & Jacoby, 1993, 1997) have only begun to be tested at the neural level. Cabeza et al. (2004) proposed their finding of increased parahippocampal and decreased hippocampal activations in old relative to young adults could potentially be evidence for increased reliance on familiarity because that trace is less affected by aging than recollection. Findings of hippocampal/ prefrontal distinctions in memory processes are also reminiscent of Jacoby's theory, with medial temporal activations reflecting automatic judgments of memory, and prefrontal activations indicating effortful strategic memory processes (Moscovitch & Winocur, 1992). Such a view would seem to suggest that older adults have less prefrontal involvement in retrieving memories, showing overall lower levels of activation in this area, and conceivably relying more strongly on hippocampal activations. Although the findings in the present review have been largely suggestive of decreased hippocampal function with age, Maguire and Frith's (2003) finding that older adults had greater hippocampal engagement for stimuli associated with their personal lives would seem to support the view that older adults rely more strongly on familiarity in making memory judgments.

Neuroimaging Findings and Memory Theories

We now question how neuroimaging findings are changing theories of memory. At present, we would argue that neuroimaging findings are used as confirmatory data for extant behaviorally based theories of memory. That is, as behavioral theories are proposed, elaborated, and revised, they now must be able to accommodate neuroimaging findings because a failure to do so would indicate an inadequate theory or framework. At the same time that behavioral theories are evolving to accommodate neuroimaging findings, we also see evidence that particular interest is directed toward developing theories of memory plasticity and change in late adulthood, and we are seeing increased interest as well in interventions to improve memory and neural function (Logan et al., 2002). Memory theories are under development based on notions of compensation (Cabeza, 2002).

Given this new extraordinary ability to measure change and remodeling of neural organization with age that has resulted from imaging tools, we expect that theories of memory will increasingly be revised to integrate mechanisms of change or improvement in function in late adulthood as a result of training, contextual manipulations, or stimulation. Even from the relatively sparse and contradictory literature presented in this review, it is abundantly clear that the relatively static decline functions that occur in long-term memory across the life span are not mirrored in a pattern of linear decline in neural activation across an array of brain structures thought to be associated with memory.

Neuroimaging findings have also reinvigorated research that addresses hypotheses suggesting memory function can be broadly trained (Kramer & Willis, 2002), that cognitive vitality can be enhanced through exercise (Colcombe & Kramer, 2003), and that cognitive and social engagement facilitate a healthy mind (Schooler & Mulatu, 2001). Because tools are at last available that provide sensitive measurement of neural function, we believe that studies of patient groups with affected memory function (e.g., from Alzheimer's disease, Parkinson's disease) will provide new insight into models of normal memory function in late adulthood.

Finally, we are convinced that the complex patterns of findings in the neuroimaging literature can only be understood through the study of individual differences along with studies that systematically manipulate variables that increase or decrease difficulty of encoding in a systematic fashion. This will permit subjects to be categorized according to behavioral patterns of function (e.g., Glisky, Polster, & Routhicoux's 1995 battery for characterizing subjects in terms of frontal and hippocampal function) as well as neural patterns, such as bilaterality (Cabeza, 2002) or decreased neural selectivity (Logan et al., 2002; Park et al., in press).

Despite the many concerns we have expressed regarding interpretation of results from the neuroimaging literature, neuroimaging techniques have provided remarkable excitement and stimulation for the study of aging and memory. Memory theorists have fertile new ideas for development and measurement of conceptual models. We predict that cognitive neuroscience will be the dominant perspective from which theories of aging and memory evolve over the next decade.

References

Anderson, N. D., Craik, F. I. M., & Naveh-Benjamin, M. (1998). The attentional demands of encoding and retrieval in younger and older adults: 1. Evidence from divided attention costs. *Psychology and Aging, 13*, 405–423.

Anderson, N. D., Iidaka, T., Cabeza, R., Kapur, S., McIntosh, A. R., & Craik, F. I. M. (2000). The effects of divided attention on encoding and retrieval related brain activity: A PET study of younger and older adults. *Journal of Cognitive Neuroscience, 12*, 775–792.

Bäckman, L., Almkvist, O., Andersson, J., Nordberg, A., Windblad, B., Reineck, R., & Långström, B. (1997). Brain activation in young and older adults during implicit and explicit retrieval. *Journal of Cognitive Neuroscience, 9*, 378–391.

Baltes, P. B., & Lindenberger, U. (1997). Emergence of a powerful connection between sensory and cognitive functions across the adult life span: A new window to the study of cognitive aging? *Psychology and Aging, 12*, 12–21.

Bartlett, J. C., Leslie, J. E., Tubb, A., & Fulton, A. (1989). Aging and memory for pictures of faces. *Psychology and Aging, 4*, 276–283.

Brewer, J. B., Zhao, Z., Desmond, J. E., Glover, G. H., & Gabrieli, J. D. E. (1998). Making memories: Brain activity that predicts how well visual experience will be remembered. *Science, 281*, 1185–1187.

Cabeza, R. (2002). Hemispheric asymmetry reduction in older adults: The HAROLD model. *Psychology and Aging, 17*, 85–100.

Cabeza, R., Anderson, N. D., Houle, S., Mangels, J. A., & Nyberg, L. (2000). Age-related differences in neural activity during item and temporal-order memory retrieval: A positron emission tomography study. *Journal of Cognitive Neuroscience, 12*, 197–206.

Cabeza, R., Anderson, N. D., Locantore, J. K., & McIntosh, A. R. (2002) Aging gracefully: Compensatory brain activity in high-performing older adults. *Neuroimage, 17*, 1394–1402.

Cabeza, R., Daselaar, S. M., Dolcos, F., Prince, S. E., Budde, M., & Nyberg, L. (2004). Task-independent and task-specific age effects on brain activity during working memory, visual attention, and episodic retrieval. *Cerebral Cortex, 14*, 364–375.

Cabeza, R., Grady, C. L., Nyberg, L., McIntosh, A. R., Tulving, E., Kapur, S., Jennings, J.M., Houle, S., & Craik, F. I. M. (1997). Age-related differences in neural activity during memory encoding and retrieval: A positron emission tomography study. *Journal of Neuroscience, 17*, 391–400.

Cabeza, R., McIntosh, A. R., Tulving, E., Nyberg, L., & Grady, C. L. (1997). Age-related differences in effective neural connectivity during encoding and recall. *Neuroreport, 8,* 3479–3483.

Chalfonte, B. L., & Johnson, M. K. (1996). Feature memory and binding in young and older adults. *Memory and Cognition, 24,* 403–416.

Cherry, K. E., & Park, D. C. (1993). Individual difference and contextual variables influence spatial memory in younger and older adults. *Psychology and Aging, 8,* 517–526.

Cohen, N. J., Ryan, J., Hunt, C., Romine, L., Wszalek, T., & Nash, C. (1999). Hippocampal system and declarative (relational) memory: Summarizing the data from functional neuroimaging studies. *Hippocampus, 9,* 83–98.

Colcombe, S., & Kramer, A. F. (2003). Fitness effects on the cognitive function of older adults: A meta-analytic study. *Psychological Science, 14,* 125–130.

Craik, F. I. M (1986). A functional account of age differences in memory. In F. Klix & H. Hagendorf (Eds.), *Human memory and cognitive capabilities, mechanisms, and performances* (pp. 409–422). North Holland, The Netherlands: Elsevier.

Craik, F. I. M., & Byrd, M. (1982). Aging and cognitive deficits: The role of attentional resources. In F. I. M. Craik & T. A. Salthouse (Eds.), *The handbook of aging and cognition* (pp. 51–110). Hillsdale, NJ: Erlbaum.

Craik, F. I. M., Byrd, M., & Swanson, J. M. (1987). Patterns of memory loss in three elderly samples. *Psychology and Aging, 2,* 79–86.

Craik, F. I. M., Govoni, R., Naveh-Benjamin, M., & Anderson, N. D. (1996). The effects of divided attention on encoding and retrieval processes in human memory. *Journal of Experimental Psychology: General, 125,* 159–180.

Craik, F. I. M., & Lockhart, R. S. (1972). Levels of processing: A framework for memory research. *Journal of Verbal Learning and Verbal Behavior, 11,* 671–684.

Craik, F. I. M., & McDowd, J. M. (1987). Age differences in recall and recognition. *Journal of Experimental Psychology: Learning, Memory, & Cognition, 13,* 474–479.

Craik, F. I. M., & Simon, H. (1980). Age differences in memory: The roles of attention and depth of processing. In L. W. Poon, J. L. Fozard, L. Cermak, D. Arenberg, & L. W. Thompson (Eds.), *New directions in memory and aging: Proceedings of the George Talland memorial conference* (pp. 95–112). Hillsdale, NJ: Erlbaum.

Daselaar, S. M., Veltman, D. J., Rombouts, S. A., Lazeron, R. H., Raaijmakers, J. G., & Jonker, C. (2003). Neuroanatomical correlates of episodic encoding and retrieval in young and elderly subjects. *Brain, 126,* 43–56.

Daselaar, S. M., Veltman, D. J., Rombouts, S. A., Raaijmakers, J. G., & Jonker, C. (2003). Deep processing activates the medal temporal lobe in young but not elderly adults. *Neurobiology of Aging, 24,* 1005–1011.

Demb, J. B., Desmond, J. E., Wagner, A. D., Baidys, C. J., Glover, G. H., & Gabrieli, J. D. E. (1995). Semantic encoding and retrieval in the left inferior prefrontal cortex: A functional MRI study of task difficulty and process specificity. *Journal of Neuroscience, 15,* 5870–5878.

Dixon, R. A., Simon, E. W., Nowak, C. A., & Hultsch, D. F. (1982). Text recall in adulthood as a function of level of information, input modality, and delay interval. *Journal of Gerontology, 37,* 358–364.

Eysenck, M. W. (1974). Age differences in incidental learning. *Developmental Psychology, 10,* 936–941.

Frieske, D. A., & Park, D. C. (1999). Memory for news in young and old adults. *Psychology and Aging, 14,* 90–98.

Glisky, E. L., Polster, M. R., & Routhicaux, B. C. (1995). Double dissociation between item and source memory. *Neuropsychology, 9,* 229–235.

Grady, C. L., Bernstein, L. J., Beig, S., & Siegenthaler, A. L. (2002). The effects of encoding task on age-related differences in the functional neuroanatomy of face memory. *Psychology and Aging, 17*, 7–23.

Grady, C. L., McIntosh, A. R., Horwitz, B., Maisog, J. M., Ungerleider, L. G., Mentis, M. J., Pietrini, P., Schapiro, M. B., & Haxby, J. V. (1995). Age-related reductions in human recognition memory due to impaired encoding. *Science, 269*, 218–221.

Grady, C. L., McIntosh, A. R., Rajah, M. N., Beig, S., & Craik, F. I. M. (1999). The effects of age on the neural correlates of episodic encoding. *Cerebral Cortex, 9*, 805–814.

Gutchess, A. H., Welsh, R. C., Hedden, T., Bangert, A., Minear, M., Liu, L., & Park, D. C. (in press). Aging and the neural correlates of successful picture encoding: Frontal activations compensate for decreased medial temporal activity. *Journal of Cognitive Neuroscience.*

Hasher, L., & Zacks, R. T. (1979). Automatic and effortful processes in memory. *Journal of Experimental Psychology: General, 108*, 356–388.

Hasher, L., & Zacks, R. T. (1988). Working memory, comprehension, and aging: A review and new view. In G. H. Bower (Ed.), *The psychology of learning and motivation* (Vol. 22, pp. 193–225). San Diego, CA: Academic Press.

Hedden, T., & Park, D. C. (2001). Aging and interference in verbal working memory. *Psychology and Aging, 16*, 666–681.

Hedden, T., & Park, D. C. (2003). Contributions of source and inhibitory mechanisms to age-related retroactive interference in verbal working memory. *Journal of Experimental Psychology: General, 132*, 93–112.

Hultsch, D. F., MacDonald, S. W. S., Hunter, M. A., Levy-Bencheton, J., & Strauss, E. (2000). Intraindividual variability in cognitive performance in older adults: Comparison of adults with mild dementia, adults with arthritic, and healthy adults. *Neuropsychology, 14*, 588–598.

Iidaka, T., Sadato, N., Yamada, H., Murata, T., Omori, M., & Yonekura, Y. (2001). An fMRI study of the functional neuroanatomy of picture encoding in younger and older adults. *Cognitive Brain Research, 11*, 1–11.

Jennings, J. M., & Jacoby, L. L. (1993). Automatic versus intentional uses of memory: Aging, attention, and control. *Psychology and Aging, 8*, 283–293.

Jennings, J. M., & Jacoby, L. L. (1997). An opposition procedure for detecting age-related deficits in recollection: Telling effects of repetition. *Psychology and Aging, 12*, 352–361.

Johnson, M. K., Hashtroudi, S., & Lindsay, S. D. (1993). Source monitoring. *Psychological Bulletin, 114*, 3–28.

Kausler, D. H. (1990). Automaticity of encoding and episodic memory processes. In E. Lovelace (Ed.), *Aging and cognition: Mental processes, self-awareness, and interventions* (pp. 29–67). Oxford, U.K.: North-Holland.

Kelley, W. M., Miezin, F. M., McDermott, K. B., Buckner, R. L., Raichle, M. E., Cohen, N. J., Ollinger, J. M., Akbudak, E., Conturo, T. E., Snyder, A. Z., & Petersen, S. E. (1998). Hemispheric specialization in human dorsal frontal cortex and medial temporal lobe for verbal and nonverbal memory encoding. *Neuron, 20*, 927–936.

Kramer, A. F., & Willis, S. L. (2002). Enhancing the cognitive vitality of older adults. *Current Directions in Psychological Science, 11*, 173–176.

Kukull, W. A., Higdon, R., Bower, J. D., McCormick, W. C., Teri, L., Schellenberg, G. D., van Belle, G., Jolley, L., & Larson, E. B. (2002). Dementia and Alzheimer disease incidence: A prospective cohort study. *Archives of Neurology, 59*, 1737–1746.

Launer, L. J., Andersen, K., Dewey, M. E., Letenneur, L., Ott, A., Amaducci, L. A., Brayne, C., Copeland, J. R. M., Dartigues, J.-F., Kragh-Sorensen, P., Lobo, A., Martinez-Lage, J. M., Stijnen, T., & Hofman, A. (1999). Rates and risk factors for dementia and Alzheimer's disease: Results from EURODEM pooled analyses. *Neurology, 52*, 78–84.

LaVoie, D., & Light, L. L. (1994). Adult age differences in repetition priming: A meta-analysis. *Psychology and Aging, 9,* 539–553.

Li, S.-C., Aggen, S. H., Neselroade, J. R., & Baltes, P. B. (2001). Short-term fluctuations in elderly people's sensorimotor functioning predict text and spatial memory performance: The MacArthur Successful Aging Studies. *Journal of Gerontology, 47,* 100–116.

Light, L. L. (1991). Memory and aging: Four hypotheses in search of data. *Annual Review of Psychology, 42,* 333–376.

Lindenberger, U., & Baltes, P. B. (1994). Sensory functioning and intelligence in old age: A strong connection. *Psychology and Aging, 9,* 339–355.

Logan, J. M., Sanders, A. L., Snyder, A. Z., Morris, J. C., & Buckner, R. L. (2002). Under-recruitment and non-selective recruitment: Dissociable neural mechanisms associated with aging. *Neuron, 33,* 827–840.

Lustig, C., Snyder, A. Z., Bhakta, M., O'Brien, K., McAvoy, M., Raichle, M. E., Morris, J. C., & Buckner, R. L. (2003). Functional deactivations: Change with age and dementia of the Alzheimer type. *Proceedings of the National Academy of Sciences of the United States of America, 100,* 504–514.

Madden, D. J., Turkington, T. G., Provenzale, J. M., Denny, L. L., Hawk, T. C., Gottlob, L. R., & Coleman, R. E. (1999). Adult age differences in functional neuroanatomy of verbal recognition memory. *Human Brain Mapping, 7,* 115–135.

Maguire, E. A., & Frith, C. D. (2003). Aging affects the engagement of the hippocampus during autobiographical memory retrieval. *Brain, 126,* 1511–1523.

Mason, S. E. (1979). Effects of orienting task on the recall and recognition performance of subjects differing in age. *Developmental Psychology, 15,* 467–469.

May, C. P., Hasher, L., & Kane, M. J. (1999). The role of interference in memory span. *Memory and Cognition, 27,* 759–767.

Miller, E. K., & Cohen, J. D. (2001). An integrative theory of prefrontal cortex function. *Annual Review of Neuroscience, 24,* 167–202.

Morcom, A. M., Good, C. D., Frackowiak, R. S., & Rugg, M. D. (2003). Age effects on the neural correlates of successful memory encoding. *Brain, 126,* 213–229.

Moscovitch, M., & Winocur, G. (1992). The neuropsychology of memory and aging. In F. I. M. Craik & T. A. Salthouse (Eds.), *The handbook of aging and cognition* (pp. 315–372). Hillsdale, NJ: Erlbaum.

Nystrom, L. E., Braver, T. S., Sabb, F. W., Delgado, M. R., Noll, D. C., & Cohen, J. D. (2000). Working memory for letters, shapes, and locations: fMRI evidence against stimulus-based regional organization in human prefrontal cortex. *NeuroImage, 11,* 424–446.

Park, D. C. (2000). The basic mechanisms accounting for age-related decline in cognitive function. In D. C. Park & N. Schwarz (Eds.), *Cognitive aging: A primer* (pp. 1–21). Philadelphia, PA: Psychology Press.

Park, D. C., Lautenschlager, G., Hedden, T., Davidson, N. S., Smith, A. D., & Smith, P. (2002). Models of visuospatial and verbal memory across the adult life span. *Psychology and Aging, 17,* 299–320.

Park, D. C., Polk, T. A., Mikels, J. A., Taylor, S. F., & Marshuetz, C. (2001). Cerebral aging: Integration of brain and behavioral models of cognitive function. *Dialogues in Clinical Neuroscience: Cerebral Aging, 3,* 151–165.

Park, D. C., Polk, T., Park, R., Minear, M., Savage, A., & Smith, M. R. (in press). Aging reduces neural specialization in ventral visual cortex. *Proceedings of the National Academy of Sciences of the United States of America.*

Park, D. C., & Puglisi, J. T. (1985). Older adults' memory for the color of matched pictures and words. *Journal of Gerontology, 40,* 198–204.

Park, D. C., Puglisi, J. T., & Lutz, R. (1982). Spatial memory in older adults: Effects of intentionality. *Journal of Gerontology*, *37*, 330–335.

Park, D. C., Puglisi, J. T., & Smith, A. D. (1986). Memory for pictures: Does an age-related decline exist? *Psychology and Aging*, *1*, 11–17.

Park, D. C., Royal, D., Dudley, W., & Morrell, R. (1988). Forgetting of pictures over a long retention interval in old and young adults. *Psychology and Aging*, *3*, 94–95.

Park, D. C., & Shaw, R. (1992). Effect of environmental support on implicit and explicit memory in young and old adults. *Psychology and Aging*, *7*, 632–642.

Park, D. C., Smith, A. D., Dudley, W. N., & Lafronza, V. N. (1989). Effects of age and a divided attention task presented during encoding and retrieval on memory. *Journal of Experimental Psychology: Learning, Memory, and Cognition*, *15*, 1185–1191.

Park, D. C., Smith, A. D., Lautenschlager, G., Earles, J., Frieske, D., Zwahr, M., & Gaines, C. (1996). Mediators of long-term memory performance across the life span. *Psychology and Aging*, *11*, 621–637.

Park, D. C., Smith, A. D., Morrell, R. W., Puglisi, J. T., & Dudley, W. N. (1990). Effects of contextual integration on recall of pictures in older adults. *Journal of Gerontology: Psychological Sciences*, *45*, 52–58.

Park, D. C., Welsh, R. C., Marshuetz, C., Gutchess, A. H., Mikels, J., Polk, T. A., Noll, D. C., & Taylor, S. F. (2003). Working memory for complex scenes: Age differences in frontal and hippocampal activations. *Journal of Cognitive Neuroscience*, *15*, 1122–1134.

Poldrack, R. A., Wagner, A. D., Prull, M. W., Desmond, J. E., Glover, G. H., & Gabrieli, J. D. E. (1999). Functional specialization for semantic and phonological processing in the left inferior prefrontal cortex. *Neuroimage*, *10*, 15–35.

Rabinowitz, J. C. (1984). Aging and recognition failure. *Journal of Gerontology*, *39*, 65–71.

Rabinowitz, J. C. (1986). Priming in episodic memory. *Journal of Gerontology*, *41*, 204–213.

Raz, N. (2000). Aging of the brain and its impact on cognitive performance: Integration of structural and functional findings. In F. I. M. Craik & T. A. Salthouse (eds.), *Handbook of Aging and Cognition* (pp. 1–90). Mahwah, NJ: Erlbaum.

Raz, N., Gunning-Dixon, F. M., Head, D., Dupuis, J. H., & Acker, J. D. (1998). Neuroanatomical correlates of cognitive aging: Evidence from structural magnetic resonance imaging. *Neuropsychology*, *12*, 95–114.

Reuter-Lorenz, P. A., Jonides, J., Smith, E., Hartley, A., Miller, A., Marshuetz, C., & Koeppe, R. (2000). Age differences in the frontal lateralization of verbal and spatial working memory revealed by PET. *Journal of Cognitive Neuroscience*, *12*, 174–187.

Rosen, A. C., Prull, M. W., O'Hara, R., Race, E. A., Desmond, J. E., Glover, G. H., Yesavage, J. A., & Gabrieli, J. D. E. (2002). Variable effects of aging on frontal lobe contributions to memory. *Neuroreport*, *13*, 2425–2428.

Salthouse, T. A. (1994). The nature of the influence of speed on adult age differences in cognition. *Developmental Psychology*, *30*, 240–259.

Salthouse, T. A. (1996). The processing-speed theory of adult age differences in cognition. *Psychological Review*, *103*, 403–428.

Salthouse, T. A., & Babcock, R. L. (1991). Decomposing adult age differences in working memory. *Developmental Psychology*, *27*, 763–776.

Salthouse, T. A., Mitchell, D. R., Skovronek, E., & Babcock, R. L. (1989). Effects of adult age and working memory on reasoning and spatial ability. *Journal of Experimental Psychology: Learning, Memory, and Cognition*, *15*, 507–516.

Schacter, D. L., Savage, C. R., Alpert, N. M., Rauch, S. L., & Albert, M. S. (1996). The role of hippocampus and frontal cortex in age-related memory changes: A PET study. *Neuroreport*, *7*, 1165–1169.

Schonfield, D., & Robertson, B. A. (1966). Memory storage and aging. *Canadian Journal of Psychology, 20*, 228–236.

Schooler, C., & Mulatu, M. S. (2001). The reciprocal effects of leisure time activities and intellectual functioning in older people: A longitudinal analysis. *Psychology and Aging, 16*, 466–506.

Simon, E. (1979). Depth and elaboration of processing in relation to age. *Journal of Experimental Psychology: Human Learning and Memory, 5*, 115–124.

Smith, A. D. (1977). Adult age differences in cued recall. *Developmental Psychology, 13*, 326–331.

Smith, A. D., Park, D. C., Cherry, K., & Berkovsky, K. (1990). Age differences in memory for concrete and abstract pictures. *Journal of Gerontology: Psychological Sciences, 35*, 205–209.

Smith, A. D., Park, D. C., Earles, J. L. K., Shaw, R. J., & Whiting, W. L. (1998). Age differences in context integration in memory. *Psychology and Aging, 13*, 21–28.

Spencer, W. D., & Raz, N. (1995). Differential effects of aging on memory for content and context: A meta-analysis. *Psychology and Aging, 10*, 527–539.

Stebbins, G. T., Carrillo, M. C., Dorfman, J., Dirksen, C., Desmond, J. E., Turner, D. A., Bennett, D. A., Wilson, R. S., Glover, G., & Gabrieli, J. D. E. (2002). Aging effects on memory encoding in the frontal lobes. *Psychology and Aging, 17*, 44–55.

Stern, C. E., Corkin, S., Gonzalez, R. G., Guimaraes, A. R., Baker, J. R., Jennings, P. J., Carr, C. A., Sugiura, R. M., Vedantham, V., & Rosen, B. R. (1996). The hippocampal formation participates in novel picture encoding: evidence from functional magnetic resonance imaging. *Proceedings of the National Academy of Sciences of the United States of America, 93*, 8660–8665.

Tulving, E., Kapur, S., Craik, F. I. M., Moscovitch, M., & Houle, S. (1994). Hemispheric encoding/retrieval asymmetry in episodic memory: Positron emission tomography findings. *Proceedings of the National Academy of Sciences of the United States of America, 91*, 2012–2015.

Wagner, A. D., Schacter, D. L., Rotte, M., Koutstaal, W., Maril, A., Dale, A. M., Rosen, B. R., & Buckner, R. L. (1998). Building memories: Remembering and forgetting of verbal experiences as predicted by brain activity. *Science, 281*, 1188–1191.

Zacks, R., & Hasher, L. (1997). Cognitive gerontology and attentional inhibition: A reply to Burke and McDowd. *Journal of Gerontology: Psychological Sciences, 52B*, 274–283.

10

The Neural Basis of Age-Related
Declines in Prospective Memory

Robert West

Prospective memory represents the realization of intentions that must be delayed over minutes, hours, or days in the absence of an external cue or prompt (Kvavilashvili & Ellis, 1996; Meacham & Leiman, 1975). Examples of common intentions might include returning a phone call to a colleague following the completion of a conversation or retrieving a jacket from the cleaners on your way home from work. Failures of prospective memory reflect one form of absent-mindedness (Schacter, 2001), a topic that has been of interest to authors over the last 100 years (G. Cohen, 1989; Freud, 1901). This chapter provides an overview of recent advances in our understanding of the cognitive and neural mechanisms supporting prospective memory within the context of the effects of aging on the realization of delayed intentions.

Following the landmark publication of Einstein and McDaniel (1990), there has been a steady increase in the number of studies devoted to understanding the effects of aging on the cognitive processes and neural mechanisms supporting prospective memory. Much of the early work examining this relationship was motivated by the counterintuitive finding that age-related differences in prospective memory were often small and not significant (Einstein & McDaniel, 1990; West, 1988). The observation of robust age-related differences in prospective memory in later studies has led researchers to investigate the boundary conditions under which spared and impaired prospective memory is observed in older adults (see McDaniel & Einstein, 2000) and to explore the cognitive and neural loci of age-related declines in prospective memory (Kidder et al., 1997; Kliegel, McDaniel, & Einstein, 2000; West & Covell, 2001).

The importance of identifying the source of age-related declines in prospective memory in healthy older adults and those with age-associated pathological conditions is illustrated in the findings of two studies. First, a population-based study that included approximately 12,000 individuals aged 65 years and older revealed poor prospective memory in some participants who obtained perfect scores on measures of free recall and mental status (Huppert, Johnson, & Nickson, 2000). These findings may indicate that age-related declines in the processes recruited during performance of tasks measuring mental status, episodic memory, and prospective memory follow somewhat different trajectories within the older adult population. Second, another study revealed that caregivers rated the prospective memory errors of patients with Alzheimer's disease (AD) as more frustrating than the episodic memory errors of these patients (G. Smith et al., 2000), leading to the suggestion that prospective memory errors may be one source of tension in the patient–caregiver relationship.

The goals of this chapter are threefold: (1) to provide an overview of current models of prospective memory within the context of the cognitive aging literature, (2) to provide a review of findings related to the neural basis of prospective memory, and (3) to examine the neural basis of age-related declines in prospective memory.

Models of Prospective Memory

Multicomponent Models

Multicomponent models of prospective memory hold that the realization of delayed intentions is supported by prospective and retrospective components responsible for the recognition that some intention is to be realized and the recovery of the relevant intention from memory (McDaniel & Einstein, 1992). The noticing-plus-search model reflects one example of a multicomponent model that seeks to specify the functional characteristics of the prospective and retrospective components of prospective memory (Einstein & McDaniel, 1996). In this model, noticing is thought to reflect a familiarity-based process that supports the detection of prospective memory cues when they are encountered in the environment; in contrast, directed search is thought to reflect a more consciously controlled process that serves to attribute meaning to cues that are recognized. Findings from a number of studies indicate that the success of prospective memory is modulated by the relative distinctiveness between prospective memory cues and stimuli presented in the ongoing activity (Brandimonte & Passolunghi, 1994; Einstein & McDaniel, 1990), consistent with the idea that noticing is a relatively automatic process.

However, other data clearly indicate that attentional processes contribute to the detection of prospective memory cues (West, Herndon, & Crewdson, 2001). A number of investigators have reported that the efficiency of prospective memory is modulated by the context within which a cue is embedded (e.g., Marsh, Hicks, & Hancock, 2000), and that this effect reflects a failure to detect prospective memory cues rather than an inability to retrieve from memory the intention associated with the cue (West & Craik, 2001). Also, age-related differences in the prospective component of memory for intentions tend to be greater than age-related differences in the retrospective component of memory for intentions (A. L. Cohen, West, & Craik, 2001). This last finding seems inconsistent with the idea that an automatic process supports the detection of prospective memory cues because automatic processes are thought to be relatively immune to the effects of aging (Hasher & Zacks, 1979).

Automatic Associative Model

The automatic associative model has been offered as an alternative to the noticing-plus-search model (Guynn, McDaniel, & Einstein, 2001). This model represents an adaptation of Moscovitch's (1994) working-with-memory model to the area of prospective memory. In the automatic associative model, the realization of an intention takes place when a prospective memory cue is focally attended and interacts with a memory trace representing the cue–intention association; the intention is then automatically delivered to consciousness and realized.

A number of findings are consistent with predictions derived from the automatic associative model. For instance, the probability of prospective responding is reduced when the context in which a prospective memory cue is presented changes from the formation to the realization of the intention and when the cue is initially processed to a relatively shallow level (McDaniel, Robinson-Riegler, & Einstein, 1998). Also, the ability to retrieve the intention associated with a given cue is modulated more strongly by the degree of semantic association between the cue and intention than the perceptual characteristics of the cue (Cohen et al., 2001). Consistent with these findings, the benefit of prospective memory reminders is greater when individuals are asked to consider both the cue and intention, presumably fostering greater associative or elaborative processing, than when individuals are asked to consider the cue or intention in isolation (Guynn, McDaniel, & Einstein, 1998).

Findings from the cognitive aging literature provide support for the automatic associative model. Age-related differences in memory for intentions are small when there is a preexisting association between the prospective memory cue and intention and larger when there is no a priori relationship between the cue and intention (A. L. Cohen, West, & Craik, 2001). Also, older adults are known to form less-elaborate intentions than are younger adults, and this may in turn result in failures of prospective memory (Kliegel, McDaniel, & Einstein, 2000). Furthermore, elaborative or extended processing of the cue–intention association reduces, and possibly eliminates, age-related differences in prospective memory (Chasteen, Park, & Schwarz, 2001).

Controlled Attention Model

The controlled attention model of prospective memory is founded on the idea that the realization of an intention requires the allocation of controlled or effortful attentional processing. This model is represented in the writings of a number of authors, who have provided supporting evidence using a variety of manipulations to modulate the allocation of attentional resources (Einstein et al., 1997; Marsh & Hicks, 1998; R. E. Smith, 2003). For instance, the division of attention during the ongoing activity can reduce the efficiency of prospective memory (Einstein et al., 1997; Otani et al., 1997).

The contribution of controlled attention to prospective memory has also been considered in studies in which response time for the ongoing activity performed in isolation is compared to response time for the ongoing activity when a prospective demand is added to the task (Burgess, Quayle, & Frith, 2001; R. E. Smith, 2003). In these studies, there is typically a marked increase in response time when both prospective and ongoing components of the task are performed relative to when the ongoing activity is performed in isolation. Furthermore, R. E. Smith (2000) reported that this slowing of response time was correlated with individual differences in working memory capacity. Other work examining the contribution of different components of working memory to prospective memory has demonstrated that occupying the central executive, but not the articulatory loop or visuospatial sketchpad, leads to a disruption of prospective memory (Marsh & Hicks, 1998).

The idea that aging is associated with a reduction in the efficiency of attentional or processing resources has a long history in the cognitive aging literature (e.g., Craik & Byrd, 1982). However, studies that have examined the contribution of controlled attention to age-related declines in prospective memory have provided somewhat mixed results. Some evidence is consistent with the controlled attention model, revealing larger age-related differences in prospective memory when attention is divided (Einstein et al., 1997) and when working memory load is high (Kidder et al., 1997). However, other work has failed to reveal an effect of divided attention on prospective memory in either younger or older adults (Einstein et al., 2000).

Mirroring these experimental findings, work that has examined the correlations among age, prospective memory, and measures of processing resources has produced variable results. West and Craik (2001) observed significant correlations between prospective memory and measures of processing resources (i.e., speed, inhibition, and working memory) and found that the relationship between age and prospective memory was no longer significant when variance shared with processing resource variables was statistically controlled. In contrast, other investigators have not observed significant relationships among prospective memory, age, and measures of processing resources (Cherry & LeCompte, 1999; Kidder et al., 1997; Park et al., 1997).

The Neural Basis of Prospective Memory

Functional Neuroimaging

Functional neuroimaging studies have revealed that a distributed network that includes structures in the frontal and parietal cortices, the hippocampus, and the thalamus supports prospective memory. The first study using positron emission tomography (PET) to examine the functional neuroanatomy of prospective memory compared neural activity during a scan in which individuals performed an ongoing activity and realized a simple intention to activity during a scan that simply required performance of the ongoing activity (Okuda et al., 1998). This comparison revealed significant activation in several cortical and subcortical regions, including right dorsolateral and ventrolateral prefrontal, the left frontal pole, medial frontal and anterior cingulate, and the left parahippocampal gyrus.

The use of only two conditions in the study of Okuda et al. (1998) make it difficult to ascertain the functional characteristics of those neural structures that were activated during task performance. However, a study by Burgess, Quayle, and Frith (2001) that included three conditions provided some insight into the functional characteristics of the neural structures recruited during prospective remembering. In the isolation condition, individuals performed one of three ongoing activities in the absence of a prospective demand. In the expectation condition, individuals were told that prospective memory cues could appear, however, no cues were presented. In the execution condition, individuals were told that prospective memory cues could appear, and cues were presented in 20% of the trials. By including the expectation and execution conditions, the investigators were able to identify neural structures that were differentially activated by the maintenance of an intention (i.e., isolation vs. expectation and execution conditions) and the realization of an intention (i.e., expectation vs. execution conditions). The comparison of the isolation condition to the other conditions revealed bilateral activation in the frontal-polar and precuneus regions and in the right lateral prefrontal and parietal regions. This finding led to the suggestion that these neural structures are involved in the maintenance of intentions over a delay (Burgess, Quayle, & Frith, 2001). In contrast, the comparison of the expectation and execution conditions revealed activation in the right thalamus and deactivation in the right middle frontal gyrus (Burgess, Quayle, & Frith, 2001). This finding led to the suggestion that these structures are particularly involved in the realization or execution of intentions.

Neuropsychology

Studies of neuropsychological patients have served both to identify a number of neurological (e.g., traumatic brain injury or TBI, focal brain lesions, multiple sclerosis) and psychiatric (i.e., schizophrenia, Korsakoff's disease, ecstasy abuse) conditions that have a negative impact on the efficiency of prospective memory and define some of the factors that contribute to disrupted prospective memory in these groups of individuals. Work with patients who sustained focal and diffuse lesions revealed that damage to structures within the frontal and temporal lobes can disrupt prospective memory (Palmer & McDonald, 2000; Cockburn, 1995; Shum, Valentine, & Cutmore, 1999). Complimenting the findings of lesion studies, work with psychiatric patients may provide some degree of insight into the neuropharmacology of prospective memory (Heffernan et al., 2001; Kondel, 2002).

Studies of patients with focal and diffuse lesions indicated that structures within the frontal and medial temporal regions support discrete processes subserving prospective memory. Damage to the frontal lobe disrupts different types of prospective memory (i.e., time, event, and activity based; Shum, Valentine, & Cutmore, 1999) and is often associated with a profound impairment of prospective memory accompanied by the relative sparing of other cognitive and intellectual abilities (Burgess & Shallice, 1997).

For instance, Bisiacchi (1996) reported data for two patients who had sustained a TBI and were grossly impaired on tasks measuring both time- and event-based prospective memory; in contrast, these patients performed within the normal-to-superior range on measures of planning, reasoning, general intelligence, episodic memory, and short-term memory. Cockburn (1995) described a patient with damage to the medial frontal lobe who possessed a similar neuropsychological profile. This patient performed well on most tests of memory, reasoning, and intellectual ability and even on some tests of prospective memory; however, a profound impairment of prospective memory was revealed when active disengagement from an ongoing activity was required for an intention to be realized.

Other work indicated that distinct subregions within the frontal lobe may support different aspects of prospective memory. Patients with damage to the right dorsolateral prefrontal cortex appear to be specifically impaired in the formation of intentions; patients with damage to the left frontal pole form adequate intentions that go unrealized during task performance (Burgess et al., 2000).

In summary, damage to the frontal lobes can produce impairment on a variety of different prospective memory tasks. The impairment may result from disruptions in the ability to form intentions, maintain preparatory attention, and disengage from the ongoing activity when a cue is encountered.

The contribution of the medial temporal lobe to prospective memory is less clear than that of the frontal lobe. Patients who have undergone temporal lobe resection as a treatment for epilepsy perform poorly on prospective memory tasks (Palmer & McDonald, 2000); however, this deficit may arise from a concomitant disruption of episodic memory as these patients also perform poorly on measures of retrospective memory. Other evidence for an association between prospective memory and episodic memory is revealed by the results of a study in which prospective memory impairment in patients with multiple sclerosis was attributed to failures of episodic memory (Bravin et al., 2000). A role of the medial temporal lobe in prospective memory is also supported by data indicating that disruptions of prospective memory are observed in patients with mild cognitive impairment (Huppert & Beardsall, 1993), a possible precursor of AD, which has been associated with medial temporal lobe pathology (Jack et al., 1997).

A limited number of studies have examined the effects of psychiatric disorders on the efficiency of prospective memory; still, these studies provide initial insight into the neuropharmacological foundation of prospective memory. Kondel (2002) reported that the intention superiority effect (i.e., faster response times to words associated with intentions) was disrupted in patients with schizophrenia who demonstrated impairments of executive function relative to patients with schizophrenia possessing intact executive function. This finding may indicate that the dopamine or serotonin systems play a role in efficient prospective memory because schizophrenia is associated with abnormalities in aspects of both these systems.

Further evidence for the involvement of these neurotransmitter systems in prospective memory is found in a study that examined self-reported memory failures in users of ecstasy (Heffernan et al., 2001), a drug that is known to be toxic to serotonergic and dopaminergic neurons (Ricaurte et al., 2002). In this study, users of ecstasy reported higher levels of prospective memory errors, but not cognitive failures, than matched controls; this deficit was related to a concomitant impairment of executive functions.

Electrophysiology

Studies utilizing event-related potentials (ERPs) to examine the neural basis of prospective memory have been concerned with identifying the neural correlates of the
processes that support prospective memory, examining the specificity of these processes to prospective memory, and exploring the functional characteristics of the
neural correlates of prospective memory. Work related to process identification has
revealed a number of modulations of the ERPs associated with different aspects of
the formation (i.e., formation slow wave [FSW]; West & Ross-Munroe, 2002) and
realization (i.e., N300, prospective positivity, realization slow wave [RSW]; West,
Herndon, & Crewdson, 2001; West & Ross-Munroe, 2002) of intentions. Work related to process specification has revealed that modulations of the ERPs associated
with prospective memory can be dissociated from modulations of the ERPs associated with target selection and categorization and recollection of a previous episode.
Other work has served to define the functional characteristics of modulations of the
ERPs associated with the detection of prospective cues and the recollection of delayed intentions.

Two studies have examined modulations of the ERPs associated with the formation of intentions. These studies revealed that the formation of intentions is associated with a FSW over the frontal-polar region of the scalp that begins around 500
ms after the onset of a stimulus indicating that an intention should be formed (figure
10.1a; West & Ross-Munroe, 2002). The FSW reflects greater negativity for trials
in which the intention is later realized than trials in which the intention goes unrealized. The time course and topography of the FSW are similar when the prospective
memory cue is defined by color (West & Ross-Munroe, 2002) or word identity
(West, Herndon, & Ross-Munroe, 2001), leading to the suggestion that it reflects
conceptual level or elaborative processing during the formation of an intention. This
proposal is based on evidence from studies indicating that elaborative or deep processing of information within the context of episodic memory encoding is associated
with slow wave activity over the anterior frontal region of the scalp (Mangels, Picton, & Craik, 2001; Rugg, 1995).

The detection of a prospective memory cue is associated with a phasic negativity
(N300) over the occipital-parietal region of the scalp (figure 10.1b; West & Ross-
Munroe, 2002). The N300 is elicited by prospective cues that are defined by letter
case (West, Herndon, & Crewdson, 2001), color (West & Ross-Munroe, 2002), and
letter (West & Wymbs, 2003) or word identity (West & Krompinger, in press),
indicating that it is not bound to the perceptual characteristics of the cues. The N300
is associated with prospective cues that elicit a prospective response (i.e., prospective
hits) and not prospective cues that fail to elicit a prospective response (i.e., prospective misses; West & Ross-Munroe, 2002). This finding indicates that the N300 is
specifically related to the detection of a prospective cue and does not merely reflect
a response to the distinctiveness of the prospective cues (West, Herndon, & Crewdson, 2001).

The realization of an intention following the detection of a prospective cue is
associated with a sustained positivity over the parietal region of the scalp that appears to reflect two functionally distinct processes: recollection positivity and pro-

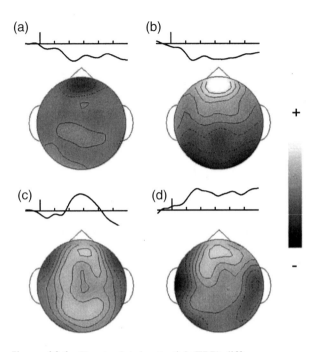

Figure 10.1. Event-related potential (ERP) difference waves from 200 ms before stimulus onset to 1200 ms after stimulus onset and topographic maps as viewed from the top of the head for younger adults: *a*, formation slow wave reflecting greater negativity for realized than unrealized intentions; *b*, N300 reflecting greater negativity for prospective memory hit trials than prospective memory miss or ongoing activity trials; *c*, prospective positivity reflecting greater positivity for prospective memory hit trials than ongoing activity trials; *d*, realization slow wave reflecting greater positivity for prospective memory hit trials than prospective memory miss or ongoing activity trials. The vertical bar indicates stimulus onset and reflects +2 μV.

spective positivity. The recollection positivity reflects a sustained positivity over the parietal region of the scalp between 400 ms and 800 ms after cue onset that is greater in amplitude for prospective hits than prospective misses and is similar in time course and topography to the recognition old–new effect (figure 10.1c).

The functional characteristics of the recollection positivity have been examined in a study using Partial Least Squares (Lobaugh, West, & McIntosh, 2001; McIntosh et al., 1996) technique to compare the neural correlates of prospective memory, recognition memory, and cued recall (West & Krompinger, in press). In this study, the recollection positivity was associated with a latent variable that contrasted prospective hits and recognition hits with ongoing activity trials and prospective lures (experiment 1) and prospective hits and cued-recall hits with ongoing activity trials, prospective lures, and prospective misses (experiment 2). Together these findings led to the suggestion that the recollection positivity reflects the activity of a neural mechanism that supports the recollection of a previously studied episode in prospective and retrospective memory tasks (West & Krompinger, in press).

Like the N300, the prospective positivity is elicited when cues are defined by a number of different stimulus attributes (West & Ross-Munroe, 2002; West, Herndon, & Ross-Monroe, 2001). The prospective positivity is elicited by prospective hits and not by prospective misses when unique prospective cues are used for each block of trials, indicating that it is associated with successful prospective remembering (West & Krompinger, in press).

The functional significance of the prospective positivity is not clearly understood. It has been dissociated from the P3 (West et al., 2003; West & Wymbs, 2003), indicating that it is not specifically related to target categorization (Kok, 2001) or updating working memory (Donchin & Coles, 1988). One possibility is that the prospective positivity represents a neural correlate of the directed search process described in the noticing-plus-search model of prospective memory (Einstein & McDaniel, 1996), representing the activity of a neural mechanism that serves to monitor or coordinate the action that is specified following recollection of an intention associated with a prospective cue. Consistent with this proposal, West et al. (2003) observed that the amplitude of the prospective positivity was modulated by the need for output monitoring being greater when the task included three cue–intention pairings relative to when a single cue–intention pairing was used.

In addition to the N300, recollection positivity, and prospective positivity, prospective cues can elicit an RSW (West & Ross-Munroe, 2002). The RSW reflects sustained positivity over the frontal region of the scalp that begins between 400 ms and 500 ms after onset of the prospective memory cue and differentiates prospective hits from prospective misses and ongoing activity trials (figure 10.1d; West, Herndon, & Ross-Monroe, 2001; West & Ross-Munroe, 2002). The functional characteristics of the RSW have not been explored, making it difficult to know what process is reflected by this modulation. However, given the finding that prospective memory impairment following frontal lobe injury can result from an inability to disengage from the ongoing activity (Cockburn, 1995), it seems reasonable to suggest that the RSW reflects the activity of a neural mechanism supporting this disengagement process.

The Neural Basis of Age-Related Decline in Prospective Memory

Neuropsychology, Aging, and Prospective Memory

The neuropsychological foundation of age-related declines in prospective memory has been explored in an interesting study examining the relationship between individual differences in prospective memory and various neuropsychological tests associated with frontal and medial temporal lobe function (McDaniel et al., 1999). In this study, individuals were classified according to their performance on tasks sensitive to frontal and medial temporal lobe function (i.e., high frontal/high temporal, high frontal/low temporal, low frontal/high temporal, low frontal/low temporal), and then group differences on a measure of prospective memory were examined. The results of this study revealed that high frontal function was associated with better prospective memory than low frontal function; in contrast, individual differences in medial temporal lobe function were not significantly related to prospective memory (figure 10.2).

Complimenting these findings, correlational analyses from a second study revealed that the relationship between age and prospective memory was attenuated when variance shared with measures sensitive to frontal lobe function (i.e., self-ordered pointing and Stroop tasks) was statistically controlled (West & Craik, 2001). These findings are also consistent with the frontal lobe theory of aging, by which age-related differences across a number of different domains of cognition are thought to arise from declines in the functional integrity of the prefrontal cortex (West, 1996; but see Greenwood, 2000) or the frontostriatal system (Rubin, 1999).

The failure to observe a significant relationship between individual differences on measures sensitive to medial temporal lobe function and prospective memory in older adults is consistent with other evidence examining the effects of aging on medial temporal lobe structures. Based on an extensive meta-analysis that examined age-related changes in brain volume across cortical, limbic, and subcortical regions, Raz (2000) concluded that the effects of normal aging on the prefrontal cortex tend to be greater than the effects of aging on the medial temporal lobe. An interesting finding of Raz's review was that the medial temporal lobe revealed the greatest degree of between-study variation in the magnitude of the effect of age of any structure that was considered.

One possible explanation for the increased variability in medial temporal lobe volume reported across studies is that some samples may have included individuals with preclinical AD (Raz, 2000), thereby confounding the effects of aging with age-associated pathology known to adversely affect the medial temporal lobe (Jack et al., 1997). Within the context of aging and prospective memory, this idea dovetails

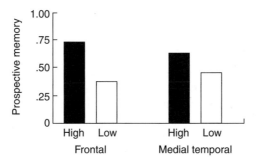

Figure 10.2. Percentage of correct prospective responses for individuals high or low on frontal lobe function or medial temporal lobe function. (Adapted from McDaniel et al., 1999.)

nicely with the findings of Huppert and Beardsall (1993), who observed a prospective memory deficit in individuals with mild cognitive impairment.

Finally, the finding that individual differences in tasks associated with frontal lobe, but not medial temporal lobe, functions are correlated with the efficiency of prospective memory in older adults seems consistent with evidence indicating that disruptions of prospective memory in healthy older adults are more likely to result from a failure to detect prospective cues than from an inability to retrieve intentions from memory (Dobbs & Rule, 1987; West & Craik, 2001).

Event-Related Potentials, Aging, and Prospective Memory

Studies using ERPs to examine the neural basis of age-related differences in prospective memory have revealed that aging affects modulations of the ERPs elicited during both the formation and the realization of intentions (West & Covell, 2001; West, Herndon, & Covell, 2003). West, Herndon, and Covell (2003) observed that the amplitude of the FSW, which is elicited during the formation of simple intentions, is attenuated in older adults (figure 10.3a). This finding is consistent with predictions derived from the automatic associative model (Guynn, McDaniel, & Einstein, 2001) and with behavioral data indicating that older adults form less-elaborate intentions than younger adults (Kliegel, McDaniel, & Einstein, 2000), and that age-related

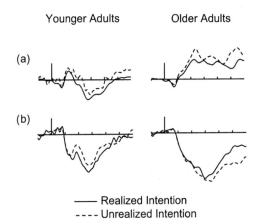

Younger Adults   Older Adults

(a)

(b)

——— Realized Intention
- - - - Unrealized Intention

Figure 10.3. Grand average event-related potentials (ERPs) for realized (solid line) and unrealized (broken line) intention trials in younger and older adults from 200 ms before stimulus onset to 1200 ms after stimulus onset: *a*, the formation slow wave at electrode Af3 over the anterior frontal region that is greater in amplitude for younger than older adults; *b*, the temporal-parietal slow wave at the left mastoid that is greater in amplitude for older than younger adults. The vertical bar reflects +2 μV.

differences in prospective memory are greatest when the prospective memory cue and intention are not semantically related (A. L. Cohen, West, & Craik, 2001).

In addition to the age-related reduction in the amplitude of the FSW, a temporal-parietal slow wave (TPSW) has been observed in older adults, but not younger adults, that reflects greater positivity for later realized intentions than later unrealized intentions (figure 10.3b; West, Herndon, & Covell, 2003). This finding led to the proposal that the TPSW may reflect some degree of functional reorganization on the part of older adults to compensate for a reduced ability to engage in elaborative processing during the formation of intentions. This proposal was based on recent evidence from studies using functional neuroimaging methods to examine the effects of aging on episodic memory, in which differential activation in older and younger adults has been interpreted as reflecting compensatory processing by older adults (see Cabeza, 2002). The results of further analyses of these data examining the relationship between individual differences in the amplitude of the TPSW and the accuracy and latency of prospective responding in older adults is inconsistent with the idea that this modulation reflects compensatory processing. The results of these analyses revealed that there is a strong negative correlation between the amplitude of the TPSW and the accuracy of prospective responding and a strong positive correlation between the amplitude of the TPSW and response time for correct prospective responses (figure 10.4). These findings indicate that the amplitude of the TPSW is greatest for those older adults who are least accurate and slowest when later making prospective responses and represents the opposite of what would be expected based on the compensation hypothesis. Furthermore, these findings lead to the suggestion that enhanced neural activity in older adults relative to younger adults may, in some instances, reflect maladaptive rather than compensatory processing (Buckner, 2002).

The findings of behavioral studies indicated that the failure to detect prospective memory cues can contribute to age-related declines in prospective memory (e.g., West & Craik, 2001). Based on these findings, it would be expected that aging would be associated with a reduction in the amplitude of the N300 that is related to the detection of prospective cues. This hypothesis has been confirmed in two studies in which the amplitude of the N300 was reduced in older adults relative to younger

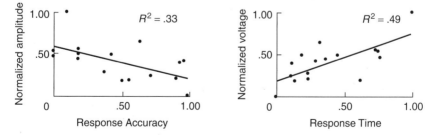

Figure 10.4. Scatterplots representing the correlation between the temporal-parietal slow wave and response accuracy and response time for older adults. Note that the amplitude of the temporal-parietal slow wave is greatest for those older adults who were least accurate and slowest.

adults (figure 10.5a; West & Covell, 2001; R. West, Herndon, & Covell, 2003). The effect of aging on the N300 appears to result from the disruption of an attentional process that facilitates the detection of prospective cues, in agreement with predictions derived from the controlled attention model of prospective memory. This idea is based on the finding that the N300 is significant in older adults over the left, but not right, hemisphere and evidence from studies of younger adults indicating that the influence of attention on the N300 is greater over the right than the left hemisphere (West, Herndon, & Crewdson, 2001). These findings may also be consistent with the automatic associative model, in which focal attentive processing of the prospective cue is thought to be required for the cue to interact with a memory trace representing the cue–intention association and give rise to the recovery of an intention from memory (Guynn, McDaniel, & Einstein, 2001).

The effect of aging on the prospective positivity has been variable in previous research. West and Covell (2001) reported that the amplitude of the parietal positivity was reduced in older adults; in contrast, West, Herndon, and Covell (2003) found that there was no difference in the amplitude of the parietal positivity in younger and older adults when contrasting prospective memory hits and ongoing activity trials (figure 10.5b). The discrepancy between the findings of these reports may reflect differences in the perceptual salience of the prospective cues used in the two studies. West and Covell (2001) used a highly salient cue (i.e., uppercase vs.

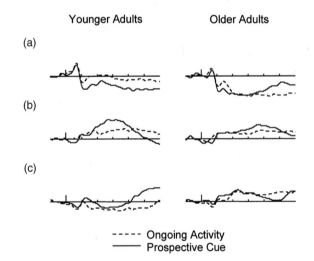

Figure 10.5. Grand average event-related potentials (ERPs) for prospective memory hit (solid line) and ongoing activity (broken line) trials for younger and older adults from 200 ms before stimulus onset to 1200 ms after stimulus onset: *a*, the N300 at electrode Po9 over the occipital-parietal region; *b*, the prospective positivity at electrode Pz; and *c*, the realization slow wave at electrode Af4 over the anterior frontal region. The vertical bar reflects +2 μV.

lowercase letters) that probably resulted in the P3 and prospective positivity contributing to the ERPs over the parietal region of the scalp between 400 and 800 ms after onset of the prospective cues; in contrast, West, Herndon, and Covell (2003) used a less-salient cue (i.e., one of six colors presented over the course of the task), probably resulting in the P3 contributing minimally to parietal activity in this study. Supporting this interpretation, other evidence indicated that the contribution of the P3 to parietal activity within the context of prospective memory tasks is reduced when nonsalient relative to salient cues are used (West et al., 2003), and extensive evidence indicated that the amplitude of the P3 is reduced in older adults (see Friedman, Kazmerski, & Fabiani, 1997).

The amplitude of the RSW is attenuated in older adults (figure 10.5c; West, Herndon, & Covell, 2003). If the RSW is taken to reflect the activity of those processes supporting disengagement from the ongoing activity, the attenuation of this modulation in older adults may indicate that aging is associated with a disruption in the ability to disengage from the ongoing activity. This proposal is consistent with data indicating that there are age-related differences in the efficiency of task switching (Kray & Lindenberger, 2000); however, more work is required before this hypothesis can be accepted because the functional significance of the RSW is poorly understood (West & Ross-Munroe, 2002).

Issues

The work reviewed in this chapter reveals that there has been considerable progress in the understanding of prospective memory and the effects of aging on those processes supporting the realization of delayed intentions. Behavioral studies have served to define the boundary conditions under which age-related differences in prospective memory are observed and provided the foundation for initial theory-building efforts in the area of prospective memory. Evidence from studies using functional neuroimaging, neuropsychological, and electrophysiological methodologies provide a preliminary sketch of the functional neuroanatomy underlying prospective memory. However, as is the case in most areas of science, this increased understanding has served to illuminate a number of unresolved issues that will challenge researchers in the coming years.

Knowledge of the functional neuroanatomy supporting the formation and realization of intentions remains quite limited. This can be appreciated by a quick survey of the literature, revealing only three published studies using PET and five published studies using ERPs. This state of affairs will certainly change in the coming years with increased interest in prospective memory and methodological advances. Two methodological advances that should foster the success of this effort are the development of a corpus of prospective memory tasks applicable to studies using electrophysiological and functional magnetic resonance imaging (fMRI) methodologies (West, Herndon, & Ross-Munroe, 2000) and emerging analytic methods in fMRI that allow investigators to separate state-related neural activity associated with the maintenance of intentions during a delay from item-related neural activity associated with the processing of prospective cues (e.g., Reynolds, West, & Braver, 2003).

Evidence from a number of studies has led to the suggestion that aging is associated with a decline in the ability to maintain contextual information over relatively brief intervals, contributing to age-related differences in working memory (Braver et al., 2001) and selective attention (West, 2004). Within the context of prospective memory, Einstein et al. (2000) also demonstrated that there are pronounced age-related differences in the success of prospective memory when the realization of an intention must be delayed for even a brief period following the detection of a prospective cue. Limited work has examined the neural basis of this disruption of context processing in the areas of working memory and selective attention, but not in the area of prospective memory. Continuing efforts will serve to determine whether there is a common underlying neurocognitive locus of age-related declines in the efficiency of context processing across these conceptually related domains of cognition.

One final unresolved question that has received intermittent attention in the literature is the degree to which declines in the efficiency of prospective memory may serve to distinguish the effects of normal aging and age-associated pathology. There is some evidence that declines in prospective memory emerge prior to declines in episodic memory in patients with mild cognitive impairment (Huppert & Beardsall, 1993). However, there is sufficient variation in the structure of tasks used to assess these forms of memory that it is difficult to determine whether this effect arises from differences in the sensitivity of the processes supporting episodic and prospective memory to age-associated pathological conditions or from differences in task demands across prospective and episodic memory tasks.

Conclusions

The evidence presented in this review indicates that the formation and realization of intentions are supported by a distributed neural network that involves structures within the frontal and parietal cortices, the medial temporal lobe, and the thalamus (Burgess et al., 2001; Okuda et al., 1998). Furthermore, different neural structures are associated with distinct cognitive processes. Various regions of the frontal lobes are differentially involved in the formation of intentions (i.e., right dorsolateral prefrontal cortex; Burgess et al., 2000), the maintenance of intentions (i.e., frontal pole, Burgess et al., 2000; Burgess, Quayle, & Frith, 2001), and possibly the realization of intentions (right middle frontal gyrus (MFG); Burgess, Quayle, & Frith, 2001). In contrast, the medial temporal lobe may play a greater role in remembering the contents of intentions (Palmer & McDonald, 2000).

Age-related declines in prospective memory result from a decrease in the efficiency with which older adults form intentions (Kliegel, McDaniel, & Einstein, 2000; West, Herndon, & Covell, 2003) and a reduced ability on the part of older adults to attentionally modulate the neural structures that support the detection of prospective cues (West & Covell, 2001). In contrast, the ability to retrieve intentions from memory that have been adequately encoded seems to contribute little to age-related differences in prospective memory (West & Craik, 2001). When considered within the context of evidence from neuropsychological and functional neuroimaging studies, the effects of aging on prospective memory appear to result from a decline in the functional integrity of neural mechanisms that are mediated by the frontal lobes and support intention formation, maintenance of intentions over time, and detection of prospective memory cues.

References

Bisiacchi, P. S. (1996). The neuropsychological approach in the study of prospective memory. In M. Brandimonte, G. O. Einstein, & M. A. McDaniel (Eds.), *Prospective memory: Theory and applications* (pp. 297–318). Mahwah, NJ: Erlbaum.

Brandimonte, M. A., & Passolunghi, M. C. (1994). The effect of cue-familiarity, cue-distinctiveness, and retention interval on prospective remembering. *The Quarterly Journal of Experimental Psychology, 47A*, 565–587.

Braver, T. S., Barch, D. M., Keys, B. A., Carter, C. S., Cohen, J. D., Kaye, J. A., Janowsky, J. S., Taylor, S. F., Yesavage, J. A., Mumunthaler, S., Jagust, W. J., & Reed, B. R. 2001. Context processing in older adults: Evidence for a theory relating cognitive control to neurobiology in healthy aging. *Journal of Experimental Psychology: General, 130*, 746–763.

Bravin, J. H., Kinsella, G. J., Ong, B., & Vowels, L. (2000). A study of performance of delayed intentions in multiple sclerosis. *Journal of Clinical and Experimental Neuropsychology, 22*, 418–429.

Buckner, R. (2002, April). Age-related changes in neural activity during episodic memory. Paper presented at the Symposium on Neuroscience, Aging and Cognition, San Francisco, CA.

Burgess, P. W., Quayle, A., & Frith, C. D. (2001). Brain regions involved in prospective memory as determined by positron emission tomography. *Neuropsychologia, 39*, 545–555.

Burgess, P. W., & Shallice, T. (1997). The relationship between prospective and retrospective memory: Neuropsychological evidence. In M. A. Conway (Ed.), *Cognitive models of memory* (pp. 247–272). Cambridge, MA: MIT Press.

Burgess, P. W., Veitch, E., de Lacy Costello, A., & Shallice, T. (2000). The cognitive and neuroanatomical correlates of multitasking. *Neuropsychologia, 38*, 848–663.

Cabeza, R. (2002). Hemispheric asymmetry reduction in older adults: The HAROLD model. *Psychology and Aging, 17*, 85–100.

Chasteen, A. L., Park, D. C., & Schwarz, N. (2001). Implementation intentions and facilitation of prospective memory. *Psychological Science, 12*, 457–461.

Cherry, K. E., & LeCompte, D. C. (1999). Age and individual differences influence prospective memory. *Psychology and Aging, 14*, 60–76.

Cockburn, J. (1995). Task interruption in prospective memory: A frontal lobe function. *Cortex, 31*, 87–97.

Cohen, A. L., West, R., & Craik, F. I. M. (2001). Modulation of the prospective and retrospective components of memory for intentions in younger and older adults. *Aging, Neuropsychology, and Cognition, 8*, 1–13.

Cohen, G. (1989). *Memory in the real world*. Hillsdale, NJ: Erlbaum.

Craik, F. I. M., & Byrd, M. (1982). Aging and cognitive deficits: The role of attentional resources. In F. I. M. Craik & S. Trehub (Eds.), *Aging and cognitive processes* (pp. 191–211). New York: Plenum.

Dobbs, A. R., & Rule, G. (1987). Prospective memory and self-reports of memory abilities in older adults. *Canadian Journal of Psychology, 41*, 209–222.

Donchin, E., & Coles, M. G. (1988). Is the P300 component a manifestation of context processing? *Behavioral and Brain Sciences, 11*, 357–427.

Einstein, G. O., & McDaniel, M. A. (1990). Normal aging and prospective memory. *Journal of Experimental Psychology: Learning, Memory, and Cognition, 16*, 717–726.

Einstein, G. O., & McDaniel, M. A. (1996). Retrieval processes in prospective memory: Theoretical approaches and some new empirical findings. In M. Brandimonte, G. O. Einstein, & M. A. McDaniel (Eds.), *Prospective memory: Theory and applications* (pp. 115–142). Mahwah, NJ: Erlbaum.

Einstein, G. O., McDaniel, M. A., Manzi, M., Cochran, B., & Baker, M. (2000). Prospective memory and aging: Forgetting intentions over short delays. *Psychology and Aging, 15*, 671–683.

Einstein, G. O., Smith, R. E., McDaniel, M. A., & Shaw, P. (1997). Aging and prospective memory: The influence of increased task demands at encoding and retrieval. *Psychology and Aging, 12*, 479–488.

Freud, S. (1901). *The psychopathology of everyday life.* London: Penguin.

Friedman, D., Kazmerski, V., & Fabiani, M. (1997). An overview of age-related changes in the scalp distribution of P3b. *Electroencephalogram and Clinical Neurophysiology, 104*, 498–513.

Greenwood, P. M. (2000). The frontal aging hypothesis evaluated. *Journal of the International Neuropsychological Society, 6*, 705–726.

Guynn, M. J., McDaniel, M. A., & Einstein, G. O. (1998). Prospective memory: When reminders fail. *Memory and Cognition, 26*, 287–298.

Guynn, M. J., McDaniel, M. A., & Einstein, G. O. (2001). Remembering to perform intentions: A different type of memory? In H. D. Zimmer, R. L. Cohen, M. J. Guynn, J. Engelkamp, R. Kormi-Nouri, & M. A. Foley (Eds), *Memory for action: A distinct form of episodic memory?* (pp. 25–48). Oxford, U.K.: Oxford University Press.

Hasher, L., & Zacks, R. T. (1979). Automatic and effortful processes in memory. *Journal of Experimental Psychology: General, 108*, 356–388.

Heffernan, T. M., Jarvis, H., Rodgers, J., Scholey, A. B., & Ling, J. (2001). Prospective memory, everyday cognitive failures and central executive function in recreational users of Ecstasy. *Human Psychopharmacology Clinical and Experimental, 16*, 607–612.

Huppert, F. A., & Beardsall, L. (1993). Prospective memory impairment as an early indicator of dementia. *Journal of Clinical and Experimental Neuropsychology, 15*, 805–821.

Huppert, F. A., Johnson, T., & Nickson, J. (2000). High prevalence of prospective memory impairment in the elderly and in early-stage dementia: Findings from a population-based study. *Applied Cognitive Psychology, 14*, S63–S81.

Jack, C. R., Peterson, R. C., Xu, Y. C., Waring, S. C., O'Brien, P. C., Tangalos, E. G., Smith, G. E., Ivnik, R. J., & Kokmen, E. (1997). Medial temporal atrophy on MRI in normal aging and very mild Alzheimer's disease. *Neurology, 49*, 786–794.

Kidder, D. P., Park, D. C., Hertzog, C., & Morrell, R. W. (1997). Prospective memory and aging: The effects of working memory and prospective memory task load. *Aging, Neuropsychology, and Cognition, 4*, 93–112.

Kliegel, M., McDaniel, M. A., & Einstein, G. O. (2000). Plan formation, retention, and execution in prospective memory: A new approach and age-related differences. *Memory and Cognition, 28*, 1041–1049.

Kok, A. (2001). On the utility of P3 amplitude as a measure of processing capacity. *Psychophysiology, 38*, 557–577.

Kondel, T. K. (2002). Prospective memory and executive function in schizophrenia. *Brain and Cognition, 2*, 405–410.

Kray, J., & Lindenberger, U. (2000). Adult age differences in task switching. *Psychology and Aging, 15,* 126–147.

Kvavilashvili, L., & Ellis, J. (1996). Varieties of intention: Some distinctions and classifications. In M. Brandimonte, G. O. Einstein, & M. A. McDaniel (Eds.), *Prospective memory: Theory and applications* (pp. 23–51). Mahwah, NJ: Erlbaum.

Lobaugh, N. J., West, R., & McIntosh, A. R. (2001). Spatiotemporal analysis of experimental differences in event-related potential data with partial least squares. *Psychophysiology, 38,* 517–530.

Mangels, J. A., Picton, T. W., & Craik, F. I. M. (2001). Attention and successful episodic encoding: An event-related potential study. *Cognitive Brain Research, 11,* 77–95.

Marsh, R. L., & Hicks, J. L. (1998). Event-based prospective memory and executive control of working memory. *Journal of Experimental Psychology: Learning, Memory, and Cognition, 24,* 336–349.

Marsh, R. L., Hicks, J. L., & Hancock, T. W. (2000). On the interaction of ongoing cognitive activity and the nature of an event-based intention. *Applied Cognitive Psychology, 14,* S29–S41.

McDaniel, M. A., & Einstein, G. O. (1992). Aging and prospective memory: Basic findings and practical applications. *Advances in Learning and Behavioral Disabilities, 7,* 87–105.

McDaniel, M. A., & Einstein, G. O. (2000). Strategic and automatic processes in prospective memory retrieval: A multiprocess framework. *Applied Cognitive Psychology, 14,* S127–S144.

McDaniel, M. A., Glisky, E. L., Rubin, S. R., Guynn, M. J., & Routhieaux, B. C. (1999). Prospective memory: A neuropsychological study. *Neuropsychology, 13,* 103–110.

McDaniel, M. A., Robinson-Riegler, B., & Einstein, G. O. (1998). Prospective remembering: Perceptually driven and conceptually driven processes? *Memory and Cognition, 26,* 121–134.

McIntosh, A. R., Bookstein, F. L., Haxby, J. V., & Grady, C. L. (1996). Spatial pattern analysis of functional images using partial least squares. *Neuroimage, 3,* 143–157.

Meacham, J. A., & Leimen, B. (1975). Remembering to perform future actions. In U. Neisser (Ed.), *Memory observed* (pp. 327–336). San Francisco: Freeman.

Moscovitch, M. (1994). Memory and working with memory: Evaluation of a component process model and comparisons with other models. In D. L. Schacter & E. Tulving (Eds.), *Memory systems* (pp. 269–310). Cambridge, MA: MIT Press.

Okuda, J., Fujii, T., Yamadori, A., Kawashima, R., Tsukiura, T., Fukatsu, R., Suzuki, K., Masatoshi, I., & Fukuda, H. (1998). Participation of the prefrontal cortices in prospective memory: Evidence from a PET study in humans. *Neuroscience Letters, 253,* 127–130.

Otani, H., Landau, J. D., Libleman, T. M., St. Louis, J, P., Kazen, J. K., & Throne, G. W. (1997). Prospective memory and divided attention. *Memory, 5,* 343–360.

Palmer, H. M., & McDonald, S. (2000). The role of frontal and temporal lobe processes in prospective memory. *Brain and Cognition, 44,* 103–107.

Park, D. C., Hertzog, C., Kidder, D. P., Morrell, R. W., & Mayhorn, C. B. (1997). Effect of age on event-based and time-based prospective memory. *Psychology and Aging, 12,* 314–327.

Raz, N. (2000). Aging of the brain and its impact on cognitive performance: Integration of structural and functional findings. In F. I. M. Craik & T. A. Salthouse (Eds.), *The handbook of aging and cognition* (2nd ed., pp. 1–90). Mahwah, NJ: Erlbaum.

Reynolds, J., West, R., & Braver, T. (2003, March). Differentiation of prospective memory and working memory using a mixed state and event-related fMRI design. Poster presented at the meeting of the Cognitive Neuroscience Society, New York, NY.

Ricaurte, G. A., Yuan, J., Hatzidimitriou, G., Cord, B. J., & McCann, U. D. (2002). Severe dopaminergic neurotoxicity in primates after a common recreational dose regimen of MDMA ("ecstasy"). *Science, 297,* 2260–2263.

Rubin, D. C. (1999). Frontal-striatal circuits in cognitive aging: Evidence for caudate involvement. *Aging, Neuropsychology, and Cognition, 6,* 241–259.

Rugg, M. D. (1995). ERP Studies of memory. In M. D. Rugg, & M. G. H. Coles (Eds.), *Electrophysiology of mind: Event-related brain potentials and cognition* (pp. 132–170). Oxford, U.K.: Oxford University Press.

Schacter, D. (2001). *The seven sins of memory: How the mind forgets and remembers.* Boston, MA: Houghton Mifflin.

Shum, D., Valentine, M., & Cutmore, T. (1999). Performance of individuals with severe long-term traumatic brain injury on time-, event-, and activity-based prospective memory tasks. *Journal of Clinical and Experimental Neuropsychology, 21,* 49–58.

Smith, G., Della Sala, S., Logie, R. H., & Maylor, E. A. (2000). Prospective and retrospective memory in normal ageing and dementia: A questionnaire study. *Memory, 8,* 311–321.

Smith, R. E. (2000, July). Successful initiation of intentions required capacity. Paper presented at the First International Conference on Prospective Memory, Hatfield, U.K.

Smith, R. E. (2003). The cost of remembering to remember in event-based prospective memory: Investigating the capacity demands of delayed intention performance. *Journal of Experimental Psychology: Learning, Memory, and Cognition, 29,* 347–361.

West, R. (2004). The effects of aging on controlled attention and conflict processing in the Stroop task. *Journal of Cognitive Neuroscience, 16,* 103–113.

West, R., & Covell, E. (2001). Effects of aging on event-related neural activity related to prospective remembering. *Neuroreport, 12,* 2855–2858.

West, R., & Craik, F. I. M. (2001). Influences on the efficiency of prospective memory in younger and older adults. *Psychology and Aging, 16,* 682–696.

West, R., Herndon, R. W., & Covell, E. (2003). Neural correlates of age-related declines in the formation and realization of delayed intentions. *Psychology and Aging, 18,* 461–473.

West, R., Herndon, R. W., & Crewdson, S. J. (2001). Neural activity associated with the realization of a delayed intention. *Cognitive Brain Research, 12,* 1–10.

West, R., Herndon, R. W., & Ross-Munroe, K. (2000). Event-related neural activity associated with prospective remembering. *Applied Cognitive Psychology, 14,* S115–S126.

West, R., Herndon, R. W., & Ross-Munroe, K. (2001, March). Event-related neural activity associated with prospective remembering. Poster presented at the Cognitive Neuroscience Society Annual Meeting, New York, NY.

West, R., & Krompinger, J. (in press). Neural correlates of prospective and episodic memory. *Neuropsychologia.*

West, R., & Ross-Munroe, K. (2002). Neural correlates of the formation and realization of delayed intentions. *Cognitive, Affective, & Behavioral Neuroscience, 2,* 162–173.

West, R., & Wymbs, N. (2003). Is detecting prospective cues the same as selecting targets? An ERP study. Manuscript submitted for publication.

West, R., Wymbs, N., Jakubek, K., & Herndon, R. W. (2003). Effects of intention load and background context on prospective remembering: An event-related brain potential study. *Psychophysiology, 40,* 260–276.

West, R. L. (1988). Prospective memory and aging. In M. M. Gruneberg, P. E. Morris, & R. N. Sykes (Eds.), *Practical aspects of memory: Current research and issues. Volume 2. Clinical and educational implications* (pp. 119–125). Chichester, UK: Wiley.

West, R. L. (1996). An application of prefrontal cortex function theory to cognitive aging. *Psychological Bulletin, 120,* 272–292.

III

CLINICAL AND APPLIED ISSUES

11

Three Principles for Cognitive Aging Research

Multiple Causes and Sequelae,
Variance in Expression and Response,
and the Need for Integrative Theory

Randy L. Buckner

Consider three very different individuals. Each is about 80 years of age and representative of older adults all of us are likely to know. One is actively engaged in social life, reads the paper daily, and debates her children on political issues at holidays. The second, still active in life, is a bit less flexible in thinking and is aware that he is not quite as quick as when he retired. The third is in a nursing home and does not recognize her family members when they come to visit. All have led roughly similar lives, as far as can be easily discerned, and all were unaware of their divergent futures the decade before. Why are these individuals so different?

Consider further the patterns shown in figure 11.1 (E. H. Rubin et al., 1998). Each panel represents longitudinal measures of cognitive ability in a different individual. One individual shows prolonged cognitive stability; the others decline rapidly after a period of stability. And, among those who decline, they do so at quite different ages. Why is there so much variability in the age of onset of prominent cognitive decline?

Perhaps most perplexing is the variance that presents itself when variance should be at bay. Consider the disease CADASIL (cerebral autosomal dominant arteriopathy with subcortical infarcts and leukoencephalopathy). CADASIL is a genetic form of dementia often characterized by severe executive dysfunction (see Kalimo, Ruchoux, et al., 2002, for review). It is an autosomal dominant disease, which means that if an individual inherits the relevant gene, he or she will show the associated age-dependent pathology.

In CADASIL, the pathology is white matter damage, with some suggestion of preferential influence on anterior brain regions. Individuals with CADASIL typically show cognitive problems at about the age of 40. Nonetheless, even though CADASIL

267

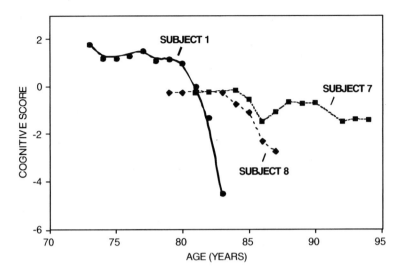

Figure 11.1. Longitudinal cognitive function is displayed for three individuals with quite different progression. Cognitive function in subject 1 is stable at a high level until about 80 years of age, when a rapidly accelerating cognitive decline begins. Subject 8, who begins in the average cognitive range, shows a similar profile, with rapid cognitive decline beginning near the age of 85 years. Subject 7, who initially overlaps with subject 8, shows largely intact cognitive function well into her 10th decade. A central question of this chapter is why such diverse cognitive profiles occur across older adults. (Data from E. H. Rubin et al., 1998.)

is genetically obligated, some individuals experience prominent symptoms as early as 30 years, but others as late as 60 years (Kalimo, Ruchoux, et al., 2002; Desmond, 2002). In one pair of identical twins, the first began experiencing prominent symptoms at 39 years of age, and the second is still free of cognitive symptoms a decade later (Kalimo, Viitanen, et al., 2002).

This chapter discusses why variance might exist in cognitive decline, organizing the discussion into three principles. The first principle is that multiple, co-occurring causal mechanisms contribute to cognitive decline in aging. Different causes, because of their distinct underlying mechanisms, have separate anatomical and physiological patterns. An individual's cognitive presentation will be the outcome of the sum and interactions among these multiple causal mechanisms. The second principle is that variability exists in the expression of causal mechanisms across individuals and in individuals' responses to them. This is a particularly intriguing principle because it suggests that identifying causal mechanisms, and the degree to which individuals are affected, will only partially explain the variance in cognitive decline. The other part of the explanation will come from the active mechanisms of compensation and responses that individuals adopt. The final principle is that causal mechanisms should be studied within integrative theories that span different levels of organization—from the genetic to the behavioral. This final principle stems from a speculation that some answers to questions about cognitive decline will only be appreciated through explorations that span multiple levels of description. A contemporary example, associated with recruitment patterns observed in imaging studies, is discussed as a target for integrative theory.

One final note, perhaps to be considered a disclaimer, is that this chapter is written to stimulate thought and not as a didactic review. Examples are drawn to illustrate broad principles and highlight considerations for future debate. Rare forms of genetically linked dementias, common genetic variations in neurotrophic factors, stroke, and ideas about how tumor suppression affects aging are some of the bases for discussion.

Principle 1: Multiple, Co-Occurring Causal Mechanisms Contribute to Cognitive Decline in Aging

From the outset, cognitive decline should be explored from the perspective that distinct age-associated mechanisms likely exist. Mechanisms may differ in cause, in physiological and anatomical target, and in resulting cognitive sequelae. For example, the broad distinction between frontal and executive change associated with aging likely originates from a different set of mechanisms than those that produce amnesic-like symptoms in Alzheimer's disease.

Strong evidence already exists for multiple causal mechanisms that associate with cognitive decline. A good example of an isolated mechanism is that linked to the disease CADASIL, mentioned in the introduction (see Kalimo, Rouchoux, et al., 2002). CADASIL was originally noted in the mid 1970s. Individuals showed symptoms of an inherited progressive dementia that associated with multiple, often small, infarcts (infarcts are lesions to the brain such as observed in stroke). Later genetic analysis narrowed its origin to chromosome 19 (Tournier-Lasserve et al., 1993) and its specific locus to a Notch3 mutation (Joutel et al., 1996). Today, there are over 100 different families known to have CADASIL originating from more than 25 distinct mutations that all affect the Notch3 gene.

Of interest, although the specific pathological mechanisms are still debated, the general form of the mechanism of cognitive decline in CADASIL has been tentatively suggested. Notch3 is a gene expressed in the smooth muscle, including the smooth muscle that surrounds small vessels (arterioles). In patients with CADASIL, there appears to be an age-associated degeneration of the smooth muscle surrounding vessels that regulate blood flow, resulting in white matter damage and, eventually, focal infarcts and stroke. Frontal and subcortical regions connected to frontal cortex show some preferential vulnerability. Progressive dementia, often including executive symptoms, is a common outcome. Animal models of CADASIL also suggest vascular alterations are potentially the causal mechanism (Ruchoux et al., 2003).

The relevance to the present chapter is that CADASIL presents a rare picture of all levels of a mechanism that causes cognitive decline. Causal mechanisms are physical events that begin with specific origins and come to influence the physiology of the brain. Their effect on the nervous system is to lead to cognitive decline. The causal mechanism in CADASIL is a genetic mutation that, through its influence on vessel function, leads to dementia. To date, CADASIL has been the focus of over 300 empirical and review articles and is perhaps a best-case scenario for study because it is a dominant (single-gene) trait, expresses as a severe behavioral change, and has clear brain changes that can be visualized with magnetic resonance imaging (MRI). In contrast, the mechanisms associated with more typical cognitive decline likely originate from multiple genes and environmental factors, express often (but not always) as subtle cognitive changes, and do not have easily discernible markers in brain-imaging studies (at least as fully analyzed to date).

Consider, for example, the distinction between cognitive decline preferential for deficits in declarative memory and that hallmarked by deficits in cognitive (executive) function (e.g., Glisky, Polster, & Routhieaux, 1995). Distinct causal mechanisms, or families of causal mechanisms, seem the likely origin of the separate cognitive profiles. Prominent declarative memory impairment associated with Alzheimer's disease and certain forms of mild cognitive impairment may relate to build up of amyloid (extracellularly) and tau (intracellularly) in a pathological form (Golde, Eckman, & Younkin, 2000; Selkoe, 2001). One causal hypothesis is that amyloid deposits (plaques) lead to neuronal dysfunction and cell death. Pathology begins prominently in the medial temporal lobe and spreads outward to the association cortex over time (Braak & Braak, 1991, 1997). The preferential vulnerability of medial temporal structures in the early stage of the disease may be why prominent initial symptoms are memory impairment and why MRI studies so consistently find medial temporal atrophy in patients with dementia of the Alzheimer type (Jack et al., 1992; Killiany et al., 1993; see Jack & Petersen, 2000 for review). Symptoms advance to eventual global compromise as the disease progresses to include widespread regions of cortex.

In contrast, preferential executive dysfunction may relate to anterior white matter damage and infarcts to subcortical structures. One causal hypothesis is that vascular compromise (small-vessel disease), perhaps associated with hypertension, induces white matter damage, including small infarcts (DeCarli & Scheltens, 2002; Pugh & Lipsitz, 2002). Anterior white matter and subcortical structures may be preferentially vulnerable and can be visualized as white matter hyperintensities and small infarcts on MRI. Preferential frontal atrophy of gray matter may also be associated (e.g., Raz et al., 1997) as well as striatal damage (D. C. Rubin, 1999), although such links have not been firmly established. As a result of microstructural damage to white matter, small infarcts, and associated effects on gray matter, frontal-striatal systems are compromised, and impairments in executive function and cognitive control result.

The main point of this first section is that multiple causal mechanisms contribute to cognitive decline in aging—not simply variations on the same mechanism. Two more subtle points are also embedded. The cognitive sequelae that result from these mechanisms will not necessarily fully dissociate at the behavioral level. Separate mechanisms not only will show different patterns and preferential effects, reflective of their anatomic targets and progressive course, but also may converge to interfere with similar tasks. For example, pathology associated with Alzheimer's disease has a general progression from the medial temporal lobes outward and affects frontal association cortex in later stages (Braak & Braak, 1991, 1997). By the time dementia of the Alzheimer type is typically diagnosed, or even before its clinical diagnosis, there is already pathology present in frontal cortex in the form of senile plaques (Price et al., 1991). It is thus not surprising that, although amnesialike symptoms reflecting medial temporal damage are the hallmark of the mechanism, deficits on tasks that tap cognitive (executive) control are also prominent (Balota & Faust, 2001; Parasuraman & Haxby, 1993). The mechanism does not respect boundaries that affect only one class of task or one family of cognitive process. Separate causal mechanisms likely manifest as anatomically diffuse pathology with complex patterns of progression. Expectations about the specificity of cognitive presentation should follow from the diffuse underlying effects. Syndromes with diffuse effects will likely be particularly relevant to understanding age-associated causal mechanisms that involve changes in neurotransmitter and receptor properties (such as the possibility that dopamine systems alter with age; Arnsten et al., 1994; Volkow et al., 2000; Backman et al., 2000).

A second subtle point stems from the possibility of co-occurring causal mechanisms. I have avoided this topic until now with the goal of first making a case for the possibility of separate mechanisms. However, it is important to fully embrace the level of complexity faced: Any individual's brain may be simultaneously experiencing the effects of multiple age-associated causal mechanisms. Causal mechanisms may sum or interact. Within the clinical setting, this is directly relevant to mixed-etiology dementia (Barker et al., 2002; Neuropathology Group of the Medical Research Council, 2001) or the concept of cofactors such as the augmentation of cognitive symptoms in patients with dementia of the Alzheimer type who also show white matter damage. Cognitive aging research is also faced with the daunting complexities that arise from interactions between co-occurring mechanisms.

Wu et al. (2002), for example, explored the influence of only hippocampal atrophy, only white matter hyperintensities, or their co-occurrence on the presence of severe cognitive decline (dementia). As noted above, growing evidence indicates hippocampal atrophy and white matter hyperintensities reflect distinct age-associated causal mechanisms. However, despite their potentially separate origins, they interacted to contribute more severe cognitive decline than either would be expected to elicit in isolation. Specifically, individuals with hippocampal atrophy *and* high levels of white matter hyperintensities were more likely to exhibit severe cognitive symptoms than the sum of their individual risk levels.

One solution, which may have merit for initial explorations, is to isolate individuals with the cleanest cognitive profiles. Removing individuals with early-stage dementia of the Alzheimer type, for example, may be a strategy for exploring executive-type symptoms that arise from vascular compromise and white matter damage. After all, the level of impairment associated with one causal mechanism may overshadow that from another. However, it is also clearly important to consider mixed cases and explore larger subject samples that allow discovery of how different causal mechanisms interact and whether they correlate with one another. Variance in cognitive decline will undoubtedly be the sum and interactions of multiple, distinct causal mechanisms. Some causal mechanisms may by chance, or by exploitation of related vulnerabilities, converge to target similar brain systems with synergistic effects. Frontal-striatal systems, for example, seem to be preferentially vulnerable to age-associated mechanisms that target white matter degeneration, neurotransmitter changes, gray matter volume, and functional activation patterns. These observed changes are unlikely the diverse effects of a single causal mechanism, but do express themselves in overlapping brain systems.

The concept of multiple co-occurring causal mechanisms is different from the related idea that certain processes, such as processes that cause Alzheimer's disease, have variability in how they affect one person or the next. For example, Kanne et al. (1998) showed that the relative anatomical distribution of cored senile plaques—a neuropathological indicator of Alzheimer's disease—associated with cognitive performance. Increased burden in frontal association cortex was negatively correlated with a neuropsychological test factor sensitive to frontal dysfunction. The regional variation in density of plaque burden in this example is not what is meant here by multiple co-occurring causal mechanisms. Rather, implications associated with the variable presentation of a single mechanism, or process, are considered separately in the next section.

Principle 2: Older Individuals Vary in Their Expression of Causal Mechanisms and in Their Level of Productive Response to Them

A long-appreciated facet of cognitive aging is that some individuals show greater and earlier deficit than others. Although part of this variance is likely because of differences in causal mechanism as outlined in principle 1, a substantial portion will reflect variance within a single mechanism. Some individuals will progress their expression slowly and others rapidly; dependent on the specific mechanism, age of onset will likely vary. All of these points have been made previously in the literature. In this section, the implications of within-mechanism variance are explored. In addition, a facet of variance that has been less well appreciated is explored that focuses on an individual's response to change.

For discussion purposes, some preliminary findings associated with CADASIL are again relevant. Individuals with CADASIL markedly differ in terms of whether they express symptoms of the disease, including cognitive decline, even though the disease is genetically determined. The extreme example is the twin pair of Kalimo, Viitanen, and colleagues (2002). One twin shows severe symptoms, and the other does not. The two twins did, however, differ in terms of the global presentation of the severity of their white matter damage. Desmond (2002) turned to a contrast between first cousins with CADASIL to gain further insight into this puzzle. Both were about 60 years of age and showed similar levels of severe white matter abnormality on MRI. Yet, one showed significant cognitive symptoms, and the other did not. A difference between the two was the presence and specific locations of small infarcts, which were present in the impaired individual and presumed to associate with his stepwise decline. These examples illustrate variance in cognitive presentation that likely originates from within the same underlying mechanism. Individual expression patterns are influenced by the rate and the exact locations of the causal mechanism's effect.

In this regard, it is appropriate to make a distinction between two kinds of expression differences. The first I refer to as core differences in level of expression and the second as randomness in expression pattern. By core differences in level of expression (burden), it is meant that different individuals may vary in their overall level of expression. In some forms of white matter abnormality, this may relate to the level of hypertension or an individual's susceptibility to hypertension. Some individuals will show considerably more white matter damage than others. The concept of core differences in levels of expression has been considered in virtually all discussions of age-associated mechanisms of cognitive decline, from those associated with hypertension-induced white matter damage, to CADASIL, to Alzheimer's disease. As another example, neuropathological measures have suggested that, across individuals, there are marked differences in the numbers of senile plaques, cored senile plaques, and neurofibrillary tangles (Braak & Braak, 1991, 1997; Price et al., 1991). These differences may link to if, and when, severe cognitive decline in the form of dementia will appear.

Randomness in expression pattern is a separate source of variation. Two individuals with roughly the same rates of expression may show different cognitive profiles simply because damage, or an induced lesion, just happens to occur in a more relevant brain area or white matter track or just happens to co-occur coincident with another lesion that augments its effect. The small, ill-placed lesions in the patient with CADASIL may be an example of such a situation. There is not much more to say on this point other than significantly different methods from those that have traditionally been employed will be required to make progress. Counting the numbers of small lesions, or the general quantity of white matter burden, may fall short of predicting cognitive decline from individual to individual. General trends across individuals should be apparent as more damage is likely also to include more relevant damage. However, attention to specific anatomical distributions of expression patterns, particularly at early stages of progression, will likely be required to relate cognitive decline to a causal mechanism's contribution. The study by Kanne et al. (1998) described under principle 1 is an example of varied expression of Alzheimer's disease pathology correlating with the specific pattern of cognitive impairment. It seems likely that these kinds of observation will become increasingly common.

Response to Age-Associated Change

To this point in the chapter, variance from individual to individual has only been considered in the context of age-associated damage. To summarize the preceding sections, there are multiple age-associated mechanisms that cause neural (brain) change, and variable levels of change can be caused by each mechanism. However, a qualitatively different sort of variance may also be present and associate with an individual's response to changes in brain structure and function. The basic idea here is that detrimental age-associated changes are not passively received. As we age, and as compromises are accumulated, active responses will be initiated to compensate. Baltes (1997) nicely defined compensation as a "response to loss in means (resources) used to maintain success or desired levels of functioning (outcomes)."

The central question here is to identify productive responses and determine how variance in response from individual to individual links to cognitive performance. Recent brain imaging work provided an example of the identification of what might be a productive form of compensatory response.

Increased recruitment of brain regions in older adults has been repeatedly observed and recently considered within a compensation framework (for reviews, see Grady & Craik, 2000; Reuter-Lorenz, 2002; Cabeza, 2002). The basic finding is that older adults, in a variety of cognitive tasks, show increased activation, as measured by positron emission tomography (PET) or functional MRI (fMRI), compared to younger controls. Increased recruitment has been demonstrated in individuals with dementia of the Alzheimer type (Becker et al., 1996; Grady et al., 2003), individuals genetically at risk for Alzheimer's disease (Bookheimer et al., 2000), individuals with CADASIL (Reddy et al., 2002), individuals with stroke (Buckner et al., 1996), and older adults without any known clinical syndrome (Cabeza et al., 1997; Reuter-Lorenz et al., 2000; Logan et al., 2002). Thus, increased recruitment of brain regions appears to be a general response to conditions of neural compromise or strain.

What is the evidence that increased recruitment is a productive response? A series of studies suggested a link between increased activation levels and better task performance (Cabeza et al., 2002; Rosen et al., 2002; Grady et al., 2003). Cabeza and colleagues, for example, selected two groups of older adults, those who performed similarly to younger adults on a battery of memory tests and those who performed worse. Bilateral activation of frontal cortex was observed in the older adults who performed well, in contrast to unilateral activation in those who performed badly, suggesting activation increases were compensatory in the older adults. This kind of finding goes against the alternative possibility that bilateral frontal recruitment is directly caused by (and not a productive response to) detrimental changes in aging (Cabeza, 2002; Logan et al., 2002). However, such relations raise the perplexing question of how to interpret correlations between performance and activation changes.

Consider the model outlined in figure 11.2, which stems from discussions with my colleague Cindy Lustig. Included in the model are three components: (1) the level of underlying age-associated structural change, (2) the functional response to change, and (3) behavioral performance. The model is deceptively simple for a subtle reason: The model predicts both positive relations between behavior and activation levels and negative relations. It will depend on who, among the sample, is carrying the variance and whether the compensatory response is able to maintain performance levels on the task in question. This is not an obvious point, so it is worth discussing in some detail (see also Cabeza, 2001, for a related discussion of this issue).

Age is associated with underlying causal mechanisms that are detrimental to brain function. For discussion, consider the extreme case of stroke. Individuals suffering stroke will show cognitive impairment relative to young adults or other healthy older adults. For this reason, strong negative correlations will exist between measures of stroke and cognitive performance. As noted by several studies, patients with stroke often show increased activation in intact brain regions relative to healthy individuals (see plate 11.1 in the color insert, for example) (Buckner et al., 1996; Rosen et al., 2000). For the moment, let us assume the observed activation increase is compensa-

(a)   **COMPENSATION**
       (PRODUCTIVE RESPONSE)

(b)   **DISRUPTION**
       (PART OF THE PROBLEM)

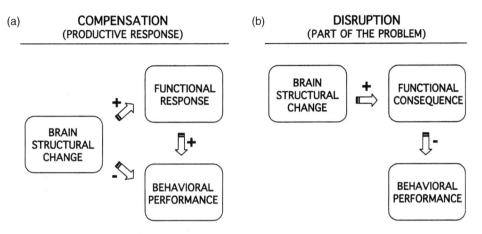

Figure 11.2. Two alternative models of how increased activation might associate with cognitive aging: *a*, compensation model hypothesizes that increased activation is a productive functional response to brain changes and alleviates cognitive decline; *b*, disruption model hypothesizes that increased activation is itself a consequence of, and not a response to, detrimental age-associated change. Operationally, the two models primarily differ in terms of whether increased activation serves as a positive moderating variable on performance or itself is a causal negative variable.

tory and, for discussion, assume that it is similar to the phenomenon of additional recruitment in aging.

What kind of correlation between increased activation and performance is expected? The relation is predicted to be negative if all of the older adults are sampled. This is because, on average, healthy individuals will show the least additional recruitment and the best performance. On average, individuals suffering stroke will show the greatest additional recruitment and the worst performance. This negative correlation is misleading (to some degree) because increased activation reflects a positive response to the stroke and allows performance to be maintained at a higher level than would otherwise occur. The relation is negative in this example because the presence of additional activation is a proxy marker for stroke. However, if *only* patients with comparable strokes are considered, the predicted relation will be positive and reflect the compensatory nature of the response. This is because, on average, individuals showing the productive compensatory response will perform better than those who do not. In this example, increased activation is a classic moderator variable and requires interactions to be explored to reveal its true influence (Cohen et al., 2003).

Grady and colleagues (2003) reported a study that demonstrated these kinds of complex activation–performance relations. In their study, individuals with early-stage dementia of the Alzheimer type showed greater extent of recruitment in diverse cortical regions, including frontal cortex, in contrast to healthy older adults. The individuals with dementia performed significantly worse than the healthy older adults. However, when performance correlations were examined within the dementia group, more extensive recruitment correlated with better performance. In other words, the best performance was obtained in healthy individuals with the relatively most circumscribed recruitment pattern. Nonetheless, within the demented group, expanded recruitment appeared to associate with a compensatory response.

A further variable also comes into play: the specific behavioral measure. Compensatory abilities in individuals with stroke are usually only partial. One patient, for example, who showed right hemisphere activation during typically left-lateralized language tasks, could perform at near-normal levels on some language tasks, but failed miserably on others (Buckner et al., 1996). In particular, the patient was near floor for tasks that required inhibition of already-retrieved responses. The implication is that, for some tasks, performance may correlate positively with increased activation because the tasks are those that inherently can benefit from compensation. Performance on other tasks may correlate negatively because all they will measure is the extent of damage. In these instances, additional recruitment at the functional level may serve as a rough proxy for the amount of damage. Examples of interactions involving task and specific behavioral measures have yet to emerge in the literature, but are nonetheless worth considering.

Findings of activation increases in aging raise many questions. First, why are older adults adopting an alternative functional activation pattern? In other words, what, specifically, is being compensated? In instances of stroke, the relevant lesion is clear; in instances of "healthy" aging, the candidates are numerous and more subtle. Second, if compensation occurs because some form of degeneration has taken place, then where are the performance decrements in these older adults? Presumably, there will be some tasks for which older adults cannot fully compensate. Compensatory mechanisms are expected to be productive, but have their limits. Finally, why are some older adults showing compensatory activation patterns, and others are not? It is in this last question that a small paradox emerges. The older adults, who are performing the worst, show activation patterns that are most similar to that of younger adults, who perform well. One might naively expect that the best situation would be to show minimal change with aging.

In the next section, motivated by the questions here, theories of cognitive aging are discussed that target the complex relations among causal mechanisms, underlying age-associated change, responses to change, and cognition.

Principle 3: Causal Mechanisms Should Be Studied Within Integrative Theories That Span Different Levels of Organization, from the Genetic to the Behavioral

Churchland and Sejnowski (1991) articulated the important points that neural structures can be studied at molecular through systems levels, different methods observe phenomenon at distinct levels, and organization at smaller levels influences organization at larger levels. In this section, a conceptually related point is made in the context of age-associated cognitive decline: Cognitive change in aging is the outcome of multiple organization levels that require interdependent study. Changes at one level influence changes at other levels. Perhaps most relevant to this discussion, some phenomenon observed at one level will likely only be understood in relation to changes observed at other levels. I return to this last point, which directly relates to the utility of integrative theory, at the end of the chapter, but first focus on how integrative theories of cognitive aging might be pursued.

What are the steps required to develop multilevel theories of cognitive aging? A first step, which is perhaps obvious but is nonetheless mentioned for completeness, is the didactic characterization of age-associated change at the various levels of organization. What are the myriad cognition changes that associate with age? What are the morphological changes that are observed at the cellular level? What are the macroscopic structural changes that are observed in MRI images, such as whole-brain and regional volume reductions, white matter hyperintensities, and regional patterns of cortical thinning? What is the distribution and rate of change in neuro-transmitter systems with aging? How are older adults' functional activation patterns different from those of younger adults? The answers to these questions provide the necessary building blocks for integrative theories. Considerable progress has already been made in answering these questions, but the endeavor of characterization is a moving target as methods to visualize more sophisticated aspects of behavior and anatomy are in continual development.

A second step is the attempt to relate observations across levels of organization and behavior. Here is where many contemporary studies have focused their efforts. A notable example of progress comes from the work of Raz and colleagues, who have systematically explored the relation between structural-level organization (regional volume differences) and cognitive differences (see Raz, 2000, for review). Many studies, mentioned already, have explored relations between brain activation patterns and behavioral performance. Clinically oriented studies have long sought to relate pathological, metabolic, structural, and genetic findings to disease diagnosis (e.g., see Kemper, 1994, for a review of numerous pathological findings in aging and dementia). In addition, links between macroscopic structural changes in white matter and underlying cellular-level changes have been described (e.g., see DeCarli & Scheltens, 2002).

Nonetheless, relations between most forms of age-associated change are unknown, even within similar levels of organization and especially between different neural levels and behavior. Park et al. (2001) set the tone for more expansive exploration. In their thought-provoking review, they listed a number of behavioral findings in cognitive aging with tentative relations to neural findings. Their stated goal was to relate behavioral findings about cognitive aging to their neural underpinnings. I would like to add to Park and colleagues' suggestion: Relations between all levels of organization from molecular, to cellular, to systems, to behavioral, should be explored.

An important aspect of this endeavor will be to look for family resemblances among different correlates of aging within and between levels of organization. Do certain kinds of change cluster (e.g., anterior white matter lesions and frontal volumetric decline)? Do other kinds of change form independent factors (anterior white matter change and medial temporal lobe atrophy)? Do certain genes correlate with change at multiple levels of description? How do clusters within levels of description associate with behavioral correlates? As more descriptive information is available on large samples of subjects, patterns among variables should suggest meaningful relations. Hypotheses will continue to emerge that relate observations at one level of organization to others and such relations to age-associated changes in cognition.

The final step is just beginning and involves the development of full-fledged integrative theories of cognitive aging that describe causal mechanisms across multiple levels. CADASIL represents one example for which this goal is rapidly being achieved. However, the approach taken to understand CADASIL applies only to a limited set of situations. One approach to development of integrative theories, represented by the syndrome of CADASIL, is to focus opportunistically on the rare genetic variations that robustly influence biological pathways and, in turn, behavior. Prominent examples of such bottom-up approaches in aging research have come from genetic mutations that obligate dementia in familiar forms of Alzheimer's disease (Goate et al., 1991) or place individuals at genetic risk for developing late-onset Alzheimer's disease (Corder et al., 1993). Identification of genes in these instances, against the background of histological and behavioral correlates of dementia, has led to understanding the proteins affected by the genes and in turn the cellular and systems-level disruptions that occur.

The potential for understanding causal mechanisms of cognitive change from genetic anomalies, or variation in simple polymorphisms, should not be underestimated. To find genetic anomalies, we will have to be on the lookout for outliers. Rare individuals that deviate from expectations may be more informative than the numerous individuals that find homes within the general population. Leverage might come from any of the observational levels. Genes could arise that explain exceptional longevity, systematic changes in white matter, or perhaps even usual cognitive slowing. Mutants that affect longevity in model systems, such as the worm *Caenorhabditis elegans*, may also provide candidates (Hekimi & Guarente, 2003). The important point is that, once identified, genetic mutations and variations that lead to age-associated change can be used to understand the organizational levels that are disrupted. Variation in the general population may not arise from the same specific mutations as the identified anomalies, but may share family resemblance or similarity in causal mechanisms.

Subtle genetic variations may also provide important avenues for exploration, but will require distinct research methods. Egan and colleagues (2003) provided an informative example of how such explorations might be undertaken and their potential utility. In exploring factors associated with psychiatric illness, they studied a human genetic variation of the BDNF val66met polymorphism. BDNF, or brain-derived neurotrophic factor, is associated with a number of ongoing cellular processes believed to relate to memory, cellular regeneration, and cell survival. The BDNF polymorphism refers to the common genetic variation by which some individuals have one form of the gene (*val*) and others a second form (*met*). Of importance, Egan et al. showed that memory performance (as measured by standard neuropsychological tests) was significantly lower in individuals with a *met/met* genotype compared to those with either *val/met* or *met/met* genotypes. Using a preparation for culturing hippocampal neurons that expressed either *val* or *met* variants of BDNF, they further demonstrated activity-dependent BDNF secretion was lower in cells expressing the *met* form. The implication, albeit still speculative, is that common genetic variation in the BDNF gene may cause physiologically significant differences in cellular processes associated with memory. It is probable that further study of this particular association will show the putative link to be incomplete. Nonetheless, the approach is groundbreaking and stands as model for a future generation of studies.

Use of genetic markers in cognitive aging research confronts a number of challenges that are common to studies of complex systems that span levels of analysis and have multiple interacting components embedded. Among these challenges are those that stem from the complexity by which gene-to-physiology relations are almost certain to work. Genes may code for proteins that are used by many different systems and even in multiple ways during distinct periods of development. Moreover, protein interactions and feedback make it unlikely that a single gene causes a simple, single effect. The Notch3 gene, which as noted is tied closely to CADASIL, is expressed in numerous forms of embryonic and adult tissue. Not surprisingly, severe cognitive decline, as discussed in this chapter, is only one of the consequences of having CADASIL. Expectations about how genetic observations will influence cognitive aging research must consider these features. Perhaps, for the near term, only subsets of possible genetic markers will be useful because of their fortuitous simplicity or because of their association to theoretically relevant aging processes.

A related challenge comes with the sheer number of possible human genetic variations that can be studied. Of the tens of thousands of already-identified human genetic polymorphisms, which are the best candidates for exploration? One possible approach is more or less a shotgun approach, using methods such as quantitative trait loci (QTL) or other exploratory genetic approaches. QTL analysis, as applied to aging, asks which genetic segments are correlated with aging processes, independent of reason. Other approaches are constrained functionally. For example, even prior to understanding how they might cause variance in aging, some genes may be better candidates because of their relevance to aging processes, begging the question of why we age at all. Some causes of age-associated change are linked inextricably to our time on earth. For example, more hazards are encountered the longer we live. However, even within relatively guarded environments, different species undergo stereotyped aging trajectories that likely stem directly from their genetic makeup (Troen, 2003). Why do we live to about 80 years of age and mice to about 2 years?

Fundamental aging mechanisms may originate from the manner in which cells divide and repair themselves and maintain physiological processes across cell generations. One avenue that has been actively explored recently is the rival pressures of avoiding cancer and extending life. For a species to gain its fitness advantage through an extended life span, survival and reproduction depends on a balance between tissue replacement during aging and the risk of cancer. Renewable tissues not only allow damage to be repaired, but also convey a risk of cancer because cell proliferation allows mutations to arise and consequent development of malignant tumors. As a result, molecular bases of tumor-suppressor mechanisms become a rich source of candidate genes that may influence aging (e.g., see Campisi, 2003). For this reason, in addition to exploring candidate genes that have functional properties that relate to the kinds of deficit observed in aging (such as the plausible link made between BDNF and its putative role in cognitive memory function), we should also target genetic variations that relate to our fitness as an organism that fills a niche with a lengthy, but not infinite, life cycle (figure 11.3).

Integrative theories may also arise from brute-force approaches to data exploration. Imagine a database that contained 10,000 participants ranging in age from 6 to 100 years and who underwent extensive cognitive and behavioral testing, clinical evaluation, MRI imaging, functional imaging, and numerous molecular imaging techniques that identified proteins associated with cell death, regional amyloid and tau burden, and neurogenesis, to name a few. Imagine further that these participants were tracked longitudinally, had case histories that included measures of their life-long health patterns, including blood pressure and any atypical (or perhaps even typical) illnesses. Blood for genetic analysis was routinely obtained, and the group of participants included a high percentage of twins and family members. Moreover, individuals enrolled in this fantasy database were willing to volunteer for additional hypothesis-directed studies on a week's notice. Although this database clearly does not exist, it stirs ideas about how integrative theories might be constructed *if* such data were available.

If large-scale data sets were available, relations among multiple organizational levels could be explored and hypotheses about relations tested. In the context of newly observed functional imaging correlates of aging, this need is particularly acute. Consider two competing theories of why older adults recruit additional brain regions (see figure 11.2). Theory one (derived from a compensation model) proposes that the observed functional correlate is a productive response to detrimental changes associated with aging. Embedded in this theory are a number of hypotheses. For

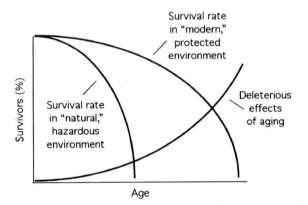

Figure 11.3. Causal mechanisms associated with aging may stem from processes associated with species fitness. Deleterious effects of aging may manifest when the life span has been extended (via modern, protected environments) beyond that selected for by our evolutionary lineage. Core processes associated with cellular regeneration, repair, and tumor suppression may provide important targets for insights into cognitive aging.

example, activation increases, among older adults of similar brain state, should correlate positively with performance. In addition, the need for compensation should correlate with some underlying change in brain morphology or other physiological marker associated with age. Some forms of brain change may be responsive to mediation by compensatory responses and others less response. Finally, the theory encourages exploration of factors that associate with why some individuals show functional compensation and others do not.

An alternative theory (derived from a disruption model) proposes that the observed correlate is itself a reflection of dysfunctional coordination among multiple, potentially competing brain regions. Contrasted to a compensation theory, a disruption theory would predict that increased activation should correlate negatively with performance and do so proportionately or additively in connection with observable structural change. This last theory encourages exploration of factors that associate with why some individuals are less susceptible to structural change and the mechanism by which structural change leads to disruption. All of these explorations require constraints across levels of observation. Observations at the behavioral, structural, and functional levels are individually, or even in pairs, insufficient to tease these hypotheses apart. The full theoretical description requires interrelations among all three, and the deeper questions about underlying causal mechanisms and interactions with genetics and environmental factors require even further description.

Large-scale databases of the form described above are not presently available. However, databases that have acquired data across multiple organization levels are already in place through efforts like the Betula project of Sweden (Nilsson et al., 1997), among others. Past efforts have tended not to focus on imaging data (whether structural MRI or functional) that are amenable to automated quantitative analysis, placing some limitations on what can be derived. However, I am personally optimistic that brute-force approaches that meld large samples of multiple data types will come to be a dominant contributor to theoretical progress in cognitive aging research.

One reason for this optimism is that cognitive aging research has a long tradition of exploring relations among variables and factors that influence behavior. Salthouse and Ferrer-Caja (2003; see also Salthouse, 1996), for example, systematically explored a series of possible models to identify factors that explain performance on a wide range of behavioral tasks (for another notable example, see Lindenberger & Baltes, 1994). The approach and specific findings of Salthouse and colleagues are relevant to this chapter in multiple ways. First, by formalizing possible relations among variables and testing between possibilities, they exemplify the kind of rigor that will be required to explore relations between levels of organization in integrative theories of cognitive aging. By including data from multiple levels of organization, rather than data from within only one level of analysis, leverage is gained because basic biological principles place strong constraints on how one level of organization might affect another. Furthermore, their results suggest specific goals that integrative theories should be able to achieve. For example, their results suggest a common influence of age on many task forms, including reasoning, memory, spatial, and speed abilities, and another to account for additional age-related effects on memory. If successful, formal integrative theories should, from the identification of causal mechanisms, explain clustering and patterning at the behavioral level.

In ending this chapter, it is worthwhile to return to the overarching goal of understanding the variance in cognitive aging. The fundamental assumption is that the varied cognitive states of older individuals are caused by the many age-associated brain changes that are taking place, their responses to these changes, how they sum and interact, and how the experiences and external interactions in a person's life influence these changes. Full description of why some individuals present in one manner and others quite differently will require that theories and measurement span multiple levels of organization—from the genetic to the behavioral. This chapter, in an imperfect manner, begins to set a framework for establishing such relations.

Acknowledgments   I thank Cindy Lustig for extensive discussion that led to many of the ideas articulated here and Jamie Parker for help with manuscript preparation. Susan Fitzpatrick, Denise Head, Avi Snyder, and Anthony Fotenos also provided valuable discussion. I am supported by the Howard Hughes Medical Institute and by grants from the James S. McDonnell Foundation, the Alzheimer Association, and the National Institutes of Health.

References

Arnsten, A. F., Cai, J. X., Murphy, B. L., & Goldman-Rakic, P. S. (1994). Dopamine D_1 receptor mechanisms in the cognitive performance of young adult and aged monkeys. *Psychopharmacology, 116*, 143–151.

Backman, L., Ginovart, N., Dixon, R. A., Wahlin, T. B., Wahlin, A., Halldin, C., et al. (2000). Age-related cognitive deficits mediated by changes in the striatal dopamine system. *American Journal of Psychiatry, 157*, 635–637.

Balota, D. A., & Faust, M. E. (2001). Attention in dementia of the Alzheimer's type. In F. Boller & S. F. Cappa (Eds.), *Handbook of neuropsychology: Volume 6. Aging and dementia* (2nd ed., pp. 51–80). Amsterdam, The Netherlands: Elsevier.

Baltes, P. (1997). On the complete architecture of human ontogeny: Selection, optimization, and compensation as a function of developmental theory. *American Psychologist, 52*, 366–380.

Barker, W. W., Luis, C. A., Kashuba, A., Luis, M., Harwood, D. G., Loewenstein, D., et al. (2002). Relative frequencies of Alzheimer disease, Lewy body, vascular and frontotemporal dementia, and hippocampal sclerosis in the State of Florida Brain Bank. *Alzheimer Disease and Associated Disorders, 16*, 203–212.

Becker, J. T., Mintun, M. A., Aleva, K., Wiseman, M. B., Nichols, T., & DeKosky, S. T. (1996). Compensatory reallocation of brain resources supporting verbal episodic memory in Alzheimer's disease. *Neurology, 46*, 692–700.

Bookheimer, S. Y., Strojwas, M. H., Cohen, M. S., Saunders, A. M., Pericak-Vance, M. A., Mazziotta, J. C., et al. (2000). Patterns of brain activation in people at risk for Alzheimer's disease. *New England Journal of Medicine, 343*, 450–456.

Braak, H., & Braak, E. (1991). Neuropathological staging of Alzheimer-related changes. *Acta Neuropathology, 81*, 261–268.

Braak, H., & Braak, E. (1997). Staging of Alzheimer-related cortical destruction. *International Psychogeriatrics, 9*(Suppl. 1), 257–261.

Buckner, R. L., Corbetta, M., Schatz, J., Raichle, M. E., & Petersen, S. E. (1996). Preservedspeech abilities and compensation following prefrontal damage. *Proceedings of the National Academy of Sciences of the United States of America, 93*, 1249–1253.

Cabeza, R. (2001). Functional neuroimaging of cognitive aging. In R. Cabeza & A. Kingstone (Eds.), *Handbook of functional neuroimaging of cognition* (pp. 331–376). Cambridge, MA: MIT Press.

Cabeza, R. (2002). Hemispheric asymmetry reduction in older adults: The HAROLD model. *Psychology and Aging, 17*, 85–100.

Cabeza, R., Anderson, N. D., Locantore, J. K., & McIntosh, A. R. (2002). Aging gracefully: Compensatory brain activity in high-performing older adults. *NeuroImage, 17*, 1394–1402.

Cabeza, R., Grady, C. L., Nyberg, L., McIntosh, A. R., Tulving, E., Kapur, S., et al. (1997). Age-related differences in neural activity during memory encoding and retrieval: A positron emission tomography study. *Journal of Neuroscience, 17*, 391–400.

Campisi, J. (2003). Cancer and ageing: Rival demons? *Nature Reviews Cancer, 3*, 339–349.

Churchland, P. S., & Sejnowski, T. J. (1991). Perspectives on cognitive neuroscience. In R. G. Lister & M. J. Weingartner (Eds.), *Perspectives on cognitive neuroscience* (pp. 3–23). New York: Oxford University Press.

Cohen, J., Cohen, P., West, S. G., & Aiken, L. S. (2003). *Applied multiple regression/correlation analysis for the behavioral sciences* (3rd ed.). Mahwah, NJ: Erlbaum.

Corder, E. H., Saunders, A. M., Strittmatter, W. J., Schmechel, D. E., Gaskell, P. C., Small, G. W., et al. (1993). Gene dose of apolipoprotein E type 4 allele and the risk of Alzheimer's disease in late onset families. *Science, 261*, 921–923.

DeCarli, C., & Scheltens, P. (2002). Structural brain imaging. In T. Erkinjuntti & S. Gauthier (Eds.), *Vascular cognitive impairment* (pp. 433–457). London: Martin Dunitz, Ltd.

Desmond, D. W. (2002). Cognition and white matter lesions. *Cerebrovascular Diseases, 13*(Suppl. 2), 53–57.

Egan, M. F., Kojima, M., Callicott, J. H., Goldberg, T. E., Kolachana, B. S., Bertolino, A., et al. (2003). The BDNF val66met polymorphism affects activity-dependent secretion of BDNF and human memory and hippocampal function. *Cell, 112*, 257–269.

Glisky, E. L., Polster, M. R., & Routhieaux, B. C. (1995). Double dissociation between item and source memory. *Neuropsychology, 9*, 229–235.

Goate, A., Chartier-Harlin, M. C., Mullan, M., Brown, J., Crawford, F., Fidani, L., et al. (1991). Segregation of a missense mutation in the amyloid precursor protein gene with familial Alzheimer's disease. *Nature, 349*, 704–706.

Golde, T. E., Eckman, C. B., & Younkin, S. G. (2000). Biochemical detection of Aβ isoforms: Implications for pathogenesis, diagnosis, and treatment of Alzheimer's disease. *Biochimica et Biophysica Acta, 1502*, 172–187.

Grady, C. L., & Craik, F. I. M. (2000). Changes in memory processing with age. *Current Opinions in Neurobiology, 10*, 224–231.

Grady, C. L., McIntosh, A. R., Beig, S., Keightley, M. L., Burian, H., & Black, E. (2003). Evidence from functional neuroimaging of a compensatory prefrontal network in Alzheimer's disease. *Journal of Neuroscience, 23*, 986–993.

Hekimi, S., & Guarente, L. (2003). Genetics and the specificity of the aging process. *Science, 299*, 1351–1354.

Jack, C. R., Jr., & Petersen, R. C. (2000) Structural imaging approaches to Alzheimer's disease. In L. F. M. Scinto & K. R. Daffner (Eds.), *Early diagnosis and treatment of Alzheimer's disease* (pp. 127–148) Totowa, NJ: Humana Press.

Jack, C. R., Jr., Petersen, R. C., O'Brien, P. C., & Tangalos, E. G. (1992). MR-based hippocampal volumetry in the diagnosis of Alzheimer's disease. *Neurology, 42*, 183–188.

Joutel, A., Corpechot, C., Ducros, A., Vahedi, K., Chabriat, H., Mouton, P., et al. (1996). Notch3 mutations in CADASIL, a hereditary adult-onset condition causing stroke and dementia. *Nature, 383*, 707–710.

Kalimo, H., Ruchoux, M. M., Viitanen, M., & Kalaria, R. N. (2002). CADASIL: A common form of hereditary arteriopathy causing brain infarcts and dementia. *Brain Pathology, 12*, 371–384.

Kalimo, H., Viitanen, M., Carlstrom, C., Nordberg, A., & Bronge, L. (2002). CADASIL in monozygotic twins. *Neuropathology & Applied Neurobiology,* 28, 151.

Kanne, S. M., Balota, D. A., Storandt, M., McKeel, D. W., & Morris, J. C. (1998). Relating anatomy to function in Alzheimer's disease: Neuropsychological profiles predict regional neuropathology 5 years later. *Neurology, 50*, 979–985.

Kemper, T. L. (1994). Neuroanatomical and neuropathological changes during aging and dementia. In M. L. Albert & J. E. Knoefel (Eds.), *Clinical neurology of aging* (2nd ed., pp. 3–67). New York: Oxford University Press.

Killiany, R. J., Moss, M. B., Albert, M. S., Sandor, T., Tieman, J., & Jolesz, F. (1993). Temporal lobe regions on magnetic resonance imaging identify patients with early Alzheimer's disease. *Archives of Neurology, 50*, 949–954.

Lindenberger, U., & Baltes, P. B. (1994). Sensory functioning and intelligence in old age: A strong connection. *Psychology and Aging, 9*, 339–355.

Logan, J. M., Sanders, A. L., Snyder, A. Z., Morris, J. C., & Buckner, R. L. (2002). Underrecruitment and nonselective recruitment: Dissociable neural mechanisms associated with aging. *Neuron, 33*, 827–840.

Neuropathology Group of the Medical Research Council Cognitive Function and Aging Study. (2001). Pathological correlates of late-onset dementia in a multicentre, community-based population in England and Wales. *The Lancet, 357*, 169–175.

Nilsson, L. G., Backman, L., Emgrund, K., Nyberg, L., Adolfsson, R., Bucht, G., et al. (1997). The Betula Prospective Cohort Study: Memory, health, and aging. *Aging, Neuropsychology, and Cognition, 4*, 1–32.

Parasuraman, R., & Haxby, J. V. (1993). Attention and brain function in Alzheimer's Disease: A review. *Neuropsychology, 7*, 242–272.

Park, D. C., Polk, T. A., Mikels, J. A., Taylor, S. F., & Marshuetz, C. (2001). Cerebral aging: Integration of brain and behavioral models of cognitive function. *Dialogues in Clinical Neuroscience, 3*, 151–165.

Price, J. L., Davis, P. B., Morris, J. C., & White, D. L. (1991). The distribution of tangles, plaques, and related immunohistochemical markers in healthy aging and Alzheimer's disease. *Neurobiology of Aging, 12*, 295–312.

Pugh, K. G., & Lipsitz, L. A. (2002). The microvascular frontal-subcortical syndrome of aging. *Neurobiology, 23*, 421–431.

Raz, N. (2000). Aging of the brain and its impact on cognitive performance: Integration of structural and functional findings. In F. I. M. Craik & T. A. Salthouse (Eds.), *The handbook of aging and cognition* (2nd ed., pp. 1–90). Mahwah, NJ: Erlbaum.

Raz, N., Gunning, F. M., Head, D., Dupuis, J. H., McQuain, J., Briggs, S. D., et al. (1997). Selective aging of the human cerebral cortex observed in vivo: Differential vulnerability of the prefrontal gray matter. *Cerebral Cortex, 7*, 268–282.

Reddy, H., De Stefano, N., Mortilla, M., Federico, A., & Matthews, P. M. (2002). Functional reorganization of motor cortex increases with greater axonal injury from CADASIL. *Stroke, 33*, 502–508.

Reuter-Lorenz, P. A. (2002). New visions of the aging mind and brain. *Trends in Cognitive Sciences, 6*, 394–400.

Reuter-Lorenz, P. A., Jonides, J., Smith, E. E., Hartley, A., Miller, A., Marshuetz, C., et al. (2000). Age differences in the frontal lateralization of verbal and spatial working memory revealed by PET. *Journal of Cognitive Neuroscience, 12*, 174–187.

Rosen, A. C., Prull, M. W., O'Hara, R., Race, E. A., Desmond, J. E., Glover, G. H., et al. (2002). Variable effects of aging on frontal lobe contributions to memory. *Neuroreport*, *13*, 2425–2428.

Rosen, H. J., Petersen S. E., Linenweber, M. R., Snyder, A. Z., White, D. A., Chapman, L., Dromerick, A. W., Fiez, J. A., Corbetta, M. D. (2000). Neural correlates of recovery from aphasia after damage to left inferior frontal cortex. *Neurology*, *55*, 1883–1894.

Rubin, D. C. (1999). Frontal-striatal circuits in cognitive aging: Evidence for caudate involvement. *Aging, Neuropsychology, and Cognition*, *6*, 241–259.

Rubin, E. H., Storandt, M., Miller, J. P., Kinscherf, D. A., Grant, E. A., Morris, J. C., et al. (1998). A prospective study of cognitive function and onset of dementia in cognitively healthy elders. *Archives of Neurology*, *55*, 395–401.

Ruchoux, M. M., Domenga, V., Brulin, P., Maciazek, J., Limol, S., Tournier-Lasserve, E., et al. (2003). Transgenic mice expressing mutant Notch3 develop vascular alterations characteristic of cerebral autosomal dominant arteriopathy with subcortical infarcts and leukoencephalopathy. *American Journal of Pathology*, *162*, 329–342.

Salthouse, T. A. (1996). Constraints on theories of cognitive aging. *Psychonomic Bulletin and Review*, *3*, 287–299.

Salthouse, T. A., & Ferrer-Caja, E. (2003). What needs to be explained to account for age-related effects on multiple cognitive variables? *Psychology and Aging*, *18*, 91–110.

Selkoe, D. J. (2001). Alzheimer's disease: Genes, proteins, and therapy. *Physiological Reviews*, *81*, 741–766.

Tournier-Lasserve, E., Joutel, A., Melki, J., Weissenbach, J., Lathrop, G. M., Chabriat, H., et al. (1993). Cerebral autosomal dominant arteriopathy with subcortical infarcts and leukoencephalopathy maps to chromosome 19q12. *Nature Genetics*, *3*, 256–259.

Troen, B. R. (2003). The biology of aging. *Mount Sinai Journal of Medicine*, *70*, 3–22.

Volkow, N. D., Logan, J., Fowler, J. S., Wang, G. J., Gur, R. C., Wong, C., et al. (2000). Association between age-related decline in brain dopamine activity and impairment in frontal and cingulate metabolism. *American Journal of Psychiatry*, *157*, 75–80.

Wu, C. C., Mungas, D., Eberling, J. L., Reed, B. R., & Jagust, W. J. (2002). Imaging interactions between Alzheimer's disease and cerebrovascular disease. *Annals of the New York Academy of Sciences*, *977*, 403–410.

12

Functional Connectivity During Memory Tasks in Healthy Aging and Dementia

Cheryl L. Grady

Memory failure is a common complaint of older people. However, age-related memory losses are very task dependent; performance on some tasks drops substantially with increasing age, whereas performance on other tasks shows essentially no change across the adult years. Older individuals have particular difficulty with *episodic memory*, defined as the conscious recollection of events that have occurred in a person's experience (Tulving, 1983). Age-related difficulties in this type of memory may be related to deficits in encoding the new material (Craik & Byrd, 1982), as well as to reductions in the ability to retrieve previously learned information (Burke & Light, 1981). Within episodic memory, performance on recognition tasks can be relatively maintained with age, whereas free recall is consistently reduced (Craik & Jennings, 1992; Craik & McDowd, 1987). In contrast, semantic memory, or the accumulation of knowledge about the world, is maintained in older adults (Craik & Jennings, 1992). In terms of short-term memory function, working memory tasks show substantial age-related declines (for reviews see Balota, Dolan, & Duchek, 2000; Zacks, Hasher, & Li, 2000), but other closely related short-term memory tasks (e.g., span measures) show little change (Craik & Jennings, 1992).

Dysfunction in episodic memory also is a hallmark of Alzheimer's disease (AD) and is one of the earliest and most devastating symptoms (Grady et al., 1988; Jacobs et al., 1995; Price et al., 1993; Zec, 1993). Delayed memory is affected to a greater extent than is immediate memory, although the latter is clearly impaired as well (Hart et al., 1988; Moss et al., 1986; Welsh et al., 1991). This early impairment of episodic memory in AD is consistent with the damage to medial temporal structures, including the hippocampus and entorhinal cortex, that is thought to occur early in the disease (Braak, Braak, & Bohl, 1993; Kemper, 1994). Unlike healthy aging, semantic memory also is impaired early in AD, although to a lesser extent than episodic memory (Chan, Butters, & Salmon, 1997; Chertkow & Bub, 1990; Ober & Shenaut, 1999). This deficit usually manifests as a loss of access to specific information about object attributes (Binetti et al., 1995; Giffard et al., 2001; Hodges, Salmon, & Butters, 1992).

In recent years, functional neuroimaging has been used to study how these differences in memory between young and old adults and between healthy older adults and patients with AD are expressed in terms of brain activity while performing a variety of tasks. These experiments have revealed a number of interesting differences in brain activity, the most notable of which is increased activity in prefrontal cortex in older adults compared to younger adults and in AD patients compared to age-matched controls. The major challenge facing researchers in this field is how to interpret these differences, either in the framework of existing theories of cognitive aging, such as reduced inhibitory function (Hasher & Zacks, 1988), or in terms of new theories that might emerge from this work.

The majority of the neuroimaging studies focused on aging have used the subtraction technique to examine how activity in the brain is modulated by task. That is, brain activity during a memory task is compared to activity during a baseline condition in the hopes that processes of little interest could be subtracted out, leaving only brain activity caused by the processes of primary interest to the investigators. With this type of approach, activity can be examined throughout the brain, although the statistical inferences are made on each region separately.

Other approaches exist, however, that take the view that cognition is the result of the integrated activity of dynamic brain networks rather than the action of any region or regions acting independently. This view has resulted in the application of multivariate techniques to image analysis to reveal the regions comprising these networks and to illuminate the functional interactions among them (Friston et al., 1993; Horwitz, 1994; McIntosh, 1999). These functional interactions are known as *functional connectivity*, that is, how activity in a specific brain region is correlated with activity in the rest of the brain. Functional connectivity analysis allows us to go beyond the examination of how activity changes in a given brain area and to begin to understand the complex interplay of activity in areas distributed throughout the brain.

The purpose of this chapter is to review briefly the functional neuroimaging studies of memory in young adults, older adults, and patients with dementia that have used the traditional univariate subtraction approach, and to show how examination of functional connectivity can be useful in identifying between-group differences not possible with univariate approaches. The focus is on changes involving prefrontal cortex and the hippocampus because these areas are thought by some to be particularly vulnerable to aging, and much of the neuroimaging literature on memory has focused on these regions.

Neuroimaging Studies of Memory in Young Adults

It was noted early that prefrontal activity during encoding of new information was seen mainly in the left hemisphere, whereas retrieval of previously learned information was accompanied by increased activity in right prefrontal areas. This so-called hemispheric encoding/retrieval asymmetry (HERA) (Tulving et al., 1994) has been found for a number of different types of stimuli, including verbal and nonverbal (for reviews, see Cabeza & Nyberg, 2000; Nyberg, Cabeza, & Tulving, 1996). The pattern is far from an absolute one, however, as encoding-related activity in some areas of prefrontal cortex is modulated by type of material, such that it is left lateralized for words and right lateralized for faces (Kelley et al., 1998; McDermott, Buckner, et al., 1999). In addition, although the prefrontal region is consistently activated during episodic memory retrieval, usually the anterior portions of prefrontal cortex near the frontal poles, activation is sometimes found only in the right hemisphere (Buckner et al., 1996, 1998; Duzel et al., 1999; Grasby et al., 1993; Haxby et al., 1996; Kohler et al., 1998; Nyberg et al., 2000; Tulving, Kapur, Markowitsch, et al., 1994) and sometimes in both hemispheres (Andreasen et al., 1995; Becker et al., 1994; Blaxton et al., 1996; Dalla Barba et al., 1998; Kohler et al., 2000; McDermott, Ojemann, et al., 1999; Rugg et al., 1996; Schacter, Alpert, et al., 1996).

However, although most would agree that right prefrontal cortex plays a role in memory retrieval, the precise nature of this role is still under debate. Activity in this region has been attributed to retrieval mode (Lepage et al., 2000), retrieval monitoring (Allan et al., 2000; Fletcher et al., 1998; Henson, Shallice, & Dolan, 1999), retrieval effort (Schacter, Alpert, et al., 1996), retrieval success (McDermott et al., 2000; Rugg et al., 1996), retrieval context (Wagner, Desmond, et al., 1998), or a combination of these effects (Grady, McIntosh, et al., 2001).

Other areas besides prefrontal regions are also active during both encoding and retrieval. For example, medial temporal cortex is active during encoding (e.g., Haxby et al., 1996; C. E. Stern et al., 1996; Wagner, Schacter, et al., 1998) and during some retrieval conditions, particularly during retrieval of autobiographical memories (Ryan et al., 2001). Parietal regions, notably the precuneus, also are active during retrieval (Haxby et al., 1996; Moscovitch et al., 1995; Schmidt et al., 2002). In addition, there have been reports of a "subsequent memory effect" in which activity in medial temporal and prefrontal regions during encoding was greater for items that subsequently were correctly recognized compared to forgotten items (Brewer et al., 1998; Fernandez et al., 1999; Kirchhoff et al., 2000; Otten, Henson, & Rugg, 2001; Strange et al., 2002; Wagner, Schacter, et al., 1998).

Working memory (WM), like episodic memory, is accompanied by activity in the prefrontal cortex, typically in dorsolateral prefrontal areas. Prefrontal activity is consistently seen during WM tasks for both visual (e.g., D'Esposito et al., 1998; Haxby et al., 2000) and auditory stimuli (Martinkauppi et al., 2000; Schumacher et al., 1996; Zatorre, Evans, & Meyer, 1994). However, like the debate over the role of prefrontal cortex in episodic memory, there has been debate over which areas are active and which aspect of working memory tasks is mediated by this frontal activity. Some have taken a process-oriented view and proposed that ventral portions of prefrontal cortex are involved in maintaining information in working memory, and that dorsal areas mediate manipulation of information (e.g., D'Esposito et al., 1999; Owen et al., 1998). Others have stressed a ventral/dorsal dissociation on the basis of stimulus specificity, that is, identifying object features versus object location (Courtney et al., 1998).

Neuroimaging Studies of Memory in Older Adults

When brain activity in young and older adults is compared on a task, there are at least three possible outcomes in a given brain area: (1) Young and old groups could have equivalent brain activity, (2) older adults could show less activity, or (3) old adults could show greater activity. Reduced activity in the elderly can reasonably be assumed to reflect a reduced level of functioning, particularly when accompanied by poorer performance on the task. During episodic encoding, older adults generally have reduced activity in the left prefrontal regions prominently active in the young.

For example, older adults showed less activation of left prefrontal and temporal regions during a face-encoding task compared to younger adults (Grady et al., 1995, 2002). Similarly, old adults showed less activation in left prefrontal and temporal regions during encoding of verbal paired associates (Cabeza et al., 1997). This finding was replicated by Anderson et al. (2000), who showed that divided attention during encoding and aging both reduced encoding-related activity in left prefrontal cortex. The results of these studies suggest that the reductions in memory accuracy with age in part may be caused by a reduction in the ability to engage in elaborative encoding that is mediated by left prefrontal cortex.

The underrecruitment of left prefrontal areas in older adults during encoding can be ameliorated when meaningful visual stimuli, such as pictures of objects, are used as the to-be-remembered stimuli (Grady et al., 1999). This also has been reported when older adults are required to use semantically driven encoding strategies (Logan et al., 2002), although this has not been found consistently (Stebbins et al., 2002). In a study by Logan et al. (2002), older adults showed less left prefrontal activity than did younger adults during shallow perceptual encoding, but equivalent activity during deeper semantic encoding. Similarly, Grady et al. (1999) found that older and younger adults showed equal left prefrontal activity during semantic encoding, particularly for pictures of objects. These results suggest that older adults, under some conditions, can show levels of prefrontal activity during encoding equivalent to those seen in younger adults.

During retrieval, the picture is somewhat different. Recognition of faces in both young and old adults is accompanied by increased activity in right prefrontal and parietal cortices, with little or no difference in the magnitudes of these activations (Grady et al., 1995, 2002). Right prefrontal activity also is seen during verbal retrieval in both young and old adults during cued recall (Cabeza et al., 1997) and recognition (Cabeza et al., 1997; Madden, Turkington, et al., 1999). Sometimes, however, right prefrontal activity is reduced in the older group during cued recall (Anderson et al., 2000) or is in a different location compared to young adults (Schacter, Savage, et al., 1996). Thus, if the results are examined in terms of reduced frontal activity in the elderly, the findings are consistent with the idea that older individuals may have difficulty with both stages of memory, but that the encoding stage may be especially problematic.

In contrast to reductions in brain activation, which imply a reduction in processing resources, a number of investigators have now reported increased utilization of some brain regions by older adults during memory tasks, primarily in prefrontal regions during episodic memory retrieval. Studies of both verbal (Backman et al., 1999; Cabeza et al., 1997, 2000; Madden, Turkington, et al., 1999) and nonverbal retrieval (Grady et al., 2002) have found bilateral prefrontal activity in older adults, whereas young adults generally showed right prefrontal activation in these experiments. Interestingly, some of the left prefrontal areas with increased activity during retrieval in older adults are those that show decreased activity during encoding. Thus, older adults may not engage left prefrontal cortex consistently during encoding, but often do so during retrieval and to a greater extent than do young adults. This suggests that the cognitive processes mediated by left prefrontal regions during memory tasks are not necessarily unavailable to the elderly, but are utilized differently.

Differential utilization of prefrontal cortex with age also has been found in working memory experiments. Several recent studies of working memory for letters using similar paradigms found decreased activity in the left prefrontal cortex (Jonides et al., 2000) and in the bilateral dorsolateral prefrontal cortex in older adults compared to younger adults (Rypma & D'Esposito, 2000; Rypma et al., 2001). One of these (Rypma & D'Esposito, 2000) also showed that this age-related difference was seen only when participants made their responses to a memory probe and not during encoding or the 10-s retention period that preceded presentation of the probe, indicating that the age deficit may be selective to particular phases of a working memory task.

Other working memory studies have shown increases as well as decreases in activation in older adults. One such experiment involved short-term recognition of unfamiliar faces using a delayed match-to-sample paradigm (Grady et al., 1998). When the delayed recognition conditions were compared to a baseline condition, both young and old adults had activation of occipitotemporal and prefrontal cortices bilaterally. However, young adults had greater activation of the right ventral prefrontal cortex, and old individuals showed greater activation in the left dorsolateral prefrontal cortex. In addition, the older adults had greater activity during the working memory tasks in the occipital cortex.

Reuter-Lorenz and colleagues (2000) examined working memory for verbal and spatial information. They found that young adults had lateralized prefrontal activity during these tasks, in the left hemisphere during the verbal task and in the right hemisphere during the spatial task. Older adults, on the other hand, had bilateral prefrontal activity during both tasks, similar to the reports of bilateral prefrontal activity in the elderly during episodic retrieval discussed above.

Finally, a meta-analysis compared brain activity in young and old adults in three face-processing experiments: episodic memory, working memory, and degraded face perception (Grady, 2002). Activity was contrasted between the memory tasks or the difficult perceptual task and control face-processing tasks that did not require memory or perceptual degradation. The older adults had increased bilateral prefrontal activity in both memory and degraded perceptual tasks (plate 12.1; see color insert). In contrast, prefrontal activity was task specific in young adults and was increased only during the memory tasks and not during the difficult perceptual task. This suggests that prefrontal activation in older adults reflects greater use of executive functions at lower levels of task demand or in a more generalized fashion across tasks than would be necessary for activation of this area in young adults.

Medial temporal lobe regions also showed age-related differences in memory-related activity, primarily reductions. Reduced activity in the anterior hippocampus has been reported in older adults during face encoding (Grady et al., 1995) and during a task of working memory for objects and their locations (Mitchell et al., 2000), both of which also resulted in poorer performance in the older group. In contrast, anterior hippocampal activity during encoding of pictured objects was maintained in the elderly, and recognition of these items also was equivalent to that seen in young adults (Grady et al., 1999). Activity in the posterior hippocampal region and parahippocampal gyrus in older adults was reported to be maintained during memory tasks, even if their performance is lower than that seen in young adults (Backman et al., 1997; Schacter, Savage, et al., 1996). These results, taken together, would suggest that anterior regions of the hippocampus are sensitive to age-related changes, and that activity in this region might be more closely tied to memory ability in the elderly than activity in posterior regions.

Correlational Approaches to Image Analysis

The studies reviewed above were generally concerned with assessing how activity in certain brain areas was modulated across task conditions by the different cognitive processes under study. There are additional types of information inherent in imaging data sets that can be assessed using correlations or covariance analyses. One useful approach is to compare individual differences in performance on the experimental task with differences in brain activity. In the context of aging research, it is important to look not only at how levels of activity in various brain regions change with age, but also at how these changes in activity have an impact on task performance. This has been done by correlating brain activity in specified brain regions or across the whole brain with measures of task accuracy or reaction time. These correlations can then be compared in young and old adults to see if the brain regions that facilitate performance change with age.

Assessment of the covariance among brain areas can be done using multivariate approaches and functional connectivity analyses. Multivariate approaches, such as principal component analysis or partial least squares (Friston et al., 1993; McIntosh, 1999; Moeller & Strother, 1991), are used to identify a group of brain areas that shows the same pattern of functional changes during the experimental tasks. Groups of regions thus identified can be thought of as the networks that underlie cognitive processing. Functional connectivity is another type of network-based approach and involves assessing how activity in a given region covaries with activity in other areas of the brain during a task (Friston et al., 1993; Horwitz, 1994; McIntosh, 1999). This type of correlation can be done on a pairwise region basis or across the whole brain, and it requires no assumptions about how the influence of one region on another is actually brought about. Effective connectivity, on the other hand, is a related type of analysis that models the way brain areas influence one another and tests whether the model fits the data at hand (Aertsen et al., 1989; Friston, 1994; McIntosh & Gonzalez-Lima, 1994).

In a practical sense, the two ways of assessing connectivity can be thought of as measuring correlations among a group of brain regions (functional connectivity) and decomposing this correlation matrix to determine the direction of influences (i.e., from one region to another) and the magnitude of these influences (effective connectivity). Thus, connectivity approaches emphasize the functional interactions among brain areas and the ways in which these interactions mediate cognitive processing rather than the activity in any individual brain region. The following sections review age-related differences in brain–behavior correlations and functional or effective connectivity.

Age-Related Differences in Brain–Behavior Correlations

Age-related differences in brain activity can be assessed further by measuring correlations between activity in a particular region or regions and individual differences in memory performance. Della-Maggiore et al. (2000) measured brain activity in young and old adults during memory for visual patterns over very short time intervals (0.5 and 4 s) and found that hippocampal activity was positively correlated with performance in both young and older adults. That is, as hippocampal activity increased, memory performance improved in both groups. Under other conditions, however, activity in the hippocampus may not be correlated with the ability of older adults to recognize previously encountered stimuli.

In an experiment of face memory, activity in the hippocampus and ventral prefrontal cortex during encoding was positively correlated with subsequent recognition accuracy in young adults, but not old adults (Grady et al., 2002). In contrast, the older group showed correlations between recognition performance and activity in dorsolateral prefrontal and parietal cortices during encoding. This difference in correlational pattern suggests a ventral-to-dorsal shift with age in the cognitive resources utilized to facilitate memory ability. Similarly, Madden, Gottlob, et al. (1999) reported that activity in the right prefrontal cortex was correlated with reaction time measures in both old and young adults during a retrieval task, but that this correlation also was present in the older adults during encoding, suggesting that this region may mediate other aspects of task performance in addition to retrieval in the elderly. Other brain areas also showed correlations with performance in the old, but not the young, group, such as parahippocampal gyrus and temporoparietal regions, indicating a wider recruitment of areas in the elderly to support performance.

Working memory studies have shown inconsistent results in terms of age differences in how frontal lobe activity is correlated with memory task performance. Rypma and D'Esposito (2000) found that increasing activity in the dorsolateral prefrontal cortex during a verbal working memory task was associated with faster response times in the elderly, but slower responses in young adults. Opposite results have been reported during a face working memory task (Grady, 2002; Grady et al., 1998), in that increased activity in the dorsolateral prefrontal cortex, mainly in the left hemisphere, was associated with slower responding in the older adults and faster response times in the young adults (plate 12.2; see color insert). These studies were different in terms of both stimuli and procedures, so it is difficult to compare them directly. Nevertheless, it seems clear that the relation between brain activity and memory task performance, in prefrontal cortex and elsewhere, is both complex and sensitive to the effects of age.

Connectivity Studies in Aging

The functional connectivity approach has not been applied widely to the study of brain function in aging, but has provided some intriguing glimpses into the kinds of age differences that can be revealed with this type of approach. Cabeza and colleagues (1997) followed up their study of age-related differences in episodic memory by examining the effective connectivity of prefrontal regions that were active during encoding and retrieval. Consistent with their left prefrontal activation seen during encoding and right frontal activation during retrieval, young adults showed strong positive functional interactions of left prefrontal regions and other areas during encoding, with a shift to interactions involving predominantly right prefrontal regions during retrieval. In contrast, the functional interactions of prefrontal regions in older adults were bilateral during retrieval, suggesting that age-related changes in neural activation during retrieval tasks are partly caused by changes in effective connectivity in the neural network underlying the task.

In the article by Della-Maggiore et al. (2000), mentioned in the Age-Related Differences in Brain–Behavior Correlations section, activity in the right hippocampus was positively correlated with memory in both young and old adults. However, examination of the functional and effective connectivity of this region showed that the brain areas where activity covaried with activity in the hippocampus were quite different in young and old adults. Specifically, older adults showed larger functional connections between the hippocampus and frontal and temporal regions than did the younger adults. These connectivity differences were seen despite the fact that the two groups were equivalent in performance on the task. This result indicates that similar behavioral outcomes do not necessarily imply that the brain networks supporting that behavior will be the same.

Using a similar approach, Grady, McIntosh, and Craik (2003) examined the functional connectivity of the hippocampus during encoding of words and objects in young and old adults. During encoding, right hippocampal activity was more active during object encoding than word encoding in both groups (Grady et al., 1999) and was positively correlated with subsequent recognition performance in young and old. However, the functional interactions of the right hippocampus differed with age. In young adults, hippocampal activity was correlated with activity in ventral prefrontal and extrastriate regions (figure 12.1a). In contrast, older adults showed correlations between hippocampal activity and dorsolateral prefrontal and parietal regions (figure 12.1b). This pattern of ventral/dorsal age differences was found for both words and objects. Of particular interest was that activity in these ventral and dorsal networks as a whole was correlated with better subsequent recognition performance in young and old groups, respectively. This was assessed using a multivariate approach to

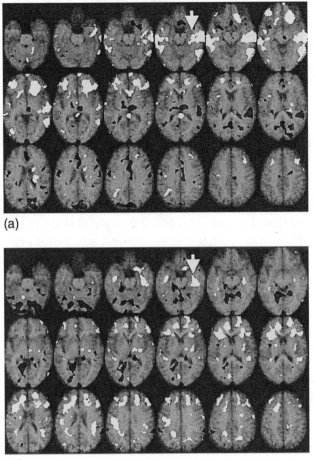

(a)

(b)

Figure 12.1. Brain areas where activity during object encoding was significantly correlated with activity in right hippocampus and with subsequent recognition performance in *a*, young adults, and *b*, old adults, are shown on standard magnetic resonance images (MRIs; slices ranging from −28 mm to +40 mm relative to the anterior-posterior commissure [AC-PC] line). The right hippocampal region used for the functional connectivity analyses is indicated by the white arrows. Increased activity in the white areas in panel *a* was significantly associated with increased object recognition accuracy ($r = .91$) and activity in the hippocampus ($r = .79$) in the young adults, but not in the old. Increased activity in the white areas in panel *b* was significantly associated with increased object recognition accuracy ($r = .64$) and activity in the hippocampus ($r = .84$) in the old adults, but not in the young. (Data from Grady, McIntosh, and Craik, 2003.)

determine simultaneously those brain areas in which activity was correlated both with activity in the hippocampus and with recognition accuracy. Thus, connectivity among hippocampus, ventral prefrontal, and visual cortices during encoding supported subsequent recognition in younger adults, whereas in older adults connectivity among hippocampus, dorsolateral prefrontal, and parietal regions supported memory. This ventral/dorsal distinction suggests a shift in the cognitive resources utilized with age from more perceptually based processes to those involved in executive and organizational functions and is similar to the brain–behavior correlations noted during face memory (discussed in a separate section). Further, the results of this study provided evidence that these alterations in functional connectivity have an impact on memory performance. That is, the types of cognitive processes engaged to facilitate memory, and the networks that subserve them, may undergo alterations across the life span.

The results of this study and of Della Maggiore et al.'s 2000 work both showed that more information about memory-related brain activity can be obtained by examining the functional interactions among brain regions, and that in some cases this type of analysis can demonstrate age-related differences when more traditional comparisons of activity across task conditions do not show such differences. For example, activity in the medial temporal regions during semantic object encoding in the experiment by Grady, McIntosh, and Craik (2003) was similar between young and old adults. In addition, in both studies a positive correlation between hippocampal activity and performance was found in young and old groups. Thus, if only task-related modulations of activity in the hippocampus had been examined, or even just the behavioral correlations, it could have been concluded that there were no age differences involving this region. However, the functional connectivity analyses showed that the way in which the hippocampus interacted with other brain areas, particularly in the prefrontal cortex, was markedly different between young and old. This is important because it suggests that the integrated function of medial temporal and prefrontal areas changes as a function of age, even if behavioral changes reflecting dysfunction in these areas are relatively independent of one another (Glisky, Polster, & Routhieaux, 1995). These results also suggest that a lack of age differences in brain activity should be interpreted cautiously because these differences may be revealed by some types of analysis, but not others.

Neuroimaging Studies of Memory in Alzheimer's Disease

Functional neuroimaging studies carried out in the resting state have shown that the parietal cortices important for memory function are affected relatively early in the course of AD (Foster et al., 1984; Friedland et al., 1985; Haxby et al., 1985; Jagust et al., 1988; McGeer et al., 1990). In contrast, metabolic measures in frontal cortex usually are reduced later in the course of the disease (Chase, 1987; Grady et al., 1990). In addition, activity in specific brain areas known to participate in semantic and episodic memory in healthy individuals (e.g., Cabeza & Nyberg, 2000) is related to memory ability in AD patients. For example, semantic processing in patients with AD is correlated with activity in left hemisphere lateral temporal, parietal, and prefrontal regions (Desgranges et al., 1998; Grossman et al., 1997) and with activity in the left anterior prefrontal cortex (Saykin et al., 1999). Episodic memory in patients with AD is correlated with activity in temporoparietal regions (Desgranges et al., 1998; Grady et al., 1988) and in medial temporal regions (Desgranges et al., 1998; Eustache et al., 2001).

Similar to the work reviewed here on healthy aging, functional neuroimaging studies of those with early AD have found increased prefrontal activity during some cognitive tasks compared to older controls (Backman et al., 1999; Becker et al., 1996; Saykin et al., 1999; Woodard et al., 1998). In two studies of word recall, mildly demented patients showed increased activity in most of the areas activated in healthy elderly controls, although they failed to show activation in the hippocampus (Backman et al., 1999; Becker et al., 1996). However, the patients showed increased activity compared to controls in some regions of prefrontal cortex, particularly in the left hemisphere. This additional increase in prefrontal activation in the patients was interpreted as a compensatory reallocation of cognitive resources during the memory task, although the patients were significantly impaired in performance on the word memory tasks.

A study of overt verbal rehearsal of word lists also found that prefrontal cortex was utilized to a greater degree in the patients compared to age-matched controls during the rehearsal phase, although activity in other areas, such as the premotor cortex, was reduced (Woodard et al., 1998). This increased prefrontal activation was accompanied by normal rehearsal rates in the patients, but their ability to remember the words later was impaired.

Thus, all of these experiments suggested that, early in the course of AD, prefrontal activation is maintained and may even be increased above normal levels in some memory tasks. However, this redistribution of cognitive resources may not be sufficient to maintain performance at normal levels.

Studies of Functional Connectivity and Alzheimer's Disease

Examination of functional connectivity and network interactions also has been enlightening in the study of brain activity in patients with AD. In one study (Y. Stern et al., 2000), a network approach was used to examine brain activity in patients and healthy controls during the performance of a serial verbal recognition task in which study list size (SLS) was adjusted so that each subject recognized words at 75% accuracy. In the healthy older adults, higher SLS was associated with the recruitment of a network of brain areas involving left the anterior cingulate and anterior insula. Three patients also expressed this network; however, in the remaining patients, higher SLS was associated with the recruitment of an alternate network that included the left posterior temporal cortex and the posterior cingulate. Activity in this alternate network was unrelated to memory performance in the healthy controls. The use of an alternate brain network in some of the patients with AD may be a way of compensating for processing deficits. In addition, the authors suggested that the appearance of this alternate network may indicate a point at which brain disease has irreversibly altered brain function.

In addition to showing different functional networks during cognitive tasks, patients with AD also show increases or decreases in functional connections between specific brain regions compared to healthy older controls. Increased functional connectivity among regions in prefrontal cortex has been reported in patients with AD during a perceptual matching task, along with decreased correlations between prefrontal and posterior regions (Horwitz et al., 1995).

Another experiment examined functional interactions between prefrontal and medial temporal areas in AD patients during a delayed match-to-sample task for faces (Grady, Furey, et al., 2001) to examine the hypothesis that damage to medial temporal areas occurring early in the disease (e.g., Braak, Braak, & Bohl, 1993; Jack et al., 1997) would result in reduced connectivity. Controls showed increased activity in bilateral prefrontal and parietal cortex, with increasing delay between the presentation of a sample face and two choice faces. The patients had increased activity in the right prefrontal cortex and anterior cingulate with increasing delay. Increased activity in the right prefrontal cortex was associated with better memory performance in both groups. In controls, activity in the right prefrontal cortex was positively correlated with blood flow in the left prefrontal cortex, bilateral extrastriate and parietal areas, and the right hippocampus. In patients, activity in the right prefrontal cortex was correlated mainly with other prefrontal regions, but not with the hippocampus.

These results support the idea of a functional disconnection between prefrontal cortex and hippocampus in AD and suggest that memory breakdown in early AD is related to a reduction in the integrated activity within a distributed network that includes these two areas. Interestingly, the patients, but not the controls, showed increased activity in the left amygdala during the task, which also was associated with better face memory performance, suggesting that the patients may have processed the emotional content of the faces to a greater degree than did the controls. Further, the positive association between amygdala activity and memory performance in the patients suggests a possible compensatory role for an emotion-related network of regions.

A more recent study focused on the behavioral consequences of the increased functional connectivity in the frontal lobes of AD patients during semantic and episodic memory tasks (Grady, McIntosh, et al., 2003). Both patients and healthy elderly controls had increased activity in a region of the left ventrolateral prefrontal cortex during the tasks compared to a baseline task. However, the functional connectivity of this region differed markedly between groups. Controls recruited a left hemisphere network of regions, including prefrontal and temporal cortices in both the semantic and episodic tasks, whereas patients engaged a network involving bilateral dorsolateral prefrontal and posterior cortices (figure 12.2).

To determine the impact of this alternate network in the patients, the correlation between activity in the network as a whole and accuracy of task performance was assessed (Grady, McIntosh, et al., 2003). This was done by identifying those areas significantly correlated with both performance accuracy and activity in left prefrontal cortex. This analysis showed that activity in the network of regions expressed in the patients was indeed correlated with better performance on both the semantic and episodic tasks. That is, those patients who were able to engage bilateral frontal and

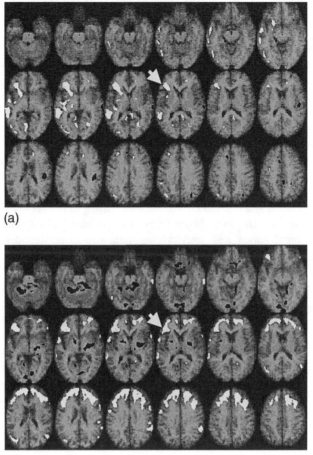

(a)

(b)

Figure 12.2. Functional connectivity of left ventrolateral prefrontal cortex (indicated by white arrows) during semantic and
episodic memory tasks is shown on standard magnetic resonance
images (MRIs) as in figure 12.1: *a*, connectivity in a group of
healthy older controls; *b*, connectivity in a group of mildly demented patients with Alzheimer's disease. The left frontal region
used for the analysis is indicated by white arrows. Positive correlations with the left frontal area are shown in white, and negative
correlations are shown in black. (Data from Grady et al., 2003.)

temporal regions to a greater degree also were able to perform more accurately on the tasks. This provides direct evidence that patients with AD can utilize additional neural resources in the prefrontal cortex, presumably those mediating executive functions, to compensate for losses caused by the degenerative process of the disease.

Issues

As stated in this chapter, the challenge presented by the data reviewed here is how to interpret recruitment of additional or different brain activity in the elderly or in patients with dementia. In some cases, this recruitment occurs during a task that the older adults are able to perform as well as young adults, leading to the suggestion that recruitment of additional areas is compensatory (Cabeza et al., 1997; Grady et al., 1994). On the other hand, others have reported differential patterns of activity in young and old adults, including greater activation of prefrontal cortex in the elderly, despite the fact that the older group performs less well on the task (Madden, Turkington, et al., 1999; Smith et al., 2001). In other experiments, direct comparison of the relation between brain activity and task performance has found that different brain areas are associated with better task performance in old compared to young adults (Grady, McIntosh, & Craik, 2003; McIntosh et al., 1999), suggesting that successful memory performance depends on the function of different sets of brain regions as we age. Still other studies have reported that activity in the same brain area can have different consequences depending on age (Grady, 2002; Rypma & D'Esposito, 2000).

This rather complex body of evidence suggests several possibilities that have yet to be clearly distinguished. First, there is some evidence to suggest that older adults might be able to recruit brain areas, particularly dorsolateral prefrontal cortex, during certain tasks to compensate for reduced activity elsewhere in the brain. As a consequence of this compensation, task performance is maintained or improved.

On the other hand, the dorsolateral prefrontal cortex increases its activity when tasks emphasize executive functions (e.g., D'Esposito et al., 1995, 1999) or become more difficult (e.g., Braver et al., 1997; Grady et al., 1996). It is possible, then, that increased prefrontal activity in the elderly under some conditions may reflect greater need or use of executive functions at lower levels of task demand than would be necessary for activation of this area in young adults. In this case, the increased activity in prefrontal cortex might not be related at all to performance on the particular task, but would reflect a type of nonselective recruitment in older adults (Logan et al., 2002).

It is also possible that greater recruitment of some brain areas could represent a failure of inhibition in older adults that would be associated with worse performance. There is no evidence for this in the prefrontal cortex in terms of accuracy of performance, although prefrontal activity has been associated with slower reaction times in the elderly (Grady, 2002).

In short, there a number of ways that different recruitment of specific brain areas could be interpreted in older adults or patients with AD, and the mechanism may vary with the particular task demands under study. Clearly, the best way to resolve this issue in the future is to systematically relate behavioral performance with brain activity and/or connectivity.

There are other aspects of age-related changes in brain activity that are still unclear. One question is whether changes in brain activity with age indicate that young and old adults use different cognitive processes to carry out the same task, even if they presumably follow the same set of instructions, or whether over time different brain areas come to be used for the same cognitive process. That is, does a given cognitive process become represented differently in the brain as we age? Another way of expressing this question is to ask if these differences seen in brain activity with age are changes in how cognition is carried out or changes in strategy use by older adults. In some sense, the answer to this question may not be a critical one because cognitive strategies and the brain activity that mediates them are very closely intertwined. Researchers in the field of functional neuroimaging routinely make inferences from cognitive strategy to brain area and vice versa, and it is not clear if the two can be separated.

A more reasonable question to ask may be which comes first, the change in brain function necessitating a change in strategy or a change in strategy that is reflected in brain activity. Unfortunately, it may be very difficult to distinguish between these two alternatives except by longitudinal studies. This raises an additional question as to when in the life span these changes occur. It is likely that the differences in brain activity seen in older adults have developed gradually over time, but it is not known at what age these changes would begin. It is conceivable that our brains are continually changing over the life span with new experiences and as new information is acquired, and that the effects of advanced age are just a part of this evolution. Longitudinal studies would address this problem, but given the difficulty of doing these, studying a middle-aged group along with a young and old sample would begin to address this issue.

Finally, there are issues specific to connectivity studies that have yet to be resolved. For example, results to date indicate that older adults engage different brain networks even when their performance on the task in question is statistically equivalent to that seen in young adults. This raises the question of whether old and young groups will *always* be different in terms of their cognitive networks or whether there are some task conditions in which these would be the same. It is possible, and perhaps likely, that for simple perceptual or sensorimotor tasks, such as pressing a button to a specified stimulus, the recruited network would not differ with age, but this has not been tested. It is clear there must be constraints on the degree to which networks can be altered, as well as aspects that remain invariant with age, but these limits have not been determined. In addition, most tasks involve more than one cognitive process as well as motor components, so that multiple networks are probably active simultaneously. Little is known about how these processes and networks interact with one another in young adults, much less in older adults.

Another interesting question is the extent to which the network alterations seen in older adults are caused by changes in the function of the brain regions themselves or to changes in the white matter tracts that connect the regions. That is, communication between cortical regions could be reduced or altered because the neurons in the regions themselves have altered function or because the fibers that connect them are damaged or less efficient. Changes with age in white matter, and the impact of these on cognition, are well documented (e.g., DeCarli et al., 1995; Garde et al., 2000; Gunning-Dixon & Raz, 2000; Pfefferbaum et al., 2000), but how these changes affect functional connectivity of gray matter regions during cognitive tasks is unknown.

Conclusions

It is clear from this volume that the cognitive neuroscience of aging is a complex but exciting area of study. Functional neuroimaging has provided some intriguing insights and provided us with some new challenges as well. The use of network approaches to image analysis has, in particular, provided information about how brain areas work together to mediate memory function and how these networks change with age or with degenerative brain disease. Perhaps the most important use of this approach is to examine how changes in the functional organization of these networks have had an impact on the ability of individuals to remember new information. Evidence to date would suggest that increased recruitment of the dorsolateral prefrontal cortex and functional interactions between dorsolateral prefrontal and medial temporal regions are associated with better memory performance in older adults. These alterations in the memory networks may thus be compensatory, at least for some types of tasks. The clear goals of future research will be to understand the task conditions that promote this compensation, the role of the various brain areas in aiding memory function, and how these compensatory mechanisms can be elicited to enhance rehabilitation efforts.

Acknowledgments   This work was supported in part by the Canadian Institutes of Health Research and the Alzheimer Society of Canada.

References

Aertsen, A. M., Gerstein, G. L., Habib, M. K., & Palm, G. (1989). Dynamics of neuronal firing correlation: Modulation of "effective connectivity." *Journal of Neurophysiology*, *61*, 900–917.

Allan, K., Dolan, R. J., Fletcher, P. C., & Rugg, M. D. (2000). The role of the right anterior prefrontal cortex in episodic retrieval. *Neuroimage*, *11*, 217–227.

Anderson, N. D., Iidaka, T., Cabeza, R., Kapur, S., McIntosh, A. R., & Craik, F. I. M. (2000). The effects of divided attention on encoding- and retrieval related brain activity: A PET study of younger and older adults. *Journal of Cognitive Neuroscience*, *12*, 775–792.

Andreasen, N. C., O'Leary, D. S., Arndt, S., Cizadlo, T., Hurtig, R., Rezai, K., et al. (1995). Short-term and long-term verbal memory: A positron emission tomography study. *Proceedings of the National Academy of Science of the United States of America*, *92*, 5111–5115.

Backman, L., Almkvist, O., Andersson, J., Nordberg, A., Winblad, B., Reineck, R., et al. (1997). Brain activation in young and older adults during implicit and explicit retrieval. *Journal of Cognitive Neuroscience*, *9*, 378–391.

Backman, L., Andersson, J. L. R., Nyberg, L., Winblad, B., Nordberg, A., & Almkvist, O. (1999). Brain regions associated with episodic retrieval in normal aging and Alzheimer's disease. *Neurology, 52,* 1861–1870.

Balota, D. A., Dolan, P. O., & Duchek, J. M. (2000). Memory changes in healthy older adults. In E. Tulving & F. I. M. Craik (Eds.), *The Oxford handbook of memory* (pp. 395–409). New York: Oxford University Press.

Becker, J. T., Mintun, M. A., Aleva, K., Wiseman, M. B., Nichols, T., & DeKosky, S. T. (1996). Compensatory reallocation of brain resources supporting verbal episodic memory in Alzheimer's disease. *Neurology, 46,* 692–700.

Becker, J. T., Mintun, M. A., Diehl, D. J., Dobkin, J., Martidis, A., Madoff, D. C., et al. (1994). Functional neuroanatomy of verbal free recall: A replication study. *Human Brain Mapping, 1,* 284–292.

Binetti, G., Magni, E., Cappa, S. F., Padovani, A., Bianchetti, A., & Trabucchi, M. (1995). Semantic memory in Alzheimer's disease: An analysis of category fluency. *Journal of Clinical and Experimental Neuropsychology, 17,* 82–89.

Blaxton, T. A., Bookheimer, S. Y., Zeffiro, T. A., Figlozzi, C. M., Gaillard, W. D., & Theodore, W. H. (1996). Functional mapping of human memory using PET: Comparisons of conceptual and perceptual tasks. *Canadian Journal of Experimental Psychology, 50,* 42–56.

Braak, H., Braak, E., & Bohl, J. (1993). Staging of Alzheimer-related cortical destruction. *European Neurology, 33,* 403–408.

Braver, T. S., Cohen, J. D., Nystrom, L. E., Jonides, J., Smith, E. E., & Noll, D. C. (1997). A parametric study of prefrontal cortex involvement in human working memory. *NeuroImage, 5,* 49–62.

Brewer, J. B., Zhao, Z., Desmond, J. E., Glover, G. H., & Gabrieli, J. D. E. (1998). Making memories: Brain activity that predicts how well visual experience will be remembered. *Science, 281,* 1185–1187.

Buckner, R. L., Koutstaal, W., Schacter, D. L., Wagner, A. D., & Rosen, B. R. (1998). Functional-anatomic study of episodic retrieval using fMRI. I. Retrieval effort versus retrieval success. *NeuroImage, 7,* 151–162.

Buckner, R. L., Raichle, M. E., Miezin, F. M., & Petersen, S. E. (1996). Functional anatomic studies of memory retrieval for auditory words and visual pictures. *Journal of Neuroscience, 16,* 6219–6235.

Burke, D. M., & Light, L. L. (1981). Memory and aging: The role of retrieval processes. *Psychological Bulletin, 90,* 513–546.

Cabeza, R., Anderson, N. D., Houle, S., Mangels, J. A., & Nyberg, L. (2000). Age-related differences in neural activity during item and temporal-order memory retrieval: A positron emission tomography study. *Journal of Cognitive Neuroscience, 12,* 197–206.

Cabeza, R., Grady, C. L., Nyberg, L., McIntosh, A. R., Tulving, E., Kapur, S., et al. (1997). Age-related differences in neural activity during memory encoding and retrieval: A positron emission tomography study. *Journal of Neuroscience, 17,* 391–400.

Cabeza, R., & Nyberg, L. (2000). Imaging cognition II: An empirical review of 275 PET and fMRI studies. *Journal of Cognitive Neuroscience, 12,* 1–47.

Chan, A. S., Butters, N., & Salmon, D. P. (1997). The deterioration of semantic networks in patients with Alzheimer's disease: A cross-sectional study. *Neuropsychologia, 35,* 241–248.

Chase, T. N. (1987). Cortical glucose utilization patterns in primary degenerative dementia of the anterior and posterior types. *Archives of Gerontology and Geriatrics, 6,* 289–297.

Chertkow, H., & Bub, D. (1990). Semantic memory loss in dementia of Alzheimer's type. What do various measures measure? *Brain, 113*(Part 2), 397–417.

Courtney, S. M., Petit, L., Maisog, J. M., Ungerleider, L. G., & Haxby, J. V. (1998). An area specialized for spatial working memory in human frontal cortex. *Science, 279,* 1347–1351.

Craik, F. I. M., & Byrd, M. (1982). Aging and cognitive deficits: The role of attentional resources. In F. I. M. Craik & S. Trehub (Eds.), *Aging and cognitive processes* (pp. 191–211). New York: Plenum Press.

Craik, F. I. M., & Jennings, J. M. (1992). Human memory. In F. I. M. Craik & T. A. Salthouse (Eds.), *The handbook of aging and cognition* (pp. 51–110). Hillsdale, NJ: Erlbaum.

Craik, F. I. M., & McDowd, J. M. (1987). Age differences in recall and recognition. *Journal of Experimental Psychology: Learning, Memory and Cognition, 13,* 474–479.

Dalla Barba, G., Parlato, V., Jobert, A., Samson, Y., & Pappata, S. (1998). Cortical networks implicated in semantic and episodic memory: common or unique? *Cortex, 34,* 547–561.

DeCarli, C., Murphy, D. G., Tranh, M., Grady, C. L., Haxby, J. V., Gillette, J. A., et al. (1995). The effect of white matter hyperintensity volume on brain structure, cognitive performance, and cerebral metabolism of glucose in 51 healthy adults. *Neurology, 45,* 2077–2084.

Della-Maggiore, V., Sekuler, A. B., Grady, C. L., Bennett, P. J., Sekuler, R., & McIntosh, A. R. (2000). Corticolimbic interactions associated with performance on a short-term memory task are modified by age. *Journal of Neuroscience, 20,* 8410–8416.

Desgranges, B., Baron, J. C., de la Sayette, V., Petit-Taboue, M. C., Benali, K., Landeau, B., et al. (1998). The neural substrates of memory systems impairment in Alzheimer's disease. A PET study of resting brain glucose utilization. *Brain, 121*(Part 4), 611–631.

D'Esposito, M., Aguirre, G. K., Zarahn, E., Ballard, D., Shin, R. K., & Lease, J. (1998). Functional fMRI studies of spatial and nonspatial working memory. *Cognitive Brain Research, 7,* 1–13.

D'Esposito, M., Detre, J. A., Alsop, D. C., Shin, R. K., Atlas, S., & Grossman, M. (1995). The neural basis of the central executive system of working memory. *Nature, 378,* 279–281.

D'Esposito, M., Postle, B. R., Ballard, D., & Lease, J. (1999). Maintenance versus manipulation of information held in working memory: An event-related fMRI study. *Brain and Cognition, 41,* 66–86.

Duzel, E., Cabeza, R., Picton, T. W., Yonelinas, A. P., Scheich, H., Heinze, H. J., et al. (1999). Task-related and item-related brain processes of memory retrieval. *Proceedings of the National Academy of Science of the United States of America, 96,* 1794–1799.

Eustache, F., Desgranges, B., Giffard, B., de la Sayette, V., & Baron, J. C. (2001). Entorhinal cortex disruption causes memory deficit in early Alzheimer's disease as shown by PET. *NeuroReport, 12,* 683–685.

Fernandez, G., Brewer, J. B., Zhao, Z., Glover, G. H., & Gabrieli, J. D. (1999). Level of sustained entorhinal activity at study correlates with subsequent cued-recall performance: A functional magnetic resonance imaging study with high acquisition rate. *Hippocampus, 9,* 35–44.

Fletcher, P. C., Shallice, T., Frith, C. D., Frackowiak, R. S., & Dolan, R. J. (1998). The functional roles of prefrontal cortex in episodic memory. II. Retrieval. *Brain, 121*(Part 7), 1249–1256.

Foster, N. L., Chase, T. N., Mansi, L., Brooks, R., Fedio, P., Patronas, N. J., et al. (1984). Cortical abnormalities in Alzheimer's disease. *Annals of Neurology, 16,* 649–654.

Friedland, R. P., Budinger, T. F., Koss, E., & Ober, B. A. (1985). Alzheimer's disease: Anterior-posterior and lateral hemispheric alterations in cortical glucose utilization. *Neuroscience Letters, 53,* 235–240.

Friston, K. J. (1994). Functional and effective connectivity: A synthesis. *Human Brain Mapping, 2,* 56–78.

Friston, K. J., Frith, C. D., Liddle, P. F., & Frackowiak, R. S. J. (1993). Functional connectivity: The principal-component analysis of large (PET) data sets. *Journal of Cerebral Blood Flow and Metabolism, 13*, 5–14.

Garde, E., Mortensen, E. L., Krabbe, K., Rostrup, E., & Larsson, H. B. (2000). Relation between age-related decline in intelligence and cerebral white- matter hyperintensities in healthy octogenarians: A longitudinal study. *Lancet, 356*, 628–634.

Giffard, B., Desgranges, B., Nore-Mary, F., Lalevee, C., de la Sayette, V., Pasquier, F., et al. (2001). The nature of semantic memory deficits in Alzheimer's disease: New insights from hyperpriming effects. *Brain, 124*(Part 8), 1522–1532.

Glisky, E. L., Polster, M. R., & Routhieaux, B. C. (1995). Double dissociation between item and source memory. *Psychology and Aging, 9*, 229–235.

Grady, C. L. (2002). Age-related differences in face processing: A meta-analysis of three functional neuroimaging experiments. *Canadian Journal of Experimental Psychology, 56*, 208–220.

Grady, C. L., Bernstein, L., Siegenthaler, A., & Beig, S. (2002). The effects of encoding task on age-related differences in the functional neuroanatomy of face memory. *Psychology and Aging, 17*, 7–23.

Grady, C. L., Furey, M. L., Pietrini, P., Horwitz, B., & Rapoport, S. I. (2001). Altered brain functional connectivity and impaired short term memory in Alzheimer's disease. *Brain, 124*, 739–756.

Grady, C. L., Haxby, J. V., Horwitz, B., Sundaram, M., Berg, G., Schapiro, M. B., et al. (1988). Longitudinal study of the early neuropsychological and cerebral metabolic changes in dementia of the Alzheimer type. *Journal of Clinical and Experimental Neuropsychology, 10*, 576–596.

Grady, C. L., Haxby, J. V., Schapiro, M. B., Gonzalez-Aviles, A., Kumar, A., Ball, M. J., et al. (1990). Subgroups in dementia of the Alzheimer type identified using positron emission tomography. *Journal of Neuropsychiatry and Clinical Neurosciences, 2*, 373–384.

Grady, C. L., Horwitz, B., Pietrini, P., Mentis, M. J., Ungerleider, L. G., Rapoport, S. I., et al. (1996). The effect of task difficulty on cerebral blood flow during perceptual matching of faces. *Human Brain Mapping, 4*, 227–239.

Grady, C. L., Maisog, J. M., Horwitz, B., Ungerleider, L. G., Mentis, M. J., Salerno, J. A., et al. (1994). Age-related changes in cortical blood flow activation during visual processing of faces and location. *Journal of Neuroscience, 14*, 1450–1462.

Grady, C. L., McIntosh, A. R., Beig, S., & Craik, F. I. M. (2001). An examination of the effects of stimulus type, encoding strategy, and functional connectivity on the role of right prefrontal cortex in recognition memory. *NeuroImage, 14*, 556–571.

Grady, C. L., McIntosh, A. R., Beig, S., Keightley, M. L., Burian, H., & Black, S. E. (2003). Evidence from functional neuroimaging of a compensatory prefrontal network in Alzheimer disease. *Journal of Neuroscience, 23*, 986–993.

Grady, C. L., McIntosh, A. R., Bookstein, F., Horwitz, B., Rapoport, S. I., & Haxby, J. V. (1998). Age-related changes in regional cerebral blood flow during working memory for faces. *NeuroImage, 8*, 409–425.

Grady, C. L., McIntosh, A. R., & Craik, F. I. (2003). Age-related differences in the functional connectivity of the hippocampus during memory encoding. *Hippocampus, 13*, 572–586.

Grady, C. L., McIntosh, A. R., Horwitz, B., Maisog, J. M., Ungerleider, L. G., Mentis, M. J., et al. (1995). Age-related reductions in human recognition memory due to impaired encoding. *Science, 269*, 218–221.

Grady, C. L., McIntosh, A. R., Rajah, M. N., Beig, S., & Craik, F. I. M. (1999). The effects of age on the neural correlates of episodic encoding. *Cerebral Cortex, 9*, 805–814.

Grasby, P. M., Frith, C. D., Friston, K. J., Bench, C., Frackowiak, R. S. J., & Dolan, R. J.

(1993). Functional mapping of brain areas implicated in auditory-verbal memory function. *Brain, 116,* 1–20.

Grossman, M., Payer, F., Onishi, K., White-Devine, T., Morrison, D., D'Esposito, M., et al. (1997). Constraints on the cerebral basis for semantic processing from neuroimaging studies of Alzheimer's disease. *Journal of Neurology, Neurosurgery, and Psychiatry, 63,* 152–158.

Gunning-Dixon, F. M., & Raz, N. (2000). The cognitive correlates of white matter abnormalities in normal aging: A quantitative review. *Neuropsychology, 14*(2), 224–232.

Hart, R. P., Kwentus, J. A., Harkins, S. W., & Taylor, J. R. (1988). Rate of forgetting in mild Alzheimer's-type dementia. *Brain and Cognition, 7,* 31–38.

Hasher, L., & Zacks, R. T. (1988). Working memory, comprehension, and aging: A review and a new view. In G. H. Bower (Ed.), *The psychology of learning and motivation* (Vol. 22, pp. 193–225). San Diego, CA: Academic Press.

Haxby, J. V., Duara, R., Grady, C. L., Rapoport, S. I., & Cutler, N. R. (1985). Relations between neuropsychological and cerebral metabolic asymmetries in early Alzheimer's disease. *Journal of Cerebral Blood Flow and Metabolism, 5,* 193–200.

Haxby, J. V., Petit, L., Ungerleider, L. G., & Courtney, S. (2000). Distinguishing the functional roles of multiple regions in distributed neural systems for visual working memory. *NeuroImage, 11,* 145–156.

Haxby, J. V., Ungerleider, L. G., Horwitz, B., Maisog, J. M., Rapoport, S. I., & Grady, C. L. (1996). Storage and retrieval of new memories for faces in the intact human brain. *Proceedings of the National Academy of Science of the United States of America, 93,* 922–927.

Henson, R. N. A., Shallice, T., & Dolan, R. J. (1999). Right prefrontal cortex and episodic memory retrieval: A functional MRI test of the monitoring hypothesis. *Brain, 122,* 1367–1381.

Hodges, J. R., Salmon, D. P., & Butters, N. (1992). Semantic memory impairment in Alzheimer's disease: Failure of access or degraded knowledge? *Neuropsychologia, 30,* 301–314.

Horwitz, B. (1994). Data analysis paradigms for metabolic-flow data: Combining neural modeling and functional neuroimaging. *Human Brain Mapping, 2,* 112–122.

Horwitz, B., McIntosh, A. R., Haxby, J. V., Furey, M., Salerno, J., Schapiro, M. B., et al. (1995). Network analysis of PET-mapped visual pathways in Alzheimer type dementia. *NeuroReport, 6,* 2287–2292.

Jack, C. R., Jr., Petersen, R. C., Xu, Y. C., Waring, S. C., O'Brien, P. C., Tangalos, E. G., et al. (1997). Medial temporal atrophy on MRI in normal aging and very mild Alzheimer's disease. *Neurology, 49,* 786–794.

Jacobs, D. M., Sano, M., Dooneief, G., Marder, K., Bell, K. L., & Stern, Y. (1995). Neuropsychological detection and characterization of preclinical Alzheimer's disease. *Neurology, 45,* 957–962.

Jagust, W. J., Friedland, R. P., Budinger, T. F., Koss, E., & Ober, B. (1988). Longitudinal studies of regional cerebral metabolism in Alzheimer's disease. *Neurology, 38,* 909–912.

Jonides, J., Marshuetz, C., Smith, E. E., Reuter-Lorenz, P. A., Koeppe, R. A., & Hartley, A. (2000). Age differences in behavior and PET activation reveal differences in interference resolution in verbal working memory. *Journal of Cognitive Neuroscience, 12,* 188–196.

Kelley, W. M., Miezin, F. M., McDermott, K. B., Buckner, R. L., Raichle, M. E., Cohen, N. J., et al. (1998). Hemispheric specialization in human dorsal frontal cortex and medial temporal lobe for verbal and nonverbal memory encoding. *Neuron, 20,* 927–936.

Kemper, T. L. (1994). Neuroanatomical and neuropathological changes during aging and in dementia. In M. L. Albert & E. J. E. Knoepfel (Eds.), *Clinical neurology of aging* (2 ed., pp. 3–67). New York: Oxford University Press.

Kirchhoff, B. A., Wagner, A. D., Maril, A., & Stern, C. E. (2000). Prefrontal-temporal circuitry for episodic encoding and subsequent memory. *Journal of Neuroscience, 20,* 6173–6180.

Kohler, S., Moscovitch, M., Winocur, G., Houle, S., & McIntosh, A. R. (1998). Networks of domain-specific and general regions involved in episodic memory for spatial location and object identity. *Neuropsychologia, 36,* 129–142.

Kohler, S., Moscovitch, M., Winocur, G., & McIntosh, A. R. (2000). Episodic encoding and recognition of pictures and words: Role of the human medial temporal lobes. *Acta Psychologica, 105,* 159–179.

Lepage, M., Ghaffar, O., Nyberg, L., & Tulving, E. (2000). Prefrontal cortex and episodic memory retrieval mode. *Proceedings of the National Academy of Science of the United States of America, 97,* 506–511.

Logan, J. M., Sanders, A. L., Snyder, A. Z., Morris, J. C., & Buckner, R. L. (2002). Under-recruitment and nonselective recruitment: Dissociable neural mechanisms associated with aging. *Neuron, 33,* 827–840.

Madden, D. J., Gottlob, L. R., Denny, L. L., Turkington, T. G., Provenzale, J. M., Hawk, T. C., et al. (1999). Aging and recognition memory: Changes in regional cerebral blood flow associated with components of reaction time distributions. *Journal of Cognitive Neuroscience, 11,* 511–520.

Madden, D. J., Turkington, T. G., Provenzale, J. M., Denny, L. L., Hawk, T. C., Gottlob, L. R., et al. (1999). Adult age differences in the functional neuroanatomy of verbal recognition memory. *Human Brain Mapping, 7,* 115–135.

Martinkauppi, S., Rama, P., Aronen, H. J., Korvenoja, A., & Carlson, S. (2000). Working memory of auditory localization. *Cerebral Cortex, 10,* 889–898.

McDermott, K. B., Buckner, R. L., Petersen, S. E., Kelley, W. M., & Sanders, A. L. (1999). Set- and code-specific activation in frontal cortex: An fMRI study of encoding and retrieval of faces and words. *Journal of Cognitive Neuroscience, 11,* 631–640.

McDermott, K. B., Jones, T. C., Petersen, S. E., Lageman, S. K., & Roediger, H. L. (2000). Retrieval success is accompanied by enhanced activation in anterior prefrontal cortex during recognition memory: An event-related fMRI study. *Journal of Cognitive Neuroscience, 12,* 965–976.

McDermott, K. B., Ojemann, J. G., Petersen, S. E., Ollinger, J. M., Snyder, A. Z., Akbudak, E., et al. (1999). Direct comparison of episodic encoding and retrieval of words: An event-related fMRI study. *Memory, 7,* 661–678.

McGeer, E. G., Peppard, R. P., McGeer, P. L., Tuokko, H., Crockett, D., Parks, R., et al. (1990). 18-Fluorodeoxyglucose positron emission tomography studies in presumed Alzheimer cases, including 13 serial scans. *Canadian Journal of the Neurological Sciences, 17,* 1–11.

McIntosh, A. R. (1999). Mapping cognition to the brain through neural interactions. *Memory, 7,* 523–548.

McIntosh, A. R., & Gonzalez-Lima, F. (1994). Structural equation modeling and its application to network analysis in functional brain imaging. *Human Brain Mapping, 2,* 2–22.

McIntosh, A. R., Sekuler, A. B., Penpeci, C., Rajah, M. N., Grady, C. L., Sekuler, R., et al. (1999). Recruitment of unique neural systems to support visual memory in normal aging. *Current Biology, 9,* 1275–1278.

Mitchell, K. J., Johnson, M. K., Raye, C. L., & D'Esposito, M. (2000). fMRI evidence of age-related hippocampal dysfunction in feature binding in working memory. *Cognitive Brain Research, 10,* 197–206.

Moeller, J. R., & Strother, S. C. (1991). A regional covariance approach to the analysis of functional patterns in positron emission tomographic data. *Journal Cerebral Blood Flow and Metabolism, 11,* A121–A135.

Moscovitch, M., Kapur, S., Kohler, S., & Houle, S. (1995). Distinct neural correlates of visual long-term memory for spatial location and object identity: A positron emission tomography study in humans. *Proceedings of the National Academy of Science of the United States of America, 92,* 3721–3725.

Moss, M. B., Albert, M. S., Butters, N., & Payne, M. (1986). Differential patterns of memory loss among patients with Alzheimer's disease, Huntington's disease, and alcoholic Korsakoff's syndrome. *Archives of Neurology, 43,* 239–246.

Nyberg, L., Cabeza, R., & Tulving, E. (1996). PET studies of encoding and retrieval: The HERA model. *Psychonomic Bulletin and Review, 3,* 135–148.

Nyberg, L., Persson, J., Habib, R., Tulving, E., McIntosh, A. R., Cabeza, R., et al. (2000). Large scale neurocognitive networks underlying episodic memory. *Journal of Cognitive Neuroscience, 12,* 163–173.

Ober, B. A., & Shenaut, G. K. (1999). Well-organized conceptual domains in Alzheimer's disease. *Journal of the International Neuropsychological Society, 5,* 676–684.

Otten, L. J., Henson, R., & Rugg, M. D. (2001). Depth of processing effects on neural correlates of memory encoding. *Brain, 124,* 399–412.

Owen, A. M., Stern, C. E., Look, R. B., Tracey, I., Rosen, B. R., & Petrides, M. (1998). Functional organization of spatial and nonspatial working memory processing within the human lateral frontal cortex. *Proceedings of the National Academy of Science of the United States of America, 95,* 7721–7726.

Pfefferbaum, A., Sullivan, E. V., Hedehus, M., Lim, K. O., Adalsteinsson, E., & Moseley, M. (2000). Age-related decline in brain white matter anisotropy measured with spatially corrected echo-planar diffusion tensor imaging. *Magnetic Resonance in Medicine, 44,* 259–268.

Price, B. H., Gurvit, H., Weintraub, S., Geula, C., Leimkuhler, E., & Mesulam, M. (1993). Neuropsychological patterns and language deficits in 20 consecutive cases of autopsy-confirmed Alzheimer's disease. *Archives of Neurology, 50,* 931–937.

Reuter-Lorenz, P. A., Jonides, J., Smith, E. E., Hartley, A., Miller, A., Marshuetz, C., et al. (2000). Age differences in the frontal lateralization of verbal and spatial working memory revealed by PET. *Journal of Cognitive Neuroscience, 12,* 174–187.

Rugg, M. D., Fletcher, P. C., Frith, C. D., Frackowiak, R. S. J., & Dolan, R. J. (1996). Differential activation of the prefrontal cortex in successful and unsuccessful memory retrieval. *Brain, 119,* 2073–2084.

Ryan, L., Nadel, L., Keil, K., Putnam, K., Schnyer, D., Trouard, T., et al. (2001). Hippocampal complex and retrieval of recent and very remote autobiographical memories: Evidence from functional magnetic resonance imaging in neurologically intact people. *Hippocampus, 11,* 707–714.

Rypma, B., & D'Esposito, M. (2000). Isolating the neural mechanisms of age-related changes in human working memory. *Nature Neuroscience, 3,* 509–515.

Rypma, B., Prabhakaran, V., Desmond, J. E., & Gabrieli, J. D. (2001). Age differences in prefrontal cortical activity in working memory. *Psychology and Aging, 16,* 371–384.

Saykin, A. J., Flashman, L. A., Frutiger, S. A., Johnson, S. C., Mamourian, A. C., Moritz, C. H., et al. (1999). Neuroanatomic substrates of semantic memory impairment in Alzheimer's disease: Patterns of functional MRI activation. *Journal of the International Neuropsychological Society, 5,* 377–392.

Schacter, D. L., Alpert, N. M., Savage, C. R., Rauch, S. L., & Albert, M. S. (1996). Conscious recollection and the human hippocampal formation: Evidence from positron emission tomography. *Proceedings of the National Academy of Science of the United States of America, 93,* 321–325.

Schacter, D. L., Savage, C. R., Alpert, N. M., Rauch, S. L., & Albert, M. S. (1996). The role of hippocampus and frontal cortex in age-related memory changes: A PET study. *NeuroReport, 7,* 1165–1169.

Schmidt, D., Krause, B. J., Mottaghy, F. M., Halsband, U., Herzog, H., Tellmann, L., et al.

(2002). Brain systems engaged in encoding and retrieval of word-pair associates independent of their imagery content or presentation modalities. *Neuropsychologia, 40,* 457–470.

Schumacher, E. H., Lauber, E., Awh, E., Jonides, J., Smith, E. E., & Koeppe, R. A. (1996). PET evidence for an amodal verbal working memory system. *NeuroImage, 3,* 79–88.

Smith, E. E., Geva, A., Jonides, J., Miller, A., Reuter-Lorenz, P., & Koeppe, R. A. (2001). The neural basis of task-switching in working memory: Effects of performance and aging. *Proceedings of the National Academy of Sciences of the United States of America, 98,* 2095–2100.

Stebbins, G. T., Carrillo, M. C., Dorfman, J., Dirksen, C., Desmond, J. E., Turner, D. A., et al. (2002). Aging effects on memory encoding in the frontal lobes. *Psychology and Aging, 17,* 44–55.

Stern, C. E., Corkin, S., Gonzalez, R. G., Guimaraes, A. R., Baker, J. R., Jennings, P. J., et al. (1996). The hippocampal formation participates in novel picture encoding: Evidence from functional magnetic resonance imaging. *Proceedings of the National Academy of Science of the United States of America, 93,* 8660–8665.

Stern, Y., Moeller, J. R., Anderson, K. E., Luber, B., Zubin, N. R., DiMauro, A. A., et al. (2000). Different brain networks mediate task performance in normal aging and AD: Defining compensation. *Neurology, 55,* 1291–1297.

Strange, B. A., Otten, L. J., Josephs, O., Rugg, M. D., & Dolan, R. J. (2002). Dissociable human perirhinal, hippocampal, and parahippocampal roles during verbal encoding. *Journal of Neuroscience, 22,* 523–528.

Tulving, E. (1983). *Elements of episodic memory.* New York: Oxford University Press.

Tulving, E., Kapur, S., Craik, F. I. M., Moscovitch, M., & Houle, S. (1994). Hemspheric encoding/retrieval asymmetry in episodic memory: Positron emission tomography findings. *Proceedings of the National Academy of Science of the United States of America, 91,* 2016–2020.

Tulving, E., Kapur, S., Markowitsch, H. J., Craik, F. I. M., Habib, R., & Houle, S. (1994). Neuroanatomical correlates of retrieval in episodic memory: Auditory sentence recognition. *Proceedings of the National Academy of Science of the United States of America, 91,* 2012–2015.

Wagner, A. D., Desmond, J. E., Glover, G. H., & Gabrieli, J. D. (1998). Prefrontal cortex and recognition memory. Functional-MRI evidence for context-dependent retrieval processes. *Brain, 121*(Part 10), 1985–2002.

Wagner, A. D., Schacter, D. L., Rotte, M., Koutstaal, W., Maril, A., Dale, A. M., et al. (1998). Building memories: Remembering and forgetting of verbal experiences as predicted by brain activity. *Science, 281,* 1188–1191.

Welsh, K., Butters, N., Hughes, J., Mohs, R., & Heyman, A. (1991). Detection of abnormal memory decline in mild cases of Alzheimer's disease using CERAD neuropsychological measures. *Archives of Neurology, 48,* 278–281.

Woodard, J. L., Grafton, S. T., Votaw, J. R., Green, R. C., Dobraski, M. E., & Hoffman, J. M. (1998). Compensatory recruitment of neural resources during overt rehearsal of word lists in Alzheimer's disease. *Neuropsychology, 12,* 491–504.

Zacks, R. T., Hasher, L., & Li, K. Z. H. (2000). Human memory. In F. I. M. Craik & T. A. Salthouse (Eds.), *The handbook of aging and cognition* (2nd ed., pp. 200–230). Mahwah, NJ: Erlbaum.

Zatorre, R. J., Evans, A. C., & Meyer, E. (1994). Neural mechanisms underlying melodic perception and memory for pitch. *Journal of Neuroscience, 14,* 1908–1919.

Zec, R. F. (1993). Neuropsychological functioning in Alzheimer's disease. In R. W. Parks, R. F. Zec, & R. S. Wilson (Eds.), *Neuropsychology of Alzheimer's disease and other dementias* (pp. 3–80). New York: Oxford University Press.

13

Cognitive Training in Healthy Aging
A Cognitive Neuroscience Perspective

Lars Nyberg

> In the long run, assessment of maximum reserve capacity aspires to iden-
> tify biological boundaries of the plasticity of development.
>
> —P. B. Baltes (1987, p. 618)

A theoretical perspective on life span development holds that there is much plasticity in the course of development, with *plasticity* defined as within-person variability designating the potential for various forms of behavior or development (Baltes, 1987). The results from a number of studies provide empirical evidence that sizable plasticity is evident in old age. On the other hand, there seems to be substantial age differences in plasticity, such that the potential to benefit from certain forms of intervention is greater in younger age. As illustrated by the quotation above, it is therefore important to search for potential as well as constraints and to identify biological boundaries of plasticity.

This chapter is written along these lines. The first part of the review section is concerned with studies of the effectiveness of various forms of cognitive training on the performance of younger and older adults. The second part of the review presents results from structural and functional neuroimaging studies that may speak to the issue of which neurobiological factors explain reduced plasticity in older age. Finally, in the concluding section, some important and unresolved issues for future research are highlighted.

Review of Empirical Studies

It should be noted that this review is selective rather than comprehensive. By presenting the results of relevant studies, the goal of the review is fourfold, to illustrate (1) the potential for plasticity in older age, (2) limitations of plasticity in older age,

(3) cognitive explanations of reduced plasticity in older age, and (4) neuroanatomical correlates of reduced plasticity in older age.

Potential for Plasticity in Older Age

A large-scale study illustrates the existence of plasticity in older age (Ball et al., 2002). In this study, 2832 persons between 65 and 94 years of age were assigned to one of four different groups. Three of the groups involved intervention, and the fourth was a control group. Each intervention group received 10 sessions of intervention. All of the interventions were conducted in small group settings over 5- to 6-week periods. Sessions 1–5 involved strategy instruction and practice, and the remaining 5 sessions involved additional practice on the acquired strategy.

One form of intervention consisted of memory training, specifically verbal episodic memory. The memory training involved learning of various mnemonic strategies for remembering episodic information, such as word lists and text material. Examples of such strategies included learning to organize information into meaningful categories and forming visual images and mental associations. The exercises were done on laboratorylike tasks (e.g., recalling a list of nouns) as well as on more real-life type of tasks (e.g., recalling a shopping list).

The second form of intervention consisted of reasoning training. This training was focused on the ability to solve problems that follow a serial pattern. As in the memory training, laboratory-like (e.g., identifying the pattern in a number series) as well as real-life (e.g., understanding travel schedules) tasks were used. The participants were taught strategies to identify patterns in the various sequences presented.

The third form of intervention consisted of speed-of-processing training. This training was focused on visual search skills and fast identification of visual information in a divided attention setting. The participants received training on computerized speed tasks, and difficulty was successively increased when the participants received certain levels of criterion performance.

For about 60% of the participants in each group, booster training was offered 11 months after the initial training. The booster training was given in four 75-min sessions over a 2- to 3-week period.

To evaluate the effects of the interventions, a number of outcome measures were used. These could be divided into two basic categories: proximal (cognitive abilities) and primary (daily function). Cognitive abilities tested memory, reasoning, and speed of processing (each ability domain was measured by two to three tests). Daily function was assessed by tests of everyday problem solving, everyday speed, activities of daily living, and driving habits.

It was hypothesized that each intervention group would perform better than the other groups on their primary and proximal outcomes (e.g., training on speed of processing would lead to better outcome on proximal and primary tests of speed of processing than, for example, memory training). In addition, it was hypothesized that booster training would lead to enhanced performance. The study produced a multitude of results, but, briefly, the results supported the hypotheses. In particular, the results from the proximal outcome measures were strong, and positive intervention effects on these measures were seen after 2 years. A possible reason for weaker intervention effects on the primary outcome measures is that there were minimal functional declines over the 2-year period (many performed at ceiling). Longer follow-up may reveal positive effects of the intervention on the primary measures as well.

The results of the Ball et al. (2002) study clearly support the effectiveness and duration of cognitive training interventions in improving targeted cognitive abilities. These results converge with those from a previous meta-analysis of the effectiveness of memory training for the elderly (Verhaeghen, Marcoen, & Goossens, 1992). Based on the results of their analysis, Verhaeghen and colleagues concluded that "it is obvious that even in old age memory remains plastic" (p. 248). This conclusion appears solid because it was based on a total sample of 1,539 persons with an estimated mean age of 69 years. Of interest is that, in comparison with mere retesting or placebo treatment, the performance was enhanced reliably more by mnemonic training. The studies that were included in the meta-analysis used a variety of treatments, such as concentration and attention training, external memory techniques, and problem solving. A comparison of the effectiveness of different mnemonics suggested that they did not differ much in how effective they were at enhancing the performance. It should be noted, though, that almost all mnemonics were imagery based, which may have contributed to the similarities in effect size across type of mnemonic.

Taken together, as shown in the above-discussed studies and in several others as well (see Glisky & Glisky, 1999; Stigsdotter Neely, 1994), there is robust evidence for the potential for plasticity in older age. I now turn to constraints on plasticity.

Limitations of Plasticity in Older Age

Verhaeghen and Marcoen (1996) followed up their 1992 meta-analysis and presented a meta-analytic review of the size of memory training gains for older and younger adults. The results showed that the effect sizes (pre- to posttreatment) were significantly greater for the younger adults (see figure 13.1).

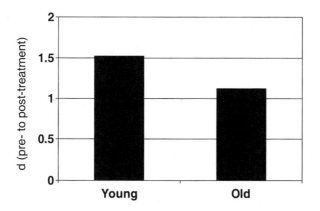

Figure 13.1. Age differences in the magnitude of pre- to posttest gain following memory training. (Based on Verhaeghen & Marcoen, 1996.)

Most of the studies in Verhaeghen and Marcoen's (1996) review involved training in the method of loci (e.g., Bower, 1970). This method involves learning to visualize a series of mental landmarks (e.g., places along one's route to work). When the landmarks have been acquired, to-be-remembered information is linked to the various loci at the time of encoding. At test, the landmarks are mentally revisited in order, and the information associated with each locus is retrieved. Both younger and older adults benefit from the method of loci (i.e., serial recall is substantially enhanced when the loci method is used), thus demonstrating plasticity. However, as summarized by Verhaeghen and Marcoen's review, age differences in memory performance tend to be greater after than before acquisition of the loci mnemonic (see figure 13.2).

Baltes and Kliegl (1992) addressed the question of whether the magnification of age differences in performance after training would exist after extensive training. That is, would older adults be able to catch up with additional practice? The answer to this question was negative. Even after a very extensive training program (38 testing and training sessions distributed over more than 1 year), age differences were considerably larger than at pretest. Based on this outcome, Baltes and Kliegl concluded: "Despite sizable developmental reserve capacity in old age, there is a robust, if not irreversible, negative age difference in some basic components of the mind relevant for the use of the method of loci in achieving superior levels of memory performance" (p. 124).

Cognitive Explanations for Reduced Plasticity in Older Age

Verhaeghen and Marcoen (1996) conducted a study on the ability of 76 older (age range 60–87 years) and 63 younger (age range 18–25 years) adults to use the method of loci. The association of the ability to use and benefit from the loci method with scores on a number of potential explanatory variables was tested. The explanatory

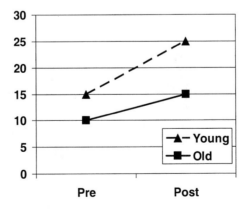

Figure 13.2. Schematic illustration of magnification of age differences in memory performance after memory training.

variables included measures of speed of mental processing, verbal and visual working memory, associative memory, spatial ability, and vividness of imagery. In addition, information concerning more specific information was gathered, including strategy use (how consistent the method of loci was used) and number of list rehearsals.

One important result was that, whereas all younger adults consistently applied the method of loci, a substantial proportion of the older adults did not comply with the instructions. Specifically, when the study time was relatively short (2 min for 25 words), 17 of the older adults (22%) did not use the loci method. When more time was allowed for study, the proportion of nonusers decreased, but even when the study time was as long as 6 min, a nonnegligible minority of the older adults (>5%) did not use the method. Importantly, those who did not use the method showed smaller gains from the intervention than did those who used the method. Thus, an important reason for magnification of age differences after memory training seems to be that some older adults do not use the mnemonic at posttest.

Path analysis was used to specify the mechanisms of plasticity in the method of loci. This analysis was limited to "users," that is, the noncompliant older adults were excluded (59 older adults were included). The results showed that several age-sensitive variables were associated with plasticity. Specifically, in both age groups, associative episodic memory had the largest influence on plasticity, number of list rehearsals was second strongest, and speed was the third most important influence. In addition, in the younger group, visual working memory had an extra effect on plasticity. It was proposed that this effect may have been related to the self-reported higher quality of the images in the young group—more visual working memory space may be necessary to form detailed images.

Taken together, the results of the Verhaeghen and Marcoen (1996) study provide evidence that noncompliance (not using the relevant strategy) and several age-related variables (associative memory, speed, and working memory) explain adult age differences in treatment gain after instruction in the loci mnemonic (see figure 13.3). This outcome can be related to the long-standing debate in the cognitive aging literature on whether age-related memory deficits are caused by a failure to engage in appropriate cognitive operations (a production deficit) or whether they reflect limita-

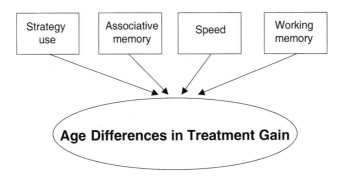

Figure 13.3. Factors influencing age differences in treatment gain after instruction in the loci mnemonic.

tions in the basic resources available for task-relevant cognitive processing (a processing deficit). As indicated by Verhaeghen and Marcoen's results, at least for plasticity, the answer may be that negative age differences reflect both a production and a processing deficiency.

The notion that processing and production deficits have a joint influence on age differences in plasticity is in good agreement with the results from other studies. For example, in a study in which older and younger adults received extensive practice on a noun pair task in which they could use a visual scanning strategy or a memory retrieval strategy, Rogers, Hertzog, and Fisk (2000) presented evidence that older adults are slower to switch to a more efficient strategy (memory retrieval). Rogers and colleagues noted that one reason why some older adults deferred use of the retrieval strategy may have been that they found it difficult to use that particular strategy (i.e., a production failure). Furthermore, they noted that age differences in speed of processing likely also played a role, and they suggested that age differences in production could indeed be caused by differences in processing speed. A similar argument was made in a study by Verhaeghen and Marcoen (1994). They concluded that age differences in using efficient strategies could be accounted for by age differences in basic cognitive processes. The interaction between processing and production factors in explaining age differences in plasticity is illustrated in figure 13.4.

In summary, the results from cognitive studies indicate that the magnification of age differences after memory training is a reflection of both a production and a processing deficit in older age that jointly contribute to negative age differences in treatment gain. Next, possible neural correlates of these deficits are discussed.

Neuroanatomical Correlates of Reduced Plasticity in Older Age

Processing Deficit

The findings from several imaging studies speak to the issue of neural correlates of an age-related processing deficit. The term *processing deficit* is used broadly to refer

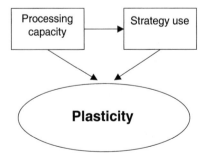

Figure 13.4. Interaction between processing and production factors in explaining age differences in plasticity.

to speed of information processing, as well as to executive functions such as working memory, inhibition, and task switching. Both speed (e.g., Salthouse, 1996) and executive functioning (e.g., Zacks, Hasher, & Li, 2000) decline with advancing age, and it has been shown that speed and working memory independently explain considerable portions of age-related variance in long-term memory function (Park et al., 1996; see also Park et al., 2002).

Results from different studies converge on an association between age-related changes in frontal cortex and a processing deficit. In one study (Rypma & D'Esposito, 2000), verbal working memory was studied with event-related functional magnetic resonance imaging (fMRI). Older and younger subjects encoded two or six letters and held these in mind during a 12-s interval. They were then presented with single letters and determined whether the letter was part of the memory set. A significant age group effect was observed in the dorsolateral prefrontal cortex (DLPFC), in which younger subjects showed greater activity during the six-letter condition. This difference was only seen during the retrieval phase. No age differences at all were seen in ventrolateral frontal cortex.

The results of the Rypma and D'Esposito study further indicated that age-related changes in DLPFC may lead to a generalized age-related slowing of behavior. Regression analyses of subjects' reaction times (RTs) during responding and activity in DLPFC showed a positive correlation for young subjects and a negative correlation for older subjects. That is, greater DLPFC activity was associated with slower performance for younger adults, but faster performance for older adults. This opposite activation–performance relationship could be a result of a reduction in neural activity in DLPFC with increasing age. In turn, in older age, higher neural activation levels may be required for achieving optimal response discriminability. In contrast, in younger age, lower levels of activity will lead to optimal performance.

The association between speed and activity in DLPFC that was indicated by the Rypma and D'Esposito (2000) findings is consistent with analyses of the relation between speed and regional brain volume. For example, Raz and colleagues (1999) collected data on regional brain volume from 60 adults between 19 and 77 years old and found a significant association between the volume of the DLPFC and speed of cognitive performance. Both DLPFC volume and speed correlated with chronological age, and path analyses suggested that age influenced DFPFC volume, which in turn influenced cognitive performance.

In addition to DLPFC, age-related decreases in speed have been related to thalamic volume (Van Der Werf et al., 2001). In a sample of 57 adults ranging in age from 21 to 82 years, structural MRI revealed a significant decrease in thalamic volume with increasing age. Critically, across the age span, the thalamic volume reduction was found to correlate with reduced cognitive speed. The authors noted that the prefrontal cortex, thalamus, and basal ganglia are part of parallel circuits involved in speeded processing, and interruption of these circuits at any level may underlie age-related reductions in speed of processing.

Further evidence for an association between age-related changes in frontal cortex and a processing deficit comes from studies of the Wisconsin Card Sorting Test (WCST). The WCST is a much-used test of executive functions and is assumed to tax complex processes such as reasoning, shifting, and working memory. A positron emission tomographic (PET) study of a modified version of the WCST found that young adults showed significantly greater activity in DLPFC than older adults (Nagahama et al., 1997). In addition, there was a strong negative correlation between number of preservative errors and DLPFC activity, suggesting that impaired set-shifting ability in older age is caused by DLPFC dysfunction. Similar results were obtained in a PET study of 41 adults between 18 and 80 years of age (Esposito et al., 1999). There was a significant negative correlation between age and percentage correct for the WCST, and during WCST performance significant age-related reductions in DLPFC activity were observed.

Production Deficit

There is less-direct evidence on the neural correlates of an age-related production deficit. Studies comparing age-related differences in the neural correlates of recall and recognition may be one relevant source. Age differences in memory performance are more pronounced on recall tests than on tests of recognition (Nyberg, Maitland, et al., 2003), which may be because of the fact that the demands on self-initiated retrieval processes are greater in recall than in recognition (Craik, 1983). Thus, differential effects of aging on the neural correlates of recall and recognition could be a reflection of a greater need for self-initiated production during recall. There is some evidence that young and old adults perform recall and recognition tasks in different ways with differences in the associated patterns of brain activity (Cabeza et al., 1997). However, in the study by Cabeza et al., performance differences between recall and recognition were attenuated to make the comparison cleaner. It is therefore difficult to relate age differences in the neural correlates of recall and recognition to a production deficiency during recall for the elderly. It can nevertheless be noted that one of the regions that was more active during recall than during recognition for younger, but not older, adults was located in the cerebellum. In turn, this finding can be related to observations in a PET study by Bäckman and colleagues (1997) that young, but not old, adults showed increased cerebellar activation during a recall test. The authors discussed this observation in the context of age-related deficiencies in self-initiated retrieval operations.

Additional results that speak to the issue of the neural correlates of an age-related production deficit come from an age-comparative PET study of episodic encoding (Grady et al., 1999). This study examined brain activity while older and younger adults encoded pictures and words using different encoding strategies (intentional encoding; deep incidental encoding; shallow incidental encoding). Multivariate analyses indicated that a network of brain regions, including left prefrontal and medial temporal regions, was similarly recruited by younger and older adults during deep processing and intentional learning of pictures. Other encoding networks showed significant age differences. It was concluded that, for older adults, engagement of critical encoding regions can occur under conditions that provide much support for memory performance (e.g., encoding of pictures under conditions that encourage elaboration). Under less-supportive conditions, when the needs for self-initiated production of relevant strategies are greater, older adults may fail to recruit the optimal brain network.

Related findings were obtained in an fMRI study by Logan et al. (2002). It was found that younger adults activated frontal regions to a greater extent than older adults during self-initiated, intentional encoding. In contrast, during deep incidental encoding, the degree of frontal activity was comparable for younger and older adults. This observation suggested that the age-related activity reduction during intentional encoding stemmed from a difficulty in spontaneously recruiting available frontal resources.

A final example that is relevant in the context of neural correlates of a production deficit in older age is a PET study on the neural correlates of memory training in adulthood and aging (Nyberg, Sandblom, et al., 2003). In that study, the neural correlates of acquiring and using the method of loci were examined. It was found that both younger and older adults could acquire the mnemonic. However, consistent with the findings of the behavioral studies that were discussed in the section on cognitive explanations for reduced plasticity, the younger adults benefited more from the mnemonic. In fact, half of the older adults did not benefit at all from the mnemonic. The other half did benefit, but did not reach the same level of performance as the younger adults.

At the neural level, when word encoding with the loci mnemonic was compared with a control condition that involved nonguided encoding, it was found that the younger and the older adults who did benefit from the mnemonic showed increased activity in posterior occipitoparietal brain regions. In keeping with related observations (e.g., Maguire et al., 2003), it was proposed that posterior activity was related to spatial imagery processes recruited when the loci method is used for word encoding. The absence of significant posterior activity of the older adults who did not benefit from the mnemonic suggested that they did not recruit these processes (i.e., a production deficit). In addition, it was found that the younger adults showed a significant activity increase in the DLPFC. Such activity was not seen for the older adults and may reflect a frontal processing deficit. The relation of frontal and posterior brain regions to age-related processing and production deficiencies during use of the loci mnemonic is illustrated in figure 13.5.

Issues

The data reviewed in this chapter support the following general conclusions: (1) There is potential for plasticity in older age; (2) younger adults benefit more from training than older adults; (3) reduced plasticity in older age reflects both a processing and a production deficit; and (4) the processing deficit is associated with age-related changes in frontal cortex, whereas the neural correlates of production deficits seem to be task specific.

The fourth conclusion, particularly the part about production deficiencies, is the most tentative as it is based on much fewer, and more indirect, observations than the other conclusions. Indeed, to my knowledge, only one study on neural correlates of training effects involving both younger and older adults has been conducted (Nyberg, Sandblom, et al., 2003). Hence, a significant issue for future neuroimaging research is to conduct more age-comparative studies of various forms of intervention.

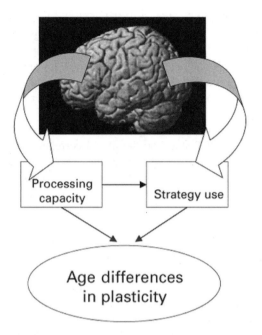

Figure 13.5. Relation of frontal and posterior brain regions to age-related processing and production deficiencies during use of the loci mnemonic.

The suggested link among age-related reductions in plasticity, processing deficiencies, and changes in DLPFC functioning in advanced age may be related to Baltes and Kliegl's (1992) conclusion of a "robust, if not irreversible, negative age difference in some basic components of the mind" (p. 124) (see the Limitations of Plasticity in Older Age section). If true, this would seem to suggest that it is not very fruitful to focus training programs in older age on trying to overcome the processing deficit. Indeed, in the Ball et al. (2002) study (see the Potential for Plasticity in Older Age section), speed-of-processing training was found to substantially improve the postintervention performance on speed tests, but did not improve the performance on tests of reasoning and memory. This lack of transfer is consistent with the bulk of empirical findings from cognitive training studies (Glisky & Glisky, 1999). Thus, although process-oriented interventions may have some general performance-enhancing effects for some individuals, age-related structural brain changes may set severe limitations on the effectiveness of such training.

Training aimed at overcoming production deficits in specific cognitive domains seems like a more fruitful strategy. As noted in the review section, intervention effects in the elderly are sizable and can, for example, correspond to the magnitude of expected decline in memory over a 6- to 7-year interval (Ball et al., 2002). Indeed, the episodic memory performance of persons in their 70s after simple forms of encoding support (enactment) can be as high as that for persons in their 30s after nonguided intentional encoding (Rönnlund et al., 2003). Thus, a major challenge is to encourage older adults to use the skills and techniques that have been trained or to overcome the perseverance effect that hinders the use of new strategies (Verhaeghen & Marcoen, 1996). How to accomplish this is not clear and may differ depending on the particular strategies, but as noted by Verhaeghen and Marcoen (1996), it may involve unlearning of previously unstated (suboptimal) routines. Moreover, in older age there is increased interindividual variability in cognitive ability that, at least in part, may be attributable to interindividual variability in brain aging (Glisky & Glisky, 1999). As noted by Glisky and Glisky, for this reason it may be necessary to tailor interventions to the individual. If this is done, it is likely that production deficiencies in older age will decrease.

In conclusion, for cognitive functions there seem to be certain biological boundaries of the plasticity of development (cf., Baltes, 1987), but it is nevertheless clear that the aging brain has a tremendous capacity (see also Reuter-Lorenz, 2002). Therefore, rather than comparing the degree of training effects for younger and older adults, future intervention studies should focus on (1) finding optimal interventions for older individuals, (2) finding ways of supporting the use of trained techniques, and (3) assessing the transfer of positive training effects on basic cognitive functions to relevant real-world outcomes (cf., Ball et al., 2002).

References

Bäckman, L., Almkvist, O., Andersson, J., Nordberg, A., Reineck, R., Winblad, B., & Långström, B. (1997). Brain activation in young and older adults during implicit and explicit retrieval. *Journal of Cognitive Neuroscience*, 9, 378–391.

Ball, K., Berch, D. B., Helmers, K. F., Jobe, J. B., Leveck, M. D., Marsiske, M., Morris, J. N., Rebok, G. W., Smith, D. M., Tennstedt, S. L., Unverzagt, F. W., & Willis, S. L. (2002). Effects of cognitive training interventions with older adults: A randomized controlled trial. *Journal of the American Medical Association*, 13, 2271–2281.

Baltes, P. B. (1987). Theoretical propositions of life-span developmental psychology: On the dynamics between growth and decline. *Developmental Psychology*, 23, 611–626.

Baltes, P. B., & Kliegl, R. (1992). Further testing of limits of cognitive plasticity: Negative age differences in a mnemonic skill are robust. *Developmental Psychology*, 28, 121–125.

Bower, G. H. (1970). Analysis of a mnemonic device. *American Scientist*, 58, 496–510.

Cabeza, R., Grady, C. L., Nyberg, L., McIntosh, A. R., Tulving, E., Kapur, S., Jennings, J. M., Houle, S., & Craik, F. I. M. (1997). Age-related differences in neural activity during memory encoding and retrieval: A positron emission tomography study. *Journal of Neuroscience*, 17, 391–400.

Craik, F. I. M. (1983). On the transfer of information from temporary to permanent memory. *Philosophical Transactions of the Royal Society of London*, B302, 341–359.

Esposito, G., Kirby, G. S., Van Horn, J. D., Ellmore, T. M., & Faith Berman, K. (1999). Context-dependent, neural system-specific neurophysiological concomitants of ageing: Mapping PET correlates during cognitive activation. *Brain*, 122, 963–979.

Glisky, E. L., & Glisky, M. L. (1999). Memory rehabilitation in the elderly. In D. T. Stuss, G. Winocur, & I. Robertson (Eds.), *Cognitive neurorehabilitation* (pp. 347–361). Cambridge, U.K.: Cambridge University Press.

Grady, C. L., McIntosh, A. R., Rajah, N., Beig, S., & Craik, F. I. M. (1999). The effects of age on the neural correlates of episodic encoding. *Cerebral Cortex*, 9, 805–814.

Logan, J. M., Sanders, A. L., Snyder, A. Z., Morris, J. C., & Buckner, R. L. (2002). Under-recruitment and nonselective recruitment: Dissociable neural mechanisms with aging. *Neuron*, *33*, 827–840.

Maguire, E. A., Valentine, E. R., Wilding, J. M. & Kapur, N. (2003). Routes to remembering: The brains behind superior memory. *Nature Neuroscience*, *6*, 90–95.

Nagahama, Y., Fukuyama, H., Yamauchi, H., Katsumi, Y., Magata, Y., Shibasaki, H., & Kimura, J. (1997). Age-related changes in cerebral blood flow activation during a card sorting test. *Experimental Brain Research*, *114*, 571–577.

Nyberg, L., Maitland, S. B., Rönnlund, M., Bäckman, L., Dixon, R. A., Wahlin, Å., & Nilsson, L.-G. (2003). Selective adult age differences in an age-invariant multi-factor model of declarative memory. *Psychology and Aging*, *18*, 149–160.

Nyberg, L., Sandblom, J., Jones, S., Stigsdotter Neely, A., Petersson, K. M., Ingvar, M., & Bäckman, L. (2003). Neural correlates of training-related memory improvement in adulthood and aging. *Proceedings of the National Academy of Sciences of the United States of America*, *100*, 13,728–13,733.

Park, D. C., Polk, T. A., Mikels, J. A., Taylor, S. F., & Marshuetz, C. (2002). Cerebral aging: Integration of brain and behavioral models of cognitive function. *Dialogues in Clinical Neuroscience: Cerebral Aging*, *3*, 151–165.

Park, D. C., Smith, A. D., Lautenschlager, G., Earles, J. G., Frieske, D., Zwahr, M., & Gaines, C. L. (1996). Mediators of long-term memory performance across the life span. *Psychology and Aging*, *11*, 621–637.

Raz, N., Briggs, S. D., Marks, W., & Acker, J. D. (1999). Age-related deficits in generation and manipulation of mental images: II. The role of dorsolateral prefrontal cortex. *Psychology and Aging*, *14*, 436–444.

Reuter-Lorenz, P. A. (2002). New visions of the aging mind and brain. *Trends in Cognitive Sciences*, *6*, 394–400.

Rogers, W. A., Hertzog, C., & Fisk, A. D. (2000). An individual difference analysis of ability and strategy influences: Age-related differences in associative learning. *Journal of Experimental Psychology: Learning, Memory, and Cognition*, *26*, 359–394.

Rönnlund, M., Nyberg, L., Bäckman, L., & Nilsson, L.-G. (2003). Memory for subject-performed tasks, verbal tasks, and cognitive activities: Parallel age-related deficits. *Aging, Neuropsychology, and Cognition*, *10*, 182–201.

Rypma, B., & D'Esposito, M. (2000). Isolating the neural mechanisms of age-related changes in human working memory. *Nature Neuroscience*, *3*, 509–515.

Salthouse, T. A. (1996). The processing-speed theory of adult age differences in cognition. *Psychological Review*, *103*, 403–428.

Stigsdotter Neely, A. (1994). Memory training in late adulthood. Doctoral dissertation, Department of Clinical Neuroscience and Family Medicine, Karolinska Institute, Stockholm.

Van Der Werf, Y., Tisserand, D. J., Visser, P. J., Hofman, P. A. M., Vuurman, E., Uylings, H. B. M., & Jolles, J. (2001). Thalamic volume predicts performance on tests of cognitive speed and decreases in healthy aging: A magnetic resonance imaging-based volumetric analysis. *Cognitive Brain Research*, *11*, 377–385.

Verhaeghen, P., & Marcoen, A. (1994). The production deficiency hypothesis revisited: Adult age differences in strategy use as a function of processing resources. *Aging and Cognition*, *1*, 323–338.

Verhaeghen, P., & Marcoen, A. (1996). On the mechanisms of plasticity in young and older adults after instruction in the method of loci: Evidence for an amplification model. *Psychology and Aging*, *11*, 164–178.

Verhaeghen, P., Marcoen, A., & Goossens, L. (1992). Improving memory performance in the aged through mnemonic training: A meta-analytic study. *Psychology and Aging, 7,* 242–251.

Zacks, R. T., Hasher, L., & Li, K. Z. H. (2000). Human memory. In F. I. M. Craik & T. A. Salthouse (Eds.), *The handbook of aging and cognition* (pp. 293–358). Mahwah, NJ: Erlbaum.

IV

MODELS IN COGNITIVE
NEUROSCIENCE OF AGING

14

Age-Related Changes
in Hemispheric Organization

Sander Daselaar
Roberto Cabeza

What are the implications for cognition of the fact that we have two cerebral hemispheres? Although this is one of the most fundamental questions in cognitive neuroscience, no definite answer is presently available. For more than a century, researchers have wondered why we have two hemispheres, how they differ, and how they interact with each other. Anatomical and functional asymmetries have been identified, and different models of hemispheric interaction have been proposed. Studies using positron emission tomography (PET) and functional magnetic resonance imaging (fMRI) have revitalized this research domain by discovering new hemispheric asymmetries. Moreover, these studies have identified changes in the lateralization of brain activity as a function of population variables, such as aging. In fact, the most consistent finding in functional neuroimaging studies of cognitive aging is a reduction in the lateralization of prefrontal activations. This is not the first time that aging has been associated with changes in lateralization; for many years, cognitive aging psychologists discussed the possibility that the right hemisphere ages faster than the left. In general, however, these ideas have not been informed by theories regarding hemispheric specialization and interaction. The goal of this chapter is to address this disconnection and to link the topic of lateralization and aging to general issues regarding hemispheric organization.

The chapter has three main sections. The first section focuses on hemispheric organization. It reviews evidence concerning hemispheric specialization, at both anatomical and functional levels, and then describes three views of hemispheric interaction: insulation, inhibition, and cooperation. The second section describes two models concerning age-related changes in lateralization: the right hemiaging model and the age-related asymmetry reduction model. Evidence supporting each model is reviewed, and the two models are compared. Finally, the third section links the first two by considering how age-related asymmetry reductions relate to the three views of hemispheric interaction and models of hemispheric specialization.

Hemispheric Organization

Hemispheric Specialization

It has been well established that the two hemispheres of the brain are anatomically and functionally asymmetric. Differences in gross anatomy have been found in several brain regions, including the planum temporale (Galaburda, Sanides, & Geshwind, 1978; Pieniadz & Naeser, 1984; Teszner et al., 1972; von Economo & Horn, 1930), the pars triangularis (Albanese et al., 1989; Foundas et al., 1996), the sylvian fissure (Eberstaller, 1884; Rubens, Mahowald, & Hutton, 1976; Witelson & Kigar, 1992), and the globus pallidus (Kooistra & Heilman, 1988). These anatomic asymmetries were confirmed using structural MRI (Pujol et al., 2002; Raz et al., 1997; Steinmetz et al., 1990; Watkins et al., 2001). There is also evidence that the gray/white matter ratio is greater in the left than in the right hemisphere (Good et al., 2001; Gur et al., 1980; Pujol et al., 2002), a difference that could account for some of the effects of aging on lateralization discussed in this chapter.

Subtler anatomical differences include the distribution of pyramidal cells in the posterior superior temporal gyrus (Galuske et al., 2000) and the extent of dendritic branching in left hemisphere speech areas (Scheibel et al., 1985). Hemispheric asymmetries can also be found in neurotransmitter systems. For example, the number of dopamine receptors in the striatum is greater in the left hemisphere (Glick, Ross, & Hough, 1982; Wagner et al., 1983), whereas the number of noradrenergic neurons in ventrolateral thalamic nuclei is greater in the right hemisphere (Oke et al., 1978).

These structural asymmetries between the two hemispheres are accompanied by functional differences. Distinctions regarding specializations attributed to the left versus right hemispheres include verbal versus spatial (Gazzaniga, 1970), local versus global (Navon, 1983), categorical versus coordinate (Kosslyn et al., 1989), positive versus negative emotions (Hellige, 1993), and production versus monitoring (Cabeza, Locantore, & Anderson, 2003). Here, we focus on two distinctions that are particularly relevant to the effects of aging on lateralization: the verbal/spatial and the production/monitoring distinctions.

Verbal Versus Spatial

It is generally accepted that the left hemisphere is more involved in verbal processing, whereas the right hemisphere is more involved in spatial processing (Hellige, 1993). The left hemisphere's specialization for language has been known for more than a century. In 1861, Paul Broca noted that lesions in a left opercular frontal area were associated with difficulties in speaking but not in comprehending language; in 1874, Carl Wernicke found that lesions in the left posterior temporal area led to severe comprehension problems. Because damage to the right hemisphere was hardly ever found to lead to speech and language problems, it was concluded that, at least in right-handed people, the left hemisphere is critical to language functions.

Studies of split-brain patients have further increased our understanding of the specialized functions of the two hemispheres. A consistent finding in these studies is that right-handed patients are capable of solving visuospatial tasks with their left hand (right hemisphere), but not with their right hand (left hemisphere), and the opposite occurs with verbal tasks (Gazzaniga, 1970). Hence, the studies of split-brain patients provided evidence for a strong right hemisphere spatial specialization, which is complementary to the dominance of the left hemisphere for language processes.

Production Versus Monitoring

Functional asymmetries have also been reported in episodic memory, which refers to memory for personally experienced past events (Tulving, 1983). Functional neuroimaging studies have shown that the left prefrontal cortex (PFC) is more involved in episodic encoding, whereas the right PFC is more involved in episodic retrieval, a pattern known as the hemispheric encoding/retrieval asymmetry (HERA) model (Nyberg, Cabeza, & Tulving, 1996; Tulving et al., 1994). Left PFC activity during encoding has been attributed to semantic processing, which is strongly associated with the left PFC (for a review, see Cabeza & Nyberg, 2000) and is known to enhance encoding (Craik & Lockhart, 1972). The role of the right PFC activity in retrieval has been attributed to verification and checking operations (Allan et al., 2000; Fletcher et al., 1998; Henson, Shallice, & Dolan, 1999; Rugg et al., 1998). Even if not as pronounced and frequent as during encoding, left PFC activations are sometimes found during retrieval (Nolde, Johnson, & Raye, 1998), possibly reflecting semantic generation operations (Cabeza, McIntosh, et al., 1997).

Combining preexistent ideas regarding the roles of the left and right PFC during episodic retrieval, the production/monitoring hypothesis states that the left PFC is more involved in semantically guided information production than the right PFC, whereas the right PFC is more involved in monitoring and verification of information than is the left PFC (Cabeza, Locantore, & Anderson, 2003).

The production/monitoring was tested by comparing PFC activity during recall and recognition tasks (Cabeza, Locantore, & Anderson, 2003). Whereas production processes are more critical for recall than for recognition, monitoring processes are more critical for recognition than for recall. Consistent with the production/monitoring hypothesis, the left PFC was more activated for recall than for recognition, whereas the right PFC was more activated for recognition than for recall (see plate 14.1 in the color insert). There is also evidence that the production/monitoring distinction generalizes beyond episodic memory retrieval. In fMRI studies that directly compared brain activity during episodic retrieval, verbal working memory, and visual attention (Cabeza, Dolcos, et al., 2002, 2003), a left PFC region was activated by both episodic retrieval and working memory, whereas a right PFC region was activated by episodic retrieval and visual attention. Thus, semantically guided production processes mediated by the left PFC may be shared by cognitive functions in which meaningful information is manipulated, and monitoring processes mediated by the right PFC may be shared by cognitive functions in which external or internal information is evaluated.

Hemispheric Interaction

Although functional neuroimaging studies have provided support for hemispheric specialization by revealing lateralized activation patterns, they have also shown that, in most cognitive tasks, both hemispheres are recruited (Cabeza & Nyberg, 2000). This does not imply that each hemisphere is equally competent, or that either could do the task alone, but rather that there is some sort of distribution of processing demands between two interacting hemispheres (Banich, 1998). On the other hand, there are conditions in which unilateral processing may be more efficient, and activity in one of the hemispheres must be suppressed. These alternatives have originated three different views about interhemispheric interaction (see figure 14.1): hemispheric insulation, hemispheric inhibition, and hemispheric cooperation.

Hemispheric Insulation

The hemispheric insulation view states that reducing communication between the two hemispheres can improve performance by reducing interference. According to the functional cerebral distance model (Kinsbourne & Hicks, 1978), interference among tasks that are unrelated and performed concurrently will be minimized when they are each performed by functionally distant cerebral regions, such as those in different hemispheres. Following this model, it has been suggested that, in some conditions, the corpus callosum can act as an inhibitory barrier, so that computations performed by each hemisphere can be insulated within each hemisphere to prevent potentially harmful interhemispheric intrusions (Liederman & Meehan, 1986).

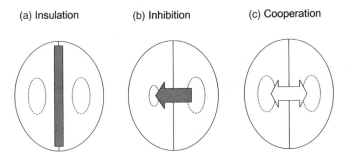

Figure 14.1. Three models of hemispheric interaction: *a*, insulation, with diminishing interhemispheric communication through callosal shielding to reduce interference between hemispheres; *b*, inhibition, for which stimulation of one hemisphere suppresses activity in the other hemisphere; *c*, cooperation, in which the two hemispheres collaborate when solving complex tasks.

This idea was tested in one study in which participants named upright and inverted letters presented within one visual field or divided across visual fields. A bilateral advantage was observed when upright and inverted letters were presented in different visual fields, but not when they were mixed across fields, consistent with the idea that hemispheric insulation helped in reducing interference (Merola & Liederman, 1990).

In another study (Liederman & Meehan, 1986), subjects were briefly shown three numbers with the instruction to add the central number to the top number and to subtract the central number from the bottom number. The results showed that there were fewer errors when the addition problem was directed to one visual field and the subtraction problem was directed to the other visual field. Again, the authors' explanation was that the two tasks were carried out by different hemispheres, thereby reducing hemispheric interference.

Hemispheric Inhibition

According to the hemispheric inhibition account, stimulus-driven activity in one hemisphere tends to suppress—through colossal interactions—activity in the other hemisphere (Chiarello & Maxfield, 1996). When the hemispheres are equally active, attention is oriented medially (Kinsbourne, 1973). When one hemisphere is more strongly activated, it will suppress the orienting tendency of the other hemisphere, causing attention to shift to the side contralateral to the more activated hemisphere.

Fink et al. (2000) found support for the interhemispheric suppression hypothesis using PET. In their study, subjects were instructed to read out columns of three characters that were presented either to one or to both visual hemifields. Characters were reported less frequently in one hemisphere when words were simultaneously presented to the other hemisphere than in the case of unilateral presentation. Furthermore, this extinction pattern was found not only at a behavioral level, but also at a neural level. They found that presentation of a competing stimulus resulted in decreased activity in the contralateral occipital cortex.

Hemispheric Cooperation

The hemispheric cooperation view states that, when computational demands are high, collaboration between the two hemispheres is more advantageous than within-hemisphere processing. This view is supported by behavioral, functional neuroimaging, and split-brain evidence. Behavioral studies have typically used a split-field methodology in which the stimuli necessary for reaching a decision (e.g., two letters in a letter identity judgment) are presented in different visual fields (left vs. right) or in the same visual field (e.g., both in the left visual field). In the first condition, the two hemispheres must communicate to make the decision (cross-hemisphere processing), whereas in the second condition, the decision can be reached within a single hemisphere (within-hemisphere processing). The typical finding is that, as task complexity increases, cross-hemisphere processing is associated with better performance than within-hemisphere processing. This effect has been observed for a variety of tasks, including summation (Banich & Belger, 1990), ordinal (Banich &

Belger, 1990), and spelling (Banich et al., 1990) tasks. Moreover, the effect has been observed not only for visual, but also for auditory and tactile stimuli (Passarotti et al., 2002).

The hemispheric cooperation view is also supported by functional neuroimaging evidence. In a PET study, Jonides and collaborators (1997) investigated an n-back task in which memory load and complexity were varied by manipulating the number of letters that had to be maintained in working memory. The results showed that symmetry of activity increased as a function of complexity. In another study, Pollmann & von Cramon (2003) used fMRI to study the neural correlates of letter identity and shape matching. Previously, Banich and colleagues (Banich & Belger, 1990) had reported a bilateral advantage for a condition in which subjects had to match the identity of two letters (both a-a and A-a: same), but not for an easier condition in which they merely had to match the shape of the two letters (i.e., a-a: same, A-a: different). For the identity-matching task, Pollman et al. found that unilateral relative to bilateral presentation led to increased activation in the contralateral side of the ventral occipital cortex. This increase went along with an ipsilateral increase of activation in homologous areas. Furthermore, these activations were reduced during bilateral presentation. Such a sharing of hemispheric resources was not seen for letter shape matching. These findings suggest that the bihemispheric processing advantage for letter identity matching already occurs in the visual processing stage.

A final line of evidence comes from the study of split-brain patients. These patients generally display greater performance deficits relative to controls as task complexity increases (Kreuter, Kinsbourne, & Trevarthen, 1972), suggesting that interhemispheric communication is more critical for complex tasks.

One plausible explanation of the advantage of cross-hemispheric processing under high processing demands is that it allows information to be spread across a larger number of processing units (neurons). Moreover, cooperation between hemispheres not only allows subcomponents of a task to be handled by different processors (hemispheres), but also allows processing in parallel (Banich, 1998). In contrast, when a task is simple enough to be handled by a single hemisphere, cross-hemispheric processing is not efficient. Cross-hemispheric processing requires the transmission of information through the corpus callosum, which consists of about 200 million white matter axons, which are only partly myelinated. When interhemispheric interactions occur along thin unmyelinated callosal fibers, they may take as long as 100–300 ms (Ringo et al., 1994). Thus, for very simple tasks, dividing processing across the hemispheres is not cost effective. Consistent with this idea, hemifield studies have found that, in the case of simple tasks, within-hemisphere processing yields better performance than cross-hemisphere processing (Banich, 1998; Weissman & Banich, 2000).

Appraisal

A problem when evaluating empirical support for the three views is that some findings can be accommodated by more than one view. For example, bilateral advantage may be interpreted as evidence of hemispheric collaboration by the cooperation view (Banich, 1998), but as evidence of hemispheric independence by the insulation view

(Liederman & Meehan, 1986). In some cases, the former account seems more reasonable.

For instance, Brown and Jeeves (1993) presented their subjects with a letter match task, in which letters were presented either unilaterally or bilaterally, while recording event-related potentials. Bilateral advantage, both in terms of accuracy and response times, was associated with faster left-to-right interhemispheric transfer times as measured by the visually evoked response. Thus, bilateral advantage was accompanied by more efficient, rather than obstructed, interhemispheric communication.

Also, Berryman and Kennelly (1992) assessed interhemispheric correlations between measures obtained in visual half-field bar graph and word judgment tasks. They found positive interhemispheric correlations for error rates and variance in response times, which increased as memory load increased. This indicated that interhemispheric communication becomes greater when processing load increases.

Together, these findings indicate that, in line with the hemispheric cooperation and inhibition views, bilateral advantages reflect greater interhemispheric coordination rather than isolation (Chiarello & Maxfield, 1996). Thus, although there is evidence supporting insulation and inhibition views, the weight of the evidence seems to favor the cooperation view.

Models of Aging and Lateralization

In this section, we briefly review two models concerning age-related changes in lateralization: the right hemiaging model, which is based mainly on behavioral findings, and the hemispheric asymmetry reduction in older adults (HAROLD) model, which is based primarily on neuroimaging findings.

The Right Hemiaging Model

The right hemiaging model states that the right hemisphere is more sensitive to the harmful effects of aging than the left hemisphere (Dolcos, Rice, & Cabeza, 2002). Thus, this view predicts that age-related cognitive decline should be more pronounced on cognitive functions associated with the right hemisphere, such as spatial processing, than on those associated with the left hemisphere, such as verbal processing. The right hemisphere may be more sensitive to aging because it has a smaller gray/white matter ratio than the left hemisphere (Good et al., 2001; Gur et al., 1980; Pujol et al., 2002). However, the right hemiaging model is primarily based on behavioral rather than neurobiological evidence. Below, we briefly review behavioral studies concerning verbal/spatial and sensorimotor functions.

Verbal/Spatial

One of the most consistent findings in the cognitive aging literature has been that, in intelligence tests (e.g., Wechsler), the scores on the verbal subtests are largely age invariant, whereas the scores of visuospatial subtests show pronounced age-related decline (Goldstein & Shelly, 1981). In line with these findings, Klisz (1987) found that performance of elderly subjects was similar to that of patients with right hemisphere damage when tested with a neuropsychological test battery developed to diagnose lateralized brain injury.

However, comparisons between the effects of aging on verbal and spatial processing have been plagued by confounds. First, verbal skills are usually measured by assessing overlearned vocabulary, whereas spatial skills are typically measured by assessing performance on novel tasks unrelated to preexisting knowledge (Meudell & Greenhalgh, 1987). Thus, it is possible that age-related decline is more pronounced on tasks that do not rely on preexistent knowledge regardless of whether stimuli are verbal or spatial (Gerhardstein, Peterson, & Rapcsak, 1998).

To address this confound, Meudell and Greenhalgh (1987) investigated a task that required the use of verbal and spatial reasoning rather than recall of previously learned information. In line with the hemiaging model, they found that old adults exhibited larger deficits on spatial than on verbal tasks.

Still, there are other confounding aspects that need to be controlled, such as type of response, attentional demands, and task complexity. To address these confounds, Schear and Nebes (1980) compared retrieval of seven letters versus retrieval of their locations in a matrix, and they found similar age effects on both tasks. Likewise, Elias and Kinsbourne (1974) compared the speed with which young and old adults made categorical judgments about two verbal stimuli or two nonverbal stimuli and found similar age-related slowing in both conditions.

Finally, Park and colleagues (2002) compared performances on well-matched visuospatial and verbal tasks across the life span in the domains of short-term memory, working memory, and episodic memory. As illustrated by figure 14.2, their results are inconsistent with the right hemiaging model: Performance declined with aging at a similar rate in verbal and visuospatial tasks. Interestingly, though, they did not find any age-related decline in general verbal knowledge tasks (see figure 14.2d), in agreement with the idea that crystallized intelligence does not deteriorate with age.

The results of studies using split-field paradigms are inconsistent and difficult to interpret. Several studies (e.g., Clark & Knowles, 1973; Johnson et al., 1979) reported an age-related recall decline for digits presented to the left ear (right hemisphere), but not for digits presented to the right ear (left hemisphere). However, verbal dichotic listening studies that controlled for peripheral hearing deficits reported no age-related asymmetry differences (Borod et al., 1983; Ellis, 1990; Nebes, Madden, & Berg, 1983). Likewise, Cherry, Hellige, and McDowd (1995) and Nebes, Madden, and Berg (1983) did not observe age-related changes in hemispheric asymmetry when verbal information was presented tachistoscopically to the left and right hemisphere.

Moreover, the interpretation of studies in which older adults were impaired in processing verbal stimuli presented to the right hemisphere is complicated by the lateralization of linguistic functions. According to some views (e.g., Zaidel, 1986), when verbal information is presented to the right hemisphere, the stimulus may not be detected and may be directed to the dominant left hemisphere via the corpus callosum, with a possible loss of features. Aging is associated with declines in callosal volume and white matter integrity (Abe et al., 2002; Hopper et al., 1994; Sullivan et al., 2002; Weis et al., 1993). Thus, age-related deficits in processing verbal stimuli

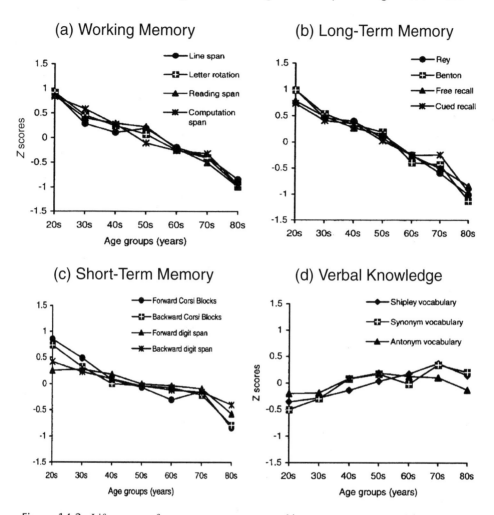

Figure 14.2. Life span performance measures: *a*, working memory measures (visuospatial and verbal); *b*, long-term memory measures (visuospatial and verbal); *c*, short-term memory measures (visuospatial and verbal); *d*, verbal knowledge measures. (Adapted from Park et al., 2002.)

presented to the right hemisphere could reflect a decline of callosal transport rather than differential aging of the right hemisphere.

Sensorimotor Processing

The right hemiaging hypothesis has also been investigated in sensorimotor processing. Weller and Latimer-Sayer (1985) used a tactile stimulation task (i.e., pegboard) to investigate changes in manipulative skill as a function of age and found evidence supporting the right hemisphere hypothesis. They showed left-hand (right hemisphere) abilities declined more rapidly with age than right hand (left hemisphere) abilities. However, other studies have shown that age differences in left- and right-hand motor skill are dependent on task demands (Meudell & Greenhalgh, 1987; Mitrushina et al., 1995).

The Hemispheric Asymmetry Reduction in Older Adults Model

The HAROLD model states that, under similar conditions, PFC activity tends to be less lateralized in older than in younger adults (Cabeza, 2002). The model is supported by functional neuroimaging, electrophysiological, and behavioral evidence in the domains of episodic memory, semantic memory, working memory, perception, and inhibitory control. Because this evidence has been reviewed elsewhere (Cabeza, 2002), here we briefly mention a few functional neuroimaging findings in the domains of episodic memory, working memory, and sensorimotor processing, including some findings published after the publication of the model (Maguire & Frith, 2003; Morcom et al., 2003).

Episodic Memory

As mentioned, activations during episodic memory tend to be right lateralized (Tulving et al., 1994). Consistent with this pattern, Cabeza, Grady, et al. (1997) found that young adults showed right PFC activations during word pair cued recall. In contrast, during the same task, older adults showed significant activations in both right and left PFC. This bilateral pattern of PFC in older adults was interpreted as compensatory: To counteract cognitive decline, older adults recruited both hemispheres in a task in which young adults recruited mainly one hemisphere. Age-related asymmetry reductions during episodic retrieval have been also found in other tasks, including word stem cued recall (Bäckman et al., 1997), word recognition (Madden et al., 1999), and face recognition (Grady et al., 2002). Thus, HAROLD during episodic retrieval has been demonstrated for both recall and recognition tasks and for both verbal and nonverbal materials.

Moreover, age-related asymmetry reductions during episodic memory have also been found during encoding (Logan et al., 2002; Morcom et al., 2003; Stebbins et al., 2002). Older adults show a lack of hemispheric asymmetry even when they are provided with encoding strategies that raise their PFC activity to the level of young adults (Logan et al., 2002; Morcom et al., 2003; Stebbins et al., 2002), suggesting that HAROLD reflects a change in cognitive architecture rather than a difference in cognitive strategies. Morcom et al. (2003) investigated the effect of aging on the neural correlates of episodic encoding by comparing study phase activity for items that were remembered versus forgotten in a subsequent recognition task. The remembered-minus-forgotten contrast yielded left PFC activity in young adults, but bilateral PFC activity in older adults. In sum, HAROLD during episodic memory has been found during both encoding and retrieval.

Working Memory

In young adults, PFC activity tends to be left lateralized for verbal working memory and right lateralized for spatial working memory (for a review, see Smith & Jonides, 1999). Consistent with this pattern, Reuter-Lorenz et al. (2000) found that, in young adults, PFC activity during a delayed response task was significant in the left hemisphere when the stimuli were letters, but in the right hemisphere when the stimuli were spatial locations. In contrast, older adults tested under identical conditions showed significant PFC activity bilaterally for both verbal and spatial stimuli. This finding suggests that HAROLD can be observed not only for process-related asymmetries (e.g., encoding vs. retrieval), but also for stimuli-related asymmetries (e.g., verbal vs. spatial).

In another working memory study, Dixit et al. (2000) found an age-related asymmetry reduction in PFC activity during an n-back task. Interestingly, older participants in this study were under 50 years of age, suggesting that age-related asymmetry reductions develop in middle age. At the same time, other evidence mentioned in the concluding section of the chapter suggests that HAROLD becomes more pronounced with advancing age (Logan et al., 2002; Nielson, Langenecker, & Garavan, 2002).

Sensorimotor Processing

In a study by Grady et al. (1994), PFC activity during face matching was found in the right hemisphere in young adults, but in both hemispheres in old adults. Grady and colleagues (2000) replicated this finding in both normal and degraded face matching. A study that investigated brain activity during finger tapping (Calautti, Serrati, & Baron, 2001) showed—as expected—that both young and older adults had sensorimotor activity in the contralateral hemisphere. In addition, older adults showed more activity than younger adults in the right dorsal PFC during right-hand tapping. Thus, age-related asymmetry reductions can be found not only for higher order cognitive processes, such as episodic and working memory, but also for more simple sensorimotor processes.

Appraisal

Whereas evidence for the right hemiaging model has been mixed, evidence for the HAROLD model has been largely consistent. Although no study has explicitly compared the two models, some of the aforementioned functional neuroimaging findings are consistent with HAROLD, but inconsistent with the right hemiaging model. Conditions in which PFC activity is right lateralized in young adults are not useful for comparing the two models because both models predict an age-related reduction in lateralization. In contrast, when PFC activity is left lateralized in young adults, the right hemiaging model predicts an increase in hemispheric asymmetry, whereas the HAROLD model predicts a decrease. The results of three functional neuroimaging studies of episodic encoding/semantic retrieval (Logan et al., 2002; Morcom et al., 2003; Stebbins et al., 2002) supported the prediction of the HAROLD model. In all these studies, younger adults showed greater activity in the left than in the right PFC, and this difference was reduced in older adults, a finding in direct opposition to the right hemiaging model.

One way of harmonizing the two models is to assume that HAROLD applies to PFC, whereas the right hemiaging model applies to other brain regions. However, there is some evidence that age-related asymmetry reductions may occur in brain regions outside the PFC. For example, Nielson, Langenecker, and Garavan (2002) found that parietal activity during a go/no-go inhibition task was right lateralized in young adults (see also Garavan, Ross, & Stein, 1999), but bilateral in older adults. Likewise, Grady et al. (2000) found an age-related reduction in the lateralization of parietal and temporal activity during face memory. Moreover, two fMRI studies of simple reaction time tasks found age-related asymmetry reductions in the primary motor cortex (Hutchinson et al., 2002; Mattay et al., 2002).

Finally, the fMRI study by Maguire and Frith (2003) suggested that HAROLD may also occur in subcortical regions. This study investigated the effects of aging on the neural correlates of remembering real-life autobiographical events. As illustrated by plate 14.2 (see color insert), young adults selectively recruited the left hippocampus (plate 14.2a), whereas older adults activated both the left and the right hippocampus (plate 14.b). In summary, available evidence is more consistent with the HAROLD model than with the right hemiaging model.

Aging and Hemispheric Organization

In the first section of the chapter, we considered ideas about hemispheric organization, including alternatives regarding hemispheric specialization (verbal vs. spatial, production vs. monitoring) and hemispheric interaction (cooperation, insulation, and inhibition). In the second section of the chapter, we described two models concerning the effects of aging on lateralization and concluded that available evidence supports the idea of age-related asymmetry reductions. Linking previous sections, this section considers how age-related asymmetry reductions relate to models of hemispheric interaction and hemispheric specialization.

Aging and Hemispheric Interaction

In the first section, we discussed three models of hemispheric interaction: cooperation, insulation, and inhibition. Next, we consider these three models in relation to aging. Because hemispheric cooperation has received most attention in recent functional neuroimaging studies of aging, we consider this model last.

Age-Related Decline in Hemispheric Insulation: The Dedifferentiation View

The hemispheric insulation model posits that confining cognitive processes within one hemisphere is sometimes necessary to reduce potentially harmful interhemispheric cross talk (Liederman & Meehan, 1986). If it is assumed that unilateral activation patterns reflect an insulation mechanism, then bilateral activity in older adults may be interpreted as a breakdown of such a mechanism. According to this view, bihemispheric recruitment in older adults would not reflect functional compensation, but a failure to keep neural activity confined within a single hemisphere. Consistent with this idea, the dedifferentiation view proposes that bilateral activation patterns in older adults reflect a difficulty in recruiting specialized neural mechanisms (e.g., Li & Lindenberger, 1999).

The process of dedifferentiation during aging is the counterpart of the process of differentiation during childhood. In the child development literature, *differentiation* refers to the process through which a global cognitive capacity branches into a series of specialized cognitive abilities (Garret, 1946). During aging, cognitive functions may again begin to rely on similar executive or organizing resources (Balinsky, 1941; Baltes & Lindenberger, 1997). In other words, the differentiation achieved during childhood is reversed by a process of dedifferentiation during aging.

The dedifferentiation account is supported by evidence that correlations among different cognitive measures, and between cognitive and sensory measures, tend to increase with age (Balinsky, 1941; Baltes & Lindenberger, 1997). These results suggest that older adults recruit similar sets of cognitive operations for very different tasks. The dedifferentiation view is also consistent with fMRI evidence that children can show bilateral activation patterns that resemble those seen in older adults. For example, Moses et al. (2002) investigated a global/local paradigm of children between 12 and 14 years old. The children were divided into two groups based on their reaction time. Whereas the group with faster reaction times displayed the expected pattern of right-lateralized activity for global processing and left-lateralized activity for local processing, the group with slower response times showed bilateral activity patterns for both global and local conditions. One possible explanation is that children with faster reaction times had already shifted from undifferentiated bilateral processing toward a more efficient hemispheric specialization, whereas children with slower reaction times were relying on the undifferentiated bilateral processing. By analogy, this evidence suggests that bilateral activity in older adults reflect a failure to recruit a more efficient unilateral network.

Age-Related Decline in Hemispheric Inhibition: The Competition View

According to the hemispheric inhibition model, activity may suppress activity in the other hemisphere through colossal interactions (Chiarello & Maxfield, 1996). If it is assumed that aging impairs hemispheric communication, then bilateral recruitment in older adults may be interpreted as an age-related decline in hemispheric inhibition. In other words, older adults show greater activity in the hemisphere less activated by younger adults not because they are compensating, but because they are failing to inhibit inefficient or irrelevant activity in the hemisphere less appropriate for task performance. Bilateral recruitment in older adults, then, would reflect a decline in the normal competition between hemispheres.

This competition view has been proposed by Buckner and collaborators (Buckner & Logan, 2002) and is supported by two main kinds of evidence. First, this view is supported by evidence that aging is associated with a decline in the anatomical integrity of the corpus callosum (Abe et al., 2002; Hopper et al., 1994; Sullivan et al., 2002; Weis et al., 1993). Using diffusion tensor imaging (DTI), Abe et al. (2002) found that the integrity of white matter tracts in the genu of the corpus callosum declined significantly with age. Using volumetric MRI methods, Sullivan et al. (2002) found that aging was associated with a substantial decline in callosal volume. If it is assumed that the two hemispheres compete with or inhibit each other, then a decline in callosal integrity could lead to a decline in interhemispheric inhibition and to the appearance of inadequate activations in the less-relevant hemisphere.

Second, the competition view is supported by functional neuroimaging evidence that activity in the less-relevant hemisphere occurs early during processing but then disappears, suggesting an inhibition mechanism. Konishi, Donaldson, and Buckner (2001) conducted a meta-analysis of data from three separate fMRI studies of word and face encoding. In line with previous studies, they found that PFC activity was mostly left lateralized during word encoding and mostly right lateralized during face encoding. Interestingly, at the onset of word blocks, there was a transient activation in the right frontal cortex. The authors proposed that this transient activation might be indicative of a competition between left and right frontal regions, which are specialized, respectively, in verbal and nonverbal processing. In this view, the right frontal region that will not be used for the verbal encoding task is nonetheless initially activated. The rapid extinction of this activation would then be indicative of an active inhibition by the left hemisphere. If this interhemispheric inhibition mechanism is impaired in older adults (e.g., because of callosal decline), then the activity in the less-relevant hemisphere would not be extinguished and would lead to a bilateral activation pattern.

Age-Related Increase in Hemispheric Cooperation: The Compensation View

The hemispheric cooperation model states that when task demands are high, collaboration between the two hemispheres is more advantageous than within-hemisphere processing (e.g., Banich & Belger, 1990; Brown & Jeeves, 1993; Weissman & Banich, 2000). If it is assumed that under the same conditions task demands are greater for older than for younger adults, then age-related bihemispheric recruitment may be explained as an increase in interhemispheric cooperation. This is the basic idea underlying the compensation view of bilateral activity in older adults: To counteract cognitive decline, older adults recruit both hemispheres during task conditions for which young adults recruit primarily one hemisphere (Cabeza, Anderson, et al., 2002; Cabeza, Grady, et al., 1997). The compensation view is supported by different kinds of evidence, including behavioral data, recovery from brain damage, activity–performance correlations, and comparisons between high- and low-performing older adults.

Behavioral Data Behavioral evidence for the compensation view can be found in the results of studies investigating interhemispheric cooperation using the split-field method. For example, Reuter-Lorenz, Stanczak, and Miller (1999) investigated the effects of aging on a task in which subjects matched two letters projected either to the same visual field (hemisphere) or to the opposite visual field (hemisphere). In the first condition, matching can be done within hemispheres, whereas in the second condition, matching must be done across hemispheres. As illustrated by figure 14.3a, this manipulation was crossed with three levels of difficulty: low (physical matching with one distracter), medium (physical matching with three distracter letters), and high (name matching with three distracters).

The critical results were reaction time differences between within- and across-hemisphere conditions (see figure 14.3b). In young adults, the within-hemisphere condition was faster when difficulty was low, the across-hemisphere condition was faster when difficulty was high, and the two conditions yielded similar speed when difficulty was medium. These results are consistent with the idea that, at high levels of difficulty, the benefits of engaging resources from both hemispheres outweigh the

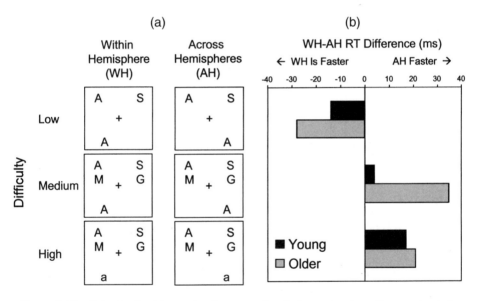

Figure 14.3. Behavioral evidence showing across-hemisphere advantages for complex tasks in young and older subjects. *a*, Task design: Subjects were submitted to physical and identity match trials. In the physical match trials, the target letter physically matched one of the probes. In the identity match trials, the target letter had the same name as one of the probes. The figure illustrates within-hemisphere (WH) and across-hemisphere (AH) trial types. For WH trial types, the target and probe were presented within the same visual field, in which case a match could be detected without the need for hemispheric interactions. For AH trials, the target and probe were presented to opposite hemispheres, in which case match detection required the two hemispheres to interact. *b*, Difference scores indicate the relative AH advantage in accuracy for younger and older adults for each of the three difficulty levels. The scores were calculated by subtracting the average percentage correct for WH trials from the average percentage correct for the AH trials. The results indicate that older adults benefit more from bihemispheric processing than young adults. (Adapted from Reuter-Lorenz, Stanczak, and Miller, 1999.)

costs of interhemispheric communication (Banich, 1998). In old adults, the benefits of bihemispheric processing were evident in the medium difficulty condition, in which young adults did not show a bilateral advantage. In other words, older adults may benefit from cross-hemispheric processing at levels of task difficulty for which intra-hemispheric processing seem to be enough in young adults. Thus, these results suggested that older adults may rely more heavily on interhemispheric cooperation than younger adults, and hence that the age-related increase in bilateral recruitment observed in may functional neuroimaging studies reflects a form of functional compensation.

Recovery From Brain Damage   The compensation view is also supported by evidence that recovery from unilateral brain damage sometimes involves bilateral recruitment. Reasoning by analogy, it may be argued that if bilateral recruitment can ameliorate cognitive deficits caused by brain damage, such a mechanism could also help counteract cognitive deficits caused by age-related cerebral decline. Although the sudden, specific effects of brain damage are quite different from the slow, diffuse effects of age-related neural decline, it is reasonable to assume that some forms of brain plasticity can attenuate the effects of neural injuries of different nature and from different sources.

Evidence that recovery of motor function after unilateral damage is facilitated by the recruitment of homologous regions in the unaffected hemisphere has been found with a variety of techniques, including cortical potentials (Honda et al., 1997), Doppler ultrasonography (Silvestrini et al., 1998), xenon-133 (Brion, Demeurisse, & Capon, 1989), PET (Di Piero et al., 1992), fMRI (Feydy et al., 2002), and transcranial magnetic stimulation (Butefisch et al., 2003). For example, Feydy et al. (2002) longitudinally studied a group of stroke patients with an affected upper limb. Three fMRI sessions were performed over a period of 1 to 6 months after stroke. Patients with sparing of the primary motor cortex showed an initial recruitment of additional ipsilateral and contralateral motor areas, but this gradually developed toward a pattern of activation restricted to the contralateral sensorimotor cortex. However, in patients with primary motor lesions, a persistent recruitment of ipsilateral activity was typically found.

The involvement of the healthy hemisphere has also been observed during the recovery of language abilities, again using a variety of methods, including finger tapping (Klingman & Sussman, 1983), cortical potentials (Thomas et al., 1997), Doppler ultrasonography (Silvestrini et al., 1998), xenon-133 (Demeurisse & Capon, 1991), PET (Buckner et al., 1996; Engelien et al., 1995; Ohyama et al., 1996; Weiller et al., 1995), and fMRI (Cao et al., 1999; Thulborn, Carpenter, & Just, 1999). For example, Cao et al. (1999) reported a positive correlation between bilateral PFC recruitment during verb generation and picture-naming tasks and recovery of language functions after left hemisphere stroke. A longitudinal study using Doppler ultrasonography also found that, after a period of speech therapy, word fluency in a group of aphasics was associated with a bilateral increase in flow velocity (Silvestrini et al., 1998).

Activity–Performance Correlations   More direct evidence for the compensation view of age-related bihemispheric recruitment has been provided by studies that measured correlations between brain activity and task performance. As mentioned in the preceding section, Reuter-Lorenz et al. (2000) investigated the effect of aging on performance on a working memory task with three difficulty levels. They found that older adults who displayed a bilateral pattern of PFC activity were faster in the verbal working memory task than those who did not display the pattern.

This kind of evidence suggesting that bilateral activity is beneficial for performance raises a question: If bihemispheric recruitment enhances performance, why do young adults not take advantage of this mechanism? A possible answer to this question was provided by a study by Rypma and D'Esposito (2000). In this study, the correlation between PFC activity and speed in a working memory task was positive in older adults, but negative in younger adults. In other words, in the older group, those participants showing greater PFC activity were faster than those showing less PFC activity, whereas in the young group, participants showing greater PFC activity were slower than those showing less PFC activity. The authors suggested that younger and older adults could be at different points of a sigmoid curve relating neural activity and performance such that the level of neural activity for optimal performance is higher for older adults than it is for young adults. Thus, one possible answer to the question here is that bilateral activity is efficient for older adults, but not for young adults.

Although activity–performance correlations represent very valuable evidence for the compensation view, they have two limitations. First, activity–performance correlations can be ambiguous. Although it would be expected that activations that are positively correlated with better performance are beneficial (compensatory) whereas those that are negatively correlated with performance are detrimental, this is not necessarily the case. To explain this point with an analogy, let us consider walking stick use in the older adult population. Even though walking stick use is obviously compensatory, the correlation between walking stick use and walking performance is likely to be negative for the simple reason that a walking stick is used only by those adults who have difficulties walking.

Second, activity–performance correlations cannot be easily generalized to different experimental conditions. In functional neuroimaging experiments, activations are extremely sensitive to experimental conditions; hence, differences between individuals who show more or less activity in a particular cognitive task are highly specific to the nature of the task. One way of addressing this issue is to distinguish between high- and low-performing individuals not on the basis of the same task associated with the activation of interest, but on the basis of a battery of neuropsychological tasks that are standardized and therefore generalizable. Studies that used this approach are described in the next section.

High- Versus Low-Performing Elderly   Direct evidence for the compensation account has come from three neuroimaging studies that distinguished between high- and low-performing elderly adults (Cabeza, Anderson, et al., 2002; Daselaar et al., 2003b; Rosen et al., 2002). In Cabeza, Anderson, et al.'s (2002) study, two groups were selected from a larger sample of older adults before scanning, one group that performed as well as a young group in a battery of memory tests (old-high group) and another group that performed significantly worse than the young group (old-low group). The two groups of older adults and the group of young adults were then scanned during a source memory task, which was previously shown to be associated with right PFC activity in young adults (Cabeza, Locantore, & Anderson, 2003). As illustrated by plate 14.3 (see color insert), the results clearly supported the compensation hypothesis: Old-low participants showed no reduction in lateralization (plate 14.3b), whereas old-high participants showed a bilateral activation pattern (plate 14.3c). This finding suggests that the old-low participants recruited similar PFC regions as young adults, but used them inefficiently, whereas old-high participants compensated for age-related memory decline by reorganizing the episodic retrieval network. In contrast, the results in plate 14.3 are inconsistent with the dedifferentiation and competition views, which predict the asymmetry reduction, as other forms of age-related neurocognitive decline, should be more pronounced in low-performing than in high-performing older adults.

Similar results were reported in fMRI studies by Rosen et al. (2002) and Daselaar et al. (2003b). As in Cabeza, Anderson, et al.'s (2002) study, Rosen et al. used standardized memory tasks to select high- and low-performing older adults from a larger sample. Young, old-high, and old-low participants were scanned during deep (manufactured vs. natural) and shallow (uppercase vs. lowercase) verbal encoding conditions. As illustrated by figure 14.4a, old-low participants showed decreased activity in the left and right PFC compared to young controls, whereas old-high participants showed preserved left PFC activity and increased RPFC activity. Thus, this study extended the finding of Cabeza, Anderson, et al. from episodic retrieval to episodic encoding.

Finally, Daselaar et al. (2003b) also compared groups of high- and low-performing old adults on a verbal encoding/recognition task; the groups were divided post hoc based on their memory scores. As illustrated by figure 14.4b, during the seman-

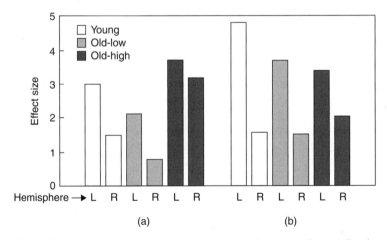

Figure 14.4. Reduced hemispheric asymmetry during semantic encoding in high-performing elderly compared to young and old-low adults. Bars indicate effect sizes in left and right prefrontal cortex. (From [a] Rosen et al., 2002; [b] Daselaar et al., 2003b.)

tic encoding task (pleasant/unpleasant decisions), all groups showed left-lateralized activation patterns, but PFC activity was slightly less lateralized in the low-performing elderly and even less so in the high-performing elderly.

Appraisal

Overall, evidence for the compensation view is much stronger than evidence for the dedifferentiation and competition views. Moreover, findings supporting dedifferentiation and competition are problematic in other ways. For example, the notion that children move from bilateral to unilateral activation patterns to development is supported mainly by one study (Moses et al., 2002) and is very indirect. In fact, this finding is not inconsistent with the notion that bilateral recruitment in older adults is not compensatory. Actually, it could be argued that bilateral processing is more efficient than unilateral when processing resources are low, either because they have not developed yet or because they have declined with aging.

As for the competition view, a serious problem is that the basic assumption that the two hemispheres tend to inhibit each other is controversial in and of itself. Although the notion that the two hemispheres compete with each other in young adults is consistent with some evidence, particularly in the spatial attention domain (Kinsbourne, 1973), it has not received much empirical support in other domains (Chiarello & Maxfield, 1996). On the contrary, evidence from several different domains tends to support that the two hemispheres do not compete but collaborate during the performance of cognitive tasks, particularly when tasks more complex or difficult (Banich, 1998; Berryman & Kennelly, 1992; Brown & Jeeves, 1993; Weissman & Banich, 2000). Moreover, the competition account has not been tested directly in older adults; hence, it remains highly speculative. In sum, the compensation view is at present the most convincing account of age-related asymmetry reductions.

Aging and Hemispheric Specialization

If one accepts the compensation view of age-related asymmetry reductions, then it is reasonable to ask which specific cognitive operations are recruited for compensation. For example, if older adults recruit bilateral PFC regions during a task that activates mainly right PFC regions in young adults, it may be asked how cognitive operations mediated by the left PFC can enhance performance in a task primarily dependent on the right PFC. This kind of question brings us back to distinctions regarding the specialization of the left and right hemispheres, such as the verbal versus spatial and the production versus monitoring distinctions.

Verbal Versus Spatial

On the basis of the verbal versus spatial/pictorial hypothesis, speculation could be that bilateral activity in older adults reflects the recruitment of verbal processing to compensate for deficits in spatial/pictorial processing and vice versa. Consistent with this idea, age-related asymmetry reductions may appear as an attenuation of differences in stimulus-related lateralization patterns. In the aforementioned working memory study by Reuter-Lorenz et al. (2000), young adults showed significant activity in the left PFC during a verbal working memory task (letter maintenance) and in the right PFC during a spatial working memory task (location maintenance), whereas older adults showed significant PFC activity bilaterally in both tasks. Thus, the argument could be that older subjects compensated for deficits in spatial working memory by recruiting verbal working memory processes (e.g., coding screen locations with verbal labels) and for deficits in verbal working memory by recruiting spatial/pictorial working memory processes (e.g., paying attention to visual features of the letters).

The main problem of this account is that it cannot easily account for age-related asymmetry reductions in conditions in which the lateralized activation patterns in young adults are not stimulus related, such as the one in Reuter-Lorenz et al.'s (2000) study, but process related. As reviewed, PFC activity in young adults tends to be left lateralized during encoding and right lateralized during retrieval (Nyberg, Cabeza, & Tulving, 1996; Tulving et al., 1994), whereas older adults may show a more bilateral pattern of PFC activity because of additional recruitment of the right PFC during encoding and left PFC during retrieval. Because age-related right PFC increases during encoding and age-related left PFC increases during retrieval have been found for the same kind of stimuli, namely words, they cannot be accommodated by the verbal/spatial account. In contrast, they could be explained by an account of a process-related lateralized pattern, such as the production/monitoring hypothesis.

Production Versus Monitoring

According to the production/monitoring hypothesis, the left PFC is more involved in semantically guided information production processes, whereas the right PFC is more involved in verification and monitoring processes (Cabeza, Locantore, & Anderson, 2003). On the basis of this hypothesis, it could be speculated that bilateral activity in older adults reflects the recruitment of monitoring processes to compensate for production deficits and vice versa. Consistent with this idea, in a study (Cabeza et al., 2004) in which young adults showed a left PFC activation during working memory (i.e., production) and a right PFC activation during attention (i.e., monitoring), older adults showed bilateral PFC activity in both conditions (see plate 14.4 in the color insert). This bilaterality occurred because older adults recruited right PFC during verbal working memory and left PFC during visual attention. Given our account of the lateralization pattern of young adults based on the production/monitoring hypothesis, these results suggest that older adults compensated for deficits in production processes by recruiting additional monitoring processes, and for deficits in production processes by recruiting additional production processes.

The strengths and weaknesses of the production/monitoring account of compensation are the reverse of the ones of the verbal/spatial account. Generally, the production monitoring account can explain age-related asymmetry reductions when lateralization patterns in young adults are process related, as in the Cabeza et al. study (2004), but has difficulties explaining these reductions when lateralization patterns in young adults are stimulus related, as in Reuter-Lorenz et al.'s (2000) study.

One way to address the limitations of both verbal/spatial and production/monitoring accounts is to assume that compensatory recruitment of contralateral PFC regions may involve different kinds of processes depending on the task. In other words, older adults may compensate for deficits in processes mediated by the left PFC by recruiting processes mediated by the right PFC and vice versa, but the specific kinds of cognitive operations recruited vary across tasks. The strength of this view is that it can account for the wide variety of conditions for which age-related asymmetry reductions have been observed. On the other hand, the weakness of this view is that, compared to verbal/spatial and production/monitoring accounts, it is very vague and difficult to falsify. At any rate, as noted next, before any of these accounts can be tested further research is necessary to clarify the relationship between compensation-related activity in older adults and specific changes in cognitive performance.

Conclusions

The goal of this chapter was to link recent behavioral and neuroimaging findings on hemispheric lateralization and aging to general ideas about hemispheric organization. In the first section, we described anatomical differences between the left and right hemispheres of the brain and addressed the verbal/spatial and production/monitoring accounts of hemispheric specialization. In addition, we described three different models of hemispheric interaction: insulation, inhibition, and cooperation. Although supporting evidence was presented for each of these models, overall the findings favored the cooperation view.

In the second section, two models of age-related changes in hemispheric lateralization were addressed: the right hemiaging model and the HAROLD model. The first model states that the right hemisphere is more sensitive to the harmful effects of aging than the left hemisphere, resulting in greater dependence on left hemisphere processing in elderly adults. In contrast, the HAROLD model states that elderly are more likely to rely on both hemispheres in conditions in which unilateral recruitment is sufficient in young adults. Whereas evidence for the first account has been very inconsistent, the findings in support of the HAROLD model are rapidly accumulating and have consistently been reported in the domains of working memory, episodic memory, attention, inhibitory control, and sensorimotor processing.

In the third part of the chapter, we linked the first two sections by discussing three different accounts of age-related asymmetry reductions in relation to the different hemispheric interaction models addressed at the beginning of the chapter. The first account, the dedifferentiation view, proposes that asymmetry reductions reflect a failure to recruit specialized neural mechanisms mediated by either the left or the right hemisphere. This idea fits with an age-related impairment in hemispheric insulation processes. The second account, the competition view, asserts that bilateral recruitment in older adults reflects an age-related reduction in normal hemispheric inhibition. Finally, the compensation view states that age-related asymmetry reductions are compensatory and reflect greater cooperation between the hemispheres.

Whereas the first two accounts mainly have a theoretical basis, there is substantial experimental support for the compensation view. A first line of evidence comes from studies that found a positive correlation between asymmetry reductions and cognitive performance in elderly adults (Reuter-Lorenz et al., 2000; Rypma & D'Esposito, 2000). Other important evidence comes from three neuroimaging studies (Cabeza, Anderson, et al., 2002; Rosen et al., 2002; Daselaar et al., 2003b) that directly compared high- and low-performing older adults. In each of these studies, reduced hemispheric asymmetry was specific to the high-performing elderly adults. Hence, at present, the compensation view clearly is the most convincing account of age-related asymmetry reductions.

On a final note, it is important to mention that, even though valuable insights regarding aging and hemispheric organization have already been gained from the research described in this chapter, there are still some issues to be resolved concerning the prevalence of asymmetry reductions across the life span. For instance, the results of several fMRI studies (Daselaar et al., 2003a; Logan et al., 2002; Nielson, Langenecker, & Garavan, 2002; Stebbins et al., 2002) suggest that asymmetry reductions are more pronounced in "old-old adults" (75–80 years of age) than in "young-old adults" (i.e., 60–70 years of age). This could imply that asymmetry reductions are associated with more advanced forms of neurocognitive decline. In agreement with this idea, using PET, Bäckman et al. (1999) found evidence of bilateral recruitment during cued recall in a group of patients with mild Alzheimer's dementia (AD), but not in a group of healthy elderly controls.

It is also worth noting that this evidence is not inconsistent with the compensation view of HAROLD. For example, it is possible that bilateral recruitment is beneficial to performance only when cognitive demands are high. Cognitive demands may be high when the task is difficult enough or when cognitive resources have been reduced by factors such as healthy aging and dementia. This suggests that, whether bilateral recruitment is found in healthy elderly compared to young or in AD compared to healthy aging, it would depend on the particular combination of task demands and available cognitive resources. Thus, finding greater bilateral recruitment in AD than in healthy aging does not imply that bilateral recruitment is not compensatory because it is possible that among participants with AD, those who show greater bilateral recruitment perform better than those who do not.

This is exactly what a study by Grady et al. (2003) found. They used PET to investigate brain activity during encoding (living/nonliving judgments about objects and words) and a subsequent recognition memory in patients with mild AD and healthy elderly controls. During both tasks, bilateral PFC recruitment was observed in the AD group, but not in the healthy controls. In accordance with the compensation account, bihemispheric recruitment in patients with AD was positively correlated with recognition accuracy.

At any rate, given the number of factors that seem to modulate the occurrence of bilateral recruitment, further progress is unlikely to occur unless these factors are investigated one by one, keeping other factors constant. An improvement for future studies on this topic would be to compare different age groups within the same study using a range of tasks taken from different cognitive domains with differing levels of task difficulty. Such an approach may ultimately clarify the role of the various factors that contribute to the phenomenon of hemispheric asymmetry reductions.

References

Abe O, Aoki S, Hayashi N, Yamada H, Kunimatsu A, Mori H, et al. (2002) Normal aging in the central nervous system: Quantitative MR diffusion-tensor analysis. Neurobiol Aging; 23: 433–441.

Albanese E, Merlo A, Albanese A, Gomez E. (1989) Anterior speech region. Asymmetry and weight-surface correlation. Arch Neurol; 46: 307–310.

Allan K, Dolan RJ, Fletcher PC, Rugg MD. (2000) The role of the right anterior prefrontal cortex in episodic retrieval. Neuroimage; 11: 217–227.

Bäckman L, Almkvist O, Andersson J, Nordberg A, Winblad B, Reineck R, et al. (1997) Brain activation in young and older adults during implicit and explicit retrieval. J Cogn Neurosci; 9: 378–391.

Bäckman L, Andersson J, Nyberg L, Winblad B, Nordberg A, Almkvist O. (1999) Brain regions associated with episodic retrieval in normal aging and Alzheimer's disease. Neurology; 52: 1861–1870.

Balinsky B. (1941) An analysis of the mental factors of various groups from nine to sixty. Gen Psychol Monogr; 23: 191–234.

Baltes PB, Lindenberger U. (1997) Emergence of a powerful connection between sensory and cognitive functions across the adult life span: A new window to the study of cognitive aging? Psychol Aging; 12: 12–21.

Banich MT. (1998) The missing link: The role of interhemispheric interaction in attentional processing. Brain Cogn; 36: 128–157.

Banich MT, Belger A. (1990) Interhemispheric interaction: How do the hemispheres divide and conquer a task? Cortex; 26: 77–94.

Banich MT, Goering S, Stolar N, Belger A. (1990) Interhemispheric processing in left- and right-handers. Int J Neurosci; 54: 197–208.

Berryman ML, Kennelly KJ. (1992) Letter memory loads change more than visual-field advantage: Interhemispheric coupling effects. Brain Cogn; 18: 152–168.

Borod J, Obler L, Albert M, Stiefel S. (1983) Lateralization for pure tone perception as a function of age and sex. Cortex; 19: 281–285.

Brion JP, Demeurisse G, Capon A. (1989) Evidence of cortical reorganization in hemiparetic patients. Stroke; 20: 1079–1084.

Broca P. (1861) Remarque sur le siege de la faculte du langage articule, suivies d'une observation d'aphemie. Bull Soc Anthropol; 6: 330–357.

Brown WS, Jeeves MA. (1993) Bilateral visual field processing and evoked potential interhemispheric transmission time. Neuropsychologia; 31: 1267–81.

Buckner RL, Corbetta M, Schatz J, Raichle ME, Petersen, SE. (1996) Preserved speech abilities and compensation following prefrontal damage. Proc Natl Acad Sci USA; 93: 1249–1253.

Buckner RLL, Logan JM (2002) Frontal contributions to episodic memory encoding in the young and the elderly. In Parker AW, EL, Bussey TJ, eds. The cognitive neuroscience of memory: Encoding and retrieval. New York: Psychology Press; pp. 59–82.

Butefisch CM, Netz J, Wessling M, Seitz RJ, Homberg V. (2003) Remote changes in cortical excitability after stroke. Brain; 126: 470–481.

Cabeza R. (2002) Hemispheric asymmetry reduction in older adults: The HAROLD model. Psychol Aging; 17: 85–100.

Cabeza R, Anderson ND, Locantore JK, McIntosh AR. (2002) Aging gracefully: Compensatory brain activity in high-performing older adults. Neuroimage; 17: 1394–1402.

Cabeza R, Daselaar SM, Dolcos F, Prince S, Budde M, Nyberg L. (2004) Age-related differences in brain activity during working memory, visual attention, and episodic memory: Task-independent versus task-specific effects. Cereb Cortex; 14(4): 364–375.

Cabeza R, Dolcos F, Graham R, Nyberg L. (2002) Similarities and differences in the neural correlates of episodic memory retrieval and working memory. Neuroimage; 16: 317–330.

Cabeza R, Dolcos F, Prince SE, Rice HJ, Weissman DH, Nyberg L. (2003) Attention-related activity during episodic memory retrieval: A cross-function fMRI study. Neuropsychologia; 41: 390–399.

Cabeza R, Grady CL, Nyberg L, McIntosh AR, Tulving E, Kapur S, et al. (1997) Age-related differences in neural activity during memory encoding and retrieval: A positron emission tomography study. J Neurosci; 17: 391–400.

Cabeza R, Locantore JK, Anderson ND. (2003) Lateralization of prefrontal activity during episodic memory retrieval: Evidence for the production-monitoring hypothesis. J Cogn Neurosci; 15: 249–259.

Cabeza R, McIntosh AR, Tulving E, Nyberg L, Grady CL. (1997) Age-related differences in effective neural connectivity during encoding and recall. Neuroreport; 8: 3479–3483.

Cabeza R, Nyberg L. (2000) Imaging cognition II: An empirical review of 275 PET and fMRI studies. J Cogn Neurosc; 12: 1–47.

Calautti C, Serrati C, Baron J-C. (2001) Effects of age on brain activation during auditory-cued thumb-to-index opposition: A positron emission tomography study. Stroke; 2001: 139.

Cao Y, Vikingstad EM, Paige George K, Johnson AF, Welch KMA. (1999) Cortical language activation in stroke patients recovering from aphasia with functional MRI. Stroke; 30: 2331–2340.

Cherry BJ, Hellige JB, McDowd JM. (1995) Age differences and similarities in patterns of cerebral hemispheric asymmetry. Psychol Aging; 10: 191–203.

Chiarello C, Maxfield L. (1996) Varieties of interhemispheric inhibition, or how to keep a good hemisphere down. Brain Cogn; 30: 81–108.

Clark LE, Knowles JB. (1973) Age differences in dichotic listening performance. J Gerontol; 28: 173–178.

Craik FIM, Lockhart RS. (1972) Levels of processing: A framework for memory research. J Verbal Learn Verbal Behav; 11: 671–684.

Daselaar SM, Veltman DJ, Rombouts SA, Raaijmakers JG, Jonker C. (2003a) Deep processing activates the medial temporal lobe in young but not in old adults. Neurobiol Aging; 24: 1005–1011.

Daselaar SM, Veltman DJ, Rombouts SARB, Raaijmakers JGW, Jonker C. (2003b) Neuroanatomical correlates of episodic encoding and retrieval in young and elderly subjects. Brain; 126: 43.

Demeurisse G, Capon A. (1991) Brain activation during a linguistic task in conduction aphasia. Cortex; 27: 285–294.

Di Piero V, Chollet FM, MacCarthy P, Lenzi GL, Frackowiak RS. (1992) Motor recovery after acute ischaemic stroke: A metabolic study. J Neurol Neurosurg Psychiatry; 55: 990–996.

Dixit NK, Gerton BK, Dohn P, Meyer-Lindenberg A, Berman KF. (2000) Age-related changes in rCBF activation during an N-back working memory paradigm occur prior to age 50. Neuroimage; 5(part 2): S94.

Dolcos F, Rice HJ, Cabeza R. (2002) Hemispheric asymmetry and aging: Right hemisphere decline or asymmetry reduction. Neurosci Biobehav Rev; 26: 819–825.

Eberstaller O. (1884) Zur Oberflachen Anatomie der Grosshirn Hemisphaeren. Wien Med.; 7: 479, 642, 644.

Elias MF, Kinsbourne M. (1974) Age and sex differences in the processing of verbal and nonverbal stimuli. J Gerontol; 29: 162–171.

Ellis RJ. (1990) Dichotic asymmetries in aging and alcoholic subjects. Alcohol Clin Exp Res; 14: 863–871.

Engelien A, Silbersweig D, Stern E, Huber W, Doring W, Frith C, et al. (1995) The functional anatomy of recovery from auditory agnosia. A PET study of sound categorization in a neurological patient and normal controls. Brain; 118: 1395–1409.

Feydy A, Carlier R, Roby-Brami A, Bussel B, Cazalis F, Pierot L, et al. (2002) Longitudinal study of motor recovery after stroke: Recruitment and focusing of brain activation. Stroke; 33: 1610–1617.

Fink GR, Driver J, Rorden C, Baldeweg T, Dolan RJ. (2000) Neural consequences of competing stimuli in both visual hemifields: A physiological basis for visual extinction. Ann Neurol; 47: 440–446.

Fletcher PC, Shallice T, Frith CD, Frackowiak RJ, Dolan RJ. (1998) The functional roles of prefrontal cortex in episodic memory II: Retrieval. Brain; 121: 1249–1256.

Foundas AL, Leonard CM, Gilmore RL, Fennell EB, Heilman KM. (1996) Pars triangularis asymmetry and language dominance. Proc Natl Acad Sci USA; 93: 719–722.

Galaburda AM, Sanides F, Geschwind N. (1978) Human brain. Cytoarchitectonic left-right asymmetries in the temporal speech region. Arch Neurol; 35: 812–817.

Galuske RA, Schlote W, Bratzke H, Singer W. (2000) Interhemispheric asymmetries of the modular structure in human temporal cortex. Science; 289: 1946–1949.

Garavan H, Ross TJ, Stein EA. (1999) Right hemispheric dominance of inhibitory control: an event-related functional MRI study. Proc Natl Acad Sci USA; 96: 8301–8306.

Garret HL. (1946) A developmental theory of intelligence. Am Psychol; 1: 372–378.

Gazzaniga MS. (1970) The bisected brain. New York: Appleton.

Gerhardstein P, Peterson MA, Rapcsak SZ. (1998) Age-related hemispheric asymmetry in object discrimination. J Clin Exp Neuropsychol; 20: 174–185.

Glick SD, Ross DA, Hough LB. (1982) Lateral asymmetry of neurotransmitters in human brain. Brain Res; 234: 53–63.

Goldstein G, Shelly C. (1981) Does the right hemisphere age more rapidly than the left? J Clin Neuropsychol; 3: 65–78.

Good CD, Johnsrude IS, Ashburner J, Henson RNA, Friston KJ, Frackowiak RSJ. (2001) A voxel-based morphometric study of ageing in 465 normal adult human brains. Neuroimage; 14: 21–36.

Grady CL, Bernstein LJ, Beig S, Siegenthaler AL. (2002) The effects of encoding task on age-related differences in the functional neuroanatomy of face memory. Psychol Aging; 17: 7–23.

Grady CL, Maisog JM, Horwitz B, Ungerleider LG, Mentis MJ, Salerno JA, et al. (1994) Age-related changes in cortical blood flow activation during visual processing of faces and location. Journal of Neuroscience; 14: 1450–1462.

Grady CL, McIntosh AR, Beig S, Keightley ML, Burian H, Black SE. (2003) Evidence from functional neuroimaging of a compensatory prefrontal network in Alzheimer's disease. J Neurosci; 23: 986–993.

Grady CL, McIntosh AR, Horwitz B, Rapoport SI. (2000) Age-related changes in the neural correlates of degraded and nondegraded face processing. Cogn Neuropsychol; 217: 165–186.

Gur RC, Packer IK, Hungerbuhler JP, Reivich M, Obrist WD, Amarnek WS, et al. (1980) Differences in the distribution of gray and white matter in human cerebral hemispheres. Science; 207: 1226–1228.

Hellige JB. (1993) Hemispheric asymmetry: What's right and what's left? Cambridge, MA: Harvard University Press.

Henson RA, Shallice T, Dolan RJ. (1999) Right prefrontal cortex and episodic memory retrieval: A functional MRI test of the monitoring hypothesis. Brain; 122: 1367–1381.

Honda M, Nagamine T, Fukuyama H, Yonekura Y, Kimura J, Shibasaki H. (1997) Movement-related cortical potentials and regional cerebral bllod flow in patients with stroke after motor recovery. J Neurol Sci; 146: 117–126.

Hopper KD, Patel S, Cann TS, Wilcox T, Schaeffer JM. (1994) The relationship of age, gender, handedness, and sidedness to the size of the corpus callosum. Acad Radiol; 1: 243–248.

Hutchinson S, Kobayashi M, Horkan CM, Pascual-Leone A, Alexander MP, Schlaug G. (2002) Age-related differences in movement representation. Neuroimage; 17: 1720–1728.

Johnson RC, Cole RE, Bowers JK, Foiles SV, Nikaido AM, Patrick JW, et al. (1979) Hemispheric efficiency in middle and later adulthood. Cortex; 15: 109–119.

Jonides J, Schumacher EH, Smith EE. (1997) Verbal working memory load affects regional brain activation as measured by PET. J Cogn Neurosci; 9: 462–475.

Kinsbourne M. (1973) The control of attention by interaction between the cerebral hemispheres. In Kornblum S, ed. Attention and performance IV. New York: Academic Press; pp. 239–256.

Kinsbourne M, Hicks RE. (1978) Functional cerebral space: A model for overflow, transfer, and interference effects in human performance. In Kinsbourne M, ed. Asymmetrical function of the brain. Cambridge, UK: Cambridge University Press; pp. 345–362.

Klingman KC, Sussman HM. (1983) Hemisphericity in aphasic language recovery. J Speech Hearing Res; 26: 249–256.

Klisz D. (1987) Neuropsychological evaluation in older persons. In Storandt MS, Siegler IC, Elias MF, eds. The clinical psychology of aging. New York: Plenum; pp. 71–95.

Konishi S, Donaldson DI, Buckner RL. (2001) Transient activation during block transition. Neuroimage; 13: 364–374.

Kooistra CA, Heilman KM. (1988) Motor dominance and lateral asymmetry of the globus pallidus. Neurology; 38: 388–390.

Kosslyn SM, Koenig O, Barrett A, Cave CB, Tang J, Gabrieli JD. (1989) Evidence for two types of spatial representations: Hemispheric specialization for categorical and coordinate relations. J Exp Psychol Hum Percept Perform; 15: 723–735.

Kreuter C, Kinsbourne M, Trevarthen C. (1972) Are deconnected cerebral hemispheres independent channels? A preliminary study of the effect of unilateral loading on bilateral finger tapping. Neuropsychologia; 10: 453–461.

Li S-C, Lindenberger U. (1999) Cross-level unification: A computational exploration of the link between deterioration of neurotransmitter systems dedifferentiation of cognitive abilities in old age. In Nilsson L-G, Markowitsch HJ, eds. Cognitive neuroscience of memory. Seattle, WA: Hogrefe and Huber; pp. 103–146.

Liederman J, Meehan P. (1986) When is between-hemisphere division of labor advantageous? Neuropsychologia; 24: 863–874.

Logan JM, Sanders AL, Snyder AZ, Morris JC, Buckner RL. (2002) Under-recruitment and nonselective recruitment: Dissociable neural mechanisms associated with aging. Neuron; 33: 827–840.

Madden DJ, Gottlob LR, Denny LL, Turkington TG, Provenzale JM, Hawk TC, et al. (1999) Aging and recognition memory: Changes in regional cerebral blood flow associated with components of reaction time distributions. J Cogn Neurosci; 11: 511–520.

Maguire EA, Frith CD. (2003) Aging affects the engagement of the hippocampus during autobiographical memory retrieval. Brain; 126: 1511–1523.

Mattay VS, Fera F, Tessitore A, Hariri AR, Das S, Callicott JH, et al. (2002) Neurophysiological correlates of age-related changes in human motor function. Neurology; 58: 630–635.

Merola JL, Liederman J. (1990) The effect of task difficulty upon the extent to which performance benefits from between-hemisphere division of inputs. Int J Neurosci; 51: 35–44.

Meudell PR, Greenhalgh M. (1987) Age related differences in left and right hand skill and in visuo-spatial performance: Their possible relationships to the hypothesis that the right hemisphere ages more rapidly than the left. Cortex; 23: 431–445.

Mitrushina M, Fogel T, D'Elia L, Uchiyama C, et al. (1995) Performance on motor tasks as an indication of increased behavioral asymmetry with advancing age. Neuropsychologia; 33: 359–364.

Morcom AM, Good CD, Frackowiak RS, Rugg MD. (2003) Age effects on the neural correlates of successful memory encoding. Brain; 126: 213–229.

Moses P, Roe K, Buxton RB, Wong EC, Frank LR, Stiles J. (2002) Functional MRI of global and local processing in children. Neuroimage; 16: 415–424.

Navon D. (1983) How many trees does it take to make a forest? Perception; 12: 239–254.

Nebes RD, Madden DJ, Berg WD. (1983) The effect of age on hemispheric asymmetry in visual and auditory identification. Exp Aging Res; 9: 87–91.

Nielson KA, Langenecker SA, Garavan H. (2002) Differences in the functional neuroanatomy of inhibitory control across the adult life span. Psychol Aging; 17: 56–71.

Nolde SF, Johnson MK, Raye CL. (1998) The role of prefrontal cortex during tests of episodic memory. Trends Cogn Sci; 2: 399–406.

Nyberg L, Cabeza R, Tulving E. (1996) PET studies of encoding and retrieval: The HERA model. Psychonomic Bull Rev; 3: 135–148.

Ohyama M, Senda M, Kitamura S, Ishii K, Mishina M, Terashi A. (1996) Role of the nondominant hemisphere and undamaged area during word repetition in poststroke aphasics. Stroke; 27: 897–903.

Oke A, Keller R, Mefford I, Adams RN. (1978) Lateralization of norepinephrine in human thalamus. Science; 200: 1411–1413.

Park DC, Lautenschlager G, Hedden T, Davidson NS, Smith AD, Smith PK. (2002) Models of visuospatial and verbal memory across the adult life span. Psychol Aging; 17: 299–320.

Passarotti AM, Banich MT, Sood RK, Wang JM. (2002) A generalized role of interhemispheric interaction under attentionally demanding conditions: Evidence from the auditory and tactile modality. Neuropsychologia; 40: 1082–1096.

Pieniadz JM, Naeser MA. (1984) Computed tomographic scan cerebral asymmetries and morphologic brain asymmetries. Correlation in the same cases post mortem. Arch Neurol; 41: 403–409.

Pollmann SZ, von Cramon DY. (2003) The neural basis of the bilateral distribution advantage. Exp Brain Res; 221: 322–333.

Pujol J, Lopez-Sala A, Deus J, Cardoner N, Sebastian-Galles N, Conesa G, et al. (2002) The lateral asymmetry of the human brain studied by volumetric magnetic resonance imaging. Neuroimage; 17: 670–679.

Raz N, Gunning FM, Head D, Dupuis JH, McQuain J, Briggs SD, et al. (1997) Selective aging of the human cerebral cortex observed in vivo: Differential vulnerability of the prefrontal gray matter. Cereb Cortex; 7: 268–282.

Reuter-Lorenz P, Jonides J, Smith ES, Hartley A, Miller A, Marshuetz C, et al. (2000) Age differences in the frontal lateralization of verbal and spatial working memory revealed by PET. J Cogn Neurosci; 12: 174–187.

Reuter-Lorenz PA, Stanczak L, Miller AC. (1999) Neural recruitment and cognitive aging: Two hemispheres are better than one, especially as you age. Psychol Sci; 10: 494–500.

Ringo JL, Doty RW, Demeter S, Simard PY. (1994) Time is of the essence: A conjecture that hemispheric specialization arises from interhemispheric conduction delay. Cereb Cortex; 4: 331–343.

Rosen AC, Prull MW, O'Hara R, Race EA, Desmond JE, Glover GH, et al. (2002) Variable effects of aging on frontal lobe contributions to memory. Neuroreport; 13: 2425–2428.

Rubens AB, Mahowald MW, Hutton JT. (1976) Asymmetry of the lateral (sylvian) fissures in man. Neurology; 26: 620–624.

Rugg MD, Fletcher PC, Allan K, Frith CD, Frackowiak RSJ, Dolan RJ. (1998) Neural correlates of memory retrieval during recognition memory and cued recall. Neuroimage; 8: 262–273.

Rypma B, D'Esposito M. (2000) Isolating the neural mechanisms of age-related changes in human working memory. Nat Neurosci; 3: 509–515.

Schear JM, Nebes RD. (1980) Memory for verbal and spatial information as a function of age. Exp Aging Res; 6: 271–281.

Scheibel AB, Paul LA, Fried I, Forsythe AB, Tomiyasu U, Wechsler A, et al. (1985) Dendritic organization of the anterior speech area. Exp Neurol; 87: 109–117.

Silvestrini M, Cupini LM, Placidi F, Diomedi M, Bernardi G. (1998) Bilateral hemispheric activation in the early recovery of motor function after stroke. Stroke; 29: 1305–1310.

Smith EE, Jonides J. (1999) Neuroscience—Storage and executive processes in the frontal lobes. Science; 283: 1657–1661.

Stebbins GT, Carrillo MC, Dorfman J, Dirksen C, Desmond JE, Turner DA, et al. (2002) Aging effects on memory encoding in the frontal lobes. Psychol Aging; 17: 44–55.

Steinmetz H, Rademacher J, Jancke L, Huang YX, Thron A, Zilles K. (1990) Total surface of temporoparietal intrasylvian cortex: Diverging left-right asymmetries. Brain Lang; 39: 357–372.

Sullivan EV, Pfefferbaum A, Adalsteinsson E, Swan GE, Carmelli D. (2002) Differential rates of regional brain change in callosal and ventricular size: A 4-year longitudinal MRI study of elderly men. Cereb Cortex; 12: 438–445.

Teszner D, Tzavaras A, Gruner J, Hecaen H. (1972) L'asymétrie droite-gauche du planum temporale: à propos de l'étude anatomique de 100 cerveaux [Right-left asymmetry of the planum temporale; apropos of the anatomical study of 100 brains]. Rev Neurol (Paris); 126: 444–449. (In French)

Thomas C, Altenmuller E, Marckmann G, Kahrs J, Dichgans J. (1997) Language processing in aphasia: Changes in lateralization patterns during recovery reflect cerebral plasticity in adults. Electroencephalogr Clin Neurophysiol; 102: 86–97.

Thulborn KR, Carpenter PA, Just MA. (1999) Plasticity of language-related brain function during recovery from stroke. Stroke; 30: 749–754.

Tulving E. (1983) Elements of episodic memory. Oxford: Oxford University Press.

Tulving E, Kapur S, Craik FIM, Moscovitch M, Houle S. (1994) Hemispheric encoding/retrieval asymmetry in episodic memory: Positron emission tomography findings. Proc Natl Acad Sci USA; 91: 2016–2020.

von Economo C, Horn L. (1930) Uber Windungsrelief, Masseund Rindenarchitektonik der Supratemporalflache, ihre individuellen und ihre Seitenunterschiede. Ztg Neurol Psychiatr; 130: 678–657.

Wagner HN Jr, Burns HD, Dannals RF, Wong DF, Langstrom B, Duelfer T, et al. (1983) Imaging dopamine receptors in the human brain by positron tomography. Science; 221: 1264–1266.

Watkins KE, Paus T, Lerch JP, Zijdenbos A, Collins DL, Neelin P, et al. (2001) Structural asymmetries in the human brain: A voxel-based statistical analysis of 142 MRI scans. Cereb Cortex; 11: 868–877.

Weiller C, Isensee C, Rijntsjes M, Huber W, Müller S, Bier D, et al. (1995) Recovery from Wernicke's aphasia: A positron emission tomography study. Ann Neurol; 37: 723–732.

Weis S, Kimbacher M, Wenger E, Neuhold A. (1993) Morphometric analysis of the corpus callosum using MR: Correlation of measurements with aging in healthy individuals. AJNR Am J Neuroradiol; 14: 637–645.

Weissman DH, Banich MT. (2000) The cerebral hemispheres cooperate to perform complex but not simple tasks. Neuropsychology; 14: 41–59.

Weller MP, Latimer-Sayer DT. (1985) Increasing right hand dominance with age on a motor skill task. Psychol Med; 15: 867–872.

Wernicke C. (1874) Der Aphasische Symptomencomplex: Eine Psychologische Studie auf Anaomischer Basis. Breslau, Germany: Cohn and Welgert.

Witelson SF, Kigar DL. (1992) Sylvian fissure morphology and asymmetry in men and women: Bilateral differences in relation to handedness in men. J Comp Neurol; 323: 326–340.

Zaidel E. (1986) Callosal dynamics and right hemisphere language. In Lepore F, Ptito M, Jasper HH, eds. Two hemispheres—One brain: Functions of the corpus callosum. New York: Liss; pp. 435–459.

15

Neurocomputational Perspectives Linking Neuromodulation, Processing Noise, Representational Distinctiveness, and Cognitive Aging

Shu-Chen Li

It is because something of exterior objects penetrates in us that we see forms and that we think.

—Epicurus, *Letter to Herodotus*

Men judge things according to the organization of their brain.

—Benedict de Spinoza, *Ethics* I

So thou through windows of thine age shalt see.

—William Shakespeare, *Sonnet* III

The foregoing series of quotations together capture the view that neurocognitive representations of mental experiences are dynamically co-constructed by the brain and its world through continual contextual and experiential tunings that occur throughout life, including old age. Couched within this conception, this chapter addresses neurocomputational approaches that examine the relation between cognitive aging deficits and aging-related attenuation of neuromodulation affecting neural activity representation and information transfer within and between cortical regions.

Following a brief overview on how to conceptualize "representation" in the context of cognitive neuroscience of aging or life span development (Baltes, Staudinger, & Lindenberger, 1999), the bulk of this chapter is devoted to a selective, rather than comprehensive, review of recent computational approaches to neuromodulation and their applications in cognitive aging research. A cross-level integrative theoretical link is highlighted: Deficient neuromodulation leads to noisy neural information processing, which in turn might result in less-distinctive cortical representation and various subsequent behavioral manifestations of commonly observed cognitive aging deficits. The brain is an open system and life span cognitive development is a dynamic, cumulative process that shapes the neurocognitive representations of ongoing interactions with the environment and sociocultural contexts through experiences (S.-C. Li, 2003; S.-C. Li & Lindenberger, 2002). Therefore, not only feed-upward effects from neural mechanisms to cognition and behavior, but also downward contextual and experiential influences on neurocognitive processing should be investigated. The last section of this chapter presents a set of simulations exploring the utility of neurocomputational models for investigating the trade-offs between aging-related deficiency in neuromodulation and contextual tuning of cortical representational distinctiveness.

Traditionally, the issue of *representation* has been a central topic in both philosophical inquiries as well as scientific investigations of mental experiences. Philosophers, cognitive and developmental psychologists, and neuroscientists have all been pursuing questions regarding the relations between the brain and its inner and outer world. For instance, how does the external world get to be represented in the brain? How do phylogenetic, developmental, and individual differences in the brain's inner world (i.e., differences or changes in the brain's structural and functional organization, as well as its neurochemical mechanisms) affect the ways with which the outer world is experienced? How do experiences taking place in the environmental, sociocultural contexts at the macrolevels and neurobiological changes at the microlevels together progressively co-construct the brain–world relation during phylogeny and ontogeny?

Co-Constructed Neurocognitive Representations of Environment and Experience Interactions

Although theoretical perspectives differ greatly in their views about the nature of representation, most share the assumption that mental experiences involve some kind of internal mediating states that carry information (see Markman & Dietrich, 2000, for review). With the aim of facilitating cross-level integration (cf. Churchland & Sejnowski, 1988) in mind, it is arguably more fruitful to consider these internal mediating states as co-constructed neurocognitive representations of ongoing environment and experience interactions that occur cumulatively throughout the life span, including old age (cf. Baltes, Reuter-Lorenz, & Rösler, in press; G. M. Edelman, 2001). Co-constructed neurocognitive representations defined as such more easily integrate neural epigenetic (Changeux, 1985; G. M. Edelman, 1987) and constructivist (Quartz & Sejnowski, 1997), developmental dynamic (e.g., Thelen & Smith, 1994; van Geert, 1998), perceptual (e.g., S. Edelman, 1998, 2001), cognitive (e.g., Palmer, 1978), conceptual (e.g., Gärdenfors, 2000), and situational/embodied (e.g., Clark, 1999) views of representation. As for integrating neurocognitive aging phenomena across levels—a goal shared by the research reviewed in this volume— the dynamic interplay between aging-related neurobiological changes at one level and environmental, experiential influences at another level are brought to the foreground by the notion of co-constructivism.

Computational Approaches to Neuromodulation of Cortical Function

This section reviews computational approaches in the study of neuromodulation of cortical function. Theories of the morphofunctional architecture of the brain emphasize the importance of connectivity and communication between cellular elements (Shepherd, 1991). Cortical functioning is implemented by the brain's structural and functional organization. Furthermore, the neurochemical processes therein influence the dynamical properties of cortical information processing by affecting ongoing neural activity representation and information transfer within and between cortical regions. Specifically, the present synaptic plasticity hypothesis was first enunciated by Ramón y Cajal (1894). In his Croonian Lecture to the Royal Society in 1894, Ramón y Cajal proposed the idea: "Mental exercise facilitates a greater development of . . . the nervous collaterals in the part of the brain in use. In this way, preexisting connections between groups of cells could be reinforced" (as cited in Squire & Kandel, 1999, p. 35). The synaptic processes of memory were formulated (e.g., Hebb, 1949) and discovered (e.g., Bliss & Lømo, 1973; Kandel & Tauc, 1964; Wigström & Gustafsson, 1981). Since then, a great variety of neurochemical singling mechanisms have been identified. It is now known that these mechanisms are very much involved in tuning the intercellular as well as interregional communications that support the brain's ongoing representations of currently perceived environmental stimulations or past experiences regenerated in current contexts.

Neurochemical influences on cortical function involve both neurotransmission operating through more constrained synaptic connections and neuromodulation acting mostly through indirect and more diffused second-messenger pathways (see Hasselmo, 1995; Zoli et al., 1998, for reviews). The anatomical characteristics of neuromodulatory innervation involving the neuromodulators, such as acetylcholine (ACh), norepinephrine (NE), serotonin (5-HT), and dopamine (DA), tend to be spatially diffuse, with extensive innervation of cortical regions arising from localized subcortical nuclei. Given such relatively broad neuromodulatory influences, it has been suggested that computational neural networks are particularly suitable for theoretical investigations of general principles of on-line, dynamic neuromodulation of cortical functioning (Hasselmo, 1995).

Modeling Neuromodulation With Respect to Different Specificity and Functionality

Neuromodulatory effects have been computationally modeled with respect to different levels of specificity and types of functionality (see Doya, Dayan, & Hasselmo, 2002; Fellous & Linster, 1998, for reviews). At the level of chemical kinetics, neuronal processes can be described as a chain of chemical reactions with their kinetics quantitatively determined by Markovian models. Modeled as such, neuromodulatory phenomena are not distinguished from other chemical reactions at the intracellular, membrane, and synaptic levels (e.g., Destexhe, Mainen, & Sejnowski, 1994). At a higher level of abstraction, neuromodulatory effects have also been modeled in terms of regulating the signal-to-noise ratio of synaptic transmission in different variants of neural networks (e.g., Cohen & Servan-Schreiber, 1992; Doya, 2002).

Focusing on working memory and attentional functions of the prefrontal cortex (PFC), a model captured the role of neuromodulation as a dynamic gating process that stabilizes or destabilizes cortical representations of ongoing experiences (O'Reilly et al., 2002). There are also other approaches that model neuromodulation of memory processes by specifying particular learning rules or activity-dependent changes (Cartling, 1999; Camperi & Wang, 1998; Lisman, Fellous, & Wang, 1998).

Besides these relatively valence-neutral views of signal tuning, neuromodulation has been conceptualized as experience-dependent regulation that enables the organisms to function adaptively in different contexts. At this level, neuromodulatory effects have been modeled as value-dependent selection (or categorization) of patterns of ongoing cortical processing that are associated with context-specific adaptive behaviors, such as behaviors leading to better rewards (e.g., Friston et al., 1994; Montague, Dayan, & Sejnowski, 1996) or better error processing (e.g., Holroyd & Coles, 2002) in a given environment.

In summary, without directly changing the structural complexity of the network itself, most models capture neuromodulation as the dynamic on-line regulation of neurocomputational complexity that affects neurocognitive representations of ongoing experience and environment interactions. During normal aging, attenuated neurochemical mechanisms are not necessarily coupled with severe global neuroanatomical degeneration. Although structural alterations in the numbers of neurons and synapses are less severe in comparison to pathological aging, reductions in transmitter contents and receptors affect the efficacy of intercellular communication and play roles in the milder cognitive declines observed in normal aging (see Morrison & Hof, 1997; Peters, 2002, for review). Computational models of neuromodulation that focus on on-line dynamic regulation of functional complexity, rather than on altering structural complexity per se, are thus suitable for studying the relations between aging-related declines in neuromodulation and cognition.

Aging and Neuromodulation

Along with neurochemical changes, brain aging involves structural losses in neurons and the connections between them (see Schneider & Rowe, 1996, for general review). Severe, progressive neuroanatomical degeneration resulting from cell death and reduced synaptic density is typical for pathological aging (e.g., of Alzheimer's disease). As for normal aging, the volumes of various cortical regions also show slightly declining trends. The most substantial shrinkage is observed in the PFC, in which the evidence for a relation between volume shrinkage and aging deficit in working memory functions is more consistently found (Head et al., 2002; Raz, 2000; see also chapter 2, this volume).

Parallel to the less-severe neuroanatomical changes, the milder cognitive declines that occur during normal aging are likely to be due to neurochemical shifts in still relatively intact neural circuitry (Morrison & Hof, 1997). Such neurochemical shifts affect the efficacy of signal transmission, which in turn regulates neural activity within and across cell assemblies. Various transmitter systems are affected by aging and have implications for cognitive declines associated with pathological and normal aging. For instance, the transmitter ACh is important for long-term memory consolidation. It plays a specific role in the memory deficit of retaining new information of patients with Alzheimer's disease (Hasselmo, 1999). Furthermore, for an understanding of the neurochemical circuits of the aging brain, it is important to consider both the effects of various transmitters independently and the interactions between multiple transmitters, such as the recently discovered interaction of glutamate with other transmitters (e.g., DA, gamma-amino butyric acid [GABA], and ACh; Segovia et al., 2001).

Deficient Dopaminergic Neuromodulation

Among various neuromodulatory systems, the monoamines (e.g., 5-HT and the catecholamines, particularly DA) are promising neurochemical correlates of normal cognitive aging for several reasons. First, there is evidence of about 7% to 11% reduction per decade in DA D_2 receptors during normal aging, starting at about 20 years of age in the nigrostriatal region (Wong et al., 1997). There is now also evidence of D_2 receptor loss in various other extrastriatal regions (Kaasinen et al., 2000; see also chapter 3, this volume), such as the anterior cingulate cortex (13%), frontal cortex (11%), hippocampus (10%), and the amygdala (7%). D_1 receptor loss as well has been observed in the striatum (Giorgi et al., 1987) and the frontal cortex (de Keyser et al., 1990; Zahrt et al., 1997).

Note, however, the evidence thus far for aging-related declines in transmitter content and receptors has been based on cross-sectional findings derived from relatively small samples. Although the cohort effect, which is known to be a common confound in cross-sectional behavioral findings, may not have as strong an influence at the level of transmitter mechanisms, a mortality-related selection effect could be a possible confound affecting the extent of aging-related receptor loss observed in cross-sectional data. Future longitudinal data are necessary for the more direct assessment of aging-related changes in transmitter mechanisms.

Second, besides the trends of aging-related declines of DA receptors in different brain regions across the adult life span, there is also more direct experimental evidence for functional relationships between deficient dopaminergic modulation and cognitive deficits. For instance, deficient dopaminergic modulation was associated with increased response speed and reaction time fluctuation in old rats (MacRae et al., 1988). Drugs that facilitated dopaminergic modulation alleviated working memory deficits in old monkeys (Arnsten et al., 1994; Arnsten & Goldman-Rakic, 1985). In humans, aging-related attenuation of the striatal D_2 receptor binding mechanism was statistically associated with age differences in processing speed and episodic memory (Bäckman et al., 2000).

Third, on the one hand, cognitive aging deficits have been attributed, at least in part, to the dysfunction of the PFC (West, 1996). On the other hand, research over the last two decades has suggested that DA plays important roles (e.g., Gao, Wang, & Goldman-Rakic, 2003) in modulating how well the PFC utilizes briefly activated cortical representations to circumvent constant reliance on environmental cues and to selectively regulate attention toward relevant stimuli and appropriate responses (see Arnsten, 1998, for review).

Taken together, deficient dopaminergic modulation is implicated in cognitive aging deficits; however, many details of this neuromodulation–cognition link await further explication. Firm understanding of the relations between neuromodulation and cognition may require the influence of the contexts within which ongoing individual mental experiences occur to be considered as well. Computational approaches to neuromodulation of cortical function provide general frameworks for theoretical investigations of the relations between cognition and aging-related declines in neuromodulation as well as of the interactions between neuromodulatory and contextual tunings of neurocognitive representations.

Modeling Aging Neuromodulation and Cognition

Aging affects several facets of cognitive processing. People's abilities to activate, represent, and maintain information in mind, to attend to relevant but ignore irrelevant information, and to process information promptly all decline with advancing age (see Craik & Salthouse, 2000, for a general review). Aging-related decline in working memory function has been found in various tasks accessing memory span.

Other than the more "traditional" memory capacity view, working memory has been decomposed into processes for representing and maintaining context information. These processes, which support both mnemonic and attentional control functions, are also compromised by aging (Braver et al., 2001). However, it should be underscored that, whereas different aspects of episodic memory, such as working memory, recall, and recognition, show different degrees of aging-related declines, systems and processes involved in knowledge-based semantic memory seem to be preserved selectively (Nyberg et al., 2003). Aging-related declines in attentional mechanisms have also been found in various selective attention and interference tasks (McDowd & Shaw, 2000). Last, but not least, there is also ample evidence for aging-related slowing in many speeded tasks (Salthouse, 1996).

Building on the various approaches to model neuromodulation that have been developed in computational neuroscience, there have been a few computational theories aimed specifically at exploring computational principles relating aging-related decline of dopaminergic modulation with cognitive aging. For instance, with respect to the ability of monitoring the valence of behavioral consequences, a model related weakened phasic activity of the mesencephalic DA system with aging-related deficit in error processing that is expressed as reduced error-related negativity in event-related brain potential waveforms (Nieuwenhuis et al., 2002). Another theory focused on the functional interactions between dopaminergic modulation and the PFC, specifically the dorsal lateral PFC, to capture the effect of aging on context representation and maintenance (Braver et al., 2001).

In the remaining sections, the phenomena of aging neuromodulation and cognition are integrated within a cross-level framework. This theory addresses neural signal processing at a high level of abstraction and aims to elucidate a potential sequence of functional relations from deficient dopaminergic modulation to reduced neural information-processing fidelity, with ensuing consequences for cortical representational distinctiveness and various behavioral manifestations of cognitive aging (e.g., S.-C. Li, Lindenberger, & Frensch, 2000).

As mentioned, neuromodulation can be modeled with respect to different specificity and functionality. DA's modulatory effects are diverse, depending on the cortical regions and receptor types. However, a general feature of the net effect of dopaminergic modulation in decreasing background firing rate and enhancing the excitability of target neurons has been well documented. It is, hence, generally conceptualized that DA alters the signal-to-noise ratio of neural information processing, thus regulating neurons' response sensitivity to afferent signals (see Gu, 2002, for review; O'Donnell, 2003; Volkow et al., 2001).

Servan-Schreiber, Printz, and Cohen (1990) proposed that one way to model this effect is by adjusting the gain G parameter of the sigmoidal (or logistic) activation function in neural networks (figure 15.1a shows the effect of G on the activation function). This approach models DA's potentiation effects on postsynaptic neurons' responsivity to other afferent inputs without considering the details of concentration- and/or voltage-dependent influences. Nonetheless, physiological data showed that such a gain gating mechanism coupled with a negative bias of the sigmoid activation function capture the nonlinear, gain-mediated cortical stimulus–response relations resembling those modulated by the catecholamines (Cohen & Servan-Schreiber, 1992; Freeman, 1979). There are other approaches using recurrent networks to more specifically model voltage-dependent dopaminergic modulation of the PFC neurons' memory fields and delayed activity (e.g., Durstewitz, Kelc, & Güntürkün, 1999; Lisman, Fellous, & Wang, 1998; Seamans et al., 2001).

Figure 15.1. (Facing Page) Simulations of gain modulation, neuromodulation, and aging. *a*, The *S*-shaped logistic activation function at different values of *G*. Physiological evidence suggests that the logistic function with a negative bias captures the function relating the strength of an input signal to a neuron's firing rate, with its steepest slope around the baseline firing rate. Reducing mean *G* flattens the activation function such that a unit becomes less responsive. Aging-related decline of dopaminergic modulation can be simulated by sampling values of *G* from a distribution with a lower mean. *b*, *G* and the variability of activation across processing steps. Reducing mean *G* (0.8 and 0.3 for the young and old networks, respectively) increases the temporal variability of a unit's response to an identical input signal (set to 4.0) across 1000 trials. *c*, Internal activation patterns across five hidden units of one young and one old network in response to four different stimuli (S1 to S4). The internal representations of the four stimuli are much less differentiable in the old than in the young network. (Adapted from S.-C. Li et al., 2000, with permission. Copyright 2000 Elsevier Science.)

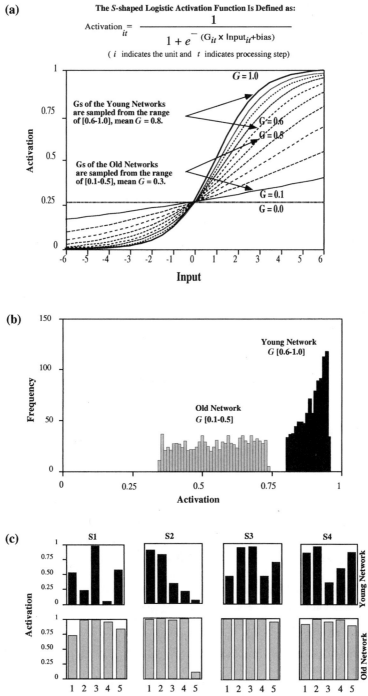

(a)

The *S*-shaped Logistic Activation Function Is Defined as:

$$\text{Activation}_{it} = \frac{1}{1 + e^{-(G_{it} \times \text{Input}_{it} + \text{bias})}}$$

(*i* indicates the unit and *t* indicates processing step)

G = 1.0

Gs of the Young Networks
are sampled from the range
of [0.6-1.0], mean *G* = 0.8.

G = 0.6

G = 0.8

Gs of the Old Networks
are sampled from the range
of [0.1-0.5], mean *G* = 0.3.

G = 0.1

G = 0.0

Activation

Input

(b)

Frequency

Young Network
G [0.6-1.0]

Old Network
G [0.1-0.5]

Activation

(c)

S1   S2   S3   S4

Young Network

Old Network

Activation

Units at the Hidden Layer

In sum, despite differences in implementation details, a common feature shared by many computational models of dopaminergic modulation is its functional effect of tuning the signal-to-noise ratio (or sharpening the selections) of relevant signals. Thus far, the strength of neurocomputational models is in the theoretical impetus they provide for linking the extensive evidence on the role of neuromodulators in behavioral tasks to the physiological evidence on the effects of neuromodulation. The downside of the computational approach, however, is that it is often hard to decide between alternative models, particularly when the models are postulated at a high level of abstraction to gain generality, but ignore specificities.

From Deficient Neuromodulation to Increased Neuronal Noise and Less-Distinctive Representation

A classical hypothesis about cognitive aging at the neurobiological level is aging-related increase of neuronal noise (Welford, 1965). However, thus far mechanisms leading to the increasing neuronal noise and its proximal and distal consequences are still not clearly understood. Simulating aging-related decline of dopaminergic neuromodulation by attenuating the G parameter in neural networks suggests a possible chain of mechanisms that relate deficient neuromodulation to increased neuronal noise and less-distinctive cortical representations that are either within or across processing pathways (S.-C. Li, Lindenberger, & Sikström, 2001).

Reduced Responsivity and Increased Neuronal Noise

Reducing the G parameter simulates aging-related attenuation of dopaminergic modulation by decreasing the slope and flattening the nonlinearity of the S-shaped logistic activation function (i.e., make it more linear) such that a unit's average responsivity to excitatory and inhibitory input signals is reduced (figure 15.1a). Put differently, the unit becomes less selective in responding to different stimulus inputs. Computationally, the effect of decreasing the G parameter is interchangeable with decreasing the initial weights (i.e., a computational analog of initial synaptic connectivity) and learning rate (i.e., a computational analog of neural adaptivity) of the network (Thimm, Moerland, & Fiesler, 1996). Conceptually, however, the G parameter manipulation is, arguably, more parsimonious in the sense that it captures neuromodulatory effects on synaptic connectivity and neural plasticity rather than treating these two properties as primitives that still need to be explained.

When the values of a unit's G are randomly chosen (i.e., stochastic G manipulation; S.-C. Li et al., 2000) from a set of values with a lower average (i.e., mean G reduction, but keeping the range of the distribution constant), the unit's response to a given external signal fluctuates more across discrete time steps. This implies decreased signal transmission fidelity (figure 15.1b). In other words, a given amount of random variations in G—simulating random fluctuations in DA transmitter substance because of probabilistic transmitter release or stochasticity in receptor binding efficacy (Hessler, 1993)—generates more haphazard activation during signal processing if the average of the processing units' Gs is reduced. This sequence of computational effects depicts a potential neurochemical mechanism for aging-related increase in neural noise: As aging attenuates neuromodulation, the impact of transmitter fluctuations caused by probabilistic transmitter release and other sources of neuronal noise (e.g., background spiking activity) on the overall level of haphazard neuronal activity is amplified in the aging brain.

Reduced Representational Distinctiveness

Furthermore, the simulations show that, as reduced responsivity leads to increased intranetwork random activation variability, another subsequent effect is a decrease in the distinctiveness of the network's internal representations. Low representational distinctiveness means that the activation profiles formed across the network's hidden units for different stimuli are less readily differentiable from each other.

Figure 15.1c shows the internal activation patterns across units at the hidden layer of a "young" (higher mean G in the top row) and an "old" (lower mean G in the bottom row) network in response to four input signals. As shown, the internal representations are less distinctive (patterns representing different memory events are less differentiable from each other) in the old than in the young network. In everyday terms, this effect implies that, as people age, neurocognitive representations of different events and their associated contexts, such as the various conversations held with different individuals during a day, become less distinct and thus more likely to be confused with one another.

Indeed, the distinctiveness of memory episodes has been featured as a basic heuristic of memory (Schacter et al., 2001). Arguably, in tasks for which the level of retrieval support is low (such as recall) people need to rely more heavily on the distinctiveness of the internal representations of remembered events for their memory performance, whereas when external cognitive support is high (such as recognition), the overall distinctiveness of self-initiated internal representations plays a lesser role. In episodic memory, it has been suggested that aging-related deficits in self-initiated processing and encoding operations (Craik, 1983; Bäckman, 1989) contribute to the greater sensitivity of recall compared to recognition to aging (e.g., Nyberg et al., 2003).

The set of simulations presented here also provides a possible computational specification for an earlier hypothesis proposed at the information-processing level. Previously, Craik (1983) suggested that, because of reduced attentional resources, older persons process information less elaborately than young people do and therefore have less-distinctive memory traces. Couched within the cross-level integrative framework, the simulation suggests that deficient dopaminergic modulation of the PFC's attention regulation mechanisms might be the neural correlate of old people's less-elaborate, less-distinctive neurocognitive representations of experienced events, although it should be underscored that in this case the memory "trace" is not to be viewed as a static representation. Remembering is not necessarily the act of retrieving an exact replica of a static memory trace stored in the past; rather, it is the "dialing up" of activity patterns across neural assemblies when current circumstances demand the on-line reconstruction of past experiences in current contexts (cf. G. M. Edelman, 2001).

In summary, a potential biological implication of these theoretical effects could be that, as people age, declining dopaminergic modulation reduces cortical neuron responsivity and increases neural noise in the aging brain. Consequently, neuronal activity representations elicited by different stimuli and contexts become less differentiated, although the relative susceptibility of context and content memory to aging may be different. Current empirical findings suggest that the context of the memory episodes is more sensitive to aging than the memory content itself (see Spencer & Raz, 1995, for review).

Neurocognitive representations of concurrent exogenous and endogenous events (e.g., perception and sensation) and later reinstatements of these events (e.g., memory and action) are the primitives of subsequent information processing carried out by various neural circuits. It has been argued that perceptual, motor, and memory processes all involve the binding together of multiple representations of stimulus features, task goals, and contexts (Johnson, 1992; Nadel et al., 2000; Treisman, 1998; Wolpert, Ghahramani, & Flanagan, 2001). Deficient neuromodulation causing less-distinctive representations of different events and contexts may therefore have far-reaching consequences for various facets of cognitive and sensorimotor processing.

This observation, however, should not be taken as suggesting a general aging effect in the usual sense that one process or one factor is mainly responsible for most cognitive aging deficits. Even if a given process accounts for most of the individual differences attributable to aging, it is helpful to take a cross-level perspective because the processes and mechanisms of aging occur at multiple levels and are hierarchically related. Whereas neuromodulatory influences on cortical functions are relatively general, as indicated by the anatomical characteristics of broad neuromodulatory cortical innervation, different neuronal circuitry and brain regions may still exhibit differential patterns of aging (Raz, 2000). Furthermore, various aspects of cognitive processing require neurocognitive representations of environment and experience interactions to different degrees. Therefore, albeit similar neuromodulatory mechanisms may be involved, brain aging at the neurochemical level is embodied in different anatomical regions that could be affected by aging and be involved in different cognitive processes to varying degrees.

The theoretical link as described above has been tested in a series of simulations that captured a range of behavioral human cognitive aging phenomena, such as adult age differences in learning rate, asymptotic performance, interference susceptibility, and complexity cost. Furthermore, besides these aging effects on performance level, the simulations of aging-related declines in neuromodulation could also account for aging-related increases in intra- and interindividual variability and in ability dedifferentiation (S.-C. Li et al., 2000). With increasing age, not only does old people's cognitive performance become more variable across test trials (i.e., intraindividual variability), but also their performance tends to differ from each other more (i.e., interindividual variability), and different cognitive abilities become more correlated (i.e., ability dedifferentiation; e.g., S.-C. Li et al., 2004). More recent simulations tested the theoretical link with respect to three other aspects of cognitive aging phenomena: optimal level of neuromodulation and memory capacity, as well as adult age differences in working memory and in the coactivation of different neurocognitive processes.

Optimal Neuromodulation, Representational Distinctiveness, and Memory Capacity

Most research has focused on the facilitation effects of dopaminergic neuromodulation. More recent findings, however, showed that an excessively high level of DA D_1 receptor stimulation impairs prefrontal working memory function (Murphy et al., 1996). By piecing together evidence from studies with varying levels of DA receptor stimulation, it was suggested that dopaminergic modulation exhibited an inverted U-shaped dose-by-performance curve (Arnsten, 1998): Working memory performance is impaired by either too little or too much receptor stimulation. Whereas there have been empirical studies examining the details of receptor dynamics with respect to deficient and excessive stimulation, the implications of these two aspects of nonoptimal neuromodulation at the representational level are still not clear.

In a set of simulations, we explored the effects of varying levels of neuromodulation on representational distinctiveness and memory capacity. Manipulating mean G across a wide range of values to simulate a wide level of dopaminergic modulation showed that the network's memory span displays an inverted-U curve. Memory span was reduced when deficient dopaminergic modulation was simulated by very low mean G or when excessive dopaminergic modulation was simulated by very high mean G. The reduced memory span at the performance level was coupled with an expression of less-distinctive internal pattern representation. When mean G was very low or very high, the internal representations of the stimulus patterns were less distinctive, with more units nonselectively participating in representing many different stimuli. In other words, the units were less selective in their representations of different experienced events (see S.-C. Li & Sikström, 2002, for details).

At the behavioral level, not only does memory capacity decrease with aging, but also it increases as children develop (Cowan et al., 1999; Fry & Hale, 2000). There are many empirical and theoretical studies suggesting that aging-related declines in memory functions are in part related to aging-related decline in dopaminergic modulation. Researchers have also begun to investigate the relation between the development of memory and neuromodulation in children (e.g., Diamond, 1996; Levitt et al., 1997). The above simulations suggest that it is possible to consider child cognitive development, at least in part, as the development of neuromodulation of cortical representational distinctiveness and specificity.

Neuromodulation and Adult Age Differences in Working Memory

Aging-related decline in working memory is a well-established phenomenon (see Grady & Craik, 2000, for review). One paradigm often used for accessing working memory function is the n-back task, which manipulates the on-line memory load. As a series of stimuli is presented, the memory load is manipulated by whether the memory response deals with the current item (0-back), the item in the immediately preceding trial (1-back), or the item presented two trials ago (2-back), and so on. Empirical evidence shows that, in comparison to people in their 30s and 40s, old people in their 70s performed significantly worse when the memory load was increased from the 0-back condition to the 1-back or 2-back condition (Dobbs & Rule, 1989).

We have also investigated the effect of reducing mean G in simulating negative adult age differences in the n-back task. In line with the empirical findings, our simulation results showed that, across a range of manipulated mean G, memory performance of the networks with a lower mean G, simulating aging-related deficit in neuromodulation, is more affected by increasing memory load (S.-C. Li & Sikström, 2002).

Deficient Neuromodulation and Increased Co-Activation of Processes

The computational effects of reduced representational distinctiveness because of lowering mean G also generalize to networks with multiple processing modules. Using a network architecture similar to a model of Stroop interference (Cohen, Dunbar, & McClelland, 1990), a dual-module network with separate processing pathways for verbal and spatial memory was set up to explore the effect of aging-related decline of neuromodulation on functional processing specificity. Simulation results showed that reducing the mean G of units within the two processing modules led to extensive activation overlap across the two processing pathways. In other words, with attenuated G simulating deficient neuromodulation, processes designated to different modules became coactivated in the old networks (S.-C. Li & Sikström, 2002).

Furthermore, when the activation patterns of young networks (plate 15.1a; see color insert) are compared to those of old networks with better or poorer performance, an effect of old networks' performance level found in empirical studies (e.g., Cabeza et al., 2002; Reuter-Lorenz et al., 2000) was also observed. Although high-performing old networks showed medium level of within-module activation and a clear pattern of cross-module coactivation (plate 15.1b), the low-performing old networks overall showed a lower level of within-module activation and no pattern of cross-module coactivation (plate 15.1c). In Cabeza et al.'s (2002) empirical findings, the old lower performers did not show particularly low activation, however. The simulations did not capture all details of the empirical finding in this case.

This set of results is of particular interest in light of neuroimaging evidence suggesting that cognitive processes carried out more specifically by different brain regions in young adults coactivate multiple brain regions in old people. For instance, people in their 60s and beyond showed bihemispheric (bilateralized) activity when retrieving or performing verbal and spatial working memory tasks, whereas the brain activities relating to these tasks are more lateralized in young adults (see Cabeza, 2002; Reuter-Lorenz, 2002, for reviews). It seems that, in response to aging-related decline in brain efficacy and integrity, "apparently nominal cognitive tasks" (i.e., tasks with seemingly identical requirements) are implemented differently in the aging brain.

Currently, these data are primarily interpreted in terms of a compensation view postulating that the increase in bilateral activation (or reduction in activation asymmetry across hemispheres) in old adults may be one way to compensate for neurocognitive deficits. There is some evidence supporting the interpretation. For example, it has been found that older adults who displayed bilateral activation were faster in a verbal memory task than those who did not (Reuter-Lorenz et al., 2000). Also, source memory performance of old adults with bilateral activity was better than that of those without (Cabeza et al., 2002; see also chapter 14, this volume).

However, the issue of whether the more diffused functional distribution of cortical activation is always adaptively compensatory or reflects nonselective recruitment (Logan et al., 2002) requires more systematic studies examining such effects in terms of within- and cross-hemispheric processes as well as in different domains of functioning. When the phenomena are not specific with respect to bihemispheric coactivation, but with respect to the specificity of topographical functional representations in general, there is also some evidence suggesting that more diffuse topographical distribution of cortical activation might not always be associated with better performance.

For instance, it was found that the receptive fields of the hind-paw representation in the sensorimotor cortex excited by tactile stimulation are large and highly overlapping in old rats, but relatively small and focused in young rats. At the behavioral level, in comparison to young rats, the old rats, however, showed sensorimotor deficits (Spengler, Godde, & Dinse, 1995; Godde et al., 2002). Or, consider a different example: Using an electroencephalogram (EEG) to measure responses elicited by elementary cognitive processing, it was demonstrated in young adult samples that individuals who performed better on a reasoning test showed more focused and specific patterns of cortical activation than individuals who scored lower on the test (Neubauer, Freudenthalter, & Pfurtscheller, 1995; Neubauer, Sange, & Pfurtscheller, 1999).

At present, very little is known about the details of how the reorganization of the more diffused functional circuitry is neurocognitively implemented. The association found between striatal D_2 receptor availability and glucose metabolism in the frontal cortex (Volkow et al., 2000) raises the question of whether neuromodulation at the synaptic level might be related to aging-related changes in cortical reorganization. Aging-related declines in neuromodulation could be one aspect of neurocognitive deficits needing compensation at both the cortical and behavioral levels. Attenuating the G parameter causing less-distinctive internal representations and increased coactivation of different processing pathways suggests that aging-related changes in cortical reorganization might, in part, be related to aging-related changes in neuromodulation. The simulation results presented in plate 15.1 also suggest that reducing mean G, which simulates the aging deficit in dopaminergic modulation, could result either in a coactivation of processes that in turn produces better performance or in overall low activation that leads to poor performance.

At the computational level, these effects are the results of differential initial weight configurations that map onto smoother (in the case of high performers) or rougher (in the case of low performers) stimulus–response spaces. At the current stage, the differences in initial weight configurations are treated as primitives of the

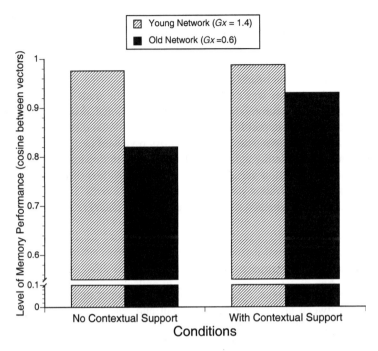

Figure 15.2. Memory performance of young and old networks under conditions with or without contextual support. The mean G of the young and old networks were 1.4 and 0.6, respectively.

support, however, the level of representational distinctiveness of the old network was much enhanced.

Relations Between Aging Neuromodulatory, Cognitive, and Sensorimotor Processes

Thus far, this chapter has reviewed computational approaches focusing mainly on relating aging neuromodulation with cognitive aging deficits. However, aging-related declines have also been commonly observed in sensory (see Stevens et al., 1998, for review) and sensorimotor processes (see Ferrandez & Teasdale, 1996, for review). Aging-related declines in cognitive and sensorimotor processing might be related to each other. For instance, it has been found that an aging-related increase in intraindividual variability in sensorimotor performance is negatively related to old people's memory performance (S.-C. Li et al., 2000). Studies employing dual-task paradigms usually found aging-related increases in dual-task costs in both the cognitive and sensorimotor domains (K. Z. H. Li et al., 2001; see K. Z. H. Li & Lindenberger, 2002, for review; Lindenberger, Marsiske, & Baltes, 2000).

Two parallel conceptual explanations have been proposed to understand aging-related increase in the association between cognitive and sensorimotor processes. At the information-processing level, as an extension of an earlier proposal that the need

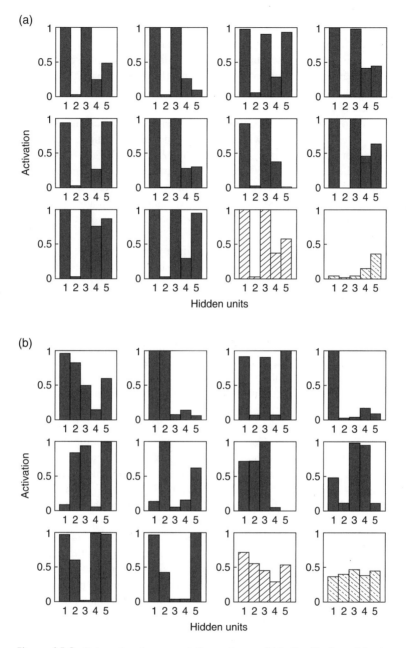

Figure 15.3. International representation patterns of 10 stimuli of an old network under conditions *a*, without, or *b*, with, contextual support. Within each panel, the units' averaged activation and variance of activation across 10 stimuli are plotted in two minipanels at the lower right-hand corner (averages are plotted in the left of the two minipanels, whereas the variances are plotted in the right panel).

for attentional resource in sensorimotor performance increases in old age (Craik & Byrd, 1982), it was proposed that, with increasing age, simple sensory and motor aspects of behavior need more cognitive control (Lindenberger et al., 2000). Another explanation addresses this relationship at the neurobiological level, suggesting that aging-related strengthening of the sensory–cognitive link could be the behavioral manifestation of aging-related declines in neurobiological mechanisms that compromise brain integrity across a wide range of functional circuitry, thereby affecting multiple sensory and cognitive systems (Baltes & Lindenberger, 1997). These two accounts parallel each other. Whereas it may be the case that simple sensorimotor tasks require more attention and cognitive control in old age, it is also the case that neurobiological mechanisms involved in attentional regulation and executive control, particularly the neuromodulatory processes reviewed in this chapter, are compromised during aging.

Motor learning and sensorimotor processing involve complex and dynamic neural computations that integrate multiple sensory inputs and motor commands (Wolpert, Ghahramani, & Flanagan, 2001). There is evidence that different neural substrates support different forms of motor learning (Doya, 2000). The dopaminergic systems in the basal ganglia regulate reward learning (Schultz, Dayan, & Montague, 1997). Furthermore, the dysfunctions of these systems are related to movement disorders, addiction, and problems with processing reinforcement signals.

The specific involvement of neuromodulation in aging-related sensorimotor deficits is most clearly exemplified in Parkinson's disease (PD). It has been suggested that the difficulty of patients with PD in switching between movement sequences is related to declines in dopaminergic modulation of the direct inhibitory and indirect excitatory pathways of the basal ganglia motor loop (Bar-Gad & Bergman, 2001; Onla-or & Winstein, 2001). Computational approaches to motor (e.g., Onla-Or & Winstein, 2001; Toffano-Nioche, Beroule, & Tassin, 1998) and cognitive (Amos, 2000; Monchi, Taylor, & Dagher, 2000) deficits of PD commonly involve parameterizations that model dopaminergic modulation. For instance, in models of Parkinson's motor deficits, it has been assumed that sensorimotor patterns associated with movements are represented in neural pathways, just like other perceptual or regenerated memory patterns. Successful executions of motor movements involve dynamic matching and synchrony between internal representations of the acquired motor movements and the concurrent on-line proprioceptive information (Toffano-Nioche, Beroule, & Tassin, 1998). Dopaminergic modulation of motor programming in the basal ganglia has been modeled either as regulating the balance between the direct and indirect pathways of the motor loop, or, at a functional level, as regulating the match between internal representations of motor sequences and ongoing proprioceptive stimuli.

So far, most computational models of aging have focused on either cognitive or sensorimotor aging deficits. Given the seeming involvement of neuromodulation in both aging cognitive and sensorimotor deficits, in the future large-scale network models with submodules capturing functional cortical circuitry for cognitive and sensorimotor processing could serve as general neurocomputational frameworks for investigating the interactions among aging neuromodulatory, cognitive, and sensorimotor processes (see S.-C. Li & Dinse, 2002, for review).

Conclusions

Aging-related changes in the dynamical properties of cortical function could be related not only to neuroanatomical degeneration, but also to declines in neurochemical processes affecting pattern representation and information transfer within and between cortical regions. Specifically, cognitive aging may be related to declines in dopaminergic modulation in the PFC and in other subcortical regions. Details regarding the involvement of neuromodulation in cognitive aging deficits remain to be investigated. Pieces of the puzzle are emerging in various subfields. When considered within an integrative neurocomputational framework, various facets of cognitive aging phenomena, such as adult age differences in learning rate, susceptibility to interference, costs of processing complexity, working memory, and processing specificity, may be related to the decline in dopaminergic neuromodulation.

Furthermore, aging studies reviewed here have mainly focused on the neurobiological effects of aging and their expressions at the cognitive and behavioral levels; however, the recent emergence of biocultural co-constructive views on cognition and adaptive behavior (e.g., Baltes & Singer, 2001; see Baltes, Reuter-Lorenz, & Rösler, in press; S.-C. Li, 2003, for reviews) hints at another important direction for future research: the investigation of feed-downward experiential and environmental influences on the aging neurocognitive processes. Neurocomputational models with their dynamic adaptive properties that depend jointly on network parameters, input-output mapping, and training history provide suitable frameworks for investigating the interactions among neuromodulation, environmental support (Craik & Anderson, 1999), and sociocultural context (Park & Gutchess, 2002) that continuously tune the neurocognitive representations throughout life span development.

Acknowledgments   The preparation of this manuscript was sponsored by the support of the Max Planck Institute for Human Development to the author. I also thank Thomas Elbert for bringing my attention to Bao, Chan, and Merzenich's (2001) findings of VTA dopamine neurons affecting long-range cortical remodeling. Amy Michéle's assistance in language and style editing is also greatly appreciated.

References

Amos, A. A. (2000). Computational model of information processing in the frontal cortex and basal ganglia. *Journal of Cognitive Neuroscience, 12*, 505–519.

Arnsten, A. F. T. (1998). Catecholamine modulation of prefrontal cortical cognitive function. *Trends in Cognitive Sciences, 2*, 436–447.

Arnsten, A. F. T., Cai, J. X., Murphy, B. L., & Goldman-Rakic, P. S. (1994). Dopamine D_1 receptor mechanisms in the cognitive performance of young adult and aged monkeys. *Psychopharmacology, 116*, 143–151.

Arnsten, A. F. T., & Goldman-Rakic, P. S. (1985). Alpha 2-adrenergic mechanisms in prefrontal cortex associated with cognitive declines in aged non-human primates. *Science, 230*, 1273–1276.

Bäckman, L. (1989). Varieties of memory compensation by older adults in episodic remembering. In L. W. Poon, D. C. Rubin, & B. A. Wilson (Eds.), *Everyday cognition in adulthood and late life* (pp. 509–544). Cambridge, UK: Cambridge University Press.

Bäckman, L., Ginovart, N., Dixon, R. A., Wahlin, T. B. R., Halldin, C., & Farde, L. (2000). Age-related cognitive deficits mediated by changes in the striatal dopamine system. *American Journal of Psychiatry, 157,* 635–637.

Baltes, P. B., & Lindenberger, U. (1997). Emergence of a powerful connection between sensory and cognitive functions across the adult life span: A new window to the study of cognitive aging? *Psychology and Aging, 12,* 12–21.

Baltes, P. B., Reuter-Lorenz, P., & Rösler, F. (Eds.). (in press). *Brain, mind, and culture: From interactionism to biocultural co-construction.* New York: Cambridge University Press.

Baltes, P. B., & Singer, T. (2001). Plasticity and the aging mind: An exemplar of the biocultural orchestration of brain and behavior. *European Review, 9,* 59–76.

Baltes, P. B., Staudinger, U. M., & Lindenberger, U. (1999). Lifespan psychology: Theory and application to intellectual functioning. *Annual Review of Psychology, 50,* 471–507.

Bao, S., Chan, V. T., & Merzenich, M. M. (2001). Cortical remodelling induced by activity of ventral tegmental dopamine neurons. *Nature, 412,* 79–83.

Bar-Gad, I., & Bergman, H. (2001). Stepping out of the box: Information processing in the neural networks of the basal ganglia. *Current Opinion in Neurobiology, 11,* 689–695.

Bliss, T. V. P., & Lømo, T. (1973). Long-lasting potentiation of synaptic transmission in the dentae area of the anaesthetized rabbit following stimulation of the perforant path. *Journal of Physiology, 232,* 331–356.

Braver, T. S., Barch, D. M., Key, B. A., Carter, C. S., Cohen, J. D., Kaye, J. A., et al. (2001). Context processing in older adults: Evidence for a theory relating cognitive control to neurobiology in healthy aging. *Journal of Experimental Psychology: General, 130,* 746–763.

Cabeza, R. (2002). Hemispheric asymmetry reduction in older adults: The Harold model. *Psycholology and Aging, 17,* 85–100.

Cabeza, R., Anderson, N. D., Locantore, K. J., & McIntosh, A. R. (2002). Aging gracefully. Compensatory brain activity in high-performing older adults. *Neuroimage, 17,* 1394–1402.

Camperi, M., & Wang, X. J. (1998). A model of visuospatial working memory in prefrontal cortex: Recurrent network and cellular bistability. *Journal of Computational Neuroscience, 5,* 383–405.

Cartling, B. (1999). Control of resolution and perception in working memory. *Behavioral Brain Research, 100,* 255–271.

Changeux, J.-P. (1985). *Neuronal man.* New York: Oxford University Press.

Churchland, P. S., & Sejnowski, T. J. (1988). Perspectives on cognitive neuroscience. *Science, 242,* 741–745.

Clark, A. (1999). An embodied cognitive science? *Trends in Cognitive Sciences, 3,* 345–351.

Cohen, J. D., Dunbar, K., & McClelland, J. L. (1990). On the control of automatic processes: A parallel distributed processing model of the Stroop effect. *Psychological Review, 97,* 332–361.

Cohen, J. D., & Servan-Schreiber, D. (1992). Context, cortex, and dopamine: A connectionist approach to behavior and biology in Schizophrenia. *Psychological Review, 99,* 45–77.

Cowan, N., Saults, J. S., Nugent, L. D., & Elliott, E. M. (1999). The microanalyses of memory span and its development in childhood. *International Journal of Psychology, 34,* 353–358.

Craik, F. I. M. (1983). On the transfer of information from temporary to permanent memory. *Philosophical Transactions of the Royal Society London B, 302,* 341–359.

Craik, F. I. M., & Anderson, N. D (1999). Applying cognitive approach to problems of aging.

In D. Gopher and A. Koriat (Eds.), *Attention and performance XVII* (pp. 583–615). Cambridge, MA: MIT Press.

Craik, F. I. M., & Byrd, M. (1982). Aging and cognitive deficits: The role of attentional resources. In F. I. M. Craik and S. Trehub (Eds.), *Aging and cognitive processes* (pp. 191–211). New York: Plenum.

Craik, F. I. M., & Salthouse, T. A. (Eds.). (2000). *The handbook of aging and cognition.* Mahwah, NJ: Erlbaum.

de Keyser J., de Backer, J. P., Vauquelin, G., & Ebinger, G. (1990). The effect of aging on the D_1 dopamine receptors in human cortex. *Brain Research, 528*, 308–310.

Destexhe, A., Mainen, Z. F., & Sejnowski, T. J. (1994). Synthesis of models for excitable membranes, synaptic transmission and neuromodulation using a common kinetic formalism. *Journal of Computational Neuroscience, 1*, 195–230.

Diamond, A. (1996). Evidence for the importance of dopamine for prefrontal cortex functions early in life. *Philosophical Transactions of The Royal Society of London: Biological Sciences, 351*, 1483–1493.

Dobbs, A. R., & Rule, B. G. (1989). Adult age differences in working memory. *Psychology and Aging, 4*, 500–503.

Doya, K. (2000). Complementary roles of basal ganglia and cerebellum in learning and motor control. *Current Opinion in Neurobiology, 19*, 732–739.

Doya, K. (2002). Metalearning and neuromodulation. *Neural Networks, 15*, 495–506.

Doya, K., Dayan, P., & Hasselmo, M. E. (Eds.). (2002). Special issue 2002: Computational models of neuromodulation. *Neural Networks, 15*, 475–774.

Durstewitz, D., Kelc, M., & Güntürkün, O. (1999). A neurocomputational theory of the dopaminergic modulation of working memory functions. *Journal of Neuroscience, 19*, 2807–2822.

Edelman, G. M. (1987). *Neural Darwinism: The theory of neuronal group selection.* New York: Basic Books.

Edelman, G. M. (2001). Building a picture of the brain. In G. M. Edelman and J.-P. Changeux (Eds.), *The brain* (pp. 37–70). London: Transaction Publishers.

Edelman, S. (1998). Representation is representation of similarities. *Behavioral and Brain Sciences, 21*, 449–498.

Edelman, S. (2001). Neural spaces: A general framework for the understanding of cognition? *Behavioral and Brain Sciences, 21*, 664.

Fellous, J.-M., & Linster, C. (1998). Computational models of neuromodulation. *Neural Computation, 10*, 771–805.

Ferrandez, A.-M., & Teasdale, N. (1996). (Eds.). *Changes in sensory motor behavior in aging.* New York: Elsevier Science.

Freeman, W. J. (1979). Nonlinear gain mediating cortical stimulus-response relations. *Biological Cybernetics, 33*, 243–247.

Friston, K. J., Tononi, G., Reeke, G. N., Sporns, O., & Edelman, G. M. (1994). Value-dependent selection in the brain-simulation in a synthetic neural model. *Neuroscience, 59*. 229–243.

Fry, A. F., & Hale, S. (2000). Relationships among processing speed, working memory, and fluid intelligence in children. *Biological Psychology, 54*, 1–34.

Gao, W. J., Wang, Y., & Goldman-Rakic, P. S. (2003). Dopamine modulation of perisomatic and peridendritic inhibition in prefrontal cortex. *Journal of Neuroscience, 23*, 1622–1630.

Gärdenfors, P. (2000). *Conceptual spaces: The geometry of thought.* Cambridge, MA: MIT Press.

Giorgi, O., Calderini, G., Toffano, G., & Biggio, G. (1987). D1 dopamine receptors labeled with ³H-SCH 23390: Decrease in the striatum of aged rats. *Neurobiology of Aging, 8*, 51–54.

Godde, B., Berkefeld, T., David-Jürgens, M., & Dinse, H. R. (2002). Age-related changes in primary somatosensory cortex of rats: Evidence for parallel degenerative and plastic-adaptive processes. *Neuroscience and Biobehavioral Reviews, 26*, 743–752.

Grady, C. L., & Craik, F. I. M. (2000). Changes in memory processing with age. *Current Opinion of Neurobiology, 10*, 224–231.

Gu, Q. (2002). Neuromodulatory transmitter systems in the cortex and their role in cortical plasticity. *Neuroscience, 111*, 815–835.

Hasselmo, M. E. (1995). Neuromodulation and cortical function: Modeling the physiological basis of behavior. *Behavioural Brain Research, 67*, 1–27.

Hasselmo, M. E. (1999). Neuromodulation: Acetylcholine and memory consolidation. *Trends in Cognitive Sciences, 3*, 351–359.

Head, D., Raz, N., Gunnin-Dixon, F., Williamson, A., & Acker, J. D. (2002). Age-related differences in the course of cognitive skill acquisition: The role of regional cortical shrinkage and cognitive resources. *Psychology and Aging, 17*, 72–84.

Hebb, D. O. (1949). *The organization of behavior*. New York: Wiley.

Hessler, N. A., et al. (1993). The probability of transmitter release at a mammalian central synapse. *Nature, 366*, 569–572.

Holroyd, C. B., & Coles, M. G. H. (2002). The neural basis of human error processing: Reinforcement learning, dopamine, and the error-related negativity. *Psychological Review, 109*, 679–709.

Johnson, M. K. (1992). MEM: Mechanisms of recollection. *Journal of Cognitive Neuroscience, 4*, 268–280.

Kaasinen V., Vilkman, H., Hietala, J., Nagren, K., Helenius, H., Olsson, H., et al. (2000). Age-related dopamine D₂/D₃ receptor loss in extrastriatal regions of the human brain. *Neurobiology of Aging, 21*, 683–688.

Kandel, E. R., & Tauc, L. (1964). Mechanism of prolonged heterosynaptic facilitation. *Nature, 202*, 145.

Levitt, P., Harvey, J. A., Friedman, E., Simansky, K., & Murphy, H. (1997). New evidence for neurotransmitter influences on brain development. *Trends in Neuroscience, 20*, 269–274.

Li, K. Z. H., & Lindenberger, U. (2002). Relations between aging sensory/sensorimotor and cognitive functions. *Neuroscience and Biobehavioral Reviews, 26*, 777–784.

Li, K. Z. H., Lindenberger, U., Freund, A. M., & Baltes, P. B. (2001). Walking while memorizing: A SOC study of age-related differences in compensatory behavior under dual-task conditions. *Psychological Science, 12*, 230–237.

Li, S.-C. (2003). Biocultural orchestration of developmental plasticity across levels: The interplay of biology and culture in shaping the mind and behavior across the life span. *Psychological Bulletin, 129*, 171–194.

Li, S.-C., Aggen, S., Nesselroade, J. R., & Baltes, P. B. (2000). Short-term fluctuations in elderly people's sensorimotor functioning predict text and spatial memory performance. *Gerontology, 47*, 100–116.

Li, S.-C., & Dinse, H. R. (Eds.). (2002). Special issue: Aging of the brain, sensorimotor, and cognitive processes. *Neuroscience and Biobehavioral Reviews, 26*, 729–859.

Li, S.-C., & Lindenberger, U. (2002). Co-constructed functionality instead of functional normality [commentary]. *Behavioral and Brain Sciences, 25*, 761–762.

Li, S.-C., Lindenberger, U., & Frensch, P. A. (2000). Unifying cognitive aging: From neuromodulation to representation to cognition. *Neurocomputing, 32–33*, 879–890.

Li, S.-C., Lindenberger, U., Hommel, B., Aschersleben, G., Prinz, W., & Baltes, P. B. (2004).

Lifespan transformations in the couplings among intellectual abilities and constituent cognitive processes. *Psychological Science, 15,* 155–163.

Li, S.-C., Lindenberger, U., & Sikström, S. (2001). Aging cognition: From neuromodulation to representation. *Trends in Cognitive Sciences, 5,* 479–486.

Li, S.-C., & Sikström, S. (2002). Intergrative neurocomputational perspectives on cognitive aging, neuromodulation, and representation. *Neuroscience and Biobehavioral Reviews, 26,* 795–808.

Lindenberger, U., Marsiske, M., & Baltes, P. B. (2000). Memorizing while walking: Increase in dual-task costs from young adulthood to old age. *Psychology and Aging, 15,* 417–436.

Lisman, J. E., Fellous, J. M., & Wang, X. J. (1998). A role for NMDA-receptor channels in working memory. *Nature Neuroscience, 1,* 273–275.

Logan, J. M., Sanders, A. L., Snyder, A. Z., Morris, J. C., & Buckner, R. L. (2002). Under-recruitment and nonselective recruitment: Dissociable neural mechanisms associated with aging. *Neuron, 33,* 827–840.

MacRae, P. G., Spirduso, W. W., & Wilcox, R. E. (1988). Reaction time and nigrostriatal dopamine function: The effect of age and practice. *Brain Research, 451,* 139–146.

Markman, A. B., & Dietrich, E. (2000). Extending the classical view of representation. *Trends in Cognitive Sciences, 4,* 470–475.

McDowd, J. M., & Shaw, R. J. (2000). Attention and aging: A functional perspective. In F. I. M. Craik and T. A. Salthouse (Eds.), *The handbook of aging and cognition* (pp. 221–292). Mahwah, NJ: Erlbaum.

Monchi, O., Taylor, J. G., & Dagher, A. (2000). A neural model of working memory processes in normal subjects, Parkinson's disease and schizophrenia for fMRI design and predictions. *Neural Networks, 13,* 953–973.

Montague, P. R., Dayan, P., & Sejnowski, T. J. (1996). A framework for mesencephalic dopamine systems based on predictive Hebbian learning. *Journal of Neuroscience, 16,* 1936–1947.

Morrison, J. H., & Hof, P. R. (1997). Life and death of neurons in the aging brain. *Science, 278,* 412–429.

Murphy, B. L., Arnsten, A. F. T., Goldman-Rakic, P. S., & Roth, R. H. (1996). Increased dopamine turnover in the prefrontal cortex impairs spatial working-memory performance in rats and monkeys. *Proceedings of National Academy of Sciences USA, 93,* 1325–1329.

Nadel, L., Samsonovich, A., Ryan, L., & Moscovitch, M. (2000). Multiple trace theory of human memory: Computational, neuroimaging, and neuropsychological results. *Hippocampus, 10,* 352–368.

Neubauer, A. C., Freudenthalter, H. H., & Pfurtscheller, G. (1995). Intelligence and spatiotemporal patterns of event-related desynchronization (ERD). *Intelligence, 20,* 249–266.

Neubauer, A. C., Sange, G., & Pfurtscheller, G. (1999). Psychometric intelligence and event-related desynchronization during performance of a letter matching task. In G. Pfurtscheller and F. H. Lopes da Silva (Eds.), *Event-related desynchronization and related oscillatory EEG phenomena of the awake brain. Handbook of EEG and clinical neurophysiology, revised series* (pp. 219–231). Amsterdam, The Netherlands: Elsevier.

Nieuwenhuis, S., Ridderinkhof, K. R., Talsma, D., Coles, M. G. H., Holroyd, C., Kok, A., et al. (2002). A computational account of altered error processing in older age: Dopamine and error-related processing. *Cognitive, Affective, and Behavioral Neuroscience, 2,* 19–36.

Nyberg, L., Maitland, S. B., Rönnlund, M., Bäckman, L., Dixon, R. A., & Wahln, A. (2003). Selective adult age differences in an age-invariant multifactor model of declarative memory. *Psychology and Aging, 18,* 149–160.

O'Donnell, P. (2003). Dopamine gating of forebrain neural ensembles. *European Journal of Neuroscience, 17*, 429–435.

Onla-Or, S., & Winstein, C. J. (2001). Function of the "direct" and "indirect" pathways of the basal ganglia motor loop: Evidence from reciprocal aiming movements in Parkinson's disease. *Cognitive Brain Research, 10*, 239–232.

O'Reilly, R. C., Noelle, D. C., Braver, T. S., & Cohen, J. D. (2002). Prefrontal cortex and dynamic categorization tasks: Representational organization and neuromodulatory control. *Cerebral Cortex, 12*, 246–257

Palmer, S. E. (1978). Fundamental aspects of cognitive representation. In E. Rosch and B. B. Lloyd (Eds.), *Cognition and categorization* (pp. 259–302). Hillsdale, NJ: Erlbaum.

Park, D. C., & Gutchess, A. (2002). Aging, cognition, and culture: A neuroscientific perspective. *Neuroscience and Biobehavioral Reviews, 26*, 859–867.

Peters, A. (2002). Structural changes that occur during normal aging of primate cerebral hemispheres. *Neuroscience and Biobehavioral Reviews, 26*, 733–741.

Quartz, S. R., & Sejnowski, T. J. (1997). The neural basis of cognitive development: A constructivist manifesto. *Behavioural and Brain Sciences, 20*, 537–596.

Raz, N. (2000). Aging of the brain and its impact on cognitive performance: Integration of structural and functional findings. In F. I. M. Craik and T. A. Salthouse (Eds.), *The handbook of aging and cognition* (pp. 1–90). Mahwah, NJ: Erlbaum.

Reuter-Lorenz, P. A. (2002). New visions of the aging mind and brain. *Trends in Cognitive Sciences, 6*, 394–400.

Reuter-Lorenz, P. A., Jonides, J., Smith, E. E., Hartley, A., Miller, A., Marchuetz, C., et al. (2000). Age differences in the frontal lateralization of verbal and spatial working memory revealed by PET. *Journal of Cognitive Neuroscience, 12*, 174–187.

Salthouse, T. A. (1996). The processing-speed theory of adult age differences in cognition. *Psychological Review, 103*, 403–428.

Schacter, D. L., Cendan, D. L., Dodson, C. S., & Clifford, E. R. (2001). Retrieval conditions and false recognition: Testing the distinctiveness heuristic. *Psychonomic Bulletin and Reviews, 8*, 827–833.

Schneider, E. L., & Rowe, J. W. (Eds.). (1996). *Handbook of the biology of aging*. New York: Academic Press.

Schultz, W., Dayan, P., & Montague, P. R. (1997). A neural substrate of prediction and reward. *Science, 275*, 1593–1599.

Seamans, J. K., Gorelova, N., Durstewitz, D., & Yang, C. R. (2001). Bidirectional dopamine modulation of GABAergic inhibition in prefrontal cortical pyramidal neurons. *Journal of Neuroscience, 21*, 3628–3638.

Segovia, G., Porras, A., Del Arco, A., & Mora, F. (2001). Glutamatergic neurotransmission in aging: A critical perspective. *Mechanisms of Ageing and Development, 122*, 1–29.

Servan-Schreiber, D., Printz, H., & Cohen, J. D. (1990). A network model of catecholamine effects: Gain, signal-to-noise ratio, and behavior. *Science, 249*, 892–895.

Shepherd, G. M. (1991). *Foundations of the neuron doctrine*. New York: Oxford University Press.

Spencer, W. D., & Raz, N. (1995). Differential effects of aging on memory for content and context: A meta-analysis. *Psychology and Aging, 10*, 527–539.

Spengler, F., Godde, B., & Dinse, H. R. (1995). Effects of aging on topographic organization of somatosensory cortex. *NeuroReport, 6*, 469–473.

Squire, L. R., & Kandel, E. R. (1999). *Memory: From mind to molecules*. New York: Scientific American Library.

Stevens, J. C., Cruz, L. A., Marks, L. E., & Lakatos, S. (1998). A multimodal assessment of sensory threshold in aging. *Journals of Gerontology, 53B*, 263–272.

Thelen, E., & Smith, L. B. (1994). *A dynamic approach to the development of cognition and action*. Cambridge, MA: MIT Press.

Thimm, G., Moerland, P., & Fiesler, E. (1996). The interchangeability of learning rate and gain in backpropagation neural networks. *Neural Computation, 8*, 451–460.

Toffano-Nioche, C., Beroule, D., & Tassin, J.-P. (1998). A functional model of some Parkinson's disease symptoms using a guided propagation network. *Artificial Intelligence and Medicine, 14*, 237–258.

Treisman, A. (1998). Feature binding, attention and object perception. *Philosophical Transactions of Royal Society London: B, 353*, 1295–1306.

van Geert, P. (1998). A dynamic systems model of basic developmental mechanisms: Piaget, Vygotsky, and beyond. *Psychological Review, 105*, 634–677.

Volkow, N. D., Chang, L., Wang, G. J., Fowler, J. S., Lenoido-Yee, M., Franceschi, D., et al. (2000). Association between age-related decline in brain dopamine activity and impairment in frontal and cingulate metabolism. *American Journal of Psychiatry, 157*, 75–80.

Volkow, N. D., Wang, G. J., Fowler, J. S., Logen, J., Gerasimov, M., Maynard, L., et al. (2001). Therapeutic doses of oral methylphenidate significantly increase extracellular dopamine in the human brain. *Journal of Neuroscience, 21*, 1–5.

Welford, A. T. (1965). Performance, biological mechanisms and age: A theoretical sketch. In A. T. Welford and J. E. Birren (Eds.), *Behavior, aging, and the nervous system* (pp. 3–20). Springfield IL: Thomas.

West, R. L. (1996). An application of prefrontal cortex function theory to cognitive aging. *Psychological Bulletin, 120*, 272–292.

Wigström, H., & Gustafsson, B. (1981). Increased excitability of hippocampal unmyelinated fibers following conditioning stimulation. *Brain Research, 229*, 507–513.

Wolpert, D. M., Ghahramani, Z., & Flanagan, J. R. (2001). Perspectives and problems in motor learning. *Trends in Cognitive. Sciences, 5*, 487–494.

Wong, D. F., et al. (1997). Quantification of neuroreceptors in the living brain: III. D2-like dopamine receptors: Theory, validation and changes during normal aging. *Journal of Cerebral Blood Flow and Metabolism, 17*, 316–330.

Zahrt, J., Taylor, J. R., Mathew, R. G., & Arnsten, A. F. T. (1997). Supranormal stimulation of dopamine D_1 receptors in the rodent prefrontal cortex impairs spatial working memory performance. *Journal of Neuroscience, 17*, 8528–8535.

Zoli, M., Torri, C., Ferrari, R., Jansson, A., Zini, I., Fuxe, K., & Agnati, L. F. (1998). The emergence of the volume transmission concept. *Brain Research Review, 26*, 136–157.

Author Index

Subject Index

RETURN TO: **FONG OPTOMETRY LIBRARY**

490 Minor Hall • 642-1020

LOAN PERIOD	1	2	3
1 MONTH			
	4	5	6

All books may be recalled after 7 days.
Renewals may be requested by phone or, using GLADIS,
type **inv** followed by your patron ID number.

DUE AS STAMPED BELOW.

This book will be held
in OPTOMETRY LIBRARY
until _____ APR - 5 2005

MAY 1 8 2005